The Institute of Chartered Accountants in England and Wales

BUSINESS PLANNING: TAXATION
Finance Acts 2015

For exams in 2016

Study Manual

www.icaew.com

Business Planning: Taxation
The Institute of Chartered Accountants in England and Wales

ISBN: 978-1-78363-210-7

Previous ISBN: 978-0-85760-990-8

First edition 2013
Fourth edition 2015

British Library Cataloguing-in-Publication Data
A catalogue record for this book is available from the British Library

Originally printed in the United Kingdom by Polestar Wheatons on paper
obtained from traceable, sustainable sources.

Polestar Wheatons
Hennock Road
Marsh Barton
Exeter
EX2 8RP

Welcome to ICAEW

I am delighted that you have chosen ICAEW to progress your journey towards joining the chartered accountancy profession. It is one of the best decisions I also made.

The role of the accountancy profession in the world's economies has never been more important. People making financial decisions need knowledge and guidance based on the highest technical and ethical standards. ICAEW Chartered Accountants provide this better than anyone. They challenge people and organisations to think and act differently, to provide clarity and rigour, and so help create and sustain prosperity all over the world.

As a world leader of the accountancy and finance profession, we are proud to promote, develop and support over 144,000 chartered accountants worldwide. Our members have the knowledge, skills and commitment to maintain the highest professional standards and integrity. They are part of something special, and now, so are you. It's with our support and dedication that our members and hopefully yourself, will realise career ambitions, maintain a professional edge and contribute to the profession.

You are now on your journey towards joining the accountancy profession, and a highly rewarding career with endless opportunities. By choosing to study for our world-leading chartered accountancy qualification, the ACA, you too have made the first of many great decisions in your career.

You are in good company, with a network of over 26,000 students around the world made up of like-minded people, you are all supported by ICAEW. We are here to support you as you progress through your studies and career; we will be with you every step of the way, visit page x to review the key resources available as you study.

I wish you the best of luck with your studies and look forward to welcoming you to the profession in the future.

Michael Izza
Chief Executive
ICAEW

Contents

1 Introduction

ACA qualification

The ICAEW chartered accountancy qualification, the ACA, is a world-leading professional qualification in accountancy, finance and business.

The ACA has integrated components that give you an in-depth understanding across accountancy, finance and business. Combined, they help build the technical knowledge, professional skills and practical experience needed to become an ICAEW Chartered Accountant.

Each component is designed to complement each other, which means that you can put theory into practice and you can understand and apply what you learn to your day-to-day work. Progression through all the elements of the ACA simultaneously will enable you to be more successful in the workplace and exams.

The components are:

- Professional development
- Ethics and professional scepticism
- 3-5 years practical work experience
- 15 accountancy, finance and business modules

To find out more on the components of the ACA and what is involved in training, visit your dashboard at icaew.com/dashboard.

2 Business Planning: Taxation

The full syllabus and technical knowledge grids can be found within the module study guide. Visit icaew.com/dashboard for this and more resources.

2.1 Module aim

The aim of this paper is:

To enable candidates to apply technical knowledge and professional skills to identify and resolve taxation issues that arise in the context of preparing tax computations and to advise on tax-efficient strategies for businesses and individuals.

Candidates will be required to use technical knowledge and professional judgement to identify, explain and evaluate alternative tax treatments and to determine the appropriate solutions to taxation issues, giving due consideration to the needs of clients and the interaction between taxes. The commercial context and impact of recommendations will need to be considered in making such judgements, as will ethical and legal issues.

The examiners have stated that in the examination all references to HMRC are to HM Revenue and Customs.

2.2 Method of assessment

The Business Planning: Taxation module will be examined using traditional paper based assessments. The paper-based exam will be 2.5 hours in length. This exam will contain questions requiring the use of communication, judgement and evaluation skills as well as an ability to understand the interaction of different taxes.

The exam will consist of three questions. One question will be an integrated scenario of approximately 40 marks which will cover a range of taxes as well as including tax planning. Ethics and law may be tested in any of the three questions.

The exam will be open book and will permit candidates to take any written or printed material into the exam hall subject to practical space restrictions.

2.3 Specification grid

This grid provides a general guide as to the subject matter within this module and assessment coverage over a period of time.

	Weighting (%)
Ethics and law	5 – 10
Taxation of corporate entities	35 – 45
Taxation of owner-managed businesses	20 – 30
Personal taxation	15 – 25

This grid provides guidance on the relative weighting between knowledge and skills:

	Weighting (%)
Knowledge	25 – 35
Skills	65 – 75

3 Permitted Texts

3.1 At the Professional and Advanced Levels there are specific texts that you are permitted to take into your exams with you. All information for these texts, the editions that are recommended for your examinations and where to order them from, is available on www.icaew.com/permittedtexts.

Professional Level Examinations	Permitted Text
Audit and Assurance	✓
Financial Accounting and Reporting	✓
Tax Compliance	✓
Business Strategy	✗
Financial Management	✗
Business Planning: Banking/Insurance/Taxation	No restrictions

Advanced Level Examinations	
Corporate Reporting	No restrictions
Strategic Business Management	No restrictions
Case Study	No restrictions

Business Planning: Banking/Insurance/Taxation and the Advanced Level exams have no restrictions so you may take any hard copy materials in to these exams that you wish, subject to practical space restrictions.

Although the examiners use the specific editions listed to set the assessment, you **may** use a different edition of the text at your own risk. If you use a different edition within your exams, you should note this inside your answer booklet, at the beginning of the question.

This information, as well as what to expect and what is and is not permitted in your exams is available in the Instructions to Candidates. You will be sent this with your exam admission details and it is also available on our website; www.icaew.com/exams.

3.2 Business Planning: Taxation

To ensure that you are up to date with the relevant content of Finance (No. 2) Act 2015, a supplement has been produced and will be dispatched with your Business Planning: Taxation Question Bank. The supplement will cover relevant examinable material introduced by the second Finance Act, and should be used in conjunction with the recommended edition of the permitted text. There are no restrictions within the Business Planning: Taxation exam and so we recommend that you take the supplement into your exam with you. Relevant examinable rates and allowances from Finance (No. 2) Act 2015 will also be included within the exam paper.

4 Key Resources

Student support team

Our student support team are here to help you as much as possible, providing full support throughout your studies.

T +44 (0)1908 248 250
F +44 (0)1908 248 069
E studentsupport@icaew.com

Student website

The student area of our website provides the latest information, guidance and exclusive resources to help you progress through the ACA. Find everything you need (from sample paper to errata sheets) at icaew.com/dashboard.

Online student community

The online student community provides support and practical advice – wherever you are, whenever you need it. With regular blogs covering a range of work, life and study topics as well as a forum where you can post your questions and share your own tips. Join the conversation at icaew.com/studentcommunity.

Tuition

The ICAEW Partner in Learning scheme recognises tuition providers who comply with our core principles of quality course delivery. If you are receiving structured tuition with an ICAEW Partner in Learning, make sure you know how and when you can contact your tutors for extra help. If you are not receiving structured tuition and are interested in classroom, online or residential learning , take a look at our recognised Partner in Learning tuition providers in your area, on our website icaew.com/dashboard.

Faculties and Special Interest Groups

Faculties and special interest groups support and develop members and students in areas of work and industry sectors that are of particular interest.

Our seven faculties provide knowledge, events and essential technical resources. Register to receive a complimentary e-magazine from one faculty of your choice each year throughout your studies.

Our 12 special interest groups provide practical support, information and representation within a range of industry sectors. Register to receive free provisional membership of one group each year throughout your studies.

Find out more about faculties and special interest groups at icaew.com/facultiesandsigs.

Library & Information Service

The Library & Information Service is ICAEW's world-leading accountancy and business library.

The library provides access to thousands of resources online and a document delivery service, you'll be sure to find a useful eBook, relevant article or industry guide to help you. Find out more at icaew.com/library.

Finance Act 2015 update

This summary contains details of the Finance Act 2015, enacted on 26 March 2015. A supplement will be issued with the Question Bank detailing the examinable content of Finance (No. 2) Act. At the time of going to print Finance (No. 2) Act had not been enacted.

This summary also contains details of legislation previously enacted which comes into effect for the tax year 2015/16.

PERSONAL TAX

1 Income tax allowances

The following are the new allowances for 2015/16:

	£
Personal allowance if born after 5 April 1938	10,600
Personal allowance if born before 6 April 1938	10,660
Income limit for personal allowances (if born before 6 April 1938)	27,700

The blind person's allowance for 2015/16 is £2,290.

For married and civil partnership couples, the married couple's allowance is £8,355 if either spouse was born before 6 April 1935 (ie aged 81 or over at 5 April 2016). The married couple's allowance provides a tax reduction at the rate of 10%, so the maximum tax reduction is £835.50.

The income limit for personal allowances for 2015/16 for those born before 6 April 1938 is £27,700. If the individual's adjusted net income exceeds this amount, first the personal allowance is reduced by £1 for every £2 of excess adjusted net income. The personal allowance cannot be reduced below £10,600 (unless it is tapered as a result of having adjusted net income in excess of £100,000 (see below)). If there is any further excess income, a similar reduction is made against the married couple's allowance. The minimum amount of married couple's allowance for 2015/16 is £3,220.

'Adjusted net income' is after deducting trading losses, gross Gift Aid donations and gross personal pension contributions paid by the individual (rather than an employer).

1.1 Tapering of the personal allowance

If an individual's adjusted net income for 2015/16 exceeds £100,000, the personal allowance is reduced by £1 for every £2 excess income. The personal allowance of an individual with adjusted net income of £121,200 in 2015/16 is reduced to £nil. This gives a marginal rate of tax of 60% for adjusted net income between £100,000 and £121,200.

In addition, if the income which takes a taxpayer over £100,000 is *earned* income then national insurance at 2% is also payable, making the marginal rate of tax 62%.

Individuals who earn more than £100,000 pa continue to pay tax plus NI at 42% but for each extra £2 earned, lose £1 of personal allowance for income tax purposes only. So they pay 42% on the extra £2 earned and lose the nil rate of tax on £1, ie extra tax and NI of £0.84 on the £2 of additional income, and extra tax of £0.40 on the £1 no longer receiving a personal allowance for income tax purposes. This gives total extra tax and NI of £1.24 on £2 of income which, as a percentage, is 62%.

Worked example: Tapering of the personal allowance

Josephine, age 35, earns £85,000 a year (salary and benefits). She also receives £16,000 interest from her bank account and UK dividends of £11,700. She makes a donation of £800 to charity via Gift Aid and contributes £500 a month to her personal pension.

Requirement

What personal allowance is she entitled to for 2015/16?

Solution

	£	£
Basic PA		10,600
Less reduction		
Total income £(85,000 + 20,000 + 13,000)	118,000	
Less:		
Gift Aid donation £800 × 100/80	(1,000)	
Personal pension contribution £500 × 12 × 100/80	(7,500)	
Net adjusted income	109,500	
Less limit	(100,000)	
	9,500	
× ½		(4,750)
Personal allowance		5,850

1.2 Marriage allowance

From 2015/16 if a spouse/ civil partner has income below the level of the personal allowance they can elect to transfer unused personal allowance up to £1,060 (ie 10% of the basic personal allowance) to their spouse/ civil partner provided the recipient is a basic rate taxpayer. The marriage allowance is not available where either spouse/ civil partner is entitled to the married couples allowance.

2 Income tax rates and bands

2.1 Starting rate

The starting rate for savings income is reduced to 0% from 2015/16 (previously 10%). The starting rate band is increased significantly to £5,000. This is only available if the individual's non-savings income is below this amount.

2.2 Basic rate

The basic rate of tax is 20% for both non-savings income and savings income.

Dividend income within the basic rate band is taxable at 10%. This liability is covered by the tax credit attaching to the dividend.

The basic rate band limit has been reduced from £31,865 in 2014/15 to £31,785 in 2015/16.

2.3 Higher rate

Between £31,785 and £150,000, the higher rate of tax is 40% for non-savings and saving income.

The higher rate for dividend income is 32.5%. The effective tax rate for higher rate taxpayers is 25% of the amount actually received (ie the cash dividend).

2.4 Additional rate

In 2015/16 for taxable income exceeding £150,000, dividends are taxable at the 'additional dividend rate' of 37.5%, while other income is taxable at the 'additional rate' of 45%. This gives an effective tax rate on dividends for additional rate taxpayers of 30.56%.

Worked example: Additional rate band

During 2015/16 Andrea earns a salary of £170,000 and receives bank interest of £30,000 and dividend income of £18,000.

Requirement

What is Andrea's income tax payable for 2015/16?

Solution

Andrea's tax payable is:

	Non-savings £	Savings £	Dividends £
Employment income	170,000		
Bank interest £30,000 × 100/80		37,500	
Dividends £18,000 × 100/90			20,000
Less personal allowance*	(Nil)		
Taxable income	170,000	37,500	20,000
Tax liability			
£31,785 @ 20%	6,357		
£(150,000 – 31,785) = £118,215 @ 40%	47,286		
£(170,000 – 150,000) = £20,000 @ 45%	9,000		
£37,500 @ 45%	16,875		
£20,000 @ 37.5%	7,500		
Tax liability	87,018		
Less tax deducted at source:			
Dividend tax credit	(2,000)		
Interest	(7,500)		
Tax payable	77,518		

*Note Andrea's personal allowance is reduced to £nil as her net adjusted income is above £121,200. The net tax payable on the dividend is £5,500, which is 30.56% of the £18,000 cash dividend received.

2.5 Application of tax rate bands

There is no change to the order in which different types of income are taxed. Income is still taxed in the order of non-savings income, savings income then dividend income. However, remember that if an individual's non-savings income exceeds the starting rate limit, the starting rate for savings will not be available for savings income.

Worked example: Application of tax rate bands

James is 49. In 2014/15 he earns a salary of £850 from a part time job and receives bank interest of £6,400 and dividends of £166,500.

Requirement

What is James's income tax liability for 2015/16?

Solution

	Non-savings income	Savings income	Dividends	Total
	£	£	£	£
Employment income	850			850
Bank interest £6,400 × 100/80		8,000		8,000
Dividends £166,500 × 100/90			185,000	185,000
Net income	850	8,000	185,000	193,850
Less personal allowance (net income >£121,200)	(Nil)			(Nil)
Taxable income	850	8,000	185,000	193,850

Tax liability	£
£850 × 20%	170
£(5,000 – 850) = £4,150 × 0%	–
£(8,000 – 4,150) = £3,850 × 20%	770
£(31,785 – 8,000 – 850) = £22,935 × 10%	2,294
£(150,000 – 31,785) = £118,215 × 32.5%	38,420
£(185,000 – 22,935 – 118,215) = £43,850 × 37.5%	16,444
Tax liability	58,098

3 Savings and investments

3.1 Individual Savings Accounts (ISAs)

From 6 April 2015 the maximum amount that an individual can save in an ISA increases from £15,000 to £15,240. The investment can be in cash and cash like equity products and/ or stocks, shares and insurance products, split in any proportion. However, an individual can pay into a maximum of one cash ISA and one stocks and shares ISA each year.

If an individual dies on/after 3 December 2014 a tax-free amount up to the value held in their ISA at death can be added to their surviving spouse's/civil partner's ISA - in addition to that spouse's own ISA allowance.

3.2 Junior ISAs

The maximum amount that can be paid into a JISA or a CTF each year increases from £4,000 to £4,080 from 6 April 2015.

3.3 'Help to buy ISAs'

From Autumn 2015 a 'Help to Buy ISA' is available to help first time buyers save for a new home. Individuals can save up to £12,000 and receive a 25% bonus when the home is purchased. Accounts will be limited to one per person rather than one per property, so those buying together can each receive a bonus.

3.4 Venture capital schemes

3.4.1 Excluded activities

From 6 April 2015 companies generating electricity from renewable sources carry on excluded activities for venture capital purposes.

3.4.2 Entrepreneurs' relief on deferred gains

An individual can claim entrepreneurs' relief on a gain which has been deferred under the EIS rules, when the gain eventually becomes chargeable.

Entrepreneurs' relief is available on the deferred gain if it qualified for the relief at the time of the original disposal, the original disposal took place on/ after 3 December 2014 and the claim is made within one year of the 31 January following the tax year that the original gain accrued.

4 Employment income

4.1 Company cars and vans

4.1.1 2015/16

- Cars that emit between 0 and 50g/km of CO_2 have a taxable benefit percentage of 5%.

- Cars that emit between 51 and 75g/km of CO_2 have a taxable benefit percentage of 9%.

- Cars that emit between 76 and 94g/km of CO_2 have a taxable benefit percentage of 13%.

- The basic car and fuel benefit percentage is 14% for cars with emissions between 95g/km and 210g/km, with a 1% increase for every 5g/km in excess of 95g/km. The maximum has increases to 37%.

- From 6 April 2015 the car fuel benefit charge is based on an increased figure of £22,100 (£21,700 in 2014/15).

To summarise, the car benefit percentages for petrol cars applicable for 2015/16 are as follows:

Emissions	Car benefit percentage
0 – 50g/km	5%
51 – 75g/km	9%
76 – 94g/km	13%
95 – 209g/km	14% + 1% for every 5g/km in excess of 95g/km
210g/km or more	37%

Worked example: Changes in company car rules in 2015/16

John is provided with a fuel efficient Renault Clio by his employer for the 2015/16 tax year. The car has a list price of £19,600 and a CO_2 emissions figure of 84g/km. His employer pays for all private petrol.

Jo's company car during 2015/16 is a 1 Series BMW which has a list price of £24,670 and CO_2 emissions of 150g/km. Her employer also pays for all of her private petrol.

Both John and Jo are higher rate taxpayers.

Requirement

What is the additional tax payable by John and Jo in 2015/16 compared to 2014/15?

Solution

	2015/16		2014/15		Extra tax in 2015/16
	Car	Fuel	Car	Fuel	@ 40%
John	£19,600 × 13% = **£2,548**	£22,100 × 13% = **£2,873**	£19,600 × 11% = **£2,156**	£21,700 × 11% = **£2,387**	**£351**
Jo	£24,670 × 25%* = **£6,168**	£22,100 × 25% = **£5,525**	£24,670 × 23%** = **£5,674**	£21,700 × 23% = **£4,991**	**£411**

$* \left(\frac{150-95}{5} = 11\% + 14\% \right)$ $** \left(\frac{150-95}{5} = 11\% + 12\% \right)$

4.1.2 2016/17 and later years

From 6 April 2016 the basic car and fuel benefit percentage increases from 5% to 7% for cars emitting 50g/km or below, from 9% to 11% for cars emitting between 51 and 75g/km and 13% to 15% for cars emitting between 76 and 94g/km. In addition the 3% diesel supplement will be removed from that date.

4.1.3 Company vans

The van benefit charge increases from £3,090 to £3,150 for 2015/16.

The van fuel benefit charge also increases from £581 to £594.

The exemption for zero emission vans is removed from 2015/16. If there is insignificant private use the benefit is nil, otherwise it is

$$\text{appropriate percentage} \times \text{cash equivalent}$$

For 2015/16 the appropriate percentage is 20% (40% 2016/17; 60% 2017/18; 80% 2018/19; 90% 2019/20), and the cash equivalent is £3,150.

4.2 Official rate of interest

The official rate of interest which applies, for example, when calculating the taxable benefit of a low interest loan from an employer, reduces to 3.00% (from 3.25%) for 2015/16.

4.3 Other benefits issues

4.3.1 Abolition of £8,500 threshold

From 6 April 2016 the £8,500 limit for benefits will be abolished. From that point all employees will be subject to tax and national insurance contributions on their benefits and expenses in the same way.

4.3.2 Exemption for reimbursed deductible expenses

Currently if an employer pays or reimburses deductible expenses and benefits (eg professional subscriptions) they either apply for a dispensation or must include the expense on the employee's P11D. In the latter case the employee then claims a deduction via the tax return. From 2016/17 such expenses are exempt, thus simplifying the administration of such benefits and expenses.

4.3.3 Real time collection of tax on benefits

From 2016/17 there will be an option for employers to deal with certain benefits, such as cars, medical insurance and gym membership, via the payroll rather than by completion of a P11D after the year end.

5 Pension schemes – drawing a pension

From 6 April 2015, individuals are able to draw their pensions however they wish once they reach the requisite age. This may include drawing the whole amount as a lump sum, or drawing the tax free amount as a lump sum and then buying an annuity (a regularly, usually monthly, income for life) or buying a flexible income drawdown product.

In practice, the receipt of pension benefits under the new rules is complex, but in simplistic terms the following tax treatment applies. Apart from the tax free lump sum of up to 25% all other income taken from the pension is taxed as non-savings income at the individual's marginal rate of tax. Therefore, drawing the whole amount as a lump sum in one tax year may give rise to a large income tax liability if the taxpayer's income then extends beyond the basic or higher rate limits.

6 National insurance contributions

6.1 Class 1

For 2015/16 the Class 1 primary rate paid by employees remains at 12% and the additional rate above the upper earnings limit remains at 2%.

The Class 1 secondary rate paid by employers remains 13.8%.

The lower earnings limit increases to £112 per week (£486 per month) and the upper earnings limit increases to £815 per week (£3,532 per month) and the upper accruals point remains at £770 per week (£3,337 per month).

The primary earnings threshold (for employees) has been increased for 2015/16 to £155 per week (£672 per month), and the and secondary earnings threshold (for employers) to £156 per week (£676 per month). Both were £153 in 2014/15.

From 2015/16 employers only need to pay class 1 secondary contributions in respect of employees aged under 21 if their earnings exceed the upper secondary threshold of £815 per week (£3,532 per month).

Worked example: Primary & secondary Class 1 NIC

An employer has the following four employees:

1. Employee 1: £70 per week
2. Employee 2: £455 per week
3. Employee 3: £500 per week
4. Employee 4: £1,000 per week

Requirement

Calculate the weekly primary and secondary Class 1 NIC due in 2015/16 and 2014/15 for the above non contracted out employees. All employees are over 21 years old except employee 3 who is 19 years old.

Solution

Employee contributions

	2015/16		2014/15	
EE 1:	£Nil (below PT)		£Nil (below PT)	
EE 2:	£(455 – 155) × 12% =	**£36.00**	£(455 – 153) × 12% =	**£36.24**
EE 3:	£(500 – 155) × 12% =	**£41.40**	£(500 – 153) × 12% =	**£41.64**
EE 4:	£(815 – 155) × 12% =	£79.20	£(805 – 153) × 12% =	£78.24
	£(1,000 – 815) × 2% =	£3.70	£(1,000 – 805) × 2% =	£3.90
		£82.90		**£82.14**

Employer contributions

	2015/16		2014/15	
EE 1:	£Nil (below ST)		£Nil (below ST)	
EE 2:	£(455 – 156) × 13.8% =	**£41.26**	£(455 – 153) × 13.8% =	**£41.68**
EE 3:	£Nil (below £815 UST for under 21s)		£(500 – 153) × 13.8% =	**£47.89**
EE 4:	£(1,000 – 156) × 13.8% = **£116.47**		£(1,000 – 153) × 13.8% =	**£116.89**

6.2 Class 1A and 1B

Only employers pay Class 1A NICs (on employees' taxable benefits) and Class 1B (on amounts included in PAYE Settlement Agreements (PSAs)). The rates for both remain at 13.8% for 2015/16.

6.3 Class 2

For 2015/16, the equivalent weekly contribution increases to £2.80.

A small earnings exception applies where **accounting** profits are below £5,965.

The method of paying class 2 contributions is changing. In 2015/16 the class 2 contributions are paid with the self-assessment balancing payment for the year ie by 31 January 2017.

6.4 Class 3

For 2015/16, voluntary Class 3 contributions increase to £14.10 per week.

6.5 Class 4

For 2015/16, the annual lower profits limit increases to £8,060 and the annual upper profits limit rises to £42,385.

The rates of Class 4 NICs remain at 9% between the lower and upper limits and 2% above the upper limit.

Worked example: Class 4 NIC

Simon is self employed and has taxable profits of £75,000 for 2015/16.

Requirement

Calculate Simon's total NIC liability for the year.

Solution

	£	£
Class 2		
£2.80 × 52		146
Class 4		
£(42,385 – 8,060) @ 9%	3,089	
£(75,000 – 42,385) @ 2%	652	
		3,741
Total NICs		3,887

6.6 NIC employment allowance

For 2015/16 any business that pays Class 1 NICs on its employees' or directors' earnings can again claim the £2,000 'employment allowance' as part of the normal payroll process under Real Time Information (RTI).

The claim reduces the employer Class 1 NICs due, as they arise during the tax year, by the lower of:

- The employer Class 1 NICs due, and
- Maximum of £2,000 per year.

CAPITAL GAINS TAX

1 Annual exempt amount

The annual exempt amount (AEA) increases from £11,000 to £11,100 in 2015/16. The amount available to trusts is £5,550.

2 CGT rates

For 2015/16 the CGT rates remain unchanged. An individual's capital gains falling within the basic rate band (if there is any remaining after taking the individual's taxable income into account) are taxed at 18%, while gains falling in the higher rate band or additional rate band are taxed at 28%.

However, if a disposal by an individual qualifies for entrepreneurs' relief (see below), the gains are taxed at 10%.

Taxpayers may deduct capital losses and the AEA in a way that minimises their CGT liability (although see below for interaction with entrepreneurs' relief).

Worked example: CGT rates for 2015/16

Amos has taxable income of £27,000 in 2015/16.

He realises a gain on the sale of an asset in January 2016 of £28,000, which does not qualify for entrepreneurs' relief. Amos has no capital losses in 2015/16.

Requirement

What is Amos's CGT liability?

Solution

	£	£
£(28,000 – 11,100) = £16,900		
£(31,785 – £27,000) = £4,785 @ 18%	861	
£(16,900 – £4,785) = £12,115 @ 28%	3,392	
Total CGT		4,253

Individuals who claim to use the remittance basis and are required to pay the remittance basis charge are usually taxed at a flat rate of 28%.

3 Entrepreneurs' relief

3.1 Rates and limits

There are no changes to the entrepreneurs' relief rates and limits in 2015/16. Where individuals or trustees make qualifying gains on or after 6 April 2011, the lifetime limit for entrepreneurs' relief is £10 million. This gives a potential total lifetime tax saving of £1.8 million.

If an individual or trustee made a qualifying disposal in excess of the previous limits before 6 April 2011, no additional relief is available for any excess gain above the old limit(s). However, if the individual or trustee makes further qualifying gains on or after 6 April 2011, he can claim relief on up to £10 million in total.

When establishing an individual's CGT rate(s), gains qualifying for entrepreneurs' relief are set against any unused basic rate band before non qualifying gains.

Current and historic limits are as follows:

Date	Lifetime limit
6 April 2011 – present	£10 million
23 June 2010 – 5 April 2011	£5 million
6 April 2010 – 22 June 2010	£2 million
6 April 2008 – 5 April 2010	£1 million

3.2 Entrepreneurs' relief on deferred gains

As mentioned above, entrepreneurs' relief is available on gains deferred due to EIS where the original disposal was of a qualifying asset on/after 3 December 2014.

3.3 Denying entrepreneurs' relief on disposals of goodwill

With effect from 3 December 2014, when a sole trader or a member of a partnership transfers their business to a close company, of which they are a 'related party', then internally-generated goodwill is not eligible for entrepreneurs' relief. This is aimed to remove the unfair advantage afforded to a person who set up an unincorporated business compared to one who originally set up as a company.

However it can be claimed by a retiring partner in a firm who does not hold any stake in the successor company.

3.4 Associated disposals

The conditions for an asset to be an associated disposal are:

- The individual is disposing of the whole or part of his interest in a partnership, or the disposal of shares in a company (ie there is a material disposal);

- The disposal is made as part of the individual's withdrawal from the business of the partnership or company; and

- The assets being sold have been used for the purpose of the business for one year prior to the date of the material disposal of business assets or the cessation of the business of the partnership or company.

From 18 March 2015 'material', for the first of these conditions is defined as at least a 5% shareholding or at least a 5% share in the assets of the partnership.

4 Valuation of quoted shares

From 6 April 2015 the valuation of quoted shares and securities for capital gains tax purposes is changed to a 'half-up' basis ie at the end of the date of disposal the lower of the two prices on the stock exchange daily official list plus half of the difference between the two prices.

Note, the valuation of quoted shares and securities for inheritance tax purposes remains at the lower of quarter-up and mid bargain.

INHERITANCE TAX

1 Nil rate band

As previously announced, the nil rate band will remain frozen at £325,000 until 2017/18.

2 Exemptions – decorations and medals

From 3 December 2014 the exemption for awards is extended to include those received by any member of the armed services from overseas.

PERSONAL TAX – OVERSEAS MATTERS

1 Remittance basis for overseas earnings

From 2015/16, the remittance basis charge (RBC) remains at £30,000 where an individual has been UK resident for seven out of the last nine years, but has increased from £50,000 to £60,000 for those resident for 12 of the last 14 years. In addition there is a new RBC of £90,000 for an individual who has been resident for 17 out of the last 20 years.

2 Non-UK residents and UK residential property

From 6 April 2015 a capital gains tax charge arises on the disposal of UK residential property by non-UK resident persons. This applies to non-UK resident:

- individuals (plus the personal representatives of a non-UK resident individual)
- trusts, and
- companies controlled by five or fewer persons.

The taxable gain is that part of the gain arising after 5 April 2015, based on the market value at that date. Alternatively an election can be made for the total gain over the whole period of ownership to be time apportioned and only the post 5 April 2015 gain charged to tax. The rate of capital gains tax applying to a non-UK resident company in 2015/16 is 20%.

The gain may be subject to principal private relief if qualifying conditions are met. These broadly require the non-UK resident individual to spend a minimum of 90 nights in the property over the year.

This also applies to disposals in the overseas part of a split year.

BUSINESS TAX

1 Capital allowances for plant and machinery

1.1 The annual investment allowance

The annual investment allowance (AIA) is £200,000 per 12 month period for expenditure from 1 January 2016 (as amended by the Summer budget). This follows the temporary increase to £500,000 from 6 April 2014 (1 April 2014 for companies) until 31 December 2015.

Levels of AIA which are examinable in 2016 are:

Dates	AIA
6 April 2010 – 5 April 2012 (1 April 2010 – 31 March 2012 for companies)	£100,000 pa
6 April – 31 December 2012 (1 April – 31 December 2012 for companies)	£25,000 pa
1 January 2013 – 31 March 2014	£250,000 pa
1 April 2014 – 31 December 2015	£500,000 pa
From 1 January 2016	£200,000 pa

Where an accounting period straddles a date on which the limit changes, the maximum AIA is calculated using the pro rated amounts for each part of the accounting period. However the maximum which can be claimed in respect of expenditure incurred after 31 December 2015 is $n/12 \times £200,000$, where 'n' is the number of months in the accounting period after 31 December 2015. The AIA was £500,000 per annum prior to 1 January 2016 so for a nine month period of account ending on 31 March 2016, the maximum AIA that could be allocated to expenditure incurred in March 2016 would be £50,000.

Worked example: AIA where AP straddles 31 December 2015

Nigel prepares accounts for the year to 31 March 2016. In June 2015 he acquired machinery for £320,000 and in February 2016, he acquired machinery for £105,000.

What is the maximum annual investment allowance available to Nigel for the year ended 31 March 2016, how is it allocated to the acquisitions made in the year, and what is the balance of expenditure (if any) eligible for writing down allowance?

Solution

The AIA must be time apportioned around 31 December 2015.

	£
Period 1.4.15 to 31.12.15: 9/12 × £500,000	375,000
Period 1.1.16 to 31.3.16: 3/12 × £200,000	50,000
Maximum AIA for year ended 31.12.14	425,000
Acquisition – June 2015	320,000
Less AIA (maximum £425,000 – no other restriction)	(320,000)
Balance transferred to main pool	–
Acquisition – February 2016	105,000
Less AIA (not exceeding £50,000)	(50,000)
Balance eligible for WDA (transferred to main pool)	55,000

1.2 First year allowances

The 100% first year allowance for new low CO_2 emission and electrically propelled cars has been extended to 31 March 2018.

From April 2015 the emissions threshold below which vehicles are eligible for the FYA is reduced from 95g/km to 75g/km.

1.3 Interaction of capital allowances

Consideration must be given to the most efficient way of using the AIA available. Certain expenditure may qualify for more than one type of allowance.

The AIA gives relief for 100% of the expenditure in the year of acquisition but is limited to a maximum annual amount of £200,000 (£500,000 prior to January 2016) which is lost if it is not claimed in full. In order to maximise the allowances available the AIA should be allocated against assets in the following order:

(1) Assets which would otherwise only qualify for WDA at 8% (special rate expenditure)
(2) Assets which would otherwise only qualify for WDA at 18%.

Worked example: Comprehensive capital allowances computation

Cactus Ltd has TWDVs b/f on 1 January 2015 as follows:

Main pool – £324,400
Special rate pool – £127,500

During its accounting period for the three months ended 31 March 2015, Cactus Ltd made the following acquisitions and disposals:

- Items relating to the special rate pool – £88,000 (purchased 04.01.15)
- Plant and machinery which is qualifying energy saving technology – £6,000 (purchased 01.02.15)
- Plant and machinery – £49,000 (purchased 01.03.15)

In its year ended 31 March 2016, Cactus Ltd made the following acquisitions and disposals:

- Computer equipment – £272,000 (purchased 01.05.15)
- Office equipment – £75,750 (purchased 01.02.16)
- Car with CO_2 emissions of 120g/km – £26,000
- Car with CO_2 emissions of 73g/km – £14,000
- Car with CO_2 emissions of 180g/km – £38,000

Requirement

Calculate Cactus Ltd's maximum entitlement to capital allowances for each accounting period.

Solution

AIA

Three months ended 31 March 2015

Cactus Ltd is entitled to an AIA for its three month period ended 31 March 2015 of £500,000 × 3/12 = £125,000.

The AIA should always be offset against the special rate pool in priority to the main pool. The first £88,000 of the AIA should therefore be set against the £88,000 special rate pool expenditure. The energy saving technology is eligible for a first year allowance of 100% and therefore should receive no AIA. The remaining £37,000 should therefore be set against the £49,000 of main pool expenditure incurred on 1 March 2015.

Year ended 31 March 2016

Cactus Ltd is entitled to an AIA for its year ended 31 March 2016 of:

1 April 2015 – 31 December 2015:	£500,000 × 9/12	=	£375,000
1 January 2016 – 31 March 2016:	£200,000 × 3/12	=	£ 50,000
Total AIA for the year			£425,000

Cars are not eligible for the AIA. A maximum of £425,000 (being the pro rata amount of the AIA) may be offset against expenditure incurred prior to 31 December 2015. A maximum of £50,000 may be offset against expenditure incurred on or after 1 January 2016. Therefore the maximum AIA which can be claimed is £272,000 on the expenditure incurred on 1 May 2015 of £272,000 and £50,000 on the expenditure incurred on 1 February 2016, giving a total AIA claimed of £322,000 despite actual expenditure on qualifying main pool assets being £347,750.

The total capital allowances available to Cactus Ltd for each accounting period will be as follows:

	Main pool £	Special rate pool £	Total allowances £
3m to 31 March 2015			
Bal b/f	324,400	127,500	
Main pool eligible for ECA	6,000		
ECA @ 100% (Note)	(6,000)		6,000
Eligible for AIA			
– Special rate pool		88,000	
– Main pool not eligible for ECA	49,000		
AIA	(37,000)	(88,000)	125,000
	336,400	127,500	
WDA 18% × 3/12 / 8% × 3/12	(15,138)	(2,550)	17,688
WDV c/f	321,262	124,950	
			148,688
Year to 31 March 2016			
Additions eligible for FYA @ 100%	14,000		
New low emission car	(14,000)		14,000
Eligible for AIA – computer equipment	272,000		
AIA (Max £425,000)	(272,000)		272,000
Eligible for AIA – office equipment	75,750		
AIA (Max £50,000)	(50,000)		50,000
Additions not eligible for AIA – cars	26,000	38,000	
	373,012	162,950	
WDA 18% / 8%	(67,142)	(13,036)	80,178
WDV c/f	305,870	149,914	
			416,178

Note

In the three months to 31 March 2015 the AIA and the WDA are prorated, but the ECA is not.

CORPORATION TAX AND DIVERTED PROFITS TAX

1 Corporation tax rates

The following table summarises the corporation tax rates for the current and previous financial years, which you may need for computational purposes or for tax planning questions:

Financial year	Main rate	Small profits rate	Standard fraction	Marginal rate
2015	20%	N/A	N/A	N/A
2014	21%	20%	1/400	21.25%
2013	23%	20%	3/400	23.75%
2012	24%	20%	1/100	25.00%
2011	26%	20%	3/200	27.50%
2010	28%	21%	7/400	29.75%
2009	28%	21%	7/400	29.75%

From 1 April 2015 all corporation tax profits are taxed at the main rate of 20%, irrespective of the size of company.

Worked example: Corporation tax rates

Enjo Ltd has a year end of 31 December 2015. Calculate the company's corporation tax liability assuming it has no FII and its taxable total profits are:

(a) £230,000

(b) £600,000

(c) £2.3 million

Solution

For FY 2014 the upper and lower corporation tax limits are £1.5 million and £300,000 respectively.

(a) Enjo Ltd is a small profits company in FY 2014 and its tax liability is calculated as follows:

	£
FY 2014: £230,000 × 3/12 × 20%	11,500
FY 2015: £230,000 × 9/12 × 20%	34,500
CT liability	46,000

As there is no change in the rate of tax charged this can be calculated as:

	£
£230,000 × 20%	46,000

(b) Enjo Ltd is a marginal relief company in FY 2014 and its tax liability is calculated as follows:

	£
FY 2014: £600,000 × 3/12 × 21%	31,500
Less: 1/400 × £(1,500,000 – 600,000) × 3/12	(563)
FY 2015: £600,000 × 9/12 × 20%	90,000
CT liability	120,937

(c) Enjo Ltd is a main rate company and its tax liability is calculated as follows:

	£
FY 2014: £2.3m × 3/12 × 21%	120,750
FY 2015: £2.3m × 9/12 × 20%	345,000
CT liability	465,750

When determining the optimum use of losses, companies should consider that a prior year claim to FY 2014 where relief will be at the marginal rate (21.25%) or the main rate (21%) will give more relief than a current year claim in FY 2015 at the unified main rate (20%).

Worked example: Corporation tax rates and use of losses

XY Ltd owns 100% of Z Ltd. XY Ltd's recent results are as follows:

	Y/e 31.3.15 £	Y/e 31.3.16 £
Trading profits	500,000	Nil
Other income and gains	200,000	20,000
Taxable total profits	700,000	20,000

XY Ltd has a tax adjusted trading loss for the year ended 31 March 2016 of £600,000.

Z Ltd's recent results are as follows:

	Y/e 31.3.15 £	Y/e 31.3.16 £
Trading profits	1,800,000	640,000
Other income and gains	200,000	200,000
Taxable total profits	2,000,000	840,000

Requirement

Explain the optimum use of XY Ltd's losses.

Solution

For FY 2014 the upper and lower corporation tax limits are £750,000 and £150,000 respectively (as there are two associated companies). The two companies pay corporation tax at the following rates for each accounting period:

	XY Ltd		Z Ltd	
	Y/e 31.3.15	Y/e 31.3.16	Y/e 31.3.15	Y/e 31.3.16
	£	£	£	£
Trading profits	500,000	Nil	1,800,000	640,000
Other income and gains	200,000	20,000	200,000	200,000
Taxable total profits	700,000	20,000	2,000,000	840,000
FY	FY 2014	FY 2015	FY 2014	FY 2015
CT rate	21.25% then 20%	20%	N/A	20%

The optimum use of the loss would be to carry back as much as possible to the prior year such that XY Ltd's taxable total profits are reduced to the adjusted lower limit of £150,000. However, a company may not make a carry back claim until it has made a current year claim.

Once £550,000 of losses are offset in XY Ltd's prior year, tax will then only be saved at 20%. The balance of £30,000 of losses can then either be surrendered to Z Ltd or relieved in XY Ltd in the year ended 31 March 2015. Group relief can only be offset against profits arising in a corresponding accounting period and therefore cannot be carried back to Z Ltd's profits for the year ended 31 March 2015 even though this would save tax at a higher rate.

Assume that a decision is made to relieve some losses in Z Ltd (although this produces the same amount of tax relief as a carry back claim). As a current year/prior year claim is all or nothing, to prevent the whole loss from being offset against XY Ltd's prior year profits, a group relief claim should be made first. Therefore £30,000 can be offset against Z Ltd's profits for the year ending 31 March 2016, then £20,000 of the loss should be offset in XY Ltd against its current year profits, and finally £550,000 of the loss should be offset against its profits in the prior year. The total tax saved is:

	£
£30,000 @ 20% =	6,000
£20,000 @ 20% =	4,000
£550,000 @ 21.25% =	116,875
Total tax saved is	126,875

This saves more tax than a surrender of the whole loss to Z Ltd which would have saved tax at just 20%.

2 Research and development

2.1 Consumable materials

From 1 April 2015 relief for consumable materials is restricted if the consumable is incorporated into an item which becomes part of normal production. For the purposes of the exam it is assumed that all consumables are qualifying expenditure, unless stated otherwise.

2.2 Additional deduction for SMEs

The rate of additional deduction for small to medium sized enterprises (SME's) has increased to 130%, up from 125%, resulting in a total deduction of 230% of qualifying expenditure. This rate applies to qualifying expenditure incurred on or after 1 April 2015.

2.3 Above the line R&D tax credits for large companies

The amount of the above the line credit for large companies has increased from 10% to 11% for expenditure incurred on/ after 1 April 2015.

3 Intangible fixed assets

A package of measures to act as a disincentive to incorporate for tax purposes have been taken to align the treatment of incorporated businesses with those that do not incorporate, or those that initially set up as a company.

One of these measures relates to the treatment of internally-generated goodwill on incorporation. Neither the unincorporated business nor that initially set up as a company can get relief for internally-generated goodwill, whereas relief has been available after incorporation.

For incorporations on or after 3 December 2014 relief is generally restricted to nil for internally-generated goodwill where there is continuing economic ownership (eg on incorporation).

4 Diverted profits tax (DPT)

4.1 Relevant scenarios

'Google tax' or DPT is introduced, from 1 April 2015, to tackle artificial/ contrived arrangements. DPT was developed in response to a number of high profile multinational entities who have avoided UK tax.

DPT applies in either of the following situations, unless both parties are SMEs:

- Arrangements avoiding a UK permanent establishment (PE).
  A person ('the avoided PE') is carrying on activity in the UK in connection with supplies of goods and services by a non-UK resident company to customers in the UK, and the detailed conditions are met ('the first rule'); or

- Transactions with a 'lack of economic substance'.
  Where a company which is taxable in the UK creates a tax advantage using certain arrangements which lack economic substance, and the detailed conditions are met ('the second rule').

The DPT is calculated as 25% of 'taxable diverted profits'.

4.2 Arrangements avoiding a UK PE

This rule applies where all of the following conditions are met:

- There is a non-UK resident company carrying on a trade;
- A person ('the avoided PE') is carrying on an activity in the UK in connection with supplies of services, goods or other property by the non-UK resident company;
- It is 'reasonable to assume' that the activity of the avoided PE is designed to ensure the non-UK resident company does not carry on a trade in the UK for corporation tax purposes; and
- The 'mismatch condition' or the 'tax avoidance condition' is met.

The 'mismatch condition' broadly means that as a result of an increase in expenses the reduction in tax by one connected party is significantly larger than the increase in liability of the other connected party, and the arrangement was designed for tax purposes.

The 'tax avoidance' condition applies if the arrangements are in place with a main purpose of avoiding/ reducing the charge to corporation tax.

4.3 Transactions with a 'lack of economic substance'

This rule applies where all of the following conditions are met:

- There is a UK resident company or a UK PE of a non-UK resident company carrying on a trade;

- The company has an arrangement by way of a transaction or series of transactions with another person;

- The two parties are connected (defined as for transfer pricing);

- The 'mismatch condition' is met.

The other party to the arrangements will usually be a non-UK resident person although it equally applies if they are UK resident.

VALUE ADDED TAX

1 Registration and deregistration limits

The following changes have been made:

- The registration limit from 1 April 2015 is £82,000.

- The deregistration limit from 1 April 2015 is £80,000.

- The registration and deregistration threshold for relevant acquisitions from other EU Member States from 1 April 2015 is £82,000.

2 Changes in VAT rate

The standard rate of VAT has fluctuated over the past few years:

- 1 April 1991 to 30 November 2008   17.5%
- 1 December 2008 to 31 December 2009   15%
- 1 January 2010 to 3 January 2011   17.5%
- 4 January 2011   20%

For the purposes of the exams you should use the correct rate of VAT based on the date of the transaction.

STAMP TAXES

1 Stamp duty land tax (SDLT)

The rates of SDLT for residential property changed on 4 December 2014.

Stamp duty land tax on the purchase price, lease premium or transfer value is calculated as a percentage of chargeable consideration according to the following table:

%	Residential	%	Non-residential
0	£Nil – £125,000	0	£Nil – £150,000[2]
2[1]	£125,001 – £250,000	1	£150,001 – £250,000
5[1]	£250,001 – £925,000	3	£250,001 – £500,000
10[1]	£925,001 – £1,500,000	4	£500,001 or more
12[1]	£1,500,001 and over		

Note:

1   Prior to 4 December 2014 the rates and limits for residential property were as for non- residential property, except that the first threshold was £125,000 (rather than £150,000) and additional rates of 5% and 7% applied to residential property in excess of £1m and £2m respectively.

Prior to 4 December 2014 once the rate of SDLT was determined, the rate then applied to the whole of the consideration, not just the amount over the relevant threshold.

From 4 December 2014 there is no change for non-residential property. However for residential property SDLT applies to consideration at the relevant rate for each threshold.

From 1 April 2015 SDLT is replaced by Land and Buildings Transaction Tax (LBTT) in Scotland. This will not be tested in the Business Planning: Taxation exam.

HIGH VALUE DWELLINGS OWNED BY COMPANIES

1 Annual tax on enveloped dwellings (ATED)

The annual rates of tax that apply to high value residential properties physically located in the UK and owned by a company (or certain other corporate entities such as unit trusts, or partnerships which have corporate entities as partners) have increased as follows:

Property value	2015/16 £	2014/15 £
More than £1 million up to £2 million	7,000	N/A
More than £2 million up to £5 million	23,350	15,400
More than £5 million up to £10 million	54,450	35,900
More than £10 million up to £20 million	109,050	71,850
More than £20 million	218,200	143,750

A further charge of £3,500 will be introduced from 1 April 2016 for properties valued at more than £500,000 and up to £1,000,000.

2 Capital gains tax charge on ATED-related gains

From 6 April 2015, the threshold for the 28% capital gains tax charge on the disposal of high value dwellings that are subject to ATED (s.2B TCGA 1992) has been reduced to include properties valued at more than £1,000,000 (previously £2,000,000).

The charge will be further extended to properties valued at more than £500,000 from 6 April 2016.

TAX ADMINISTRATION

1 Tax avoidance schemes

1.1 Accelerated payment notice

Finance Act 2014 introduced accelerated payment notices, ie where arrangements disclosed under the DOTAS rules are in dispute, any tax potentially due if the scheme is rejected by HMRC may have to be paid up front by the taxpayer, who can claim it back if he is ultimately successful.

Finance Act 2015 adds an additional situation where an accelerated payment notice can be issued. This is where a company utilises a tax advantage from an arrangement and then surrenders all or part of this as group relief (having the effect of the advantage not having been surrendered).

1.2 HMRC information powers

In addition to HMRC being able to require an introducer to identify any person who provided them with information relating to the scheme, they now may also be required to identify any person with whom they have made any marketing contact in relation to the scheme.

1.3 Confidentiality

Protection for persons wishing voluntarily to provide information to HMRC concerning failures to comply with DOTAS has been introduced.
This action will not be a breach of the duty of confidentiality or any other restriction on disclosure. This provision extends to accountants and tax advisers in relation to their clients.

1.4 User penalties

From 26 March 2015, where a scheme user fails to report a SRN to HMRC the penalties have been increased to:

- £5,000 per scheme (previously £100) - ie each scheme to which the failure relates) for a first occasion

- £7,500 per scheme (previously £500) on the second occasion within three years - whether or not it relates to the same scheme involved in the previous occasion, and

- £10,000 per scheme (previously £1,000) on the third and subsequent occasions - whether or not the failure relates to schemes involved in a previous occasion

CHAPTER 1

Ethics

Introduction

Examination context

Topic List

Learning objectives

- Give advice which is appropriate, technically correct, and within the law and the ICAEW Code of Ethics ☐

- Identify and communicate ethical and professional issues in giving tax planning advice ☐

- Recognise and explain the relevance, importance and consequences of ethical and legal issues ☐

- Recommend and justify appropriate actions where ethical dilemmas arise in a given scenario ☐

- Design and evaluate appropriate ethical safeguards ☐

- Recognise and advise when a tax-avoidance scheme is notifiable to HMRC and distinguish between avoidance and evasion and explain their consequences ☐

Specific syllabus references for this chapter are 1e, 2e, 3a, 3b, 3c and 3d.

Syllabus links

In Chapter 1 of your Principles of Taxation and Tax Compliance study manuals, which you should review, you learned about ethical, legal and regulatory issues in relation to tax work. This specifically included elements of the IESBA Code of Ethics for Professional Accountants and ICAEW Code of Ethics as well as Professional Conduct in Relation to Taxation and the CCAB anti-money laundering guidance.

In this chapter we extend this knowledge and in particular your skills by giving consideration to more complex scenarios. These require you to identify issues embedded in the information given and to exercise professional scepticism.

The requirement for taxpayers (both individuals and corporations) to disclose their use of tax avoidance schemes is one way to ensure that tax avoidance is highlighted to HMRC. The general anti-abuse rule, and the approach adopted by the courts in relation to certain kinds of tax planning, are also relevant to counteracting tax avoidance by all taxpayers.

Examination context

In the examination candidates may be required to:

- Recognise and explain the relevance, importance and consequences of ethical and legal issues

- Recommend and justify appropriate actions where ethical dilemmas arise in a given scenario design and evaluate appropriate ethical safeguards

- Recognise and advise when a tax-avoidance scheme is notifiable to HMRC and distinguish between avoidance and evasion and their consequences

within the context of taxation; and

- Determine whether a scheme is within the scope of the DOTAS regime

- Explaining the types of advice that could lead to being designated as a promoter for DOTAS purposes, and the regulations in relation to a failure to comply

- Explain the implications of a requirement to disclose a scheme within the DOTAS regime

Where ethical dilemmas arise, candidates will be required to apply the five fundamental principles and guidance in the IESBA and ICAEW codes to recommend and justify appropriate, legal actions.

1   Fundamental principles, threats and safeguards

> ## Section overview
>
> - The IESBA and ICAEW Codes establishes the fundamental principles of professional ethics for accountants. These are integrity, objectivity, professional competence and due care, confidentiality and professional behaviour.
>
> - Professional accountants need to identify, evaluate and respond to threats to compliance with the five fundamental principles. Such threats may be self-interest threats, self-review threats, advocacy threats, familiarity threats or intimidation threats.
>
> - The professional accountant must then seek to apply safeguards to eliminate the threats or reduce them to an acceptable level. If this is impossible, the professional accountant must remove themself from the situation.

1.1   Identifying fundamental principles and threats

Professional accountants have a responsibility to act in the public interest as well as considering their client or employer. Their actions reflect on the accountancy profession as a whole. Increasing public and media focus on taxation bring an increased scrutiny on the trustworthiness of accountants working in taxation.

The Codes require professional accountants to comply with the five fundamental principles. Identifying instances where threats arise to the fundamental principles is necessary if the professional accountant is to handle ethical issues appropriately.

Interactive question 1: Fundamental principles   [Difficulty level: Exam standard]

Jacob, a professional accountant, worked as a financial controller in business. He was asked by a newly appointed director to transfer a substantial sum of money into an off-shore bank account. Jacob asked for an explanation and was told by the director that it was a payment for work done. However the director was not able to provide any supporting documentation. Jacob later received an email instructing that a payment be made and confirming that it related to legitimate expenses. As a result the payment was made but Jacob informed the managing director of his concerns. Shortly afterwards Jacob was made redundant. Three months later an insolvency practitioner was appointed as administrator and contacted Jacob to seek details relating to this transaction.

Requirement

Identify the fundamental principles that Jacob needs to consider prior to any discussion with the administrator and outline any questions needed to establish whether these are threatened.

See **Answer** at the end of this chapter.

1.2   Threats

Professional accountants are obliged to evaluate any threats as soon as they know, or should be expected to know, of their existence.

Both qualitative and quantitative factors should be taken into account in considering the significance of any threat.

1.3   Safeguards

Safeguards that may eliminate or reduce such threats to an acceptable level fall into two broad categories:

- Safeguards created by the profession, legislation or regulation, eg education, continuing professional development requirements, professional monitoring and disciplinary procedures.

- Safeguards in the work environment.

Certain safeguards may increase the likelihood of identifying or deterring unethical behaviour, eg effective, well-publicised complaints systems which enable colleagues, employers and members of the public to draw attention to unprofessional or unethical behaviour, and an explicitly stated duty to report breaches of ethical requirements.

The nature of the safeguards to be applied will vary depending on the circumstances.

A professional accountant may encounter situations in which threats cannot be eliminated or reduced to an acceptable level. In such situations, the professional accountant shall decline or discontinue the specific professional service involved or, when necessary, resign from the engagement or employment.

Worked example: Threats and safeguards   [Difficulty level: Exam standard]

You have just been asked to enter into negotiations to quote for undertaking some tax work for a potential client. The fee that you quote is significantly less than the fee quoted by one of your competitors.

Requirement

Discuss the potential threat to compliance with the fundamental principles arising from the level of fees quoted, and the safeguards to be adopted to reduce the threat.

Solution

There may be a self-interest threat to professional competence and due care if the fee quoted is so low that it is difficult to perform the tax work in accordance with relevant technical and professional standards.

Safeguards to be adopted should include:

* Making the client aware of the terms of the engagement, especially the basis of charging fees and the services covered by those fees.

* Assigning appropriate time and qualified staff to the task.

In addition, to ensure professional behaviour is maintained, care should be taken not to make disparaging references or unsubstantiated comparisons to the competitors who have quoted for the same work.

2 Conflicts of interest

Section overview

* The Code requires a professional accountant to take reasonable steps to avoid, identify and resolve conflicts of interest. Both actual and perceived conflicts must be considered.

* Examples of situations in which a conflict may arise include conflicts between a client's interests and those of the firm, financial involvements between the client and the firm, acting for both a husband and wife in a divorce settlement or a company and for its directors personally or two competing businesses, and secondment to HMRC.

2.1 The threat of a conflict of interest

The fundamental principle of objectivity requires professional accountants to ensure that bias, conflict of interest or undue influence of others do not override professional or business judgements. A professional accountant must take reasonable steps to identify circumstances that could pose a conflict of interest.

A conflict may arise between the firm and the client or between two conflicting clients being managed by the same firm.

2.2 Safeguards

Whatever the circumstances giving rise to the conflict, safeguards should ordinarily include the professional accountant notifying all known relevant parties of the conflict.

Further steps will vary depending on the matter giving rise to the conflict.

Where a conflict of interest poses a threat to one or more of the fundamental principles that cannot be eliminated or reduced to an acceptable level through the application of safeguards, the professional accountant should conclude that it is not appropriate to accept a specific engagement or that resignation from one or more conflicting engagements is required.

3 Ethical conflict resolution

Section overview

- A professional accountant may need to resolve a conflict in applying the fundamental principles.

- When initiating either a formal or informal conflict resolution process, a professional accountant should consider the relevant parties, ethical issues involved, fundamental principles related to the matter in question, established internal procedures and alternative courses of action.

- Having considered the six recommended factors, and followed the suggested steps, if the conflict cannot be resolved the professional accountant should, where possible, refuse to remain associated with the matter creating the conflict.

3.1 Conflict resolution process

If having considered the recommended factors, the matter remains unresolved, the professional accountant should consult with other appropriate persons within the firm for help in obtaining resolution. Where a matter involves a conflict with, or within, an organisation, a professional accountant should also consider consulting with those charged with governance of the organisation such as the board of directors.

It is advisable for the professional accountant to document the issue and details of any discussions held or decisions taken concerning that issue.

If a significant conflict cannot be resolved, a professional accountant may wish to obtain professional advice from the relevant professional body or legal advisors, and thereby obtain guidance on ethical and legal issues without breaching confidentiality.

If, after exhausting all relevant possibilities, the ethical conflict remains unresolved, a professional accountant should, where possible, refuse to remain associated with the matter creating the conflict. The professional accountant may determine that, in the circumstances, it is appropriate to withdraw from the engagement team or specific assignment, or to resign altogether from the engagement or the firm.

Worked example: Factors in ethical conflict resolution [Difficulty level: Exam standard]

You are an ICAEW Chartered Accountant employed by a large accountancy firm but currently on a six-month secondment to a client. You report to a relatively new financial controller named Jo Soames (who has trained in tax but is not an accountant). She has drafted the corporation tax returns of the group of companies, and included the effects of some new measures implemented in the recent Finance Act. She has asked you to look at the tax returns to ascertain whether the new measures proposed work in favour of the group.

Jo has asked the following in an email:

'We need a report to the Board of Directors that shows how these new measures will work, as I previously indicated to the Board that they are likely to be favourable for the group. Are there any particular companies within the group which would benefit? If we focus on these in the report, that would be helpful.

You may not have realised, but I'm not actually particularly knowledgeable about corporation tax – when I joined I exaggerated my knowledge and experience to get the post. I'm therefore hoping you'll write most of the report? – which we can then say we prepared together.'

Requirement

Prepare notes which document any ethical implications for yourself arising from Jo Soames's email and state the actions you should take.

Solution

I will need to consider the following points:

The relevant facts and the ethical issues, the fundamental principles related to the issue, the internal procedures available, alternative courses of action.

The relevant facts and identification of the ethical issue

1   Jo deceived her employer when applying for her post

Jo has confessed to telling an untruth during her interview. The extent of corporation tax knowledge needed in her role may be more than she has, however this is not clear. It is possible that that this was not the deciding factor for her obtaining her post. Therefore in respect of this comment, other than being careful when considering information that Jo provides in the future, there is no ethical conflict for me to resolve.

2   Jo is prepared to take credit for work she has not done

Jo is not a qualified chartered accountant therefore she is not bound by the fundamental principles in the ICAEW code of ethics. However I must consider my own position if I am party to the deception and consider the ICAEW ethical principles as follows:

Objectivity – If I allow Jo to influence me in this matter, I may not be capable of acting objectively in the future.

I am clearly facing a self-interest threat and an intimidation threat since Jo is ultimately my immediate superior and I am on a temporary secondment. Should I not do as she asks, my secondment may be terminated.

3   Jo is looking to complete a report which may not show the true picture

Jo is not a qualified chartered accountant therefore she is not bound by the fundamental principles in the ICAEW code of ethics. However I must consider my own position if I am party to the deception and consider the ICAEW ethical principles as follows:

Integrity – If I allow Jo to influence me and produce a report which does not show the true picture and either omits or conceals facts and conclusions which would result from proper, unbiased reporting on the whole group of companies, this would be a breach of integrity.

This is again a self-interest threat and a possible intimidation threat.

A sensible safeguard to put in place is that I insist on reporting fairly on all group companies . If this was not established at the outset of the secondment, it should be now.

The parties involved

The group could incur extra tax costs and penalties if Jo acts beyond her capability in taxation resulting in badly prepared computations, and/or reports to the board without giving proper and accurate guidance on the implications of the new measures. My employer and I would also be exposed to risk of being associated with work that was of insufficient quality or at worst, untruthful.

The internal procedures available, alternative courses of action

Initially I should inform Jo that I am not prepared to be part of her deception and that she should not put her name to the work I have prepared. I should suggest she seek further training and discuss the issue of her lack of corporate taxation knowledge with her line manager. If she refuses I should seek to identify any internal procedures within the group for reporting my concerns.

I may also speak to my line manager at my employer firm. I should consider carefully whether I wish to continue to work with Jo or whether I ask for the secondment to be cut short.

4 Disclosure of information and confidentiality

Section overview

- A professional accountant has a duty to respect the confidentiality of information acquired as a result of professional and business relationships.

- In limited circumstances, a professional accountant may disclose client information to third parties without the client's permission.

4.1 When to disclose

A professional accountant may disclose confidential information if:

- Disclosure is permitted by law and is authorised by the client or the employer.

- Disclosure is required by law, for example:

  - Production of documents or other provision of evidence in the course of legal proceedings, or

  - Disclosure to the appropriate public authorities of infringements of the law, eg under anti-money laundering legislation (see Section 7).

- There is a professional duty or right to disclose, when not prohibited by law:

  - To comply with the quality review of a member body or professional body
  - To respond to an inquiry or investigation by a member body or regulatory body
  - To protect the professional interests of a professional accountant in legal proceedings
  - To comply with technical standards and ethics requirements

4.2 Factors to consider regarding disclosure

In deciding whether to disclose confidential information, professional accountants should consider the following:

- Whether the interests of all parties, including third parties whose interests may be affected, could be harmed if the client or employer consents to the disclosure of information by the professional accountant.

- Whether all the relevant information is known and substantiated, to the extent it is practicable to do so. When the situation involves unsubstantiated facts, incomplete information or unsubstantiated conclusions, professional judgment should be used in determining the type of disclosure to be made, if any.

- The type of communication that is expected and to whom it is addressed; in particular, professional accountants should be satisfied that the parties to whom the communication is addressed are appropriate recipients.

- Whether the information is privileged, for example under legal professional privilege.

- The legal and regulatory obligations and the possible implications of disclosure for the professional accountant.

- That all facts have been confirmed and recorded.

Worked example: Disclosure of information – factors to consider

You have just obtained Ms Kopanovic as a client. She has a source of income which may or may not be taxable depending on her personal circumstances which are uncertain.

Requirement

Discuss the ethical considerations you must bear in mind when deciding whether to disclose the income on her tax return.

Solution

The fundamental principle at stake here is confidentiality.

There is a possible legal obligation to disclose the source to HMRC which may override this, but the situation is unclear.

You must use your professional judgement, based on all facts. If disclosure is not to be made the exact reasons for non-disclosure should be recorded and Ms Kopanovic advised of the reason for this.

If you decide that disclosure is legally required, your client should be notified. If she does not accept the advice, it may be that the engagement letter in place authorises disclosure anyway. If not, and if permission to disclose is withheld, you should decide whether you can continue to act for Ms Kopanovic.

5 Irregularities

Section overview

- Part B of both the IESBA Code and the ICAEW Code illustrates how the fundamental principles are applied in certain situations for professional accountants in public practice.

- One of the illustrations given in part B contains details relating to conflicts of interest.

5.1 Irregularities in a client's tax affairs

Definition

Irregularities: all errors, whether made by the client, the member, HMRC or any other party in a client's tax affairs ranging from the innocent to those that may amount to fraud.

5.2 Irregularities leading to overpayment of tax

A professional accountant may become aware of possible irregularities in the client's tax affairs. The client should be informed as soon as possible. Where the irregularity has resulted in a tax overpayment, the client should be advised about making a repayment claim and have regard to any relevant time limits.

5.3 Irregularities leading to underpayment of tax

A mistake made by HMRC may give rise to an underpayment of tax or an over-repayment of tax. Correcting such mistakes made by HMRC may cause expense to a member and thereby to his clients. In some circumstances, clients or accountants may be able to claim for additional professional costs incurred and compensation from HMRC.

An accountant dealing with an irregularity must bear in mind the legislation on money laundering and may need to consider whether the irregularity could give rise to a circumstance requiring notification to the firm's professional indemnity insurers. In such a situation it may be acceptable for a professional accountant to disclose the irregularity to the authorities without giving rise to a breach of confidentiality.

Records should be kept of discussions and advice regarding irregularities.

Interactive question 2: Reporting irregularities   [Difficulty level: Exam standard]

You have just received the following email from your client.

> 'I am preparing the latest VAT return. I cannot see that there has been any adjustment to reflect a change in use of the company's computer training building. Mark Charles, the finance director has told me that it is unlikely that HMRC will pick up the change in use and to ignore it for now but if notice of an inspection by HMRC is received we will pay the outstanding VAT on the next return before the VAT inspector arrives. However, I am worried we will be open to penalties.
>
> The amount of VAT is in the region of £80,000 – please could you advise me on how to report this matter.'

Requirement

Discuss the action you should take and the advice you should give to your client.

See **Answer** at the end of this chapter.

6 Client acceptance and regulatory requirements

Section overview

- Particular procedures are needed when taking on new clients including issuing an engagement letter.

- The ICAEW requires practising members to hold professional indemnity insurance.

- Professional accountants are subject to the Data Protection Act.

- Particular responsibilities are placed on anyone undertaking the role of Senior Accounting Officer in a qualifying company.

6.1 Client and engagement acceptance

Before accepting a new client, a professional accountant in public practice shall determine whether acceptance would create any threats to compliance with the fundamental principles. Potential threats to integrity or professional behaviour may be created from, for example, questionable issues associated with the client (its owners, management or activities). A professional accountant in public practice shall evaluate the significance of any threats and apply safeguards when necessary to eliminate them or reduce them to an acceptable level.

The fundamental principle of professional competence and due care imposes an obligation on a professional accountant in public practice to provide only those services that the professional accountant in public practice is competent to perform. Before accepting a specific client engagement, a professional accountant in public practice shall determine whether acceptance would create any threats to compliance with the fundamental principles. For example, a self-interest threat to professional competence and due care is created if the engagement team does not possess, and cannot acquire, the competencies necessary to properly carry out the engagement.

6.2 Engagement letter

The contractual relationship should be governed by an appropriate letter of engagement in order that the scope of both the client's and the professional accountant's responsibilities are made clear.

The letter should explain the scope of the client's and the accountant's responsibilities in each case, including limitations in or amendments to that role. In the *Mehjoo* case, based on the engagement letter, the obligation to provide tax planning advice was limited. However an implied duty of care to provide tax planning advice had been created, as the professional accountant had done so on prior occasions.

Every contractual relationship should be covered; if the member acts for a partnership and also for one or more of the partners, then the partnership and each partner acted for are separate clients for the purposes of these guidelines. Likewise, if the member acts for a husband and wife, each is a separate client.

Authority to disclose information in certain circumstances should be considered for inclusion in the engagement letter. For example when

- An HMRC error has come to light, and HMRC need to be notified.
- Disclosure is required by law.
- There is a professional duty or right to disclose, when not prohibited by law.

See Section 4.1.

6.3 Responsibility for tax returns

This section is new.

Professional Conduct in Relation to Taxation reiterates that the client retains responsibility for the accuracy of a tax return. The accountant is merely an agent when performing tax compliance work such as preparing and submitting a tax return on behalf of a client. The client is required to sign the return prior to its submission. The client's attention should be drawn to their responsibility for the accuracy and completeness of the return.

The accountant should obtain written evidence of the client's approval of the return. This is particularly relevant as an increasing number of returns are submitted online.

On occasions a professional accountant may sign tax returns for a client, for example when acting as:

- Liquidator, receiver, administrator, executor, director or attorney

- A VAT representative for a 'non-established taxable person' (NETP) or as VAT agent

    As a VAT agent the client retains responsibility for the returns and paying on time. As a VAT representative for a NETP the accountant is jointly and severally liable for the VAT debts. The accountant should consider whether this is sensible, and instead consider only being a VAT agent.

6.4 Professional indemnity insurance

Every qualified member of the ICAEW who is in public practice and resident in the United Kingdom or Republic of Ireland is required to have professional indemnity insurance (PII).

The ICAEW's PII Regulations sets the minimum amount of indemnity as follows:

- If the gross fee income of a firm is less than £600,000, the minimum limit of indemnity must be equal to two and a half times its gross fee income, with a minimum of £100,000.

- Otherwise, the minimum is £1.5 million.

Employed members will normally be covered by their employer's insurance policy. The PII regulations apply to individual members but in practical terms professional indemnity insurance usually covers their practising entity, for example their partnership or their sole practice.

A member ceasing to be in public practice should ensure that cover remains in place for at least two years. It is recommended that members consider maintaining cover for six years after they cease to practise.

It is important that insurers are notified promptly when specific circumstances arise ie:

- When a claim is made, or there is a situation that may give rise to a claim
- Possibly where there is an irregularity

6.5 Data protection

Anyone who handles personal information has a number of legal obligations to protect that information under the Data Protection Act 1998.

Every organisation that processes personal information must notify the Information Commissioner's Office (ICO) unless it is exempt, and be entered onto the ICO's register of data controllers. The only exemption at all applicable to practising firms of accountants would be where computers are not used in any way to process or store any client information, records or correspondence.

Failure to notify is a strict liability criminal offence.

The eight data protection principles include requirements to ensure that data held is accurate, up to date, securely stored, and used for a specified, lawful purpose.

6.6 Data security and online access

This section is new

Professional Conduct in Relation to Taxation advises that precautions should be taken to prevent unauthorised access to client information on computer or online and refers to HMRC's guidelines. For instance:

- Access credentials such as passwords should be kept safe from unauthorised use and computers should be physically secure.

- Passwords should be changed regularly: HMRC's recommends at least once every three months.

- Any unusual or unexpected activity on clients' online HMRC records should be reported to HMRC immediately.

- Suspicious emails appearing to be from HMRC should be forwarded to HMRC's phishing team and it is important to avoid clicking on links in these, or opening attachments.

Consideration is also needed as to how a client is to authorise a return for electronic filing by the accountant.

6.7 Accountability of senior accounting officers

Senior accounting officers of qualifying companies (generally large companies) are required to take reasonable steps to establish and monitor accounting systems within their companies that are adequate for the purposes of accurate tax reporting.

Qualifying companies are required to notify HMRC of the name of their senior accounting officer (SAO). The SAO is required to:

- Certify annually that the accounting systems in operation are adequate for the purposes of accurate tax reporting, or

- Specify the nature of any inadequacies.

A qualifying company is defined as a company with a turnover of greater than £200 million and/or a balance sheet total of greater than £2 billion.

Penalties may be charged for failure to:

(a) Establish and maintain appropriate tax accounting arrangements.

(b) Provide an annual certificate to HMRC or for providing a certificate that contains a careless or deliberate inaccuracy.

(c) Notify HMRC of the name of the SAO.

In each case the penalty is £5,000. In the case of (c) the penalty is payable by the company in the other cases the SAO is personally liable for the penalty.

Worked example: Senior Accounting Officer   [Difficulty level: Exam standard]

You are a tax adviser working for a firm of ICAEW Chartered Accountants. You are experienced in UK tax matters but have limited international tax knowledge at present.

Salvador Mica's 100% owned UK resident company, Noche Ltd, is a client of your firm and part of your client portfolio. Salvador himself has lived for many years in the UK, but remains domiciled in the non-EEA country of Somnambularia. Noche Ltd has a profitable UK trade with profits of over £250 million in the last year, but over half its total income derives from dividends from Somnambularia-resident companies, although the dividend income remains in Somnambularia.

Noche Ltd's new finance director (FD), Paolo Lunedi, has contacted your manager about some concerns he has over the way in which the company is disclosing its UK-taxable profits (**Exhibit 1**).

Requirement

Provide a briefing note for your manager in reply to Paolo Lunedi's concerns (**Exhibit 1**), which:

(i) Outlines Paolo's responsibilities as Senior Accounting Officer;
(ii) Analyses the ethical issues raised; and
(iii) Identifies the appropriate action to be taken.

Exhibit 1

Extract from a note of telephone conversation with Paolo Lunedi FD of Noche Ltd.

Paolo rang us about some concerns he is having over the tax affairs of Noche Ltd. He made the following points:

As FD of Noche Ltd he is concerned about his accountability as the newly-nominated Senior Accounting Officer (SAO) of the company.

He is worried that maybe the overseas dividends should be included in the UK CT return. He asked the financial manager about this and was told there is a treaty between the UK and Somnambularia which means these dividends are exempt from any tax. He wasn't satisfied with this, but when he raised the issue with Salvador, Salvador instructed him to ignore it.

Solution

Briefing Note for your manager
Re: Paolo Lunedi's concerns

As Senior Accounting Officer (SAO) of Noche Ltd, a company with revenue of more than £200 million, you will be required to:

- Certify the adequacy of the accounting systems for the purposes of accurate tax reporting and specify the nature of any inadequacies.

Because Paolo has been nominated as the SAO, he would be personally liable for a penalty of £5,000 should he either:

- Fail to establish and maintain appropriate tax accounting arrangements; or
- Provide a certificate that contains a careless or deliberate inaccuracy.

Given the issue raised about the overseas dividends, Paolo may be concerned that if he does not ensure that there is no need for these to appear on the UK return (whether or not they are taxable) this would have two important implications for him, he cannot be sure that tax legislation is being complied with. He cannot carry out actions that are illegal and he has to have regard to the Fundamental Principles of Professional Ethics for Accountants.

Given the concerns Paolo has raised with us we need to identify

- If there is a treaty which grants a relevant exemption
- Whether information relating to the overseas dividends should appear on the UK return
- Whether any voluntary disclosure might be advisable
- Whether any change is needed to current or past returns

before taking any action.

If, on investigation, it appears that the non-taxation and non-disclosure treatment is correct, documentation should be maintained to support this.

Otherwise, Paolo needs to discuss this matter with the Board of Directors of Noche and, if they will not comply with the UK law, he will have to consider his position as FD and SAO. He may wish to seek advice from the ICAEW confidential ethics helpline and/or take legal advice. If the issue cannot be resolved he will need to consider resigning from his position with the company.

This will also be an ethical problem for us. Now we are aware of the issue we will have to ensure that the corporation tax computations are prepared in line with the law and if not, we will have to advise the client, in writing, of our concerns. If we do not reach a satisfactory conclusion on this issue with the client we will have to consider resigning from the engagement.

7 Anti-money laundering

Section overview

- The ICAEW Members' Regulations and guidance includes anti-money laundering guidance.

- This guidance has been prepared to assist professional accountants in complying with their obligations in relation to the prevention, recognition and reporting of money laundering.

- Failure to take account of the guidance could have serious legal, regulatory or professional disciplinary consequences.

7.1 Offences and penalties

The term money laundering is used for a number of offences involving the proceeds of crime or terrorist funds. It now includes possessing, or in any way dealing with, or concealing, the proceeds of any crime.

Where a professional accountant suspects that a client is involved in money laundering he should report this to his Money Laundering Reporting Officer (MLRO) on an internal report or directly to the National Crime Agency (NCA) in the form of a suspicious activity report (SAR).

Penalties for money-laundering offences include an unlimited fine and/or

- Up to 14 years for the main money laundering offences
- Up to 5 years for failure to disclose or for tipping off
- Up to 2 years for contravention of the systems requirements of the Regulations

7.2 Defences

There are several possible defences against a charge of failure to report:

- The individual does not actually know or suspect money laundering has occurred and has not been provided by his employer with the training required, although this is then an offence on the part of the employer.

- The privilege reporting exemption ie where the professional accountant is exempt from making a report where his knowledge or suspicion came in privileged circumstances. This may be when asked to give tax advice on the interpretation or application of specific tax law, or where a confidential communication takes place between the client the accountant and the client's solicitor predominantly for use with actual or pending litigation.

- There is reasonable excuse for not making a report.

- It is known, or reasonably believed that the money laundering is occurring outside the UK, and is not unlawful under the criminal law of the country where it is occurring.

7.3 Anti-money laundering procedures

All 'relevant' businesses, including those providing accounting and tax services, need to maintain the following procedures:

- Register with an appropriate supervisory authority.

- Appoint a Money Laundering Reporting Officer (MLRO) and implement internal reporting procedures.

- Train staff to ensure that they are aware of the relevant legislation, know how to recognise and deal with potential money laundering, how to report suspicions to the MLRO, and how to identify clients.

- Establish appropriate internal procedures relating to risk assessment and management to deter and prevent money laundering, and make relevant individuals aware of the procedures.

- Carry out customer due diligence on any new client and monitor existing clients to ensure the client is known and establish areas of risk. The amount of due diligence is based on the principle of 'Know your client' (KYC). In higher risk cases the depth of due diligence should be increased, for example using internet searches and possibly subscribing to certain databases. It may extend to procedures regarding politically exposed persons such as checking against lists of persons subject to sanctions.

- Verify the identity of new clients and maintain evidence of identification and records of any transactions undertaken for or with the client.

- Report suspicions of money laundering to the National Crime Agency (NCA), using a suspicious activity report (SAR).

7.4 Reporting

This section has been rewritten.

7.4.1 Protected disclosure

The money laundering legislation requires an accountant to disclose confidential information without client consent in certain circumstances. In order to disclose confidential information, the accountant must have knowledge or suspicion, or reasonable grounds for knowledge or suspicion, that a person has committed a money-laundering offence. Disclosure without reasonable grounds for knowledge or suspicion will increase the risk of a business or an individual being open to an action for breach of confidentiality.

A professional accountant with knowledge or suspicion of money laundering must make a report. If the accountant works for a firm with a Money Laundering Reporting Officer (MLRO), then an internal report must be made direct to the MLRO.

The MLRO is then responsible for deciding whether the information contained in an internal report needs to be relayed to NCA in the form of an external report, a SAR, and if so, for compiling and despatching the SAR. There are specific offences applying to MLROs failing to make a report where one is needed.

An accountant in sole practice needing to make a report would be required to submit a SAR direct to NCA.

7.4.2 Authorised disclosure

An accountant has a defence against a money laundering offence by seeking the consent of the NCA to undertake an activity which the accountant suspects may constitute a money laundering offence. This is done by submitting an 'authorised disclosure'.

An authorised disclosure may be made:

- Before the prohibited act has been carried out.

- Whilst doing the prohibited act – provided when the accountant started the act he did not know or suspect it related to money laundering.

- After committing the act – provided there was good reason for not reporting earlier and the report was made of his own initiative as soon as possible.

The authorised disclosure method can be a good way of the authorities securing the money laundered assets.

7.5 Supervisory bodies

The 2007 Regulations require all businesses to be supervised by an appropriate anti-money laundering supervisory authority.

The ICAEW is one of the approved supervisory authorities for the accountancy sector. Accountants not regulated by one of the approved bodies will be supervised by HMRC.

The ICAEW conducts monitoring visits to firms overseen. This is typically once every eight years for small firms or annually for large or high-risk firms.

After the first monitoring visit to a firm, and provided the ICAEW are satisfied that the firm has addressed any matters identified as unsatisfactory, the firm will receive written confirmation that it may use the legend 'A member of the ICAEW Practice Assurance scheme'.

Worked example: Irregularity and money laundering

Sribani Paintal is an employer with a growing business. She is a new tax client of your firm, which has already completed its client acceptance procedures.

Sribani handled the payroll herself for the last two tax years and has recently attended a meeting to discuss handing this over to you. It is 6 April, and your firm has agreed to advise Sribani from the current tax year onwards.

You now become aware that Sribani regularly hands out cash bonuses to employees as a reward for hard work. These have been ignored in the past for payroll purposes, although they appear as a deduction in the business accounts as 'miscellaneous staff expenses'.

Sribani says she thought it was acceptable to do this as long as the payments were in cash. You have pointed out that this is incorrect. Sribani is willing to have these amounts declared going forward, but is not willing to contact HMRC regarding prior years' undeclared payments. She cannot understand why you are concerned about these given that you are not responsible for previous years.

Requirement

Comment on the ethical considerations raised by the handover of Sribani's payroll to your firm.

Solution

By omitting to declare taxable employee income for PAYE, Sribani is paying too little income tax and national insurance which is illegal. She should be informed of the need to amend previous payroll information and payments, in writing. She should also be informed of the possible interest payment on underpaid tax and also penalties, which are influenced by her behaviour. This may possibly have been careless omission at the time, but now that she has been informed a correction is needed, continuing delay becomes deliberate.

The fact that this related to years for which your firm is not responsible does not make it acceptable to ignore the omissions.

If Sribani continues to refuse to deal with the omissions, the engagement letter should be checked for any agreed conditions under which the firm may disclose information to HMRC.

Consideration should also be given as to whether the firm should give notice that it is ceasing to act for Sribani. HMRC should then be informed of the decision not to act, without reasons.

Continued failure to make good the underpaid tax and NICs would be tax evasion, the underpayments being proceeds of crime for money laundering purposes. A report should be made to the MLRO for consideration as to whether a SAR should be submitted.

8 Tax planning, tax avoidance and tax evasion

Section overview

- Tax evasion is illegal and tax avoidance is legal.

- Tax evasion could lead to prosecution for both the client and his accountant.

- Tax avoidance is liable to be countered by specific anti-avoidance rules included in particular pieces of legislation, by the GAAR, and by the application of the *Ramsay* doctrine in the courts.

This section has been rewritten

8.1 Tax planning

Taxpayers may try to minimise their tax in various ways. These range from an individual with several capital gains using the annual exempt amount in the most beneficial way, to a multinational group of companies locating its headquarters in a country with a low rate of corporation tax.

Some tax planning is uncontroversial. HMRC should not question a large pension contribution made to reduce a taxpayer's liability, provided this is within the limits set out. The Government offers various tax-saving incentives to encourage investment, including NISA accounts for individuals and Research and Development relief for companies.

8.2 Tax avoidance

There is no single definition of tax avoidance. The meaning has changed in recent years, but tax avoidance includes only legal methods of reducing the tax burden. It includes structuring taxpayers' affairs to make use of available reliefs. However, it also includes taking advantage of unintended loopholes in the legislation.

Examples of tax avoidance might include:

- Use of posthumous deed of variation to reduce inheritance tax by amending a taxpayer's will after their death

- A group of companies shifting profits to a country with a low rate of corporation tax

In the past HMRC has responded to major tax avoidance schemes by changing legislation as the scheme has come to its attention. However there is a general presumption that the effect of the changes cannot be backdated.

The courts can take a purposive approach to deny the tax benefits sought from some planning transactions by applying the *Ramsay* doctrine. In addition, the general anti-abuse rule (or GAAR – see next section) can apply to deny tax benefits sought from abusive transactions.

In recent years there has also been a requirement for promoters of certain tax avoidance schemes to disclose their schemes to HMRC, and for taxpayers to disclose details of which schemes they have used. This may enable HMRC to take action more rapidly to close the loopholes.

HMRC's booklet 'Tempted by Tax Avoidance' indicates signposts that should warn tax payers away from abusive or aggressive tax avoidance schemes. These include:

- The tax benefits are out of proportion to any real economic activity, expense or investment risk;
- There are artificial or contrived arrangements; and
- The scheme involves money going round in a circle back to where it started.

The *Ramsay* doctrine and the disclosure of tax avoidance scheme rules are considered later in this chapter.

8.3 Tax evasion

Tax evasion is illegal. It consists of seeking to mislead HMRC by either:

- Suppressing information to which HMRC is entitled, for example by:

    - Failing to notify HMRC of a liability to tax;
    - Understating income or gains; or
    - Omitting to disclose a relevant fact (eg duality of a business expense).

    OR,

- Providing HMRC with deliberately false information, for example by:

    - Deducting expenses that have not been incurred; or
    - Claiming capital allowances on plant that has not been purchased.

Minor cases of tax evasion are generally settled out of court via the payment of penalties. However, there is a statutory offence of evading income tax that can be dealt with in a magistrates court.

Serious cases of tax evasion, particularly those involving fraud, continue to be the subject of criminal prosecutions which may lead to fines and/or imprisonment on conviction.

Furthermore, tax evasion offences will fall within the definition of money laundering and in certain cases individuals may be prosecuted under one of the money laundering offences. This includes both the under declaring of income and the over claiming of expenses.

Thus where an accountant is aware of or suspects that a client has committed tax evasion, he himself may commit an offence under money laundering legislation if he has in any way facilitated the evasion. Even if the accountant was not involved in the tax evasion itself, failure to report such a suspicion is also an offence.

8.4 Distinguishing tax evasion from tax avoidance

The distinction between tax evasion and avoidance should be obvious, as a taxpayer engaged in avoidance has no intention of misleading HMRC. However, the distinction between acceptable avoidance, unacceptable avoidance and evasion has become rather blurred in recent years.

The accountant should take particular care in situations where a client believes that a tax avoidance measure has been successful and so does not submit a tax return, or does submit a return but without disclosing a particular transaction.

Note that the fact that a taxpayer is not acting illegally does not mean that steps taken to minimise tax will necessarily be acceptable to HMRC.

Interactive question 3: Tax avoidance scheme [Difficulty level: Intermediate]

You have received the following query from your HR manager.

> **EMAIL**
> **From:**   HR manager Pontbau
> **To:**   Financial controller
>
> We are putting together a fact sheet for employees who are going to be asked to work in Rania.
>
> I have heard from a friend who works in Rania that some non-Ranian workers minimise their Ranian tax liability by arranging for their salary to be paid into an overseas bank account. This apparently avoids the attention of the Ranian tax authorities. Although I am told this is not strictly illegal, it does not sound very ethical to me. However, I have a duty to provide our employees with appropriate advice when they are sent to work in Rania.
>
> Should the fact sheet include advice on this method of minimising Ranian tax? Please give me explanations for your answer since we do not seem to have a policy for this particular issue and I want to update the firm's Human Resources manual.

Requirement

Prepare a response to this email.

See **Answer** at the end of this chapter.

8.5 Measures to deter tax avoidance and evasion

Increasingly further regulation/self-regulation is introduced to deter tax avoidance measures and prevent tax evasion. Anti-avoidance measures appear throughout the text such as rules relating to a 'major change in nature or conduct of a trade', controlled foreign companies (CFCs) and the world wide debt cap (WWDC). Each Finance Act typically introduces additional anti-avoidance measures, often arising as a result of disclosures.

8.5.1 Banking code of practice

The Banking Code of Practice is a voluntary code with statutory underpinning that discourages banks from either devising and promoting tax avoidance or providing facilities and loans etc to undertake tax avoidance. While non-statutory, it is likely to be used increasingly and could be expanded more generally eg to accountants and tax advisers.

8.5.2 Government contracts

Since 2013 there has been a requirement for companies bidding for large government contracts to disclose their tax history, so that their conduct regarding tax evasion and avoidance can be considered as part of the bidding process.

9 GAAR, the *Ramsay* doctrine and BEPS

Section overview

- The GAAR applies for income tax, corporation tax, capital gains tax, IHT, SDLT and the annual tax on enveloped dwellings.

- Applies if it is reasonable to conclude that tax avoidance was one of the main purposes of a transaction, and it was not a reasonable course of action in response to the relevant tax provisions.

- Includes cases where the effect of the transaction is inconsistent with the principles on which the tax provisions are based, cases where there are contrived or abnormal steps, and transactions intended to exploit shortcomings in the legislation.

- Just and reasonable adjustments are to be made to counteract the benefit of the planning.

- In addition to the GAAR, the courts have developed a purposive approach to interpreting tax legislation (the *Ramsay* doctrine) which makes some tax planning schemes ineffective.

- The OECD and G20 countries are devising an action plan to tackle international tax avoidance, the base erosion and profit shifting (BEPS) plan.

9.1 General anti-abuse rule (GAAR)

9.1.1 Overview

The general anti-abuse rule (GAAR) applies to arrangements entered into on or after 17 July 2013.

It is intended to counter the tax advantages sought from the most aggressive tax avoidance arrangements, and can therefore be relevant to almost all taxpayers. It is intended to act as a deterrent to discourage taxpayers from using such arrangements.

It applies for income tax, corporation tax, capital gains tax, IHT, SDLT and the annual tax on enveloped dwellings. National insurance contributions are now also included under different tax provisions.

9.1.2 When the GAAR applies

The GAAR is based on the 'double reasonableness test' such that it applies to arrangements if:

- It is reasonable to conclude that obtaining a tax advantage was one of the main purposes of the arrangements, and

- The arrangements are abusive.

Arrangements are abusive if they cannot reasonably be regarded as a reasonable course of action in relation to the relevant tax provisions. Whether they are reasonable is determined having regard to whether:

- The results of the arrangements are consistent with the principles and objectives on which the relevant tax provisions are based;

- There are contrived or abnormal steps; and

- The arrangements are intended to exploit shortcomings in the tax legislation.

Factors which are likely to indicate that arrangements are abusive are cases that result in:

(a) Significantly less income, profits or gains;

(b) Significantly greater deductions or losses; or

(c) A claim for the repayment or crediting of tax (including foreign tax) that has not been, and is unlikely to be, paid.

unless it is reasonable to assume that this was the intended result of the legislation (ie the fact that R&D tax credits are more than the economic cost incurred is intended by the legislation: in that case, the fact that the deduction is more than the economic cost does not of itself indicate that the related transactions are abusive).

A transaction is unlikely to be abusive if it was based on established practice which HMRC had publicly indicated it had accepted (this is likely to be through statements in bulletins and the HMRC manuals).

Where the GAAR applies, just and reasonable adjustments are made (in relation to one or more of the taxes falling within the GAAR) to counteract the tax advantage.

In litigation the burden of proof, in demonstrating that arrangements are abusive, falls on HMRC. However, where the tax to which the GAAR relates falls within the self-assessment rules, any adjustments should be self-assessed. Failure to include them in a return is likely to lead to penalties for an incorrect return (and possibly also late payment penalties and interest on late paid tax).

The GAAR does not include a clearance procedure. However if clearance has been given under other provisions that a particular rule will apply, the GAAR will not be applied to override that treatment.

Unusually, the GAAR legislation requires a court which is considering the interpretation of the GAAR to consider:

- HMRC's guidance in relation to the GAAR, and
- The opinion of the GAAR advisory panel about the particular transaction.

The GAAR advisory panel is an independent panel of tax experts which includes tax professionals working both as advisors and in house. As well as giving opinions on cases which are taken to court, it also reviews and approves the HMRC guidance on the interpretation of the GAAR.

The initial guidance includes the following points:

- Transactions such as the straightforward use of ISAs, or EIS reliefs, or the patent box rules would not be within the scope of the rules. The GAAR would, however, apply where such reliefs are claimed as a result of contrived transactions where the taxpayer does not bear the economic risk envisaged by the provision.

- Where complex transactions are entered into to avoid a disproportionate tax charge which would have applied to a more straightforward transaction, this GAAR will not generally apply. In such cases the transactions are not an unreasonable response to the legislation.

- The fact that tax advice has been sought is not of itself an indication that an arrangement is abusive.

- Technically the GAAR applies 'after' all other anti-avoidance rules have been applied. However, HMRC can still choose to challenge blatantly abusive transactions with the GAAR, without first needing to demonstrate that there are no other provisions which apply.

Worked example: GAAR

Finance Act 2017 introduces new rules relating to the taxation of insect farming. Tax advisers identify flaws with the transitional rules, which mean that multiple tax deductions can be obtained where qualifying colonies are acquired in the transitional period and transferred between group companies. The HMRC guidance on the material, and the related parliamentary material, indicates that the transitional provisions are intended to ensure that amounts are only taxed or relieved once.

Beeline Brothers Ltd (a company formed by a collective of artisan beekeepers) forms three subsidiary companies in July 2017, and seeks to take advantage of this loophole by making four intra-group transfers of the bee colonies which it acquires before its year end on 31 August 2017.

Requirement

Explain whether the GAAR will apply to these transactions, and if it does what effect it will have.

Solution

It seems that the only reason for forming the subsidiary companies and making multiple transfers of the hives is to obtain multiple tax deductions, so it would be reasonable to conclude that obtaining a tax advantage was one of the main purposes of the arrangements.

The GAAR will therefore apply if the arrangements are abusive. It seems likely here that they are, because they are intended to exploit shortcomings in the tax legislation, and are clearly not consistent with the principles and objectives underlying the relevant tax rules, meaning that they cannot be reasonably be regarded as a reasonable course of action in relation to the provisions in question. This is supported by the fact that the company was seeking to obtain deductions which were several times the underlying economic cost.

Just and reasonable adjustments would therefore have to be made to counteract the tax advantage. Given that this seems to be a genuine trading company, which acquired trading assets, this is likely to mean that the additional deductions sought are denied but that relief is still allowed for the original acquisition of the hives.

9.2   Advice to clients in the light of the GAAR

Where the GAAR applies, tax planning arrangements will be ineffective and clients should be advised accordingly.

Measures which may be considered within and accountancy practice to deal with the GAAR include:

*   Training

*   Protocols to ensure the quality and consistency of treatment. If a member is unsure or does not have the expertise to advise he may wish to seek specialist input externally or refer the client to a specialist adviser

*   Awareness raising with clients through client alerts etc may be appropriate, especially for clients whose affairs may be more complex or who may undertake planning with other advisers

*   Caveat language to use in advice on the GAAR to explain that the GAAR is new with no precedent (or little precedent as some precedents begin to emerge) and there is therefore a level of uncertainty as to how it will be applied, so that the member cannot guarantee that it will not be applied

*   Transmittal letters for returns might refer to the GAAR for clients whose affairs may be more complex or who may undertake planning with other advisers

*   Updating existing knowledge materials to ensure that they refer to the GAAR where appropriate

*   Reviewing any existing planning in place/offerings which might be affected by the GAAR

9.3   The *Ramsay* doctrine

Even before the introduction of the GAAR, the UK courts struck down some planning schemes by effectively ignoring elements of transactions which have no commercial purpose or effect. This is again relevant to all taxpayers.

The courts have struck down planning schemes by applying purposive construction to the relevant statutory provisions. This approach has been summarised as follows:

> 'The ultimate question is whether the relevant statutory provisions, construed purposively, were intended to apply to the transaction, viewed realistically.'

> Ribeiro PJ, in *Collector of Stamp Revenue v Arrowtown Investments Ltd* (2003). This is a Hong Kong stamp duty case, but it has been widely quoted in the UK courts.

In a tax context, this approach is often referred to as the '*Ramsay* doctrine', after *Ramsay v IRC* (1982) which was one of the first tax cases to which it was applied.

In *Ramsay* the taxpayers had a tax avoidance scheme consisting of a circular series of pre-planned transactions, designed to create two debts due to the taxpayer. The scheme ensured that one debt produced a gain for the taxpayer and the other an equivalent loss. This would leave the taxpayer in a neutral financial position. The aim of the scheme was to create the gain as a tax exempt gain, but the loss as tax deductible. If the scheme had been successful the taxpayer could have set off this loss against other 'real' gains.

The House of Lords refused to allow the loss, with one of the judges commenting that capital gains tax was a 'tax on gains […] not a tax on arithmetical differences.'

In *Ramsay* and some of the other early cases, this approach was expressed as only applying to tax avoidance schemes. However, later cases have now developed the approach so that it is clear that it can also apply in other cases. It is still most often applied to tax avoidance schemes, but this is because they often involve transactions or terms which have little or no commercial purpose or effect.

Later cases have also demonstrated that the *Ramsay* doctrine cannot be applied to counteract all tax avoidance even when it includes transactions or terms which have no commercial effect. In particular, there have been several cases where the courts have concluded that the planning which had been undertaken was consistent with the purpose of the legislation. There have also been cases where the courts have decided that the legislation was formulated in such a way that it was not possible to discern its purpose. This has been primarily in areas where there are complicated statutory rules to determine the amounts which are taxed, which do not relate to commercial ideas of profits or losses.

The different conclusions can be seen from considering some of the decided cases. However around 80% of tax avoidance cases are being won by HMRC and a surprising number are being won on the basis that the cases do not pass the fundamental principles, for example was there a trade, rather than a specific application of anti-avoidance legislation.

- In *Furniss v Dawson* (1984), the taxpayer arranged for shares in a company which they wished to sell to be transferred to an Isle of Man company by way of share for share exchange, with the Isle of Man company selling the shares to the intended buyer on the same day. Under the law at the time, this was intended to defer the gain until the taxpayers sold the shares in the Isle of Man company. However, the House of Lords concluded that the transaction was in substance a sale directly from the taxpayer to the buyer, and it was taxed on that basis.

- In *Craven v White* (1988), there was also a share for share exchange of shares which were later on-sold. However, in that case there were two possible buyers, and the negotiations with the one who eventually bought the shares had been broken off at the time of the share for share exchange. In that case a majority of the House of Lords concluded that the commercial uncertainty which meant that it was possible that the foreign holding company would have been left holding the shares, meant that they could not ignore the share for share exchange. The taxpayer therefore succeeded.

- In *Macniven v Westmoreland Investments Ltd* (2001), a subsidiary of a pension scheme had large amounts of interest accrued on loans from the pension scheme, which were not tax deductible until paid. It therefore entered into a new loan with the pension scheme to obtain the funds to pay the interest and obtain the deduction. The cash went round in a circle, and the company was left with the same amount of debt as before, albeit under different loan agreements. The House of Lords concluded that the legislation required that the interest should be paid because that meant that a withholding requirement arose. As this was the case regardless of where the cash came from to make the payment, the taxpayer succeeded in claiming the interest deduction.

- In *Barclays Mercantile Business Finance Ltd (BMBF) v Mawson* (2004), the House of Lords reached a similar conclusion in relation to a collateralised leasing scheme. The arrangements in that case were very complex, but the cash went round in a circle. The court concluded that the taxpayer (a bank leasing company) did in fact incur expenditure on the provision of plant and machinery as a result of which the plant and machinery belonged to it. The Capital Allowances Act made no provision about the funding of the expenditure, and considered only the position of the taxpayer claiming the allowances, so the claim for capital allowances succeeded.

- This contrasts with the conclusion in *HMRC v Tower McCashback LLP* (2011), in which the Supreme Court concluded that a claim for first year allowances on software was excessive. The software was acquired by partnerships in which individuals had provided 25% of the funds, with 75% provided by way of interest free loan from a company related to the company which had developed the software. Looking at the transactions as a whole, the court concluded that only 25% of the amounts which the partnership had paid were in fact paid for the software rights. One of the key differences between the two cases was that in *BMBF* there was no suggestion that the assets which had been acquired were worth less than the amount paid.

- In *IRC Comms v Scottish Provident Institution* (2004) the taxpayer had entered into options to buy and sell gilts in order to benefit from a one-sided deduction under the transitional rules when the derivative contracts rules were first introduced. The two options were net settled, so that the taxpayer never actually owned the gilts. Although the options were priced so that there was a risk that the scheme would not in fact be completed as planned, the House of Lords concluded that this did not prevent it from looking at the arrangements as a single composite whole. On that basis the taxpayer did not in fact have an entitlement to acquire gilts within the meaning of the statute, so the planning failed.

- In *Mayes v HMRC* (2010) the Court of Appeal concluded that it could not strike out a planning scheme which used life assurance policies because the statute set out a formula which did not try to approximate to the actual economic profit or loss which an individual taxpayer made. A similar conclusion was reached by the Special Commissioners in *Campbell v IRC* (2004) in relation to a claim for a loss under the Relevant Discounted Securities rules.

- In *Halifax plc v C&E Commissioners* (2006) the European Courts of Justice for the first time recognised the principle of abuse of rights in relation to VAT. The bank set up a separate company to facilitate the building of a call centre. The arrangements were designed to enable the Halifax to reclaim more VAT than if it had claimed directly. The Court ruled that where avoidance is so extreme a scheme is deemed to be abusive.

The *Ramsay* doctrine therefore means that there will often be uncertainty as to whether more aggressive tax avoidance transactions will be successful, in addition to the risk that the GAAR will apply.

9.4 Base erosion and profit shifting (BEPS)

This section is new.

9.4.1 Overview

In 2013 the OECD and the G20 countries drew up the base erosion and profit shifting (BEPS) plan to address concerns that current principles of taxation are not keeping up with the global nature of modern business. Several G20 countries felt that companies have structured intra-group contractual arrangements to artificially reduce income in certain countries. The increasing fluid movement of capital and rise of the digital economy can leave gaps that can be exploited and lead to double non-taxation.

9.4.2 BEPS actions

The OECD is currently consulting on 15 actions to tackle the problem of BEPS.

Some of these are already dealt with sufficiently using current UK tax legislation, such as:

- CFC provisions (Chapter 16)
- Transfer pricing rules (including interest deductions) (Chapter 16)
- Anti-arbitrage rules to tackle hybrids

In addition Finance Act 2015 introduced diverted profits tax in support of the BEP actions. This is aimed at multinationals who artificially shift profits offshore and is expected to yield £1.3bn by 2019/20. It is considered in more detail in Chapter 16.

Other issues are still to be tackled including identifying and addressing the main challenges facing international tax rules in relation to the digital economy. A report on this area is due to be released in December 2015 and is not available at the time of writing.

10 Disclosure of tax avoidance schemes

Section overview

- Certain tax avoidance schemes must be notified to HMRC, generally by the promoter but in some cases by the taxpayer. Taxpayers using such schemes must quote the scheme reference number on their tax returns.

- DOTAS applies to all the direct taxes and to all taxpayers. Separate rules apply to VAT, SDLT on non-commercial property and inheritance tax.

- Schemes must be notified where it provides a tax advantage which is a main benefit of the scheme and the scheme falls within one of the hallmarks specified.

- Disclosure must normally be made by the scheme promoter.

10.1 Introduction

The Disclosure of Tax Avoidance Schemes regime (DOTAS) gives HMRC early warning of schemes involving aggressive tax planning, details of how they work, and information about who has used them.

The regime covers all direct taxes. The regulations focus on income tax, corporation tax, capital gains tax, national insurance contributions, financial product and employment product schemes, as well as separate rules that apply to VAT, stamp duty land tax on non-commercial property and inheritance tax.

Tax avoidance schemes are promoted and used by a relatively small number of businesses and individuals. The number of disclosures of avoidance schemes has fallen steadily with only 40 schemes disclosed in 2013/14, down from 84 in 2012/13 and from more than 600 in 2005/06. However, the amounts of tax at risk from avoidance and protected by DOTAS are considerable. The government believes that £300 million in tax was recovered in relation to a single transaction (relating to the buying in of connected party debt) which was blocked by retrospective changes to the loan relationship rules announced in February 2012, prompted by a DOTAS disclosure. DOTAS remains an important weapon and now is a potential trigger of a follower or accelerated payment notice.

10.2 Schemes within the DOTAS regime

A scheme only needs to be notified to HMRC where:

- It will or might be expected to enable any person/company to obtain a 'tax advantage'

- Which is, or might be expected to be, the main benefit or one of the main benefits of the arrangement, and

- The scheme falls within at least one of the specified descriptions or 'hallmarks'.

A tax advantage can include relief from or repayment of tax, deferral of payment of tax or the avoidance of any obligation to deduct or account for tax.

10.3 Hallmarks

The scheme must have one of the 'hallmarks' of avoidance. Some of these are designed to capture new and innovative arrangements. Others are designed to capture areas of specific concern. These include schemes that are well known or commonly used.

If a scheme falls within at least one of the following 'hallmarks' then disclosure is required under DOTAS:

(a) Confidentiality – where the promoter or user would want to keep a scheme confidential from other promoters or from HMRC.

(b) Premium fee – where a fee charged is, to a significant extent, attributable to the tax advantage or to any extent contingent upon obtaining the tax advantage.

(c) Standardised tax products – catches 'shrink-wrapped' schemes where a client purchases a prepared tax product that requires little, if any, modification. However, a number of standard products are exempt from disclosure under this hallmark (eg approved share option schemes).

(d) Certain loss schemes – applies to loss schemes which are designed so that they generate trading losses for wealthy individuals that can then be offset against income tax and capital gains tax liabilities or generate a repayment.

(e) Leasing arrangements – applies to leases with a cost of at least £10 million for a period of at least two years.

10.4 Disclosure

Disclosure must normally be made by the scheme promoter within five days of the scheme being made available. However, overseas schemes and schemes designed 'in-house' (where the advantage is to be obtained by a business that is not a small or medium enterprise) must be notified by the user of the scheme within thirty days of the scheme being implemented.

Different rules apply for Stamp Duty Land Tax (SDLT) schemes.

Persons who introduce scheme promoters to clients must identify who the promoter is.

10.5 Promoters

A promoter is a person who, in the course of 'relevant business' (that is, any trade, profession or business which involved the provision to other persons of taxation services), is responsible for the design, organisation or management of the proposed arrangements, or the marketing or promotion of schemes designed by someone else.

There are two general exceptions from being a promoter: certain group companies and the employees of promoters. A person involved in the design of the arrangements cannot be a promoter if one of three tests is passed:

- The benign test (non-designer tax advisers)
- The non-adviser test (conveyancers)
- The ignorance test (spectator tax advisers)

A person who introduces a scheme promoter to clients is an introducer.

10.6 SDLT regime

The Scheme Reference Number (SRN) system of the disclosure regime also applies to stamp duty land tax (SDLT) schemes.

Schemes involving residential property exceeding £1m in value have also been brought within the regime, which previously only applied to non-residential property exceeding £5m.

None of the main regime hallmarks apply to SDLT schemes, although there is a 'white list' of arrangements that do not need to be disclosed.

10.7 Administration

Registration of the scheme is made on form AAG 1 which provides details of the scheme, type of transactions, expected tax consequences and relevant statutory provisions.

Upon receipt of the form HMRC issues a scheme reference number (SRN) which must be passed to the scheme user, who will report its use of the scheme on its tax return or form AAG 4.

Within 30 days of the end of each calendar quarter promoters must provide HMRC with a quarterly list of clients to whom they have issued SRNs. The client must provide the promoter with additional information, such as their national insurance number or unique taxpayer reference number, to include on the quarterly list. A failure by the client to provide the information will result in penalties, as set out in Section 5.9 (b) below.

10.8 HMRC information powers

Information powers enable HMRC to:

- Require an introducer to identify any person who provided them with information relating to the scheme and any person with whom they have made any marketing contact in relation to the scheme;

- Enquire into the reasons why a promoter has not disclosed a scheme;

- Resolve disputes and enforce disclosure in appropriate cases;

- Call for more information where a disclosure is incomplete;

- Require a promoter to provide information to identify a client(s), where HMRC suspects that the reported clients are not the only parties to a scheme; and

- Require further information about notifiable proposals or arrangements to be provided within 10 working days ie information in excess of the prescribed information or if the prescribed information is incomplete.

10.9 Penalties

Broadly, penalties for failure to comply with a DOTAS obligation without a reasonable excuse (see below) fall into three categories:

(a) Disclosure penalties

Penalties apply for failure to comply with a disclosure obligation, with a maximum daily penalty of £600 where no disclosure notice has been issued. This penalty runs from the date the failure to

Ethics   25

C
H
A
P
T
E
R

1

disclose occurred, with the total amount determined by the Tribunal, taking into account the fees earned (for a promoter) or the tax saving sought (by the client).

Where a disclosure notice has been issued, but not complied with within ten days, the maximum daily penalty is £5,000.

(b) Information penalties

These apply to all other failures to comply with DOTAS except for those covered by (c) below. A Tribunal may determine an initial penalty of up to £5,000. HMRC may impose a daily penalty, not exceeding £600, for each day that the failure to provide information continues after an initial penalty has been determined.

(c) User penalties

Where a scheme user fails to report a SRN to HMRC the penalties are:

- £5,000 per scheme (ie each scheme to which the failure relates) for a first occasion);

- £7,500 per scheme on the second occasion within three years (whether or not it relates to the same scheme involved in the previous occasion); and

- £10,000 per scheme on the third and subsequent occasions (whether or not the failure relates to schemes involved in a previous occasion)

Prior to 26 March 2015 penalties were £100, £500 and £1,000 respectively.

10.10 Reasonable excuse

There is no penalty for failure to comply with the DOTAS rules if the taxpayer has a 'reasonable excuse'. What constitutes such an excuse varies according to the nature of the failure and the type and circumstances of the person concerned as there is no statutory definition of 'reasonable excuse'.

Generally, HMRC considers a reasonable excuse to be an unusual event that is either unforeseeable or beyond the person's control (for example, serious illness) that formed an 'insurmountable obstacle to timely compliance'.

10.11 Follower and accelerated payment notices

10.11.1 Follower notice

For rulings on or after the date that Finance Act 2014 receives Royal Assent HMRC may issue a 'follower notice' to a taxpayer with an open enquiry or appeal where tax arrangements have been shown in a relevant judicial ruling not to give the asserted tax advantage ie giving a taxpayer notice that they should settle their case once a tribunal or court has concluded in another party's litigation.

10.11.2 Accelerated payment notice

This measure gives HMRC the power to issue a notice requiring an accelerated payment of an amount in dispute whilst an enquiry is in progress or there is an open appeal. HMRC plan to issue over 50,000 of these notices over the first few years of their existence.

A taxpayer is required to pay the amount of an asserted tax advantage to HMRC on receipt of an 'accelerated payment notice'. The notice can be given in the following cases:

- Where a follower notice is issued;

- Where the tax arrangements are disclosable under the DOTAS rules;

- Where HMRC is taking counteraction under the GAAR; or

- Where a company utilises a tax advantage from an arrangement and then surrenders all or part of this as group relief (having the effect of the advantage not having been surrendered)

The notice requires the tax payer to pay the tax in dispute within 90 days, or a further 30 days where the taxpayer asks HMRC to reconsider the 'follower notice' or the amount of the payment notice. In addition to raising tax issues these may have an impact on professional indemnity insurance for advisers.

10.12 High risk promoters

HMRC aims to change the behaviour of certain high risk promoters, their intermediaries and clients. A promoter who triggers a threshold condition is issued with a conduct notice for a period of up to two years. There are eleven threshold conditions that include deliberate tax defaulters, dishonest tax agents and criminal offences (such as fraudulent evasion of income tax).

Breach of the conduct notice may lead to a promoter being monitored by HMRC. There is a right of appeal against the monitoring notice. A monitored promoter is subject to specific information powers and penalties of up to £1 million. In addition HMRC can name the promoter and require it to inform its intermediaries and clients. The naming includes information on why the conduct notice was breached. Clients of a monitored promoter are subject to an extended assessing period of 20 years, if any tax is lost, for failure to pass on the reference number supplied by the monitored promoter.

10.13 Confidentiality

This section is new.

Finance Act 2015 enables persons to be protected if they voluntarily provide information or documents to HMRC which they suspect may assist HMRC in determining whether there has been a breach of any DOTAS rules.

Such a disclosure of information will not be a breach of a person's duty of confidentiality or any other restriction on disclosure. This provision extends to accountants and tax advisers in relation to their clients.

11 Answering ethics exam questions

Section overview

- At this level, ethics questions are embedded in the scenario and will require you to think about the information you have been given in order to apply your knowledge and judgement to the scenario.

- You may be expected to challenge the information given. At the very least you should query what you have been told.

- In answering exam questions you must use the scenario and identify the relationship with the client, the source of the information and the issues.

Ethics in this paper is integrated into the scenario. In answering exam questions you must use the scenario and identify the relationship with the client, the source of the information and the issues. You will need to apply your knowledge and exercise judgement, including where appropriate considering whether the information you have been given is correct.

Definition

Professional scepticism: an attitude that includes a questioning mind, being alert to conditions which may indicate possible misstatement due to error or fraud, and a critical assessment of audit evidence.

Here we use a question from a previous Business Reporting exam to illustrate how best to tackle an ethics question in in the Business Planning: Taxation paper. The full solution to this question is reproduced in the revision question bank.

The following are extracts from Question 2 from the July 2010 the Business Reporting paper:

The relationship with the client is in the scenario:

'TTR's engagement letter with Pepper Art Ltd was revised to reflect the client's responsibilities to file all returns on behalf of the group and to communicate directly with HMRC. Under this revised engagement letter, TTR has agreed **to review, and adjust if necessary, Pepper Art's corporation tax return and those of Spaceway and DeliverUK, but it has no authority to communicate with HMRC** on behalf of the clients.'

In this scenario the accountant has no authority to communicate with HMRC. However the accountant does have reporting responsibilities under anti-money laundering legislation. A common weakness in candidates' answers was to confuse the reporting duties under the accountant's relationship with the client and the anti-money laundering legislation. Poor answers included comments such as:

'We should tell HMRC anyway because it's a crime'

'We should tell HMRC without tipping off the client'

Good answers recognised that anti-money laundering legislation requires the firm to report the matter to NCA not HMRC.

The source of the information

The source of the information is Jim Jones, a **financial controller** of Pepper Art Ltd, **reporting comments from the managing director**.

Poor answers failed to apply professional scepticism to the source of the information. Is Jim Jones telling the truth? Candidates often did not question the information presented in the question which is the first stage in ethical conflict resolution. Only the good answers identified the need to request further evidence to support Jim Jones' assertions.

The issues

The issues are embedded in the information:

'Software support charges

In January 2010 the computer network crashed and the managing director **asked a friend** who has a software support business **to assist** us in restoring the system. **The friend asked for £50,000 for the work but would not supply an invoice**. Pepper Art paid him in full but the managing director thought it would not be correct to claim tax relief on this item. Therefore I have disallowed this in the adjustment to profit calculation.'

Weak answers tended to overreact to the scenario and immediately accused the 'friend' and the managing director of tax evasion. However, the software support charge may be valid and therefore more information is required from the client to substantiate the deduction. A good answer would also recognise that the failure to supply an invoice may also be indicative of the quality of the accounting records and therefore undermine the accuracy of the information supplied to the accountant for review.

'Tax repayment

Pepper Art received a corporation tax repayment of £230,000. I have checked through the correspondence you sent to us last year and we were expecting a refund of only £23,000. This is obviously great for the company's cash flow. **The managing director has told me that we should keep quiet about this overpayment as it is HMRC's fault** for being so inefficient. The **excess part of the repayment has been credited to other operating income** in the financial statements.'

Poor answers immediately condemned the managing director as a thief. A good answer identified that the responsibility of the professional accountant is to establish the facts and then advise client on the appropriate course of action.

Summary

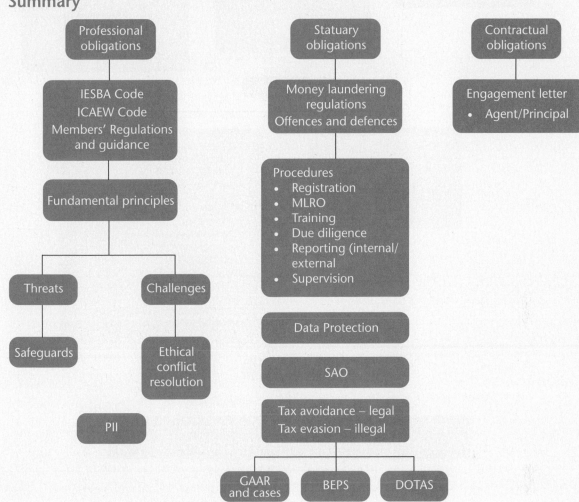

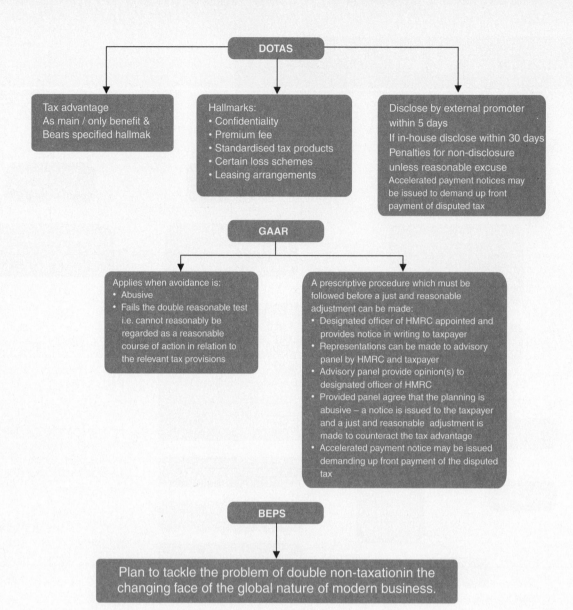

DOTAS

Tax advantage
As main / only benefit &
Bears specified hallmak

Hallmarks:
• Confidentiality
• Premium fee
• Standardised tax products
• Certain loss schemes
• Leasing arrangements

Disclose by external promoter
within 5 days
If in-house disclose within 30 days
Penalties for non-disclosure
unless reasonable excuse
Accelerated payment notices may
be issued to demand up front
payment of disputed tax

GAAR

Applies when avoidance is:
• Abusive
• Fails the double reasonable test
  i.e. cannot reasonably be
  regarded as a reasonable
  course of action in relation to
  the relevant tax provisions

A prescriptive procedure which must be
followed before a just and reasonable
adjustment can be made:
• Designated officer of HMRC appointed and
  provides notice in writing to taxpayer
• Representations can be made to advisory
  panel by HMRC and taxpayer
• Advisory panel provide opinion(s) to
  designated officer of HMRC
• Provided panel agree that the planning is
  abusive – a notice is issued to the taxpayer
  and a just and reasonable adjustment is
  made to counteract the tax advantage
• Accelerated payment notice may be issued
  demanding up front payment of the disputed
  tax

BEPS

Plan to tackle the problem of double non-taxationin the
changing face of the global nature of modern business.

Self-test

Answer the following questions.

1   You have acted for two sole trader clients for many years. They have just set up a company together as a separate enterprise each owning 50% of the shares. The clients have asked that you continue to act for them individually as well as acting for the company.

Explain the nature of the conflict of interest and how the conflict can be managed.

2   You work as a tax assistant for a firm of ICAEW chartered accountants. You have been reviewing the previous year's submitted corporation tax return of a new client prior to commencing work on the current year's return. You discovered that the client had claimed additional relief for research and development on some non-qualifying expenditure. The client is not willing to amend the corporation tax return as the client feels that it relates to a relatively small amount and 'it makes a change for it to go in our favour'.

Explain the ethical implications of this situation for your firm.

3   Several months ago your firm prepared financial statements and a forecast for a client, Trumpton Ltd, based on a trial balance provided by the client. These financial statements and forecasts were sent, with our consent, as support for a loan application to the company's bank.

The finance director of Trumpton Ltd recently informed you that the company had been sent notice of a large claim against a contract, between the time of sending in the application and hearing the result of the application. This resulted in the profit being overstated by £300,000. The directors decided not to inform the bank of this as they had not known the information at the time of submitting the application.

The loan application was subsequently declined by the bank, therefore the bank did not actually suffer as a result of the incorrect information.

Explain the ethical issues arising from the information provided by the finance director.

4   Your firm acts as tax advisors to both Huw and Ffion

Ffion is a designer. She won a significant premium bond prize and set up a sole trade two years ago.

Huw has already invested £500,000 in Ffion's business which she will be incorporating soon. She already has nearly 200 employees and needs to take on more in the immediate future.

During a meeting regarding his personal tax return, Huw mentions that he is willing to invest a further amount in the new company provided this will qualify for EIS relief. He asks you not to tell Ffion as he does not want her to count on the extra funds.

5   You have developed a scheme relating to employment benefits that could help one of your larger corporate clients to save a substantial amount of national insurance contributions. Your fee for arranging the scheme is 40% of the national insurance savings made by the company.

Explain your obligations and your client's obligations relating to the scheme.

6   **CAT Ltd**

CAT Ltd has been trading in the UK for a number of years. It is part of a large international conglomerate. The group directors have been specifically targeted with minimising the group's overall global tax liability. The UK directors have therefore adopted an aggressive policy to minimise the taxation paid in the UK. All director bonuses are dependent on an annual effective corporate tax rate in each country of no more than 5%. The UK directors have undertaken the following three strategies as the key methods to minimise the UK corporation tax liability:

- CAT Ltd makes payments to a Dutch subsidiary for use of its intellectual property rights in the UK. These payments represent 6% of total revenue and are allowable expenses in the UK. The Dutch subsidiary has negotiated a very low effective corporate tax rate with the Dutch authorities.

- In addition, CAT Ltd purchases its supplies of raw materials via a Swiss subsidiary which is also highly profitable but pays corporation tax at a very low rate in Switzerland. The cost of the raw materials CAT Ltd purchases is recognised as a valid expense in the UK and equates to 5% of revenue.

- CAT Ltd has started to purchase its business premises. It is shifting its property portfolio from a rental portfolio to an owned portfolio. Allowable property costs currently represent 50% of revenue. The properties will be owned by CAT Ltd but then leased to an offshore company before being leased back to CAT Ltd. CAT Ltd will then make substantial payments of rent to the offshore company. The leases involved will have a cost in excess of £10m and will have terms of between three and ten years.

CAT Ltd's tax advisers have recommended all three strategies. The first two strategies have been running for three years and have been referred to in the published financial accounts. The charges made for the intellectual property and the raw materials strategies were at a flat rate based on the time the advisers spent working on each strategy.

Requirement

Explain which of the three strategies, if any, fall within the DOTAS regime and explain what penalties, if any, are due for the consequential non-disclosure of their existence by CAT Ltd or its advisers to HMRC.

Now go back to the Learning objectives in the Introduction. If you are satisfied you have achieved these objectives, please tick them off.

Technical reference

Legislation

IESBA Code of Ethics for Professional Accountants

ICAEW Members' My guide to regulations: Code of Ethics

ICAEW Members' My guide to regulations : Professional conduct in relation to taxation

ICAEW Members' My guide to regulations: Anti-money laundering guidance for the accountancy sector (CCAB guidance dated August 2008)

ICAEW Professional indemnity insurance regulations and guidance 2014

Serious Organised Crime and Police Act 2005

Money Laundering Regulations 2007

ICAEW: Professional conduct in relation to taxation – guidance published 1 May 2015

All references are Corporation Tax Act 2010 *(CTA 2010)* unless otherwise stated

GAAR	ss.203 – 212 FA 2013
DOTAS	
Requirement to disclose	s.306 FA 2004
Hallmarks	Paras 6-13 SI 2006/1543
Penalties	s.98C TMA 1970

Other references

The main source of guidance from HMRC on dealing with errors by it is 'Complaints' fact sheet. This is found at www.gov.uk/government/publications/putting-things-right-how-to-complain-factsheet-cfs

Information Commissioner's Office www.ico.org.uk/

ICAEW information centre and technical helpline service+44 (0)1908 248 250 www.icaew.com/members/advisory-helplines-and-services

> This technical reference section is designed to assist you when you are working in the office. It should help you to know where to look for further information on the topics covered in this chapter.

Answer to Interactive question 1

Jacob must adhere to all five fundamental principles. In this situation he needs to consider the following fundamental principles in particular:

- Integrity – Were the actions that he took, and any conversation with the administrator, unfair, untruthful or dishonest in any way?

- Objectivity – Where is the boundary between his duty to his former employer and the administrator?

- Confidentiality – Are there proper grounds for disclosing the information?

Answer to Interactive question 2

Reporting the VAT irregularity

The potential error is large and therefore cannot simply be adjusted on the next VAT return.

Having established the facts are correct, the client should be advised to make a voluntary disclosure of the error (by either a Form 652 or by writing to HMRC) and to pay the VAT due.

HMRC may reject disclosure of errors made after the date an inspection visit has been arranged if it is considered that disclosure is prompted solely by the visit or by enquiries made by HMRC prior to the visit. Therefore Mark Charles' suggestion has no validity.

The client should be advised of the consequences of not making a disclosure, in particular that:

(a) Should HMRC discover the irregularity, a penalty for the submission of an incorrect return will be charged. The penalty will be greater where the error has been deliberately concealed.

(b) Having knowledge of the irregularity without acting upon it may be construed as a criminal offence or a civil fraud.

(c) Interest may accrue up to the time the VAT is paid.

Ethical issues for the adviser's firm

If the client declines to disclose, the firm should confirm the above advice in writing and consider whether it is appropriate to continue to act in respect of VAT affairs or indeed all affairs. The fundamental principle of integrity requires that a chartered accountant is not associated with omitting information which leads to less VAT being paid.

Clients with an inappropriate attitude to compliance with tax law may not be appropriate clients for the firm.

Money laundering

All facts should be confirmed and recorded.

Fiscal offences can also amount to money laundering. Tax evasion is a crime. Consideration should be given to whether there is an obligation to make a report via the Money Laundering Reporting Officer to NCA.

Where a report is made, the client must not be informed where this would be considered 'tipping off'. Advising the client to stop breaking the law by evading tax does not amount to 'tipping off'.

Detailed file notes should be maintained of all discussions regarding this matter.

Our firm does not agree with the clients' view regarding the potential irregularity and this needs to be made clear to the client in writing and recorded on our files.

Email to: HR manager
From: Financial controller

Ethical issue regarding tax avoidance scheme

There is a potential conflict in this situation between Pontbau's duty as an employer to provide appropriate advice to employees sent to work in Rania, Pontbau's duty to comply with the law whether that is UK or overseas, and personal ethics on whether it is appropriate to avoid tax by circumventing the substance of tax law.

In addition, it is a concern that the firm does not have written procedures which consider this ethical problem.

Before advising on this issue certain steps should be considered to ascertain the facts:

- Pontbau should obtain professional tax advice from a reputable firm in Rania which can advise on legal means of minimising the employees' tax liabilities in Rania.

- This advice should be considered by Pontbau at an appropriate level of seniority to consider the opinion given to ensure that the advice matches with the company's corporate policy on working in other tax jurisdictions and to ensure that there are no potential conflicts.

Resolving the problem of personal ethics conflicting with the workplace is a very difficult issue. The ICAEW code of ethics sets out five fundamental principles which act as a framework. Relevant to this scenario are the principles of integrity, requiring a professional accountant to be straightforward and honest in business and professional relationships; and professional behaviour, requiring that a professional accountant should comply with relevant laws and regulations and should avoid any action that discredits the profession.

I would advise you to consult your professional body's code of ethics to ascertain your position and responsibilities in this matter.

As a priority, a project to review all Pontbau's procedures manuals in respect of HR and other functions should be implemented and also review of training to ensure that ethics is incorporated at all levels within the organisation.

1   At this point in time there is no reason to suggest that you should not act for all three clients. However, if your firm acts for all three separate clients the principle of confidentiality must be maintained for each client. The clients must also be informed that you may need to cease to act if future conflict arises.

2   By claiming R&D relief that is not due, the client is evading tax which is illegal. The client should be informed of the need to amend the tax return, in writing. The client should also be informed of the possible interest payment on underpaid tax and also penalties, which are also influenced by The client's behaviour, which appears to be deliberate.

   If the client continues to refuse to amend the return, the engagement letter should be checked for any agreed conditions under which the firm may disclose information to HMRC.

   Consideration should also be given as to whether the firm should cease to act. HMRC should then be informed of the decision not to act, without reasons.

   As the client has filed the tax return, the tax evasion means that the client has paid less tax than should have been paid and therefore this constitutes proceeds of crime for money laundering purposes. A report should be made to the MLRO with consideration as to whether a SAR should be submitted.

3   The issue is whether the firm is required to disclose information to a third party (the bank) without threatening the fundamental principle of confidentiality. Part A of the ICAEW ethical code contains a section on confidentiality which states that a professional accountant may disclose confidential information if permitted by law and is authorised by the client to do so. Accountants may be required to disclose information by law eg to produce certain documents for a court case or under anti-money laundering regulations or to comply with quality review procedures.

   In this particular circumstance, there would appear to be no legal requirement to disclose information to the bank without the client's permission.

   The fact that the loan application was refused in this instance would not influence the decision whether to report under anti-money laundering regulations which the firm would have to do if it believed that the client is engaged in money laundering. Since the client has not benefited from the falsification of the financial statements there would appear to be no requirement to make a report under POCA. However further consideration should be given to this issue by the firm's money laundering officer.

   The issue clearly has wider implications for the client relationship.

   There are clearly now grounds for mistrusting the client and this has implications for the accuracy of information supplied to the firm for the purpose of filing accurate tax returns. The directors are required to submit accurate returns to HMRC on the company's behalf. The firm should therefore be sceptical of information provided and should verify where possible any explanations given to the firm by the directors.

4   Even without considering Huw's comment about not revealing to Ffion his intended further investment, there is a clear conflict of interest arising if working for both Huw and Ffion which the firm must address.

   Your firm must check that they have engagement letters for both parties and that these do not exclude working for the other party.

   You must notify both Huw and Ffion that the firm acts for them both and ensure that this is reflected in the respective engagement letters and if necessary that the engagement letters are revised.

   Appropriate safeguards should be set up to ensure that client's confidentiality is maintained and the independence of the advice is preserved.

These safeguards should include informing the clients of the potential conflict of interest; using separate teams within the firm; or indeed deciding that working for both clients is not possible if the quality of advice and confidentiality is to be assured.

Although you could advise Huw to be transparent in his relationship with Ffion and to give her the chance to fulfil the criteria for EIS investment, the number of employees being one criterion, he has a right to confidentiality.

If you personally have knowledge of both parties' plans, it may be appropriate for Ffion and Huw both to be handed over to separate teams who have not known them previously. It is difficult to imagine the threat to your objectivity could be overcome otherwise, unless the firm were to cease entirely to act for either client.

5   The scheme appears to have one of the hallmarks (premium fee hallmark) that require the scheme to be disclosed to HMRC. As the promoter you will be required to disclose full details of the scheme to HMRC within five days of making it available to the client.

Your client is required to disclose the scheme number on all relevant correspondence with HMRC, and particularly on corporation tax and PAYE returns affected by the scheme.

6   **CAT Ltd**

DOTAS Scope

Schemes must be notified to HMRC where they allow a user to obtain a tax advantage as the main benefit or one of the main benefits of the scheme and which bear at least one of the prescribed hallmarks.

Therefore unless the scheme bears one of the prescribed hallmarks it need not be notified to HMRC even if it does convey a tax advantage to its user.

In terms of the three strategies used by CAT Ltd, the first two strategies did not require a premium fee to be paid to the advisers and their use has been fully disclosed in the company accounts so presumably cannot be considered to be confidential. It would therefore appear that none of the prescribed hallmarks apply to either of these two schemes and that they do not need to be disclosed under the DOTAS regime.

The third strategy relates to leasing arrangements for which there is a specific hallmark which these leases fulfill. It would appear that there is a definite tax advantage from the scheme's use and therefore this strategy is within DOTAS and should have been disclosed to HRMC.

Administration

As the scheme was designed by an external adviser, it should have been reported to HMRC within five days of the scheme being made available to CAT Ltd. The advisers would then have been sent a scheme reference number (SRN) which should have been passed on to CAT Ltd. The advisers are liable to a maximum daily penalty of £600 for failing to disclose the scheme.

CAT Ltd should make clear its use of the scheme on its tax return. Failure to do so will result in a penalty of £5,000.

CHAPTER 2

Income tax and NIC

Introduction

Examination context

Topic List

Summary and Self-test

Technical reference

Answers to Interactive questions

Answers to Self-test

Introduction

Learning objectives

Tick off

- Determine, explain and calculate the tax liabilities for individuals including income tax and national insurance ☐

- Advise and calculate the impact of tax efficient schemes including NISAs, enterprise investment schemes, seed enterprise investment schemes and venture capital trusts ☐

- Calculate tax liabilities for individuals including income tax and national insurance contributions ☐

- Identify legitimate tax planning measures to minimise tax liabilities ☐

The specific syllabus references for this chapter are 1f, 1t, 1v, 2a.

Syllabus links

NIC and the income tax computation were covered in your Tax Compliance study manual. The reliefs available for those investing in NISAs and venture capital are new to you.

Examination context

A professional adviser acting for an individual looks for tax planning opportunities to suggest a wide range of tax efficient investments, such as NISAs and venture capital schemes.

In the examination candidates may be required to:

- Give advice to an individual about investments in NISAs

- Give advice to an individual about investments in enterprise investment schemes, seed enterprise investment schemes and venture capital trusts

Better candidates have previously been able to pick up valuable marks by offering advice on tax efficient investments.

1 Revision from Tax Compliance

Section overview

- Primary class 1 NIC contributions are paid by employees on their gross employment income received in cash. Secondary class 1 contributions are paid by employers on their employees' gross employment income received in cash.

- Class 1A NIC contributions are payable by employers on taxable benefits provided to employees.

- Class 1B NIC contributions are payable by employers on the grossed-up value of earnings in a PAYE settlement agreement.

- Class 2 NIC contributions are paid by the self-employed at a fixed weekly rate.

- Class 4 NIC contributions are based on taxable trading income.

- Trading losses are deemed to be carried forward to set against future trading income for class 4 NIC purposes.

- Some forms of income are exempt from income tax, eg income from NISAs, certain VCT dividends, Premium Bond winnings.

- Income received net must be shown gross in the income tax computation.

- Taxable income is Net Income less the Personal Allowance.

- Different rates of tax apply to non-savings income, savings and dividend income.

- In the Business Planning: Taxation exam you may still be required to calculate an individual's income tax liability or income tax payable. It is therefore important that you have a good grasp of the income tax topics encountered in your previous studies.

1.1 Class 1 NIC contributions

Gross employment income received in cash or readily convertible assets is subject to primary class 1 NIC contributions paid by employees and secondary class 1 contributions paid by employers. To recap what you learnt at Professional Stage:

- Class 1 contributions are based on the employee's earnings period – weekly, monthly or annually.

- No contributions are due on earnings below the earnings threshold.

- For primary contributions only, there is an upper earnings limit above which contributions are due at a lower rate.

- There are lower class 1 contributions payable if an individual is contracted out of the Additional State Pension. It is no longer possible to contract out through a money purchase occupational or personal pension scheme.

- From 6 April 2015, where an employee is under 21 years old, the rate of employer contributions is reduced to 0% for earnings up to the upper secondary threshold (and 13.8% as normal above that limit).

- Directors have an annual earnings period.

- Employers can claim the employment allowance to reduce class 1 secondary contributions payable to HMRC by £2,000 pa.

1.2 Class 1A and Class 1B NIC contributions

Class 1A contributions are payable by employers, on taxable benefits provided to employees. Note that employees do not pay national insurance contributions on their non-cash earnings ie taxable benefits.

Class 1B contributions are payable by employers on the grossed-up value of earnings included in a PAYE settlement agreement.

A PAYE settlement agreement is one between an employer and HMRC where the employer pays income tax on small employee benefits and expense payments as one amount. This means that it is not necessary to keep separate records of such amounts or enter them on forms P11D or P9D.

1.3 Class 2 NIC contributions

A self-employed individual aged between 16 and state pension age is required to pay flat weekly rate class 2 contributions (£2.80 per week for 2015/16). Payments start on the individual's 16th birthday and cease on attaining state pension age. This is currently age 65 for men. It was age 60 for women but is being increased to 65 in steps over the eight years from 6 April 2010, prior to a further increase for both men and women.

No contributions are payable if the individual's profits are below the small profits threshold (£5,965 for 2015/16) and an application for exemption is made.

1.4 Class 4 NIC contributions

In addition to the flat rate class 2 liability, self-employed individuals may be liable to pay class 4 NICs based on their taxable trading income as liable to income tax. An individual is liable to pay class 4 contributions if aged 16 or over at the start of the tax year. He ceases to be liable if he has reached state retirement age at the start of the tax year. In a partnership, each partner is responsible for paying his own class 2 and class 4 contributions based on his own share of partnership profits.

For income tax purposes there are various ways in which an individual may utilise any trading losses (see Chapter 4). For the purposes of calculating class 4 liability, losses allowed under carry forward trade loss relief, early trade loss relief and trade loss relief against general income are set only against trading income of the individual. This means that any relief for a loss allowed for income tax purposes against non-trading income can be carried forward for class 4 purposes and set off against trading income in future years. Thus the treatment of a loss for IT and NIC purposes may differ.

Worked example: NIC for the self-employed

Jasper is a sole trader. He makes up accounts to 5 April each year.

In the year ended 5 April 2015, Jasper made a trading loss of £(20,000). He made a claim to set off the loss against property income in 2014/15 under s.64 ITA 2007.

In the year ended 5 April 2016, Jasper had taxable trading income of £58,000.

Requirement

Calculate the total national insurance contributions payable by Jasper for 2015/16.

Solution

	£
Class 2 contributions	
52 × £2.80	146
Class 4 contributions	
y/e 5.4.16	
Taxable trading income for class 4	
(£58,000 – £20,000) = £38,000	
(£38,000 – 8,060) × 9%	2,695
Total NICs for 2015/16	2,841

1.5 Pro forma income tax computation

The proforma income tax computation is as follows:

A Taxpayer, Income tax computation – 2015/16

	Non-savings income £	Savings income £	Dividend income £	Total £
Income				
Employment income/Trading income	X			
Interest (gross)		X		
Dividends			X	
Property income	X			
Total income	X	X	X	X
Qualifying interest payments/gift of assets to charity	(X)			(X)
Net income before losses	X			X
Reliefs				
Losses	(X)			(X)
Net income	X	X	X	X
Personal allowance	(X)			(X)
Taxable income	X	X	X	X

	£
Tax	
Non-savings income @ 20/40/45%	X
Savings income @ 0/20/40/45% (Note)	X
Dividends @ 10/32.5/37.5%	X
	X
Less tax reducers (ie VCT relief, EIS relief, relief for married couples)	(X)
	X
Less DTR	(X)
Income tax liability	X
Less tax deducted at source	(X)
Add income tax retained on patent royalties paid net of BRIT	X
Income tax payable	X

Notes: Starting rate band of 0% for non-savings income up to £5,000 (2014/15: 10% up to £2,880). The starting rate band is not available if non-savings income exceeds £5,000.

From 2014/15 up to £1,060 of unused personal allowance can be transferred to an individual's spouse/civil partner, and is treated as a tax reducer at 20% by the transferee. It is only available if the transferee is a basic rate taxpayer, and neither is claiming the married couples allowance.

Tax is calculated for each source of taxable income at the applicable rate and any income tax reducers can then be deducted.

Patent royalties paid in relation to a trade must be paid net of the basic rate of tax ie 20%. The gross amount is then deducted from trading profits and the income tax retained is added to the income tax liability of the payer. Note that copyright royalties are outside the scope of this syllabus.

1.6 Exempt income

The main types of exempt income are:

- Interest on National Savings Certificates

- Income from New Individual Savings Accounts (NISAs)

- Dividends received on shares held in a Venture Capital Trust (VCT) subject to conditions

- Betting, lottery and Premium bond winnings

- Some social security benefits such as universal credit, housing benefit and child benefit

- The first £30,000 of statutory redundancy pay and compensation received for loss of employment (see Chapter 3) [Hp80]

- First £4,250 of gross annual rents from letting under the rent-a-room scheme

- Scholarships

- Interest received from HMRC on overpaid tax

Income tax and NIC   43

2 New Individual Savings Accounts (NISAs)

Section overview

- NISAs can contain cash, shares and insurance products.
- An individual may invest in a cash NISA and/or a stocks and shares NISA.
- Income and gains on NISA investments are exempt from tax.
- Junior ISAs are available for children not eligible for a Child Trust Fund.

2.1 Investing in an NISA

NISAs are available to individuals aged 18 or over. Cash-only NISAs are also available to 16 and 17 year olds.

An individual can invest in either or both of the two different types of an NISA:

- Cash and cash like equity products, eg investment of cash in bank and building society accounts;

- Qualifying stocks and shares and insurance products, eg investment on any worldwide stock exchange including shares and securities, gilt-edged securities, unit trusts and investment trusts and investment in insurance products

The investments in the two types of NISA can be with the same or different providers.

From 3 December 2014, if an individual's spouse or civil partner dies, a tax-free amount up to the value held in the dead spouse's NISA at death can be added to the surviving spouse's NISA (an addition to their own NISA allowance).

2.2 Limits on NISA investment

There are conditions attached to the amounts that can be invested in each tax year. [Hp40]

The following conditions apply for 2015/16:

- The annual subscription limit is £15,240.

- An individual can invest up to £15,240 in cash and cash like equity products and/or stocks, shares and insurance products, split in any proportion. However the individual can only pay into a maximum of one cash NISA and one stocks and shares NISA each year.

- Individuals aged 16 and 17 can invest up to £15,240 in a cash NISA, but cannot open a stocks and shares NISA.

2.3 Tax reliefs for NISAs

All income (interest, dividends, insurance proceeds) is exempt from income tax.

All gains and losses on disposals of assets (eg shares) are exempt from capital gains tax.

In Autumn 2015 a 'Help to Buy ISA' will be made available to help first time buyers save for a new home. Individuals can save up to £12,000 and receive a 25% bonus when the home is purchased. Accounts will be limited to one per person rather than one per property, so those buying together can each receive a bonus.

2.4 Junior ISAs

Junior ISAs are available to any UK resident child under the age of eighteen who is not eligible for a Child Trust Fund (CTF). Currently, Junior ISAs are not available to children who already have an existing CTF. Children can hold up to one cash and one stocks and shares Junior ISA at any one time. The annual limit for contributions to Junior ISAs is a combined total of £4,080 for 2015/16. There is no minimum annual contribution.

Any cash put into a Junior ISA is locked in until the child is eighteen and then it will, by default, become an adult NISA. At the age of eighteen the child can withdraw money from the NISA without losing the tax exemption.

Tax relief for Junior ISAs is the same as for adult NISAs (Section 2.3 above).

3 Venture capital

Section overview

- An individual can invest up to £1,000,000 in new shares in a qualifying Enterprise Investment Scheme (EIS) company and receive tax relief at 30%. Income tax relief will be withdrawn if the shares are sold within three years.

- Gains on EIS shares held for at least three years are exempt.

- A gain on the disposal of any asset may be deferred if reinvested in EIS shares.

- An individual can also invest up to £100,000 in new shares in a qualifying Seed Enterprise Investment Scheme (SEIS) company and receive tax relief at 50%. A SEIS company must have been trading for less than two years at the time when the shares are issued, and not have previously issued EIS or VCT shares. Income tax relief will be withdrawn if the shares are sold within three years.

- Gains on SEIS shares held for at least three years are exempt.

- A gain on the disposal of any asset may be exempt if reinvested in SEIS shares. The maximum relief is 50% of the value of the SEIS investment.

- An individual can invest up to £200,000 in new shares in a qualifying Venture Capital Trust (VCT) company and receive tax relief at 30%. Income tax relief will be withdrawn if the shares are sold within five years.

- Gains on VCT shares are always exempt and losses are never allowable.

Providing venture capital is a high risk/high return investment. The government encourages venture capital investments in certain circumstances by providing tax relief for both individuals and companies.

Three such schemes currently apply:

- Enterprise Investment Scheme (EIS)
- Seed Enterprise Investment Scheme (SEIS)
- Venture Capital Trust (VCT)

3.1 Enterprise Investment Scheme (EIS)

Tax relief is available to an individual under the EIS if he subscribes for new fully paid-up shares in a qualifying company wholly for cash. The shares must either be ordinary shares, or other classes of shares as long as the amount of the dividend paid on the shares is at the discretion of the company.

3.1.1 Qualifying company

A qualifying company is an unquoted company which must have a permanent establishment in the UK, carries on a qualifying trade and:

- Does not control any other company (except for qualifying 90% subsidiaries) and it is not under the control of another company

- Its gross asset value before the share issue does not exceed £15 million (and £16 million immediately after the share issue)

- It has fewer than 250 full-time equivalent employees at the date of issue

- It has raised no more than £5 million under EIS and VCT schemes (see later in this chapter) in the previous 12 months

A qualifying trade is one carried on commercially with a view to profit and excludes activities such as dealing in commodities, dealing in property, certain financial services and certain companies generating energy from renewable sources. The company must use the money raised from the share subscription for the purpose of the qualifying trade generally within two years of the date of the share issue. Money raised cannot be used to invest in shares, unless they are shares of a 90% subsidiary which in turn invests in a qualifying trade.

The issuing company must not be 'in difficulty' at the date of issue of the shares. A firm is regarded as being in difficulty where it is unable, whether through its own resources or with the funds it is able to obtain from its owner/shareholders or creditors, to stem losses which, without outside intervention by the public authorities, will almost certainly condemn it to going out of business in the short or medium term.

3.1.2 Income tax relief under the EIS

The maximum amount of investment on which a qualifying individual can obtain relief in any tax year is £1,000,000. [Hp41] There is no minimum qualifying investment.

The taxpayer is entitled to a deduction from his income tax liability equal to the lower of:

- 30% × amount invested under the EIS scheme; and
- The amount which reduces his income tax liability to nil.

Relief is normally given in the tax year that the investment is made. However, a taxpayer can claim to carry back his investment, up to the usual limit which applied in that year, to the previous tax year, thus accelerating the timing of the tax relief.

Income tax relief will be withdrawn if the investor disposes of the EIS shares within three years of issue. Income tax relief is withdrawn by bringing the relief given back into charge in the tax year in which the disposal is made.

Income tax relief is only given for the investment in shares. Any dividends subsequently received on the shares are taxable in the normal way.

3.1.3 Qualifying individual

A qualifying individual is one who is not connected with the company at any time in the period from two years before the issue (or from incorporation if later) to three years after the issue. An individual is connected with the company broadly if he (either alone or with his associates) holds more than 30% of the ordinary shares or can exercise more than 30% of the voting rights in the company or he is an employee or a non-qualifying director of the company.

A qualifying director is, broadly, one who only receives reasonable remuneration (including any benefits) from the company.

For EIS purposes, associates include spouse, civil partner, parent, grandparent, child and grandchild.

For EIS income tax relief purposes, the investor need not be UK resident.

3.1.4 Capital gains tax exemption under the EIS

Any gains arising are exempt provided the EIS relief has not been withdrawn. [Hp100]

The capital gain exemption does not apply if the investor disposes of the EIS shares within three years of issue.

If a capital loss arises on the disposal, it is allowable regardless of when it is realised.

In calculating a loss on the disposal of EIS shares themselves, the cost of the shares is reduced by the amount of EIS income tax relief attributable to the shares disposed of.

Share loss relief is available for a loss arising on the disposal of EIS shares. This means it can be set against general income of the same and/or preceding year.

3.1.5 Reinvestment relief under the EIS

Capital gains tax reinvestment relief is available where an investment is made under the EIS scheme. To qualify for reinvestment relief, the investor must be UK resident at the time the gain is realised and at the time the shares are purchased. There is no requirement for income tax relief to be claimed, and the annual investment limit does not apply.

Where any asset is disposed of and new EIS shares are subscribed for within 12 months before and 36 months after the date of the disposal, the chargeable gain arising on the disposal of the asset may be deferred until the later disposal of the EIS shares. [Hp42]

The maximum amount of relief available is the lower of:

- The amount of the gain; and
- The subscription cost of the new shares.

Partial claims are possible, thus providing tax planning opportunities. The relief operates by deferring the amount of the gain for which the relief claimed and taxing only the remainder of the gain.

On the disposal of EIS shares, a gain or loss may arise on the EIS shares. In addition, the amount of the gain for which reinvestment relief was claimed becomes chargeable on the disposal of the EIS shares.

Where the original disposal takes place on/ after 3 December 2014, and would have been eligible for entrepreneurs' relief at that time, then entrepreneurs' relief can be claimed on the deferred gain when it is charged to tax. If the original disposal took place prior to 3 December 2014, entrepreneurs' relief is not available on the deferred gain.

Interactive question 1: Deferring a gain
[Difficulty level: Intermediate]

On 4 July 2015 Rex, who is aged 42, sold all of his shares in Rex Ltd realising a gain of £95,000.

On 4 October 2015 he subscribed £100,000 for ordinary shares in Caesar Ltd, an unquoted trading company. These shares qualified for EIS relief.

Rex has taxable income for 2015/16 of £80,000.

Requirements

How much reinvestment relief should Rex claim, assuming he makes no other disposals in 2015/16?

See **Answer** at the end of this chapter.

The deferred gain will crystallise if:

- The new shares are disposed of, other than by way of an intra-spouse/civil partner transfer;
- Within three years the investor, or spouse/civil partner if he/she now owns the shares, becomes non UK resident (other than if working abroad on a full-time contract for less than three years); or
- Within three years the shares cease to be eligible shares or the company ceases to be a qualifying company.

Interactive question 2: Crystallising a deferred gain
[Difficulty level: Intermediate]

Renata owns 75% of the shares in Rene Ltd and works full time for the company. She sold all of her shares for £349,984 in June 2013. The shares were bought in August 1966 for £125,000. The gain on the disposal of the shares was £124,000. Renata made no other disposals in 2013/14. Reinvestment relief of £113,100 was claimed by Renata in 2013/14 in respect of the subscription of shares in Star Ltd.

In August 2014 Renata subscribed for a 25% ordinary shareholding in Star Ltd, an unquoted UK trading company, for £250,000. The shares qualified for EIS relief.

In September 2015 Renata sold her Star Ltd shares for £320,000.

Requirements

Compute the chargeable gain arising in 2015/16, assuming Renata claimed reinvestment relief in August 2014.

See **Answer** at the end of this chapter.

3.2 Seed Enterprise Investment Scheme (SEIS)

In a scheme which is aimed at investors in small start-up companies, tax relief is available to an individual under the SEIS if he subscribes for new fully paid-up ordinary shares in a qualifying company wholly for cash.

Many of the scheme conditions are similar to those for EIS, but there are a number of important differences.

3.2.1 Qualifying company

As for EIS, a qualifying company is an unquoted company which must: have a permanent establishment in the UK; carry on a qualifying trade; not control any other company (except for qualifying 90% subsidiaries); not be or have been under the control of another company (excluding a company formation agent if the company was formed as an 'off-the-shelf' company); and not be in 'difficulty'.

A qualifying trade is one carried on commercially with a view to profit and excludes activities such as dealing in commodities, dealing in property, certain financial services and certain companies generating energy from renewable sources.

However, to qualify for SEIS:

- The company's trade must be 'new', in that it must have been carried on for less than two years before the share issue;

- Its gross asset value before the share issue must not exceed £200,000;

- It must have fewer than 25 full-time equivalent employees at the date of issue; and

- It must not have previously raised funds through the EIS or VCT schemes, or raise more than £150,000 (on a cumulative basis) under SEIS.

Funds raised under SEIS must be invested in its new qualifying trade within three years of the share issue. A company which has raised funds under SEIS can go on to raise further funds under EIS or VCT schemes, so long as it has spent at least 70% of its SEIS funds before doing so.

3.2.2 Income tax relief under the SEIS

The maximum amount of investment on which a qualifying individual can obtain relief in any tax year is £100,000, with no minimum investment required. [Hp 42]

The taxpayer is entitled to a deduction from his income tax liability equal to the lower of:

- 50% × amount invested under the SEIS scheme; and
- The amount which reduces his income tax liability to nil.

Relief is normally given in the tax year that the investment is made, although a taxpayer can claim to carry back his investment to the previous tax year. No relief can be claimed until the company has spent at least 70% of the funds invested. The investor needs a compliance certificate issued by the company to be able to claim the relief, and this cannot be issued until 70% of the funds have been spent.

Income tax relief will be withdrawn if the investor disposes of the SEIS shares within three years of issue, or receives value from the company in certain forms. Unlike for EIS, SEIS income tax relief is withdrawn by adjusting the assessment for the year in which the relief was originally claimed.

As for EIS, income tax relief is only given for the investment in shares. Any dividends subsequently received on the shares are taxable in the normal way.

3.2.3 Qualifying individual

As for EIS, a qualifying individual is one who is not connected with the company at any time in the period from two years before the issue (or from incorporation if later) to three years after the issue. An individual is connected with the company broadly if he (either alone or with his associates) holds more than 30% of the ordinary shares or can exercise more than 30% of the voting rights in the company or he is an employee or a non-qualifying director of the company.

A qualifying director is, broadly, one who only receives reasonable remuneration (including any benefits) from the company.

For SEIS purposes, associates include spouse, civil partner, parent, grandparent, child and grandchild.

For SEIS income tax relief purposes, the investor need not be UK resident.

3.2.4 Capital gains tax exemption under SEIS

The capital gains treatment is the same as for EIS shares. Any gains arising are exempt provided the SEIS relief has not been withdrawn.

The capital gain exemption does not apply if the investor disposes of the SEIS shares within three years of issue.

If a capital loss arises on the disposal, it is allowable regardless of when it is realised.

In calculating a loss on the disposal of SEIS shares themselves, the cost of the shares is reduced by the amount of SEIS income tax relief attributable to the shares disposed of.

Share loss relief is available for a loss arising on the disposal of SEIS shares provided the company has remained a qualifying trading company. This means it can be set against general income of the same and/or preceding year.

3.2.5 Reinvestment relief under SEIS

Where an individual makes a gain on the disposal of an asset, it is completely exempt from CGT if he also makes a qualifying SEIS investment during that same year. The maximum relief which can be claimed is 50% of the value of the investment, so in order for a gain to be exempt in full the SEIS investment needs to be twice the value of the gain.

Note that EIS deferral and SEIS reinvestment relief cannot be claimed in respect of the same expenditure.

The maximum amount of reinvestment relief available is the lower of:

- The amount of the gain; and

- 50% of the subscription cost of the new shares which qualify for SEIS relief (maximum 50% × £100,000).

Where an election is made to treat an SEIS investment as made in the previous tax year for income tax purposes, the investment is also treated as made in the previous tax year for the purposes of SEIS reinvestment relief.

Where SEIS income tax relief is reduced or withdrawn (for example, on a sale at a profit within three years of the shares being issued), the reinvestment relief is withdrawn to the same extent. This is done as an adjustment to the original capital gains tax calculation for the relevant year.

The combined effect of the CGT holiday and the income tax relief offers relief of up to 64% depending on the rate of capital gains tax that would have applied.

Worked example: SEIS reinvestment relief

In September 2015 Beverley invested £50,000 in shares qualifying for SEIS relief, which she intends to keep as a long term investment. In January 2016 she disposed of a holiday home, realising a gain of £68,500.

Beverley had taxable income of £95,000 in 2015/16.

Requirements

(a) Calculate Beverley's capital gains tax liability for 2015/16, assuming that she made no other taxable disposals.

(b) Explain the effect of selling the SEIS shares in January 2020.

Solution

(a) Capital gains tax liability

	£
Gain before reliefs	68,500
Less SEIS reinvestment relief (50% × £50,000)	(25,000)
Gain after reliefs	43,500
Annual exempt amount	(11,100)
Taxable gain	32,400

Capital gains tax 28% × £32,400 = £9,072

(b) On a disposal in January 2020, there would be no gain on the disposal of the SEIS shares because they have been held for more than three years. The gain which was subject to reinvestment relief is not crystallised because the SEIS relief is an exemption rather than a deferral.

3.3 Venture Capital Trusts (VCT)

An individual can obtain an investment in a wide variety of unquoted investments by holding readily marketable quoted shares in a VCT.

3.3.1 Investment in a VCT

A VCT is a company quoted on the Stock Exchange, approved by HMRC, with income derived wholly or mainly from shares and securities in unquoted companies. The companies in which the VCT invests must have:

- Fewer than 250 full-time equivalent employees at the date of the issue.
- Raised no more than £5 million under EIS and VCT schemes in the previous 12 months.

If a VCT invests in a company which has breached the annual investment limit then the fund will cease to be treated as a VCT. Previously, a breach only affected that particular investment. Funds will therefore need to monitor companies in which they invest more closely.

An individual is eligible for relief if he is at least 18 and subscribes for new ordinary shares in a venture capital trust. The maximum permitted investment for income tax relief is £200,000 per tax year. [Hp 44] The individual may invest more than this amount in a VCT, but will not receive tax relief on any further investment.

3.3.2 Income tax relief for investment in a VCT

The taxpayer is entitled to a deduction from his income tax liability equal to the lower of:

- 30% × amount invested; and
- The amount which reduces the income tax liability to nil.

The tax relief is only available in the tax year the investment is made.

The VCT tax relief is given before any EIS tax relief.

Income tax relief will be withdrawn if the investor disposes of the VCT shares within five years of issue. Income tax relief is withdrawn by bringing the relief given back into charge in the tax year in which the disposal is made.

Dividends received from a VCT are exempt if they relate to shares acquired within the £200,000 permitted maximum per tax year. This relief applies even if the shares are sold within five years of issue.

3.3.3 Capital gains tax relief for investment in a VCT

Any capital gain is exempt and any loss is not allowable on the disposal of VCT shares, whenever the shares are disposed of. Although shares must be held for five years to benefit from income tax relief, there is no holding period for capital gains tax relief.

Worked example: EIS & VCT

In June 2015 Joe won £60,000 on the National Lottery. He wished to invest this money tax efficiently and, following professional advice, he subscribed £40,000 for an EIS investment in June 2016. He wishes to carry back the investment to 2015/16. Joe also subscribed £20,000 to a VCT in August 2016.

Joe has asked you to calculate his tax liabilities for 2015/16 and 2016/17 and has given you the following information:

	2015/16 £	2016/17 £
Salary	60,000	60,000
Dividends received from EIS investment		3,600
Distribution from VCT		2,800

Requirements

(a) Calculate Joe's income tax liabilities for 2015/16 and 2016/17.
(b) Explain the effect of selling his EIS and VCT shares in either May or September 2019.

Assume tax rates and allowances for 2015/16 apply in future years.

Solution

(a) **Income tax computations**

				2015/16 £	2016/17 £
Salary				60,000	60,000
Dividends					
EIS (£3,600 ×100/90)					4,000
VCT – exempt				–	–
Net income				60,000	64,000
PA				(10,600)	(10,600)
Taxable income				49,400	53,400
Income tax					
£	£			£	£
31,785	31,785	@ 20%		6,357	6,357
17,615	17,615	@ 40%		7,046	7,046
–	4,000	@ 32½%			1,300
49,400	53,400			13,403	14,703
Less EIS relief £40,000 × 30%				(12,000)	
Less VCT relief £20,000 × 30%					(6,000)
Income tax liability				1,403	8,703

(b) **Effect of selling EIS and VCT shares**

- Disposal of EIS shares

  (i) If the EIS shares are sold within three years of their issue

      – A gain or loss can arise
      – The income tax relief given of £12,000 will be clawed back

  (ii) If the shares are sold after three years

      – Any gain is exempt
      – No recovery of income tax relief takes place
      – Any capital loss is allowed but reduced by the income tax relief given

- Disposal of VCT shares

  No gain/loss arises on disposal of the VCT shares regardless of how long the shares are held.

  However, if sold within five years of issue (May or September 2019) the income tax relief given is clawed back.

3.4 Summary of venture capital rules

EIS	SEIS	VCT
• Subscribe for new, fully paid up ordinary shares in a qualifying company for cash	• Subscribe for new, fully paid up ordinary shares in a qualifying company for cash	• Subscribe for new, ordinary shares in a quoted company that invests in qualifying companies (a VCT)
Qualifying company	**Qualifying company**	**Qualifying company**
• Unquoted UK Co with a qualifying trade	• Unquoted UK Co with a 'new' qualifying trade • 'New'= the trade has been carried on for less than 2 years	• As for EIS
Qualifying trade	**Qualifying trade**	**Qualifying trade**
• Commercially trading with view to a profit • NOT dealing in commodities/ property/financial services/ generating energy from renewable sources • Does not control (except qualifying 90% subs)/not under control of another Co. • Gross assets of no more than £15 million before (£16 million after) the share issue • <250 full time EEs • Raised no more than £5 million under EIS and VCT in past 12 months • Co uses money within 2 years of share issue	• Mainly as for EIS with the following differences • Gross assets of no more than £200,000 before the share issue • <25 full time EEs • Not previously raised funds under EIS or VCT • Raised no more than £150,000 under SEIS • Co uses money within 3 years of share issue	• <250 full time EEs • Raised no more than £5 million under EIS and VCT in past 12 months
Income tax relief	**Income tax relief**	**Income tax relief**
• Tax reducer max £1 million [Hp41] × 30% (reduce IT to nil, no repayment) • Tax relief in tax yr of investment or c/back to previous tax year • Claw back of IT relief if sold within 3 years (via special assessment) • Dividends taxable • Can use share loss relief to offset capital gains against income of current year and/or prior year	• Tax reducer max £100,000 [Hp42] × 50% (reduce IT to nil, no repayment) • Tax relief in tax year of investment or c/back to previous tax year • No relief can be claimed until the company has spent at least 70% of the funds invested • Claw back of IT relief if sold within 3 years (by adjusting the assessment for the year of relief) • Dividends taxable • Can use share loss relief to offset capital losses against income of current year and/or prior year	• Tax reducer max £200,000 [Hp44] × 30% (reduce IT to nil, no repayment) • Tax relief in tax year of investment – no c/back • Claw back of relief if sold within 5 years (via special assessment) • Dividends exempt • VCT relief given first, then EIS relief and then SEIS relief

EIS	SEIS	VCT
CGT Exemption	**CGT Exemption**	**CGT Exemption**
• Gain exempt if held for three years [Hp42]	• As for EIS	• Gain exempt from CGT (no minimum holding period)
• Capital losses allowable (no minimum holding period – cost reduced by any EIS relief)		• Capital losses not allowable
• Need not be UK R for IT relief		
Qualifying investor	**Qualifying investor**	**Qualifying investor**
• Cannot be connected with company:	• As for EIS	• Age 18
– Connected = investor + associates hold >30% OSC/votes (or E'ee/non-qualifying director) in 2 years before and up to 3 years after investment		
– Qualifying director – receives reasonable remuneration (including benefits) from the Co.		
EIS reinvestment relief	**SEIS reinvestment relief**	
• Investor UKR	• Gain on disposal of an asset is EXEMPT if there is a SEIS investment during the year [Hp100]	
• Sell **any** asset	• Maximum relief is 50% of the SEIS investment. Income tax relief must also be claimed	
• Reinvest GAIN in EIS shares [Hp100]	• If the SEIS IT relief is withdrawn the reinvestment relief is also withdrawn (by adjusting the computation for the year of the original disposal)	
• 1 year before and up to 3 years after [Hp42]		
• Gain NOT taxed		
• Held over and taxed:		
– When EIS shares sold, **or**		
– If cease to be UKR < 3 years		
– If share no longer eligible <3 years, or co no longer qualifies <3 years		
• Can be connected with Co for deferral relief		

Summary

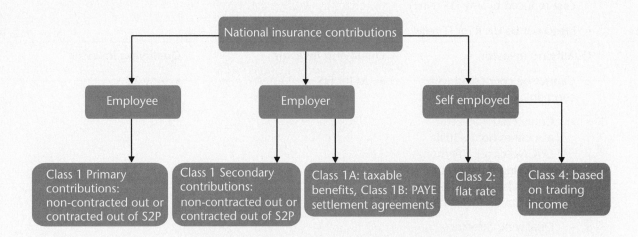

National insurance contributions

- Employee
  - Class 1 Primary contributions: non-contracted out or contracted out of S2P
- Employer
  - Class 1 Secondary contributions: non-contracted out or contracted out of S2P
  - Class 1A: taxable benefits, Class 1B: PAYE settlement agreements
- Self employed
  - Class 2: flat rate
  - Class 4: based on trading income

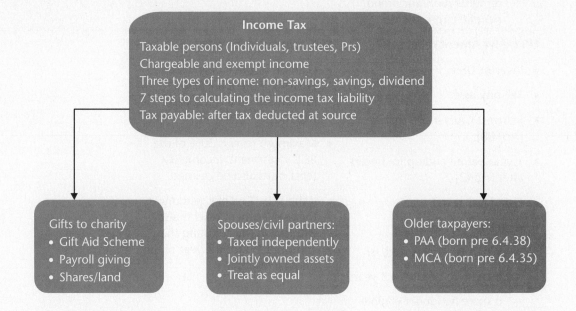

Income Tax

Taxable persons (Individuals, trustees, Prs)
Chargeable and exempt income
Three types of income: non-savings, savings, dividend
7 steps to calculating the income tax liability
Tax payable: after tax deducted at source

- Gifts to charity
  - Gift Aid Scheme
  - Payroll giving
  - Shares/land
- Spouses/civil partners:
  - Taxed independently
  - Jointly owned assets
  - Treat as equal
- Older taxpayers:
  - PAA (born pre 6.4.38)
  - MCA (born pre 6.4.35)

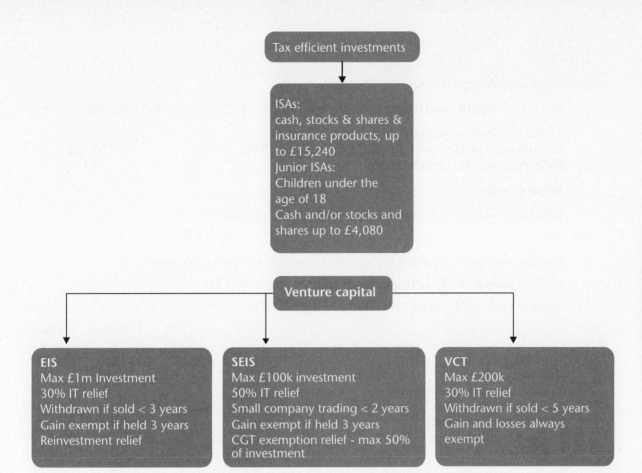

CHAPTER

2

Self-test

Answer the following questions.

1   Rosemary is aged 33 and is a full-time student. In 2015/16, she received the following income:

Scholarship from university	£350
Earnings from vacation work (gross, PAYE deducted £910)	£10,425
Dividends from UK company shares	£450

Requirement

Calculate how much tax is repayable to Rosemary.

2   Bert and Pearl are not married but have lived together for the last 10 years.

Bert was born on 1 July 1949 and Pearl was born on 29 July 1937.

In the tax year 2015/16, Bert and Pearl had the following income:

	Bert	Pearl
	£	£
Pension (gross)	24,635	13,500
(Tax deducted)	(3,100)	(973)
Building society interest received	1,080	216
Dividends received from UK companies	1,620	2,430
NISA dividends received	1,350	
Premium bond winnings		180
Property income	5,040	2,160

The property income is derived from a house which Bert and Pearl own together in the proportions 70:30.

In December 2015, Bert made a Gift Aid donation of £1,053. In March 2016, Pearl gave quoted shares worth £4,000 to a charity.

Requirement

Calculate the tax payable by Bert and Pearl.

3   Joshua is self-employed. He makes up his accounts to 5 April each year. The following information relates to 2015/16:

(1)   Joshua's taxable trading income for the year to 5 April 2016 was £20,040. In the year to 5 April 2015, he made a trading loss of £5,000. He made a claim under s.64 ITA 2007 to set the loss against savings income in 2014/15.

(2)   Joshua has two weekly paid employees, Thelma and Louise (both over 21 years old). They receive wages of £8,840 and £12,480 gross per year respectively. He also paid Thelma a bonus of £750 during the week commencing 18 December 2015.

Thelma has occasional use of a pool car from Joshua and Louise receives medical insurance cover for her family which costs Joshua £1,040 pa. Joshua also provides small benefits for both Thelma and Louise valued at £200 per year, which are covered by a PAYE settlement agreement. Thelma and Louise are members of personal pension schemes.

Requirement

Calculate all the national insurance contributions for which Joshua should account to HMRC in respect of 2015/16 and state how they will be paid.

4   Deborah has an actual income tax liability of £36,000 for 2015/16 and an estimated liability of £35,000 for 2016/17.

Deborah is considering purchasing £150,000 worth of new ordinary shares in Garden Ltd, a qualifying Enterprise Investment Scheme (EIS) company. Deborah intends to complete the purchase on 1 April 2016.

Requirement

Explain to Deborah the advantages of delaying the purchase of shares in Garden Ltd until on or after 6 April 2016.

Now, go back to the Learning objectives in the Introduction. If you are satisfied you have achieved these objectives, please tick them off.

Technical reference

References are to Income Tax Act 2007 (*ITA 2007*) unless otherwise stated

NISAs

References are to Individual Savings Account Regulations 1998 (*SI 1998/1870*) (as amended)

General conditions for accounts and subscriptions to accounts	reg.4
General investment rules	reg.6
Qualifying investments	regs.7 – 9
Exemption from tax	reg.22

EIS

IT relief	s.158
Claim for IT relief	s.202
Withdrawal of relief	s.209
Conditions	ss.162-200
Other tax reliefs	s.161
Disposal of EIS shares at a gain	s.150A TCGA 1992
Disposal of EIS shares at a loss – share loss relief	s.131
EIS CGT deferral relief	Sch 5B TCGA 1992

SEIS

IT relief	s.257AB
Claim for IT relief	s.257EA
Withdrawal of relief	s.257FA
Offset of capital losses against general income	s.131
Conditions	Ss.257B-257DN
CGT reliefs	s.257AE
Disposal of SEIS shares at a gain	s.150E TCGA 1992
Disposal of SEIS shares at a loss – share loss relief	s.131
SEIS reinvestment relief	Sch 5BB TCGA 1992

VCT

IT relief	s.263
Conditions	ss.274-332
Other tax reliefs	s.260
CGT disposal relief	s.151A TCGA 1992

HMRC manual references

National Insurance Manual (Found at www.hmrc.gov.uk/manuals/nimmanual/index.htm)

Relief Instructions Manual (Found at www.hmrc.gov.uk/manuals/remanual/RE1830+.htm)
Gift Aid relief: outline of the relief RE1830

Venture Capital Schemes Manual (Found at hmrc.gov.uk/manuals/vcmmanual/index.htm)

This technical reference section is designed to assist you when you are working in the office. It should help you to know where to look for further information on the topics covered in this chapter.

Answer to Interactive question 1

Rex could claim relief for a maximum of the lower of

(i) £95,000 = the gain otherwise chargeable
(ii) £100,000 = the cost of the new shares

Rex will restrict his claim in order to utilise his annual exempt amount.

	£
Gain before reliefs	95,000
Less reinvestment relief	(83,900)
Gain after reliefs	11,100

	£
Chargeable gain	11,100
Less annual exempt amount	(11,100)
Taxable amount	Nil

Answer to Interactive question 2

Disposal – September 2015

	£	£
Deferred gain crystallises		113,100
Sales of shares		
Proceeds (September 2015)	320,000	
Less cost (August 2014)	(250,000)	
Chargeable gain		70,000
Chargeable in 2015/16		183,100

Notes:

As the shares were held for less than three years, the income tax relief will be withdrawn and the base cost of the shares is their original cost.

If the new shares had been held for at least three years, the gain on these shares would be exempt under the EIS reinvestment rules. The deferred gain would, however, still be chargeable.

As the original disposal took place before 3 December 2014, entrepreneurs' relief is not available on crystallisation of the deferred gain (even if all conditions were fulfilled in June 2013).

1 Rosemary

Income tax repayable

	Non-savings income £	Dividend income £	Total £
Employment income	10,425		
Dividends £450 × 100/90		500	
Net income	10,425	500	10,925
Less PA	(10,425)	(175)	(10,600)
Taxable income	Nil	325	325

Scholarship is exempt from income tax.

Tax

	£
£325 × 10%	33
Less: tax credit on dividend (restricted)	(33)
Income tax via PAYE	(910)
Repayable	(910)

Notes

The tax credit on dividends is set off first to ensure that the full amount of income tax paid via PAYE is recoverable. However, the excess tax credit of £17 (£50 – £33) is not recoverable.

In addition to the dividend tax credit not being repayable, the maximum tax credit recoverable is restricted to that proportion which relates to the taxable dividend. For example where a taxpayer has £50,000 gross dividends and no other income, the taxable dividend for 2015/16 will be £39,400. The dividend tax credit will therefore be restricted to £3,940. [s.397(3) ITTOIA 2005]

2 Bert

Tax payable

	Non-savings income £	Savings (excl. dividend) income £	Dividend income £	Total £
Pension income	24,635			
Property income (N2)	5,040			
BSI £1,080 × 100/80		1,350		
Dividends £1,620 × 100/90			1,800	
Net income	29,675	1,350	1,800	32,825
Less PA	(10,600)			(10,600)
Taxable income	19,075	1,350	1,800	22,225

Notes

(1) NISA investment income is exempt from income tax.

(2) As Bert and Pearl are not married they are taxed on the property income by reference to their actual percentage ownership in the property. If they had been married, they would have been taxed on the income in equal shares unless they had made an election to be taxed on their actual ownership.

Tax

		£
£20,425 × 20%		4,085
£1,800 × 10%		180
£22,225		
		4,265

Tax liability	
Less tax deducted at source	
Dividends £1,800 × 10%	(180)
Pension tax	(3,100)
Interest £1,350 × 20%	(270)
Tax payable	715

Note: Higher rate tax relief is given for the gross Gift Aid donation of £1,316 (£1,053 × 100/80) by extension of the basic rate band. As Bert is not a higher rate taxpayer no adjustment to the computation is required.

Pearl
Tax payable

	Non-savings income	Savings (excl. dividend) income	Dividend income	Total
	£	£	£	£
Pension income	13,500			
Property Income	2,160			
BSI £216 × 100/80		270		
Dividends £2,430 × 100/90			2,700	
Less gift to charity	(4,000)			
Net income	11,660	270	2,700	14,630
Less PAA	(10,660)			(10,660)
Taxable income	1,000	270	2,700	3,970

Tax

	£
£1,000 × 20%	200
£270 × 0% (within the starting rate band)	-
£2,700 × 10%	270
£4,130	

Tax liability	470
Less tax deducted at source	
Dividend £2,700 × 10%	(270)
Pension tax	(973)
Interest £270 × 20%	(54)
Tax repayable	(827)

Premium bond winnings are exempt from income tax.

3   **Joshua – National insurance contributions accountable 2014/15**

Class 2 NICs

Payable by Joshua as self-employed person

£2.80 × 52   £146

Paid with income tax under self assessment (from 2015/16).

Class 4 NICs

Payable by Joshua as self-employed person

Taxable trading income for Class 4

(£20,040 – £5,000) = £15,040

(£15,040 – £8,060) × 9%   £628

Paid with income tax under self assessment.

Class 1 primary NICs

Deducted by Joshua from employee's gross pay.

As both employees are members of personal pension schemes, they can no longer be contracted out of the Additional State Pension. Contributions at the not contracted out rates are applicable.

	£
Thelma (£170 – £155) × 12% × 51 weeks	92
(£815 – £155) × 12% × 1 week	79
(£920 – £815) × 2% × 1 week	2
Total for Thelma	173
Louise (£240 – £155) × 12% × 52 weeks	530
Total class 1 primary NICs	703

Paid with IT via PAYE monthly

Class 1 secondary NICs

Payable by Joshua as employer

	£
Thelma (£170 – £156) × 13.8% × 51 weeks	99
(£920 – £156) × 13.8% × 1 week	105
Louise (£240 – £156) × 13.8% × 52 weeks	603
	807
Less employment allowance (max £2,000)	(807)
Total class 1 secondary NICs	Nil

Assuming that Joshua claims the employment allowance, otherwise £807 paid with IT via PAYE monthly.

Class 1A NICs

Payable by Joshua as employer

£1,040 × 13.8%   £144

Pool car is exempt benefit.

Payable in one sum by 19 July 2016 (22 July for electronic payment).

Class 1B NICs

Payable by Joshua as employer

Both employees are basic rate taxpayers so grossed up benefits subject to PAYE settlement agreement are:

$$\frac{100}{80} \times £200 = £250$$

£250 × 13.8% × 2   £69

Payable with the tax in one sum by 19 October 2016 (22 October for electronic payment).

4   EIS relief can only reduce an individual's income tax liability to nil. So Deborah will waste some of the possible income tax relief as her income tax liability in 2015/16 is less than the relief available. Excess relief cannot be carried forward.

However, it is possible to elect to treat any amount of the investment (subject to the overall maximum investment of £1,000,000) as if it were made in the previous tax year.

Thus if Deborah delayed the purchase until the start of the next tax year, she could then claim EIS relief on £120,000 of the shares in 2015/16. This would reduce her income tax bill to £nil in 2015/16.

The balance of the available relief could then be claimed in 2016/17, ie £9,000.

Deborah would then have claimed the full relief possible over the two years.

CHAPTER 3

Employee remuneration

Introduction

Examination context

Topic List

Summary and Self-test

Technical reference

Answers to Interactive questions

Answers to Self-test

Learning objectives

- Advise on the tax implications of remuneration packages including share schemes, termination payments, and allowable deductions

☐

- Calculate tax liabilities for individuals including income tax and national insurance contributions

☐

Specific syllabus references for this chapter are 1u, 1v.

Syllabus links

Taxable benefits interacts with national insurance contributions (Chapter 2) and withdrawing profits from a business (Chapter 21). Share schemes and pension schemes may also be important in a corporate transformation question.

Examination context

There are many tax-advantaged share schemes that advisers can suggest to employers in order to incentivise employees/ attract key personnel. In addition when employees are terminating their employment an accountant would aim to devise a tax-efficient exit using exempt termination payments.

In the examination candidates may be required to:

- Advise on the tax implications of different potential remuneration packages
- Advise on appropriate structures for termination packages
- Advise on the appropriateness of different share schemes for a given scenario

Candidates must ensure that they fully understand these planning issues relating to employment. Candidates must be able to apply the concepts to specific scenarios.

1 Taxable and exempt benefits

Section overview

- Some benefits are more tax efficient than others, as some are exempt whilst others are taxable.
- Employees' NIC is not payable on the provision of benefits although employer's NIC is payable on taxable benefits.

The following is a summary of the main provisions that you have met during your previous studies:

	Taxable on:	
	Employees in excluded employment	Directors and employees not in excluded employment
Assets		
Use of company's assets by employees (other than cars, vans, certain computers, mobile telephones and accommodation – see below) Benefit = 20% × original value of asset	NO	YES
Gift of company's assets to an employee	YES (second hand value)	YES (cost to employer)
Beneficial loans		
>£10,000 and interest charged at below the HMRC official rate	NO	YES
Canteen facilities (subsidised)		
If available to all employees and not provided by salary sacrifice	NO	NO
Company cars & private fuel		
List price × % (based on CO_2 emissions)	NO	YES
Childcare facilities	NO	NO (conditional)
Company vans		
Private use at flat rate of £3,150 + £594 for fuel. Travel to/from work not private use	NO	YES
Living accommodation		
Job-related	NO	NO
Not job-related	YES	YES
Facilities connected with living accommodation		
Repairs, heating etc		
• Job-related	NO	YES (10% limit)
• Not job-related	NO	YES
Medical insurance	NO	YES (unless for overseas duties)
Mobile telephone	NO	NO
Options other than share options	YES	YES

	Taxable on:	
	Employees in excluded employment	Directors and employees not in excluded employment
Payments to registered pension schemes	NO	NO
Profit sharing	YES	YES
Reasonable relocation expenses		
Removal costs, stamp duty land tax, solicitors' fees, etc	NO (but £8,000 limit)	NO (but £8,000 limit)
Recommended medical treatment		
Employer payments of up to £500 per annum to meet the cost of treatment recommended by occupational health	NO	NO
Subscriptions		
Many subscriptions may be deducted	NOT USUALLY	YES
Homeworker's additional household expenses		
Up to £4 per week with no supporting evidence	NO	NO

It is worth remembering that in a shareholder/director owned company, benefits will be taxable on the directors as if they were higher rate employees regardless of their actual level of employment income. However, there is still a tax advantage as employees do not pay national insurance contributions (NIC) on the provision of benefits. The company will pay Class 1A NIC on the provision of any taxable benefits. It may be preferable in cash terms for the company to provide certain benefits rather than pay additional salary once the NIC benefit is taken into account. It is definitely preferable if the benefit is exempt from tax.

2 Termination payments

Section overview

- Payments received on termination of employment are exempt, fully taxable or partly taxable.

- Payments arising from the contract of employment are fully taxable.

- Discretionary payments are exempt up to £30,000, taxable as specific employment income on any excess.

2.1 Types of termination payment

There are three types of payments received by an employee on the termination of employment.

Payment which are fully exempt from income tax are:

- Payments made on the death, injury or disability of the employee
- Lump sum payments under registered pension schemes

Payments which are fully taxable are:

- Payment as reward for services, eg terminal bonuses

- Compensation for loss of office which was either a contractual entitlement or there was a reasonable expectation of payment, eg many types of payments in lieu of notice (PILONs)

Payments which are fully taxable are general earnings and taxable on a receipts basis under the usual rules. This is because they arise from the contract of employment.

Payments which are partly exempt are discretionary payments (**ex gratia payments**) as compensation for loss of office. The exemption applies up to £30,000. Any excess over £30,000 is taxable. If the employee receives statutory redundancy pay in addition to a discretionary payment, the amount of statutory redundancy pay received reduces the £30,000 exemption. [Hp80]

For NIC purposes if the payment is taxable as a reward for services it will be 'earnings' for NIC purposes and subject to Class 1 contributions. However, if a payment attracts the £30,000 exemption, the whole payment is exempt from NIC.

2.2 Ex gratia payments and foreign service

There is a complete exemption from the charge to income tax if the employment includes a **substantial element of foreign service.**

For this purpose a 'substantial element of foreign service' comprises either:

- Three-quarters of the whole period of service;

- The last ten years, where the whole period of service exceeds ten years; or

- Half of the total period of service, including 10 out of the last 20 years where the whole period of service exceeds 20 years.

If there is an element of foreign service which does not qualify as 'substantial' and after applying all other exemptions (ie the £30,000 exemption), part of the termination payment is still taxable, the taxable part may be reduced by a fraction equal to:

$$\frac{\text{period of foreign service}}{\text{total length of service}}$$

Worked example: Foreign service

Jane is an employee of W Ltd. She was made redundant by her employer on 31 October 2015 and received an ex gratia termination payment of £50,000.

Jane had been employed by W Ltd for 25 years with the following pattern of employment.

Years 1 – 2   UK service
Years 3 – 13 Foreign service
Years 14 – 25   UK service

Requirements

Calculate Jane's taxable termination payment. Identify how this would have changed if Jane's foreign service had been from years 3 to 17.

Solution

Jane's total foreign service is 11 years (years 3 to 13) which does not qualify as 'substantial'. Her taxable termination payment is:

	£
Total payment	50,000
Less first £30K	(30,000)
	20,000
Less foreign service	
$\frac{11}{25} \times £20,000$	(8,800)
Taxable termination payment	11,200

If Jane's foreign service had been from year 3 to 17 it would qualify as 'substantial' as it is at least half of the total period of service, including 10 out of the last 20 years. The payment would have been fully exempt.

2.3 Taxation of discretionary termination payments

The excess of a discretionary termination payment over £30,000 is taxable as specific employment income. It is treated as the top slice of the individual's income and is taxed after savings income and dividends at the individual's highest marginal rate of tax.

Any statutory redundancy pay received uses up part of the £30,000 exemption and thereby reduces the amount of any discretionary payment that can be exempt from income tax.

Remember that a termination payment which is specific employment income is taxable when it is received by the ex-employee. This may or may not be in the year that the employment ceases.

The actual payment received by the employee is received:

- Net of income tax via PAYE if paid on leaving employment; or

- Net of the basic, higher and additional rates of tax as appropriate, if paid after the cessation of employment.

Sometimes, an ex-employee may also continue to receive benefits (eg use of a car) for some time after the termination of the employment. The value of such benefits (using the usual benefit rules) must also be taken into account when considering the £30,000 limit. Benefits are received when they are used or enjoyed.

Benefits which would be exempt under the usual benefit rules are also exempt for this purpose. The provision of counselling and outplacement services and retraining courses is an exempt benefit.

Worked example: Termination payment

Karen is an employee of V Ltd. She was made redundant by her employer on 31 December 2015.

She earned an annual salary of £34,000. She was also entitled to use of a company car, the annual benefit for which was £4,800. She was not entitled to private fuel.

Karen received a redundancy package as follows:

Statutory redundancy pay	£1,680
Discretionary payment for loss of employment	£35,200
Terminal bonus under employment contract	£6,100

Use of car until 31 March 2016.

Karen also received dividends of £3,465 in December 2015. This was her only other source of income.

Requirement

Calculate Karen's tax liability for 2015/16.

Solution

Termination payment

	£
Statutory redundancy pay	Nil
Discretionary payment for loss of employment	35,200
Terminal bonus (taxable as general earnings)	Nil
Car benefit 3/12 × £4,800	1,200
	36,400
Less exemption (£30,000 – £1,680)	(28,320)
Taxable as specific employment income	8,080

Tax liability

	Non-savings income £	Dividend income £	Termination payment £	Total £
Salary £34,000 × 9/12	25,500			
Car benefit				
£4,800 × 9/12	3,600			
Terminal bonus	6,100			
Dividends				
£3,465 × 100/90		3,850		
Termination payment			8,080	
Net income	35,200	3,850	8,080	47,130
Less PA	(10,600)			(10,600)
Taxable income	24,600	3,850	8,080	36,530

Tax

	£
£24,600 × 20%	4,920
£3,850 × 10%	385
£3,335 × 20%	667
£31,785	
£4,745 × 40%	1,898
£36,530	
Tax liability	7,870

3 Share schemes

Section overview

- Share schemes are used as a way of rewarding and incentivising employees. Certain schemes, fulfilling specific conditions and notified to HMRC, have significant tax advantages.

- Tax-advantaged schemes result in no income tax or national insurance for the employee at grant and exercise (unless EMI scheme issued at a discount). A capital gain will arise on disposal of the shares.

- Schemes that are not tax-advantaged result in neither income tax nor national insurance at grant. Income tax and national insurance is payable on exercise. Capital gains tax is payable on disposal of the shares.

- There are four main tax-advantaged schemes:
    1. Company Share Option Plan (CSOP)
    2. Enterprise Management Incentives (EMI)
    3. Save As You Earn (SAYE)
    4. Share Incentive Plan (SIP)

- The CSOP, EMI and SAYE are all share option based schemes. The SIP is a complex scheme which enables the issue of free shares (rather than share options) and/or the purchase of shares by employees out of gross pay.

3.1 Tax treatment of share schemes

Share schemes involve three stages:

- The grant of the option – when the option to buy the shares at a future date is granted to the employee.

- The exercise of the option – when the employee actually buys the shares.

- The sale of the shares.

Tax liabilities may arise at any or all of the stages of the scheme depending on its status.

The most significant difference between the terms of tax-advantaged schemes and other schemes is that for a tax-advantaged scheme, the exercise price must normally be at least equal to the market value of the shares at the date of grant. For other schemes, the exercise price may be heavily discounted or may even be nil.

3.1.1 Employers' corporation tax liabilities

This section is rewritten.

The cost of providing shares for a tax-advantaged share schemes is an allowable deduction for the purposes of corporation tax, if they are ordinary shares with no special rights and relate to:

- A listed company (or a subsidiary of a listed company); or
- A company which is not under the control of another company.

As a result, employees of a subsidiary company are usually awarded shares in the parent company to ensure a corporation tax deduction.

The deduction is the difference between the market value of the shares at exercise and the actual exercise price. It is given in the accounting period in which the employee exercises the option. For schemes which are heavily discounted (not tax-advantaged schemes), this may be a substantial deduction.

In addition the majority of running costs for a share incentive plan are also an allowable deduction for the purposes of corporation tax.

3.1.2 Employees' tax liabilities

	Grant	Exercise	Disposal
Tax-advantaged schemes	Not taxable	Not normally taxable	Subject to capital gains tax as normal
Other schemes	No tax for options granted after 01.09.03	Taxed as employment income: 　　　　　　　　£ MV on exercise　X Cost　　　　　(X) Taxable　　　　X	Capital gain on increase in value of shares since exercise date: 　　　　　　　　　£ Proceeds　　　　X Cost　　　　　(X) Amount charged to income tax on exercise　(X) ⎫ Equal to 　　　　　　　　 ⎬ MV @ Gain　　　　　　X ⎭ exercise

Therefore:

- A tax-advantaged scheme taxes all the increase in market value from the date of grant to the date of disposal as a capital gain.

- Other schemes tax the increase in value from grant to exercise as income and the increase in market value from exercise to disposal as a capital gain.

- Note that for all schemes ie tax-advantaged and other schemes (other than EMI), ownership for entrepreneurs' relief purposes runs from the date of exercise not the date of grant. Where shares are acquired by exercise of an EMI option on or after 6 April 2013 (or 6 April 2012, if an election is made), the conditions for entrepreneurs' relief are relaxed so that the normal requirement for the individual to own at least 5% of the company does not apply, and the one year ownership requirement is relaxed so that it is satisfied if one year has passed from the date of grant of the option. Entrepreneurs' relief is considered in detail in Chapter 6.

3.1.3 NIC and share schemes

If there is an income tax charge in respect of acquiring shares through a share scheme, Class 1 National Insurance Contributions (NIC) may also be due, but only if the shares are 'readily convertible assets', ie they can be sold on a stock exchange.

The NIC charge follows the income tax charge so there is never an NIC (or income tax) charge on the grant or exercise of options under a Company Share Option Plan (CSOP) or under the Save As You Earn (SAYE) scheme.

There may, however, be an NIC charge (if the shares are readily convertible assets):

(a) On the exercise of a share option that is not tax-advantaged.

(b) On the exercise of an enterprise management incentive (EMI) option if, at the date of grant, the exercise price was set at lower than market value.

(c) On the withdrawal of shares from a Share Incentive Plan (SIP) within the five-year holding period.

(d) On the receipt of free or cheap shares provided directly by the employer.

3.2 Tax-advantaged share schemes

Four main schemes exist to reward employees and enable them to benefit from substantial tax advantages. The schemes are:

- Company Share Option Plan (CSOP)
- Enterprise Management Incentives (EMI)
- Save As You Earn (SAYE)
- Share Incentive Plan (SIP)

3.2.1 CSOP and EMI

The CSOP and EMI schemes are both based on the award of share options to key employees.

3.2.2 SAYE

The SAYE scheme is a no risk savings scheme which allows employees to save a proportion of their net income each month for a period of three or five years. A share option may be issued at the start of the savings period enabling the employees to purchase shares at the end of the savings period for a fixed price. At the end of the savings period the savings can then either be taken together with a tax free bonus (ie interest), or may be used to purchase shares at the share option price.

3.2.3 SIP

SIPs are complex share plan arrangements which provide up to four different ways of providing shares (as opposed to share options) to employees.

Employers may use one, some or all of the following ways of issuing shares to reward their employees:

- **Free shares** – An employer can give up to £3,600 worth of shares a year to an employee.

- **Partnership shares** – An employee can buy shares out of pre-tax remuneration up to a value of the lower of £1,800 and 10% of salary per year.

- **Matching shares** – An employer can match the partnership shares bought by the employee by giving him up to two free shares for every partnership share purchased.

- **Dividend shares** – An employee can use dividends received from the plan shares to reinvest in further plan shares.

All shares are held in the plan in trust for the employees rather than owned personally by each employee. To benefit from the tax advantages, all the shares except partnership shares must be held in the plan for at least three years.

If an employee ceases to be employed the shares will leave the plan and then be owned by the employee personally, the tax advantages will then be lost and may be clawed back depending on how long the shares have been owned:

- Held < 3 years – income tax and NIC payable based on market value of the shares at withdrawal. For dividend shares the original dividend is taxable instead.

- Held 3 – 5 years – income tax and NIC payable based on lower of market value of the shares at withdrawal and market value at grant. Dividend shares may be removed from the plan after three years with no income tax or NI payable.

- Held > 5 years – no taxable benefit.

Capital gains tax is not payable on shares disposed of after five years if still held in the plan ie the individual is still employed. Otherwise the base cost for capital gains tax purposes is the market value at the date the shares leave the plan ie the date the employee leaves the company.

3.2.4 Summary of all four schemes

	CSOP	EMI	SAYE	SIP
Qualifying employees	Restrict to key employees only (must own ≤ 30%)	Restrict to key employees only (must own ≤ 30% and work for substantial amount of time for company)	Must be open to all (no maximum holding)	Must be open to all (no maximum) Possible to award free shares based on performance criteria
Maximum total value at grant per employee	£30k	£250k (reduced by value of any shares held under a CSOP) Company may only have £3m in issue at any one time	£10 – £500 per month may be saved per employee from net income	Free = £3.6k pa Partnership = £1.8k pa (max 10% salary) Matching = up to 2 for each partnership share Dividend = use dividends from SIP shares to buy more shares
Conditions	No discount at grant Exercisable ≥3 years and ≤10 years	May issue at a discount Exercisable ≤10 years Company must have gross assets ≤£30m, be trading, may be quoted or unquoted Company group must have <250 employees at time of grant	Maximum 20% discount	Hold for at least 3 years except partnership shares
Tax treatment at grant	No income tax or NIC	No income tax or NIC	No income tax or NIC	No income tax or NIC on issue of free or matching shares, partnership shares are purchased out of gross income, no income tax on dividends used to buy dividend shares

	CSOP	EMI	SAYE	SIP
Tax treatment at exercise	No income tax or NIC	If issued at a discount, the discount is taxable employment income: £ Exercise price X MV at grant (X) Taxable X Or the difference between the exercise price and the MV of shares at exercise, if lower	No income tax or NIC	Not applicable
Tax treatment at disposal	Normal capital gain based on proceeds less exercise price	Normal capital gain based on: £ Proceeds X Exercise price (X) Amount taxable at exercise (X) Gain X Entrepreneurs' relief requirements relaxed for EMI shares acquired on or after 6.4.2013 (6.4.2012 by election). There is no minimum 5% holding, and the one year holding period runs from the grant of the option	Normal capital gain based on proceeds less exercise price	No CGT if still held in plan at disposal ie still an employee If not in plan, base cost = MV at date left plan

Worked example: CSOP or not tax-advantaged scheme

Adrian Black, an employee, is granted an option in October 2010 to acquire 1,000 shares in his employing company, a quoted trading company, before 1 October 2016 at £8 each. When the option is exercised in November 2015 the shares are worth £20 each. Adrian sells the shares on the same day for their market value.

Adrian is a higher rate taxpayer who normally earns at least £70,000 pa and has no other capital gains in 2015/16.

Requirements

Calculate the tax charges on the exercise of the option and on the disposal of the shares assuming:

(a) The share option scheme is a Company Share Option Plan; or

(b) The scheme is not tax-advantaged.

Solution

	Company Share Option Plan £	Other share option scheme £
IT on exercise		
[1,000 × (£20 – £8)] = £12,000 × 40%	Nil	4,800
NIC on exercise – Employer's (£12,000 × 13.8%)	Nil	1,656
– Employee's (£12,000 × 2%)	Nil	240
CGT on disposal of shares		
Sale proceeds (£20 × 1,000)	20,000	20,000
Less cost (£8 × 1,000)	(8,000)	(8,000)
gain charged to IT (above)		(12,000)
Chargeable gain	12,000	Nil
Less annual exempt amount	(11,100)	
	900	
Tax thereon at 28%	252	

Interactive question 1: Share option scheme
[Difficulty level: Intermediate]

Compubuy Ltd is a trading company breaking into the e-commerce market. Its gross assets are £20 million. The market value of its ordinary shares is 125p each on 31 August 2014, at which time the company grants to Alison an option over 80,000 shares under a Enterprise Management Incentive scheme. The cost of the shares under the option is fixed at 125p per share.

Alison is a full-time employee of Compubuy Ltd and currently holds no other share options. Compubuy Ltd has £2 million of such share options currently in issue.

Requirements

Show the taxation consequences for Alison if:

(a) The option is exercised on 31 August 2017 when the market value of the shares is 350p; and
(b) The shares are then sold on 30 June 2018 for £750,000.

Assume Alison is a higher rate tax payer who always uses her capital gains tax annual exempt amount.

See **Answer** at the end of this chapter.

Interactive question 2: Income tax liability
[Difficulty level: Intermediate]

Stan Lee is the advertising manager for Spider plc, a quoted trading company. In 2015/16 he was paid a salary of £29,000 and received taxable benefits of £3,400. He is also a member of two share option schemes. His transactions in the shares of Spider plc were as follows:

*   **1 May 2015** – sold 800 shares for £3,200. The shares had been acquired for £2.50 each in February 2011 via the company's SAYE scheme.

*   **1 June 2015** – exercised share options (not tax-advantaged) to acquire 3,000 shares for £1.50 each. The options were granted in June 2013 when the value of a share in the company was £1.50 and had to be exercised before 1 June 2017. The market value of a share in the company on 1 June 2015 was £4.05.

*   **1 January 2016** – exercised options to acquire 2,000 shares for £2.80 each under the company's SAYE scheme. The market value of a share in the company on 1 January 2016 was £4.20.

His only other income in the year was bank interest received of £6,500 and dividends from UK companies of £2,970. He paid personal pension contributions of £3,360 on 1 May 2015.

Requirements

Compute the income tax liability of Stan Lee for 2015/16 and state the tax treatment of the share transactions.

See **Answer** at the end of this chapter.

3.3 Employee shareholder shares

Employees can receive shares in the company they work for in exchange for entering into an employee shareholder agreement under which they give up certain employment rights. These include rights to statutory redundancy pay and rights to claim for unfair dismissal.

In order for the agreement to be binding the employee must receive shares worth at least £2,000. There is no upper limit on the value of the shares which can be issued in consideration for entering into such an agreement.

3.3.1 Income tax treatment

Where employee shareholder shares are issued there is no income tax or NIC on the first £2,000 of shares.

3.3.2 Capital gains tax treatment

The first disposal of employee shareholder shares is exempt from capital gains tax. This applies to only the first £50,000 of shares issued to an individual by a particular employer group.

The exemption takes priority over:

- The normal tax-free disposal rule between spouses,
- The paper for paper reorganisations rules (see Chapter 6), and
- The normal share pooling rules.

If the company buys the shares back from the individual once he is no longer an employee, no part of the consideration is treated as a distribution (see Chapter 17 for details of how share buy-backs are usually treated), meaning that the capital gains tax exemption can apply to such transactions.

3.3.3 Employees with a material interest in the company

Neither the income tax nor capital gains tax exemptions apply to employee shareholder shares if at any time in the year before the shares were issued the individual, or someone connected with him, had a 25% or more interest in the company.

Worked example: Employee shareholder shares

Jonathan signs an employee shareholder agreement when he starts working for Fizzbang plc on 1 March 2016, and in consideration is issued with 1,000 employee shareholder shares with a market value of £35,000.

In January 2019 he sells the shares to an unrelated third party for £55,000.

Requirements

Explain the tax consequences of the transactions.

Solution

The value of the shares received, less the £2,000 exemption, is taxed as employment income. The taxable amount is therefore £35,000 – £2,000 = £33,000. If the shares are 'readily convertible' the same amount will be subject to NICs.

Because the value of the shares when they were issued was less than £50,000, the full gain on the disposal in January 2019 is exempt.

4 Pension schemes

Section overview

- Pension schemes provide individuals with a tax efficient method of saving in the long term.

- Pension schemes offer an alternative way for an employer to remunerate an employee in a tax efficient way.

- Employer pension contributions are an exempt benefit, deductible for corporation tax purposes and the pension fund itself is not subject to taxation.

- Although the income on retirement is taxable, it is a tax efficient way of paying employees or extracting funds from a company.

- A person may contribute to any number of personal and/or occupational pension schemes subject to an overall limit of relevant earnings or £3,600 if higher.

- Tax relief is given for individual's contributions so that a £100 contribution by a higher rate taxpayer normally only costs £60.

- The maximum contributions for which relief is available is capped at £40,000 for 2015/16.

- Unused annual allowance can be carried forward for three tax years increasing the amount of contributions on which tax relief is available.

- Pension schemes exist for small businesses/wealthy individuals which permit investment in commercial property and loans to businesses.

4.1 Overview of pension schemes

The following table summarises the pension schemes knowledge brought forward from Tax Compliance:

	Occupational Scheme	Personal Scheme
Eligible to contribute	Employees	Employed, self-employed or unemployed
Examples of scheme	Final salary/defined benefit scheme	Group personal pensions
	Money purchase/defined contribution scheme	Any privately arranged personal pension
	Small self administered schemes (SSAS)	Self invested personal pensions (SIPP)
Maximum contributions eligible for tax relief **(total employee + employer)**	**Employee contributions:** Higher of: • Total relevant earnings; and • £3,600 (gross) Relevant earnings = employment income + trading profits + income from furnished holiday accommodation **Employee and employer contributions:** Subject to the annual allowance – for 2015/16 maximum relief for total combined pension contributions is £40,000 (2013/14 and before: £50,000)	

	Occupational Scheme	Personal Scheme
Tax relief for individual's contribution	Net pay arrangements Paid from gross income Deduct from employment income	Tax relief at source Treated as paid net ie maximum cash payment = 80% of gross contribution Do not deduct from employment income, instead extend basic rate band by gross amount of contribution
Tax relief for employer contribution	Not a taxable benefit, paid gross Deductible from trading profits in year in which paid	

Contributions in excess of annual allowance limit of £40,000	• If contributions for which relief has been given in respect of an individual's schemes, including:
	
	   – All individual contributions
	   – All employer contributions
	
	exceeds the annual allowance limit, then an excess contributions charge is made.
	
	• The annual allowance limit can be increased by unused annual allowance from the three previous tax years on a FIFO basis. (See Section 4.2.1 below.)
	
	• This charge is calculated as:
	
	Marginal tax rate × (Excess of total contributions for which relief has been given over the annual allowance). (See Section 4.2.2 below.)
	
	• The charge is added to the individual's income tax liability.	

Retirement age	55 (50 pre 6 April 2010)	
Tax free lump sum on retirement (TFLS)	On retirement up to 25% of the lifetime allowance may be taken as a TFLS. The lifetime allowance is £1.25m (2013/14 and before: £1.5m) 25% of the total fund may be taken as a lump sum, but any excess over 25% of the lifetime allowance is taxable at 55%	
Annuity/Draw-down	The fund balance can either be used to buy an annuity or be subject to annual draw-downs. Any excess over the lifetime allowance taken as an annuity or as draw-downs is taxable at 25%	
Pension fund's tax liability	The pension fund itself is not subject to taxation	
Pension income	Pension income is taxable as non-savings income at 20/40/45%	

4.1.1 Employer contributions

Large one-off employer contributions may be deductible from profits over a number of accounting periods. Deductions for contributions of more than £500,000 are spread over up to four years.

4.2 Restriction of tax relief on pension contributions

4.2.1 Carry forward of unused annual allowance

An individual can carry forward unused annual allowance for three years and increase the relief available in any year on a FIFO basis. The carry forward can be from any year during which the individual was a member of a registered pension scheme, regardless of whether he made any contributions that year or had a nil pension input amount during that year.

Worked example: Carry forward of unused annual allowance

Maurice makes the following contributions into his personal pension scheme.

2012/13	£32,000
2013/14	£35,000
2014/15	£15,000

In 2015/16 Maurice makes a contribution to his pension fund of £70,000.

Requirement

Calculate the amount of any unused annual allowance remaining at 5 April 2016 for each of the tax years 2012/13 to 2015/16 showing how the gross payment of £87,500 by Maurice in 2015/16 is allocated.

Solution

	Available allowance	Allowance utilised	Allowance remaining
	£	£	£
2012/13	18,000	18,000	0
2013/14	15,000	15,000	0
2014/15	25,000	14,500	10,500
2015/16	40,000	40,000	0
		87,500	10,500

4.2.2 Annual allowance charge

If the pension input amount exceeds the annual allowance there is a charge to income tax on the individual. This might happen where the individual makes tax relievable contributions in excess of the annual allowance where his earnings exceed the amount of allowance or where the employer makes excess contributions.

The annual allowance charge will remove the tax relief received on the pension input in excess of the annual allowance. This could be in whole or part at 45%, 40% or 20% depending on the taxable income of the individual.

The tax charge is added to the individual's income tax liability for the year.

Employer contributions are not treated as earnings or taxable benefits for NIC purposes. Therefore, there is a slight advantage to the employer making contributions directly to a pension scheme instead of paying the individual the money for that individual to make contributions, even if the charge applies.

Worked example: Annual allowance charge

Julia is a member of a money purchase personal pension scheme. In the tax year 2015/16, she has taxable earnings of £275,000. During that year, she makes a contribution of £120,000 to the pension scheme and her employer makes further contributions of £130,000 to the scheme. Julia has no other taxable income in the year and has no unused pension annual allowance brought forward.

Requirement

Calculate Julia's income tax liability for 2015/16.

Solution

Julia has made a net contribution of £120,000 to the pension scheme which grosses up to (£120,000 × 100/80) = £150,000.

This is all tax-relievable since it is lower than the greater of:

- Her relevant earnings of £275,000; and
- The basic amount of £3,600.

Julia's pension contributions in excess of the annual allowance are:

	£
Individual contribution subject to tax relief	150,000
Employer contributions	130,000
Total tax relievable contributions	280,000
Less annual allowance	(40,000)
Excess contributions	240,000

Her basic and higher rate limits are increased by £150,000, as follows:

- Basic rate band: £181,785 (£31,785 + £150,000)
- Higher rate limit: £300,000 (£150,000 + £150,000)

	£
Earnings/net income	275,000
Less personal allowance (Note)	(Nil)
Taxable income	275,000

Tax	
£181,785 × 20%	36,357
£93,215 × 40%	37,286
£275,000	
Annual allowance charge	
(£300,000 – £275,000) £25,000 × 40%	10,000
(£240,000 – £25,000) £215,000 × 45%	96,750
Tax liability	180,393

Note: Julia's adjusted net income is £275,000 – £150,000 = £125,000 and therefore her personal allowance is nil.

4.3 Small self administered scheme (SSAS)

A SSAS is a special type of occupational pension scheme which is subject to most of the rules applicable to all occupational pension schemes. It is designed for small companies which are likely to be owner managed.

It may borrow up to 50% of the fund value. It may also lend up to 50% of the fund value to its own company. It may also invest up to 5% of the net pension fund in its own shares.

It may not invest in residential property unless held in a real estate investment trust (REIT) or in tangible moveable property, eg fine wines.

4.4 Self invested personal pension (SIPP)

A SIPP is a type of personal pension plan subject to all the normal rules of any personal pension plan.

Like a SSAS it may also borrow up to 50% of the fund value. However, unlike a SSAS, it may not lend money. It may purchase shares in any company without limit including those companies in which the person investing in the pension also owns shares.

It may not invest in residential property unless held in a REIT or in tangible moveable property eg fine wines.

4.5 Commercial property held by a SSAS or a SIPP

A SSAS or a SIPP may be set up specifically to hold commercial property used in the business of the sponsoring company (SSAS) or pension investor (SIPP).

The main advantage of doing so is that there is no tax paid on capital gains realised on the eventual disposal of the building as pension funds do not pay tax. In addition, the rent paid by the company/business will be deductible from trading profits and will not be taxable on the pension fund. The property will also be protected from creditors.

Interactive question 3: Pension advice   [Difficulty level: Exam standard]

Your manager has asked you to prepare some notes for a client meeting. In preparing your notes, consider the following:

- Your client has just started a new job and is 40. Current annual employment income is approximately £200,000 increasing to £500,000 in five years' time.

- The client's employer operates an occupational money purchase pension scheme. The client has no idea what a money purchase scheme is. The employer contributes 5% of salary to the scheme and employees are required to contribute 10%.

- The client is concerned about the risk of having just one pension scheme but is unsure whether he can be a member of other schemes or even whether his employer's scheme is compulsory to join.

- As he has not contributed to a scheme in the past the client would like to invest significant amounts.

- The client does not understand how tax relief is given on contributions to a pension scheme.

- The client does not understand what benefits are available on retirement nor how they are taxed.

Requirement

Prepare suitable notes for the meeting. Assume that the current date is February 2016.

See **Answer** at the end of this chapter.

Summary

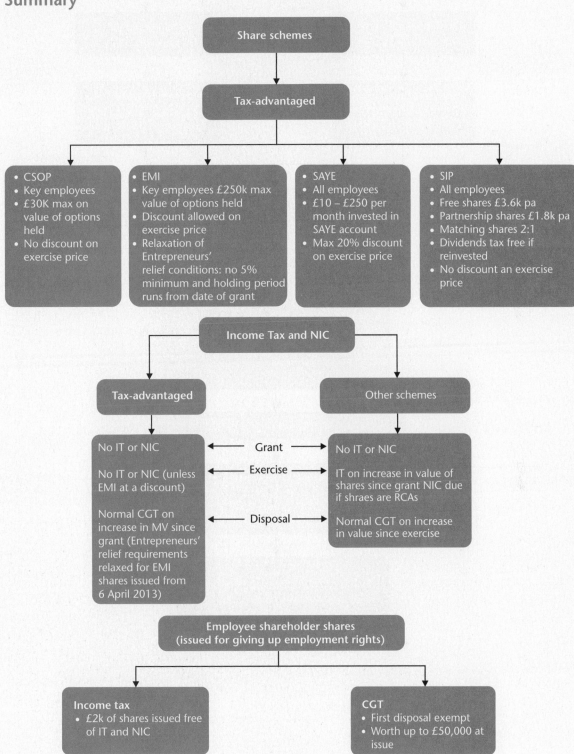

Share schemes

↓

Tax-advantaged

- **CSOP**
  - Key employees
  - £30K max on value of options held
  - No discount on exercise price

- **EMI**
  - Key employees £250k max value of options held
  - Discount allowed on exercise price
  - Relaxation of Entrepreneurs' relief conditions: no 5% minimum and holding period runs from date of grant

- **SAYE**
  - All employees
  - £10 – £250 per month invested in SAYE account
  - Max 20% discount on exercise price

- **SIP**
  - All employees
  - Free shares £3.6k pa
  - Partnership shares £1.8k pa
  - Matching shares 2:1
  - Dividends tax free if reinvested
  - No discount an exercise price

Income Tax and NIC

Tax-advantaged

No IT or NIC

No IT or NIC (unless EMI at a discount)

Normal CGT on increase in MV since grant (Entrepreneurs' relief requirements relaxed for EMI shares issued from 6 April 2013)

Other schemes

No IT or NIC

IT on increase in value of shares since grant NIC due if shraes are RCAs

Normal CGT on increase in value since exercise

← Grant →

← Exercise →

← Disposal →

Employee shareholder shares
(issued for giving up employment rights)

Income tax
- £2k of shares issued free of IT and NIC

CGT
- First disposal exempt
- Worth up to £50,000 at issue

CHAPTER 3

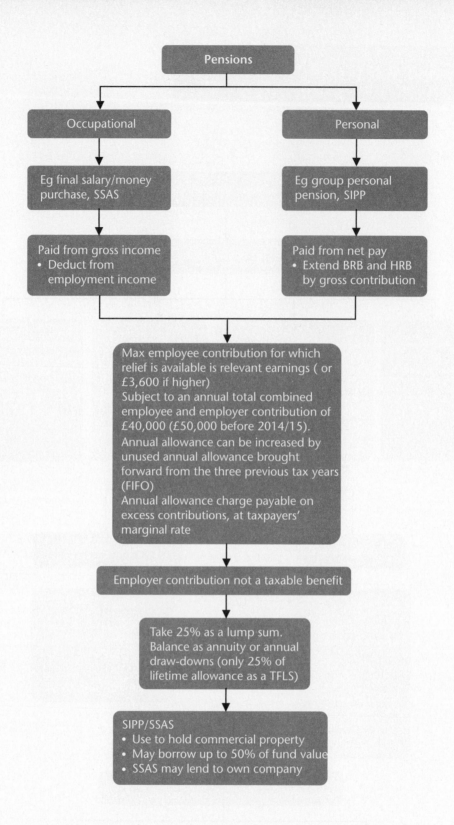

Pensions

Occupational

Personal

Eg final salary/money purchase, SSAS

Eg group personal pension, SIPP

Paid from gross income
• Deduct from employment income

Paid from net pay
• Extend BRB and HRB by gross contribution

Max employee contribution for which relief is available is relevant earnings (or £3,600 if higher)
Subject to an annual total combined employee and employer contribution of £40,000 (£50,000 before 2014/15).
Annual allowance can be increased by unused annual allowance brought forward from the three previous tax years (FIFO)
Annual allowance charge payable on excess contributions, at taxpayers' marginal rate

Employer contribution not a taxable benefit

Take 25% as a lump sum. Balance as annuity or annual draw-downs (only 25% of lifetime allowance as a TFLS)

SIPP/SSAS
• Use to hold commercial property
• May borrow up to 50% of fund value
• SSAS may lend to own company

ICAEW

Self-test

Answer the following questions.

1   Rose was made redundant by her employer on 6 June 2015.

    She received the following redundancy package:

	£
Statutory redundancy pay	3,800
Discretionary payment in cash	25,000
Market value of car – ownership transferred to Rose	6,000
Retraining course	1,500

    What is the termination payment taxable on Rose as specific employment income?

2   Mountain plc normally pays significant bonuses to its senior management team but is considering issuing share options instead. It has yet to decide the best way to issue the options.

    Mountain plc is a small, quoted trading company with total gross assets of £23m. It generally pays bonuses of approximately £30,000 per annum to each director. It has 12 full-time directors who generally remain with the company for five years and fewer than 200 other employees. None of the directors owns 5% or more of the share capital in Mountain plc.

    Requirement

    Suggest a suitable share option scheme and explain how it will be taxed.

3   Suzanne is a manager in your firm. You are a newly-qualified senior. Suzanne qualified some years ago but has not been on any up-date courses since that time. She has recently been involved in preparing a report concerning the tax-efficient extraction of funds for your firm's largest corporate client, Hill Ltd. For the year ending 31 March 2016 Hill Ltd anticipates taxable total profits of £1.3m.

    The following are extracts from Suzanne's recent report written on 6 May 2016:

    •   Directors could extract funds as share options under a tax-efficient scheme and pay tax at an effective rate of 10%.

    •   The company should consider putting extra contributions into the directors' pension fund, as this is extremely tax efficient.

    •   It would be very efficient to give staff extra benefits instead of salary increases, as neither the employee nor the company would incur national insurance contributions on these benefits.

    The partner in charge has asked you to prepare in note form any comments you have on this report, including relevant calculations. He informs you that the directors wish to extract £100,000 gross.

    Requirement

    Prepare the notes as required by the partner.

Now, go back to the Learning objectives in the Introduction. If you are satisfied you have achieved these objectives, please tick them off.

CHAPTER

3

Technical reference

Legislation

References relate to Income Tax (Earnings and Pensions) Act 2003 (*ITEPA 2003*)

Taxable and exempt benefits

The Benefits Code (general)	s.63
Vouchers	ss.73 – 96A
Living accommodation	ss.97 – 113
Expenses connected with provision of living accommodation	ss.313 – 315
Cars and fuel for private use	ss.114 – 153, 167
Vans for private use	ss.154 – 164
Employment related loans	ss.173 – 191
Assets available for private use/transfer	ss.204 – 210
Other benefits	ss.201 – 203
Exempt benefits	ss.227 – 326

Termination payments

Fully exempt termination payments	ss.406 – 407
Partly exempt termination payments	ss.403 – 404

Share schemes

Share incentive plan	ss.488 – 515 & Sch 2
Save as you earn scheme	ss.516 – 520 & Sch 3
Company share option plan	ss.521 – 526 & Sch 4
Enterprise management incentives	ss.527 – 541 & Sch 5

Pensions

References are to Finance Act 2004 (*FA 2004*)

Types of pension scheme	s.150
Tax relief for contributions by member	s.188
Annual limit for relief	s.190
Tax relief at source	s.192
Net pay arrangements	s.193
Contributions by employer	s.196
Annual allowance charge	ss.227 – 238A
Pension rules during life of member	s.165
Lump sum rules during life of member	s.166
Lifetime allowance	ss.214 – 226

HMRC manual references

Employment Income Manual (Found at www.hmrc.gov.uk/manuals/eimanual/index.htm)

Employment Related Securities Manual (Found at www.hmrc.gov.uk/manuals/ersmmanual/index.htm)

Registered Pension Schemes Manual: Main Contents – Technical pages (Found at www.hmrc.gov.uk/manuals/rpsmmanual/index.htm)

> This technical reference section is designed to assist you when you are working in the office. It should help you to know where to look for further information on the topics covered in this chapter.

Answer to Interactive question 1

(a) Exercise of EMI option

The base cost for any future disposal will be the exercise price ie 80,000 × £1.25 = £100,000. There is no income tax or NIC charge under EMI rules as the shares were not issued at a discount.

(b) Sale of shares

	£
Proceeds	750,000
Cost of shares	(100,000)
Gain	650,000

	£
Capital gains tax at 10% (Note)	65,000
A profit for Alison of (£750,000 – £100,000 – £65,000)	585,000

Note: As the shares were disposed of on/ after 6 April 2013, the option was granted more than a year before disposal and Alison works full-time for the company, entrepreneurs' relief is available.

Answer to Interactive question 2

Income tax computation – 2015/16

	Total £	Non-savings £	Savings £	Dividends £
Salary	29,000	29,000		
Benefits	3,400	3,400		
Share options (3,000 × (£4.05 – £1.50))	7,650	7,650		
Bank interest (£6,500 × 100/80)	8,125		8,125	
Dividends (£2,970 × 100/90)	3,300			3,300
Net income	51,475	40,050	8,125	3,300
Less PA	(10,600)	(10,600)		
Taxable income	40,875	29,450	8,125	3,300

Income tax

Extended basic rate band:

$$\left(£31,785 + \left[£3,360 \times \frac{100}{80}\right]\right) = £35,985$$

			£
Non-savings income	29,450	@ 20%	5,890
Savings income	6,535	@ 20%	1,307
	35,985		
Savings income	1,590	@ 40%	636
Dividends	3,300	@ 32½%	1,073
	40,875		
Income tax liability			8,906

Treatment of share transactions:

1 May 2015	The sale of shares gives rise to a capital gain.
1 June 2015	The exercise of these share options gives rise to taxable income equal to the difference between the market value of the shares and the price paid. This income will also be subject to Class 1 NIC as the shares are in a quoted trading company and are therefore readily convertible assets.
1 January 2016	There are no taxation implications when tax-advantaged share options are exercised.

Answer to Interactive question 3

You do not have to join your new employer's pension scheme; however, if your employer will not contribute to a private pension scheme you will effectively be taking a 5% pay cut if you do not join. You could alternatively start a personal pension scheme or join a personal pension scheme in addition to your employer's pension scheme.

A money purchase (or defined contribution) scheme is one where the value of your pension depends on the value of the investments in the pension scheme at the date that you purchase an annuity, ie you bear the risk of investment performance, not your employer.

You can contribute up to 100% of your earnings into pension scheme(s) and obtain tax-relief on those contributions. Your employer may also contribute to your pension scheme and this is not a taxable benefit. The total amount which may be contributed to your pension schemes is subject to an annual limit of £40,000 gross (until 2013/14: £50,000 pa). The annual allowance can be increased if there is any unused annual allowance from the three previous tax years. However, you must have been a member of a registered pension scheme in a tax year in order to have unused annual allowance. This does not appear to be the case for you for the three tax years prior to 2015/16.

You should also consider the implications of the lifetime allowance limit. This is the maximum value of the pension fund that you are allowed to build up to provide pension benefits without incurring adverse tax consequences when you take a benefit from the scheme. The lifetime allowance is currently £1,250,000.

If your fund exceeds the lifetime allowance at retirement, there will be a tax charge of 55% on funds vested to provide a lump sum and 25% on funds vested to provide a pension income. It may not therefore be advantageous to over contribute to your pension scheme such that it then exceeds the lifetime allowance at retirement.

Normally, occupational pension schemes pay contributions under 'net pay arrangements' whereby your employer deducts your pension contributions gross from your pay before applying income tax. This means that tax relief is given automatically at your highest rate of tax and no adjustment is needed in your tax return. Thus a £100 contribution will mean you will only forego £55 of net income as you will be an additional rate taxpayer.

If you join a personal pension scheme your cash contributions will be treated as having been paid net of basic rate income tax at 20%. The basic rate of income tax will be added to your pension fund directly by HMRC. Further tax relief at 25% will be given by extending the basic rate limit and higher rate limit when calculating your income tax liability for the year. You will therefore receive 45% tax relief overall and a £100 contribution will only have cost you £55.

You may not trigger your retirement benefits before age 55. At retirement you may take up to 25% of the fund value as a lump sum. However, only 25% of the lifetime allowance will be tax free. Any excess taken as a lump sum will be taxable at 55%. The balance of the fund can either be used to buy an annuity, or you can choose to make annual draw-downs directly from your pension scheme. Any amount in excess of the lifetime allowance used to purchase an annuity, or withdrawn from the pension scheme, is taxable at 25%.

An annuity will pay you an annual amount for life which will be taxable as non-savings income at 20/40/45%.

1 Termination payment

	£
Statutory redundancy pay	Nil
Discretionary payment	25,000
Car	6,000
Retraining course (exempt)	Nil
	31,000
Less exemption (£30,000 – £3,800)	(26,200)
Taxable as specific employment income	4,800

2   Given that Mountain plc is a trading company with gross assets of less than £30m, it could consider awarding share options under an enterprise management incentive (EMI) scheme to key employees. Mountain plc could only have £3m such share options in issue at any one time.

Under such a scheme it could award total shares of £250,000 per director. There would be no income tax or national insurance contributions (NIC) for either employee or employer at the time of granting the option. At exercise, ie when the shares were actually purchased, there would only be an income tax charge if the share options were granted at a discount. As Mountain plc is a quoted company, a NIC liability would also arise if the share options were granted at a discount as the shares are readily convertible assets.

At sale the gain would be calculated as proceeds less cost less the amount taxed at exercise, if any.

Alternatively, the company could use a company share option plan (CSOP) but that is less advantageous as the shares cannot be issued at a discount and the maximum amount is only £30,000. If both schemes are offered, the amount held under a CSOP is deducted from the maximum permitted under the EMI scheme.

As directors stay for five years, if their annual bonus (£30,000) were always issued in shares this would not exceed the maximum £250,000.

Any gain on the disposal of shares acquired under these schemes will be subject to capital gains tax at 28% (assuming all the directors are higher rate taxpayers).

However, entrepreneurs' relief may reduce this rate to 10%. For CSOP shares, this only applies if the shares are in a company where the employee owns at least 5% (including voting rights). This condition is not currently satisfied. However, for EMI shares issued on or after 6 April 2013, there is no minimum percentage holding, and the one year holding period is relaxed to run from the date of grant of the option rather than from the date of issue of the shares. So long as the directors are still directors or employees of the company when they sell the shares, and the company is still a trading company, entrepreneurs' relief should be available on the later sale of EMI shares.

It should be noted that there is an overall lifetime limit on entrepreneurs' relief of £10 million.

3   Share option schemes

The company could issue share option schemes under a number of tax-advantaged schemes. As it appears to be restricted to a number of key employees, a save as you earn (SAYE) or share incentive plan (SIP) would not be possible.

Hill Ltd could either use a company share option plan (CSOP) or an enterprise management incentive (EMI) scheme. Under a CSOP scheme up to £30,000 could be held by any one director at a time; under an EMI scheme the limit is £250,000. Therefore the shares could be issued under just the EMI scheme or a combination of the two schemes.

As long as the shares were not issued at a discount, there would be no income tax or employee or employer NIC either at grant of the option or on exercise of the option. If EMI share options are issued at a discount (CSOP share options must be granted at market value) then there is an employment income charge at exercise equivalent to the discount given. A NIC liability would only arise on this employment income if the shares were quoted.

To qualify for an EMI scheme, Hill Ltd would have to be a trading company with gross assets of less than £30m, have less than £3m such options already in issue and have fewer than 250 full-time employees.

Any gain on sale will be subject to tax at 28%, or 10% if entrepreneurs' relief applies. The entrepreneurs' relief conditions are relaxed for EMI shares (but not for CSOP shares), meaning that the normal 5% minimum holding requirement does not apply, and the one year holding period is treated as running from the time when the option is granted rather than from the time when the shares are issued.

The costs of setting up the tax-advantaged share scheme are allowable for corporation tax purposes.

Provided Hill Ltd is not controlled by any other company there is also a corporation tax deduction at the time of exercise, which is the difference between the market value of the shares at exercise and the actual exercise price.

Pension contributions

Pension contributions are tax efficient as:

- The company can deduct contributions as part of the salary cost in calculating taxable total profits;

- The employer's contribution is not a taxable benefit; and

- The contribution will be invested in a pension fund which is free of tax.

However, whilst there is no limit on the amount which may be paid into a pension scheme, tax relief on contributions made by the directors personally is only available on contributions made up to a maximum of relevant earnings for the year.

If the company makes contributions on behalf of the directors, the total contributions of the company and the directors are compared to the annual allowance of £40,000. An income tax charge on the excess combined contributions over £40,000 will be payable by the directors at their marginal rate of tax.

It may be possible to contribute in excess of £40,000, without incurring the income tax charge, if a director has any unused annual allowance to bring forward from the previous three tax years and has been a member of a scheme in the earlier year. Unused annual allowance will have arisen if contributions in any of the previous three tax years were below the level of the annual allowance in that year (£40,000 for 2014/15 and £50,000 for 2013/14 and earlier years). The difference between the annual allowance and the value of contributions is the amount of unused annual allowance. This is used on a FIFO basis.

Also consideration should be given to the lifetime allowance limit which is £1,250,000. Funds which exceed the lifetime limit will be subject to penalty taxation of either 25% (annuity purchased) or 55% (lump sum taken) on retirement.

Large contributions (> £500,000) may only be allowed as a deduction against profits over a number of years.

Additional benefits rather than salary

Additional benefits would be subject to employer's NIC in the same way as a salary increase would. However, benefits are not subject to employee's NIC unlike an increase in salary. So from the director's perspective it may be preferable to receive additional benefits instead of additional cash.

Some benefits may also be exempt and would therefore represent a considerable tax saving such as childcare associated benefits or mobile phones.

CHAPTER 4

Unincorporated businesses

Introduction

Examination context

Topic List

Summary and Self-test

Technical reference

Answer to Interactive question

Answers to Self-test

Introduction

Learning objectives

- Prepare suitable advice to explain tax liabilities with supporting calculations ☐

- Recommend appropriate tax-planning advice ☐

- Identify further information required to complete tax computations and finalise tax advice ☐

- Give advice which is appropriate, technically correct, and within the law and the ICAEW Code of Ethics ☐

- Explain and calculate the tax implications involved in the cessation of trade ☐

- Recognise, explain and communicate opportunities to use alternative tax treatments arising from past transactions ☐

Specific syllabus references for this chapter are 1b, 1c, 1d, 1e, 1m, 2d.

Syllabus links

The mechanics of relief for trading losses is covered in the Tax Compliance study manuals. This is extended at Business Planning: Taxation to encompass tax planning aspects including giving advice to clients on the most appropriate form of loss relief.

Examination context

The aim of the accountant advising an unincorporated trader making losses is to fulfil the client's needs. That may be to make the maximum possible tax saving, or it may be to improve cash flow by making obtaining tax repayments.

In the examination candidates may be required to:

- Calculate the trading loss available for relief in the opening years of a business

- Identify the trading loss relief options open to an individual who has a business that has been trading for many years, has just commenced trading, is ceasing to trade or is incorporating

- Calculate the taxable income of the individual after the losses are relieved, giving recommendations

The effective use of trading losses can often be a discriminating factor between better and weaker candidates.

It is important to appreciate what you are trying to achieve with loss relieving, and to write this down. If the numbers partly or fully reflect the reasoning then good marks will be obtained.

1 Revision from Tax Compliance – calculation of the trading profit/loss

Section overview

- Expenditure is generally allowable if it is incurred wholly and exclusively for the purposes of the trade.

- Capital expenditure, appropriations of profit, general provisions, non-trade debts, most entertaining and gifts, and fines and penalties are disallowable.

- Pre-trading expenditure is allowable if incurred in the seven years before trading starts.

- Current year basis (CYB) applies to a continuing business. There are special rules in the opening and closing years of a business.

- Overlap profits may be created where there is double counting in the opening years. Relief for overlap profits is given on cessation.

- Expenditure on most assets is pooled in the main pool.

- A writing down allowance (WDA) is given on the balance of the main pool at the end of the period of account. This pool has a WDA of 18% for a 12-month period.

- The tax written down value (TWDV) is carried forward to the start of the next period of account.

- First Year Allowances (FYAs) are given in the period of account in which expenditure is incurred.

- FYAs of 100% are available for expenditure on research and development capital expenditure (companies only); expenditure in an enterprise zone (companies only); low emission cars; zero emission goods vehicles; and certain energy saving and water technologies.

- A special rate pool exists to include expenditure on integral features, thermal insulation and long life assets. This pool has a WDA of 8% for a 12-month period.

- An annual investment allowance (AIA) of £500,000 for a 12-month period, for expenditure incurred from 6 April 2014 (1 April for companies) to 31 December 2015, is available to all businesses. From 1 January 2016 the AIA is £200,000 for a 12-month period .The AIA was calculated on the basis of £250,000 for a 12-month period from 1 January 2013 to 6 April 2014 (1 April for companies); £25,000 for a 12-month period from 6 April 2012 (1 April for companies) to 31 December 2012; and was £100,000 for a 12-month period before 6 April 2012 (1 April 2012 for companies). The AIA can be allocated to any pool of expenditure the business chooses.

- Any small balances, up to the small pool limit of £1,000, remaining at the end of the period of account on the main or special rate pool are eligible for a WDA of up to the amount remaining.

- Some assets are not put in the main pool but have a separate pool for each asset.

- Each asset which is partly used privately by a sole trader or partner is kept in a separate pool.

- A taxpayer may elect for most assets in the main pool to be depooled except for cars or assets with private use.

- On disposal, a balancing charge arises if too many capital allowances have been given or a balancing allowance may arise if too few capital allowances have been given.

- In the last period of account of a business, no allowances are given and all the assets are actually disposed of or deemed to have been disposed of at their market value.

- A succession election can be made to transfer assets at tax written down value on a transfer of a trade to a connected person.

- A partnership itself is not a taxable person. Each partner is liable to income tax on his share (and only his share) of the partnership taxable trading income. Similarly each partner is liable to capital gains tax on his share of any gains realised on the disposal of partnership assets.

- The CYB applies to continuing partnerships. Opening and closing year rules apply to partners who join and leave the partnership but the continuing partners remain on the CYB.

1.1 Adjustments to profit

You are already familiar with the following adjustments to profit:

Item	Treatment
Capital expenditure	Disallowable – add back. Distinguish between repairs (allowable as revenue expenditure) and improvements (disallowable as capital).
Depreciation	Disallowable – add back.
Appropriation of profit	Disallowable – add back. Examples include payment of 'salary' to sole trader or payment of his pension contributions, payment of his tax liabilities and payment of excessive salary to family member.
General provision eg for stock or debts	Disallowable – add back. Distinguish from a specific provision which is allowable.
Non-trade bad debts – specific provision or written off	Disallowable – add back. Distinguish from trade debts which are allowable.
Non-staff entertaining	Disallowable – add back. Distinguish from staff entertaining which is allowable.
Gifts	Disallowable – add back except: • Gifts to employees • Gifts of trade samples (not for resale) • Gifts to customers if they incorporate a conspicuous advertisement for the business, are not food, drink, tobacco or vouchers exchangeable for goods, and the total cost per customer is no more than £50
Donations and subscriptions	Disallowable – add back except: • Small donations to local charities • Trading stock or plant gifted to charities or UK educational establishments • Subscriptions to trade and professional associations
Fines and penalties	Disallowable – add back except: • Employee parking fines
Interest on late payment of tax	Disallowable – add back.
Legal and professional fees relating to capital	Disallowable – add back except: • Legal costs relating to renewal of short lease (up to 50 years) • Costs of registration of patent or copyright for trade use • Incidental costs of raising long-term finance
Irrecoverable VAT	If relates to disallowable expenditure: disallowable – add back.
Employment payments and pensions	Generally allowable. However, on cessation of trade, payments in addition to redundancy payments are only allowable up to 3 × statutory redundancy pay.
Leased cars	If the leased car (not motorcycle) has CO_2 emissions: • In excess of 130g/km the disallowance is 15% × hire charge • No more than 130g/km the hire charge is fully allowable

Item	Treatment
Pre-trading expenditure	Allowable deduction if incurred within seven years of the start of trade and would have been deductible after start of trade.
	Eg distinguish between rent payable before trading starts (allowable) and entertaining prospective customers (disallowable).
Trading income not shown in accounts	Eg goods are taken from the business by the owner for personal use without reimbursing the business with the full value. If nothing recorded in accounts: add back selling price. If entered at cost: add back profit.
Non trading income in accounts	Eg rental income, profit on disposal of fixed assets. Deduct.
Expenditure not shown in accounts	Eg business expenditure paid personally by the owner. Allowable and so make deduction.
Lease premium paid by trader on grant of short lease	Allowable deduction: premium taxed on the landlord as property income divided by the number of years of the lease.
Trade related patent royalties	Allowable deduction: the gross amount after grossing up for basic rate tax.

Rules which specifically deny a deduction in computing trading profits take priority over those allowing a deduction.

Traders with turnover of less than £82,000 (VAT registration limit) can choose to be taxed on the cash basis. Where this applies, loan interest in excess of £500 is not deductible (ie maximum deduction is £500) and expenditure on capital assets which qualify for plant and machinery capital allowances (excluding cars) is deducted on a cash basis. Capital allowances can be claimed on cars in the usual way.

1.2   Basis periods

Current year basis

The basic rule is called the current year basis (CYB). The basis period for the tax year is the 12-month period of account ending in that tax year.

Special rules are needed for the opening years of a business because there will not usually be a 12-month period of account ending in the tax year in which the business starts.

Opening year rules

The basis of assessment in the first tax year that a business operates is the **actual basis**. The taxable trading income for the first tax year is the taxable trading income of the business from the date of commencement to the following 5 April.

The basis of assessment in the second tax year depends on the length of the period of account ending in the second tax year. There are four possibilities:

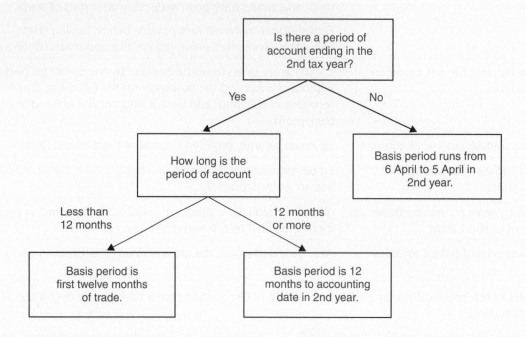

Usually, the current year basis applies to the third tax year of trading because there will be a 12-month period of account ending in that year.

Occasionally, there will not be a 12-month period of account ending in the third tax year. In this case the basis period will be the 12 months to the end of the period of account ending in the third tax year.

Cessation

The basis period for the last tax year is one of the following possibilities:

Business ends	Basis period for last tax year
Not in the first tax year	From end of basis period for the penultimate tax year to date of cessation
In the first tax year	Period for which business traded

1.3 Capital allowances

The pro forma as set out below was considered in detail in Tax Compliance. You must ensure that you could still calculate the capital allowances due to a business.

	Main pool	Special rate pool	Short life asset (Note 1)	Private use asset (Note 2)	Allowances
Period of accounts	£	£	£	£	£
TWDV b/f	X	X	X	X	
Additions eligible for FYA @ 100%					
Acquisitions (incl cars CO_2 ≤ 75g/km) (Note 3)	X				
FYA @ 100%	(X)				X
Additions eligible for AIA					
– Special rate pool		X			
– Main pool	X				
AIA (Note 4)	(X)	(X)			X
Additions (cars):					
– Cars CO_2 ≤ 130g/km	X				
– Cars CO_2 > 130g/km		X			
Less disposals (restricted to original cost)	(X)	(X)			
	X	X	X	X	
Small pools WDA (£1,000)					
WDA @ 18%	(X)		(X)	(X) × bus%	X
@ 8%		(X)			X
TWDV c/f	X	X	X	X	
Total allowances					X

Notes:

(1) A trader can elect that specific items of plant (other than cars and certain other exceptions) be kept separately from the main pool. The election should therefore be made for assets likely to be sold within eight years for less than their tax written down values (ie likely to give rise to a balancing allowance on sale).

Provided that the asset is disposed of within eight years (four years for expenditure incurred prior to 6 April 2011 (1 April 2011 for companies)) of the end of the period of account or accounting period in which it was bought (ie after nine (previously five) allowances have been taken), a balancing charge or allowance is made on its disposal. Otherwise, its tax written down value is added to the main pool at that time.

(2) All assets with private use by the proprietor have their own column, ie one per asset.

(3) Assets qualifying for FYAs are allocated to the appropriate pool as on disposal the sale proceeds must be deducted from the main pool. Prior to 6 April 2015 (1 April 2015 for companies) car with emissions of 95g/km or less were eligible for the FYA.

(4) Allocate AIA to expenditure in the following order:

(i) Special rate additions (which would otherwise only qualify for WDA at 8%)
(ii) Main pool additions (which would otherwise only qualify for WDA at 18%)

From 6 April 2010 (1 April 2010 for companies) to 5 April 2012 (31 March 2012 for companies) the AIA was £100,000. From 6 April 2012 (1 April 2012 for companies) to 31 December 2012 the AIA was £25,000 for a 12-month period. From 1 January 2013 to 5 April 2014 (1 April 2014 for companies) the AIA was £250,000 for a 12-month period. From 6 April 2014 (1 April 2014 for companies until 31 December 2015 the AIA is £500,000. From 1 January 2016 the AIA is £200,000 for a 12-month period. For accounting periods straddling April 2014 and/ or 31 December 2015 the AIA must be prorated.

1.4 Capital allowances on cessation

On the cessation of trade, all the plant and machinery in the business are disposed of or deemed to have been disposed of.

Capital allowances for the final period of account are computed as follows:

- Any items acquired in the final period are added to TWDV b/f.

- No WDAs or FYAs or AIAs are given for the final period of account.

- The disposal value of the assets in each pool is deducted from the balance, giving rise to balancing allowances or balancing charges. Any assets taken over personally by the owner are treated as sold for market value.

1.5 Capital allowances for successions

Where a trade is transferred or sold, there is a cessation of trade by the original owner. Balancing adjustments for capital allowances will arise.

If the transfer or sale is to a connected person, assets are deemed to be sold at market value.

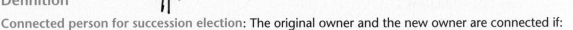

Definition

Connected person for succession election: The original owner and the new owner are connected if:

- One of them is the spouse/civil partner of the other

- One of them is a relative or the spouse/civil partner of a relative of the other

- One of them is a relative (or relative's spouse/civil partner) of the spouse/civil partner of the other

- One of them is a partnership and the other has a right to a share in that partnership

- One of them is a company and the other has control over the company

- Both of them are partnerships and another person has a right to a share in both partnerships

- Both of them are companies (or one is a company and one is a partnership) and another person has control over them

For this purpose, relatives means brothers, sisters, ancestors and lineal descendants.

However, if the trade is transferred to a connected person, a joint election can be made by the original owner and the new owner. The effect of the election is to transfer the capital assets at their tax written down value so that no balancing adjustments will arise.

This could be used on the incorporation of a business or the transfer of a business to a close relative eg a son or daughter.

If the election is made, in the final period of account of the original owner no WDAs, FYAs or AIAs are available. In the first period of the new owner only WDAs (not FYAs) are available on the assets transferred.

The election must be made within two years of the date on which the succession takes effect. [Hp164]

Worked example: Succession election

Victor is a sole trader, who has been making up accounts to 31 December each year. The TWDV of his main pool at 1 January 2015 was £24,000.

Victor transferred his business to his son Paul on 30 September 2015. Paul intends to draw up his first accounts to 31 March 2016.

A succession election is made.

Requirement

Calculate the capital allowances available to

(i) Victor in his nine months to 30 September 2015

(ii) Paul in his six months to 31 March 2016

Solution

		Allowances
	£	£
Victor		
TWDV at 1 January 2015	24,000	
No allowances in year of transfer		Nil
	24,000	
Paul (six-month period)		
Addition at 1 October 2015	24,000	
WDA @ 18% × 6/12	(2,160)	2,160
	21,840	

1.6 Partnerships

A partnership itself is not a taxable person. Each of the partners is liable to tax on his share of the taxable trading income of the partnership on the same basis as a sole trader.

The net profit or loss for the partnership for the period of account must be adjusted for tax purposes (in the same way as for a sole trader).

Capital allowances for the partnership must then be computed and deducted from the adjusted trading profit. Capital allowances are available on partnership assets and are computed as for a sole trader.

The resultant taxable trading income of the partnership for the period of account is allocated between the partners according to the profit-sharing agreement for the period of account.

The agreement may specify that one or more of the partners is entitled to a 'salary' (an allocation of profits) and/or interest on capital introduced into the partnership. These amounts are allocated first and then the remaining amount of taxable trading income is allocated in accordance with the agreed profit-sharing ratios (PSR).

Where there is a change in the profit-sharing agreement during the period of account, divide the period of account into the periods of the different profit sharing agreements. Any salaries and interest on capital as appropriate must be time-apportioned accordingly.

If a new partner joins a partnership, the opening year rules will apply to that partner, but the continuing partners will continue on the current year basis.

If a partner leaves a partnership, the closing year rules will apply to that partner, but the continuing partners will continue on the current year basis.

2 Revision from Tax Compliance – relief for trading losses

Section overview

- A trading loss arises in a period of account if there is a negative result in the taxable trading income computation.

- If there is a trading loss in a period of account, there is no taxable trading income for the tax year to which it relates.

- The trader may also claim loss relief.

- If the loss arises in the opening years such that the period of account is the basis period for more than one tax year, the loss is a trade loss in the earlier tax year only ie there is no overlap of losses.

- S.83 loss relief (carry forward) applies unless an alternative claim is made.

- Under s.83, losses must be carried forward and set against the first available trading income of the same trade.

- A claim must be made to quantify the amount of loss available.

- Under s.86, losses of an unincorporated business which is incorporated can be set against income received from the company.

- S.64 loss relief is given against general income in the tax year of the loss and/or the previous tax year.

- In addition to other reliefs, trading losses in the first four tax years of trade can be carried back and set against general income in the three tax years before the loss on a FIFO basis, under s.72.

- Loss relief under s.64, s.72 or against gains is restricted to a maximum of £25,000 where the individual is a non-active trader.

- Loss relief under s.64, s.72 or against gains is also restricted where the loss has arisen as a result of tax avoidance.

- For partners in a limited liability partnership, loss relief under s.64 and s.72 is restricted to the partner's capital contribution.

- For certain reliefs generated from 2013/14, the amount which any individual can deduct from total income is limited to the higher of £50,000 and 25% of adjusted total income. This includes loss reliefs under s.64 and s.72, to the extent that the losses are not offset against profits of the trade which generated them.

2.1 Trading losses

A trading loss arises where the computation of a trader's taxable trading income in a period of account produces a negative result.

A trading loss has two main consequences:

- The amount of taxable trading income for the tax year to which the period of account relates will be nil; and

- The trader will be eligible for tax relief for the trading loss.

Special rules apply in the opening years of a business such that losses cannot be used twice (ie no overlap losses).

The following table summarises the use of trading losses (statutory section numbers are not required but are given for ease of reference):

	s.83	s.64	s.72	s.89
Type of loss relief	Carry forward	Current year and/or prior year (in any order)	Loss in first four tax years	Terminal loss relief on cessation
Set against	Future trading profits from the same trade	General income	General income	Trading profits from the same trade
Time limits	Carries forward until fully utilised or cease to trade	Current year and/or prior year	Carry back to prior three years on a FIFO basis	Carry back to prior three years on a LIFO basis
Conditions	Automatic, cannot restrict use of loss to preserve personal allowances	Optional but 'all or nothing' Can claim in one or both years If used in both years can be set-off in any order to maximise use of personal allowances	Optional but 'all or nothing'	Optional but 'all or nothing'
Claim [Hp 27]	Need to agree the amount of loss within 4 years of end of tax year in which loss arose.	Within 12 months from 31 January following the end of the tax year in which the loss arose	Within 12 months from 31 January following the end of the tax year in which the loss arose	Within four years of the end of the last tax year in which the business operated

The pro forma as set out below was considered in detail in Tax Compliance. You should ensure that it is still familiar:

	2014/15	2015/16	2016/17
	£	£	£
Trading income	X	Nil	X
Less s.83 relief			(X)
	X	Nil	X
Other income	X	X	X
Net income	X	X	X
Less s.64 relief	(X)	(X)	—
Less PA (possibly restricted)	(X)	(X)	(X)
Taxable income	X	X	X

2.2 Trading losses on incorporation of an unincorporated business (s.86)

If an unincorporated business is transferred to a company, any unrelieved trading losses of the unincorporated business would normally be lost, as the unincorporated trader is no longer carrying on the same trade.

However s.86 provides that s.83 loss relief will apply in such a case, by setting the loss against income received from the company by the former owner as if such income were trading income.

The consideration received by the former owner of the unincorporated business for the incorporation of the business must be solely or mainly shares (at least 80% of the total consideration). The shares must be held by the former owner throughout the tax year in which loss relief is given.

Worked example: s.86 loss relief on incorporation

Sally incorporated her business on 5 April 2015. The business made a trading loss of £18,000 in 2014/15 which Sally wishes to carry forward to 2015/16.

Sally's income in 2015/16 is as follows:

	£
Salary from the new company	15,000
Dividends received from the new company	450
Dividends received from X plc (unconnected)	230

Sally received only shares as consideration on the incorporation of her business.

Requirement

Identify how much of the trading loss is relieved in 2015/16.

Solution

The trading loss is only relieved against income from the new company.

	£
Salary	15,000
Dividends (£450 × $^{100}/_{90}$)	500
Relieved in 2015/16	15,500

2.3 Partnership losses

Where a trading loss arises on the computation of a partnership taxable trading income the loss is allocated to the partners using the profit share arrangement in the same way as a profit would be allocated.

Sometimes, if the partnership makes an overall loss, the allocation of loss results in one or more of the partners making a notional profit. In this case, the loss allocation must be adjusted.

A partner with a notional profit will have a nil amount of taxable trading income.

The notional profit will then be reallocated to the remaining partners in proportion to the loss initially allocated to them.

This can also happen in reverse then the partnership makes a profit but one partner makes a notional loss. The same method of reallocation applies.

2.4 Restrictions on the use of losses

2.4.1 Non-active traders

Loss relief will be restricted in its use if it arises in a trade carried on by an individual and that individual does not devote a 'significant' amount of time (ie 10 hours per week) to the trade in the period in which the loss arises.

Where a trader does not spend a 'significant' amount of time, the loss relief will be restricted to a maximum of £25,000 when making a loss claim against total income (under s.64 or s.72) or against capital gains. The loss can be carried forward against future profits of the same trade under s.83 without restriction.

Similar rules apply to non-active partners. Sideways loss relief (ie against non-trading income) is restricted by reference to the partner's capital contribution for losses sustained in the first four years of trading. In addition, sideways loss relief is always subject to a maximum of £25,000 per annum.

2.4.2 Tax avoidance schemes

Loss relief is not available under s.64, s.72 or s.261B TCGA 1992 for offset against non-trading income or gains where the loss has arisen as a result of tax avoidance. Tax avoidance is defined as arrangements entered into with the main purpose of generating a loss to offset against non-trading income or capital gains.

2.4.3 Restriction on loss relief in a limited liability partnership

In general, the partners of an LLP are entitled to loss relief in the same way as partners in an unlimited liability partnership.

However, there is a restriction on the amount of loss that a LLP partner may claim under s.64 and s.72 against income other than that from the partnership. In this case, the loss relief cannot exceed the amount of capital that the partner has contributed to the partnership.

2.4.4 Restriction on income tax reliefs against total income

For 2013/14 and later years, there is a limit on the amount by which certain deductions from total income, including trading losses under s.64 and s.72, can reduce a taxpayer's taxable income.

The limit is the higher of

- £50,000, and

- 25% of the adjusted total income for the tax year in which the deductions are offset (this is total income, plus amounts deducted under payroll giving schemes, less the grossed up value of pension contributions to personal pension schemes made under the relief at source rules. There is no adjustment where pension contributions are made to an occupational pension scheme under net pay arrangements).

The restriction applies to any amounts offset in 2013/14 or a later year. Where a loss arises in 2013/14 or later and is offset in an earlier year (ie under a s.64 ITA 2007 prior year claim, or a s.72 ITA 2007 claim), the restriction applies in the earlier year but only in relation to the amounts which arise in 2013/14 or later.

3 Choice of loss relief

Section overview

- Loss relief reduces taxable income and so reduces the tax liability.

- Loss relief should be claimed to give the highest amount of tax saving at the earliest time.

- Additional options are available in the opening and closing years of a business which may be beneficial.

- In a partnership each partner can choose his own method of loss relief.

3.1 Choosing which loss relief to use

The aim of the taxpayer will be to choose the option which achieves the maximum tax saving at the earliest time.

Consider the following:

- The rate of income tax applying in the relevant tax years;
- The possible wastage of loss where net income is already covered by the personal allowance;
- The possible wasting of the personal allowance to achieve higher rate tax savings; and
- The projected level of future profits and tax rates.

Interactive question: Choice of loss relief
[Difficulty level: Intermediate]

Geraldine is in business preparing accounts to 30 June each year having started trading on 1 July 2005. Her recent taxable profits and (losses) have been as follows:

	£
Y/e 30 June 2015	39,000
Y/e 30 June 2016	(38,000)

Geraldine anticipates that her taxable profit will be £5,000 in the year to 30 June 2017.

She has also received gross rental income of £10,725 each year which she expects to continue.

Requirement

Using the standard formats below, explain the most tax efficient use of the trading loss, assuming rates and allowances continue unchanged in the future. Show the calculation of Geraldine's tax liability taking into account your choice of loss relief. Assume the personal allowance is £10,600 for all years.

Income tax computations – ignoring loss relief

	2015/16 £	2016/17 £	2017/18 £
Trading income			
Other income			
Net income before loss relief/net income			
Less personal allowance	( )	( )	( )
Taxable Income			
Tax	£	£	£
................./................./................. × 20%			
................./................./................. × 40%			

Loss relief options

Claim 1

....

....

Claim 2

....

Claim 3

....

....

Conclusion

Income tax computations – with loss relief

	2015/16 £	2016/17 £	2017/18 £
Trading income			
Other income			
Net income before loss relief			
Less s.64 loss relief			
Net income			
Less personal allowance	( )	( )	( )
Taxable Income			
Tax	£	£	£
................./................./................. × 20%			
................./................./................. × 40%			

See **Answer** at the end of this chapter.

3.2 Choice of loss relief in the opening and closing years of a business

In the opening years of a business a trader will also need to consider the additional option of s.72 relief against general income of the three tax years preceding the tax year of the loss on a first in first out (FIFO) basis.

This will give the earliest form of relief, and may also give the highest rate of relief, for example if the individual was previously employed with a high level of employment income. However care must be taken if there is a year of low income, as the s.72 claim relates to all three years. So a high level of saving in one year may be offset by a low level of saving in another.

In the closing years of a business s.89 terminal loss relief claim is available against trading income of the three previous years on a last in first out (LIFO) basis. However not all other options are available. Losses cannot be carried forward under s.83 when the trade ceases as there are no future trading profits of the business. An alternative is available on incorporation when losses can be carried forward under s.86 against future income generated from the company. Although a later relief, this may give relief at a higher rate.

3.3 Partners – choosing which loss relief to use

Partners are entitled to the same loss reliefs as a sole trader.

Each partner makes his own loss relief claim based on his own circumstances. For example, a partner joining a partnership may claim s.72 loss relief for losses in the first four years that he is a member of the partnership.

Similarly, a partner leaving a partnership is entitled to closing years loss relief under s.89.

Continuing partners may use loss relief under s.83 and s.64.

If a partnership is incorporated, the partners are entitled to loss relief under s.86.

Worked example: Choice of loss relief – partners

George, Harry and Imogen are in partnership. In the year ended 31 December 2015, the partnership had a taxable trading loss of £60,000. In accordance with the profit sharing arrangement this was allocated as follows:

	Total £	George £	Harry £	Imogen £
Trading loss	(60,000)	(16,000)	(18,000)	(26,000)

The following information relates to the three partners:

- George has been a partner for many years. He has £80,000 of investment income in 2015/16 arising from an investment property inherited from his uncle during the year. His income in 2014/15 was £9,000.

- Harry has also been a partner for many years. His income in 2014/15 and 2015/16 is covered by the personal allowance.

- Imogen joined the partnership on 1 January 2015. She was previously employed and had a salary of £100,000 per annum.

The partnership is expected to return to profitablility for the year ended 31 December 2016.

Requirement

Determine the most appropriate form of loss relief for each partner.

Solution

George should claim s.64 relief against his income of £80,000 in 2015/16 giving relief at 40% at an early point in time. His income in 2014/15 is covered by the personal allowance.

Harry has limited other income and no tax saving would be made by relieving profits against general income in 2014/15 and/ or 2015/16. He should therefore carry forward his loss using s.83 relief against future trading income.

Imogen has just joined the partnership so her loss is subject to the opening year rules. As she has a substantial amount of employment income in previous years she should relieve her losses under s.72.

	£
2014/15	
1.1.2015 – 5.4.2015 3/12 x £(26,000)	(6,500)
2015/16	
1.1.2015 – 31.12.2015	(26,000)
Less used in 2014/15	6,500
	(19,500)

Hence the loss of £6,500 should be relieved against total income in 2011/12, and the loss of £19,500 against total income in 2012/13.

Summary

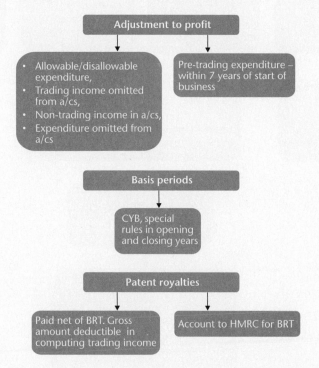

Adjustment to profit

- Allowable/disallowable expenditure,
- Trading income omitted from a/cs,
- Non-trading income in a/cs,
- Expenditure omitted from a/cs

Pre-trading expenditure – within 7 years of start of business

Basis periods

CYB, special rules in opening and closing years

Patent royalties

Paid net of BRT. Gross amount deductible in computing trading income

Account to HMRC for BRT

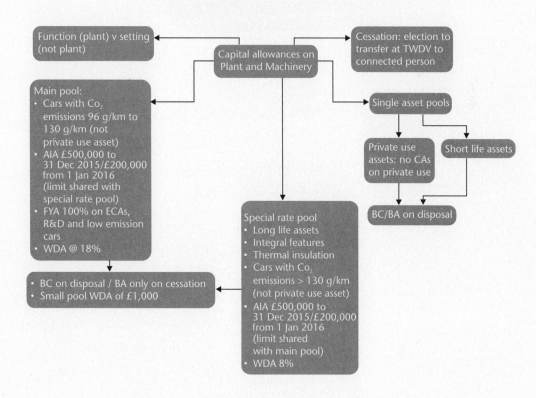

Function (plant) v setting (not plant)

Capital allowances on Plant and Machinery

Cessation: election to transfer at TWDV to connected person

Main pool:
- Cars with CO_2 emissions 96 g/km to 130 g/km (not private use asset)
- AIA £500,000 to 31 Dec 2015/£200,000 from 1 Jan 2016 (limit shared with special rate pool)
- FYA 100% on ECAs, R&D and low emission cars
- WDA @ 18%

Single asset pools

Private use assets: no CAs on private use

Short life assets

BC/BA on disposal

- BC on disposal / BA only on cessation
- Small pool WDA of £1,000

Special rate pool
- Long life assets
- Integral features
- Thermal insulation
- Cars with CO_2 emissions > 130 g/km (not private use asset)
- AIA £500,000 to 31 Dec 2015/£200,000 from 1 Jan 2016 (limit shared with main pool)
- WDA 8%

CHAPTER

4

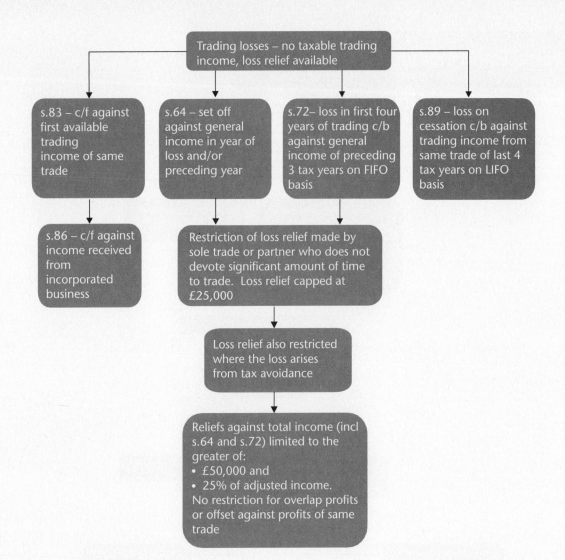

Trading losses – no taxable trading income, loss relief available

s.83 – c/f against first available trading income of same trade

s.64 – set off against general income in year of loss and/or preceding year

s.72 – loss in first four years of trading c/b against general income of preceding 3 tax years on FIFO basis

s.89 – loss on cessation c/b against trading income from same trade of last 4 tax years on LIFO basis

s.86 – c/f against income received from incorporated business

Restriction of loss relief made by sole trade or partner who does not devote significant amount of time to trade. Loss relief capped at £25,000

Loss relief also restricted where the loss arises from tax avoidance

Reliefs against total income (incl s.64 and s.72) limited to the greater of:
- £50,000 and
- 25% of adjusted income.
No restriction for overlap profits or offset against profits of same trade

Self-test

Answer the following questions.

1 Diana has been trading since 6 April 2014. Her trading results are:

	£
Period to 31 March 2015	14,905
y/e 31 March 2016	(25,945)
y/e 31 March 2017	24,170

Before starting her own business Diana was employed, earning £8,705 per year. She also has property income of £2,600 per annum.

Requirement

Set out the options available for relief of the loss and advise Diana as to the best method of obtaining loss relief, quantifying the amount of income tax saved.

Assume the personal allowance is £10,600 and the rates of tax are as for 2015/16 throughout.

2 Bert and Ernie have been in partnership for many years. In the year ended 31 March 2016, the partnership had a taxable trading loss of £100,000. Profits and losses are shared equally after allocating a £20,000 pa salary to Bert. The partnership broke even in the year ended 31 March 2015 and also expects to break even in the year ending 31 March 2016, then make substantial profits of in excess of £100,000 from 2017.Bert has other income of approximately £21,000 pa, and has cashflow problems at the present time.

Ernie has investments that generate other taxable income of £95,000 pa.

Requirement

Explain the best method of relieving losses for Bert and Ernie.

Now, go back to the Learning objectives in the Introduction. If you are satisfied you have achieved these objectives, please tick them off.

Technical reference

Legislation

Trade profits

References refer to Income Tax (Trading and Other Income) Act 2005 (*ITTOIA 2005*)

Charge to tax on trade profits	s.5

Disallowable expenditure

• Capital	s.33
• Wholly and exclusively	s.34
• Bad debts	s.35
• Unpaid remuneration	s.36
• Employee benefits	ss.38 – 44
• Business entertainment and gifts	ss.45 – 47
• Car hire	ss.48 – 50
• Penalties etc	s.54

Allowable expenditure

• Incidental costs of finance	s.58
• Redundancy payments	ss.76 – 80
• Incidental expenses re patents	s.89
• Gifts to charities etc of stock	s.108
• Pre-trading expenditure	s.57
Cash basis for small businesses	ss.25A & 31A –31F
Current year basis	s.198
Opening years	ss.199 – 201
Overlap profits	ss.204 – 205
Closing years	ss.201 – 202

Capital allowances

References relate to Capital Allowances Act 2001 (*CAA 2001*), unless otherwise stated

Qualifying activities	ss.15 – 20
Qualifying expenditure: general	ss.21 – 38
Qualifying expenditure: first year allowances	ss.39 – 49
Pooling	ss.53 – 54
Writing down allowances	s.55
First year allowances	s.52
Long life assets	ss.90 – 102
Cars costing more than £12,000	ss.74 – 82
Private use assets	ss.205 – 208
Short life assets	ss.83 – 89
Balancing adjustments	s.56
Final chargeable period	s.65
Successions	s.265
Election between connected persons	s.266
Thermal insulation of buildings	s.28
Integral features	ss.33A – 33B
Annual investment allowance	ss.38A – 38B & 51A – 51N

Small pools	s.56A
Special rate expenditure and the special rate pool	ss.104A – 104E
Fixtures	s.187A
Fixtures election	s.198
Succession election	s.266

Loss reliefs

References are to Income Tax Act 2007 (*ITA 2007*)

Carry forward against subsequent profits	ss.83 – 84
Carry forward where business transferred to company	s.86
Set off against general income	s.64
Further relief for losses in early years of trade	ss.72 – 73
Carry back of terminal losses	ss.89 – 91
Restriction on loss relief for non active traders	ss.74A & 74C
Restriction on loss relief where loss results from tax avoidance scheme	s.74ZA
Restriction on loss in LLP	s.107
Restriction on income tax reliefs against total income	s.24A

HMRC manual references

Business Income manual

(Found at www.hmrc.gov.uk/manuals/bimmanual/index.htm)

Trade: badges of trade: summary	BIM20205
Measuring the profits (general rules)	BIM30000
The relationship between tax and accountancy	BIM31000
Capital/revenue divide: introduction: overview of the guidance	BIM35001
Wholly & exclusively	BIM37000
Computation of liability: The current year basis of assessment rules: Commencement years	BIM71015
Computation of liability: The current year basis of assessment rules: Overlap relief	BIM71075
Computation of liability: The current year basis of assessment rules: Basis of assessments on cessation	BIM71025
Computation of liability: The current year basis of assessment rules: Change of accounting date: Introduction	BIM71035
Trading losses: general matters: introduction	BIM75001
Trading losses: general matters: forms of relief	BIM75005

Capital allowances manual

(Found at www.hmrc.gov.uk/manuals/camanual/Index.htm)

PMAs: Introduction: Outline	CA20006
General: Definitions: Chargeable period, accounting period and period of account	CA11510
PMA: FYA: Expenditure on which available and rates	CA23110
PMA: Short life assets: Outline	CA23610

This technical reference section is designed to assist you when you are working in the office. It should help you know where to look for further information on the topics covered in this chapter.

Answer to Interactive question

Income tax computations – ignoring loss relief

	2015/16 £	2016/17 £	2017/18 £
Trading income	39,000	Nil	5,000
Other income	10,725	10,725	10,725
Net income before loss relief/net income	49,725	10,725	15,725
Less personal allowance	(10,600)	(10,600)	(10,600)
Taxable Income	39,125	125	5,125

Tax

	£	£	£
£31,785/£125/£5,125 × 20%	6,357	25	1,025
£7,340/£NIL/£NIL × 40%	2,936	Nil	Nil
	9,293	25	1,025

Loss relief options

Claim 1

S.64 claim in 2016/17 would use £10,725 of the loss. The rest would be carried forward under s.83 against trading income in 2017/18 and subsequent years.

But since most of net income is already covered by the personal allowance in 2016/17, this claim only saves £25 and so is not recommended.

Claim 2

S.64 claim in 2015/16 – would use all of loss.

Claim would not waste any of the personal allowance, but saves £9,068 (£9,293 – (£1,125 × 20%)) in tax and generates a significant cash flow advantage at a time of difficult trading.

Claim 3

S.83 carry forward (no s.64 claim) – would use £5,000 of loss in 2017/18.

Saves tax of £1,000 (£1,025 – (£125 × 20%)). The remaining £33,000 loss would be carried forward and may generate a larger tax saving in the future, but this is a delayed benefit and the future profitability of the business is uncertain.

Conclusion

The most tax efficient use of the loss would be to claim s.64 in 2015/16.

Income tax computations – with loss relief

	2015/16 £	2016/17 £	2017/18 £
Trading income	39,000	Nil	5,000
Other income	10,725	10,725	10,725
Net income before loss relief	49,725	10,725	15,725
Less s.64 loss relief	(38,000)	Nil	Nil
Net income	11,725	10,725	15,725
Less personal allowance (restricted)	(10,600)	(10,600)	(10,600)
Taxable Income	1,125	125	5,125

Tax

	£	£	£
	225	25	1,025
£1,125/£125/£5,125 × 20%			
£Nil/£Nil/£Nil × 40%	Nil	Nil	Nil
	225	25	1,025

1 **Income tax computations – without loss relief**

	2012/13 £	2013/14 £	2014/15 £	2015/16 £	2016/17 £
Trading income	Nil	Nil	14,905	Nil	24,170
Employment income	8,705	8,705	Nil	Nil	Nil
Property income	2,600	2,600	2,600	2,600	2,600
Net income	11,305	11,305	17,505	2,600	26,770
Less personal allowance	(10,600)	(10,600)	(10,600)	(10,600)	(10,600)
Taxable income	705	705	6,905	Nil	16,170

Tax

	2012/13	2013/14	2014/15	2015/16	2016/17
£705/£705/£6,905/ NIL/£16,170 × 20%	141	141	1,381	Nil	3,234

Options available for loss relief

Claim 1 – s.64 and s.83

Against the year of the loss (2015/16). This would waste the personal allowance without saving any tax (loss used £2,600), so should not be used.

A s.64 claim can also be made for the previous year (2014/15). This would also waste the personal allowance but would save tax of £1,381 (loss used £17,505).

Balance of loss (£8,440) can be carried forward under s.83 and set against trading income in 2016/17 saving tax of £1,688 (£8,440 × 20%).

Total tax saved £3,069.

Claim 2 – s.83

£24,170 of the loss would be used in 2016/17 but most of the personal allowance of £10,600 would be wasted. The remaining loss would be carried forward to future years against trading income only. Tax saved would be £3,234.

Claim 3 – s.72

The loss could be used against net income of the three preceding years on a FIFO basis. The effect would be as follows:

2012/13

£11,305 loss used; PA of £10,600 wasted; Tax saved £141

2013/14

£11,305 loss used; PA of £10,600 wasted; Tax saved £141

2014/15

£3,335 balance of loss used; No waste of PA; Tax saved £667.

This would utilise the whole loss, saving tax of £949.

Conclusion

Carrying forward the loss saves the most tax. However this delays taking relief for the loss.

The best option is therefore probably to claim against 2014/15 net income (s.64) and carry forward the balance of the loss under s.83. This saves a slightly smaller amount of tax but will result in a tax repayment in respect of 2014/15 and is therefore better from a cash flow perspective.

2 **Partners – loss relief**

Allocation of losses

	Total £	Bert £	Ernie £
Salary	20,000	20,000	Nil
PSA	(120,000)	(60,000)	(60,000)
Trading loss	(100,000)	(40,000)	(60,000)

Bert

Approximately half of Bert's income in 2015/16 and 2014/15 is covered by his personal allowance. Relief under s.64 in 2014/15 would use £21,000 of his losses and the remaining £19,000 could be used in £2015/16. This would generate tax savings at 20% of £4,280 (£2,200 + £2,080) as follows:

	2014/15 £	2015/16 £
Income	21,000	21,000
Personal allowance	(10,000)	(10,600)
Taxable income	11,000	10,400
Tax savings at 20%	2,200	2,080

If Bert decided to carry forward the loss against trading income in 2016/17 when he is expected to be a higher rate taxpayer he would make much greater savings of £16,000 (£40,000 x 40%).

However he currently has cashflow problems so he may prefer to relief the losses now to generate a repayment.

Ernie

Ernie is a higher rate taxpayer each year therefore he will aim to relieve profits as early as possible ie under s.64 in 2014/15. His loss relief in that year is restricted to £50,000 (being higher than 25% of adjusted total income). So generating a repayment of £20,000, the additional loss of £10,000 can be relieved in 2015/16 to provided further tax savings of £4,000. Carrying forward to loss would generate the same level of relief but at a later point in time and so is not the preferred method.

CHAPTER 5

Capital gains tax

Introduction

Examination context

Topic List

Summary and Self-test

Technical reference

Answers to Interactive questions

Answers to Self-test

Learning objectives

- Calculate capital gains tax liabilities for individuals

- Identify legitimate tax planning measures to minimise tax liabilities

- Evaluate and advise on alternative tax strategies relating to changes in personal circumstances such as marriage, divorce and death

- Recognise, explain and communicate opportunities to use alternative tax treatments arising from past transactions

The specific syllabus references for this chapter are 1v, 2a, 2c, 2d.

Syllabus links

In Principles of Taxation and Tax Compliance, you learnt about some of the basic principles of chargeable gains for individuals. These included chargeable and exempt persons, disposals and assets, how to compute and use gains and losses and the charge to capital gains tax. You also learnt about the treatment of chattels and principal private residence relief.

In this chapter we review the fundamental aspects of chargeable gains and look at some other more advanced aspects of chargeable gains such as deferred consideration.

Examination context

Capital gains tax planning opportunities often arise in family situations with the passing of assets within the family unit. The use of losses in these situations is often influential.

In the examination candidates may be required to:

- Calculate gains as part of a personal tax question, often setting off gains and losses

- Identify when trading losses can be relieved against gains, and calculate the optimum form of loss relief

- Advise an individual of capital gains tax planning opportunities within the family unit

When relieving capital losses candidates often have an insufficient knowledge of the distinction between current year and brought forward losses.

Candidates often forget s.261B Taxation of Chargeable Gains Act 1992 loss relief when considering trading losses.

Family capital gains tax planning issues are vital to personal tax questions, and easy marks are available.

1 Revision from Tax Compliance – calculation of gains and losses

Section overview

- Chargeable persons include individuals, partners, and trustees. Gains realised by companies are subject to corporation tax.

- Chargeable disposals include sales and gifts.

- Death is not an occasion of charge for CGT and there is a tax-free uplift of the value of assets passed on death.

- Exempt assets include cars, some chattels and investments held in ISAs.

- Gains and losses are disposal proceeds less allowable costs.

- Part of the original cost of an asset is allowable on a part disposal based on the market values of the part sold and the part retained.

- Spouses/civil partners are taxed separately.

- Disposals between spouses/civil partners are on a no gain/no loss basis.

- An individual is connected with certain close relatives.

- Disposals to connected persons (other than a spouse/civil partner) are at market value.

1.1 Chargeable persons, disposals and assets

1.1.1 Chargeable persons

Chargeable persons include individuals, business partners, and trustees. Companies are subject to corporation tax on their chargeable gains, with the exception of certain gains relating to high value residential properties (see Chapter 19).

Some persons are specifically exempt from capital gains. These include registered charities and registered pension schemes.

1.1.2 Chargeable disposals

Chargeable disposals include:

- The sale of whole or part of an asset
- The gift of whole or part of an asset
- Receipts of capital sums on the surrender of rights over assets
- The loss or destruction of the whole or part of an asset
- Appropriation of assets to trading stock

If a taxpayer appropriates an asset to trading stock, there is a disposal of the asset at market value at the date it is taken into stock. The trader may elect for the disposal to be treated as one at neither a gain nor a loss. The cost of the asset for trading income is then adjusted for the gain or loss which would have occurred.

Exempt disposals include:

- Gifts to charities, art galleries, museums and similar institutions, provided that the asset is used for the purposes of the institution.

Death is not a disposal for capital gains tax purposes and there is a tax-free uplift of the value of assets passed on death.

1.1.3 Chargeable assets

Chargeable assets are all capital assets except those which are specifically exempted from CGT.

Chargeable assets include both tangible assets (such as land, furniture, works of art) and intangible assets (such as goodwill of a business, shares, leases).

Exempt assets include:

- Legal tender (ie cash)
- Motor cars (including vintage and classic cars)
- Wasting chattels (tangible moveable property such as furniture, moveable machinery, with a predictable life not exceeding 50 years), except assets used in a business where the owner has or could have claimed capital allowances on the assets
- Chattels which are either not wasting chattels or used in business etc, if sold for consideration which does not exceed £6,000
- Gilt-edged securities
- Qualifying Corporate Bonds (QCBs)
- National Savings Certificates and Premium Bonds
- Shares and investments held in an Individual Savings Account (ISA)

1.2 Computation of gains and losses

The disposal consideration is the sale proceeds, if the asset is sold at arm's length. If the asset is not sold at arm's length (eg a gift or sale at undervalue) the disposal consideration is generally the market value of the asset. There are a few specific exceptions for 'nil gain/nil loss' transfers, such as between spouses.

Incidental costs of disposal are deducted to give the net disposal consideration. These include legal fees, estate agents' and auctioneers' fees and advertising costs.

Allowable costs are:

- Acquisition cost of the asset (purchase price if bought, market value of asset if gifted, probate value if acquired on death)
- Incidental costs of acquisition such as legal fees, surveyors' fees, stamp duty, stamp duty land tax
- Enhancement expenditure (capital costs of additions and improvements to the asset reflected in the value of the asset at the date of disposal such as extensions, planning permission and architects' fees for such extensions)

1.3 Part disposals

The definition of a chargeable disposal includes the disposal of part of a chargeable asset.

The cost for calculation of the gain or loss is:

$$\text{Cost} \times \frac{A}{A+B}$$

where A is the market value of the part disposed of and B is the market value of the part that is retained.

Any incidental costs relating wholly to the part disposal are deductible in full.

1.4 Taxation of spouses/civil partners

1.4.1 Introduction

In general, spouses/civil partners are taxed separately as two individual taxpayers.

Each has his own annual exempt amount. Losses cannot be shared between spouses/civil partners.

Assets owned jointly between spouses/civil partners are taxed in accordance with the underlying beneficial ownership of the asset. Where a declaration of beneficial ownership has been made for income tax purposes, this will generally also apply for capital gains tax.

1.4.2 Disposals between spouses/civil partners

Disposals in a tax year between spouses/civil partners who are living together in that tax year are on a nil gain/nil loss basis.

Married couples/civil partners are treated as living together unless they are separated under a court order or deed of separation or are, in fact, separated in circumstances which make permanent separation likely. A couple will be treated as living together in a tax year if they have satisfied this condition at any time during the tax year.

The disposal value on a nil gain/nil loss disposal is cost. The transferee has a base cost equal to the original cost.

1.4.3 Tax planning for spouses/civil partners

Spouses/civil partners can organise their capital disposals to ensure that as a couple they:

- Make use of both spouses/civil partners annual exempt amounts
- Make use of any unrelieved capital losses

However, if an asset is transferred between spouses/civil partners, it is important that there is an outright unconditional disposal. In addition, the disposal proceeds should be retained by the spouse/civil partner making the ultimate disposal to the third party.

HMRC may otherwise contend (following the *Ramsay* doctrine, which is discussed in more detail in chapter 13) that there was not an actual disposal between the spouses/civil partners and treat the ultimate disposal as being made by the spouse/civil partner who originally owned the asset.

1.5 Connected persons

Definition

Connected persons: An individual is connected with his:

- Spouse/civil partner
- Relatives and their spouses/civil partners
- Spouse's/civil partner's relatives and their spouses/civil partners
- Business partners and their spouses/civil partners and relatives
- Any companies which he controls

In addition, a trustee of a settlement is connected with the trust settlor and anyone connected with the settlor.

A settlor and the trustees of his settlement are connected from the start of the trust, ie in respect of the initial property transferred to the trust. If the settlor dies, his relatives and spouse or civil partner and their relatives are no longer connected with the trustees.

For this purpose, relatives means brothers, sisters, ancestors and direct descendants.

Note that under the definition of connected persons, an individual is not connected with his aunt, uncle, niece, nephew or cousins.

A disposal by an individual to a person connected with him is always at market value at the date of the disposal.

Where a settlor puts an asset into a trust or when the trustees dispose of assets out of the trust to a beneficiary, the disposal proceeds are always deemed to be the market value. The market value is also the base cost for the recipient.

This rule does not apply to a disposal by an individual to his own spouse/civil partner as such a disposal is on a no gain/no loss basis.

2 Revision from Tax Compliance – capital gains tax payable

Section overview

- Each individual is entitled to an annual exempt amount. Trustees are entitled to half the annual exempt amount. If several trusts are created by the same settlor the available amount is divided equally between them subject to a minimum of 10% of the full individual's exempt amount.

- Current year losses are set off fully against current year gains.

- Brought forward losses are only set off to bring down gains to the annual exempt amount.

- A loss on a disposal to a connected person can only be used against gains on disposals to the same connected person.

- CGT is chargeable at 18% or 28%, depending on the individual's taxable income.

- CGT is chargeable at 10% on gains subject to entrepreneurs' relief.

- Relief can be given against chargeable gains for trading losses.

- An individual may make a claim for trading loss relief under s.64 ITA 2007 against his general income in the year of the loss and/or the previous year. In addition, he may then extend the claim for any unrelieved part of the loss to be set against his chargeable gains for the year of the loss and/or the previous year.

2.1 Annual exempt amount

Each individual is entitled to an annual exempt amount each year. For 2015/16 the annual exempt amount is £11,100 (£11,000 for 2014/15). The annual exempt amount is deducted from chargeable gains to produce gains liable to CGT (**taxable gains**). [Hp95]

If the annual exempt amount is unused in a tax year, it is wasted and cannot be used in any other tax year.

The annual exempt amount available to trustees is one half of that given to individuals, so it is £5,550 for 2015/16 (£5,500 for 2014/15). However, the full annual exempt amount is available for trustees of a bare trust or a disabled person's trust.

If several trusts are created by the same settlor, the exempt amount is divided equally between them subject to a minimum exemption per trust of one tenth of a full individual annual exempt amount (£1,110 for 2015/16).

2.2 Losses

An individual is chargeable on his chargeable gains less allowable losses.

Where an individual has losses in the same tax year as he makes gains, he must set off those same year losses to the fullest extent possible, even if this reduces the net chargeable gains below the annual exempt amount or if it produces an overall loss. An overall loss is carried forward and set off against gains in future years.

If an individual has losses brought forward from a previous tax year, he must set these against the first available net gains. However, the offset of losses brought forward is restricted so that they cannot take net gains below the level of the annual exempt amount.

2.3 Losses and connected persons

A loss incurred on a disposal to a connected person can only be set off against gains made on disposals to the same connected person in the same year or in future years.

Again, this rule does not apply to a disposal by an individual to his own spouse/civil partner since such a disposal will not give rise to a loss.

2.4 Computing capital gains tax

2.4.1 Rates of capital gains tax

Individuals are taxed on their taxable gains separately from their taxable income.

Taxable gains are taxed at the rate of 18% or 28% depending on the individual's taxable income. The rate of CGT is 28% if the individual is a higher or additional rate taxpayer. If the individual is a basic rate taxpayer then CGT is payable at 18% on an amount of taxable gains up to the amount of the individual's unused basic rate band and at 28% on the excess.

When calculating the amount of unused basic rate band it must be extended for gross Gift Aid donations and gross personal pension contributions made during the tax year.

The rate of tax for all trusts (except bare trusts and trusts for disabled persons) is 28%.

2.4.2 Entrepreneurs' relief

Entrepreneurs' relief may be available, on certain qualifying disposals, which will reduce the rate of tax on these gains to 10% (see Chapter 6).

An individual may deduct capital losses and the annual exempt amount in a way that minimises his CGT liability. Capital losses and the annual exempt amount should therefore be deducted as follows:

(1)   Firstly from gains that do not qualify for entrepreneurs' relief as they are taxed at 28% or 18%

(2)   Secondly from gains that qualify for entrepreneurs' relief, as they are taxed at 10%

When establishing an individual's CGT rate(s), any unused basic rate band is set against gains qualifying for entrepreneurs' relief before non-qualifying gains.

2.5 Relief for converted trading losses

An individual may make a claim for trading loss relief under s.64 ITA 2007 against his general income in the year of the loss and/or the previous year (see Chapter 4). In addition, he may then extend the claim for any unrelieved part of the loss to be set against his chargeable gains for the year of the loss and/or the previous year. A claim must be made against general income for a year before any remaining loss can be offset against gains arising in that same year.

The claim must be made within 12 months from 31 January following the end of the tax year in which the loss arose. [Hp113]

The relevant legislation is s.261B Taxation of Chargeable Gains Act 1992 (TCGA 1992).

The loss is treated as a current year capital loss and so cannot be restricted to preserve the annual exempt amount.

The amount of the s.261B loss is the lower of:

• The unrelieved trading loss (the **relevant amount**) ie after s.64 relief

• The current year gains less current year losses and capital losses brought forward (the **maximum amount**) ie ignoring the annual exempt amount

The maximum amount takes account of all capital losses brought forward, not restricted by the annual exempt amount. The annual exempt amount may therefore be wasted if the trading losses reduce the amount of the gains to less than £11,100.

3 Deferred consideration

Section overview

- Where consideration for a capital disposal is contingent on a future event, special rules apply.

- The consideration may be payable by instalments or may be dependent on a future event. The future payment may be known or unknown.

- Where the future payment is unknown there are two disposals.

3.1 Overview

Where some of the consideration for the sale of an asset is dependent on a future event, special rules apply. How this is taxed depends on whether the amount of future consideration is known at the time of the original asset sale.

There are three possible types of future consideration:

- **Amount payable by instalments** – If there is no actual contingency and the payment is simply by instalments, there is a single disposal calculated under normal gains rules. The proceeds used are the total proceeds receivable.

  Where consideration is payable by instalments extending over a period of more than 18 months, the taxpayer can apply for the tax to be paid in instalments. Each instalment of tax is usually 50% of each instalment of consideration, until the tax liability is paid in full.

- **Future payment(s) contingent but known** – If the contingency results in a fixed amount being paid then the amount is known at the date of sale and there is a single disposal. The future payment is included in the total proceeds at the time of sale. If the contingency is not met, the computation may subsequently be amended.

- **Future payment contingent and unknown** – If the future payment depends on some future event and the amount to be paid cannot be determined, there are two disposals.

3.2 Future payment contingent and unknown

Where the amount of the future payment cannot be ascertained at the time of sale, the right to the future consideration is treated as a separate asset known as a 'chose in action'.

At the time of the sale of the original asset, a gain is calculated using the proceeds actually received and an estimated present value of the chose in action. The receipt of the future consideration is treated as a disposal of the chose in action and gives rise to a second gain/loss.

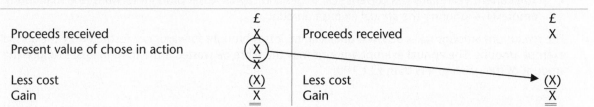

DISPOSAL OF ASSET	£	DISPOSAL OF CHOSE IN ACTION	£
Proceeds received	X	Proceeds received	X
Present value of chose in action	X		
	X		
Less cost	(X)	Less cost	(X)
Gain	X	Gain	X

For individuals only, where a loss arises on the sale of the chose in action it may be carried back and offset against the original gain on the disposal of the asset. There is no equivalent relief for companies.

The chose in action is not eligible for entrepreneurs' relief for an individual even if the gain on the original disposal is eligible for the relief.

Worked example: Future payment contingent and unknown

Cara sold business premises to a Blyth Ltd, an unconnected company, in August 2010 for £300,000 plus a percentage of the proceeds on future sale of the premises. The estimated value of the additional amount to be received by Cara was agreed with HMRC at £80,000.

Blyth Ltd sold the business premises in January 2016. As a result Cara received £75,000.

Requirement

Identify the sale proceeds for each disposal by Cara.

Solution

2010/11 – Cara sold the business premises

Sale proceeds are the proceeds actually received and the estimated present value of the chose in action ie the right to receive additional consideration ie £380,000 (£380,000 + £80,000).

2015/16 – Cara made a disposal of the chose in action ie she received the additional consideration

Sale proceeds are the consideration actually received ie £75,000. (Note this generates an allowable los available to carry back against the original gain.)

Interactive question: Contingent consideration [Difficulty level: Exam standard]

Elliot sold his shareholding in Hudson Ltd in February 2014 for £590,000 plus a right to receive an additional cash payment if Hudson Ltd met specific incremental profit targets in the following 12 months. The right was valued at £120,000 in February 2014. The shares originally cost Elliot £230,000.

Hudson Ltd made profits that resulted in an additional payment to Elliot of £140,000 in August 2015.

Requirement

Calculate the gains chargeable on Elliot.

2013/14 – sale of shares

	£
Proceeds	
Less cost	
Gain	

2015/16 – receipt of contingent consideration

	£
Proceeds	
Less cost	
Gain	

See **Answer** at the end of this chapter.

CHAPTER

5

Summary

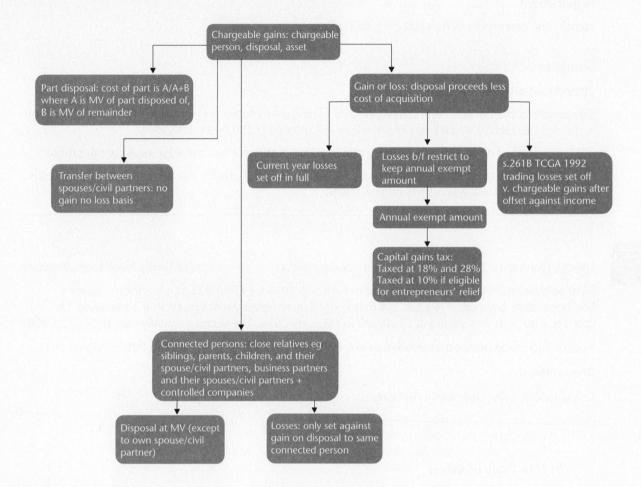

Chargeable gains: chargeable person, disposal, asset

Part disposal: cost of part is A/A+B where A is MV of part disposed of, B is MV of remainder

Transfer between spouses/civil partners: no gain no loss basis

Gain or loss: disposal proceeds less cost of acquisition

Current year losses set off in full

Losses b/f restrict to keep annual exempt amount

Annual exempt amount

Capital gains tax:
Taxed at 18% and 28%
Taxed at 10% if eligible for entrepreneurs' relief

s.261B TCGA 1992 trading losses set off v. chargeable gains after offset against income

Connected persons: close relatives eg siblings, parents, children, and their spouse/civil partners, business partners and their spouses/civil partners + controlled companies

Disposal at MV (except to own spouse/civil partner)

Losses: only set against gain on disposal to same connected person

Self-test

Answer the following questions.

1   Henrietta started trading on 1 June 2014. Her recent trading results have been as follows:

	£
y/e 31 May 2015	7,800
y/e 31 May 2016	(30,500)

In 2015/16 she had the following income and gains:

	£
Dividends from UK companies	4,200
Chargeable gain	35,000
Capital loss b/f	3,000

Henrietta makes a claim under s.64 ITA 2007 in 2015/16.

What is the s.261B TCGA 1992 loss available for use against the capital gain in 2015/16?

A   £18,033
B   £28,033
C   £32,000
D   £30,500

2   Marian acquired 980 shares in Tree plc (a 49% holding) for £63,000 in June 1999. In January 2016 Marian sold her shares to Branch plc for £244,000 in cash and the right to 20% of any profits exceeding the forecast for the year ended 31 December 2016. The value of the right to receive the additional consideration was agreed by HMRC at £8,000. Tree plc is a trading company.

Marian's actual entitlement received in January 2017 was £30,000.

Requirement

Calculate the total gains before any reliefs arising from the disposal of shares in Tree plc.

Now, go back to the Learning objectives in the Introduction. If you are satisfied you have achieved these objectives, please tick them off.

Technical reference

Legislation

References relate to Taxation of Chargeable Gains Act 1992 (*TCGA 1992*)

Chargeable persons	s.2
Annual exempt amount	s.3
Rates of tax	s.4
Computation of gains and losses	ss.15 – 17
Disposals between connected persons	s.18
Assets and disposals	s.21
Allowable deductions	ss.37 – 39
Consideration due after time of disposal (earn outs)	s.48
Disposals between spouses/civil partners	s.58
Deferred unascertainable consideration: election for treatment of loss	s.279A
Connected persons: interpretation	s.286
Capital gains tax reform	Sch 2 FA 2008

Note that the 'two disposal' treatment of unascertainable deferred consideration is not set out in statute. It was established by case law, in the case of *Marren v Ingles (54 TC 67)*

HMRC manual references

Capital gains manual

(Found at www.hmrc.gov.uk/manuals/cgmanual/index.htm)

Persons chargeable	CG10700
Chargeable assets: exemptions from capital gains charge	CG12600
Computation: introduction	CG14200
Part-disposals: general	CG12730
Part-disposals: formula for apportioning expenditure	CG12731
Deferred consideration	CG14850

Business Income manual

(Found at www.hmrc.gov.uk/manuals/bimmanual/BIM75001.htm)

Trading losses: types of relief: relief against chargeable gains	BIM75420

> This technical reference section is designed to assist you when you are working in the office. It should help you know where to look for further information on the topics covered in this chapter.

Answer to Interactive question

2013/14 – sale of shares

	£
Proceeds (£590,000 + £120,000)	710,000
Less cost	(230,000)
Gain	480,000

2015/16 – receipt of contingent consideration

	£
Proceeds	140,000
Less cost	(120,000)
Gain	20,000

If Elliot had received say £110,000 (instead of £140,000) he would have a capital loss of £10,000 in 2015/16. The loss could be carried back by Elliot and relieved against the gain arising in 2013/14.

1 A – £18,033

   Lower of:

   Relevant amount

	£
Trading income y/e 31 May 2015	7,800
Dividends £4,200 × 100/90	4,667
Net income	12,467
Less loss of 2016/17	(30,500)
Relevant amount	18,033

   Maximum amount

	£
Gains of year	35,000
Less losses brought forward	(3,000)
Maximum amount	32,000

2 **January 2016**

	£
Proceeds £(244,000 + 8,000)	252,000
Less cost	(63,000)
Gain	189,000

   January 2017

	£
Proceeds	30,000
Less cost	(8,000)
Gain	22,000

CHAPTER 6

Capital gains tax – reliefs

Introduction

Examination context

Topic List

Summary and Self-test

Technical reference

Answer to Interactive question

Answers to Self-test

Learning objectives

- Calculate capital gains tax liabilities for individuals

- Identify legitimate tax planning measures to minimise tax liabilities

- Evaluate and advise on alternative tax strategies relating to changes in personal circumstances such as marriage, divorce and death

- Recognise, explain and communicate opportunities to use alternative tax treatments arising from past transactions

The specific syllabus references for this chapter are 1v, 2a, 2c, 2d.

Syllabus links

In Tax Compliance you learnt about rollover relief, gift relief and entrepreneurs' relief.

In this chapter we review these reliefs and look at some other more advanced aspects relevant to the scenarios that you will encounter in the Business Planning: Taxation exam, such as incorporation relief and takeovers/reconstructions.

Examination context

With effective tax planning, a professional accountant should be able to mitigate the gains chargeable on a client's disposals. Several different reliefs are potentially available on the disposal of business assets.

In the examination candidates may be required to:

- Advise businesses of their taxable gains. In doing so it will be essential to identify when entrepreneurs' relief, rollover relief, gift relief or incorporation relief apply or the effect of a takeover/ reconstruction

- Calculate the reliefs where specific restrictions apply, for example some non-business use for rollover relief

This area of the syllabus is a good discriminator between candidates. The reliefs are not usually obvious in a question but need to be identified. Candidates need to identify which scenarios give rise to which reliefs and then learn to apply them.

1 Revision from Tax Compliance

Section overview

- There are various capital gains tax reliefs available which can significantly reduce the tax payable on the disposal of assets or defer the gain until a future event.

- In order to be able to offer tax planning advice you need to have a good understanding of the different reliefs available.

- Rollover relief is available when an old qualifying business asset is disposed of and a new qualifying business asset is acquired.

- The new asset must be acquired within one year before and three years after the disposal of the old asset.

- Full rollover relief is available if an amount at least equal to the disposal proceeds of the old asset is invested in the new asset.

- Gift relief is available on gifts of business assets such as assets used by a sole trader and certain shares.

- Gift relief passes the gain on disposal from the donor of the gift to the donee.

- There are restrictions on gift relief where the gift relates to shares in personal companies (donor owns at least 5% of voting rights) or where consideration is received.

- A special form of gift relief applies when there is an immediate charge to inheritance tax.

- Entrepreneurs' relief is available on the disposal of certain business assets.

- A minimum ownership period must be met in order for the relief to be available.

- The relief is given by taxing qualifying gains at the rate of 10%.

- Losses and the annual exempt amount can be set against other gains in priority gains qualifying for entrepreneurs' relief.

- There is a lifetime limit, per individual, on the value of the gains that are eligible for entrepreneurs' relief.

1.1 Replacement of business assets (rollover relief)

The relief defers payment of tax on gains on business assets whilst the trade is being carried on because the gain on the disposal of the business asset (**the old asset**) is rolled-over into the base cost of the replacement asset (**the new asset**).

The relief is available to both individuals (sole traders and partners) and companies making qualifying disposals.

Both the old asset and the new asset must be qualifying business assets, these include: [Hp99]

- Land and buildings (occupied and used for trade purposes)
- Fixed plant and fixed machinery
- Ships, aircraft and hovercraft
- Satellites, space stations and spacecraft
- Goodwill (sole traders and partners only, not companies)

The new asset must be acquired during a **qualifying time period** of one year before and three years after the date of disposal of the old asset. [Hp99]

A claim for rollover relief must be made within the later of four years of the end of the tax year (accounting period for companies) in which the gain is realised or the new asset is acquired [Hp114]. A provisional claim can be made.

1.2 How does rollover relief work?

Full relief is only available if an amount at least equal to the net disposal proceeds of the old asset is invested in the acquisition of the new asset. In this case the whole of the gain on the old asset will be rolled over into the base cost of the new asset.

If less than the net proceeds from disposal is invested in the new asset, a gain will arise at the time of the disposal of the old asset equal to the lower of:

*   The gain on disposal of the old asset; and
*   The amount not reinvested.

Any remaining gain may be rolled over.

The base cost of the new asset is reduced by the rolled over gain.

Note that a partial claim for rollover relief is not possible. If claimed, the maximum amount of gain must be deferred.

1.3 Rollover relief – special situations

1.3.1 Non-business use

When an asset has non-business use, relief is only available on the business element of the gain. The length and extent of business use through the whole period of ownership is considered.

Only the proceeds of the business element should be considered when looking at the proceeds invested in the new asset.

Where the replacement asset also has a non-business element, only consider the business element of the investment to determine the amount invested.

1.3.2 Depreciating assets

Where the replacement asset is a depreciating asset, the gain is not rolled over by reducing the cost of the replacement asset. Rather it is deferred until it crystallises on the earliest of:

*   The disposal of the replacement asset.
*   Ten years after the acquisition of the replacement asset.
*   The date the replacement asset ceases to be used in the trade (but the gain does not crystallise on the taxpayer's death).

An asset is a **depreciating asset** if it is, or within the next ten years will become, a wasting asset. Thus, any asset with an expected life of 60 years or less is covered by this definition (eg fixed plant and machinery or a building held on a lease with 60 years or less to run).

1.4 Gift relief for business assets

A claim may be made by an individual (**the donor**) for the gain arising on a gift of a business asset to be deferred until the recipient of the gift (**the donee**) disposes of the asset at a later date.

The assets that qualify for gift relief are:

*   Assets used in a business carried on by the donor or by the donor's personal company (a company in which the donor has at least 5% of the voting rights); or
*   Shares or securities in a trading company where either the shares are:
    *   Unquoted; or
    *   The company is the donor's personal company.

Gift relief is not available on the gift of shares or securities where the donee is a company.

A joint election must be made and signed by both the donor and the donee, within four years after the end of the tax year of the gift. [Hp114]

1.5 How does gift relief work?

If gift relief applies, there is no gain arising for the donor on the disposal of the asset. Therefore no capital gains tax is payable.

The donee's deemed cost of acquisition (which is the market value at the date of gift) is reduced by the amount of the gain which would have been chargeable had gift relief not applied.

1.6 Gift relief – special situations

1.6.1 Restriction for gift relief on shares in a personal company

There is a restriction on the amount of gift relief where the gifted asset is shares in a company which has been the donor's personal company at any time in the twelve months prior to the disposal.

In this case, the amount of the gain qualifying for gift relief is the gain times the fraction:

$$\frac{\text{Chargeable business assets of the company (CBA)}}{\text{Chargeable assets of the company (CA)}}$$

The value of the assets of the company used in this calculation is their market value at the date of disposal of the shares.

1.6.2 Restriction on gift relief where consideration received

Gift relief is also available where the donor makes a sale to the donee at less than market value in a bargain which is not at arm's length.

The gain on disposal will still be calculated using the market value of the asset, not the actual consideration received.

Any excess of actual consideration over the base cost of the asset is immediately chargeable. Any remaining gain is subject to gift relief.

1.6.3 Gifts with an immediate inheritance tax charge

A special type of gift relief is also available where an individual makes a gift during his lifetime and the gift is subject to an immediate inheritance tax charge.

This relief operates in the same way as gift relief for business assets, with the following differences:

- The relief is not restricted to gifts of business assets ie it is available for a gift of any chargeable asset
- As a result there is no restriction for CBA/CA
- The election for the relief only needs to be signed by the donor

1.7 Entrepreneurs' relief

Entrepreneurs' relief applies to certain disposals of business assets by individuals. It charges CGT on those disposals at a rate of 10%.

Qualifying assets

The relief is available in respect of gains on disposals by individuals of:

1   All or part of a trading business the individual carries on alone or in partnership

2   Assets of the individual's or partnership's trading business following the cessation of the business

3   Shares issued under an EMI option scheme (see Chapter 3), on or after 6 April 2013 (6 April 2012 if an election is made)

4   Shares in (and securities of) the individual's 'personal' trading company (or holding company of a trading group)

Disposals of shares

A personal trading company is one where the individual making the disposal owns at least 5% of the ordinary share capital of the company and that holding enables the individual to exercise at least 5% of the voting rights in that company.

Where there is a share disposal (either personal trading company shares or EMI shares) the individual making the disposal must be an officer or employee of the company, or of a company in the same group of companies.

If the company has substantial non-trading activities the relief could be denied.

Ownership period

The relevant business property must be owned for a period of one year ending with the date of disposal. On cessation of the business (as in (2) above) the qualifying period is the year up to cessation, and the assets must be disposed of within three years of the cessation.

For shares issued under an EMI option scheme the one year holding period runs from the date when the option is granted, not from the date the shares are acquired.

Assets owned personally but used in a business

Note that the disposal of individual assets owned by an individual but used for business purposes in a continuing trade does not qualify for relief unless it is an 'associated disposal' (see Section 1.9.1).

1.8 How does entrepreneurs' relief work?

1.8.1 Calculating the relief

Entrepreneurs' relief is claimed by [Hp 97]:

- Netting off gains and losses in respect of the business disposal (for example a number of assets may be disposed of in conjunction with a business)

- Taxing the gain at 10% (after deduction of losses and the annual exempt amount)

Losses and the annual exempt amount should be set against other gains before gains qualifying for entrepreneurs' relief.

Gains qualifying for entrepreneurs' relief are treated as the lowest slice of gains, and so reduce the amount of unused basic rate band available for other gains.

1.8.2 Lifetime limit

There is a lifetime limit on the amount on which entrepreneurs' relief may be given. The limit can apply to a number of disposals made over different tax years.

The current limit is £10 million

Gains in excess of the lifetime limit will be charged to CGT as normal ie usually at 28%.

Entrepreneurs' relief must be claimed. The time limit for the claim is 12 months from 31 January following the tax year in which the qualifying disposal is made. [Hp115]

1.9 Entrepreneurs' relief – special situations

1.9.1 Associated disposals

Where an individual qualifies for relief on a disposal of shares or on the disposal of his interest in a partnership, relief will also be available if the individual also disposes of an asset which was used in the company's (or group's) or partnership's business.

The conditions for an asset to be an associated disposal are:

- The individual is disposing of the whole or part of his interest in a partnership, or the disposal of shares in a company (ie there is a material disposal). From 18 March 2015 'material' is defined as at least a 5% shareholding or at least a 5% share in the assets of the partnership;

- The disposal is made as part of the individual's withdrawal from the business of the partnership or company; and

- The assets being sold have been used for the purpose of the business for one year prior to the date of the material disposal of business assets or the cessation of the business of the partnership or company.

For example, an individual might own shares in a company and also the premises from which the company carries on its business. The sale of the premises in addition to the shares may be an 'associated disposal' and the gain on this as well as the shares will qualify for entrepreneurs' relief.

The property will not be eligible for relief if let at market value rent to the company/partnership. Full relief is available if the property was let rent free, and partial relief applies if let at a reduced rent. This is because the asset was, to the extent it was rented, an investment. This restriction applies for periods from 6 April 2008 onwards only, ie rent received prior to that date is not relevant.

If only part of the asset was used for the business then only the proportion of the gain relating to business use will be eligible for entrepreneurs' relief.

Worked example: Associated disposals and entrepreneurs' relief

Jack disposes of his 10% shareholding in Wendle Ltd, a trading company, in February 2016. Jack had acquired the shares when he started to work for the company in January 2007. The gain before reliefs on the shares is £150,000. Jack is selling his shares as he is retiring from the company business.

At the same time Jack also sells the office building that has been used by Wendle Ltd, but which he owned outright, realising a gain of £56,400. Jack had let the office building to Wendle Ltd rent free since 2009.

Jack makes no other chargeable disposals in 2015/16 and has no capital losses brought forward.

Requirement

Calculate the capital gains tax payable on the disposals by Jack in 2015/16.

Solution

	£
Shares	150,000
Office building	56,400
Gains qualifying for relief	206,400
Less annual exempt amount	(11,100)
Taxable gain	195,300
CGT payable £195,300 × 10%	19,530

1.9.2 Entrepreneurs' relief on incorporation

This section is new.

From 3 December 2014, entrepreneurs' relief cannot be claimed in respect of goodwill where the goodwill has been disposed of to a limited company which is related to the claimant (eg on incorporation to a close company). However it can be claimed by a retiring partner in a firm who does not hold any stake in the successor company. This measure is intended to be a disincentive to incorporate purely for tax reasons and is part of a package of measures including the restriction of corporation tax relief for goodwill on incorporation (Chapter 10).

1.9.3 Interaction of gift relief and entrepreneurs' relief

Certain disposals by way of gift might meet the criteria for both gift relief and entrepreneurs' relief.

If gift relief is to be claimed it must be claimed first. Entrepreneurs' relief can then be applied if any gain remains in charge to tax. If gift relief is claimed, the maximum available relief must be claimed.

2 Incorporation relief

Section overview

- On the incorporation of a business, there would normally be a disposal of chargeable assets by the sole trader.

- Incorporation relief defers the net gain arising against the base cost of shares received on incorporation.

- Relief is only given to the extent that shares are received on incorporation.

2.1 What is incorporation relief?

A sole trader might decide to incorporate his business by transferring it to a company in exchange for shares.

Under normal rules, this would result in a disposal of the chargeable assets used in the business by the sole trader which could result in chargeable gains. Incorporation relief allows the trader to defer the gains against the value of the shares he receives from the company on incorporation.

Incorporation relief can also be used in a similar way on the incorporation of a partnership into a company.

2.2 Conditions for incorporation relief

The business must be transferred as a going concern.

All the assets of the business (or all the assets other than cash) must be transferred to the company.

The consideration received by the trader from the company must consist wholly or partly of shares.

Incorporation relief is automatically applied if these conditions are satisfied. However, an election may be made to disapply the relief.

2.3 How does incorporation relief work?

The gains and losses on the chargeable assets are computed, using the market value of the assets at the date of transfer to the company.

If the only consideration for the transfer is shares, the net gains are then deducted from the cost of the shares received.

Worked example: Incorporation relief

Pratish is a sole trader. In December 2015, he transfers his business as a going concern to a company in exchange for 70,000 shares valued at £10 each.

The assets of the business at transfer were:

Asset	MV at transfer	Cost	Acquired
Warehouse	£300,000	£120,000	May 1997
Shop	£50,000	£55,000	August 2007
Plant & machinery (all bought & sold for less than £6,000)	£100,000	£80,000	June 2004
Goodwill	£150,000	Nil	May 1997
Stock	£50,000	n/a	Various
Debtors	£40,000	n/a	Various
Cash at bank	£10,000	n/a	n/a
	£700,000		

All the assets were transferred.

Requirement

Show the base cost of the shares after incorporation relief.

Solution

Net gains on transfer

Gain on warehouse

	£
Market value	300,000
Less cost	(120,000)
Gain	180,000

Loss on shop

Market value	50,000
Less cost	(55,000)
Loss	(5,000)

Plant and machinery – exempt

Gain on goodwill

	£
Market value	150,000
Less cost	(Nil)
Gain	150,000

Stock, debtors and cash

Not chargeable assets

Net gains (£180,000 – £5,000 + £150,000)	£325,000

Base cost of shares

	£
Value of shares received 70,000 × £10	700,000
Less net gains	(325,000)
Base cost after incorporation relief	375,000

If there is other consideration for the transfer such as cash or loan stock, the gain that can be deferred is:

$$\frac{\text{Value of shares received}}{\text{Value of total consideration received}} \times \text{net gains}$$

Interactive question : Partial incorporation relief [Difficulty level: Intermediate]

Sammi is a sole trader. In March 2016, she transfers her business as a going concern to a company. The net gains on the assets transferred amount to £60,000.

Sammi receives 16,000 shares valued at £5.00 each and £10,000 of loan stock valued at its nominal value.

Requirement

Using the standard format below, show the gain chargeable on Sammi and the base cost of her shares after incorporation relief.

Gain deferred

Value of shares received	£_____
Value of loan stock received	£_____
Value of total consideration	£_____

Gain deferred:

.... × £..................... £_____

Chargeable gain

(£..................... – £.....................) £_____

Base cost of shares

	£
Value of shares received	
Less incorporation relief	( )
Base cost after incorporation relief	

See **Answer** at the end of this chapter.

Consideration in the form of cash or loans can be used to achieve a gain equal to the unused annual exempt amount. The owner will therefore receive tax free cash on incorporation.

If there is any gain remaining after incorporation relief it may be taxed at 10% if the conditions for entrepreneurs' relief are satisfied, or at 18%/28% otherwise. However if the total gains on incorporation include a gain on goodwill (to a close company), then that part of the remaining gain after incorporation relief will not be eligible for entrepreneurs' relief (from 4 December 2014). HMRC have suggested that the proportion not eligible for entrepreneurs' relief is in the same proportion as the total gains. For example in the interactive question if £20,000 of the net gains (one third) relate to goodwill, then one third of the remaining gains are not eligible for incorporation relief ie £2,222 (£6,667 × 1/3).

2.4 Summary of reliefs

	Rollover relief	Incorporation relief	Gift relief	Entrepreneurs' relief
How does it work?	Disposal of an old asset followed by acquisition of new asset. Both old and new asset must be used in trade. Reinvestment must be within 12 months before and 36 months after disposal	Transfer **all** the assets (except cash) of a business to a limited company in return for at least some shares	Gift qualifying assets – eg to company on incorporation as no need to transfer all the assets of the business	Gains eligible for ER qualify for a reduced rate of CGT at 10% Can offset losses and the AEA against non-ER assets first ER assets are treated as using up any remaining BRB in priority to non-ER assets so unlikely to then have gains taxed at 18%
What qualifies?	• Land and buildings • Goodwill • Fixed plant and fixed machinery	Assets of a business if all the assets are transferred as a going concern	• Business assets • Shares in trading co; unquoted or min 5% holding • Any asset with an immediate IHT charge	Disposal of: • Unincorporated business • Shares in trading co with min 5% holding (or EMI shares) and employee • Associated disposals owned for a period of one year ending with date of disposal

	Rollover relief	Incorporation relief	Gift relief	Entrepreneurs' relief
How much is the relief?	Where all the proceeds are reinvested the whole of the gain is eligible for rollover relief Where only some of the proceeds are reinvested, the amount not reinvested is taxed now and the balance of the gain is eligible for rollover relief Relief for business use only	If no cash received then all the gains are deferred Where some cash and some shares received, then gain deferred is: $\dfrac{\text{Shares}}{\text{Total}} \times \text{net gains}$	If no cash received then all the gains are deferred Where some cash received (sale at undervalue) restrict deferral by excess of actual proceeds over original cost Where gift of shares and co owns non-business assets restrict to: $\dfrac{\text{CBA}}{\text{CA}} \times \text{gain}$ (Unless immediate IHT charge)	Lifetime limit (currently £10m) eligible for reduced CGT rate at 10%
How is relief given?	If reinvest in depreciating asset (UEL of $\leq$ 60 years) then gain is held over and becomes chargeable on earlier of: • 10 years from date of purchase of new asset • Cease to use new asset in trade • Dispose of new asset If reinvest in non-depreciating asset then the deferred gain reduces the base cost of the new asset	Gain deferred is deducted from base cost of shares received	Gain deferred is deducted from donee's base cost of each asset	Not a deferral relief – gain will be taxed at 10% instead of 18% or 28%
Optional?	Optional – election required	Automatic but can claim to disapply so effectively optional	Optional – joint election required (unless immediate IHT charge)	Optional – election required

2.5 Interaction of reliefs

In some cases there may be more than one relief available. In this case, the reliefs are taken in the following order:

- Rollover relief for replacement of business assets [s.152] – reduces the proceeds for the asset disposed of such that it creates a nil gain, nil loss (assuming full relief). Therefore it must be first.

- Incorporation relief [s.162] – reduces the aggregate net chargeable gains and is therefore next.

- Gift relief [ss.165 & 260] – reduces each chargeable gain and is therefore next.

- SEIS reinvestment relief [s.150G & Sch 5BB] – exempts the specified part of a chargeable gain.

- EIS deferral relief [Sch 5B] – treats the gain as not arising until some future event and is therefore applied after the other reliefs which reduce the amount of the taxable gain.

- Entrepreneurs' relief [s.169H] – reduces the rate applying to the aggregate gains as already computed, ie after any other possible reliefs. Therefore it must come after the other reliefs.

3 Takeovers and reconstructions

Section overview

- Where there is a reorganisation of a company's share capital, the new shares are treated as having been acquired for the same cost and at the same date as the original shares.

- A paper for paper takeover is one where shares in one company are exchanged for shares in another company.

- There is no chargeable disposal on a paper for paper takeover. The new shares are treated as acquired at the same time and for the same cost as the original shares.

- Where mixed consideration is received ie shares plus non-cash consideration, there will be a part disposal.

- Where part of the consideration is a QCB, a gain is calculated at the time of the takeover and this gain is deferred until the subsequent disposal of the QCB. Any gain on the QCB itself will be exempt for an individual but chargeable under the loan relationship rules for a company.

This section details the technical rules concerning the chargeable gains implications of corporate takeovers and reconstructions. In Chapter 23 you will review this technical topic again from a scenario based perspective. This will ensure that you can answer exam based questions requiring you to apply this knowledge.

3.1 Paper for paper takeovers

When one company (Company A) takes over another company (Company B), Company A acquires the shares of Company B. Company A may do this in exchange for shares in itself ie Company B's shareholders swap their shares in Company B for shares in Company A. This is called a 'paper for paper' or 'share for share' takeover.

On a share for share disposal, there is no chargeable disposal on the takeover.

The shares in Company A received on the takeover by the shareholders of Company B are deemed to have been acquired at the same time and at the same cost as the original shareholdings in Company B.

Worked example: Paper for paper takeover

Derek made the following acquisitions of ordinary shares in W plc:

Date	Shares acquired	Cost £
10 August 1992	1,200	2,400
15 May 1997	Rights 1 for 2	£5 per share
8 October 2003	700	2,800

W plc was the subject of a takeover by Z plc in May 2015. Derek received 5 ordinary shares in Z plc for each share that he held in W plc.

In December 2015, Derek sold 10,000 shares in Z plc for £12,000. This was his only capital disposal in 2015/16.

Requirement

Calculate the chargeable gain on sale.

Solution

	No.	Cost £
W plc shares		
10 August 1992		
Acquisition	1,200	2,400
15 May 1997		
Rights 1:2 @ £5	600	3,000
8 October 2003		
Acquisition	700	2,800
	2,500	8,200
Z plc shares		
May 2015 Takeover 2,500 × 5	12,500	8,200
December 2015		
Disposal	(10,000)	(6,560)
c/f	2,500	1,640

Gain

	£
Disposal proceeds	12,000
Less cost	(6,560)
Chargeable gain	5,440

3.2 Shares held by an individual investor

For individuals, the above treatment is only available if the conditions in the following diagram are satisfied:

Are the following conditions satisfied?

- The new securities are issued in proportion to the old securities.

- After the takeover the acquiring company controls > 25% of the ordinary share capital or > 50% of the votes.

- The arrangements are not part of a scheme to avoid tax.

No

- HMRC can disapply the relief.

- The shareholder is treated as having made a normal disposal of the old shares and a purchase of the new shares.

- This leads to an immediate gain/loss.

Yes

- No gain arises at the time of the takeover.

- The gain arising on disposal is effectively deferred until the sale of the new securities.

The relief can also apply where, as part of a scheme of reconstruction or amalgamation:

- The new company issues shares to the shareholders of the original company in proportion to their shareholdings in the original company, and

- The old shares are either retained or cancelled.

The relief will be disapplied if the arrangements are part of a scheme to avoid tax.

There are four situations to consider where shares are sold for different forms of consideration:

Consideration	Taxation consequences
Exchange for shares of the same class	• The new shares take on the cost and acquisition date(s) of the old shares. • No gain arises until the new shares are disposed of.

Exchange for different classes of share capital	• For example where ordinary shares and preference shares are received.
	• The cost of the original shares is apportioned between the new shares by reference to the relative market values of the new shares.
	  – For new quoted shares, use the relative market values at the date of exchange.
	  – For new unquoted shares, use the relative market values at the date of the first disposal.
	• No gain arises until the new shares are disposed of.

Receipt of shares and cash	• The cost of the original shares is apportioned.
	• If the cash is ≤ 5% of the value of the total consideration, or ≤ £3,000 then
	  – No gain is charged.
	  – The cash received is deducted from the base cost of the shares.
	• Otherwise, a gain must be computed on a part disposal of the shares In respect of the cash element of the consideration.

Receipt of loan stock	• If the loan stock is a qualifying corporate bond (QCB):
	  – The cost of the original shares is apportioned between the components of the consideration received by reference to their relative market values.
	  – A gain arises in respect of the loan stock but is deferred.
	  – The deferred gain is charged when the loan stock is disposed of.
	  – Note the disposal of the loan stock itself (a QCB) is an exempt asset for capital gains purposes, for an individual.
	• If the loan stock is not a QCB, it is treated in the same way as shares.
	• Consideration left outstanding under the terms of a sale agreement does not constitute loan stock unless a loan note is issued. Consideration which is left outstanding is therefore treated in the same way as cash consideration.

Definition

Qualifying corporate bond (QCB): For individuals, a QCB is defined as:

- Sterling denominated
- Non-convertible
- Loan stock representing a normal commercial loan
- The interest upon which is neither excessive nor dependent on business performance

For a company, a QCB is a loan relationship receivable.

Worked example: Takeover with mixed consideration

Roundhouse plc is a quoted company specialising in the manufacture of health foods. The directors have accepted an offer from Hanover plc, a listed company with a large chain of health food stores, to purchase the share capital of Roundhouse plc. Its offer for each £1 ordinary share is as follows:

	Value £
1 Hanover 50p ordinary share	2.80
1 Hanover 25p preference share	1.20
Cash	4.00

Madge holds 1,000 Roundhouse plc £1 ordinary shares acquired on 1 June 2008 for £1.50 each. She does not work for the company.

The takeover is finalised on 14 August 2015.

Requirements

(a) How will the takeover be treated for tax purposes for Madge?
(b) What would the effect be of receiving loan stock instead of the cash?

Solution

(a) The cost of Madge's original shareholding is allocated as follows.

	Consideration £	Cost allocated £
1,000 50p ordinary shares	2,800	525
1,000 25p preference shares	1,200	225
Cash	4,000	750
	8,000	1,500

The receipt of cash gives rise to a gain.

	£
Proceeds	4,000
Cost	(750)
Gain	3,250

(b) What would be the effect of receiving loan stock which was a qualifying corporate bond (QCB) worth £4,000 instead of cash?

Madge would still make a gain of £3,250 but this would be deferred until disposal of the QCB.

The disposal of the QCB itself would be exempt.

What would be the effect of receiving loan stock which was not a QCB (ie loan notes convertible into shares or containing the right to repayment in a foreign currency)?

The new loan stock is treated like shares and hence is carried forward with an acquisition cost of £750 as at 1 June 2008.

On the assumption that the loan stock does not change materially in value, any future disposal would produce a gain of around £3,250.

3.3 Disapplication of paper for paper rules on a takeover

In the previous section you saw how a takeover of one company (Company B) by another company (Company A) can result in no chargeable disposal on the takeover.

It may, however, be the case that an individual's holding of the old shares in Company B would, on disposal, have been entitled to entrepreneurs' relief, but the disposal of the new shares in Company A would not.

The paper for paper takeover rules mean that only the future disposal of the Company A shares would become chargeable and the benefit of entrepreneurs' relief would be lost.

Therefore an individual may make a claim to disapply the paper for paper rules on the takeover.

On the takeover the disposal of the shares in Company B will give rise to a chargeable disposal.

The Company A shares will have a cost equal to their market value at the date of the takeover.

 ### Worked example: Disapplication of paper for paper rules on a takeover

Hamid purchased 1,000 shares in C Ltd in February 2001 as part of a management buy-out. He has worked for C Ltd since 1999. The shares cost £30,000 and C Ltd had 10,000 ordinary shares in issue.

In August 2015 C Ltd was taken over by J plc. J plc offered 8 shares in itself for every share in C Ltd. J plc had 10,000,000 shares in issue after the takeover and each share was worth £37.

Hamid plans to sell his J plc shares in September 2016 when they are expected to be worth £40 each.

Hamid has no capital losses brought forward at 6 April 2015. He expects to make other capital gains in both 2015/16 and 2016/17 sufficient to use his annual exempt amount. Hamid is a higher rate taxpayer.

Requirement

Advise Hamid on his capital gains tax payable on the takeover and on the sale of the J plc shares in September 2016 if:

(a) The paper for paper takeover rules apply.
(b) He makes a claim to disapply the paper for paper rules at the date of the takeover.

Assume that all reliefs and rates of tax for 2015/16 continue to apply for 2016/17.

Solution

(a) There will be no chargeable disposal in August 2015 when the takeover occurs. The shares in J plc will take on the cost and acquisition date of the C Ltd shares. After the takeover Hamid will own 8,000 shares in J plc.

September 2016

	£
Disposal proceeds 8,000 × £40	320,000
Less cost	(30,000)
Chargeable gain	290,000
CGT payable £290,000 × 28%	81,200

No entrepreneurs' relief is available as Hamid does not own at least 5% of the shares in J plc in the one year prior to the disposal in September 2016.

(b) There will be a chargeable disposal at the date of the takeover.

August 2015

	£
Disposal proceeds 8,000 × £37 (MV of shares)	296,000
Less cost	(30,000)
Chargeable gain	266,000
CGT payable £266,000 × 10%	26,600

Hamid has a 10% holding in C Ltd and has worked for C Ltd for the one year prior to the disposal so the gain on the disposal of the shares is eligible for entrepreneurs' relief.

September 2016

	£
Disposal proceeds 8,000 × £40	320,000
Less cost	(296,000)
Chargeable gain	24,000
CGT payable £24,000 × 28%	6,720
Total CGT payable (£26,600 + £6,720)	£33,320

There is a capital gains tax saving under option (b) of £47,880 (£81,200 – £33,320). Hamid should elect to disapply the paper for paper rules and claim entrepreneurs' relief.

3.4 Interaction between reorganisations involving qualifying corporate bonds and entrepreneurs' relief

For an individual, if QCBs are received under a takeover the normal rule is to calculate the gain in respect of the QCBs, but to defer the gain until the QCBs are disposed of. Entrepreneurs' relief may be available in certain circumstances.

Entrepreneurs' relief is only available on the reorganisation if an election is made not to defer the gain on the QCBs. If the election is made the whole gain is chargeable at the time of the takeover, and entrepreneurs' relief can then be claimed.

If the election is not made no entrepreneurs' relief is available, but the gain attributable to the QCBs can be deferred.

Summary and Self-test

Summary

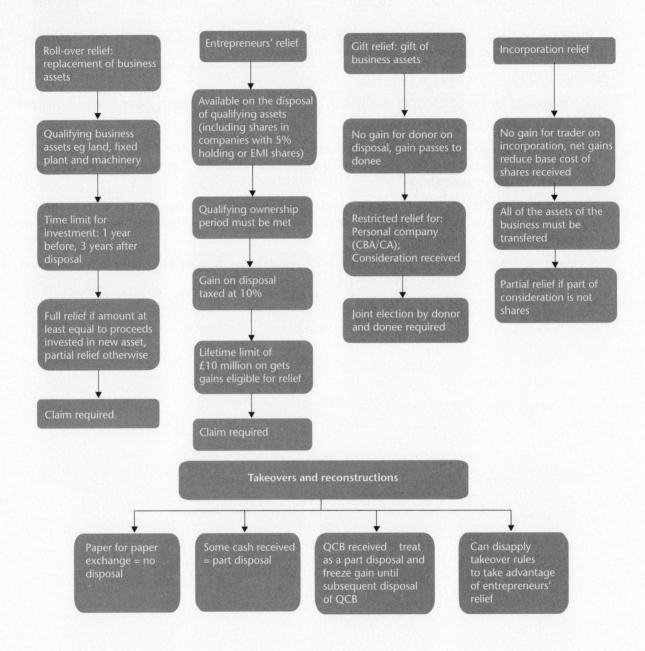

Roll-over relief: replacement of business assets

↓

Qualifying business assets eg land, fixed plant and machinery

↓

Time limit for investment: 1 year before, 3 years after disposal

↓

Full relief if amount at least equal to proceeds invested in new asset, partial relief otherwise

↓

Claim required

Entrepreneurs' relief

↓

Available on the disposal of qualifying assets (including shares in companies with 5% holding or EMI shares)

↓

Qualifying ownership period must be met

↓

Gain on disposal taxed at 10%

↓

Lifetime limit of £10 million on gets gains eligible for relief

↓

Claim required

Gift relief: gift of business assets

↓

No gain for donor on disposal, gain passes to donee

↓

Restricted relief for: Personal company (CBA/CA); Consideration received

↓

Joint election by donor and donee required

Incorporation relief

↓

No gain for trader on incorporation, net gains reduce base cost of shares received

↓

All of the assets of the business must be transfered

↓

Partial relief if part of consideration is not shares

Takeovers and reconstructions

- Paper for paper exchange = no disposal
- Some cash received = part disposal
- QCB received   treat as a part disposal and freeze gain until subsequent disposal of QCB
- Can disapply takeover rules to take advantage of entrepreneurs' relief

Self-test

Answer the following questions.

1   Jamilla incorporates her business in October 2015 and transfers all the assets of her business to the company, all of which she had owned for many years.

The net gains arising on the transfer are £52,000. Jamilla receives shares worth £90,000 and cash of £10,000.

Requirement

Calculate the gain on which incorporation relief will be given.

2   Sam buys 10,000 Acre plc ordinary shares for £200,000 on 1 December 2014. The company is taken over by Hectare plc (a quoted company) on 1 April 2016. Sam receives 4 Hectare plc ordinary shares, 2 preference shares and £8 in cash for each Acre plc share held. The value of Hectare plc ordinary and preference shares at the time of the takeover is £4.65 and £1.12 respectively. Sam is a higher rate taxpayer, has never worked for either company and has no other capital transactions in 2015/16.

Requirement

Calculate the capital gains tax payable by Sam at the time of the takeover, if any, and show the base cost of the shares held in Hectare plc.

3   Amy acquired 15,000 shares in Field plc in April 1999 for £75,000. Field plc was taken over in December 2004 by Orchard plc. Amy received 20,000 Orchard plc shares worth £126,000 and £66,000 7.5% Orchard plc loan stock 2017 valued at £82,000. The loan stock satisfies the conditions of a qualifying corporate bond.

Amy sold 75% of the loan stock in January 2016 for £30,000. Amy is a higher rate taxpayer and has never worked for either company. She has capital disposals in the year that utilise the annual exempt amount.

Requirement

Calculate any capital gains tax payable by Amy as a result of these transactions.

Now, go back to the Learning objectives in the Introduction. If you are satisfied you have achieved these objectives, please tick them off.

Technical reference

Legislation

References are to Taxation of Chargeable Gains Act 1992 (*TCGA 1992*)

Rollover relief

Deferral of gain	s.152
Classes of assets	s.155
Assets only partly replaced	s.153

Incorporation relief

Deferral of gain	s.162

Gift relief

Deferral of gain	s.165
Restriction for personal company	Sch 7 para 7

Entrepreneurs' relief

	ss.169H – 169R

Takeovers and reconstructions

Reorganisation of shares	s.127
Takeovers – paper for paper relief	s.135
Disapply paper for paper rules	s.169Q

HMRC manual references

Capital gains manual

(Found at www.hmrc.gov.uk/manuals/cgmanual/CG60201c.htm)

Rollover relief: conditions	CG60280
Transfer of a business to a company	CG65700
Gifts : gifts of business assets: introduction	CG66910
Reorganisations of share capital: introduction: general	CG51700

> This technical reference section is designed to assist you when you are working in the office. It should help you know where to look for further information on the topics covered in this chapter.

Answer to Interactive question

Gain deferred

Value of shares received 16,000 × £5	£80,000
Value of loan stock received	£10,000
Value of total consideration	£90,000

Gain deferred:

$$\frac{80,000}{90,000} \times £60,000 \qquad\qquad £53,333$$

Chargeable gain

(£60,000 – £53,333)	£6,667

Base cost of shares

	£
Value of shares received	80,000
Less incorporation relief	(53,333)
Base cost after incorporation relief	26,667

1 Gain deferred:

Value of shares received	£90,000
Value of other consideration	£10,000
Value of total consideration	£100,000

Gain on which incorporation relief given:

$$\frac{90,000}{100,000} \times £52,000 \qquad\qquad £46,800$$

2 The values for apportionment are:

	£
Ordinary shares: 10,000 × 4 × £4.65	186,000
Preference shares: 10,000 × 2 × £1.12	22,400
Cash: 10,000 × £8	80,000
	288,400

Clearly the cash element is not 'small'. There is no gain on the paper for paper exchanges, however the cash received will be treated as giving rise to a part disposal.

The base costs of the new holdings and cash are:

		Cost £
Ordinary shares	$\frac{186,000}{288,400} \times £200,000$	128,988
Preference shares	$\frac{22,400}{288,400} \times £200,000$	15,534
Cash	$\frac{80,000}{288,400} \times £200,000$	55,478
		200,000

The gain on the cash element is:

	£
Disposal proceeds	80,000
Less cost	(55,478)
Chargeable gain	24,522
Less annual exempt amount	(11,100)
Taxable gain	13,422
CGT @ 28%	3,758

3 The base cost of the Field plc shares is divided on the takeover:

	£
Orchard plc shares 126,000/(126,000 + 82,000) × £75,000	45,433
Loan stock 82,000/(126,000 + 82,000) × £75,000	29,567
	75,000

There is no gain in respect of the shares received because of the 'paper for paper' provisions. The gain of £52,433 (£82,000 – £29,567) in respect of the loan stock received is calculated at the date of the takeover and is 'frozen'.

Therefore on the sale of three-quarters of the loan stock in January 2016, three-quarters of the frozen gain becomes chargeable, ie £39,325 (£52,433 × 75%). There is no loss allowable for the decrease in value of the QCB as they are exempt assets for capital gains purposes for an individual. Therefore CGT of £39,325 × 28% = £11,011 is payable.

The advantage to the shareholder of receiving a QCB is the ability to defer the gain to a later year when perhaps the annual exempt amount will be available or a lower marginal rate of tax will apply. However, this advantage may effectively be lost where the QCB falls in value but the deferred gain is still chargeable based on its original value.

CHAPTER 7

Inheritance tax

Introduction

Examination context

Topic List

Summary and Self-test

Technical reference

Answer to Interactive question

Answers to Self-test

Learning objectives

- Calculate inheritance tax liabilities for individuals

- Advise on the taxation of foreign assets, income and gains

- Explain the implications of domicile for inheritance tax

- Identify legitimate tax planning measures to minimise tax liabilities

- Evaluate and advise on alternative tax strategies relating to changes in personal circumstances such as marriage, divorce and death

Specific syllabus references for this chapter are 1v, 1w, 1z, 2a, 2c.

Syllabus links

Inheritance tax was covered in Tax Compliance. You will now consider how deeds of variation can be used to legitimately reduce tax liabilities. In addition you will consider the gift with reservation of benefit anti-avoidance rules, and the interaction of inheritance tax and capital gains tax.

Examination context

In practice capital gains tax and inheritance tax often need to be considered together in the planning of the disposal of a client's estate. The availability of a large number of reliefs can lead to significant reduction on potential liabilities with careful planning. The accountant needs to consider the client's overall aim before putting planning measures into place, for example a desire to maximise estate passed onto grandchildren may suggest a deed of variation if a grandparent has died recently.

In the examination candidates may be required to:

- Advise on the use of business property relief and agricultural property relief in tax planning strategies for different individuals

- Advise on HMRC's approach to gifts made with reservation of benefit

- Determine how an individual's inheritance tax payable on death may be reduced by using a deed of variation

- Identify when gift relief is available on lifetime transfers

Candidates must ensure that they fully understand these planning issues relating to inheritance tax. Candidates must be able to apply the concepts to specific scenarios.

1 Revision from Tax Compliance

Section overview

- Inheritance tax applies to lifetime transfers based on the diminution in the donor's estate and to transfers on death based on the value of the death estate. Some transfers are exempt from inheritance tax.

- The value of a transfer of value is the diminution in value of the transferor's estate, usually the value of the asset transferred. Assets transferred on death are usually valued at open market value.

- A lifetime transfer of value can be a chargeable lifetime transfer (CLT) or a potentially exempt transfer (PET).

- IHT is chargeable on the death estate when an individual dies. The death estate comprises the deceased's assets less allowable debts and funeral expenses. Allowable debts are those incurred for full consideration and those imposed by law (eg tax), although in general debts are only deductible if they are in fact paid by the executors.

- Business Property Relief (BPR) and Agricultural Property Relief (APR) reduce the value of a transfer by 100% or 50%.

- BPR is available where relevant business property is held for an ownership period (usually two years).

- Relevant business property includes unincorporated business interests and unquoted shares in most trading companies.

- BPR is reduced if there are excepted assets held by an unincorporated business or a company.

- APR is available on the agricultural value of agricultural property.

- If the transferor has liabilities associated with an asset which qualifies for BPR or APR, BPR or APR is only available on the net value after deducting the liability.

- BPR and APR can be withdrawn or not given on a lifetime transfer where the transferee does not own the property as business/agricultural property at the transferor's death.

1.1 Inheritance tax

Inheritance tax applies to lifetime transfers based on the diminution in the donor's estate and to transfers on death based on the value of the death estate. Some transfers are exempt from inheritance tax:

- A transfer to a spouse/civil partner is exempt (lifetime and death).

- A transfer to a charity is exempt (lifetime and death).

- A transfer to a qualifying political party is exempt (lifetime and death).

- Lifetime transfers up to £3,000 per tax year are exempt (annual exemption). The unused exemption from the previous year may be carried forward one year and used after the annual exemption for that year.

- Lifetime transfers on the occasion of a marriage/civil partnership are exempt up to certain amounts.

- Lifetime transfers up to £250 per transferee per tax year are exempt.

- Lifetime transfers made as part of normal expenditure out of income are exempt.

1.2 Valuation of assets

The value of a transfer of value is the diminution in value of the transferor's estate, usually the value of the asset transferred. Assets transferred on death are usually valued at open market value.

For lifetime transfers where part of an asset is given away, the position before and after the transfer must be considered. The difference between the two figures is the transfer of value for inheritance tax purposes.

However, note the following with regard to the valuation of assets:

- Related property is taken into account when valuing certain assets eg unquoted shares and land held jointly.

- For lifetime transfers it may be necessary to use both the diminution in value and the related property principles to calculate the value of the transfer.

- Quoted shares are valued at the lower of ¼ up and average bargain.

  The ¼ up value is: lower quoted price + ¼ (higher quoted price less lower quoted price).

  The average bargain is the average of the highest and lowest bargain on the day.

  Note: From 6 April 2015 this is different to the valuation method for CGT purposes, which is now the '½ up value' ie lower quoted price + ½ (higher quoted price less lower quoted price).

- Unit trust units are valued at bid price.

- Proceeds of a life assurance policy owned by a person on his own life are part of his death estate.

- There is a discount for valuing land held jointly (except related property).

1.3 Lifetime transfers

A lifetime transfer of value can be a chargeable lifetime transfer (CLT) or a potentially exempt transfer (PET).

The following are CLTs:

- Gifts to a discretionary trust.
- Gifts to a **non-qualifying** interest in possession trust from 22 March 2006.

Lifetime tax is chargeable on a CLT and additional tax may be payable if the transferor dies within seven years of making the CLT. The additional tax on death is chargeable at a reduced rate if the transferor survives between three and seven years (taper relief).

The following are PETs:

- A transfer of value to another individual (other than spouse/civil partner).

- Gifts made before 22 March 2006 to either an interest in possession trust for another individual (other than spouse/civil partner) or an accumulation and maintenance trust.

A PET is treated as an exempt transfer during the lifetime of the transferor and is an exempt transfer if he survives seven years. If the transferor does not survive seven years from making a PET, it is a chargeable transfer and IHT may be payable on it, subject to taper relief.

Where a lifetime transfer falls in value between the date of the gift and the transferor's death, fall in value relief is given.

1.4 IHT on the death estate

IHT is chargeable on the death estate when an individual dies. The death estate is the sum of assets less allowable debts and funeral expenses.

Allowable debts are those incurred for full consideration and those imposed by law eg tax. Debts are only allowable if they are in fact settled by the executors, unless there is a real commercial reason why they are not paid and it is not part of a tax avoidance scheme.

Quick succession relief applies where there are two charges to IHT within five years. QSR is calculated as: [Hp121]

$$\text{Tax paid on first transfer} \times \frac{\text{net transfer}}{\text{gross transfer}} \times \text{relevant \%}$$

The net transfer is the amount actually received by the transferee after IHT. The gross transfer is the amount chargeable to IHT.

The relevant % relates to the period of time between the first transfer and the date of death:

	Relief %
One year or less	100
More than one year but not more than two years	80
More than two years but not more than three years	60
More than three years but not more than four years	40
More than four years but not more than five years	20

1.4.1 Transfer of nil rate band between spouses/civil partners

Any unused IHT nil rate band that was not utilised on a person's death transfers to the surviving spouse/civil partner, if any.

Where a claim to transfer the unused nil-rate band is made, the nil-rate band that is available when the surviving spouse or partner dies will be increased by the proportion of the nil-rate band unused on the first death.

The maximum nil-rate band available on the surviving spouse or civil partner's death is twice the nil-rate band applicable on the survivor's death, ie maximum nil-rate band in 2015/16 is
2 × £325,000 = £650,000.

1.4.2 Reduced rate for charitable giving

This section has been rewritten.

Where an individual dies and leaves at least 10% of their net chargeable estate on death to charity, the rate of IHT which applies to the balance of their estate is automatically reduced from 40% to 36% (the donation itself is exempt).

The 'net chargeable estate' is the total value of the estate after deducting all reliefs and exemptions including the nil rate band, but before deducting the value of the charitable donations (and excluding any gift with reservation of benefit).

Where an estate includes

- A free estate,

- Jointly held property (which will pass automatically to the survivor, including the family home if held as joint tenants), and

- Settled property,

these are treated as separate components of the estate and the rules apply to each component of the estate separately.

Worked example: Reduced rate – three components

Rebecca died on 17 August 2015. She had made no lifetime transfers and left a cash legacy of £60,000 to a UK registered charity with the residue to her son George.

Rebecca's death estate was valued as follows:

	£
Family home (owned jointly with her boyfriend, Dan, as joint tenants)	510,000
Cash and personal assets	300,000
Settled property (Rebecca was the life tenant of a trust set up on her fathers death)	250,000
	1,060,000
Less exempt legacy	(60,000)
	1,000,000

Requirement

Calculate the inheritance tax payable on Rebecca's death.

Solution

The death estate is allocated between the three components:

	Free estate £	Joint property £	Settled property £
Chargeable estate (exempt legacy out of free estate)	240,000	510,000	250,000
Less nil rate band 2015/16 (240:510:250)	(78,000)	(165,750)	(81,250)
Excess over nil band	162,000	344,250	168,750
Add legacy	60,000		
'Net chargeable estate'	222,000	344,250	168,750
Legacy more than 10% of free estate element			
IHT payable £162,000 x 36%	58,320		
IHT payable £344,250/£168,750 x 40%		137,700	67,500
Tax borne by	George	Dan	Trustees

Total IHT payable = £263,520

Where a donation of more than 10% has been made out of one component of the estate an election can be made to 'merge' two or more components.

In the worked example the combined value of the free estate and the joint property is £566,250 (£222,000 + £344,250) and 10% of this is £56,625 ie less than the £60,000 legacy. Therefore the 36% rate can be applied to the merged elements by election. This reduces the tax borne by Dan to £123,930 (£344,250 x 36%). Including the settled property as well would cause the 10% test to fail, so this is not beneficial.

1.5 Basis of assessment

An individual's liability to inheritance tax is determined by his domicile status:

	UK assets	Overseas assets
UK domiciled or deemed UK domiciled	Assessable	Assessable
Non-UK domiciled	Assessable	Exempt

Definition

Deemed UK domicile: An individual will be deemed to have UK domicile for IHT purposes:

*   If the individual has been resident in the UK for 17 out of the last 20 tax years (including the tax year of the chargeable transfer or death); or

*   For 36 months after ceasing to be UK domiciled under general law.

Transfers between spouses/civil partners are exempt.

Where a transfer is made by a UK domiciled person to a non-UK domiciled spouse/civil partner only the first £325,000 of the transfer is exempt (for 2012/13 and earlier years, the limit was £55,000). This is a cumulative lifetime total, and although it is fixed at the same value as the nil rate band it is entirely separate from it.

Transfers from a non-UK domicile person to a UK domicile spouse/ civil partner, or where both spouses/civil partners are non-UK domiciled are totally exempt.

An individual with a UK domiciled spouse/civil partner can elect to be treated as UK domiciled for IHT purposes (the election does not affect their income tax or CGT position). An election can be backdated by up to seven years so long as the individual's spouse/civil partner was their spouse/civil partner and was also UK domiciled on the effective date of the election, but the earliest possible effective date is 6 April 2013. If an election is made after the UK resident spouse/civil partner has died, it must be made within two years of their death. A domicile election cannot be revoked, but ceases to have effect once the non-UK domiciled individual has been non-UK resident for four successive tax years.

Where assets included in the death estate are situated abroad, additional expenses incurred of up to 5% of the value of the asset may be deducted from the value of the overseas property.

1.6 Double taxation relief

Where assets are subject to double taxation, relief is available against the UK inheritance tax liability.

DTR applies to transfers (during lifetime and on death) of assets situated overseas which may suffer tax overseas as well as IHT in the UK. Relief may be given under a treaty, but if not then the following rules apply.

DTR is given as a tax credit against the IHT payable on the overseas asset. The amount available as a tax credit is the lower of the foreign tax liability and the IHT (at the average rate) on the asset.

1.7 Location of assets

If an individual is not domiciled in the UK the location of assets becomes very important. The location of some common assets is as follows:

Type of asset	Location
Land and buildings	Where physically situated
Debt	Where the debtor resides
Life policies	Where the proceeds are payable
Registered shares and securities	Where they are registered
Bearer securities	Where the certificate of title is located at the time of transfer
Bank accounts	At the branch where the account is kept
Interest in a partnership	Where the partnership business is carried on
Goodwill	Where the business to which it is attached is carried on
Tangible property	At its physical location

1.8 Business and agricultural property reliefs

Where a transferor makes a transfer of value of an asset which qualifies as either business property or agricultural property, relief applies to reduce the value of the transfer made by either 100% or 50%.

The reliefs apply to lifetime transfers and transfers made on death. If there is any value remaining after the reliefs have been applied, the usual exemptions (eg annual exemption for a lifetime transfer) are used.

1.9 Business Property Relief (BPR) – availability of relief

In order for a transfer to qualify for BPR, there are four elements to take into account:

R   Relevant Business Property must be transferred
O   Ownership period of the transferor
S   Sale contract in place denies relief
E   Excepted assets reduce amount of relief

1.9.1 Relevant business property

The main categories of relevant business property, together with the applicable rates of relief are as follows: [Hp121]

• An unincorporated business or an interest in a business (eg a share in a partnership);	100%
• Furnished holiday accommodation which is treated as a business under IHTA 1984 and is not seen as a business of wholly or mainly holding investments.;	100%
• Shares in an unquoted company;	100%
• Securities in an unquoted company which gave the transferor control of the company immediately before the transfer;	100%
• Shares transferred from a controlling holding in a quoted company;	50%
• Land, buildings, plant and machinery owned by the transferor and used for business purposes by either:	
– A partnership in which the transferor was a partner, or	50%
– A company of which the transferor had control immediately before the transfer.	50%

Unquoted shares include shares quoted on the Alternative Investments Market (AIM).

In all categories above, the business of the sole trader, partnership or company must be a trading business.

In considering control, related property is taken into account.

Relevant business property can be held anywhere in the world.

1.9.2 Ownership period

Usually, the property transferred must have been owned by the transferor throughout the two years immediately before the transfer.

Except:

• Where the property transferred replaced other business property which together were owned for at least two years within the five years prior to the transfer

• Where property passed **on death** from a spouse/civil partner, ownership by the deceased spouse is counted as ownership by spouse/civil partner making the transfer

• Where there are successive transfers of the same property, one of which was on death and the first transfer of property qualified for relief, the second also qualifies

1.9.3 Sale contract in place

BPR does not usually apply where there is already a contract in place to sell the business property.

For example a partnership agreement often includes a provision that the interest is to be sold to the other partners on the death of a partner. In this case, no BPR will be available on the death of that partner.

However cross options enable BPR to still be available ie the deceased partner's estate have an option to force the surviving partners to buy the interest and the surviving partners have an option to force the estate to sell the interest.

1.9.4 Excepted assets

BPR does not apply to the value of excepted assets (eg large cash balances/assets held as investments) held by a business being transferred or the business of a company where shares are being transferred.

1.10 Agricultural property relief (APR) – agricultural property

APR applies to agricultural property situated in the UK, Channel Islands or Isle of Man and in the European Economic Area.

APR is given at the following rates: [Hp120]

- Property where the transferor had vacant possession immediately before the transfer or the right to obtain vacant possession within the next twelve months (extended to 24 months by extra statutory concession); 100%

- Property which is let out under a tenancy granted on or after 1 September 1995; 100%

- Property let out under a tenancy granted before 1 September 1995 which has more than twelve months to run (extended to 24 months by extra statutory concession). 50%

APR only applies to the agricultural value of the land. However, if the transferor is carrying on a business, BPR will be available to cover any additional value (eg development value).

1.10.1 Occupation/ownership period

Usually, in order to qualify for APR, the property transferred must have been either:

- Occupied by the transferor for the purposes of agriculture throughout the period of two years prior to the date of the transfer; or

- Owned by him throughout the period of seven years ending with the date of the transfer and occupied by a tenant farmer.

Occupation by a company which is controlled by the transferor is treated as occupation by the transferor.

The same exceptions apply to this APR rule as apply to the BPR rule, with the two out of five year replacement property rule being replaced by a seven out of ten year rule for property occupied by a tenant farmer.

1.10.2 Sale contract in place

APR does not apply where there is already a contract in place to sell the agricultural property unless the sale is to a company wholly or mainly in consideration for shares/securities of the company which will give the transferor control.

1.10.3 Shares in agricultural companies

APR is also available on the transfer of shares in a company where the transferor has control of the company, to the extent that the company owns agricultural property.

In this case, the company must satisfy the ownership/occupation test. The transferor must have owned the shares throughout the relevant ownership/occupation period.

1.11 BPR and APR – attributable liabilities

For transfers which take place on or after 17 July 2013, if

- The asset transferred qualifies for BPR or APR, and

- The transferor has a liability which is taken out on or after 6 April 2013 and is wholly or partly attributable to acquiring, maintaining or enhancing the asset.

BPR and/or APR only applies to the net value of the asset, after deduction of the attributable liability.

Where a liability relates only partly to assets which qualify for BPR and/or APR, and it is partly repaid, the repayment is allocated first to the part of the liability which does not relate to BPR and/or APR assets.

1.12 BPR and APR – transfers within seven years before the death of transferor

In general, BPR and/or APR will no longer apply to a lifetime transfer if the transferee does not still own the property transferred to him at the date of death of the transferor eg where the transferee has sold or gifted the property before the death of the transferor, or the transfer was of unquoted shares or securities, the shares become quoted and the transferee does not have control of the company

However replacement business or agricultural property can be treated as the original property transferred if the original property was sold before the death of the transferor and the whole of the consideration received by the transferee was used to acquire the replacement property within three years from the disposal.

If the lifetime transfer is a CLT, additional tax on death is calculated by adding back the BPR or APR which is now withdrawn. However, the value of the transfer in the cumulation remains the original value on which lifetime tax was chargeable.

If the lifetime transfer was a PET, then BPR or APR is not available on the transfer. The death tax is calculated on the unreduced value. Also, this unreduced value enters into the cumulation.

2 Payment of IHT and interest

Section overview

- Instalments can be used to pay IHT due in relation to land and buildings; unquoted shares and securities; or a business or interest in a business.

- The instalments are interest-free in relation to certain shares and securities; businesses and interests in businesses qualifying for BPR; and land eligible for APR.

- Other instalments are interest-bearing.

2.1 Payment by instalments

In some circumstances the taxpayer can make a written election to HMRC to pay the IHT due in ten equal annual instalments. Payment by instalments can be made for:

- Lifetime IHT on a CLT where the transferee pays the IHT

- Additional IHT on death on a CLT and IHT on death on a PET (but only if the transferee still owns the transferred property at the transferor's death or, in the case of a PET, his own death if earlier)

- IHT on the death estate

For lifetime transfers, the due date for the first instalment is the due date if the IHT were to be paid in one amount. In relation to the death estate, the first instalment is due at the end of the six months following the date of death. The other instalments follow at annual intervals.

The election for instalments may be made on the following property [Hp123]:

- Land and buildings
- Most unquoted shares and securities
- A business or interest in a business

If the instalment property is sold, the IHT on it immediately becomes payable in full.

Instalments may be interest-free or interest-bearing.

2.2 Interest-free instalments

Interest-free instalments are free of interest provided that each instalment is paid when due. An instalment paid late will bear interest from the due date for that instalment until the day before the IHT is paid.

Interest-free instalments are available on:

- Controlling holdings of shares and securities or holdings of unquoted shares and securities unless the company is one which does not qualify for BPR (eg investment or property trading companies)

- Businesses and interests in businesses (including partnerships) qualifying for BPR

- Land eligible for APR to the extent that its value is not reduced by APR or BPR

2.3 Interest-bearing instalments

Interest-bearing instalments carry interest on the outstanding IHT balance from the date the first instalment is due to the date each instalment is due. The interest is added to that instalment.

In addition, if an instalment is paid late it will bear interest from the due date for that instalment until the day before the IHT is paid.

Interest-bearing instalments are available on:

- Unquoted shares and securities which are either not a controlling holding or where the company is one which does not qualify for BPR (eg investment companies, property trading companies)

- Businesses and interests in businesses (including partnerships) not qualifying for BPR

- Land (other than that stated above)

3 Gifts with reservation of benefit

Section overview

- A gift with reservation of benefit occurs when a transferor transfers an asset but continues to enjoy a benefit in relation to that asset.

- A gift with reservation of benefit is a transfer of value when it is made.

- If the benefit continues until the transferor dies, the asset is also treated as part of his death estate.

- If the asset ceases to be subject to the benefit, the transferor is treated as making a PET at the date of cessation.

- If the asset could be charged twice to IHT, only the event which results in the greater charge to IHT is actually charged.

- There are exclusions from the rules where, for example, the transferor only retains a minor benefit or where he gives full consideration for the benefit.

3.1 Treatment of gifts with reservation of benefit

There are special rules which apply where a transferor makes a transfer of value but continues to enjoy some benefit from the gifted asset.

Common examples of gifts with reservation of benefit include:

- Transfer of residence – living in the property without paying full consideration for occupation

- Transfer of chattel such as a work of art – retaining possession of the chattel without paying full consideration for enjoyment

- Transfer of income producing asset such as shares – continuing to receive the income

- Transfer of any asset to a trust of which the transferor is a beneficiary

When a gift with reservation is made, the transfer of value is treated in the same way as any other transfer. So, for example, if there is a transfer to most trusts, there will be a chargeable lifetime transfer on which IHT may be payable. If there is a transfer to another individual (other than the transferor's spouse/civil partner), the transfer will be a potentially exempt transfer.

If the transferor retains the benefit in the asset transferred until his death, the asset will be treated as being part of his death estate and charged to IHT accordingly at its value at that time.

This means that there may be two charges to IHT on the same asset. There are rules which provide that only the event which results in the higher amount of IHT being payable will actually be chargeable.

Worked example: Gift with reservation of benefit

Mary gave her house to her son, Phil, on 10 June 2011 when it was worth £340,000. This was the first transfer of value that Mary had made, apart from using her annual exemption in April each year. Mary lived in the house by herself without making any payment for her occupation.

Mary died on 16 October 2015. Her death estate was £550,000 (excluding the house) which she left to Phil. The house was then worth £390,000.

Requirement

Compute the IHT payable on Mary's death.

Solution

The transfer of the house is clearly a gift with reservation of benefit.

First, look at the situation if the transfer had not been a gift with reservation of benefit:

Additional tax due on lifetime transfer

10 June 2011

	£
Gross transfer of value	340,000
Less nil rate band at death – 2015/16	(325,000)
Excess over nil band	15,000
IHT on £15,000 @ 40%	6,000

Transferor survived 4 years but not 5 years

Chargeable 60% × £6,000	3,600

Death tax due on death estate

16 October 2015

	£	£
Death estate		550,000
Nil rate band 2015/16	325,000	
Less gross transfer of value in 7 years before death (after 16 October 2008)	(340,000)	
Nil rate band available		(Nil)
Excess over nil band		550,000
IHT on £550,000 @ 40%		220,000
Total IHT payable (£3,600 + £220,000)		223,600

Next, ignore the original transfer and treat the property transferred as part of the death estate:

	£
Death estate (£550,000 + £390,000)	940,000
Less nil rate band 2015/16	(325,000)
Excess over nil band	615,000
IHT on £615,000 @ 40%	246,000

Clearly, as an appreciating asset with no other lifetime transfers, treating the property transferred as part of the death estate gives the greater amount of IHT and so this is the amount which will be taxable on Mary's death.

If the transferor ceases to retain a benefit in the asset within the seven years before his death, he is treated as making a further potentially exempt transfer of the asset at the time the reservation ceases which will be chargeable on his death. The charge is based on the value of the asset at the time of the cessation of the reservation.

Again, this may result in the asset being subject to two charges to IHT and only the event which leads to the greater amount of IHT being payable is chargeable.

Note that the 36% rate (for estates leaving at least 10% to charity) does not apply to property subject to the gift with reservation of benefit rules.

3.2 Defining gifts with reservation of benefit

Definition

Gift with reservation of benefit: Asset transferred where either:

- Possession and enjoyment of the asset is not bona fide assumed by the transferee at or before the beginning of the relevant period; or

- At any time in the relevant period the asset is not enjoyed to the entire exclusion, or virtually the entire exclusion of the transferor or of any benefit to him by contract or otherwise;

where the relevant period means the period ending on the transferor's death and beginning seven years before that time or at the date of the transfer, if later.

The term **virtually to the entire exclusion of the transferor** allows minor benefits to be disregarded. An example would be the transfer of a house which becomes the transferee's residence where the transferor subsequently:

- Stays in the property in the absence of the transferee for not more than two weeks each year; or
- Stays in the property with the transferee for less than one month each year.

The gift with reservation of benefit rules do not apply to land or chattels where the transferor gives full consideration for any right of occupation or enjoyment.

There is also an exclusion from the rules in relation to land where:

- The circumstances of the transferor changes in a way that was unforeseen at the date of the original transfer; and

- The benefit provided by the transferee represents reasonable care and maintenance of the transferor as an elderly or infirm relative.

Interactive question: Is there a gift with reservation of benefit?

[Difficulty level: Intermediate]

Consider the following situations and state whether or not there is a gift with reservation of benefit, giving brief reasons for your answer.

Situation	Answer
Hazel gives a necklace to her daughter but continues to wear it regularly without making any payment.	
Donald gives an asset to a discretionary trust of which he is a beneficiary.	
June gives her house to her daughter and goes to live in a flat. Six months later, she becomes unexpectedly ill and returns to the house to be nursed by her daughter without making any payment.	
John gives a holiday home to his son, but goes to stay there on his own for one week a year without making any payment.	
Harriet gives shares in A Ltd to her son but the dividends on the shares continue to be paid to her.	

See **Answer** at the end of this chapter.

4 Variations

Section overview

- A beneficiary can vary his entitlement on death within two years.

- If a statement is included for IHT, the variation will take effect as if the deceased had made the varied dispositions on his death.

- If a statement is included for CGT, the assets will pass at probate value to the new beneficiary.

4.1 Variation of dispositions on death for IHT

The terms of a will (or other disposition on death such as distributions on intestacy or passing of property by survivorship under a joint tenancy) may be varied by a beneficiary under the will.

For example, a beneficiary of the estate of one of his parents may decide that he wishes that his share of the estate should pass to his own children rather than to him.

If the variation is made:

- By the original beneficiary of the asset under the terms of the will;
- Within two years of the death;
- In writing;
- For no consideration in money or money's worth other than the making of another variation;
- Containing a statement that the variation is to have effect for IHT purposes;

then the inheritance tax rules apply as if the terms of variation had been made by the deceased on his death. Therefore if the new recipient is a trust, the deceased is the settlor.

If there is additional IHT payable as a result of the variation, the personal representatives of the deceased must also join in the making of the variation. In addition, notice must be given to HMRC within six months if additional IHT is due as a result of the variation. However, since most variations are made either to be tax-neutral or to result in an IHT-saving in relation to the death-estate, it is rare that this provision will apply, in practice.

Worked example: Variation for IHT

Bernard died on 17 November 2015. He had made no lifetime transfers and left the whole of his estate to his daughter Margaret.

Bernard's death estate is valued at £463,000. Margaret dies on 13 February 2016 leaving the whole of her estate to her daughter Rose. Margaret's death estate is valued at £700,000 excluding what she received on the death of her father Bernard.

Margaret had not made any lifetime transfers.

Requirement

Explain, with calculations, how tax could be saved if a deed of variation were made prior to Margaret's death to pass Bernard's estate directly to his granddaughter Rose.

Solution

First let's consider the position without a deed of variation:

Death of Bernard – 17 November 2015

	£
Chargeable estate	463,000
Less nil rate band 2015/16	(325,000)
Excess over nil band	138,000
IHT on £138,000 @ 40%	55,200

Death of Margaret – 13 February 2016

The estate of Bernard, net of the IHT paid, will form part of Margaret's death estate and therefore be charged to tax again, effectively wasting her nil rate band. However, QSR will reduce the tax bill by almost the full amount of the tax paid on the death of Bernard.

	£
Chargeable estate (£700,000 + £463,000 – £55,200)	1,107,800
Less nil rate band 2015/16	(325,000)
Excess over nil band	782,800
IHT on £782,800 @ 40%	313,120
Less QSR	
$£55,200 \times \dfrac{£407,800}{£463,000} \times 100\%$	(48,619)
	264,501
Total IHT payable (£55,200 + £264,501)	319,701

Alternative:

Death of Bernard – 17 November 2015

A deed of variation could be made which passes Bernard's estate directly to his granddaughter Rose. This will not affect the tax payable on Bernard's estate but will reduce the amount of tax payable on Margaret's death.

The deed of variation should be made before 17 November 2017 and in any event before the sole beneficiary's death, ie Margaret. It should include the statement that the variation has the effect for IHT.

	£
Chargeable estate	463,000
Less nil rate band 2015/16	(325,000)
Excess over nil band	138,000
IHT on £138,000 @ 40%	55,200

Death of Margaret – 13 February 2016

Margaret only has a death estate of £700,000, enabling her nil rate band to offset this and reduce the amount of IHT payable.

	£
Chargeable estate	700,000
Less nil rate band 2015/16	(325,000)
Excess over nil band	375,000
IHT on £375,000 @ 40%	150,000
Total IHT payable (£55,200 + £150,000)	205,200
Therefore there is a tax saving of (£319,701 – £205,200)	£114,501

The deed of variation is not necessary where a spouse/civil partner who has died leaves his/her estate to the surviving spouse, as the unused nil rate band can be transferred to the surviving spouse.

If the variation is made in favour of a trust (ie the asset passes into a trust rather than directly to a specific beneficiary) and the IHT statement is made, the deceased will be treated as being the settlor of the trust rather than the beneficiary making the variation. This means that it is possible for a beneficiary of a will to make a variation in favour of a trust of which he is also a beneficiary without a gift with reservation of benefit being made. The asset could then be utilised by the beneficiary and his children without it being treated as a gift with reservation of benefit by the beneficiary.

4.2 Variation of dispositions on death for CGT

There is a similar, but separate and more limited, provision for CGT.

If the variation is made:

- By the original beneficiary of the asset under the terms of the will;
- Within two years of the death;
- In writing;
- For no consideration in money or money's worth other than the making of another variation;
- Containing a statement that the variation is to have effect for CGT purposes;

then assets subject to the variation are treated as passing directly to the person entitled under the variation at probate value and the beneficiary making the variation does not make a disposal of the assets.

The CGT statement is independent of the IHT statement. It might be preferable for the CGT statement not to be included in the variation.

Without the CGT statement the asset will be treated as a disposal by the original beneficiary to the person entitled under the variation.

Regardless of whether a CGT variation is made, if the new recipient is a trust, the original beneficiary will be the settlor.

Worked example: Variation for CGT

Walter died on 11 August 2015 leaving his estate to his son, Matthew. The estate contained some shares in X plc valued at £100,000.

Matthew wishes to pass the shares in X plc to a trust for his children in March 2016, when they are valued at £108,000, in the most tax-efficient manner. Matthew owns no assets chargeable to CGT.

Requirement

Explain how Matthew can achieve his wishes.

Solution

Matthew should make a variation of Walter's will by 11 August 2017 passing the shares in X plc to the trust for his children.

The variation should include a statement that the variation is to have effect for IHT. This will be tax-neutral for Walter's estate as Walter will be treated as making the transfer of shares to the trust for Matthew's children, which will be a chargeable transfer in the same way that the original transfer to Matthew was chargeable. However, it will be advantageous for Matthew as otherwise he would be treated as making a chargeable transfer of £108,000 as a result of the variation.

The variation should not include the statement for CGT. The shares will pass to Matthew at probate value (£100,000) and, in the absence of a CGT statement, he will be deemed to dispose of them on the variation at a market value of £108,000. The resulting gain will be covered by his annual exempt amount which would otherwise be wasted. The trustees will have a base cost of £108,000 (rather than £100,000 had the CGT statement been made).

5 Interaction of IHT and CGT

Section overview

- Gifts on death are exempt from capital gains tax but may be liable to inheritance tax.
- A lifetime gift can be subject to both inheritance tax and capital gains tax.
- Gift relief may be available to relieve the immediate capital gains tax charge.

5.1 Gifts on death

On death inheritance tax may be payable on the death estate and on lifetime gifts made within the previous seven years.

Capital gains tax is not payable on the death estate. Donees receive assets at their probate value (market value at death), and so receive a free capital gains tax uplift in value.

5.2 Lifetime gifts – potentially exempt transfers

Potentially exempt transfers have no immediate inheritance tax charge.

The capital gains tax position depends on the asset gifted. The asset may be

- Exempt, for example cash, or
- Chargeable to capital gains tax.

If the asset is chargeable to capital gains tax, the gain is calculated using market value for the sale proceeds. The gain may be subject to gift relief if the asset is a business asset (see Chapter 6).

5.3 Lifetime gifts – chargeable lifetime transfers

A chargeable lifetime transfer may be subject to an immediate inheritance tax charge and an immediate capital gains tax charge.

To alleviate this problem, the gain arising on the transfer may be deferred using a special form of gift relief.

The asset does not have to be a business asset for this relief. The gain is not removed, it is merely deferred until the donee sells the asset.

If the asset is a business asset eligible for both types of gift relief, then this special form of gift relief takes priority. For a disposal of shares this is advantageous because, unlike for business asset gift relief, this form of gift relief makes no restriction for investment assets held by a company.

The disposal is 'immediately chargeable to tax' for this purpose if either

- There is an immediate IHT liability, or
- There would have been but for the annual exemption/nil rate band.

There is no requirement for any inheritance tax to be paid for the relief to be given. Relief is available if the value of the chargeable transfer is within the inheritance tax nil rate band. The relief also applies where the value of the chargeable transfer is **nil** because of inheritance tax business or agricultural property relief.

Worked example: IHT and CGT interaction

On 1 January 2016, Charles transferred shares worth £500,000 in Rex plc, a quoted investment company, into a discretionary trust. The shares had cost Charles £279,000 in August 2004.

Requirement

Calculate the CGT base cost of the shares for the trustees, assuming all beneficial elections are made.

Solution

The transfer into the discretionary trust is a CLT. There will be an immediate inheritance tax charge.

As a result the special form of gift relief is available.

Charles' gain on disposal:

	£
Sale proceeds (MV)	500,000
Less acquisition cost	(279,000)
Gain	221,000
Less gift relief	(221,000)
Chargeable gain	Nil

Trustees base cost:	
Market value	500,000
Less gift relief	(221,000)
Base cost	279,000

5.4 Summary of interaction between CGT and IHT

	Capital gains tax	Inheritance tax
Payable	• On all chargeable disposals by a chargeable person during his lifetime • Some assets are exempt • Not payable on death ie there is a tax free uplift to probate value when assets are transferred on death • It may be more beneficial to transfer appreciating chargeable assets on death	• On lifetime transfers which are CLTs, additional tax on PETs and CLTs within seven years of death and on all assets still owned at death • No capital assets are exempt • Some legacies are exempt eg to charities or political parties
Inter-spouse/civil partner transfers	• Transferred at nil-gain/nil-loss	• Transfers exempt both in lifetime and on death • Transfer of nil rate band between spouses/civil partners
Related property	• No such concept exists for CGT purposes • Assets are valued at their stand alone value ie if a holding of 20% of shares is transferred it will be valued as a 20% holding regardless of the total holding owned by the donor	• Assets must be valued based on the ownership of the donor plus holdings of any related property • The loss to donor must also be considered ie the diminution in the donor's estate as a result of the transfer
Lifetime transfer qualifying as a PET	• If it is a chargeable asset it will be liable to CGT unless qualifies for gift relief • s.165 TCGA 1992 gift relief applies to business assets (s.260 cannot apply as no immediate charge to IHT on a PET) • Entrepreneurs' relief may be available	• No lifetime IHT is payable • IHT may become payable on donor's death within seven years of gift • Taper relief is available if made at least seven years before death

	Capital gains tax	Inheritance tax
Lifetime transfer qualifying as a CLT	• If it is a chargeable asset it will be liable to CGT • s.260 TCGA 1992 gift relief applies to **any** asset where there is an immediate charge to IHT (even if IHT is charged at 0%) • Again, entrepreneurs' relief may be available	• Lifetime IHT is payable although possibly at 0% if covered by nil band • Further IHT may become payable on donor's death within seven years of gift • Taper relief is available if made at least three years before death
Gift with reservation of benefit	• If a chargeable disposal will be liable to CGT • If gift is a house and is not occupied by the donee, it will not qualify for PPR relief • As a house is generally an appreciating asset this may lead to a significant CGT liability on its subsequent sale as will not benefit from the free CGT uplift on death	• Will be treated as a PET or CLT and will still be treated as part of donor's death estate • Only the treatment which generates the higher tax liability will actually be payable – for an appreciating asset this will normally be by treating as part of the death estate

Summary

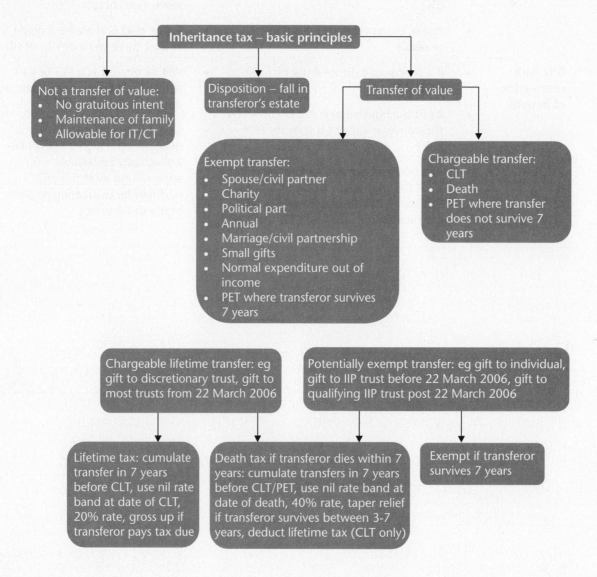

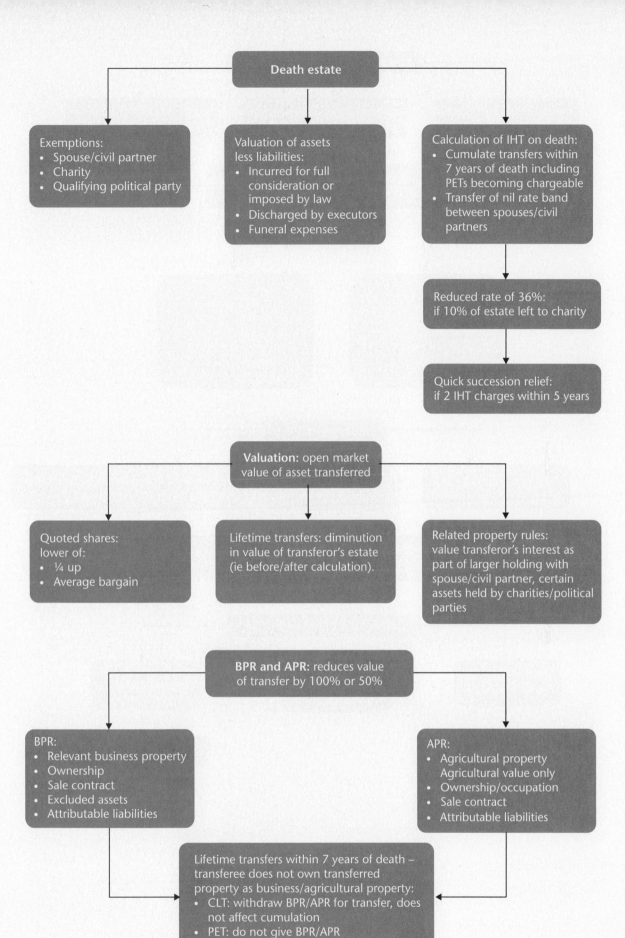

Death estate

Exemptions:
- Spouse/civil partner
- Charity
- Qualifying political party

Valuation of assets less liabilities:
- Incurred for full consideration or imposed by law
- Discharged by executors
- Funeral expenses

Calculation of IHT on death:
- Cumulate transfers within 7 years of death including PETs becoming chargeable
- Transfer of nil rate band between spouses/civil partners

Reduced rate of 36%: if 10% of estate left to charity

Quick succession relief: if 2 IHT charges within 5 years

Valuation: open market value of asset transferred

Quoted shares: lower of:
- ¼ up
- Average bargain

Lifetime transfers: diminution in value of transferor's estate (ie before/after calculation).

Related property rules: value transferor's interest as part of larger holding with spouse/civil partner, certain assets held by charities/political parties

BPR and APR: reduces value of transfer by 100% or 50%

BPR:
- Relevant business property
- Ownership
- Sale contract
- Excluded assets
- Attributable liabilities

APR:
- Agricultural property Agricultural value only
- Ownership/occupation
- Sale contract
- Attributable liabilities

Lifetime transfers within 7 years of death – transferee does not own transferred property as business/agricultural property:
- CLT: withdraw BPR/APR for transfer, does not affect cumulation
- PET: do not give BPR/APR

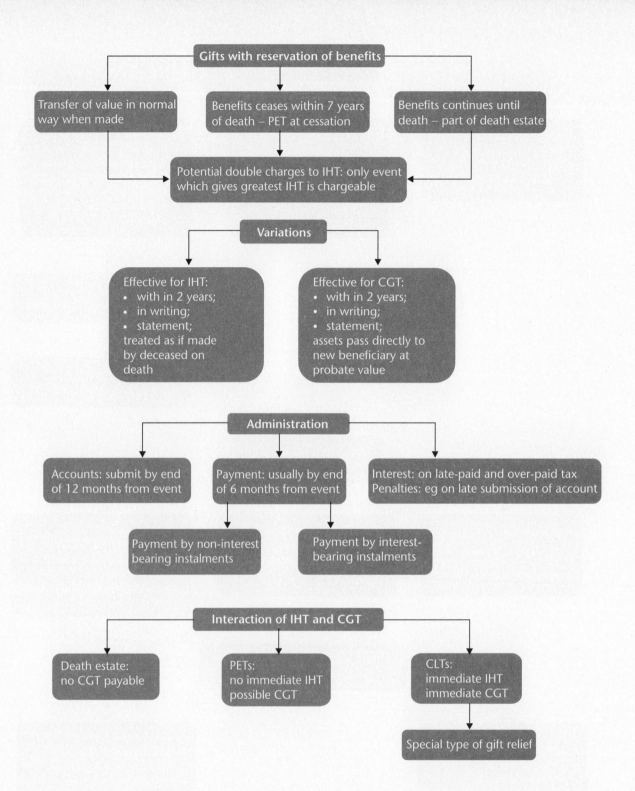

Gifts with reservation of benefits

- Transfer of value in normal way when made
- Benefits ceases within 7 years of death – PET at cessation
- Benefits continues until death – part of death estate

Potential double charges to IHT: only event which gives greatest IHT is chargeable

Variations

Effective for IHT:
- with in 2 years;
- in writing;
- statement;
treated as if made by deceased on death

Effective for CGT:
- with in 2 years;
- in writing;
- statement;
assets pass directly to new beneficiary at probate value

Administration

- Accounts: submit by end of 12 months from event
- Payment: usually by end of 6 months from event
- Interest: on late-paid and over-paid tax
  Penalties: eg on late submission of account

- Payment by non-interest bearing instalments
- Payment by interest-bearing instalments

Interaction of IHT and CGT

- Death estate: no CGT payable
- PETs: no immediate IHT possible CGT
- CLTs: immediate IHT immediate CGT

Special type of gift relief

Self-test

Answer the following questions.

1 Ivor gave his shares in L Ltd to his daughter in July 2010 when they were worth £100,000. He continued to receive the dividends from the shares until his death in August 2015. The shares were then worth £90,000.

Which **one** of the following statements is **not** true?

A Ivor's death estate includes the L Ltd shares valued at £90,000.

B Where IHT is charged twice on property which is a gift with reservation of benefit, only the event which gives the greater IHT is chargeable.

C Ivor makes a potentially exempt transfer of £100,000 in July 2010.

D There is no transfer of value in July 2010 because the transfer is a gift with reservation.

2 Judith dies on 24 June 2015 leaving her estate to her son, Derek.

Derek wishes to pass the assets in the estate to a trust for his children.

Before what date must Derek make a variation of his entitlement if it is to be effective for IHT and CGT purposes?

A 30 April 2016
B 31 January 2017
C 24 June 2017
D 30 June 2017

3 Phillip died on 5 January 2016, leaving a wife, Elizabeth, and two adult children, Beatrice and Harry, surviving him. Phillip had made the following transfers in his lifetime:

8 April 2012	Gift of 16,000 quoted shares to his nephew. On this day the shares were quoted at 550p – 602p each. There were no marked bargains.
10 July 2014	Gift of quoted shares to a discretionary trust for the benefit of his nephews and nieces. The shares were valued at £344,250. The trustees paid the IHT due at the time of the gift.
19 October 2014	Gift of £20,000 in cash to Beatrice on the occasion of her marriage.
28 November 2014	Gift to Harry of 10,000 ordinary shares in A Ltd, an unquoted manufacturing company. The company share capital immediately before the transfer was held as follows:

	No. of shares
Phillip	16,000
Elizabeth	8,000
Phillip's brother, Ralph	6,000
Phillip's sister, Amy	6,000
Phillip's father, Ronald	4,000
	40,000

Each shareholder had held his or her shares for many years.

HMRC has agreed the following values for the shares:

Holding	Value per share £
75% or more	50
More than 50% but less than 75%	40
Exactly 50%	35
More than 25% but less than 50%	30
Exactly 25%	20
Less than 25%	15

It has also been agreed with HMRC that £500,000 of the net assets of A Ltd relate to shares in unrelated companies. The total net assets of the business are worth £4m.

Phillip's death estate comprised the following assets:

	£
Personal chattels	31,500
House	860,000
Quoted shares	52,000
Cash	11,646
Life assurance policy on his own life	150,000
Shares in A Ltd	see below

In respect of the shares in A Ltd, HMRC agreed that the values in November 2014 still applied at Phillip's death and the value and composition of the company's net assets were also unchanged. At the time of Phillip's death, Harry still owned the shares given to him in November 2014.

Debts due at death (all of which were paid in full by the executors, and none of which related to the shares in A Ltd) amounted to £17,760 and the funeral expenses were £1,014.

Under his will, Phillip left his house, personal chattels and quoted shares to Elizabeth and everything else to his children.

Requirement

Compute the inheritance tax payable as a result of Phillip's death.

Now, go back to the Learning objectives in the Introduction. If you are satisfied you have achieved these objectives, please tick them off.

Technical reference

Legislation

References are to Inheritance Tax Act 1984 *(IHTA 1984)* unless otherwise stated

Business property relief

The relief	s.104
Relevant business property	s.105
Ownership period	s.106
Replacements	s.107
Successions	s.108
Successive transfers	s.109
Sale contracts	s.113
Excepted assets	s.112
Attributable liabilities	s.162B
Transfers in seven years before death	s.113A

Agricultural property relief

The relief	s.116
Ownership or occupation	s.117
Replacements	s.118
Successions	s.120
Successive transfers	s.121
Sale contracts	s.124
Attributable liabilities	s.162B
Transfers in seven years before death	s.124A

Gifts with reservation of benefit

References are to Finance Act 1986 (*FA 1986*) unless otherwise stated

Gifts with reservation	s.102
Interests in land	s.102A
Double charges relief	SI 1987/1130
Transferor returning due to unforeseen circumstances	Sch 20 para 6

Variations

Variations for IHT	s.142
Notification to HMRC	s.218A
Variations for CGT	s.62 TCGA 1992

Inheritance Tax Manual (Found at www.hmrc.gov.uk/manuals/ihtmanual/index.htm)

Agricultural relief: contents	IHTM24000
Business relief and businesses: contents	IHTM25000
Gifts With Reservation: interests in land	IHTM14360
Gifts With Reservation: exclusion of the donor	IHTM14333
Alterations to the devolution of an estate: contents	IHTM35000

This technical reference section is designed to assist you when you are working in the office. It should help you to know where to look for further information on the topics covered in this chapter.

Answer to Interactive question

Answer to Interactive question

Situation	Answer
Hazel gives a necklace to her daughter but continues to wear it regularly without making any payment.	Gift with reservation of benefit. Enjoyment of the asset is not entirely or virtually entirely to the exclusion of Hazel and she does not give full consideration.
Donald gives an asset to a discretionary trust of which he is a beneficiary.	Gift with reservation of benefit. Donald retains a benefit in the asset transferred by his position as a beneficiary of the trust.
June gives her house to her daughter and goes to live in a flat. Six months later, she becomes unexpectedly ill and returns to the house to be nursed by her daughter without making any payment.	Not a gift with reservation of benefit because: • The circumstances of the transferor change in a way that was unforeseen at the date of the original transfer; and • The benefit provided by the transferee represents reasonable care and maintenance of the transferor as an elderly or infirm relative.
John gives a holiday home to his son, but goes to stay there on his own for one week a year without making any payment.	Not a gift with reservation of benefit as John is virtually excluded from enjoyment of the property.
Harriet gives shares in A Ltd to her son but the dividends on the shares continue to be paid to her.	Gift with reservation of benefit. Harriet retains a benefit in the asset transferred because she still receives the dividends from the shares which should be payable to her son.

1   D – The statement that there is no transfer of value in July 2010 because the transfer is a gift with reservation is untrue.

   The transfer of value in July 2010 is still a PET even though there is a gift with reservation of benefit.

2   C – 24 June 2017

   A variation must be made within two years of the deceased's death.

3   **Phillip – IHT payable as a result of death**

   Death tax on lifetime transfers

   8 April 2012

   Potentially exempt transfer within 7 years of death

	£
Quoted shares	
16,000 shares @ [550p + 1/4 (602p – 550p)]	90,080
Less: annual exemption 2012/13	(3,000)
annual exemption 2011/12 b/f	(3,000)
Potentially exempt transfer now chargeable	84,080
Nil rate band 2015/16	(325,000)
Excess over nil band	Nil

   There is no IHT payable on this transfer as a result of Phillip's death.

   10 July 2014

   Chargeable lifetime transfer

	£	£
Quoted shares		344,250
Less: annual exemption 2014/15		(3,000)
annual exemption 2013/14 b/f		(3,000)
Gross chargeable transfer		338,250
Nil rate band 2015/16	325,000	
Less gross transfers of value in 7 years before CLT (after 10 July 2007)	(84,080)	
Nil rate band available		(240,920)
Excess over nil band		97,330

	£
IHT on £97,330 @ 40%	38,932
No taper relief as within 3 years of death	
Less lifetime IHT paid (W)	(2,650)
Death IHT due	36,282

   WORKING

	£
Gross chargeable transfer	338,250
Nil rate band 2014/15	(325,000)
Excess over nil band	13,250
IHT on £13,250 @ 20%	2,650

19 October 2014

Potentially exempt transfer within 7 years of death

	£	£
Cash		20,000
Less: marriage exemption		(5,000)
Potentially exempt transfer now chargeable		15,000
Nil rate band 2015/16	325,000	
Less gross transfers of value in 7 years before PET (after 19 October 2007) (£84,080 + £338,250)	(422,330)	
Nil rate band available		(Nil)
Excess over nil band		15,000
IHT on £15,000 @ 40%		£6,000

No taper relief as within 3 years of death

28 November 2014

Potentially exempt transfer within 7 years of death

	£	£
Shares in A Ltd		
Before: part of 60% holding with related property 16,000 @ £40		640,000
After: part of 35% holding with related property 6,000 @ £30		(180,000)
		460,000
Less BPR £460,000 × $\dfrac{(4{,}000{,}000 - 500{,}000)}{4{,}000{,}000}$ × 100%		(402,500)
		57,500
Nil rate band 2015/16	325,000	
Less gross transfers of value in 7 years before PET (after 28 November 2007) (£84,080 + £338,250 + £15,000)	(437,330)	
Nil rate band available		(Nil)
Excess over nil band		57,500
IHT on £57,500 @ 40%		£23,000

No taper relief as within 3 years of death

Death estate

5 January 2016

	£	£
Chattels		31,500
House		860,000
Quoted shares		52,000
Cash		11,646
Life assurance		150,000
Shares in A Ltd		
6,000 @ £30	180,000	
Less BPR £180,000 × $\dfrac{(4{,}000{,}000 - 500{,}000)}{4{,}000{,}000}$ × 100%	(157,500)	22,500
Gross estate		1,127,646
Less: debts	17,760	
funeral expenses	1,014	(18,774)
Net estate		1,108,872
Less: spouse exemption		
chattels	31,500	
house	860,000	
quoted shares	52,000	(943,500)

	£	£
Chargeable estate		165,372
Nil rate band 2015/16	325,000	
Less gross transfers of value in 7 years before death (after 5 January 2009) (£84,080 + £338,250 + £15,000 + £57,500)	(494,830)	
Nil rate band available		(Nil)
Excess over nil band		165,372
IHT on £165,372 @ 40%		£66,149

CHAPTER 8

Personal tax – international aspects

Introduction

Examination context

Topic List

    1   Revision from Tax Compliance

    2   Tax planning

Summary and Self-test

Technical reference

Answers to Interactive questions

Answers to Self-test

Learning objectives

Tick off

- Advise on the taxation of foreign assets, income and gains

- Evaluate and advise on the impact of residence, non-residence and domicile on an individual's tax liabilities

- Analyse and explain the implications of individuals leaving and coming to the UK as well as the special tax position for non-UK domiciled individuals

- Identify legitimate tax planning measures to minimise tax liabilities

- Recognise, explain and communicate opportunities to use alternative tax treatments arising from past transactions

The specific syllabus references for this chapter are 1w, 1x, 1y, 2a, 2d.

Syllabus links

Personal residence and domicile status give significant tax planning opportunities for high net worth individuals. For example, a person who has significant gains on the disposal of a business may choose to emigrate prior to disposal to minimise the UK tax paid.

Examination context

There are a number of pitfalls that may result in inflated income tax and capital gains tax liabilities if proficient tax planning is not put in place. For example for a non- domiciled client the adviser needs to consider annually whether the remittance basis will be beneficial. Additionally where a client enters or leaves the UK, during a tax year the timing of the change can have a significant impact on liabilities. The split year basis must be taken into account.

In the examination candidates may be required to:

- Advise whether an individual should make a claim for the remittance basis

- Consider the implications of a person's residence and domicile status for a potential or past transaction

- Suggest potential tax planning strategies suitable for a particular individual

1 Revision from Tax Compliance

Section overview

- An individual is domiciled in the country of his permanent home, subject to case law decisions.

- An individual's residence and domicile status will determine his liability to UK tax.

- An individual who is UK resident is subject to tax on his worldwide income.

- Certain exceptions apply for individuals who are non-UK domiciled.

- An individual who is non-UK resident is only subject to UK tax on UK income.

- An individual is UK resident if he does not meet any of the automatic overseas tests but either does meet one of the automatic UK tests or has sufficient UK ties to qualify as UK resident. An individual will always be UK resident if he has spent 183 days or more of the tax year in the UK, and will never be UK resident if he has spent fewer than 16 days in the tax year in the UK.

- Most UK resident individuals are subject to income tax on an arising or receipts basis. The income is taxed according to the type of income, ie non-savings income, savings income or dividend income.

- Where UK resident individuals are subject to income tax on a remittance basis, the income is always taxable as non-savings income.

- The residence and domicile status of an employee (and, in some cases, whether he carries out his duties in the UK or outside it and the residency of his employer) determine the tax treatment of his earnings.

- Other income from overseas sources is taxed on a similar basis to UK income. It may be charged on a remittance basis for non-UK domiciled individuals

- The remittance basis must usually be claimed and may be subject to payment of the remittance basis charge (RBC).

- Double taxation relief (DTR) is available where income is taxed in more than one country. DTR is calculated on a source by source basis as if the overseas income were taxed as the top slice of income in the UK.

- DTR is the lower of the UK tax on the overseas income and the actual overseas tax paid.

- CGT applies to individuals resident in the UK.

- If an individual is resident but not domiciled in the UK, overseas gains may be taxable on the remittance basis, ie to the extent that the gains are remitted to the UK. Individuals claiming the remittance basis cannot claim the annual exempt amount (£11,100 for 2015/16).

1.1 Domicile

A person is domiciled in the country in which he has his permanent home. Domicile is distinct from nationality or residence. A person may be resident in more than one country or have dual nationality, but under UK law he can be domiciled in only one country at a time.

A person:

- Acquires a domicile of origin at birth. This is normally the domicile of his father (or that of his mother if his father died before he was born or his parents were unmarried at his birth). Therefore it will not necessarily be his country of birth.

- Retains this domicile until he acquires a:

  – Different domicile of dependency (if, while he is under 16, the domicile of the person on whom he is legally dependent changes); or

  – Different domicile of choice.

A domicile of choice can only be acquired by individuals aged 16 or over.

To acquire a domicile of choice a person must sever his ties with the country of his former domicile and settle in another country with the clear intention of making it his permanent home. Long residence in another country is not in itself enough to prove that a person has acquired a domicile of choice; there must be evidence that he intends to live there permanently and even be buried there.

Individuals who are not UK domiciled may be taxed on a 'remittance' basis (see below).

For inheritance tax purposes there is an additional concept of 'deemed domicile', and in some cases it is also possible to make an election to be treated as domiciled in the UK for inheritance tax purposes (see Chapter 7).

1.2 Residence

A taxpayer's residence and domicile have important consequences in establishing the treatment of his UK and overseas income. Prior to 2013/14, whether a taxpayer was resident in the UK was determined by principles derived from case law. With effect from 2013/14, a new statutory residence test applies. You will only be examined on the new rules.

The rules for the statutory residence test must be considered in the order set out below. If for example one of the 'automatic overseas tests' is satisfied then the remaining rules do not need to be considered. Under the statutory residence test an individual is: [Hp219]

UK statutory residence test: flow chart for individuals

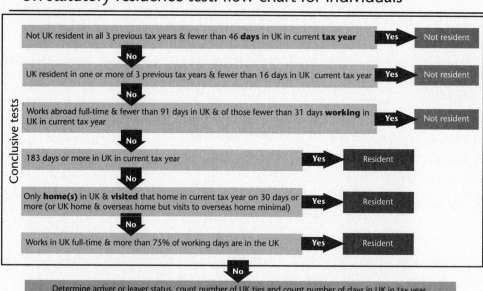

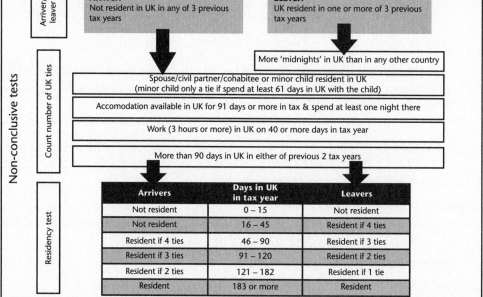

The **full-time work overseas** test is satisfied in a tax year if **all** of the following conditions are met:

- The taxpayer works an average of 35 hours a week overseas. This is calculated excluding annual leave, sick leave, gaps of up to 15 days between employments and any days when he works in the UK.

- There are no significant breaks of more than 30 days in his overseas work (excluding annual leave and sick leave).

- He has less than 31 UK work days.

- He spends no more than 90 days in the UK.

The **full-time UK work** test is satisfied if **all** of the following conditions are met:

- There is a 365-day period, all or part of which falls within the tax year, when the taxpayer works an average of 35 hours a week in the UK. This is calculated excluding annual leave, sick leave, gaps of up to 15 days between employments and days when he works overseas.

- Within that 365-day period, there are no significant breaks of more than 30 days when he does not work in the UK (excluding annual leave and sick leave).

- Within that 365-day period, the taxpayer works in the UK on more than 75% of his working days.

- There is at least one day that falls into both the 365 day period and the tax year when he does more than 3 hours' work in the UK.

1.3 Split year treatment

Where split year treatment applies, an individual is only treated as UK resident for a specified part of the tax year. He is only taxed in the UK on his worldwide income for the part of the year in which he is UK resident. For the rest of the year his UK tax liability is limited to tax on his UK source income in the same way as if he had been non-resident for the entire year (this applies to investment income as well as employment income).

Split year treatment also applies for capital gains tax purposes. If an individual realises a capital gain in the part of the year in which he is not treated as UK resident, the gain will generally only be subject to UK capital gains tax if it arises on an asset used in the trade of a UK permanent establishment.

There are different split year rules for individuals who were UK resident in the previous tax year, and for those who were not.

1.3.1 Leaving the UK

If an individual was UK resident in the previous tax year, the most important case where split year treatment applies is where he leaves for full-time work overseas. This applies where:

- The individual is not UK resident in the following tax year because he satisfies the full-time work overseas automatic overseas test, and

- The full-time work overseas conditions to be met in the part of the year after he leaves are the same as for the automatic overseas test, but the 30 UK work day and 90 days in the UK limits are reduced proportionally for the number of complete months in the tax year before the first overseas work day.

Where these conditions are met, the individual is non-resident from the day on which he first works at least three hours overseas (**not** from the date he leaves the UK).

Note that if the individual is not non-resident as a result of the full-time work overseas test for an entire tax year, split year treatment does not apply to the year in which he leaves and the general test set out above have to be applied to the year as a whole to determine whether the individual is resident or not. For overseas postings of less than two years, the date on which the period of overseas work starts is likely to be critical in determining whether the individual remains UK resident or not.

Split year treatment can also apply (subject to various conditions) where an individual was resident in the previous tax year and:

- Goes to live abroad with a partner (spouse, civil partner, or someone with whom he has been living as a spouse or civil partner) who has left for full time work overseas, or

- Is not UK resident in the following tax year, and from a time in the tax year he no longer has a UK home.

1.3.2 Arriving in the UK

If an individual was not UK resident in the previous tax year, the most important cases where split year treatment applies are where:

- He arrives to work in the UK, meaning that there is a 365 day period starting in the tax year which meets the full-time work in the UK criteria (these are the same as for the automatic UK tests). He must also not have sufficient UK ties before he starts to work in the UK (the sufficient ties tests are applied by multiplying the number of permitted days in the table in paragraph 1.2 by (the number of whole months in the year before the period of UK work begins/12)).

  The individual is UK resident from the date on which he starts to work in the UK, or

- He was not UK resident in the previous tax year because he satisfied the full-time work overseas automatic overseas test, but was UK resident in at least one of the four tax years immediately preceding the previous tax year, and is UK resident for at least part of the following tax year, and has a period (of any length) in the current year which satisfies the full-time work overseas criteria. These are the same as for the automatic overseas tests, but the 30-and 90-day limits are reduced proportionally for the number of complete months in the tax year after the last overseas work day.

  The individual is UK resident from the day after the end of the period which satisfies the full-time work overseas criteria.

The other cases where split year treatment can apply (subject to various conditions) if an individual was not UK resident in the previous tax year are:

- An individual arrives to live with a partner (spouse, civil partner, or someone with whom he has been living as a spouse or civil partner) who has returned from full time work overseas, or

- Certain cases where an individual acquires a UK home part way through the tax year, or an individual's UK home becomes his only home part way through the tax year.

Worked example: Split year treatment

Karen is an experienced executive who has been headhunted by a UK-parented group to act as their chief operating officer on an ongoing basis. She is domiciled in Germany, where she has lived for the past five years. She has never previously been UK resident, and her previous role (which she left in September 2015) did not require her to perform any duties in the UK.

Karen was appointed on 5 October 2015, made a visit to the UK from 8 to 12 October to finalise the details of her appointment, had a flat available for her use from 1 November 2015 and arrived in the UK to start work on 3 November 2015.

Her husband will remain based in their home in Germany. They have a teenage son who is at boarding school in the UK: it is anticipated that he will spend the majority of the school holidays in Germany with his father. Karen's time in the UK in 2015/16, before 5 October, comprised a total of ten days taking her son to school or collecting him, a holiday of eight nights on the Norfolk broads, and five nights on trips related to job interviews. In both of 2014/15 and 2013/14 she spent less than 30 days in the UK.

Karen has yet to determine how often she will return to Germany, but she only anticipates taking short periods of leave (no more than a week at a time) for the foreseeable future. Her new role is not expected to involve more than two weeks of overseas travel each year.

Requirement

Explain Karen's UK residence status for 2015/16 and 2016/17.

Solution

For 2015/16, Karen will not meet any of the automatic overseas tests because she will spend more than 46 days in the UK and will not meet the full-time work overseas test.

It is likely that she will meet the automatic UK test for full time UK work. She is expecting her employment to last more than 365 days, she will presumably work at least 35 hours a week, she should work in the UK on at least 75% of her working days, and there is at least one day in the year when she works for three hours in the UK.

However, the split year rule will apply, so that she is only treated as resident from 3 November 2015 (ie the date she started work) so long as she does not have sufficient UK ties in the period before that date. There are six whole months from 6 April to 3 November 2015, so the numbers of days in applying the sufficient ties tests are reduced to 6/12 of the numbers for a full year.

Karen has spent 27 nights in the UK in the first part of the year, which would mean that she would only have sufficient UK ties if she had all four ties. However, she did not spend more than 90 days in the UK in either of the two previous tax years, and the family tie is not present as she did not see her son in the UK for more than 30 days in the period before she started her UK job. She will therefore only be treated as UK resident from 3 November 2015 until the end of the tax year.

For 2016/17 she will not meet any of the automatic overseas tests, and is likely to meet the automatic UK tests both because she will spend at least 183 days in the UK and because she will again meet the full-time UK work test. On the assumption that she remains working in the UK, she will be resident for the whole year.

Interactive question 1: Residence　　　　　　　　　[Difficulty level: Exam standard]

Talya is UK domiciled, and has been UK resident for many years. She has been offered an 18 month secondment to the Paris office of the company she works for. The secondment would run from 1 January 2016 to 30 June 2017. She has been told that she would be required to return to the UK for two days every three months (ie four times a year) for work purposes. She would be expected to work at least 40 hours per week.

If she accepts the secondment, she is likely to return to the UK one weekend each month (travelling to the UK on Friday evening and back to Paris on Monday morning) and for ten days at Christmas. The rest of her annual leave for 2016 will either be spent in France or in Croatia, attending a wedding. She would also take a nine week holiday at the end of the secondment, before returning to the UK

Requirement

Explain

(a) The impact of the proposed secondment on Talya's UK residence status.

(b) How the position would change if she returned to the UK most weekends (40 weekends a year, returning on Friday night and going back to Paris on Monday morning).

(c) Whether the position would change if she made a preparatory trip to France from 6-15 December 2015, during which she spent six days working in the Paris office, before returning and working in the UK for eleven more days (she would also take a few days holiday before returning to France to start her secondment). Assume for these purposes that she only returns to the UK for one weekend each month once the secondment has started.

See **Answer** at the end of this chapter.

1.4 Overseas aspects of income tax

1.4.1 Basis of assessment

Generally, a UK resident individual is liable to UK income tax on his worldwide income, whereas a non-resident individual is liable to UK income tax only on income arising in the UK.

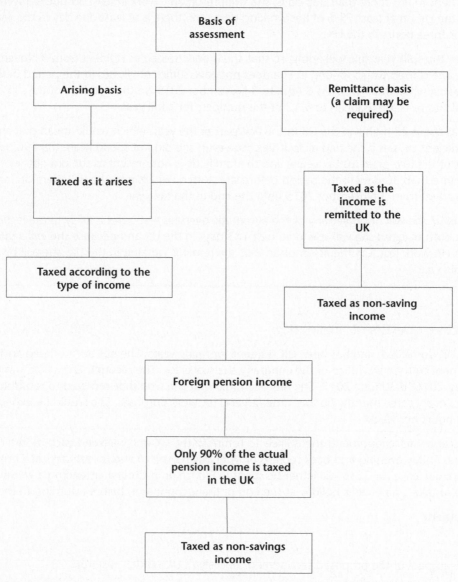

1.4.2 The remittance basis

Individuals who are resident in the UK but not domiciled in the UK may be able to use the remittance basis for their foreign income, so it is only taxed when it is brought into the UK.

Where the remittance basis applies automatically, for example where the individual has unremitted foreign income and gains of less than £2,000, the individual is entitled to income tax personal allowances and the capital gains tax annual exempt amount.

Where the remittance basis does not apply automatically, the individual must make a **claim** to use the remittance basis. Such a 'remittance basis user' (RBU) loses his entitlement to UK personal allowances and the capital gains tax annual exempt amount.

A RBU must also pay a 'remittance basis charge' RBC for 2015/16 of £30,000 per annum if he has been UK resident for at least seven out of the previous nine tax years, £60,000 per annum if he has been UK resident for 12 out of the previous 14 years or £90,000 per annum if he has been UK resident for 17 out of the last 20 years, in addition to any tax due on remitted income and gains, unless he is under 18. (Prior to 2015/16 the RBC was £30,000 per annum for seven out of the last nine years and £50,000 for 12 out of the last 14 years. There was no additional charge for 17 out of 20 years.)

Individuals who do not claim to use the remittance basis are taxed on an arising basis with full entitlement to UK personal allowance and annual exempt amount.

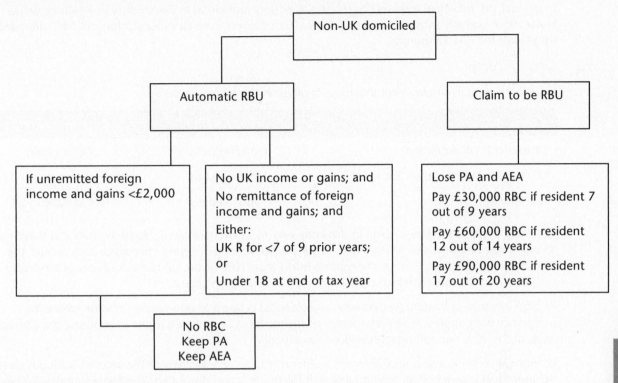

1.5 Personal allowances

Personal allowances, eg personal allowance, married couple's age allowance and blind person's allowance, may be claimed by all UK residents subject to the remittance basis rules described above. Personal allowances may only be claimed by non-UK residents if they are:

- Citizens of the EEA
- Resident in the Isle of Man or Channel Islands
- Current or former Crown servants and their widows or widowers
- Resident in certain territories with which the UK has a double tax agreement
- Former residents who have left the UK for health reasons

1.5.1 Employment income – basis of assessment

	Duties performed wholly or partly in the UK		Duties performed wholly outside the UK
	In the UK	Outside the UK	
UK resident and UK domiciled	Arising basis	Arising basis	Arising basis
UK resident but not UK domiciled	Arising basis	Arising basis*	Possible remittance basis or Arising basis
Not UK resident	Arising basis	Not taxable	Not taxable

*The remittance basis can apply where overseas workday relief applies. This applies in the tax year in which a non-UK domiciled individual comes to work in the UK, and the two following tax years, if he was non-UK resident in the three tax years before he came here to work.

A non-UK domiciled person who is resident in the UK may be taxed on 'overseas earnings' on a remittance basis provided the employer is also non-UK resident. If the employer is UK resident then the earnings will be taxed on a receipts basis.

An employer must deduct tax (under the PAYE system) if any employees are in receipt of UK taxable earnings even if the duties are performed wholly outside the UK.

In general, an individual is subject to the social security legislation in the country in which he works. However, if working abroad temporarily for a UK employer in the European Union, UK NICs are payable for at least the first 12 months.

1.5.2 Other income

Income other than employment income is taxable on the following basis:

	UK income	Overseas income
UK resident, UK domiciled	Arising basis	Arising basis
UK resident but not domiciled in the UK	Arising basis	Possible remittance basis
Non-resident	Arising basis	Not taxable in UK

Generally overseas income is taxed in the same way as its UK equivalent. However, overseas property income must be calculated separately from UK property income. Foreign dividends only receive the 10% notional tax credit if either the holding is less than 10% or the UK has a double taxation treaty with the overseas country which contains a non-discrimination clause.

Foreign investment income (ie interest and dividends) is taxed as non-savings income where the remittance basis applies. However, foreign dividends must be included in the income tax computation gross of the 10% non-refundable dividend tax credit.

Foreign pension income is taxable on UK residents. However, only 90% of the amount arising is taxed if the individual is taxed on an arising basis, ie if UK resident and domiciled. The full amount is taxable if the individual is taxed on the remittance basis.

1.6 Double taxation relief

Where overseas income is taxable both in the UK and overseas, double taxation relief (DTR) will be available. The overseas income is included in the UK income tax computation gross of any overseas taxes suffered and then DTR is calculated, on a source by source basis, as the lower of the:

- Overseas tax suffered
- UK tax on the overseas income

The steps for calculating the UK tax on overseas income are as follows:

Step 1
- Calculate the UK income tax liability (before DTR) including all sources of income gross.

Step 2
- Exclude the overseas source of income suffering the **highest** rate of overseas tax.
- Treat this source of overseas income as the top slice of income.

Step 3
- Re-calculate the UK income tax liability. The difference is the UK income tax on the excluded. overseas source of income.

Step 4
- Exclude the next source of overseas income (if applicable).

Step 5
- Repeat Step 3, now excluding both sources. The difference is the UK income tax on this second source of income.

1.7 Overseas aspects of capital gains tax

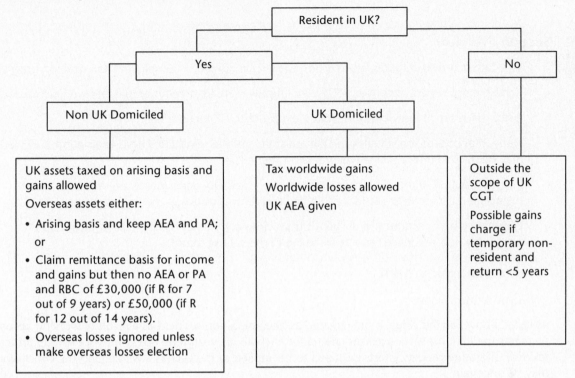

1.7.1 Basis of assessment

A liability to capital gains tax depends on an individual's residence status:

	UK gains & losses	Overseas gains & losses
UK resident and domiciled in the UK	Arising basis	Arising basis
UK resident but not UK domiciled	Arising basis	Possible remittance basis, limited relief for overseas losses
Not UK resident	Not usually taxable in UK[2]	Not taxable in UK[1]

1. Overseas gains accruing in the overseas part of a split year of residence are not charged to tax regardless of when in the year they are remitted.

2. From 6 April 2015 non-UK resident individuals, trusts and companies controlled by five or fewer persons are subject to capital gains tax on disposals of UK residential property. The taxable gain is that part of the gain arising after 5 April 2015, based on the market value at that date. Alternatively an election can be made for the total gain over the whole period of ownership to be time apportioned and only the post 5 April 2015 gain charged to tax.

   This provision includes disposals in the overseas part of a split year.

2 Tax planning

Section overview

- The date of arrival in, or departure from, the UK can impact an employee's tax position greatly.

- Certain employment expenses paid by an employer are tax free for employees working abroad.

- A non-UK resident individual has limited exposure to UK income tax.

- Non-UK domiciled individuals can take advantage of the remittance basis exemption. Calculations may be needed to determine whether this is beneficial.

- If leaving the UK 'temporarily' (for less than five years) any gains (or losses) on assets held at departure realised while outside the UK are taxed (or allowed) in the year of return.

- Remittance basis income and dividends from close companies received during a period of temporary non-residence can also be taxed in the year of return.

2.1 Overseas employment

2.1.1 Full-time work overseas

As noted above, an individual is only treated as becoming non-resident as a result of working abroad if he meets the full-time work overseas criteria for a whole tax year. If he does not work abroad for a full tax year, the other residence tests will need to be applied to the year as a whole, and the conclusion may be uncertain.

If he does meet the full-time work overseas criteria for an entire tax year:

- Subject to satisfying the UK ties test for the part of the year when he is working overseas, the split year rules should apply to treat him as non-UK resident from the day on which he starts working overseas.

- The automatic overseas tests should be met for the complete tax year(s) that he is working overseas, meaning that he is not treated as UK resident for the entire tax year.

- The split year rules should also apply in the year in which he returns to the UK, subject to the UK ties test being satisfied in the part of the year when he is working overseas and the individual not being non-resident for more than four complete tax years. He should be treated as UK resident from the day after his last day working overseas. (The split year rules may also apply if the individual is non-resident for five or more full years, but not on the basis that he is returning from full time work overseas).

As set out in sections 1.2 and 1.3, there are a number of conditions which need to be satisfies in order for a period to constitute a period of full-time work overseas. These include spending fewer than 90 days each year in the UK, and having no more than 30 UK work days a year.

This basis of assessment can be illustrated as follows:

Individual: Normally Resident in the UK (UK domiciled) – subject to the split year rules

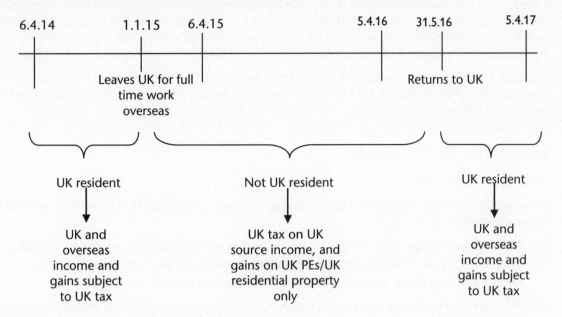

2.1.2 Relief for expenses when employed abroad

Certain expenses can be paid by an employer in respect of an employee employed overseas without creating a taxable benefit for that employee. These include:

- The cost of board and lodging abroad.

- Any number of return trips home.

- Travel expenses of his spouse/civil partner and minor children to visit him where he is abroad for 60 days or more. Only two return visits per person per year are permitted.

2.1.3 Tax planning when employed abroad

Tax planning can ensure that taxation is minimised when an employee is seconded overseas:

- Timing is important. Starting work overseas just before the end of the tax year may enable the employee to spend a complete tax year working full time overseas and so qualify as non-resident for the entire period of the full time contract.

- Where the remittance basis applies it may be prudent to separate funds so that it can be proved which monies have been remitted. Funds from a capital disposal may not be taxable even if remitted.

- Bank and building society interest may be paid gross, however no contributions to ISAs may be made whilst non-resident. Existing ISA accounts may be maintained.

- Termination payments are subject to special rules where there has been a substantial amount of overseas service (see Chapter 3).

2.2 Investment income

Individuals who certify that they are not resident in the UK can receive interest gross (rather than net of 20% tax deducted at source) from UK banks and buildings societies.

If an individual is non-resident for a complete tax year his tax liability is limited to the sum of:

- The tax deducted at source on his 'disregarded income', which is broadly his UK savings and investment income. So, his tax liability on UK dividends would be limited to the notional 10% tax credit and the liability on interest received is restricted to the 20% tax withheld at source, if paid net, plus

- The tax liability on income that cannot be 'disregarded', such as trading, employment and property income, with no personal allowances or double taxation relief taken into account.

If the level of income that cannot be disregarded is high, and the individual is entitled to a personal allowance despite being non-UK resident (see Section 1.5 – this includes all EEA citizens, and residents of certain other jurisdictions with which the UK has a double tax treaty) it may be more tax efficient for the individual to claim personal allowances and include their entire UK income in their tax computation.

Note that UK property income is never 'disregarded income', so a non-UK resident individual will always potentially be subject to full UK income tax (at the higher and additional rates where relevant) on UK property income.

2.3 Remittance basis planning

2.3.1 Remittance basis claims

As the remittance basis needs to be claimed for each tax year, those eligible to make the claim will need to decide whether to:

(i) Claim the remittance basis and pay UK tax on foreign income and gains remitted to the UK, potentially pay the £30,000, £60,000 or £90,000 remittance basis charge (RBC) and lose entitlement to personal allowances and the annual exempt amount, or

(ii) Not claim the remittance basis, pay UK tax on all foreign income and gains, receive UK personal allowances and the annual exempt amount and avoid the RBC.

Worked example: Whether to use the remittance basis

Roger has been resident in the England for tax purposes since 2006 but is not UK domiciled. In 2015/16, he has the following income:

UK trading income	£51,000
Non-UK trading income	£72,000

He remits £37,000 of his non-UK trading income into the UK. Roger realised a gain on a UK investment property of £52,000 in March 2016.

Requirement

Advise Roger whether he should claim the remittance basis in 2015/16.

Solution

Remittance basis

If Roger uses the remittance basis he will need to make a claim for it to apply and will be liable to pay the remittance basis charge (resident for at least 7 out of the last 9 years) and lose his entitlement to both the personal allowance and the annual exempt amount. Roger will be taxed on his UK income but only the world-wide income which he remits to the UK.

	£
UK trading income	51,000
Non-UK trading income remitted to the UK	37,000
Taxable income (no personal allowance as claimed for remittance basis)	88,000

His income tax liability will therefore be:	
£31,785 × 20%	6,357
£56,215 × 40%	22,486
Remittance basis charge (present for at least 7 but less than 12 years)	30,000
Income tax payable	58,843

Capital gains tax payable:	
£52,000 × 28% (no AEA as has claimed for remittance basis)	14,560
Total tax liability	73,403

Arising basis

If Roger does not make a claim for the remittance basis to apply, he will instead be taxed on his world-wide income on an arising basis.

	£
UK trading income	51,000
Non-UK trading income	72,000
Taxable income (no personal allowance as income exceeds £121,200)	123,000

His income tax liability will therefore be:

£31,785 × 20%	6,357
£91,215 × 40%	36,486
Income tax payable	42,843

Capital gains tax payable:	
(£52,000 – £11,100) × 28%	11,452
Total tax liability	54,295

Therefore Roger should not claim the remittance basis for 2015/16.

2.3.2 Investment exemption

A remittance basis taxpayer can bring funds into the UK without triggering a tax charge where he uses those funds to make an investment in the form of loans or shares in an unquoted trading company (AIM companies are treated as unlisted for these purposes) which is either UK resident or which trades in the UK through a UK permanent establishment (PE).

For this investment exemption to apply:

- The funds must be invested within 45 days of being brought into the UK.

- Where the investment is sold, the proceeds must be removed from the UK or reinvested in another qualifying investment within 45 days. Where the conditions for relief are no longer satisfied, the investment must be sold and the proceeds removed from the UK or reinvested in another qualifying asset within 90 days.

- There are rules which prevent the taxpayer or connected persons obtaining a benefit as a result of the investment.

The individual must elect for the relief by the first anniversary of 31 January following the end of the tax year in which the funds would otherwise be treated as remitted.

2.3.3 Sale exemption

Also there is no tax charge for an individual who brings assets into the UK to be sold in the UK, provided:

- He receives the entire proceeds of sale by the first anniversary of 5 January following the tax year in which the property is sold, and

- Takes the sale proceeds offshore within 45 days of receipt.

2.3.4 Overseas capital losses

If an individual has never used the remittance basis for his gains, his overseas losses are always allowable.

In the first year that an individual uses the remittance basis he can only obtain relief for his overseas capital losses if he makes an irrevocable losses election.

If he makes the losses election he must set his UK and overseas losses against his gains in the following order:

- First against remitted overseas gains
- Next against unremitted overseas gains
- Finally against UK gains

If he does not make the election in that first year he can never obtain relief for his overseas losses.

Interactive question 2: Remittance basis   [Difficulty level: Intermediate]

Kate is 29 years old. Kate has been resident in England for tax purposes since 6 April 2008 but is non UK domiciled. In 2015/16 Kate has the following income and gains:

	£
UK trading income	100,000
UK gains	15,000
Foreign trading income	80,000
Foreign gains	20,000

Requirements

(a) State whether the remittance basis would be available for Kate under each of the following scenarios either automatically or as a claim, and whether the UK personal allowances and the UK annual exempt amount would be available and if the remittance basis charge might apply.

    (i)   Kate remits all of her foreign income to the UK and all but £1,500 of her foreign gains.

    (ii)   Kate remits £10,000 of her foreign trading income to the UK and £6,000 of her foreign gains.

(b) Facts as in (a)(ii) above and Kate has been resident for the last seven tax years.

    Determine whether Kate should claim to use the remittance basis in 2015/16.

See **Answer** at the end of this chapter.

2.4   Temporary non-residence

'Temporary non residence' rules apply where an individual leaves the UK on or after 6 April 2013 for a short period and disposes of an asset, or receives certain classes of income, during that period. This is intended to prevent tax avoidance through individuals choosing to dispose of assets, or receive income where they can control the timing, while non-resident.

Where these rules apply, the income or gains in question are taxed in the tax year in which the individual returns to the UK. There is still therefore a cash flow advantage from realising a gain, or receiving income which is within the rules, while non-resident – but no overall tax advantage.

The rules apply where an individual:

- Ceases to be UK resident;

- Has been resident in the UK for at least four out of the last seven tax years; and

- Is not UK resident for a period of five years or fewer. This is any period of 60 months, and does not need to be five complete tax years.

Income and gains within the temporary non-residence rules include:

- Capital gains and losses on assets acquired when the individual was UK resident and sold while non-UK resident;

- Dividends from close companies where, at some time in the year of departure or one of the three previous tax years, the individual and his associates had a 5% interest. (Close companies are considered further in Chapter 13.) This does not apply to dividends paid out of trading profits which accrue after the individual ceases to be UK resident;

- Income relating to the writing off of loans from close companies; and

- Income taxed on the remittance basis, which has accrued during a period of UK residence but been remitted during the period of temporary non-residence.

Similar rules applied prior to 6 April 2013 for capital gains tax purposes only. However, the pre-6 April 2013 capital gains tax rules only applied where an individual was absent for a period of less than five complete tax years (not any period of five years or fewer).

Interactive question 3: Temporary non-residence [Difficulty level: Exam standard]

Paul, a higher rate taxpayer, has always been resident in England until, in January 2016, he leaves the UK to work full-time abroad. He expects to return to the UK to live on 1 May 2020. He intends to undertake the following capital transactions during his absence:

- March 2018 sell an asset for £180,000 bought in May 2009 for £65,000.
- June 2019 sell an asset for £20,000 bought in March 2016 for £50,000.

Neither of these assets is eligible for entrepreneurs' relief nor is a UK residential property.

Requirement

Draft paragraphs for a letter to Paul explaining his UK residence position for both UK income tax and UK capital gains tax purposes when he leaves the UK. You should also provide a calculation of his UK capital gains tax liability, assuming current rates and allowances continue to apply, stating when he can expect to pay any tax charge and provide advice for potentially minimising his tax liability.

See **Answer** at the end of this chapter.

Summary and Self-test

Summary

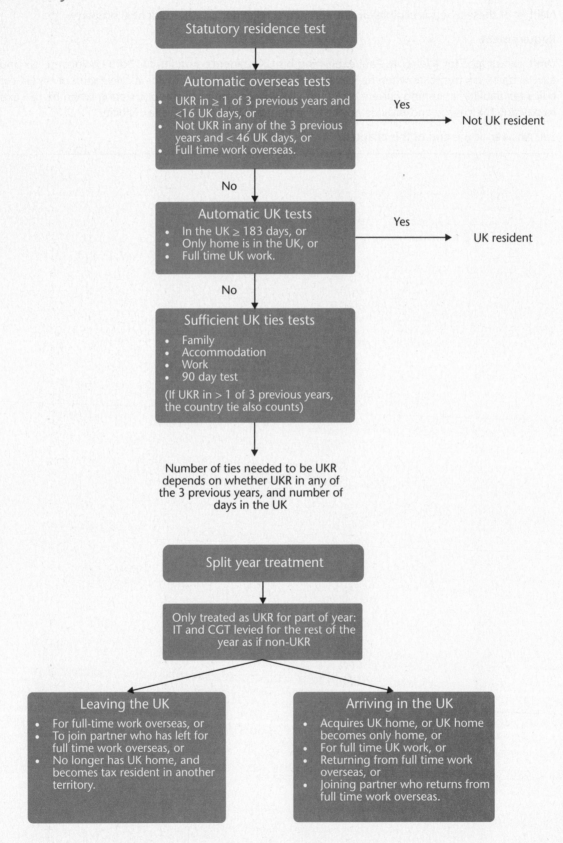

Statutory residence test

Automatic overseas tests
- UKR in ≥ 1 of 3 previous years and <16 UK days, or
- Not UKR in any of the 3 previous years and < 46 UK days, or
- Full time work overseas.

Yes → **Not UK resident**

No

Automatic UK tests
- In the UK ≥ 183 days, or
- Only home is in the UK, or
- Full time UK work.

Yes → **UK resident**

No

Sufficient UK ties tests
- Family
- Accommodation
- Work
- 90 day test

(If UKR in > 1 of 3 previous years, the country tie also counts)

Number of ties needed to be UKR depends on whether UKR in any of the 3 previous years, and number of days in the UK

Split year treatment

Only treated as UKR for part of year: IT and CGT levied for the rest of the year as if non-UKR

Leaving the UK
- For full-time work overseas, or
- To join partner who has left for full time work overseas, or
- No longer has UK home, and becomes tax resident in another territory.

Arriving in the UK
- Acquires UK home, or UK home becomes only home, or
- For full time UK work, or
- Returning from full time work overseas, or
- Joining partner who returns from full time work overseas.

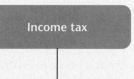

Income tax

Status	Employment income	Other income
UKR + UK D	world-wide income taxed on receipts basis	world-wide income taxed on arising basis
UKR + non-UKD	receipts basis except possibly for foreign earnings	UK income taxed on receipt basis, remittance basis may apply to overseas income
Non-UKR	UK income taxed on receipts basis otherwise exempt	UK income taxed on receipts basis otherwise exempt

- DTR available for income taxed in UK and overseas
  - Source by source basis
  - Computed as if overseas income is top-slice of income

- Remittance basis needs to be claimed if unremitted foreign income / gains > £2,000
- Otherwise tax on arising basis
- RBC of £30,000 payable if resident for 7 out of previous 9 years, £50,000 if resident for 12 out of previous 14 years
- Entitlement to UK personal allowances lost

Temporary non-residence
- ≤5 years absence
- Income received while non-UKR taxed in year of return
- Applies to loan waivers/ dividends from close companies, and remittance basis income'

CGT

Basis
- UKR + UKD
  = world-wide gains taxed
- UKR + non-UKD
  = UK gains taxed as arise, remittance basis may apply to overseas gains

- Tax year looked at as a whole unless split year treatment applies
- Temporary non-residence rules (absent ≤5 years) tax gains on pre-departure assets in year of return

Self-test

Answer the following questions.

1 Roberta is Swiss domiciled, and has a home in Switzerland which she visits most weeks. In 2015/16 she worked in the UK three days a week, spending a total of 140 days in the UK.

Roberta is single with no children, and she has a flat in the UK where she usually stays while working here. Her work pattern for the past four years has been broadly the same.

Requirement

Explain whether Roberta is UK resident in 2015/16.

2 Your client Michael, who is resident in England and domiciled in the United Kingdom, has sent you the following email.

From	Michael Morris
To	John Jenkins
Subject	Working overseas

John

I have just had a great offer to work overseas for eighteen months, which I am really keen to take up. Could you meet with me next week to discuss a few things?

I obviously need to talk through the best way to minimise any tax liabilities associated with going abroad, and have a few decisions to make. For example:

- Should I start the job on 1 January 2016 or 1 July 2016? Does it make any difference?

- My mother left me the family home two years ago when she died. I've never lived there but rent it out through a local agency. What should I do while I am away – should I sell the property before I go, whilst I am away or continue to rent it out?

- If, once overseas, I really like it and decide to make the move permanent, will my tax position alter?

If you could meet me on Friday, that would be ideal for me.

Michael

Requirement

Make brief notes for use at the forthcoming meeting you have arranged with Michael, including a list of further information you require to assist in providing final tax planning advice.

3 Nitin is based in the London office, but spends most of his time out of the office travelling overseas. He is non-UK domiciled and has been resident in England for eight years. In 2015/16 Nitin has the following income and gains:

	£
UK employment income	95,000
UK gains	25,000
Foreign trading income	125,000
Foreign gains	82,000

Nitin contributes £15,000 to his occupational pension scheme each year.

Nitin remits £24,000 of his foreign trading income and £32,000 of his foreign gains to the UK.

Requirement

Explain whether Nitin should claim the remittance basis for 2015/16.

Now, go back to the Learning outcomes in the Introduction. If you are satisfied you have achieved these outcomes, please tick them off.

Technical reference

Legislation

Overseas aspects of Income Tax

References are to Income Tax Act 2007 (*ITA 2007*) unless otherwise stated

Statutory residence test	Sch 45 FA 2013
Remittance basis	ss.809A-809Z10
Personal allowances	s.809G
Disregarded income	s.811
Overseas workday relief	s. 26A ITEPA 2003
Residence etc	ss.829-832

Overseas aspects of Capital Gains Tax

References are to Taxation of Chargeable Gains Act 1992 (*TCGA 1992*)

Residence etc	ss.9-14A
Temporary non-residence	s.10A TCGA 1992 & Sch45 FA2013 para109 et seq

HMRC manual references

Employment Income Manual (Found at www.hmrc.gov.uk/manuals/eimanual/index.htm)

Booklet HMRC6, Residence, Domicile and the Remittance basis (Found at www.hmrc.gov.uk/cnr/hmrc6.pdf)

Remittance basis (Found at www.hmrc.gov.uk/nonresidents/coming-to-the-uk.htm)

Capital gains manual (Found at www.hmrc.gov.uk/manuals/cgmanual/index.htm)

Effects of residence and domicile	CG10900+

This technical reference section is designed to assist you when you are working in the office. It should help you to know where to look for further information on the topics covered in this chapter.

Answer to Interactive question 1

(a) Her status in all three tax years affected by the secondment depends on whether she will be automatically non-resident in 2016/17 as a result of the full-time work overseas test.

She will work at least 35 hours a week overseas, is not expecting any breaks of more than 30 days, and should have only 8 UK work days (which is less than the permitted 30).

Her total days in the UK (based on days when she is in the UK at midnight) will be:

(12 × 3) for weekends + 10 for Christmas + (4 × 2) for the work visits, assuming she only stays in the UK the night before and the night after the visits start = 54 (which is less than the permitted 90).

The full-time work overseas test should therefore be met, and she should be non-UK resident for 2016/17. She will, however, need to ensure that she limits the number of her weekend and holiday days when she works in the UK, as she could conceivably exceed 30 UK workdays (ie days on which she does at least three hours work in the UK) if she did.

Split year treatment should apply to 2015/16. She will be treated as non-UK resident from the day on which she first works in Paris.

Split year treatment should also apply to 2017/18. She will be treated as UK resident from the day after her last day working in Paris (even though she will not return to the UK until nine weeks later).

(b) If she returns to the UK for 40 weekends, as well as the work visits and the ten day stay at Christmas her total UK days will be:

(40 × 3) + 10 + (4 × 2) = 138

She would therefore be in the UK for more than the permitted 90 days and would not satisfy the full-time work overseas test for 2016/17, and therefore not satisfy the requirement for split year treatment in 2015/16 or 2017/18.

Instead, she is likely to meet the automatic UK test in 2016/17 as a result of having a UK home (given the frequency of her visits at the weekend, it seems very likely that she would have one). Failing that, she would be UK resident on the basis of the sufficient ties test, because she would have been present in the UK for at least 90 days in the previous year and one tie is sufficient to make an individual resident if they are present in the UK for between 121 and 182 days in the tax year. In 2015/16 and 2017/18 she is likely to meet the automatic UK test as a result of being present for at least 183 days.

(c) The issue here is whether her period of full-time work overseas is treated as starting from the first day that she works in Paris in December 2015, or whether it starts in 2016 on the first working day of her secondment.

If the period from 6 December 2015 to 5 April 2016 is tested in the context of the full-time work overseas rules, the 30 and 90 day limits have to be reduced by 8/12 to reflect the number of months before the period of overseas work starts. These therefore become 10 and 30. As Talya would work in the UK for 11 days before returning to start her secondment, this period does not constitute a period of full-time work overseas as both the maximum number of UK workdays and the maximum break from overseas work would be exceeded.

Her residence status would therefore be as set out in (a), and she would be treated as becoming non-resident from her first day of work in Paris in January 2016.

Answer to Interactive question 2

(a) Kate is non-UK domiciled and therefore can use remittance basis for both income and gains.

   (i) As her unremitted income and gains are <£2,000 the remittance basis will apply automatically. She will be entitled to personal allowances and the annual exempt amount.

   The RBC will not apply.

   (ii) As her unremitted foreign income and gains exceed £2,000 she would need to claim the remittance basis on her self-assessment return.

   She would not be entitled to UK personal allowances or the UK annual exempt amount.

   She would need to pay the £30,000 RBC as she is 18 or over and has been resident in the UK for seven out of the last nine tax years.

(b) **Claim to use remittance basis**

Kate's taxable income:

	Non-savings income
	£
UK trading income	100,000
Non-UK trading income remitted	10,000
Taxable income (no personal allowance)	110,000

income tax liability:	
£31,785 × 20%	6,357
£78,215 × 40%	31,286
Annual tax charge on unremitted income (RBC)	30,000
	67,643

Kate's taxable gains:

	£
UK gains	15,000
Non-UK gains remitted	6,000
Taxable gains (no annual exempt amount)	21,000

CGT liability:	
£21,000 × 28%	5,880

Kate's total income tax and capital gains tax liability:

£(67,643 + 5,880)	£73,523

No remittance basis claim made

Kate's taxable income:

	Non-savings income
	£
UK trading income	100,000
Non-UK trading income	80,000
Total income	180,000
Less personal allowance (restricted as > £121,200)	Nil
Taxable income	180,000

£31,785 × 20%	6,357
£118,215 × 40%	47,286
£30,000 × 45%	13,500
	67,143

Kate's taxable gains:

	£
UK gains	15,000
Non-UK gains	20,000
	35,000
Less annual exempt amount	(11,100)
Taxable gains	23,900

CGT liability will be:

£23,900 × 28%	6,692

Kate's total income tax and capital gains tax liability:

£(67,143 + 6,692)	£73,835

Therefore Kate should claim the remittance basis for 2015/16.

Answer to Interactive question 3

UK income tax

As you are leaving the UK to work overseas, and you expect to be working full time overseas in 2016/17, you will only be treated as resident for part of 2015/16 so long as a number of conditions are met.

The conditions to be treated as working full-time overseas for the purposes of the UK residence rules are that:

- You work on average at least 35 hours a week overseas (excluding annual leave, sick leave and UK workdays);

- There are no significant breaks of more than 30 days in the tax year (excluding annual leave) when you do not work at least three hours overseas;

- You have no more than 30 UK work days in the tax year; and

- You spend fewer than 90 days in the UK in the tax year.

In 2015/16, these tests will be applied to the period starting with your first day working overseas. The 30 UK workday and 90 UK day limits will be reduced for the number of complete months before your first overseas workday. On the assumption that you start work on or after 1 January 2016, they will be reduced by 9/12, to 7 and 22.

On the assumption that these conditions are met, you will be resident in the UK until the day before you start work overseas in January 2016. You are then likely to be non-resident because you meet the full time work overseas test in 2016/17, 2017/18, 2018/19 and 2019/20. In 2020/21, you may again only be resident for part of the year (from the day after your last day working overseas), so long as the conditions for non-residence are met for the part of the year to that date.

This would mean that:

- You will be taxed in the UK on your worldwide income as it arises, and your worldwide capital gains as they are realised, up to the day you start work overseas.

- From the date you start work overseas, to the date you finish working overseas, your income and gains will be taxed as follows:

  - UK income will be taxable as it arises although you can request your bank to pay any interest to you gross. You will not be able to make contributions to any NISAs whilst you are non-resident but you can maintain any existing NISAs you have.

  - If the only UK income that you will receive whilst you are abroad is interest and dividends, then it may be preferable to not claim to receive the interest gross as your tax liability in any event will be limited to the basic rate of tax. You will then have no further tax liability due on your investment income. This is known as disregarding the income.

  - However, where your UK investment income is disregarded, any other UK income is taxable without the benefit of the personal allowance. Normally the amount of your income equal to the personal allowance is not taxed at all. Whether it is beneficial to allow your investment income to be disregarded therefore needs to be considered on a tax year by tax year basis.

- Any non-UK income will not be taxed in the UK.

- You will not be subject to UK capital gains tax.

- From the day after your last day working overseas in 2020 you will be liable to UK income tax on your worldwide income as it arises.

- Because you will be non-UK resident for less than five years, certain types of income and capital gains which arise while you are non-UK resident will be taxed on you in the year of your return to the UK (2020/21). This includes any chargeable gains arising on assets which you held at the time when you ceased to be UK resident, and certain transactions (including dividends) involving companies which are controlled by five or fewer people. Therefore the gain on the asset you intend to sell in March 2018 will be liable to UK taxation on your return as you owned the asset before you left the UK in January 2016. However, the asset that is both bought and sold during your absence will not be liable to UK capital gains tax.

You should keep a record of the time spent working abroad for your employer as it affects the tax due on any future termination payments paid by that employer. In order to support your residence position, you should also keep records of time spent in the UK, and the number of hours spent working each day.

Capital gains tax liability

Your return in May 2020 means that the gain on the asset you intend to sell in March 2018 is taxable in the UK in the tax year 2020/21 based on the rates and allowances that apply in that year. The capital gains tax liability will be due for payment on 31 January 2022. Your liability will be:

	£
UK gains (£180,000 – £65,000)	115,000
Less AEA	(11,100)
Taxable gains	103,900
CGT liability:	
£103,900 × 28%	29,092

I have assumed for this purpose that in 2020/21 you will have taxable income in excess of the basic rate band of £31,785 and that therefore all of your gains will be taxable at the higher rate of 28%. If any of the basic rate band remains after your income is taxed, then that amount of gains can be taxed at the lower rate of 18%.

Minimising tax due

The simplest way to minimise the capital gains tax liability due on your return would be to extend your period of working overseas until January 2021, so that you are non-resident for at least five years. The £29,092 capital gains tax liability would then not be due.

If this is not possible, an alternative would be to delay the sale of the second asset until just after your return to the UK in May 2020 and therefore realise an allowable loss of £30,000, saving capital gains tax of up to £8,400.

1   Roberta is present in the UK for more than 46 days, and cannot meet the full time work overseas tests. She therefore does not meet any of the automatic overseas tests which would mean she was automatically non-UK resident.

She does not appear to meet any of the automatic UK tests. In particular, because she only works in the UK three days a week she is unlikely to work here 35 hours a week on average, so the full time UK work test is not met. Because she has a home in Switzerland as well as her flat here, she is not automatically UK resident as a result of having her only home here.

However, because she has spent more than 120 days here, she will always be regarded as UK resident under the sufficient UK ties test if she has at least two UK ties (if she is resident in at least one of the three previous tax years, one UK tie would be sufficient). Because she worked in the UK for more than 40 days, had accommodation available here and spent more than 90 days here in the previous tax year, she has three UK ties. She is therefore UK resident for 2015/16.

2   **Taxation implications of working overseas**

- As he has been UK resident in the past, Michael has been liable to UK tax on his world-wide income and gains. If he is treated as non-UK resident he will only be liable to UK tax on his UK source income (and no chargeable gains, subject to the temporary non-residence rules – see below).

- If he meets the full-time work overseas criteria for a whole tax year, he will be treated as non-UK resident for income tax and capital gains tax purposes from the day on which he starts working overseas until the day after he starts working overseas. This treatment should apply if the secondment starts on 1 January, as he would be working overseas for the whole of 2016/17.

- Conditions to qualify as full-time work overseas for an entire tax year include:

    - Working overseas for an average of 35 hours/week

    - No breaks from overseas work of more than 30 days (excluding annual leave and sick leave)

    - No more than 30 days working in the UK

    - No more than 90 days in the UK (the 30 UK work days and 90 UK day limits are scaled back when testing part years)

- If he does not, and he works in the UK both in the part of 2016/17 before he leaves and the part of 2017/18 after his return, he is likely to be regarded as UK resident throughout the whole of both tax years as a result of the full-time UK work test (UK resident if at least part of a period of working in the UK for at least 365 days falls within the tax year).

In this case, income may be subject to both UK and overseas tax.

If so, double tax relief is available in one of two ways:

    - Double tax agreement – bilateral agreement between UK and country of destination setting out how income from employment is taxed and reliefs available.

    - Credit relief – where no double tax treaty exists, the UK income tax will be reduced by the lower of:

        - UK tax on overseas income; and
        - overseas tax actually paid.

- Regardless of when Michael takes up the employment, all sources of UK income will continue to be taxed in the UK.

- Further information required:

    - Likely preferred start date from Michael's point of view
    - Country of intended place of work
    - Other sources of UK income

Assessment on the rental or disposal of a UK investment property

- If the UK property is rented

    - Income received from UK property is assessed to income tax as if run as a business with a 5 April year end.

    - All expenses such as agent's fees, loan interest etc are deductible.

    - Even if resident overseas, income still assessable in UK.

    - Michael is still entitled to a personal allowance and, if no other source of income, the first £10,600 of property income will be tax free.

- If the UK property is sold

    - CGT is chargeable on all world-wide assets if an individual is UK resident (determined on the same basis as income tax, including where years are split so that an individual is only UK resident for part of a tax year). The timing of the disposal would determine when it was chargeable to CGT.

    - Thus if Michael remains UK resident throughout, or if the property is sold before his first day or after his last day working overseas, it will be liable to UK CGT.

    - If Michael is treated as being non-resident rules for disposal of UK residential property will apply. The post 5 April 2015 gain will be liable to UK CGT.

    - Any gain would be computed as proceeds less the market value at 5 April 2015, or by election the post 5 April 2015 time apportioned element of the gain calculated as proceeds less the probate value at the time of inheritance.

    - No principal private residence relief is available as Michael has never lived there.

    - CGT annual exempt amount of £11,100 is available, even if he is working abroad and the gain will be taxed at 18/28%.

- Further information required

    - Probate value of asset/market value at 5 April 2015/likely gain on sale
    - Annual rental
    - Qualifying expenses (including loan interest if applicable) of the property business

Consequences of permanent emigration abroad

- If Michael does not return to the UK, and continues to work overseas, it is likely that the full-time work overseas tests will be met which would mean that he would be treated as non-UK resident for any full tax year when he is working overseas.

- If the job started on 1 July 2016, and he remained working overseas when it ended, this may effectively change his residence status for 2016/17 as he would then as a matter of fact have a full tax year working overseas (intention isn't relevant). He would therefore be treated as non-UK resident from the day he first started work overseas as set out above.

- If the full-time work overseas tests are not met, the rest of the statutory residence test rules need to be considered.

    - Cannot be UK resident if here for fewer than 16 days in the tax year (46 days after not resident for three consecutive years).

    - If present for more, likely to need to consider the number of ties to the UK and number of days present. More likely to be UK resident if he has accommodation available here, or works in the UK on more than 40 days in a year.

- No CGT charge on disposals (other than UK residential property) while non-resident, provided period of absence includes at least five years.

- HMRC will initially not tax gains on disposal whilst abroad, but if the individual returns within five years, gains are taxed as a 're-entry charge'.

- If the individual does not return within five years, the gains are never taxed.

- Michael could seek to change his domicile to a domicile of choice. If he successfully acquires a non-UK domicile, only UK assets are chargeable to IHT, although UK domicile applies for 36 months after leaving the UK.

- Domicile of choice requires Michael to dispose of UK property and to sever ties with UK organisations, thereby illustrating his intention to lose his domicile of origin.

- At the same time he must illustrate his intention to take up a 'domicile of choice'. This would include buying a property locally and showing no intention of returning to the UK.

3 Claim to use remittance basis

Taxable income:

	Non-savings income £
UK employment income (£95,000 – £15,000)	80,000
Non-UK trading income remitted	24,000
Taxable income (no personal allowance as RBU)	104,000

Income tax liability:

£31,785 × 20%	6,357
£72,215 × 40%	28,886
Annual tax charge on unremitted income (RBC)	30,000
	65,243

As Nitin is not domiciled in the UK and has made the relevant claim, his worldwide gains are taxable in the UK on a remittance basis. However he will not receive the annual exempt amount. Nitin's taxable gains are:

	£
UK gains	25,000
Non-UK gains	32,000
Taxable gains (no annual exempt amount as RBU for IT purposes)	57,000

CGT liability:

£57,000 × 28% (HR taxpayer)	15,960

Nitin's total income tax and capital gains tax liability:

£(65,243 + 15,960)	£81,203

No remittance basis claim made

Taxable income:

	Non-savings income £
UK employment income (£95,000 – £15,000)	80,000
Non-UK trading income	125,000
Total income	205,000
Less personal allowance (restricted as > £121,200)	Nil
Taxable income	205,000

£31,785 × 20%	6,357
£118,215 × 40%	47,286
£55,000 × 45%	24,750
	78,393

Nitin's gains will be taxed on an arising basis but with the benefit of the AEA:

	£
UK gains	25,000
Non-UK gains	82,000
	107,000
Less annual exempt amount	(11,100)
Taxable gains	95,900

His CGT liability will be:

£95,900 × 28% (AR taxpayer)   26,852

Nitin's total income tax and capital gains tax liability:

£(78,393 + 26,852)   £105,245

Therefore Nitin should claim the remittance basis for 2015/16.

CHAPTER 9

The taxation of trusts

Introduction

Examination context

Topic List

Summary and Self-test

Technical reference

Answers to Interactive questions

Answers to Self-test

Introduction

Learning objectives

Tick off

- Identify the need for and advise on the use of trusts in tax planning

- Appreciate the tax implications of creating and utilising trusts and the tax implications of assets entering or leaving trusts

The specific syllabus references for this chapter are 1aa and 1bb.

Syllabus links

The income tax computation and the taxation of trusts were covered in your Tax Compliance study manual. You have also seen inheritance tax and capital gains tax earlier in this study manual, but now you will be looking at both taxes, and considering the interaction between them, in the context of trusts. There are both tax and non-tax reasons for using trusts.

Examination context

Trusts are a common tool for tax planning within a family context. They can be used effectively to ensure that family wealth is safeguarded whilst ensuring young and vulnerable family members are financially protected. If not utilised efficiently substantial tax liabilities can arise.

In the examination candidates may be required to:

- Suggest appropriate reasons for adopting a trust tax planning strategy
- Calculate the income tax payable by trustees or beneficiaries
- Identify the inheritance tax and capital gains tax implications of setting up and utilising a trust
- Identify the inheritance tax and capital gains tax implications of assets leaving a trust

1 Using trusts

Section overview

- A trust is a flexible alternative to gifting assets directly.
- A trust may be set up either during the settlor's lifetime or on their death.

1.1 Terminology

Trusts help preserve family wealth while maintaining flexibility over who should benefit.

Definitions

Trust: A trust is an arrangement under which a person, the settlor, transfers property to another person, the trustee, who must deal with the trust property on behalf of certain specified persons, the beneficiaries.

1.2 Why use a trust?

This section has been rewritten.

Trusts are useful vehicles for non-tax reasons such as to preserve family wealth, provide for those who are deemed to be incapable (minors and the disabled) or unsuitable (due to youth or poor business sense) to hold assets directly. In past years there were many tax advantages of using certain types of trusts. Many of these advantages no longer exist, but trusts remain popular vehicles for non-tax reasons.

1.2.1 Preserving family wealth

By gifting assets into trust, a settlor can ensure that they remain within his family. It is common practice for a settlor to create a trust on death such that assets can be enjoyed by his/her spouse during their lifetime, but for the assets to pass to their children or grandchildren on the spouse's death.

This prevents the spouse either selling the family assets or passing them on to somebody outside the immediate family (for example if the spouse remarries).

1.2.2 Preserving assets for minors

Trusts are useful vehicles if the beneficiary is too young to ensure the asset is properly managed. The settlor can ensure that the beneficiary has relatively limited access to the income and assets of the trust, whilst still young. The settlor can be appointed as one of the trustees to ensure the trust assets are protected.

1.2.3 Concealing ownership

In certain circumstances an individual may wish to conceal ownership of certain assets (for example ownership of shares), and can do this by use of a trust.

1.3 Will trusts

A trust may be set up in an individual's will. A discretionary trust allows flexibility about who may benefit from the trust and to what extent. This can be useful if there are beneficiaries of differing ages and whose financial circumstances may differ.

1.4 Lifetime trusts

Although gifts to trusts during lifetime can lead to an IHT charge (a chargeable lifetime transfer or 'CLT'), there can be tax benefits from setting up trusts during the settlor's lifetime.

If the cumulative total of the settlor's CLTs in any seven year period does not exceed the nil rate band, there will be no lifetime tax to pay on creation of the trust. This will also impact any further charges (the 'exit' and 'principal' charges – see below) while the trust is in existence.

CHAPTER 9

If a discretionary trust is used, the settlor can preserve maximum flexibility in the class of beneficiaries and how income and capital should be dealt with.

If the settlor is included as a beneficiary of the trust the gift will be treated as a gift with reservation.

2 Revision of income tax for trusts from Tax Compliance

Section overview

- There are two main types of trust for income tax purposes – trusts with an interest in possession and non interest in possession (ie discretionary) trusts.

- The trustees of an interest in possession trust are taxed on the income received at the basic rate applicable to that type of income – ie non-savings, savings or dividend income.

- Trustees do not deduct trust expenses from income received although expenses relating to a specific source of income are deducted from that income – eg property income expenses such as mortgage interest.

- Interest in possession beneficiaries are treated as entitled to trust income (net of expenses) as it arises. Life tenants are taxed on all the income of the trust after the deduction of tax and expenses. The life tenant will be taxed according to the type of income received by the trust – ie non-savings, interest or dividends.

- Annuitants are paid a fixed annuity each year by the trustees. The annuity is paid net of 20% tax.

- Trustees' expenses are deductible for the purposes of computing tax for discretionary trustees. Trust expenses are deducted first from dividend income.

- Discretionary trust beneficiaries are only taxable on income paid to them or applied for their benefit.

- If there is not enough tax in a discretionary trust's tax pool to cover the 45% tax credit on payments to beneficiaries, the trustees must pay the additional tax to HMRC.

- A bare trust is treated as transparent for tax purposes so any income received by the trust is taxed on the beneficiary and not the trustees.

2.1 Terminology

The way in which a trust is taxed depends on the nature of the trust itself. In order to understand the nature of the transaction it is important to have a basic understanding of English trust law (note that Scots law is different):

Definitions

Interest in possession trust: A trust where one or more of the beneficiaries has the right to receive the income of the trust (an **interest in possession**), the capital passing to another beneficiary (the remainderman) when the interest in possession comes to an end.

Discretionary trust: A trust where no beneficiary is entitled by right to any income or capital; it is left up to the discretion of the trustees which of the beneficiaries is to benefit from the trust and how they are to benefit.

Bare trust: Property in a bare trust (or 'simple' trust) is held by the trustee (or nominee) as its legal owner on behalf of the beneficiary. The beneficiary is absolutely entitled to the trust property and any income arising from it. There is no interest in possession and the trustees cannot exercise any discretion over the trust property or income.

2.2 Income tax for interest in possession trusts

2.2.1 Taxation of trustees

In a trust, assets are legally owned by trustees, for the benefit of beneficiaries. In a trust with an interest in possession, the beneficiaries are entitled to income from the trust assets as it arises. These beneficiaries are often called life tenants, as their right to the income often lasts until their deaths.

Income is taxed in the first instance on the trustees who do not have a personal allowance, nor is the trust income split into different bands of income as it is for an individual. Instead all trust income is taxed at the basic rate of tax applicable to the type of income. However, as interest is usually received net of a 20% tax credit and dividends are received with a 10% notional tax credit, these tax credits satisfy the trustees' liability for these types of income, such that no further tax is due from the trustees.

Expenses relating to specific sources of income are deducted from that income, as they are for an individual. For example, letting expenses are deducted from property income. However, there is no deduction for trust management expenses.

The trustees may have to make a fixed income payment each year, known as an annuity. This is paid to the recipient, the annuitant, net of a 20% tax credit. The trustee can deduct the gross annuity from the total trust income, from non-savings income first as a deductible payment, and must pay the 20% tax liability to HMRC.

2.2.2 Taxation of beneficiaries

The life tenant is entitled to receive the trust income once tax has been paid and expenses settled out of the net income. The beneficiary is taxed on an arising basis. Expenses are treated as paid out of dividend income in priority to other income.

The beneficiary will receive a statement of income from the trust (form R185 (Trust Income)) showing the net amounts which he is entitled to receive along with the associated tax credit (ie the tax paid by the trustees). The beneficiary will then include these amounts on his own tax return.

The income paid to the beneficiary retains its nature so if it is rental income in the trustees' hands it will be taxed as non-savings income on the beneficiary, if it is interest, as savings income and so on.

2.3 Income tax for discretionary trusts

2.3.1 Taxation of trustees

In a discretionary trust trustees have complete discretion over the distribution of trust assets. They may either pay out income or accumulate it in the trust (ie not pay it out), however they choose.

Trustees' expenses must be paid out of net income (ie after tax). Trustees of discretionary trusts can deduct the expenses in their income tax computation. However, as all figures in the computation are shown gross (ie before tax), the amount of income used to cover the expenses must be grossed up at 10% (if dividend income is used) or 20% (if savings income is used). Expenses are allocated against dividend income first, then savings income and then non-savings income.

Once expenses are deducted, discretionary trusts then have a basic rate band of £1,000. The first £1,000 of taxable income is taxed at the basic rates, ie at 20% for non-savings and savings, and 10% for dividends. As for individuals, the basic rate band is applied first to non-savings income, then savings income and finally dividends. Many smaller trusts will have no further tax to pay and will not need to file a tax return.

Where a settlor has made more than one settlement, the £1,000 is divided by the number of settlements made by the same settlor, with a minimum amount of £200 for each trust.

Any remaining income is taxed at one of two special trust tax rates. These are equivalent to the rates that additional rate taxpaying individuals pay and are therefore 45% for non-savings and savings income; and 37.5% for dividend income. These are known as the 'trust rate' and 'trust dividend rate' respectively.

Finally the income used to pay the expenses is taxed at the basic rate, depending on the type of income used to pay them, eg 10% if paid out of dividend income.

2.3.2 The tax pool

When the trustees make an income payment out of the trust to a beneficiary, the beneficiary is treated as receiving the payment net of a 45% tax credit. This means that the beneficiary must gross up the payment received by 100/55 to include as non-savings income in his income tax computation, and he will be able to deduct 45% of the gross amount as a tax credit. This applies even if the only income that the trustees have is dividend income taxed at 37.5% or income that has been taxed within the trust basic rate band.

This 45% tax credit comes from certain amounts of tax paid by the trustees. The most important of these are:

- Tax at the basic rates paid on trust income within the basic rate band

- Tax at the rate applicable to trusts (45%) on trust income

- The difference between the dividend trust and ordinary rates (ie 37.5% – 10%) = 27.5% on dividend income

This total amount of tax that is available to cover the tax credit on distributions to the beneficiaries is known as the 'tax pool'. If the trustees have paid more tax than they need to cover the tax credits, this tax is carried forward to the next tax year.

If, however, the reverse applies, ie they have paid less tax than is required to cover the tax credits, the balance required is extra tax which must be paid over to HMRC.

Note that the 10% tax credit on dividends cannot enter the tax pool as this is not real tax paid by the trustees.

2.3.3 Taxation of beneficiaries

Beneficiaries of discretionary trusts are only taxed if they receive income payments from the trust. Any payments of income to beneficiaries are made net of tax at 45% and are non-savings income for the beneficiary.

Even if all the income of the trust is dividend income the beneficiary is still treated as receiving income net of a 45% tax credit.

The trustees will provide a statement of income, R185 (Trust Income), to the beneficiaries showing the relevant figures. If the trustees have not paid sufficient tax to cover this tax credit, they must make an additional payment (see below). Beneficiaries not subject to income tax at the additional rate may obtain repayments. Additional rate taxpaying beneficiaries will have no further tax liability.

Worked example: Discretionary trust tax pool and taxation of beneficiaries

The Basket trust has a balance b/f on its tax pool at 6 April 2015 of £3,041. During the year ended 5 April 2016 it made the following receipts and payments:

	£
Receipts	
UK rental income receivable	21,340
Dividends received	1,404
Bank interest	312
Payments	
Relating to rental property	2,420
Trustees' expenses	720

Requirement

Calculate the maximum net income payment the trustees could make to Albert, a beneficiary, on 5 April 2016 without needing to make an additional payment of tax to cover the attached tax credit.

Solution

Start by calculating the balance of the tax pool for 2015/16. To do this you will first of all need to calculate the tax payable by the trust given its receipts and payments for the year:

	£	Non savings income £	Savings income £	Dividend income £
Income from UK property business	21,340			
Less letting expenses	(2,420)	18,920		
Dividends £1,404 × 100/90				1,560
Taxed interest £312 × 100/80			390	
		18,920	390	1,560
Less administration expenses (against dividends first) £720 × 100/90				(800)
Taxable income		18,920	390	760

Tax

	£
£1,000 @ 20% (non-savings income)	200
£(18,920 − 1,000 + 390) = £18,310 @ 45%	8,240
£760 @ 37.5%	285
£800 @ 10% (dividend income used to pay expenses)	80
Total tax liability	8,805
Less tax credits/paid	
£390 × 20%	(78)
£1,560 × 10%	(156)
Tax due	8,571

Next, calculate the balance of the tax pool:

	£
Tax pool brought forward as at 6 April 2015	3,041
Add tax for 2015/16 = £200 + £8,240 + (£760 @ (37.5% − 10%))	8,649
Tax available for providing credits	11,690

Remember that the dividend tax credit is notional tax and must be excluded from the computation.

If there is an available pool of £11,690 and the tax credit is 45%, then the maximum payment the trustees could make to Albert is £11,690 × 55/45 = £14,288.

Albert will then be treated as having received gross non-savings income from the trust of £14,288 + £11,690 = £25,978.

Albert will be taxed on that income at his marginal rate of tax, so unless he is an additional rate taxpayer he will receive a net repayment from HMRC on the income. If Albert is a higher rate taxpayer he will be liable to income tax of £10,391 but will be treated as having had income tax deducted at source of £11,690.

If the trustees wanted to make a payment in excess of £14,288 they would need to pay additional income tax to HMRC for 2015/16 equivalent to the additional tax credit attached.

2.4 Income tax for bare trusts

Bare trusts are treated as transparent for all tax purposes, so income arising in a bare trust is not assessed on the trustees of the trust, but instead on the beneficiary of the trust.

Bare trustees do not need to file a self-assessment return or deduct tax at source on payments to a beneficiary.

3 Inheritance tax for trusts

Section overview

- Trusts set up during lifetime since 22 March 2006, whether discretionary or interest in possession trusts, are treated as 'relevant property trusts' for IHT purposes.

- Relevant property trusts are subject to IHT on creation and during the life of the trust.

- There is a chargeable lifetime transfer when an individual sets up a relevant property trust.

- An exit charge applies when assets leave a relevant property trust.

- There is an IHT charge on every 10-year anniversary of setting up a relevant property trust.

- A life interest trust set up during the lifetime of the settlor is only a qualifying interest in possession trust if it was set up before 22 March 2006. All interest in possession trusts set up on the settlor's death are qualifying interest in possession trusts.

- The creation of a qualifying interest in possession trust may have inheritance tax implications depending on the identity of the life tenant and his relationship to the settlor.

- There may be inheritance tax implications when assets leave a qualifying interest in possession trust depending on the identity of the remainderman and his relationship to the life tenant.

- Bare trusts are transparent for IHT purposes.

3.1 IHT for relevant property trusts

Non-qualifying interest in possession trusts set up during the lifetime of the settlor on or after 22 March 2006 and all discretionary trusts are subject to the relevant property trust (RPT) regime for IHT purposes.

RPTs are subject to IHT on the following three occasions:

- When the trust is set up – a chargeable lifetime transfer (see Chapter 7)

- When property passes to a beneficiary – an 'exit' charge (see below)

- On each tenth anniversary of the creation of the trust – a 'principal' or 'ten-year' charge (see below).

3.1.1 Setting up a relevant property trust

As we saw earlier in this study manual, when an individual sets up a RPT during lifetime, it is a chargeable lifetime transfer (CLT) for inheritance tax (IHT) purposes.

Lifetime tax is chargeable on a CLT and additional tax may be payable if the transferor dies within seven years of making the CLT. The additional tax on death is chargeable at a reduced rate if the transferor survives between three and seven years (taper relief).

Where the individual sets up a RPT on death, ie via his will, the assets that enter the trust are always included in the deceased's death estate for IHT purposes, even if the beneficiary of the trust is the deceased's spouse or civil partner.

3.1.2 Overview of IHT charges on relevant property trusts

If trust property remains in the trust, it is subject to a principal charge on every tenth anniversary from the date that the trust was set up. This is often called the '10-year' charge.

If trustees pass trust property from a relevant property trust to a beneficiary, there is an IHT charge, the 'exit' charge.

Although you must have an awareness of the exit and principal charges, you are not expected to calculate the charges in the exam.

3.1.3 Exit charge before the first 10-year charge

Where a trustee passes assets to the beneficiary of a relevant property trust, the amount distributed from the trust is subject to an exit charge.

The rate of IHT is 30% of the lifetime rate (currently 20%) that would apply to an assumed transfer of the initial value of all the original property in the trust. The available nil rate band for this assumed transfer takes into account the nil rate band at the date of the exit, as reduced by the gross chargeable transfers of the settlor in the seven years before originally setting up the trust.

This IHT rate is then further reduced by adjusting by n/40, where 'n' is the number of complete quarters (ie periods of three months) that have elapsed since the trust was originally set up.

This charge applies even if the property passes to the settlor, or his spouse or civil partner.

There is no exit charge if assets leave the trust within three months of the trust being set up, ie during the first quarter (as 'n' is zero), or within two years of the death on which the trust was created.

3.1.4 Principal (10-year) charge

On every 10th anniversary of the trust being set up, there is an IHT charge on the value of the trust property at that anniversary date, plus income arising more than five years before the anniversary date and still not distributed.

The rate is 30% of the lifetime rate (currently 20%) that would apply to an assumed transfer of the property in the trust at that tenth anniversary. There is no need to adjust by n/40 as 'n' is now 40 (10 years × 4 quarters).

The available nil rate band for this assumed transfer takes into account the nil rate band at the date of the 10-year charge, as reduced by:

(i)   Transfers of the settlor in the seven years before originally setting up the trust, and
(ii)   The value of any distributions (ie 'exits') made by the trustees in the previous 10 years.

3.1.5 Exit charge after a principal charge

The rate of tax for this assumed transfer is the rate that applied at the date of the last tenth anniversary, scaled down by n/40, where n is the number of complete quarters that have elapsed since the last 10-year charge.

The rate that applied at the date of the last tenth anniversary may also have to be adjusted to take into account any change in the value of the nil rate band.

There is no exit charge if assets leave the trust within three months of a ten-year charge (as 'n' is zero).

Worked example: IHT for relevant property trusts

On 4 July 2005 Nicholas set up a discretionary trust for the benefit of his four grandchildren with shares valued at £400,000. He had previously made a gross chargeable transfer of £120,000 in September 2001.

On 4 July 2012 the trustees gave one of the beneficiaries shares valued at £150,000. On 4 July 2015 the remaining shares in the trust were valued at £600,000, and the trust had undistributed income of £20,000 that had arisen in 2008.

Requirements

Explain the inheritance tax implications of the above events. Calculations are not required.

Solution

Setting up the trust – July 2005

When Nicholas set up the discretionary trust in 2005 this was a chargeable lifetime transfer (CLT) for IHT purposes as it was a relevant property trust (discretionary trusts have always been and continue to be treated as relevant property trusts).

Two annual exemptions were available, and Nicholas would also have been able to reduce the chargeable amount by the available nil rate band (ie the nil rate band at the date of the gift less the £120,000 gross chargeable transfer made in the seven years before that gift).

Assets leaving the trust – July 2012

When the trustees gave some of the trust property (ie the shares) to one of the beneficiaries in July 2012 there was an exit charge.

This would have been based on an assumed transfer by Nicholas of all of the trust assets as valued at the time the trust was set up, less the available nil rate band (ie the nil rate band at the date of the exit as reduced by the gross chargeable transfer made in the seven years before the trust was originally set up).

The tax rate used for this assumed transfer would have been 30% × 20% × 28/40 = 4.2%. The figure '28' represents the number of complete quarters that had elapsed since the date the trust was set up to the date of the exit (ie 4 July 2005 – 4 July 2012, so 7 years × 4).

10th anniversary of setting up the trust – July 2015

On every ten year anniversary of setting up a relevant property trust there is a 10-year, or 'principal', charge.

This is based on an assumed transfer by the settlor of the current value of the trust assets still in the trust plus undistributed income from more than five years earlier (ie a total of £620,000) , as reduced by any available nil rate band, ie the nil rate band at the date of the 10th anniversary as reduced by the £120,000 gross chargeable transfer made in the seven years before the trust was originally set up and the exit from the trust in the previous 10 years (ie in July 2012).

The rate for the principal charge is 30% × 20% = 6%.

3.2 IHT for qualifying interest in possession trusts

All interest in possession (IIP) trusts set up during the lifetime of the settlor on or after 22 March 2006 are relevant property trusts for IHT purposes and are subject to the IHT charges set out above.

IIPs that were set up during lifetime before that date, or are set up on the death of the settlor, are treated differently for IHT purposes and are known as qualifying IIPs (QIIPs). The assets within a QIIP are treated for IHT purposes as if they are owned by the IIP beneficiary (ie the life tenant) and are known as 'settled property'.

The IHT consequences for both setting up a QIIP and when assets leave a QIIP are the same as if the transfers involved an individual rather than a trust.

3.2.1 Setting up a pre-22 March interest in possession trust

When an individual set up an IIP trust before 22 March 2006, the IHT treatment depended on the identity of the life tenant and whether the trust was set up during the settlor's lifetime or on his death.

IIP set up during lifetime

If the settlor set up the pre-22 March 2006 with himself as the life tenant there would have been no transfer of value as he would have actually owned the trust property directly before the transfer and would be treated as owning it for IHT purposes after the transfer.

If he had set up the pre-22 March 2006 trust for the benefit of his spouse or civil partner then the spouse exemption would have applied on the creation of the trust so no IHT would be due.

Finally, if he had set up the pre-22 March 2006 trust for another individual (eg his child) the transfer would have been a PET – exactly as it would have been had he made the transfer to his child directly.

IIP set up on death

If the trust was set up on the death of the settlor for the benefit of his spouse or civil partner, the value of the assets in the settlor's death estate would have been reduced by the spouse exemption. If, on the other hand, it had been set up on the settlor's death for the benefit of anyone else then the full value of the assets would have been fully chargeable in his death estate (subject to the availability of any reliefs, such as APR and BPR) and would have had to be included in the death estate.

3.2.2 Setting up a post-21 March 2006 qualifying IIP

It is no longer possible to set up a QIIP during lifetime. Instead, all lifetime IIP trusts are treated as relevant property trusts and setting one up is a CLT for IHT purposes (see 3.1 above).

The IHT implications of setting up a QIIP on death (an 'immediate post death interest' (IPDI) trust) are exactly the same as they were before 22 March 2006. So, the spouse exemption applies where the settlor's spouse or civil partner is the life tenant and there is a chargeable death transfer if anyone else is named as the life tenant.

3.2.3 IHT charges on QIIP trusts

QIIP ends during life tenant's lifetime

If a QIIP trust comes to an end during the lifetime of the life tenant, ie the trustees pass out the trust property so that there is nothing left in the trust, the IHT implications depend on the identity of the remainderman, ie the person who receives the trust assets, and the treatment is the same as if the life tenant has made the transfer of the assets himself.

If the assets pass to the life tenant himself, there is no transfer of value as he was treated as owning the asset for IHT purposes before the transfer and now he actually owns the asset outright.

If the assets pass to the life tenant's spouse or civil partner then the spouse exemption applies, and if the assets pass to anyone else, the life tenant is treated as making a PET of the trust assets.

QIIP ends on life tenant's death

If a QIIP trust ends on the death of the life tenant, the value of the trust assets enter the life tenant's death estate as his 'settled property' along with the value of his own directly-held assets (his 'free estate').

The treatment of the settled property for IHT purposes again depends on the identity of the remainderman so the spouse exemption will apply if the remainderman is the life tenant's spouse or civil partner, and the assets will be chargeable (subject to the availability of any reliefs such as APR or BPR) in the life tenant's death estate if the remainderman is anyone else, eg the deceased life tenant's child.

If the settled property is chargeable, IHT is calculated on the combined value of the life tenant's free estate and the settled property, and is split between the two elements proportionately. The IHT due in respect of the settled property must be paid by the trustees of the QIIP, and the tax due in respect of the free estate is paid by the executors, as normal.

Worked example: Qualifying interest in possession trust

On 4 July 2004 Oscar set up an interest in possession trust for the benefit of his son, Mason. Oscar also has a daughter, Nikki.

Mason, who is married to Lily, turned 25 on 5 June 2015 at which time his life interest came to an end under the terms of the trust deed.

Requirements

State the IHT consequences of Mason's interest in possession coming to an end assuming the remainderman of the trust who receives the trust assets is:

(a) Mason
(b) Lily
(c) Nikki

Solution

As the trust was set up before 22 March 2006 it is a QIIP trust, so when the trust ends the transfer of the assets to the remainderman would be treated as follows:

(a) There is no transfer of value if Mason is the remainderman of the trust as before the transfer he was treated as owning the assets for IHT purposes and he actually owns them after the transfer.

(b) If Lily is the remainderman of the trust, the transfer is exempt as Mason is married to Lily so the spouse exemption applies.

(c) Nikki is Mason's sister so if she is the remainderman the transfer is treated as a PET to Nikki by Mason. The PET will be exempt so long as Mason survives at least seven years from the date the trust ends.

3.3 IHT for bare trusts

A bare trust is transparent for tax purposes. Consequently, the transfer of assets to bare trustees is treated as an outright gift by the settlor to the beneficiary, so is a potentially exempt transfer (PET) for IHT purposes, and the transfer of assets by bare trustees to a beneficiary is not a transfer for IHT purposes.

A practical application of the bare trust is when a beneficiary of a trust becomes absolutely entitled to trust property (for example, when the beneficiary of a trust for a bereaved minor becomes absolutely entitled to trust property at age 18). If the trust property is not distributed at that date a bare trust will arise in favour of the beneficiary until such time as the trust fund is handed over.

4 Capital gains tax for trusts

Section overview

- A normal CGT disposal calculation is required when trustees dispose of trust assets to third parties from any type of trust.

- Trustees of all trusts (except bare trusts) are entitled to one half of an individual's annual exempt amount and their gains are always taxed at 28%.

- The creation of a trust may have both capital gains tax and inheritance tax implications.

- When an individual sets up, or adds assets to, a relevant property trust during their lifetime, there is a deemed disposal at market value for CGT purposes.

- There is also a deemed disposal at market value for CGT purposes when trustees of a relevant property trust pass trust assets to a beneficiary.

- Gift relief is available to defer the gain when any asset enters a relevant property trust, or passes out of a relevant property trust to a beneficiary, as there has also been a chargeable transfer for IHT purposes.

- When an individual set up, or added assets to, a QIIP trust before 22 March 2006 during their lifetime, there was a deemed disposal at market value for CGT purposes.

- There are no capital gains tax implications when a QIIP trust is created on death as there is no CGT on death.

- There may be a deemed disposal at market value for CGT purposes when trustees of a qualifying interest in possession trust pass trust assets to a beneficiary.

- Gift relief may be available to defer the gain when an asset passes to a beneficiary in certain circumstances.

- Bare trusts are transparent for CGT purposes.

4.1 Actual disposals by trustees

When the trustees of any type of trust make a disposal of an asset, the gain is calculated in exactly the same way as for an individual (see Chapter 5).

Once the total gains for the year have been calculated, the trustees can deduct the annual exempt amount, which is one half of that given to individuals, so it is £5,550 for 2015/16 (£5,500 for 2014/15).

If several trusts are created by the same settlor, the exempt amount is divided equally between them subject to a minimum exemption per trust of one tenth of a full individual exemption (£1,110 for 2015/16; for 2014/15 it was £1,100).

The rate of capital gains tax for all trusts is 28%.

The above rules regarding the annual exempt amount and the rate of tax do not apply to disposals from a bare trust (see below).

Interactive question 1: Trust disposal   [Difficulty level: Intermediate]

Jeremy Blend set up the Compass Discretionary Trust in May 2007. This was the only trust he had ever set up.

In June 2015 the trustees of the Compass Discretionary Trust sold a trust asset, which had a base cost of £25,000, for £100,000. This was the trustees' only disposal during the year but they also received total income during the year of £12,000.

Requirements

Calculate the trustees' capital gains tax liability for 2015/16.

See **Answer** at the end of this chapter.

4.2 CGT on gifts into and out of relevant property trusts

The creation of a relevant property trust has both capital gains tax and inheritance tax implications.

4.2.1 Gift to a relevant property trust

Gifts to relevant property trusts during lifetime

As we have already seen, where an individual sets up a trust during his lifetime on or after 22 March 2006, the trust is a relevant property trust (ie any lifetime trust except a bare trust) and there is a chargeable lifetime transfer (CLT) for IHT purposes.

In addition, the individual is treated as making a disposal of the asset entering the trust for CGT purposes, which is deemed to take place at the asset's current market value. This market value is also the base cost of the asset for the recipient (ie the trustees) when they eventually sell that asset.

The gain on this deemed disposal is only chargeable if the asset(s) entering the trust is a chargeable asset, so, for example, settling cash on the trust would not result in a gain as cash is an exempt asset for CGT purposes.

Since the individual will not have received any proceeds from the trustees with which to pay the tax, he may be able to claim gift relief to defer the gain. As there is an immediate charge to IHT when the assets enter the trust (ie the CLT), relief is available for the settlor for any asset being transferred to the trust. Any claim is made by the settlor alone, rather than jointly with the trustees as is usually the case for gift relief claims.

The trustees' base cost is reduced by the amount of any gain deferred, so a gift relief claim effectively transfers the settlor's gain to the trustees.

Gifts to relevant property trusts on death

If the trust is set up on the settlor's death there is no deemed disposal for CGT purposes as there is no CGT on death. The trustees have a base cost equivalent to the probate values of the assets, ie their market values on the date of death.

4.2.2 Assets leaving a relevant property trust

As we saw above, when trustees pass an asset from a relevant property trust to a beneficiary there is an IHT exit charge (unless the assets leave within three months of the creation of the trust or of a ten-year anniversary).

In addition, the trustees are treated as making a disposal of that trust asset for CGT purposes, which is deemed to take place at the asset's current market value.

As there is an immediate charge to IHT when the assets leave the trust (ie the exit charge), gift relief is available to the trustees for any asset being transferred out of the trust.

Interactive question 2: IHT and CGT for relevant property trusts

[Difficulty level: Intermediate]

On 7 May 2015 Christine set up an interest in possession trust for her sister, Jodie, with quoted shares worth £450,000. Her sister's children are the remaindermen of the trust. This is Christine's only lifetime transfer to date.

Christine had originally acquired the shares, which represent a 1% holding, in 2002 for £100,000.

Requirements

Explain, with calculations where relevant, the IHT and CGT consequences of the above events, assuming the parties make all available claims for relief.

See **Answer** at the end of this chapter.

4.3 CGT on gifts to and out of interest in possession trusts

There may be capital gains tax, as well as inheritance tax, implications when someone set up a qualifying interest in possession trust before 22 March 2006.

Both taxes may also apply when assets leave a QIIP trust either during the lifetime or on the death of the life tenant.

4.3.1 Gift to a QIIP trust

Pre-22 March 2006 qualifying interest in possession trust

As we saw above, setting up an interest in possession trust before 22 March 2006 was usually a PET (after that date it is a CLT and the treatment is as for other relevant property trusts above).

Where the life tenant is the settlor's spouse or civil partner, the transfer is at nil gain, nil loss.

The transfer was also a deemed disposal at market value for CGT purposes. The market value was also the base cost of the asset for the trustees when they eventually sold that asset.

As there was no immediate charge to IHT (as there is no IHT during lifetime for a PET), gift relief was only available if the gift was of qualifying business assets (see Chapter 6). If gift relief was claimed, the trustees' base cost was reduced by the amount of deferred gain.

In addition, claiming gift relief impacted the CGT position if the trust ended as a result of the life tenant's death (see below).

Qualifying interest in possession trust set up on death

There are no CGT implications of setting up a QIIP trust on death as there is no CGT on death. The trustees take the assets at their probate value (ie market value at the date of death) thus obtaining a tax-free uplift to the market value at the date of death.

4.3.2 Assets leaving a QIIP trust

Assets leaving a qualifying interest in possession trust during the life tenant's lifetime

As we saw above, when QIIP trust assets are passed to the remainderman during the life tenant's lifetime, it is usually a PET for IHT purposes (or exempt if they pass to the life tenant's spouse or civil partner).

The transfer is also a deemed disposal at market value for the trustees and gift relief is only available for qualifying business assets as there is no immediate charge to IHT.

Assets leaving a qualifying interest in possession trust on the life tenant's death

Any gain arising on assets leaving a QIIP trust on the death of the life tenant is exempt. The remainderman takes the assets at their probate value thus obtaining a tax-free uplift to the market value at the date of death.

This exemption does not apply, however, if gift relief was claimed when the property was originally transferred to the trust. Instead the lower of the actual gain and the deferred gain becomes chargeable.

However, where the life tenant's death also triggers an IHT charge because the trust assets are included in his death estate as his 'settled property' the gain can be deferred again by claiming gift relief.

Worked example: Interest in possession trusts

In September 2005 Bryan put unquoted trading company shares, valued at £50,000, into a trust for his brother, Ray, for life. This was his only lifetime gift up to that date.

The shares had cost him £1,750 in 1989. Bryan and the trustees claimed gift relief to defer the gain.

Bryan's niece, Marsha, is the remainderman of the trust.

Ray died in January 2016 when the shares were worth £63,000.

Requirement

Explain, with calculations, the IHT and CGT implications of the above events, assuming all reliefs are claimed.

Solution

September 2005 – setting up trust

As the trust was set up before 22 March 2006, it is a QIIP trust for IHT purposes. The transfer to the trust would have been a PET, so no IHT would have been paid during Bryan's lifetime, and is now completely exempt as Bryan has survived 7 years from setting up the trust.

The transfer to the trust was also a deemed disposal at market value, resulting in a gain of:

	£
Disposal by Bryan at market value	50,000
Less cost 1989	(1,750)
Gain	48,250
Less gift relief	(48,250)
Chargeable gain	Nil

Trustees' base cost:

	£
Market value	50,000
Less deferred gain	(48,250)
Base cost c/f	1,750

January 2016 – Ray's death

As the trust is a qualifying interest in possession trust, the value of the shares (£63,000) is included in Ray's death estate as his 'settled property'. If Ray has sufficient nil rate band available there may be no inheritance tax to pay.

From a CGT perspective, there is usually no CGT when the life tenant of a qualifying interest in possession trust dies, and the remainderman takes the trust assets at probate value. However, as Bryan claimed gift relief when he set up the trust, there will be a deemed disposal at market value by the trustees at the date of Ray's death.

The lower of that gain (£61,250, ie £63,000 – £1,750) and the gain that was originally deferred (£48,250) will become chargeable. In this case a gain of £48,250 will be chargeable.

As the settled property is chargeable in Ray's estate, even if it is covered by the nil rate band or BPR, then this gain can be deferred using gift relief.

4.4 Capital gains tax and bare trusts

A bare trust is effectively transparent for tax purposes.

4.4.1 Actual disposals by bare trustees

The disposal of assets by bare trustees is treated as a disposal by the beneficiary.

The full annual exempt amount is therefore available and the gain is taxed at either 18% or 28% depending on the availability of the individual beneficiary's basic rate band (see Chapter 5).

4.4.2 Setting up a bare trust

Gifts to bare trusts are always PETs, whether set up before or after 22 March 2006, ie they are treated as if they are gifts to an individual.

There is also a deemed disposal at market value by the settlor when he transfers assets to the trust.

As there is no immediate IHT charge, gift relief is only available if the asset is a qualifying business asset.

4.4.3 Assets passing to a bare trust beneficiary

The transfer of assets by bare trustees to a beneficiary is not a transfer for either IHT or CGT purposes, as the trust is transparent for tax purposes.

Consequently there is no deemed disposal at market value by the trustees and gift relief is not in point.

Summary and Self-test

Summaries

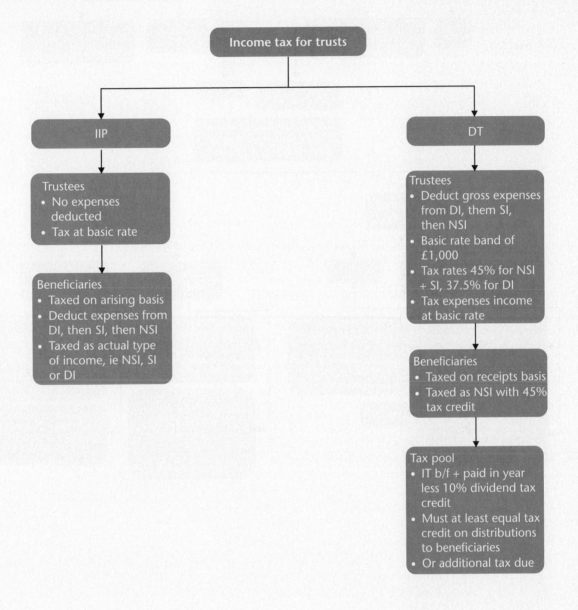

```
                        ┌─────────────────────────┐
                        │   Income tax for trusts  │
                        └─────────────────────────┘
                                    │
                 ┌──────────────────┴──────────────────┐
                 ▼                                      ▼
           ┌──────────┐                          ┌──────────┐
           │   IIP    │                          │    DT    │
           └──────────┘                          └──────────┘
                 │                                      │
                 ▼                                      ▼
```

IIP

Trustees
- No expenses deducted
- Tax at basic rate

Beneficiaries
- Taxed on arising basis
- Deduct expenses from DI, then SI, then NSI
- Taxed as actual type of income, ie NSI, SI or DI

DT

Trustees
- Deduct gross expenses from DI, them SI, then NSI
- Basic rate band of £1,000
- Tax rates 45% for NSI + SI, 37.5% for DI
- Tax expenses income at basic rate

Beneficiaries
- Taxed on receipts basis
- Taxed as NSI with 45% tax credit

Tax pool
- IT b/f + paid in year less 10% dividend tax credit
- Must at least equal tax credit on distributions to beneficiaries
- Or additional tax due

ICAEW

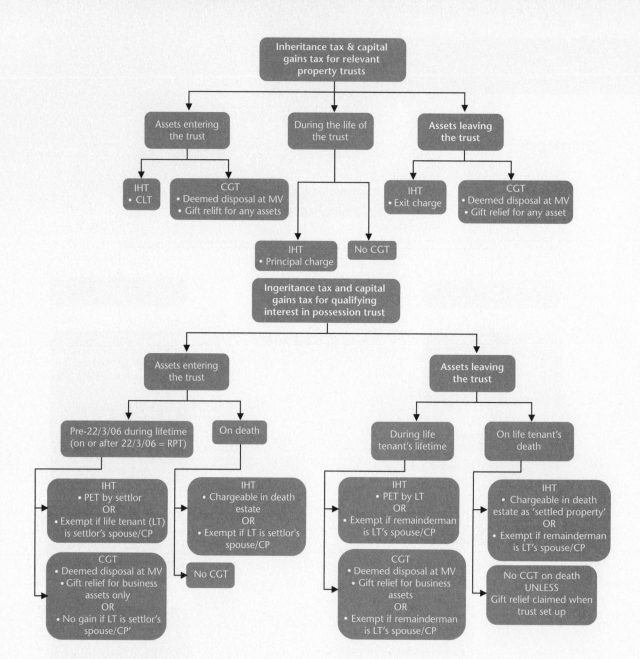

Self-test

Answer the following questions.

1   The Red interest in possession trust received the following income in 2015/16:

	£
Bank interest	540
Dividends	1,125
Gross rents	24,000

It incurred the following expenses:

	£
Expenses re rental property	3,700
Trust administration	1,300

Requirement

What is the trust's net income and the life tenant's tax position?

2   The Young Discretionary Trust received the following income in 2015/16:

	£
Dividends	4,000
Gross rents	33,000

It incurred the following expenses:

	£
Expenses re rental property	4,600
Trust administration	1,944

No distributions were made during the year.

Requirement

Calculate the trust's income tax liability.

3   The Sun Discretionary Trust

In 2015/16, the Sun trust had the following income:

	£
Property income	27,435
Interest received (paid gross)	22,300
Dividends received	36,900

Payments from the trust comprised the following:	
Allowable property expenses	6,350
Trust admin expenses	7,011

Income distributions to beneficiaries:	
George	57,000

The balance brought forward on the tax pool at 6 April 2015 was £5,800.

George has no other source of income.

Requirement

Calculate the amount of income tax payable/recoverable for George and the amount payable by the trust for 2015/16.

4   Trust capital gains tax

Harvey created a life interest trust in June 2005. This was the second trust that he had set up. Harvey did not claim gift relief at the time.

One of the trust assets was a painting valued at £25,000 in June 2005. In November 2015 the trustees disposed of the painting for £38,000. They made no other disposals during the year.

Requirement

Calculate the capital gains tax liability of the trustees.

5   The Cromwell Discretionary Trust

Peter set up the Cromwell Discretionary Trust on 1 July 2005 with cash of £250,000. The potential beneficiaries of the trust included Peter's wife, Sandra, as well as their children and grandchildren. Peter's only previous lifetime gift had been a gross chargeable transfer of £145,000 in January 2002.

The trustees immediately invested the cash in a portfolio of quoted investments and on 1 October 2009 they distributed some of the shares to Sandra.

The remaining investments are worth £400,000 in July 2015. All income generated by the trust has been distributed to the beneficiaries.

Requirement

(a) Calculate the inheritance tax and capital gains tax due from Peter on the creation of the trust in July 2005.

(b) Explain the inheritance tax and capital gains tax consequences of the distribution to Sandra in October 2009.

(c) Explain the inheritance tax and capital gains tax position for the trust in July 2015.

6   The Cromwell Life Interest Trust

Peter set up the Cromwell Life Interest Trust on 1 July 2005 with cash of £250,000. The trust deed provides for Peter's wife, Sandra, to be the life tenant of the trust and their children to take the capital on her death. Peter's only previous lifetime gift had been a gross chargeable transfer of £145,000 in January 2002.

The trustees immediately invested the cash in a portfolio of quoted investments and, in accordance with the terms of the trust, on 1 October 2009 they distributed some of the shares to Sandra.

Sandra died in July 2015.

Requirement

(a) Calculate the inheritance tax and capital gains tax due from Peter on the creation of the trust in July 2005.

(b) Explain the inheritance tax and capital gains tax consequences of the distribution to Sandra in October 2009.

(c) Explain the inheritance tax and capital gains tax position in July 2015.

Now, go back to the Learning objectives in the Introduction. If you are satisfied you have achieved these objectives, please tick them off.

Technical reference

Legislation

Income Tax

References are to Income Tax Act 2007 (*ITA 2007*) unless otherwise stated

Annuity paid net of basic rate tax	s.686 Income Tax (Trading & Other Income) Act 2005
Trust tax rates	s.479
Discretionary trust basic rate band	s.491
The tax pool	s.498

Inheritance Tax

References are to Inheritance Tax Act 1984 (*IHTA 1984*) unless otherwise stated

Exit charge	s.65(1)
Principal charge	s.64
Immediate post death interest trust	s.49A
IHT treatment of QIIP trust	ss.51 – 52

Capital Gains Tax

References are to Taxation of Chargeable Gains Act 1992 *(TCGA 1992)* unless otherwise stated

Rate of CGT	s.4(3)
Annual exempt amount	Sch 2, para 2
Settlor of a trust	s.17
Deemed disposals by trustees	s.71
Death of QIIP beneficiary	s.73
Bare trusts	s.60

HMRC manual references

Trusts, settlements and estates manual

(Found at www.hmrc.gov.uk/manuals/tsemmanual/index.htm)

Introduction to trusts	TSEM1002
Trust income and gains	TSEM3000
Ownership and income tax	TSEM9000
Relevant property trusts	IHTM42000
Settled property	IHTM16000
Trusts and capital gains tax	CG33000c

> This technical reference section is designed to assist you when you are working in the office. It should help you to know where to look for further information on the topics covered in this chapter.

CHAPTER 9

Answer to Interactive question 1

	£
Proceeds	100,000
Less cost	(25,000)
Chargeable gain	75,000
Less annual exempt amount	(5,550)
Taxable gain	69,450
Tax @ 28%	19,446

Answer to Interactive question 2

As the trust was set up after 21 March 2006 it is a relevant property trust and therefore the transfer was a CLT for IHT purposes:

	£
Transfer of value	450,000
Less annual exemptions × 2	(6,000)
	444,000
Less nil rate band	(325,000)
	119,000
Tax @ 25% (question is silent so assume settlor paid the tax)	£29,750

In addition, the transfer was a deemed disposal at market value, so Christine would have had a gain of £350,000 (£450,000 – £100,000).

This gain would have been deferred by a gift relief claim (available for any type of asset, not just business assets as there is also an immediate IHT charge), leaving Christine with no CGT due.

The trustees' base cost in the assets would have been reduced by the gift relief claimed to £100,000 (market value of £450,000 less deferred gain of £350,000).

1   Trust's net income

	Non savings income £	Savings income £	Dividend income £
Rental income (£24,000 – £3,700)	20,300		
Interest £540 × $\frac{100}{80}$		675	
Dividends £1,125 × $\frac{100}{90}$			1,250
Tax @ 20%/20%/10%	4,060	135	125
Less tax credits	–	(135)	(125)
Tax due	4,060	–	–
Trust's net income (ie after tax)	16,240	540	1,125
Less expenses	–	(175)	(1,125)
Trust's net distributable income	16,240	365	Nil

The life tenant is treated as receiving income as follows:

	Net £	Tax suffered £
Non savings income	16,240	4,060
Savings income	365	91
Dividends	Nil	Nil
	16,605	

The tax suffered on the interest income is the grossed up interest received at 20%:

$$£365 \times \frac{100}{80} = £456 \times 20\% = £91$$

2   Trust's income tax liability

	Non savings income £	Dividend income £
Rental income (£33,000 – £4,600)	28,400	
Dividends (£4,000 × 100/90)		4,444
Gross income	28,400	4,444
Less expenses of trust (£1,944 × 100/90)		(2,160)
Amount chargeable at trust rates	28,400	2,284

	£
£1,000 @ 20%	200
£28,400 – £1,000 = £27,400 @ 45%	12,330
£2,284 @ 37.5%	857
£2,160 @ 10%	216
Tax liability	13,603

3 The Sun Discretionary Trust

Trust income tax liability

	Non savings income £	Savings income £	Dividend income £
Property income £(27,435 – 6,350)	21,085		
Interest		22,300	
Dividends (£36,900 × $\frac{100}{90}$)			41,000
Admin expenses (£7,011 × $\frac{100}{90}$)			(7,790)
			33,210

Tax:	£
£1,000 @ 20%	200
£21,085 + £22,300 – £1,000 = £42,385 @ 45%	19,073
£33,210 @ 37.5%	12,454
Income to pay expenses £7,790 @ 10%	779
	32,506

Total liability:	£
Tax on income	32,506
Additional tax liability (charge re tax pool) (W)	12,430
Credit on dividends received of £36,900	(4,100)
Credit on interest (paid gross)	Nil
Income tax payable by the trustees	40,836

WORKING – Tax pool	
Pool b/f at 6 April 2015	5,800
Tax paid at 20%/45% £(200 + 19,073)	19,273
Tax paid at 37.5% less credit at 10% (£33,210 × 27.5%)	9,133
	34,206
Credit on distributions to beneficiaries (£57,000 × 45/55)	(46,636)
Additional tax to pay to HMRC by trustees	(12,430)
Tax pool c/f at 5 April 2016	Nil

George's income tax computation

	£
Trust income £57,000 × 100/(100-45)	103,636
Personal allowance £10,600 – (50% × £3,636)	(8,782)
	94,854

Income tax liability (taxed as non-savings income)	
£31,785 @ 20%	6,357
£63,069 @ 40%	25,228
Less credit on trust distribution	(46,636)
Refund due	(15,051)

4 Trust capital gains tax

	£
Proceeds	38,000
Less cost	(25,000)
Chargeable gain	13,000
Less annual exempt amount (£5,550 ÷ 2 trusts)	(2,775)
Taxable gain	10,225
Tax @ 28%	2,863

5   The Cromwell Discretionary Trust

(a)   *IHT and CGT on creation*

The trust is a relevant property trust so the transfer to the trust was a CLT for IHT purposes:

IHT	£	£
Transfer of value		250,000
Less annual exemptions × 2		(6,000)
		244,000
Less nil rate band (2005/06)	275,000	
Less gross transfers in previous 7 years	(145,000)	
		(130,000)
		114,000
Tax @ 25%		28,500

The transfer was exempt for CGT purposes as cash is not a chargeable asset.

(b)   *Transfer to Sandra*

IHT

When the trustees of a RPT transfer assets to any beneficiary (even the spouse of the settlor) there is an exit charge for IHT purposes.

The charge is based on an assumed transfer by Peter of all the assets in the trust as originally valued at the time the trust was set up, less the nil rate band at the date of the exit as reduced by Peter's gross chargeable transfers in the seven years before he set up the trust.

The tax rate used for this assumed transfer would have been 2.55%, ie 30% × 20% × 17/40. The figure '17' represents the number of complete quarters that had elapsed since the date the trust was set up to the date of the exit (ie 1.7.05 – 1.10.09, so 4 years and 3 months).

CGT

The transfer to Sandra is also a deemed disposal at market value. As there is also an IHT charge (the exit charge) the gain on any asset can be deferred by a gift relief claim. If the claim was made, Sandra's base cost for the shares would have been reduced by the amount of the gain deferred.

(c)   *IHT in July 2015*

On every ten year anniversary of setting up a relevant property trust there is a 10-year, or 'principal', charge.

The charge is based on an assumed transfer by Peter of the current value of the trust assets still in the trust (plus undistributed income from more than five year previously – nil in this instance), as reduced by any available nil rate band, ie the nil rate band at the date of the 10th anniversary as reduced by Peter's gross chargeable transfer made in the 7 years before the trust was originally set up and the exit from the trust in the previous 10 years.

The rate for the principal charge is 30% × 20% ie 6%.

There are no capital gains tax consequences of a principal charge (as nothing leaves the trust).

6   The Cromwell Life Interest Trust

(a) *IHT and CGT on creation*

The trust is a qualifying interest in possession trust so the transfer to the trust was exempt for IHT purposes as the life tenant was Peter's spouse.

The transfer was exempt for CGT purposes as cash is not a chargeable asset.

(b)   *Transfer to Sandra*

IHT

When the trustees of a qualifying interest in possession trust transfer assets to the life tenant there is no transfer of value for IHT purposes. This is because before the transfer the life tenant is treated as owning the assets and after the transfer she actually does own the assets outright, so there has been no reduction in the value of the life tenant's estate.

CGT

The transfer to Sandra is, however, a deemed disposal at market value. As there is not also an IHT charge the gain can only be deferred by a gift relief claim if the assets are qualifying business assets. This is unlikely to be the case for quoted shares which require at least a 5% shareholding.

(c) *IHT and CGT position in July 2015*

IHT

When Sandra dies in July 2015 the trust assets will be included in her death estate as her 'settled property'. As her children are the remaindermen of the trust the assets will be fully chargeable. Any tax due in respect of the settled property will need to be paid by the trustees.

CGT

There is no CGT on the death of a qualifying interest in possession trust life tenant unless gift relief was claimed when the assets entered the trust. As there was no CGT when the trust was set up, there is no gain on Sandra's death.

CHAPTER 10

Corporation tax for a single company

Introduction

Examination context

Topic List

1 Corporation tax computation

2 Research and development expenditure

3 Intangible fixed assets (IFAs)

4 Real Estate Investment Trusts (REITs) and Property Authorised Investment Funds (AIFs)

5 Companies with investment business

6 Substantial shareholding exemption

Summary and Self-test

Technical reference

Answers to Interactive questions

Answers to Self-test

Introduction

Learning objective

- Determine, explain and calculate the corporation tax liabilities for corporate entities

Specific syllabus reference for this chapter is 1f.

Syllabus links

Some of this chapter is revision from Tax Compliance – the corporation tax computation for example. These are core topics which underpin the next few chapters. You must ensure that you can complete a basic corporation tax computation before you attempt to complete a group losses question for example. The substantial shareholding exemption is examined further in a groups context in Chapter 14.

Examination context

In the examination candidates may be required to:

- Explain when an additional deduction may be made for research and development expenditure and when a tax credit may be claimed

- Explain when the disposal of a shareholding is an exempt disposal

1 Corporation tax computation

Section overview

- Corporation tax is payable by a UK resident company on its worldwide taxable total profits.
- Corporation tax is chargeable for accounting periods.
- An accounting period cannot exceed 12 months.
- Taxable total profits consists of income (Trading income, Property income, Profits on non-trading loan relationships, Miscellaneous income) and chargeable gains less qualifying donations.

1.1 Introduction

Corporation tax is payable by a UK resident company on its worldwide profits. Corporation tax is chargeable for accounting periods.

An accounting period cannot exceed twelve months. Where a company has a period of account which exceeds twelve months, it must be split into two accounting periods.

A company's corporation tax computation is based upon the figures in its accounts provided those accounts are prepared either in accordance with UK GAAP or IAS. Rules exist to prevent companies in the same group from obtaining a tax advantage from the use of IAS by one company and UK GAAP by another in relation to the same transaction.

The rest of this first section revises some of the main points that were seen at Tax Compliance. You should also refer to the summary at the beginning of this text which explains in detail the changes made by Finance Act 2015.

1.2 Computing Taxable Total Profits

You have already dealt with the basic computation of taxable total profits at Tax Compliance. Here is a summary of the main points of a taxable total profits computation:

Profit/expenditure	Treatment
Trading income	Profit for a period of account adjusted for tax purposes. No private use adjustments, no adjustments for appropriations of profit (eg an owner director's salary). Includes interest paid/received on trading loan relationships.
	Also includes the profits of an overseas permanent establishment, unless they are exempt (by election). Double taxation relief applies where profits are taxed both in the UK and the foreign country.
Property income – profits of a property business	Accruals basis for income and expenses. Interest to buy or improve let property is dealt with under loan relationships not property income.
	UK income received gross.
	Includes foreign rental income. Double taxation relief gives relief where foreign income is taxed both in the UK and the foreign country.
Non-trading loan relationships	Interest paid/received from non-trading loan relationships. Received gross. Also includes income from overseas securities.
Company distributions	Dividends from UK and foreign companies which do not fall within the exempt categories (see below).
Miscellaneous income	Received gross.

Profit/expenditure	Treatment
Chargeable gains	Generally computed as for individuals, but companies receive indexation allowance to date of disposal, but no annual exempt amount.
Qualifying donations	Qualifying charitable donations. Amount paid is the gross amount to be deducted in the computation of taxable total profits.
Exempt dividends received	Not included in taxable total profits. Includes most dividends from UK and foreign companies (see below).
	Exempt dividends received from companies which are not associated companies/ related 51% group companies are grossed up to give Franked Investment Income (FII).
	FII = cash dividend received × 100/90
	FII + taxable total profits = augmented profits
	The augmented profits figure is used to determine the corporation tax rate (up to the financial year 2014), and are also used to determine whether corporation tax should be paid in instalments

1.3 Dividends received

Dividends are taxed as follows.

- All dividends received, whether received from UK companies or overseas companies, are subject to the same rules.

- All dividends received are exempt from corporation tax if they fall within the list of exemptions.

The exemptions are different depending on whether the company receiving the dividend is defined as small.

Broadly, dividends received by small companies are exempt if:

- They are received from a UK company or a company resident in a country with which the UK has a double tax treaty with a non-discrimination clause, and

- The dividend is not paid as part of a scheme that has the obtaining of a UK tax advantage as one of its main purposes.

In addition, dividends received by a small company are exempt if they are paid out of chargeable profits which have been subject to an apportionment under the CFC rules which apply from 1 January 2013 and are not part of a scheme that has the obtaining of a UK tax advantage as one of its main purposes.

Dividends received by companies which are not small are exempt if they fall under one of five exempt categories:

- Received from a company that is controlled by the recipient, or
- Relate to non-redeemable ordinary shares, or
- Received from a portfolio holding of the share class concerned (ie <10% holding), or
- Relate to a transaction not designed to reduce UK tax (the motive test), or
- Relate to shares accounted for as liabilities which are not held for an unallowable purpose.

Definition

A small company for exempt dividend provisions: A company which has:

- Fewer than 50 employees; and

- Either:

  – An annual turnover not exceeding €10 million (approximately £8.5m); or
  – A balance sheet total not exceeding €10 million (approximately £8.5m).

Points to note:

- The exemptions available for dividends are wide ranging and therefore, in almost all cases, dividends received will be exempt dividends.

- Although exempt dividends are not chargeable to corporation tax, if they are received from companies which are not related 51% group companies (or non-associated companies until FY 2014) they are included in franked investment income. They and are therefore taken into account when determining whether to pay corporation tax in instalments and determining the rate of tax charged (until FY 2014) - see below.

1.4 Summary of capital allowances for companies

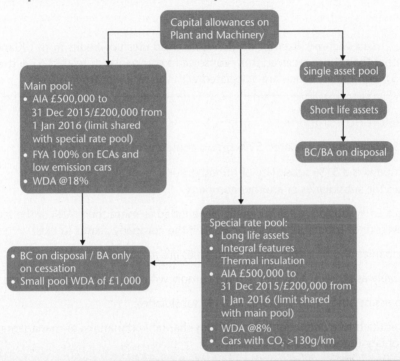

Prior to 1 April 2012 the AIA limit was £100,000 per annum. From 1 April to 31 December 2012, it was the equivalent of £25,000 for a 12-month period (pro-rated). From 1 January 2013 to 31 March 2014 it was £250,000 for a 12-month period. The £500,000 limit applies from 1 April 2014 until 31 December 2015. From 1 January 2016 the AIA is £200,000 for a 12-month period Transitional rules apply to periods straddling changes in the limit.

Within a group of companies there is only one AIA. This can be allocated in any way that the group requires.

1.5 Computation of corporation tax

In Tax Compliance you learnt that:

- Until financial year 2014 (FY2014) the rate of corporation tax depended on the augmented profits of a company and the financial year in which the accounting period falls.

- The augmented profits of a company are taxable total profits plus FII (franked investment income).

- Until FY 2014 there were two rates of corporation tax: main rate and small profits rate.

- Until FY2014 marginal relief applied where augmented profits fell between the upper and lower limits.

- Upper and lower limits were scaled down in a short accounting period.

- Upper and lower limits were apportioned between a company and its associated companies.

- From FY 2015 there is one unified main rate of corporation tax.

- Where an accounting period falls in more than one financial year and the rates/limits in those financial years are different, taxable total profits, augmented profits and the limits are time apportioned for each financial year.

The unified main rate of corporation tax in FY2015 is 20% (21% in FY 2014). The small profits rate for FY 2014 is 20% [Hp133]. The marginal rates of tax for companies with augmented profits between the upper and lower limits was 21.25% in FY 2014. These rate changes are particularly important when considering the utilisation of losses (see later in this text).

For the purposes of calculating FII the amount of the dividend received is always grossed up by a 100/90 tax credit regardless of whether it is received from a UK or overseas company. Any foreign taxes suffered on the dividend are ignored.

Definition

Franked Investment Income: Exempt dividends received plus tax credits from UK and overseas companies, other than those received from consortium companies or related 51% group companies (from FY 2015)/ companies which are associated with the recipient (to FY 2014).

1.5.1 Related 51% group companies

From FY 2015 a company is a related 51% group company of another company if:

- One company is a 51% subsidiary of the other; or
- Both are 51% subsidiaries of another company.

A company is a 51% subsidiary if it is beneficially entitled to more than 50% of the issued share capital or voting power; or distributable profits; or assets if the company ceases to exist.

Dormant companies and passive holding companies are excluded.

In order to qualify as passive, a company must comply with the following conditions:

(a) It has no assets other than shares in its 51% subsidiaries;

(b) It is not entitled to a deduction, as qualifying charitable donations or management expenses, in respect of any outgoings; and

(c) It has no income or gains other than dividends which it has distributed in full to its shareholders.

1.5.2 Associated companies – basic principles

The upper and lower limits apply to a company and its associates, and are important to determine the correct corporation tax rate until FY2014.

A company is associated with another company if:

- One company is under the control of the other; or
- Both are under common control of a third party (individual, partnership or another company).

Control means control over more than 50% of the issued share capital or voting power; or distributable profits; or assets if the company ceases to exist.

1.5.3 Associated companies – additional points

In determining the number of associated companies, the following should be considered:

- A company is associated with all of its associates' associates.

  In the following example, all of the companies are associated with each other ie four associated companies in total.

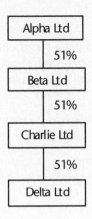

Alpha Ltd
51%
Beta Ltd
51%
Charlie Ltd
51%
Delta Ltd

- Overseas companies are included as associated companies.

- Dormant companies are excluded.

- Passive holding companies are excluded.

- Companies are associated if they are owned for only part of an accounting period.

- It is possible for two companies to be associated via ownership by an individual (unlike related 51% holding companies). If there is no substantial interdependence between the companies only the shareholdings of the individual himself are considered when determining which companies are associated.

  If there is substantial commercial interdependence between companies, HMRC will include in a person's shareholding the shares owned by all of his associates. For this purpose, a person is associated with his immediate relatives: ie his spouse/civil partner, grandparents, parents, siblings, children and grandchildren.

  Therefore, where there is substantial commercial interdependence it is possible for two companies to be associated when they would not normally be. For example where one company is owned 100% by the father, and the other company is owned 100% by the son.

  Examples of substantial interdependence include where one company gives financial support (directly or indirectly) to the other, the companies have common customers, or the businesses of the companies have or use common management/premises/equipment.

- Companies are associated where they are under the common control of the same person or persons. Consider the following examples:

  Example 1

	A Ltd	B Ltd
Mr A	50%	50%
Mr B	50%	50%

  The same two people control both companies, A Ltd and B Ltd are therefore associated.

  Example 2

	A Ltd	B Ltd
Mr A	51%	49%
Mr B	49%	51%

  Mr A controls A Ltd and Mr B controls B Ltd. The two companies are therefore controlled by different persons and will not therefore be associated.

Worked example: Associated companies

A Ltd is owned by Shaun (50%), Jenny (25%) and Gill (25%). A Ltd is a passive holding company, its only source of income is dividends received from its wholly owned trading subsidiaries. A Ltd owns 100% of B Ltd, C Ltd and D SpA (incorporated and managed and controlled in Italy).

Gill also owns 100% of the shares in P Ltd, a trading company.

Requirement

Explain how many associated companies there are.

Solution

B Ltd, C Ltd and D SpA are all associated companies as they are not dormant and are under the common control of A Ltd. A Ltd can be excluded from the number of associated companies as it is a passive holding company with dividends from its 51% subsidiaries as its sole source of income. D SpA is included regardless of where in the world it is resident.

P Ltd is not associated with B Ltd, C Ltd or D SpA as P Ltd and A Ltd are controlled by different persons. A Ltd could be controlled by either Shaun & Gill or Shaun & Jenny whereas P Ltd is controlled by Gill.

There are therefore three associated companies.

Interactive question 1: Corporation tax liability [Difficulty level: Easy]

B Ltd has one wholly owned UK subsidiary, F Ltd, and makes up its accounts to 31 December each year. For the year ended 31 December 2015, it had the following results:

	£
Trading profits before deducting interest and capital allowances	500,000
Capital allowances	19,900
Building society interest (BSI) received in the year	95,000
Chargeable gain on sale of office block	150,000
Interest received in the year on loan stock in C Ltd	61,400
Qualifying charitable donation	9,240
Interest payable on loan stock to D Ltd (Note 1)	100,000
Dividends received from F Ltd	50,000
Dividends received from Z Inc (Note 2)	20,000
Dividend paid	40,000

	BSI	C Ltd Loan stock interest
	£	£
Accrued income b/f	20,000	1,000
Accrued income c/f	25,000	3,600

Notes

(1) The funds raised from the loan stock issued to D Ltd were used to acquire plant and machinery.

(2) B Ltd owns 5% of the ordinary share capital of Z Inc, an overseas resident trading company. B Ltd is not a small company for the purposes of the exempt dividend rules.

Requirement

Calculate B Ltd's corporation tax liability for the year ended 31 December 2015.

See **Answer** at the end of this chapter.

---

2 Research and development expenditure

Section overview

- Qualifying R&D involves developing or improving the science or technology of a company's products, processes and services.

- Qualifying R&D is an allowable deduction from trading profits for companies.

- Where a company incurs qualifying R&D, it may deduct an additional amount representing 130% (small and medium companies) or 30% (large companies) of the actual expenditure.

- A small or medium sized company which has a surrenderable loss may claim a R&D tax credit of 14.5% of the surrenderable loss.

- From 1 April 2013, large companies can choose to claim a taxable 'above the line' tax credit instead of an increased deduction.

- The above the line credit is 11% of the qualifying R&D, capped at the lower of the net credit (ie after a notional 20% corporation tax deduction) and the PAYE and NIC relating to the R&D activities if it cannot be offset against the company's current period corporation tax liability.

2.1 What is research and development (R&D) expenditure?

R&D for tax purposes is defined with reference to guidelines produced by the Department for Business, Innovation and Skills.

An example of projects which would qualify as R&D are ones intended to:

- Extend overall knowledge or capability in a field of science or technology; or

- Create a process, material, device, product or service which incorporates or represents an increase in overall knowledge or capability in a field of science or technology; or

- Make an appreciable improvement to an existing process, material, device, product or service through scientific or technological changes; or

- Use science or technology to duplicate the effect of an existing process, material, device, product or service in a new or appreciably improved way.

The project must also seek to achieve an advance in overall knowledge or capability in a field of science or technology, not just the company's own state of knowledge or capability. It can include the production of a prototype, and trial production where it is needed to resolve technological uncertainty.

Routine or cosmetic improvements are not qualifying R&D.

Qualifying R&D expenditure includes revenue expenditure on:

- Staff directly or indirectly engaged on R&D
- External staff provider who provides staff to be directly engaged on R&D
- Consumable or transformable materials (see below)
- Computer software
- Power, water and fuel
- Subcontracting out R&D activities (but see further below in relation to large companies)

From 1 April 2015 relief for consumable materials is restricted if the consumable is incorporated into an item which becomes part of normal production. For the purposes of the exam it is assumed that all consumables are qualifying expenditure, unless stated otherwise.

Where staff are indirectly engaged in R&D, the expenditure only qualifies if it is specifically identifiable as a particular part of the activity of an R&D project eg training, maintenance, secretarial or payroll directly required for the R&D project. In order to qualify it must also be capable of being accounted for as R&D expenditure under UK GAAP or IAS.

2.2 Externally provided workers and subcontracted expenditure

For externally provided workers and subcontracted expenditure, only some of the expenditure may be allowable as qualifying R&D expenditure. If the workers are supplied by an unconnected company then only 65% of the payments made in respect of them will be qualifying expenditure. Where the provider is a connected company then the qualifying expenditure will be that paid up to a maximum of the provider's relevant expenditure in providing the staff. The company can elect for any company to be treated as a connected company.

Small or medium-sized entities (SMEs) can claim the large company relief (see below) where work is sub-contracted to them by a large company, or other person which would not qualify for the SME relief. The SME must either carry out the research itself, or the work must be undertaken by a research organisation (such as a university) or individual which would not qualify for the R&D relief in its own right.

2.3 Capital expenditure on R&D

In addition, capital expenditure on R&D (excluding the cost of land, if any) is also wholly allowable as a trading deduction ie 100% capital allowances are available in the year of purchase. If the capital assets are subsequently sold, the proceeds are taxed as a trading receipt.

Computer software is included in the qualifying expenditure eligible for the additional deduction from trading profits. Computer hardware is eligible for a 100% initial allowance as capital expenditure relating to R&D.

2.4 Additional deduction from trading profits for R&D expenditure

Where a company incurs qualifying R&D expenditure, it may deduct the expenditure as an allowable expense from trading profits under the usual rules. It may also take an additional deduction from trading profits. The amount of the additional deduction depends on whether the company is small/medium-sized or is a large company. There is no minimum expenditure threshold for the rules to apply.

Definition

Small or medium sized enterprise (SME) for R&D: A company which has:

- Fewer than 500 employees; and

- Either:
  - An annual turnover not exceeding €100 million (approximately £87m); or
  - An annual balance sheet total not exceeding €86 million (approximately £75m).

A company which is not within this definition is a large company.

Note that this definition is not the same as for exempt dividends. In the examination, you will be told whether a company is a SME or a large company.

A SME may take an additional 130% (125% for expenditure before 1 April 2015) deduction from trading profits although the total R&D aid per project cannot exceed €7.5m [Hp136]. Where expenditure is capped, additional relief is given at 30% (ie the large company rate of deduction). The additional deduction is only available where the SME's last accounts were prepared on a going concern basis, and the company is not in liquidation or administration.

A large company may take an additional 30% deduction from trading profits (ie 100% less than SMEs).

In general, a large company can only claim for R&D expenditure if it carries out the R&D itself. If a SME undertakes the work as a subcontractor, it can claim an additional 30% deduction (large company deduction) instead of the usual 130% (SME deduction).

Company	Additional deduction	Total allowable deduction
SME	130%	230%
Large company (or SME working as a subcontractor)	30%	130%

2.5 R&D tax credits for SMEs

If a SME has a **surrenderable loss** in an accounting period in which it is entitled to an additional deduction from trading profits, it may convert all or part of that loss into a **R&D tax credit**.

Definition

Surrenderable loss: Lower of:

- Trading loss for the accounting period after:

    - Any s.37(3)(a) CTA 2010 current period relief that could be claimed against other income and gains (regardless of whether it is actually claimed);

    - Any other loss relief actually obtained; and

    - Any amount surrendered under group relief to group or consortium members.

- 230% of the qualifying R&D expenditure.

You will learn about trading losses and group relief later on in this study manual. For the moment, we will explain how loss relief works, where relevant.

Definition

R&D tax credit for SMEs: 14.5% of the surrenderable loss.

Where the SME R&D tax credit is claimed, the trading loss carried forward is reduced by the amount of the loss surrendered to obtain the tax credit.

The SME R&D tax credit is not a taxable receipt. It will usually be paid to the company by HMRC. If the company has outstanding corporation tax, the R&D tax credit may be used to set against that liability.

Worked example: SME R&D tax credit

P Ltd is a small company. In the year to 31 March 2016, it has the following results:

	£
Trading profit (before taking into account R&D expenditure)	162,500
Qualifying R&D expenditure	270,000
Bank interest receivable	5,000
Chargeable gain	70,000

Requirement

Compute the R&D tax credit that P Ltd may claim.

Solution

Trading loss

	£
Trading profit before R&D expenditure	162,500
Less 230% R&D deduction (£270,000 × 230%)	(621,000)
Trading loss	(458,500)
Less s.37(3)(a) CTA 2010 possible claim	75,000
Adjusted trading loss	(383,500)

The company could make a claim under s.37(3)(a) CTA 2010 to set £75,000 of the trading loss against its interest income and chargeable gain for the period. This therefore reduces the amount of the loss which can be treated as a surrenderable loss.

Surrenderable loss: lower of

Adjusted trading loss	£383,500
230% R&D	£621,000
ie	£383,500

R&D tax credit:

14.5% of surrenderable loss: 14.5% × £383,500	£55,608

The losses carried forward will be reduced by £383,500.

2.6 Above the line R&D tax credits for large companies

From 1 April 2013, large companies can elect for a tax credit regime to apply to their R&D expenditure. This can also apply to SMEs where qualifying R&D work is subcontracted to them by large companies. The credit which is given under these rules is intended to be recorded 'above the line' (ie in arriving at pre-tax profits) for accounts purposes.

If an election is made, these rules apply instead of the enhanced deduction rules set out above. Once an election is made it remains in place for future periods. The tax credit rules will apply in place of the enhanced deduction rules for all large companies from 1 April 2016.

Definition

Amount of the R&D tax credit for large companies: 11% of the qualifying R&D expenditure (10% for expenditure before 1 April 2015).

The definition of R&D and the rules regarding qualifying expenditure are the same as for the deduction rules, set out in paragraphs 2.1 and 2.2 above.

The large company R&D credit is treated as follows:

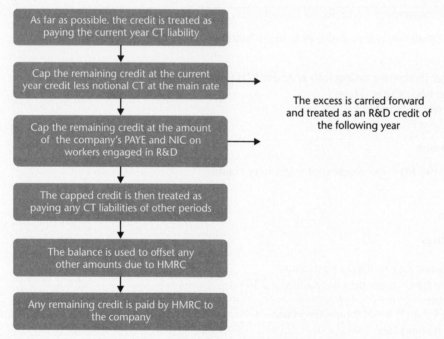

The credit is included in the calculation of the company's taxable total profits.

Notional tax amounts are offset against the CT liabilities of future periods before credits arising in the future periods.

No amounts are payable by HMRC to the company if the company is not a going concern at the time when the claim is submitted, or if the company has outstanding PAYE or NIC liabilities.

Capped amounts (regardless of which cap they arise under) are treated as credits of the next period or can be surrendered to group members (if a member of a group).

Worked example: Large company R&D tax credit

Q plc is a large company. In the year to 31 March 2016, it has qualifying R&D expenditure of £860,000. Q plc has been making trading losses for several years, and has no CT liabilities outstanding for earlier years. It also has no other liabilities to HMRC other than corporation tax on a gain of £250,000 in the year to 31 March 2016.

Its PAYE and NIC costs for employees engaged in R&D for the year to 31 March 2016 are £97,400.

Requirement

Compute the R&D tax credit that Q plc can claim assuming it has elected into the large company R&D credit regime, and explain how it will be used.

Solution

Taxable profit

Trading profit	Nil	
Chargeable gain	250,000	
TTP	250,000	
Step 1 Tax @20%	50,000	
Less ATL credit 11% × £860,000	(94,600)	
Amount remaining (after discharged liability)	(44,600)	
Step 2 CAP £94,600 – (£94,600 × 20%) = £75,680	n/a	(£44.6K< £75,680)
Step 3 CAP PAYE/NIC liabilities £97,400	n/a	(£44.6K< £97,400)
Repayable	(44,600)	

The R&D tax credit is 11% × £860,000 = £94,600. This credit is taxable but as the company is making trading losses it will not affect the CT liability in this example.

The current year CT liability is 20% of the chargeable gain, ie £50,000. First the credit pays the current year liability. The remaining credit is therefore £44,600.

The first cap is applied: the net value of the set-off amount is £75,680 (ie £94,600– 20% × £94,600), so there is no cap.

The PAYE and NIC cap is then applied to the remaining credit. As the PAYE and NIC is more than the amount of the credit, there is no cap.

£44,600 is payable by HMRC to the company.

3 Intangible fixed assets (IFAs)

Section overview

- The tax treatment of IFAs follows the accounting treatment ie debits and credits are deducted/taxed as trading expenses/income.

- An election to claim a deduction of 4% pa may be made instead of amortisation/impairment losses.

- A form of rollover relief is available where a company realises an IFA and reinvests in a new IFA.

- Indirect expenditure on IFAs may be taken into account for the purposes of reinvestment relief.

- From 1 April 2013 companies which own patents are able to elect for profits relating to patents to arise within a 'patent box'.

- A proportion of patent box profits will effectively suffer a lower rate of corporation tax.

C H A P T E R

10

3.1 The tax treatment of IFAs

The following is a summary of the treatment of IFAs acquired on or after 1 April 2002:

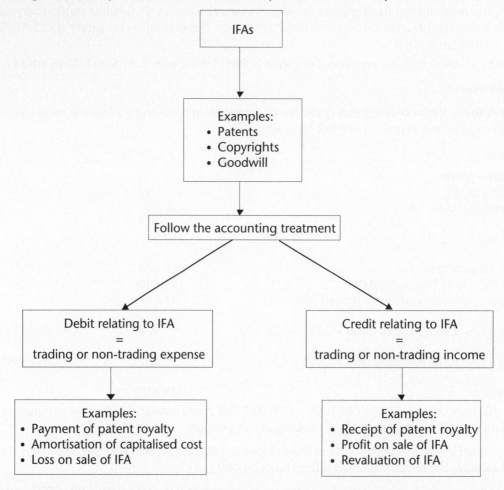

Note that goodwill includes both purchased goodwill and internally generated goodwill. Where a business was carried on before 1 April 2002 any internally generated goodwill is deemed to arise before 1 April 2002 and therefore does not fall within the IFA rules.

A net credit arising on non-trading IFAs is taxed as miscellaneous income. If a net loss arises from non-trading IFAs, all or part of it may be set against total profits of the same accounting period or group relieved. Otherwise it is carried forward and treated as a non-trading IFA debit of the following accounting period.

3.2 Treatment of IFAs

3.2.1 Alternative to the accounting treatment

Instead of following the accounting treatment, companies may elect to disallow any accounting debits arising from amortisation and impairment losses on capitalised assets and, instead, claim a straight line WDA of 4% pa. The election must be made within two years of the end of the accounting period in which the asset is created or acquired.

3.2.2 Subsequent realisation of a gain on an IFA

- A realisation occurs when an IFA

    - Is sold; or
    - Becomes valueless; or
    - Effectively ceases to exist.

The profit/loss on realisation of an IFA will be treated as follows:

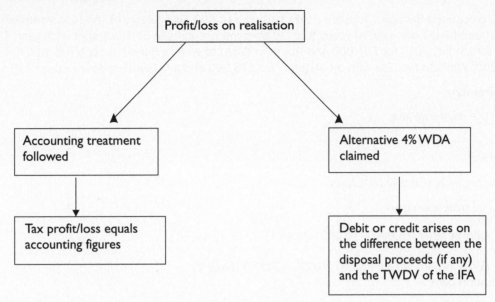

3.2.3 Goodwill acquired from a related party on incorporation

This section is new.

For incorporations on or after 3 December 2014 relief is generally restricted to nil for internally-generated goodwill where there is continuing economic ownership (eg on incorporation).

This aligns the treatment of incorporated businesses with those that do not incorporate, or those that initially set up as a company, neither of whom can get relief for internally-generated goodwill. This is intended to be a disincentive to incorporate purely for tax reasons and is part of a package of measures including the restriction to entrepreneurs' relief for goodwill on incorporation (Chapter 6).

3.3 Rollover relief for reinvestment in new IFAs

If a company makes a gain on the realisation of an IFA and re-invests in a new IFA, a claim for rollover relief may be made.

The key features of this relief are as follows:

- The relief is deducted from the cost of the new asset and from the realisation proceeds

- The reinvestment must be made within one year before and three years after the disposal

- The relief is the excess of the proceeds on realisation over the original cost

- Where the proceeds are not fully reinvested, the relief is the amount reinvested less the cost of the original asset

3.3.1 Indirect expenditure on IFAs

In rolling over gains on the realisation of IFAs, it is possible to rollover into both the:

- Direct purchase of a new IFA; and/or

- The purchase of shares in a company where the value reflects IFAs held by that company (or a subsidiary).

The acquiring company (company A) may treat the price it paid for the shares as qualifying expenditure in IFAs held by the company being acquired (company B).

The amount of deemed expenditure on IFAs is the lower of:

- The cost of acquiring the shares in company B, or
- The TWDV of the IFAs held by company B.

Worked example: IFAs and rollover relief via indirect expenditure

Bird Ltd acquired the rights to trade marks costing £10,000 on 1 July 2013. Bird Ltd writes off such costs on a straight line basis over 10 years. Bird Ltd prepares accounts to 31 December each year. The rights were sold in July 2015 for £21,000 and shares in Wire Ltd were acquired in September 2015 for £23,000. Wire Ltd has IFAs with an original cost £18,000 and a tax written down value of £13,000.

Requirement

Show the relief available.

Solution

Rollover relief is available as follows:

	£
Original realisation gain	
Proceeds	21,000
Less rollover relief (13,000 – 10,000) (Note 1)	(3,000)
	18,000
Less TWDV of Bird Ltd's IFA sold (10,000 – 2,000) (Note 2)	(8,000)
Realisation gain	10,000

The TWDV of the underlying IFAs in Wire Ltd is then reduced by the amount of rollover relief ie (£13,000 – 3,000) = £10,000

Notes:

(1) The TWDV of the underlying IFAs in Wire Ltd of £13k is less than the sale proceeds of £21k from the sale of Bird Ltd's IFAs. Full rollover relief is therefore not available. Relief is restricted to the excess of the TWDV of Wire Ltd's IFAs over the original cost of the IFAs sold by Bird Ltd.

(2) Under IAS 38/ FRS 102 (section 18) amortisation is calculated from the date the asset is first brought into use to the date it is derecognised in the accounts. Therefore amortisation is calculated as:

Y/e 31.12.13 = 10% × £10,000 × 6/12 = £500
Y/e 31.12.14 = 10% × £10,000 = £1,000
Y/e 31.12.15 = 10% × £10,000 × 6/12 = £500

Alternative:

An alternative approach is to consider how the gain would be taxed under capital gains principles. As this is more familiar to you, you may find it easier to remember:

The amount to be taxed (ie the realisation gain) follows the accounts ie proceeds less carrying value:

= £21,000 – £8,000 = £13,000

The amount of gain that would have been taxed had the IFA been taxed as a capital gain ie proceeds less cost:

£21,000 – £10,000 = £11,000

If the full proceeds of £21,000 had been reinvested the full gain of £11,000 could be rolled over and therefore only £2,000 would be taxed (£13,000 - £11,000). However as the full proceeds were not reinvested, the rollover relief needs to be restricted by the amount not reinvested ie by £8,000. Rollover relief is therefore restricted to:

£11,000 – £8,000 = £3,000

The taxable amount (ie the realisation gain) is the accounts figure less the rollover relief:

£13,000 – £3,000 = £10,000

3.4 Patent box

From 1 April 2013, companies which own patents, or exclusive licenses to exploit patents, are able to elect for the profits relating to the patents to arise within a 'patent box' which effectively suffer a lower rate of corporation tax.

In order to qualify, the company must carry on 'qualifying development' in relation to the patent, which includes both development of the patent itself or of products incorporating the patent. While the rules permit a group to be looked at as a single entity to some extent, the claimant company itself must carry on at least active management of the patents.

Where an election is made the company must calculate the deduction to be made from taxable profits:

- Determine the profit attributable to its patents (including any income from products which incorporate a patent although there is no need to split out the part which does not directly relate to the patent). The legislation provides for this to be done either by calculating the ratio of patent-related income to other income and then applying that ratio to the company's profits, or by setting up a separate profit and loss account, and

- Deduct from that profit a notional return of 10% of the costs allocated to the patent business. In most cases, a further deduction for a notional marketing royalty determined on an arm's length basis is needed. This marketing royalty deduction is either:

    - To remove a return on marketing assets used to generate relevant IP income, by deducting a notional marketing royalty for use of the assets; or

    - Provided the company's patent profits after deduction of the 10% notional return are less than a maximum amount of £3 million, it can elect to apply small claims treatment to those remaining profits. The small claims treatment removes 25% of those remaining profits as a deemed marketing return, leaving the remaining 75% (up to a maximum £1 million 'small claims threshold') inside the patent box.

A 10% effective rate of corporation tax is applied to the resulting net profit figure, by a deduction from taxable profits. The additional deduction is calculated using the formula:

RP × FY% × ((MR − IPR) ÷ MR), where:

- RP is the profits of a company's trade relevant to patent box
- FY% is the appropriate percentage for each financial year
- MR is the main rate of corporation tax
- IPR is the reduced rate of 10%

The appropriate percentage reflects the fact that the benefit is being phased in. In FY 2015 only 80% of the profits within the patent box are taxed at the 10% rate (giving a 12.0% overall rate). The proportion of patent box profits taxed at the 10% rate was 60% in FY 2013, 70% in FY 2014 and will increase to 90% in FY 2016, and 100% in FY 2017.

Worked example: Patent box

Brainstorm plc, which is a stand-alone trading company, develops and markets products incorporating patents. It has analysed its profit and loss account to determine the profits attributable to patents which qualify for the patent box regime as follows:

	y/e 31.3.16	
	£'000	£'000
Turnover	10,375	
Cost	(5,575)	
Patent box streamed profit		4,800
Other trading profits		315
Taxable total profits before patent box adjustment		5,115

A transfer pricing study has concluded that the notional marketing royalty to be deducted in computing the patent box profits is 4% of the related turnover.

Requirement

Calculate Brainstorm plc's corporation tax payable for the year ended 31 March 2016, assuming the main rate is 20% and it elects for the patent box rules to apply and for its patent box profits to be streamed.

Solution

	£'000	£'000
Taxable total profit before patent box adjustment		5,115
Patent box streamed profit	4,800	
Less 10% return on costs (10% × £5,575,000)	(558)	
Less marketing royalty (4% × £10,375,000)	(415)	
Patent box profit	3,827	
Patent box deduction £3,827,000 × 80% × ((20 – 10)/20)		(1,531)
Taxable total profits		3,584
Corporation tax payable £3,584,000 × 20%		717

4 Real Estate Investment Trusts (REITs) and Property Authorised Investment Funds (AIFs)

Section overview

- A REIT is a company with special status allowing qualifying property income and gains to be exempt from corporation tax.

- Distributions paid from such income are treated as property income of the shareholder. Individual shareholders are treated as receiving such dividends from REITs net of the basic rate of tax.

- A Property AIF (PAIF) is a form of Authorised Investment Fund, the investments of which consist of property or shares in UK REITs. An AIF can elect to come within the PAIF regime such that property income and gains are exempt from corporation tax.

4.1 REITs

A company or group can elect to become a Real Estate Investment Trust (REIT). The main advantage of making a REIT election is that qualifying property income and gains are then exempt from corporation tax. Any non-qualifying income and gains are taxable at the main rate.

In addition:

- Distributions paid by a REIT from tax exempt income or gains are taxed as if they were property income.

- Distributions paid by a REIT from taxable income or gains are taxed as a UK dividend.

4.1.1 Conditions

In order to be eligible to be a REIT, a company must have a property rental business. This includes:

- UK property businesses, and
- Overseas property businesses.

An investment by one REIT in another REIT is effectively treated as a 'good' property investment.

A number of businesses are specifically excluded, including incidental letting of property held as part of a property development trade and intra-group lettings.

The company also has to satisfy a number of other conditions relating to:

- Being quoted on either a recognised stock exchange or AIM,
- The composition of its property business(es), and the proportion of its non-exempt business, and
- Minimum distribution requirements.

4.1.2 Implications of REIT status

Making the election to become a REIT means that the property rental business carried on prior to becoming a REIT is treated for corporation tax purposes as having ceased. A new tax exempt business is treated as commencing. Therefore one accounting period ends and one accounting period commences (the new accounting period is then tax exempt).

The assets of the pre-entry business are deemed to be sold at market value and then immediately reacquired at market value by the tax exempt business.

Instead of generating balancing adjustments and chargeable gains, a notional charge is made which is taxed as miscellaneous income.

Any losses, deficits, expenses and allowances of the tax exempt and residual taxable business, if any, are ring fenced ie they must be treated separately:

- A loss from the tax exempt business may not be offset against profits of the taxable business and vice versa.

- Losses brought forward as at the date of becoming a REIT cannot be set-off against profits of the tax exempt business but may be set-off against profits of the taxable business.

- If the company ceases to be a REIT, any losses incurred whilst tax exempt cannot be carried forward and set against profits of the same trade which are now taxable.

4.1.3 Distributions by a REIT

- A distribution paid from the tax exempt business of a REIT is property income for the individual/corporate investor.

- Distributions paid to individuals or non-UK resident companies are paid net of basic rate tax. The distribution must be grossed up by 100/80.

- A distribution paid from the taxable business is a normal dividend with a notional tax credit of 10%.

- Distributions may be paid out as cash and/or as stock dividends.

4.1.4 Anti-avoidance

Companies are prevented from restructuring within their groups in order to ensure that one company meets the conditions allowing it to be re-classified as a REIT. This ensures that the regime is only available, as originally intended, to property investment businesses with third party tenants.

4.2 Property Authorised Investment Funds

A Property AIF is a form of Authorised Investment Fund, the investment portfolio of which comprises property or shares in UK REITs. An AIF that is an open-ended investment company can elect (subject to certain conditions) to come within the Property AIF regime which means that property income and gains are exempt from corporation tax.

Investors then pay tax on distributions, depending on the type of income.

4.2.1 Distributions by an AIF

A distribution paid from property income will be treated as property income for the investor.

Interest distributed by a Property AIF will be treated as savings income for an individual investor and as income from a non-trading loan relationship for a corporate investor.

Dividend income distributed to investors will be treated as such ie FII for companies or dividends subject to tax at the normal rates for individual investors.

Distributions out of property income or interest income which are paid to individual investors are paid net of basic rate income tax.

5 Companies with investment business

Section overview

- A company with investment business is permitted to deduct expenses incurred managing its investments from total profits before qualifying charitable donations relief and losses.

- Excess expenses of management may be carried forward indefinitely or surrendered via group relief.

- Anti avoidance legislation prevents the purchase of companies with excess non-trading losses and expenses in order to make use of their losses.

5.1 Introduction

Definition

Company with investment business: Means any company the business of which consists wholly or partly of making of investments.

Corporation tax is applied to companies with an investment business in the normal way. The only exception to this prior to FY2015 was a close investment holding company which was always taxed at the main rate of corporation tax.

5.2 Management expenses

A company with an investment business may also have a trade. The profits of the trade will be computed under normal trading income rules. Any overhead expenses incurred in managing the investments will be deductible as expenses of management.

Management expenses will be deducted from total profits and gains **before** qualifying charitable donations or losses provided the management expenses:

- Relate to the making of investments; and
- The investments are not held for an unallowable purpose.

An unallowable purpose is where the investment is held either:

- For a purpose which is not for a business or commercial purpose of the company eg investments held in a football club supported by one of the directors; or

- For a purpose of activities which are outside the scope of corporation tax eg where a non-resident company uses a UK branch to pay its expenses.

Expenses relating directly to other sources of income are deducted in the normal way; eg property expenses set against property income.

Non-trading loan relationships expenses and losses are dealt with under the loan relationship rules, not as an expense of management.

5.3 Excess expenses of management

Where the company's income and gains are insufficient to absorb the expenses of management, the unrelieved amount may be carried forward indefinitely. The expenses carried forward are set off against future income and gains as if they were expenses of management of that later period.

Alternatively, excess expenses of management may be group relieved in the year in which they are incurred (see later).

5.4 Changes in ownership

Where there is a change in ownership, anti-avoidance legislation prevents companies with unused expenses of management, property business losses, non-trading loan relationship deficits or non-trading losses on intangible fixed assets from being sold in order for the new owner to make use of its various losses.

The rules apply to companies with an investment business, so could also encompass trading companies with non-trading losses.

The rules are very similar to the rules on changes in ownership explained in Chapter 12 and are therefore not repeated here. There is an additional rule that the expenses of management will be lost if there is a significant increase in the company's capital after the change of ownership. For this purpose, a significant increase means that the post change capital is an increase of £1m and is at least 125% of the pre-change capital.

Where the rules apply, excess expenses of management arising prior to the change in ownership cannot be carried forward to after the change.

Interactive question 2: Excess expenses of management   [Difficulty level: Intermediate]

The principal income of Beta Ltd is derived from investments in other UK companies. It also derives income from rented properties and debenture interest. Beta Ltd's results for the eight months ended 31 October 2015 show the following:

	£
Dividends received from other UK companies	972,000
Rental income	59,400
Rental expenses	16,400
Debenture interest received	60,000

Beta Ltd incurs management expenses of £52,500 in the period. In addition, it has excess expenses of management of £23,100 as at 1 March 2015. Beta Ltd is a small company for the purposes of the exempt dividend income rules.

Requirement

Calculate the corporation tax payable by Beta Ltd for the eight months ended 31 October 2015.

See **Answer** at the end of this chapter.

6 Substantial shareholding exemption

Section overview

- The substantial shareholding exemption applies to certain disposals of shares in a trading company by a trading company.

- There must have been a holding of at least 10% for a continuous period of 12 months in the prior 2 years.

- For a company, reorganisation relief on a paper for paper exchange only applies where the substantial shareholding exemption does not apply.

6.1 Conditions

If a trading company, or member of a trading group, disposes of shares in another trading company (or holding company of a trading group) out of a **substantial shareholding**:

- Any capital gain arising is exempt from corporation tax;
- Any capital loss is not allowable.

Definition

Substantial shareholding: One where the investing company owns at least 10% of the ordinary share capital and is beneficially entitled to at least 10% of the:

- Distributable profits; and
- Assets on a winding up; and

these conditions have been satisfied for a continuous period of 12 months during the 2 years preceding the disposal.

The investing company must have been a trading company (or member of a trading group) throughout the period:

- Beginning with the start of the latest twelve month period in which the substantial shareholding conditions were satisfied; and

- Ending with the time of the disposal.

Note that for the purposes of the substantial shareholding exemption a group is made up of companies which are at least 51% subsidiaries (ie both legal and beneficial ownership is greater than 50%).

The exemption applies to the disposal of the whole or part of the substantial shareholding.

Note that it is not necessary that the shares to which the exemption applies are the ordinary shares to which the substantial shareholdings condition applies. If the substantial shareholdings condition is met in relation to ordinary shares, a sale of, say, fixed rate preference shares in the same company is exempt, irrespective of the percentage of those shares held by the disposing company, and of the period for which the preference shares have been held.

As the substantial shareholding must have been held for a continuous period of 12 months in the previous two years, it will continue to be a substantial holding for a maximum of 12 months after the holding has fallen below 10%. This allows a series of part disposals to qualify for the exemption.

Worked example: Substantial shareholding

Answer plc and Ballyhoo Ltd are trading companies. Answer plc acquired 200,000 ordinary shares (a 20% holding) in Ballyhoo Ltd on 1 January 2013.

Answer plc sold 120,000 shares on 30 June 2015. It then sold a further 30,000 shares on 31 January 2016 with the remaining shares being sold on 30 September 2016.

Requirement

Explain whether the substantial shareholding exemption applies to each of the disposals.

Solution

Shareholding history

	%
1 January 2013	20
30 June 2015	(12)
	8
31 January 2016	(3)
	5
30 September 2016	(5)
	Nil

30 June 2015

In the two year period prior to the disposal on 30 June 2015 Answer plc held at least 10% for at least 12 months. The 10% test is therefore satisfied and the substantial shareholding exemption applies to this disposal.

31 January 2016

Although Answer plc only held 8% of Ballyhoo Ltd on 31 January 2016, it had held at least 10% for a continuous period of 12 months in the previous two years (eg the 12 months ended 30 June 2015).

The substantial shareholding exemption therefore applies to disposal.

30 September 2016

Answer plc held only 5% of Ballyhoo Ltd on 30 September 2016. In addition, there is no 12 month period in the previous 24 months (1 October 2014 to 30 September 2016) when it held at least 10%.

The substantial shareholding exemption therefore does not apply to this disposal.

6.2 Share for share relief

For companies, where shares or debentures are sold to another company, the possibility of deferring some or all of the gain by taking securities rather than cash as consideration (share for share relief) depends on whether the substantial shareholding exemption (SSE) applies.

Note that the SSE does not apply to transfers that would otherwise be at nil gain/nil loss ie in the same chargeable gains group (see Chapter 14). Nor does it apply to holdings that do not fulfil the conditions ie the company:

- Is not a trading company
- The holding is less than 10%
- Or the shares have not been owned for at least 12 months in the past 2 years

The SSE takes precedence over the share for share rules if a disposal would have taken place in the absence of the share for share rules.

Worked example: SSE or share for share relief?

Company A has held 15% of the shares in company B since 1 January 2005. Company B is taken over by company C. Company A receives shares in company C in exchange for its shares in company B. Companies A and B are both trading companies.

Requirements

(a) Does the substantial shareholding exemption apply?

(b) What difference would it have made if the companies A and C had been members of the same chargeable gains group?

Solution

(a) Yes.

Company A has received shares in C in exchange for shares in B and therefore normally this would qualify under the share for share relief rules. The shares in C would then be treated as having been acquired at the same price and on the same date as the original shares in B.

However, if A had sold the shares for cash the substantial shareholding exemption would have applied. As the SSE takes precedence, A is treated as having sold its shares in B giving rise to an exempt gain or loss and having acquired the shares in C at their market value.

(b) If A and C had been in the same chargeable gains group the transfer would have been at nil gain/nil loss. The SSE does not apply to such transfers and therefore the share for share relief rules would have applied instead.

For companies, the share for share relief is only available if the conditions in the following diagram are satisfied (see Chapter 6):

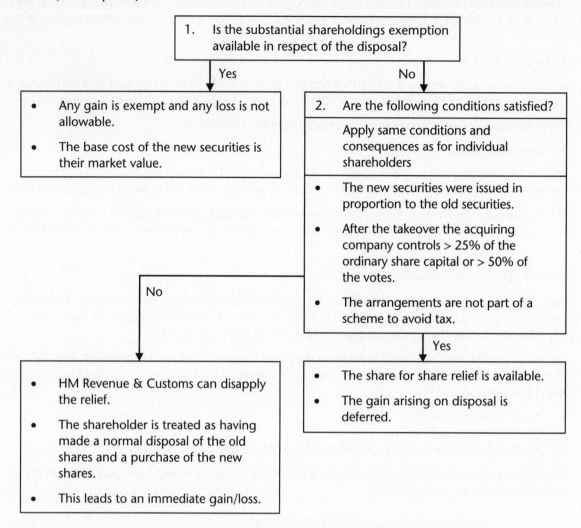

1. Is the substantial shareholdings exemption available in respect of the disposal?

Yes

No

- Any gain is exempt and any loss is not allowable.
- The base cost of the new securities is their market value.

2. Are the following conditions satisfied?

Apply same conditions and consequences as for individual shareholders

- The new securities were issued in proportion to the old securities.
- After the takeover the acquiring company controls > 25% of the ordinary share capital or > 50% of the votes.
- The arrangements are not part of a scheme to avoid tax.

No

Yes

- HM Revenue & Customs can disapply the relief.
- The shareholder is treated as having made a normal disposal of the old shares and a purchase of the new shares.
- This leads to an immediate gain/loss.

- The share for share relief is available.
- The gain arising on disposal is deferred.

The relief can also apply where, as part of a scheme of reconstruction or amalgamation:

- The new company issues shares to the shareholders of the original company in proportion to their shareholdings in the original company, and

- The old shares are either retained or cancelled.

The relief will be disapplied if the arrangements are part of a scheme to avoid tax.

The four situations to consider where shares are sold for different forms of consideration are the same as those for private investors (see Chapter 6). The only difference in the taxation of corporate investors is that QCBs are not exempt for companies. The capital profit or loss will be dealt with under the loan relationships rules rather than as a capital gain or loss.

Summary

```
                      ┌──────────────────────────┐
                      │   Charge to corporation  │
                      │ tax and taxable total profits │
                      └──────────────────────────┘
        ┌──────────────────────┼──────────────────────────┐
        ▼                      ▼                           ▼
┌───────────────┐   ┌──────────────────────┐      ┌──────────────┐
│ UK company    │   │ Accounting period:   │      │ Taxable      │
│ charged on    │   │ cannot exceed 12     │      │ total profits│
│ worldwide profits │ months              │      └──────────────┘
└───────────────┘   └──────────────────────┘
                               ▼
```

Long period of account: • 1st accounting period – 1st 12 months • 2nd accounting period – remainder	**Long period of account apportionment:** Trading profits/Property income: time apportionment Cas – prepare separate calculations for each CAP Non-trading loan relationships: accruals basis Gains/Gift Aid: actual date of disposal/payment

```
                      ┌──────────────────────────┐
                      │     Computation of CT     │
                      └──────────────────────────┘
        ┌──────────────────────┬──────────────────────────┐
        ▼                                     ▼
┌───────────────┐                    ┌──────────────┐
│   FY 2015     │                    │   FY 2014    │
└───────────────┘                    └──────────────┘
        ▼                  ┌──────────────┼──────────────┐
┌───────────────┐          ▼              ▼              ▼
│ Main rate     │
│ (unified):    │
│    20%        │
└───────────────┘
```

Main rate: 21%	Small profits rate: 20%	**Marginal relief:** between the upper and lower limits. Limits scaled down for: • Short accounting period • Associated companies

Research and Development expenditure: developing or improving science or technology of products, processes or services

Additional trading deduction 130% for SMEs 30% for large companies	**SME tax credits:** SME may surrender trading loss for tax credit of 14.5%.	Large company R&D credit • 11% of qualifying expenditure • NIC and PAYE cap can apply • Repayable net of CT deduction • Elect into the regime

Intangible fixed assets

Tax treatment:
• Follow accounting treatment
• Alternative 4% allowance available
• Trading debits or credits
	Rollover relief:
	• Needs reinvestment in:
	  – New IFA
	  – Shares in a company with IFAs
	• Relief deducted from the realisation proceeds and the cost of new IFA restriction on relief if proceeds not fully re-invested

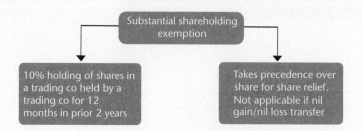

Self-test

Answer the following questions.

1   ABC Ltd, which has no associated companies/ related 51% group companies, has the following results for the year ended 30 November 2015.

	£
Trading profits before interest and royalties	275,000
Rental income net of expenses	20,000
Chargeable gain	42,000
Bank interest receivable	1,320
Patent royalties receivable from X plc	7,800
UK dividends received from shareholding of ordinary shares	18,000
Patent royalties payable to LM Ltd	4,500

Notes

(1)   The company has capital losses brought forward of £10,500.

(2)   Patent royalties receivable include £800 accrued at 30 November 2015. Both patent royalties receivable and patent royalties payable are for trade purposes.

(3)   Debenture interest of £8,000 was payable in the year on a £100,000 8% debenture issued to help finance the purchase of a new factory in 2008.

(4)   On 1 February 2015 the company sold its investment in 3½ % War Loan for £21,000. It had purchased the investment in 2006 for £19,400, and it was recorded in the company's books at cost. No interest was receivable from the War Loan during this accounting period.

Requirement

Calculate the corporation tax payable for the year ended 30 November 2015.

2   Table Ltd, an investment company, has the following results for the year ended 31 March 2016.

	£
Rental income	210,000
Building society interest	11,200
Chargeable gains	140,000
Management expenses	
Property management	56,000
General	70,000
Capital allowances	
On property	1,120
General	1,400
Qualifying charitable donations	65,800

Unrelieved expenses of management carried forward at 1 April 2015 amounted to £84,700.

Requirement

Compute the corporation tax payable for the year ended 31 March 2016.

3   The profit and loss account of Constellation Ltd for the year ended 31 March 2016 may be summarised as follows.

	£	£
Turnover		2,848,245
Less cost of sales (Note 1)		(648,269)
		2,199,976
Less expenses		
Depreciation	22,329	
Staff costs – allowable	915,762	
Other operating expenses (Note 2)	397,628	
Property costs – allowable	93,316	
		(1,429,035)
		770,941
Interest received (Note 3)		12,500
Profit from sale of quoted investments (Note 4)		80,000
Overdraft interest charges		(2,932)
Interest and penalties re VAT		(2,000)
Profit before taxation		858,509

Notes:

(1)   A general stock provision of £25,000 made during the year ended 31 March 2015 was released during the year ending 31 March 2016. This sum was credited to the profit and loss account as an adjustment to cost of sales. The provision was originally disallowed in the 2015 corporation tax computation.

(2)   Other operating expenses shown in the above profit and loss account included the following.

	£
Entertaining UK customers	24,670
Costs of obtaining bank overdraft	12,500
Legal fees re sale of quoted investments	7,850
Increase in specific bad debts	15,000
Miscellaneous allowable expenses	337,608
	397,628

(3)   Interest received was in respect of a bank deposit account as follows.

	£
Receipt 30 September 2015	5,000
Receipt 31 March 2016	7,500

Interest was paid half yearly in arrears. There was no accrued interest at 31 March 2015 or 31 March 2016.

(4)   The investments were sold on 1 September 2015 and represented a 1% shareholding. The profit arising on their sale gave rise to a chargeable gain after indexation allowance of £68,250.

(5)   During the year ended 31 March 2016 the company made the following purchases:

	£
April 2015 Three cars (each costing £8,303 and having CO_2 emissions of 150g/km)	24,909
July 2015 Commercial vehicles	160,800
July 2015 New plant (with expected life of 26 years)	369,000

The value of the main pool of plant and machinery brought forward at 1 April 2015 was £76,000.

In 2016 Constellation Ltd decided to change its accounting reference date to 30 June.

In the period ending 30 June 2016 the directors anticipate that the company's adjusted profit before deduction of capital allowances will be £230,648. Interest accrued in respect of the bank account will be £13,505 and there will be further chargeable gains of £10,095 in addition to any gains on buildings disposals.

Additions to fixed assets during this period are as follows:

	£
April 2016 Jaguar motor car (CO_2 emissions 183g/km)	32,000
May 2016 Plant (with expected life of 22 years)	281,950
June 2016 Four cars (each costing £7,025 with CO_2 emissions of 125g/km)	28,100

On 30 April 2016 Constellation Ltd disposed of a warehouse for a consideration of £194,000. The building was acquired by the company on 1 January 2011 for £150,000. In May 2016 Constellation Ltd purchased a new factory at a cost of £600,000.

Requirement

Calculate the corporation tax payable for the period 1 April 2015 to 30 June 2016 on the assumption that all beneficial reliefs are claimed by the company.

Assume the RPI for April 2016 is 260.5 Ignore VAT.

Now, go back to the Learning objectives in the Introduction. If you are satisfied you have achieved the objectives, please tick it off.

Technical reference

Legislation

References are to Corporation Tax Act 2009 (*CTA 2009*) unless otherwise stated

Corporation tax computation

Charge to corporation tax	s.2
Accounting periods	s.9
Computation of income	s.35
Marginal relief	s.19 CTA 2010
Passive holding company	s.26 CTA 2010
Attribution to persons of rights and powers of their associates	s.27 CTA 2010
Rights to be attributed	ss.450-1 CTA 2010
Exempt dividends	ss.931A-W

R&D expenditure

Entitlement	s.1044, s.1050
Qualifying R&D	s.1051 – s.1053
Subcontracted expenditure	s.1127 – s.1132
Large company credit	s.104A – s.104Y

Intangible fixed assets

Definition of Intangible Fixed Assets		s.712 – s.713
Debits:	Expenditure written off as incurred	s.728
	Amortisation	s.729
Credits:	Receipts recognised as they accrue	s.721 – s.722
	Revaluation	s.723
Goodwill: time of creation (pre April 2002 assets)		s.884

Company with investment business

Definition	s.1218
Relief for expenses of management	s.1219
Carry forward of excess expenses	s.1223
Effect of change in ownership on brought forward excess expenses	ss.677 CTA 2010

Substantial shareholding exemption

SSE	Sch 7AC TCGA 1992
Reorganisations	s.127 TCGA 1992
Paper for paper relief	s.135 TCGA 1992
SSE takes priority over paper for paper relief	s.135 TCGA 1992

Corporation tax administration

Penalty for failure to make return	Sch 55 paras 2 – 5 FA 2009
Payment by instalments	SI 1998/3175

Company Taxation Manual (Found at www.hmrc.gov.uk/manuals/ctmanual/Index.htm)

Corporate Intangibles Research and Development Manual
(Found at www.hmrc.gov.uk/manuals/cirdmanual/index.htm)

Guidance on Real Estate Investment Trusts
(Found at www.hmrc.gov.uk/manuals/greitmanual/Index.htm)

This technical reference section is designed to assist you when you are working in the office. It should help you to know where to look for further information on the topics covered in this chapter.

Answers to Interactive questions

Answer to Interactive question 1

	£
Trading income (W1)	380,100
Profit on non-trading loan relationships (W2)	164,000
Chargeable gain	150,000
	694,100
Less qualifying charitable donation	(9,240)
Taxable total profits	684,860

As the company has a 31 December year end, its accounting period straddles two financial years.
1 January 2015 – 31 March 2015 is in the financial year 2014. The rest of the accounting period is in the financial year 2015. As the rates of corporation tax have changed between the two financial years, it is necessary to calculate the corporation tax liability separately for each financial year.

	£
FY2014:	
21% × £684,860 × 3/12	35,955
Less marginal relief	
1/400 × (£750,000 – £707,082) × £684,860/£707,082 × 3/12	(26)
FY2015: 20% × £684,860 × 9/12	102,729
Corporation tax liability	138,658

WORKINGS

(1) **Trading income**

	£
Trading profits before interest and capital allowances	500,000
Less: trading loan relationship debit	(100,000)
capital allowances	(19,900)
Trading income	380,100

(2) **Profit on non-trading loan relationships**

	£	£
BSI accrued income b/f	(20,000)	
Add: cash received	95,000	
closing accrual	25,000	100,000
Loan stock income b/f	(1,000)	
Add: cash received	61,400	
closing accrual	3,600	64,000
		164,000

(3) **Calculation of augmented profits**

Two associated companies: UL = £750,000 LL = £150,000

	£
Taxable total profits	684,860
FII (£20,000 × 100/90)	22,222
Augmented profits	707,082
CT at marginal rate	

All of the dividends received are exempt from corporation tax. However, the dividends received from Z Inc are included in FII and grossed up at 100/90. The dividends received from F Ltd are from a company in which B Ltd owns more than 51% of the shares and are therefore not included in FII.

Answer to Interactive question 2

Corporation tax computation for the 8 months ended 31 October 2015

	£
Property income (£59,400 – £16,400)	43,000
Profit on non-trading loan relationship	60,000
	103,000
Less expenses of management – current period	(52,500)
– brought forward	(23,100)
Taxable total profits	27,400
Add FII (£972,000 × 100/90)	1,080,000
Augmented profits	1,107,400

Corporation tax payable

FY 2014: £27,400 × 21% × 1/8	719
FY 2015: £27,400 × 20% × 7/8	4,795
	5,514

Note that as a UK company it would have received the debenture income gross and it does not therefore need to be grossed up.

As the upper limit is prorated for the short accounting period the company is not entitled to marginal relief in FY 2014: £1,500,000 × 8/12 = £1,000,000.

1 Corporation tax computation for the year ended 30 November 2015

	£	£
Trading income (£275,000 – £8,000 + £7,800 – £4,500)		270,300
Profit on non-trading loan relationships		
Bank interest	1,320	
Loan relationship surplus (£21,000 – £19,400)	1,600	2,920
Property income		20,000
Chargeable gains	42,000	
Less capital losses b/f	(10,500)	31,500
Taxable total profits		324,720
Add franked investment income (£18,000 × $^{100}/_{90}$)		20,000
Augmented profits		344,720
Corporation tax		
FY2014:		
£324,720 × 21% × 4/12		22,730
Less marginal relief		(907)
$^1/_{400}$ × (£1,500,000 – £344,720) × $\dfrac{£324,720}{£344,720}$ × 4/12		
FY2015: £324,720 × 20% × 8/12		43,296
Corporation tax payable		65,119

It is reasonable to assume that in the absence of any specific information to the contrary that the dividends received are exempt from tax.

2 Year ended 31 March 2016

	£	£
Rents		210,000
Less: capital allowances	1,120	
property management expenses	56,000	
		(57,120)
Property income		152,880
Profit on non-trading loan relationships		11,200
Chargeable gains		140,000
		304,080
Less: general management expenses	70,000	
capital allowances	1,400	
expenses of management brought forward	84,700	
		(156,100)
		147,980
Less qualifying charitable donations relief		(65,800)
Taxable total profits		82,180
Corporation tax payable £82,180 × 20%		£16,436

3 Corporation tax computations

	12 months to 31 March 2016 £	3 months to 30 June 2016 £
Trading income (W3)	338,321	161,176
Profit on non-trading loan relationships	12,500	13,505
Chargeable gains (given/ W4)	68,250	10,095
Taxable total profits	419,071	184,776
Corporation tax (W5)		
£419,071 / £184,776 × 20%	83,814	36,955
Corporation tax payable	83,814	36,955

WORKINGS

(1) **Adjusted trading profit before capital allowances – y/e 31 March 2016**

	£	£
Net profit per accounts		858,509
Add Depreciation	22,329	
Entertaining	24,670	
Legal fees	7,850	
VAT penalties	2,000	
		56,849
Less interest received	12,500	
Profit on investment sale	80,000	
Release of provision	25,000	
		(117,500)
		797,858

(2) **Capital allowances**

	Main pool £	Special rate pool £	Total £
Y/E 31 March 2016			
WDV b/f	76,000		
Additions (AIA):			
Plant (long life asset)		369,000	
Vehicles	160,800		
Less AIA (max £425,000)	(56,000)	(369,000)	425,000
((£500,000 × 9/12) +			
(£200,000 × 3/12))			
Additions not eligible for AIA:			
Cars (special rate)		24,909	
	180,800	24,909	
WDA @ 18%	(32,544)		32,544
WDA @ 8%		(1,993)	1,993
WDV c/f	148,256	22,916	
Total allowances			459,537
3 m/e 30 June 2016			
Additions (AIA):	281,950		
Less AIA (£200,000 × $\frac{3}{12}$)	(50,000)		50,000
Additions not eligible for AIA:			
Cars	28,100	32,000	
	408,306	54,916	
Less WDA @ 18% × 3/12	(18,374)		18,374
WDA @ 8% × 3/12		(1,098)	1,098
WDV c/f	389,932	53,818	
Total allowances			69,472

(3) **Tax adjusted trading profits**

	Twelve months to 31 Mar 2016 £	Three months to 30 Jun 2016 £
Adjusted trading profit before capital allowances (W1)	797,858	230,648
Less CAs on plant and machinery (W2)	(459,537)	(69,472)
Trading income	338,321	161,176

(4) **Chargeable gains (sale of warehouse)**

	£
Proceeds (April 2016)	194,000
Less cost (January 2011)	(150,000)
Unindexed gain	44,000
Less IA (April 2016 – January 2011)	
(260.5 – 229.0) / 229.0 = 0.138	
= 0.138 × £150,000	(20,700)
Chargeable gain	23,300

This gain can be rolled over against the cost of the replacement building.

Note: For companies, indexation allowance is available and runs to the month of disposal.

Total gains are therefore £23,300 + £10,095 = £33,395, but only £10,095 chargeable.

(5) **Corporation tax rate**

The FY2015 unified tax rate of 20% applies

CHAPTER 11

Raising finance

Introduction

Examination context

Topic List

1   Loan relationships

2   Foreign exchange

3   Leases

4   Debt versus equity

Summary and Self-test

Technical reference

Answer to Interactive question

Answers to Self-test

Learning objectives

- Determine, explain and calculate the corporation tax liabilities for corporate entities

- Evaluate the tax implications of financing existing and new businesses

- Evaluate the taxation implications of returns to investors

- Evaluate and advise on tax strategies to meet business objectives

Specific syllabus references for this chapter are 1f, 1r, 1s and 2b.

Syllabus links

The basic aspects of loan relationships were covered in Tax Compliance. This chapter explores the more advanced aspects of raising finance including loan relationships, foreign exchange and using finance and operating leases.

Debt financing interacts with thin capitalisation and the worldwide debt cap which are explained in Chapter 16. Considering how to finance a business will also be critical to any restructuring or transformation of an organisation, which is explained in Chapter 23.

Examination context

Careful decision making is required when determining the best method of financing the capital structure of a business.

With careful planning foreign exchange transactions can be managed such that exchange differences on foreign assets can be matched to the foreign liabilities used to fund their acquisition.

In addition when a company raises additional finance, the accountant advising may need to consider the impact of financing methods on both the personal tax position of the investor and the corporate tax position of the company.

In the examination candidates may be required to:

- Explain the implications for the company's tax liability of loan relationship transactions

- Explain how foreign currency transactions are dealt with in calculating the company's corporation tax liability

- Determine whether a lease is a long funding lease, and how the lease is to be dealt with for tax purposes

- Explain the impact for both the investor and the company of providing equity finance and/or debt finance

1 Loan relationships

Section overview

- Under the loan relationship rules, loans may either be classified as trading or non-trading. Debits and credits relating to trading loans are allowable or taxable as trading expenses or income. Debits and credits relating to non-trading loans are allowable or taxable as non-trading loan relationships.

- Incidental costs of loan finance are also deductible under the loan relationship rules.

- A UK company receives UK interest gross.

- A net deficit on non-trading loan relationships may be group relieved; offset in the current year against total profits; offset in the previous year against profits on non-trading loan relationships; or carried forward against non-trading income.

- Any profit or loss on disposal of a qualifying corporate bond by a company is assessed under the loan relationships rules. Unless the company operates in the financial services sector, it will usually be a non-trading loan relationship.

- Where the parties to a loan are connected it must be accounted for under the amortised cost basis and loan waivers are ignored. There is no relief for impairment losses or loan waivers between connected companies but the credit in the borrower is not taxable.

1.1 Loan relationship rules

1.1.1 Accounting methods

Providing a company's accounts are prepared in accordance with IAS/ IFRS or UK GAAP, no adjustments should be required for taxation purposes for amounts which relate to loan relationships.

UK GAAP permits loans to be accounted for on the amortised cost basis (or accrual basis) or on the fair value basis.

1.1.2 Distinction between trading and non-trading purposes

The tax treatment of a loan depends on its purpose:

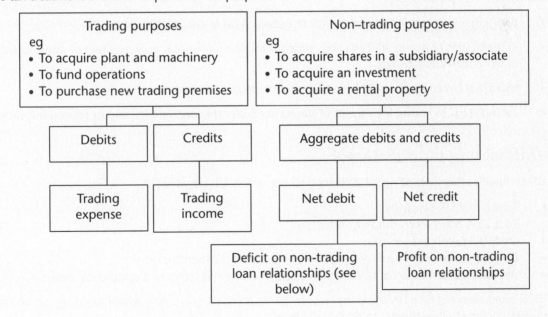

Examples of amounts which can be included as debits or credits on a non-trading loan relationship are:

Debits – examples	Credits – examples
• Interest payable	• Interest receivable
• Foreign exchange losses	• Foreign exchange gains
• Premium on a loan liability	• Discount on a loan liability
• Incidental costs	
• Interest on overdue corporation tax	
• Impairment loss on an unpaid business payment	

Interest and foreign exchange movements in respect of trade debts are dealt with under the loan relationship rules (see below). The debt itself is outside the loan relationship rules.

1.1.3 Deficit on non-trading loan relationships

A net deficit on non-trading loan relationships may be group relieved; offset in the current year against total profits; offset in the previous year against profits on non-trading loan relationships; or carried forward against non-trading income (see Chapter 12).

1.1.4 Unallowable purpose

All debits for loans which are for an unallowable purpose are excluded from the calculation of trading profits or non-trading loan relationships. A loan has an unallowable purpose if either:

*   One of its main purposes is tax avoidance; or

*   It is for a purpose which is outside the scope of UK corporation tax eg a UK branch of a non-resident company paying interest on a loan taken out for the benefit of its parent.

1.2 Incidental costs of loan finance

The incidental costs of loan finance are debits under the loan relationship rules.

Examples include the costs of:

*   Bringing a loan relationship into existence (even if these are abortive costs).

*   Entering into or giving effect to any related transaction (disposal or acquisition of rights or liabilities under a loan relationship).

*   Making payments under a loan relationship or related transaction.

*   Taking steps to ensure the receipt of payments under the loan relationship or related transaction.

1.3 Withholding tax on interest

UK companies pay interest net of 20% income tax unless it is payable:

*   To another UK company;
*   To a 25% associated company in the EU;
*   On listed Eurobonds or gilts;
*   On 'short' loans which are not capable of exceeding 12 months; or
*   Without the deduction of tax to a non-resident under the terms of a double tax treaty.

UK interest received by a UK company will always be received gross. Any withholding tax on overseas interest income will be subject to double tax relief.

1.4 Redemption/disposal of debt

It is not only the interest costs and fees in connection with borrowing that are allowable or taxable under the loan relationship rules. Any profits and losses on disposal are treated similarly.

Where a loan is sold the resulting profit or loss is treated as a debit or credit under the loan relationship rules.

1.5 Connected party loans

Two companies are connected if one is under the control of the other.

If the parties to a loan are connected, then anti-avoidance provisions exist to determine how the loan should be treated for tax purposes.

- If a UK borrowing company pays interest more than 12 months after the end of the relevant accounting period and the recipient is a connected party which is not subject to UK corporation tax, tax relief for the interest may, in certain circumstances, be delayed until actual payment. The circumstances where relief is delayed until actual payment include:

  (i)   Where the recipient company is resident in a tax haven
  (ii) Where the loan is from a participator to a close company

- Relief for impairment losses (ie bad debts) is not available to a lender in respect of a loan to a connected party.

- Loan waivers are not deductible in respect of a connected party loan, and the borrower's corresponding credit is not subject to tax.

- Trade debts (or debts incurred in respect of a property business) between connected parties are treated in the same way as non-trading loans, thus there is no relief to the creditor for impairment losses or the write off of the debt and the debtor is not taxed on its 'profit'.

1.6 Changes to IAS 39

The International Accounting Standards Board (IASB) is replacing IAS 39 with IFRS 9, with the revised draft being issued in stages. This will affect how financial instruments are accounted for. The UK's Accounting Standards Board is expected to make similar changes to FRS 102 (sections 12 and 30). The specific amendments are changes to:

- The way that financial instruments are classified and measured for accounting purposes;
- When financial instruments are recognised on the balance sheet;
- How impairment losses are quantified; and
- How hedging arrangements should be accounted for.

Given that in essence the tax treatment of loan relationships follows the accounting treatment, equivalent changes will be required to CTA 2009 in order to accommodate changes to the new UK GAAP. Finance Act 2010 inserted regulation making powers into CTA 2009 to enable new regulations to be introduced to ensure that tax law can be amended as and when these changes to GAAP are introduced. However, mandatory adoption of IFRS 9 has been delayed to accounting periods beginning on/after 1 January 2018.

2 Foreign exchange

Section overview

- Exchange differences on trading transactions are taxed as part of trading profits once they have been recognised in the income statement.

- Forex gains and losses on monetary items are dealt with under the loan relationship rules. At the end of each accounting period the company is assessed to tax on exchange gains or losses included in the income statement.

- Forex gains or losses on non-monetary items are treated for tax purposes on a realisation basis ie as capital profits.

- Where an asset is hedged, the forex gains and losses on the transaction and the hedge can generally be matched and netted off. When the hedged asset is shares, the accumulated gains and losses on the loan or derivative used to hedge it are included in the calculation of the chargeable gain rather than taxed under the loan relationship rules.

2.1 Trading transactions

A company's taxable profits are usually calculated in sterling. The exception to this is where it has a non-sterling functional currency, when its profits and losses (but not generally it's chargeable gains – see below) should be computed in that currency and then translated into sterling using the average exchange rate for the year.

When a company buys or sells goods in foreign currency, the transaction is normally converted at the actual rate at the date of the transaction. Exchange differences will arise when the transaction is settled.

These exchange differences are included in the income statement and are taxed as part of trading profits.

2.2 Monetary items

Foreign exchange (forex) gains or losses on monetary assets (receivables and cash) and monetary liabilities (payables, overdrafts and loans) are dealt with under the loan relationships rules. Gains/losses in respect of trading items are included in trading profits whilst those in respect of non-trading items are treated as debits or credits on non-trading loan relationships.

The company is assessed to tax on exchange gains or losses on current assets and liabilities even though these may be unrealised, ie where the asset has not yet been disposed of or the liability has not yet been settled.

Forex gains and losses on capital monetary items ie long term loans are only taxable or allowable where they are included in the income statement. Where the gains or losses are taken to the reserves in accordance with generally accepted accounting principles (GAAP) or international accounting standards (IAS) they are not taxable until the loan is repaid or sold.

Worked example: Foreign exchange gains and losses

K Ltd borrows NZ$750,000 in January 2015 and repays the loan in September 2016. The loan is used to finance the acquisition of a subsidiary. K Ltd's accounting period end is 31 March.

The exchange rates were as follows:

January 2015	NZ$3.0 = £1
March 2015	NZ$2.9 = £1
March 2016	NZ$2.7 = £1
September 2016	NZ$2.8 = £1

Requirement

Calculate the net non-trading loan relationship debit or credit from foreign exchange movements for the year ended 31 March 2015, 31 March 2016 and 31 March 2017.

Solution

Translation time	Exchange rate	Sterling value	Exchange difference £
January 2015	NZ$3.0 = £1	250,000	–
March 2015	NZ$2.9 = £1	258,621	(8,621) loss
March 2016	NZ$2.7 = £1	277,778	(19,157) loss
September 2016	NZ$2.8 = £1	267,857	9,921 gain

Year ended 31 March 2015 net debit £8,621 – ie reduce profits.

Year ended 31 March 2016 net debit £19,157 – ie reduce profits.

Year ended 31 March 2017 net credit £9,921 – ie increase profits.

2.3 Non-monetary items

Forex gains or losses on non-monetary assets (eg capital assets) are treated for tax purposes on a realisation basis ie as capital profits.

Chargeable gains are usually computed in sterling, with both the original cost of the asset and the proceeds being converted to sterling at spot rates. However gains on ships, aircraft and shares are computed in a company's tax currency (generally its functional currency), and converted into sterling at the spot rate on the date of the transaction.

2.4 Overseas permanent establishments (PEs)

Normally the accounts of an overseas PE are kept in the prevailing currency and then translated into sterling using the rate at the end of the period.

The only forex difference arising is the restatement of opening net assets to the closing rate. This is taken to reserves, not to the income statement.

If the local currency treatment does not apply the rate prevailing at the time transactions took place would be used, and then reconverted at settlement or at accounting period end. This would lead to forex differences in the income statement.

2.5 Hedging

Companies use both foreign currency loans and currency derivatives to hedge against foreign exchange risks in their business.

Both loans and derivatives can be used to hedge the currency risk on investments such as subsidiaries operating in a different currency. Derivatives are also used to hedge the foreign exchange risk where a company knows that it will have future expenditure or income denominated in a foreign currency.

Unless a company uses hedge accounting, it is possible for the accounting treatment of a hedge to not reflect the way in which it reduces the company's commercial risks. This is because hedging instruments are often financial assets which are accounted for at fair value through profit or loss under IAS 39, whereas hedged assets are more likely to be accounted for on an amortised cost basis.

In order for hedge accounting to be permitted under IAS 39 there must be a designated relationship between the hedged asset and hedging instrument which was documented at the time when the instrument was originally recognised, and the hedge must be between 80% and 125% effective. If these conditions are met, and a hedge fulfils the conditions to be treated as a fair value hedge, then changes in value in both the effective part of the hedging instrument and the hedged asset can be recognised in the income statement as they accrue. If the conditions are met and the hedge instead fulfils the conditions to be treated as a cash flow hedge, gains or losses on the hedging instrument can be recognised in other comprehensive income to the extent that it is effective. They are then reclassified to the income statement in the period in which the hedged transaction affects profit or loss.

Where a loan or derivative is used to hedge an investment in foreign operations (a net investment hedge), and the conditions for hedge accounting are met, this is accounted for in a similar way to a cash flow hedge.

The strict conditions mean that some transactions which are regarded as a hedge from a commercial perspective do not meet the conditions for hedge accounting. In addition, there is no obligation to adopt hedge accounting even where the conditions are met, and it is not uncommon for a company to choose not to do so because of the costs associated with documenting (and in some cases valuing) hedging relationships. Even where hedge accounting is adopted, this could still result in a tax 'mismatch' on a fair value hedge if the hedged asset was taxed on realisation under the chargeable gains rules, for example, rather than on an accounts basis.

The tax treatment of currency hedges therefore seeks to reflect the commercial nature of the hedging relationship, regardless of whether hedge accounting is adopted in the entity accounts. Where exchange differences:

- Are accounted for in other comprehensive income, or

- Arise under an arrangement which is a designated hedge for accounting purposes, or

- Arise under an arrangement where the company intends to substantially reduce the economic risk of holding the asset by entering into the hedging loan or derivative,

in general no amounts are brought into account in relation to the loan or derivative which is being used as a hedge until the transaction which it is intended to hedge is also recognised in the income statement.

The treatment of the exchange differences which are deferred under these rules depends on the nature of the transaction which has been hedged.

- Where trading transactions are hedged, the total exchange gains and losses which have not previously been taxed are brought into account as trading income or a trading deduction in the same period as that in which amounts in relation to the hedged asset are recorded in the income statement.

- Where a net investment in shares is hedged, the cumulative untaxed exchange gains and losses on the hedging instrument (for example, a currency loan) adjust the consideration when the shares are sold. Where the disposal is exempt under the substantial shareholding exemption, the foreign exchange gains and losses on the hedge are also exempt.

Worked example: Hedging

Starling Ltd has entered into two hedging transactions:

(a) A loan of 4m Euro with another group company, to hedge its investment in its Italian subsidiary Ucelli SpA. The loan was taken out when the shares were acquired on 1 January 2014, and repaid when they were sold on 1 February 2016. Although the loan was taken on in order to substantially reduce the risk of holding the shares from a commercial perspective, it was only 70% of the value of the shares when it was taken out and therefore failed to satisfy the effectiveness condition for hedge accounting. Exchange differences on the loan have been reflected in Starling Ltd's income statement as follows:

	£
Year ended 31 December 2014	157,000 gain
Year ended 31 December 2015	(45,000) loss
Period to 1 February 2016	(141,500) loss
	(29,500) loss

(b) A forward currency contract entered into in January 2015, to hedge its obligation to pay $200,000. Starling Ltd is contracted to buy $200,000 for £130,000 in March 2016, which is when the payment is due to be made. The contract has been designated as a hedge, and meets the other conditions for hedge accounting. Exchange differences on the contract, which have been recognised in other comprehensive income, are as follows:

	£
Year ended 31 December 2015	19,300 gain
Period to March 2016	(3,500) loss
	15,800 gain

Requirement

Explain which amounts are taxable in respect of the hedging transactions, and in which periods.

Solution

(a) Because the loan was intended to substantially reduce the commercial risk of holding the asset, it is treated as a hedging instrument for tax purposes even though it is not accounted for as such.

Although exchange differences are reflected in Starling Ltd's income statement in 2014 and 2015, they are not taxable until the shares are sold. At that time, the cumulative loss of £29,500 is treated as reducing the consideration for the sale of the shares in Ucelli SpA. If the sale is exempt under the substantial shareholding rules, there will be no relief for the exchange loss.

Note that in order for this treatment to apply, it is critical that Starling Ltd is able to evidence that its intention in taking on the loan was to reduce the currency risk associated with the investment. Care therefore needs to be taken in board minutes, and all other documentation relating to the loan, to ensure that the intention is properly recorded. If it is not possible to evidence the company's intention at the time when the loan is taken on, HMRC could succeed in arguing that the exchange differences should be taxed as they accrue in the normal way.

(b) No amount is taxed in the year ended 31 December 2015. The total £15,800 gain on the forward contract will be treated as taxable trading income in Starling Ltd's period ended 31 March 2016 (ie year ended 31 December 2016), matching the costs which it was used to hedge.

2.6 Summary

Foreign exchange gains or losses on	Taxation treatment if the tax hedging rules do not apply	Taxation treatment if the tax hedging rules apply
Settled trading transactions	Trading income/expense	N/A
Monetary items (receivables, cash, payables, overdrafts and loans)	Credits or debits within loan relationships as they are recorded in the accounts, as trading income or non-trading loan relationships as appropriate	Bring into account when the hedged asset/transaction is reflected in profit or loss (if the asset is shares, the exchange differences adjust the consideration for their sale)
Non-monetary items (capital assets)	Part of capital profit/loss on sale	N/A

3 Leases

Section overview

- For lessees, finance leases which were entered into before 1 April 2006 (for companies) or 6 April 2006 (unincorporated businesses) or which are not long funding leases are treated for tax purposes in the same way as they are in the financial statements provided they were prepared in accordance with IAS 17. Capital allowances are not available to the lessee. Lessors under these leases are taxed on the rents received less capital allowances.

- Operating leases which were entered into before 1/6 April 2006 or which are not long funding leases are treated for the lessee in the same way as they are in the financial statements. Capital allowances are not available to the lessee. Lessors are again taxed on the rents received less capital allowances.

- Leases which for tax purposes qualify as long funding leases entered into after 1/6 April 2006 allow the lessee to deduct the interest element from profits and claim capital allowances. The lessor is effectively taxed as if they had entered into a loan, regardless of whether the lease is accounted for as a finance lease.

A lease is defined as a contract where an asset is conveyed by the owner (lessor) to the tenant (lessee) for a fixed period of time. The tax consequences for both parties must be considered in relation to how any payments are treated and how any receipts are taxed.

3.1 Accounting treatment

Leases are classified into two types: operating leases and finance leases. The distinction between the two lies in the terms of the contract between the lessor and the lessee.

Definitions

Finance lease: A lease is classified as a finance lease if it transfers substantially all the risks and rewards incidental to ownership to the lessee. Although the asset is not legally owned by the lessee, the practicalities of the arrangement have a commercial effect similar to buying the item outright. The asset is capitalised and depreciated by the lessee. The lessee will also recognise the transaction as a liability. The lessor will recognise the transaction as a financial asset.

Operating lease: A lease is classified as an operating lease if the lessor retains substantially all the risks and rewards incidental to ownership. The asset is not capitalised and is not depreciated by the lessee. The lessee will normally expense lease rentals over the life of the lease on a straight line basis. The lessor will continue to capitalise the asset, charge depreciation and recognise the lease rentals as income.

3.2 Taxation treatment of long funding leases

3.2.1 Background

FA 2006 introduced changes to the taxation of finance and operating leases to align the tax treatment of leases and loan finance and therefore remove tax as a consideration when choosing which method of finance to use.

The rules apply to plant and machinery where the terms of the lease commence on or after 1 April 2006 for companies or on or after 6 April 2006 for unincorporated businesses.

Capital allowances on plant and machinery are available to the lessee rather than the lessor where the plant and machinery is subject to a 'long funding lease'.

The rules allow lessees to:

- Claim capital allowances on much the same amount as they would have been able to had they bought the asset, ie the capital element; and

- Receive a deduction for that part of the rentals on which capital allowances are not available, ie the interest element.

3.2.2 Definition of a long-funding lease

A long funding lease must be both 'long' and be a 'funding lease'. A lease is 'long' if it is not:

- A lease of 5 years or less, or

- A lease of between 5 and 7 years where it is a finance lease and on an annual basis lease rentals do not vary by more than 10% and the residual value implied by the lease terms is no more than 5% of the initial market value of the asset.

In addition to being a long lease, it also needs to qualify as a 'funding lease'. At least one of the following three tests must be fulfilled in order for a lease to be treated as a 'funding lease'.

(1)   The finance lease test – ie treated as a finance lease under GAAP/IAS.

(2)   The lease payments test – the present value of the minimum lease payments is at least 80% of the fair value of the plant and machinery.

(3)   The useful economic life test – the term of the lease is more than 65% of the remaining useful economic life of the plant and machinery.

3.2.3   Tax treatment of a long-funding lease

If a lessee acquires plant and machinery under a long funding lease, the lessee is treated as having incurred capital expenditure on commencement of the lease, and is treated as owning the asset throughout the duration of the lease.

The tax treatment for the different elements payable under a lease depend on the type of lease:

For long funding operating leases

•   The lessor receives no tax deduction for the capital cost of the asset.

•   The lessee claims capital allowances on the market value of the asset on the later of commencement of the lease and when the asset is first brought into use.

•   The rental payments less a tax restriction known as the 'periodic deduction' are taxable on the lessor and deductible for the lessee.

   The 'periodic deduction' is the difference between the cost of the asset at the grant of the lease and the expected residual value of the asset at the end of the lease spread over the lease term. The periodic deduction is in essence depreciation over the life of the lease. The lessor will have charged to the accounts depreciation over the life of the asset which will need to be added back for tax purposes.

For long funding finance leases

•   The lessor receives no tax deduction for the capital cost of the asset.

•   The lessee claims capital allowances on the net present value of the minimum lease payments on commencement plus any rentals paid before commencement of the lease that have not been relieved. If the lessor incurs additional expenditure resulting in increased lease payments, the present value of the increase is treated as an addition to the capital expenditure.

•   The interest element is taxable income on the lessor and a tax deductible expense for the lessee.

3.3   Taxation treatment of other leases

3.3.1   Hire purchase agreements

The purchaser may claim:

•   Capital allowances on the cash value
•   A deduction for the interest charges

3.3.2   Finance leases

For finance leases entered into prior to 1/6 April 2006 and later leases which are not long funding leases, lessees are not entitled to capital allowances but are entitled to a deduction for all their rental payments, including the capital element.

For tax purposes, the gross rentals payable by a trader are revenue in nature and allowable in computing profits. For financial reporting purposes, IAS 17 divides the rentals into an 'interest' element and a 'capital' element.

Where a finance lessee accounts for a transaction under IAS 17 the deduction of rentals equal to the finance ('interest') charge and the depreciation charge relating to the leased asset in the balance sheet will normally represent a convenient way of achieving a spread of the lessee's gross rentals which is consistent with the accruals concept.

Thus, the tax treatment for the lessee of such a finance lease mirrors its treatment under IAS 17:

- Finance costs (ie interest element) are allowed as debited to the income statement.
- Depreciation is deductible as economically equivalent to the capital payments.

However, deduction of depreciation will not be acceptable to HMRC where the depreciation rate is non-commercial or the asset has been revalued upwards. Any non-qualifying depreciation is disallowed in the tax computation.

Therefore, for pre April 2006 finance leases or short finance leases accounted for under IAS 17, there is no need to make any adjustments in computing the trade profits of the lessee.

Prior to 1/6 April 2006, under all finance leases the capital allowances were given to the lessor, usually a bank or finance company, because under the legal form of the agreement the lessor retains ownership.

Any disposal of the asset is treated as a normal disposal for capital allowances purposes and may result in a balancing adjustment for the party claiming capital allowances.

Any rebate of lease rentals paid to the lessee is a taxable receipt. The rebate will be tax deductible for the lessor.

3.3.3 Operating leases

For operating leases entered into before 1/6 April 2006 and subsequent operating leases which are not long funding leases, all the rental costs are allowable on an accruals basis.

Capital allowances are available to the lessor.

3.3.4 Leases of high emissions cars

For leases of cars with 'high' CO_2 emissions 15% of the rentals (including any irrecoverable VAT) are disallowed for tax purposes.

The restriction applies to CO_2 emissions of more than 130g/km (160g/km for leases entered into before 1/6 April 2013). This only applies where the lease is not a long funding lease.

Interactive question: Adjustment to profits [Difficulty level: Exam standard]

World In Motion plc ('WIM') is a low cost airline that operates flights within Europe. The company has been expanding for a number of years, and has not paid any dividends.

WIM plc: Income Statement for the year ended 31 March 2016 and the year ended 31 March 2015

	2016	2015
	£'000	£'000
Revenue	1,355,500	1,091,900
Cost of sales	(1,166,200)	(929,800)
Gross profit	189,300	162,100
Distribution and marketing expenses	(67,450)	(56,150)
Administration expenses	(60,900)	(56,350)
Profit from operations	60,950	49,600
Interest receivable	27,875	14,225
Interest payable	(8,220)	(3,150)
Profit before taxation	80,605	60,675
Tax	(16,121)	(12,742)
Net profit for the year	64,484	47,933

You are also given the following notes to the financial statements:

(1) WIM made rental payments under operating leases during the two years ended 31 March 2016 in relation to aircraft leased since 1 January 2011 as follows:

	2016	2015
	£m	£m
Expiring in less than one year	13.9	6.2
Expiring between two and five years	31.3	50.7
Expiring after more than five years	102.7	43.2

Of the leases expiring after more than five years, £59,500,000 worth of assets are leased under terms which qualify them as long-funding leases in the year ended 31 March 2016. Lease payments of £1,400,000 are included in cost of sales in respect of the long funding leases of which £150,000 relates to the interest element. You should assume that their tax written down value is equal to their book value.

(2) Non-cancellable payments under hire-purchase leases to pay rentals during the year ending 31 March 2017 mean that WIM is contractually committed to the acquisition of 21 new aircraft with a list price of approximately £500 million. In respect of those aircraft, deposit payments amounting to £148 million had been made as at 31 March 2016.

(3) WIM paid an interim dividend of £2 million on 1 January 2016 relating to the year ended 31 March 2016. A further dividend of £4.8 million is proposed at the year end.

(4) WIM has calculated capital allowances excluding adjustment for items in Notes 1 and 2 above as £3 million for the year ended 31 March 2016.

(5) WIM has a depreciation expense of £2.2 million for the year ended 31 March 2016.

(6) Of the interest receivable for the year ended 31 March 2016, £2 million relates to interest received on cash held on deposit. Of the interest payable for the year ended 31 March 2016, £3 million relates to a loan used to finance the acquisition of a subsidiary. The remainder of the interest payable relates to loans used to finance the acquisition of various capital assets used in the trade. Of this, £2.4 million of the interest payable relates to the aircraft purchased on hire-purchase itemised in Note 2.

(7) Included in the distribution and marketing expenses for the year ended 31 March 2016 is £645,000 of expenses relating to client entertaining and corporate hospitality. The staff annual party is also included in marketing expenses. The party cost £100,000 in total at a cost of £200 per head. The associated PAYE costs paid via the company's PAYE dispensation agreement are also included in marketing expenses. Seventy-five per cent of WIM's staff are basic rate taxpayers, 15% are higher rate taxpayers with total income of less than £90,000 and the remaining 10% are additional rate taxpayers.

Requirement

Calculate WIM plc's taxable total profits for the year ended 31 March 2016.

See **Answer** at the end of this chapter.

3.4 Summary of taxation treatment for lessors

| Accounting | Pre-April 2006 leases | Post-April 2006 leases | |
		Non-long funding leases	Long funding leases
Operating Lease (Income statement shows rent receivable less depreciation)	Tax the lease rentals and deduct capital allowances. (Add back depreciation and claim capital allowances)	Tax the lease rentals and deduct capital allowances. (Add back depreciation and claim capital allowances)	Tax the lease rentals less the periodic deduction. (Add back the depreciation and deduct the periodic deduction (may be the same if depreciation is straight line))
Finance lease (Income statement shows interest income)	Tax the lease rentals and deduct capital allowances. (Deduct the interest income included in the income statement and claim capital allowances)	Tax the lease rentals and deduct capital allowances. (Deduct the interest income included in the income statement and claim capital allowances)	Tax the interest income included in the income statement. (No tax adjustments needed)

3.5 Summary of taxation treatment for lessees

| Accounting | Pre-April 2006 leases | Post-April 2006 leases | |
		Non-long funding leases	Long funding leases
Operating Lease (Income statement shows lease rentals payable)	Deduct the lease rentals recorded in the income statement. (No tax adjustments needed).	Deduct the lease rentals recorded in the income statement. (No tax adjustments needed).	Deduct the rentals, excluding the capital element (allocated on a straight line basis), and capital allowances. (Add back the capital element of the rentals and claim capital allowances)
Finance lease (Income statement shows depreciation plus an interest charge)	Deduct the depreciation and interest charge recorded in the income statement. (No tax adjustments needed – the depreciation is **not** added back)	Deduct the depreciation and interest charge recorded in the income statement. (No tax adjustments needed – the depreciation is **not** added back)	Deduct the interest charge shown in the income statement and capital allowances. (Add back depreciation and claim capital allowances)

4 Debt versus equity

Section overview

- A distribution is not allowable as a tax deduction.

- Interest is an allowable tax expense and therefore has a lower after tax cost to the company compared to a dividend.

- However, for an individual investor, interest is taxable at a higher effective rate. For example, for a higher rate taxpayer a dividend has an effective tax rate of 25% compared to 40% for interest received by a higher rate taxpayer. For an additional rate taxpayer, a dividend will be taxed at an effective rate of 30.6% compared to a 45% tax rate for interest.

- A corporate investor may also prefer dividends as, although they might affect the rate of corporation tax payable, normally no corporation tax is actually payable on the dividend. Any gain on disposal of shares may be exempt under the substantial shareholding exemption whereas any gains on the disposal of debt are taxable under the loan relationship rules.

4.1 Distributions

A distribution includes the following:

- Any dividend paid by a company.

- Any other distribution paid out of the company's assets in respect of shares (whether in cash or otherwise).

- When securities are listed and the interest is in excess of the normal commercial rate, the excessive interest is treated as a distribution.

- The provision of certain benefits to participators of a close company.

Distributions are not deductible for tax purposes.

4.2 Taxation implications of debt versus equity financing

4.2.1 Implications for the paying company

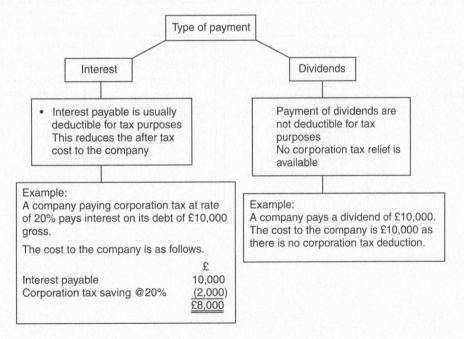

However, note that it is not permitted to pay interest to a connected company at an excessive rate of interest in order to gain a tax advantage. A company's interest deductions can also be limited with reference to its group's worldwide interest expense. Refer to the discussion of the transfer pricing rules and the worldwide debt cap in Chapter 16 for more details.

4.2.2 Implications for an individual investor

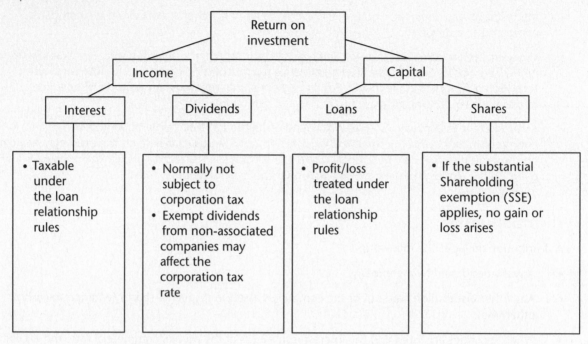

4.2.3 Implications for a corporate investor

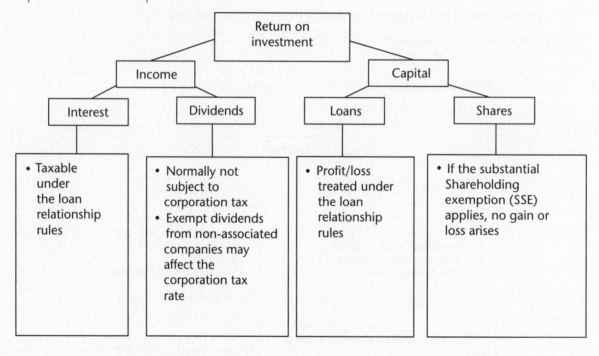

Summary and Self-test

Summary

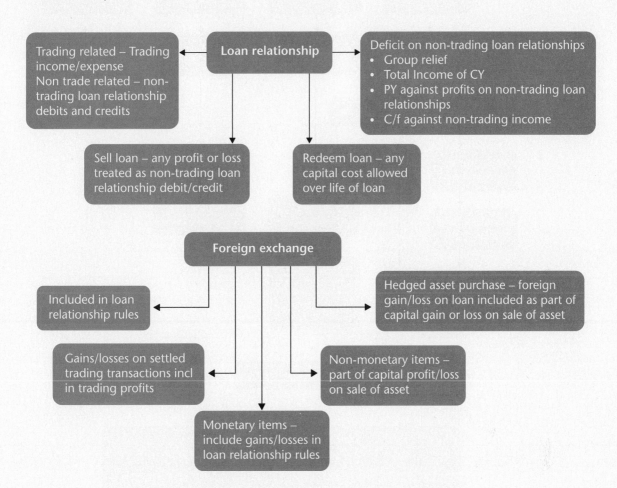

Trading related – Trading income/expense
Non trade related – non-trading loan relationship debits and credits

Loan relationship

Deficit on non-trading loan relationships
- Group relief
- Total Income of CY
- PY against profits on non-trading loan relationships
- C/f against non-trading income

Sell loan – any profit or loss treated as non-trading loan relationship debit/credit

Redeem loan – any capital cost allowed over life of loan

Foreign exchange

Included in loan relationship rules

Hedged asset purchase – foreign gain/loss on loan included as part of capital gain or loss on sale of asset

Gains/losses on settled trading transactions incl in trading profits

Non-monetary items – part of capital profit/loss on sale of asset

Monetary items – include gains/losses in loan relationship rules

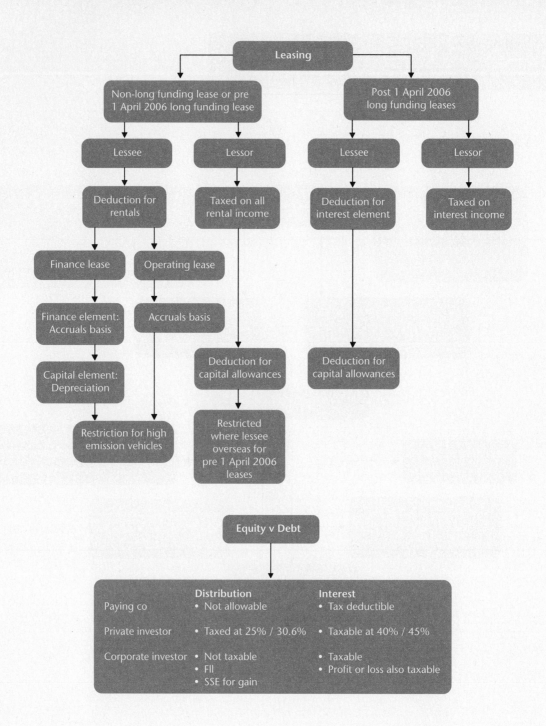

Leasing

Non-long funding lease or pre 1 April 2006 long funding lease → Lessee, Lessor

Post 1 April 2006 long funding leases → Lessee, Lessor

Lessee → Deduction for rentals
- Finance lease → Finance element: Accruals basis → Capital element: Depreciation → Restriction for high emission vehicles
- Operating lease → Accruals basis → Restriction for high emission vehicles

Lessor → Taxed on all rental income → Deduction for capital allowances → Restricted where lessee overseas for pre 1 April 2006 leases

Lessee (Post 1 April 2006) → Deduction for interest element → Deduction for capital allowances

Lessor (Post 1 April 2006) → Taxed on interest income

Equity v Debt

	Distribution	Interest
Paying co	• Not allowable	• Tax deductible
Private investor	• Taxed at 25% / 30.6%	• Taxable at 40% / 45%
Corporate investor	• Not taxable • FII • SSE for gain	• Taxable • Profit or loss also taxable

Self-test

Answer the following questions

1   Z Ltd is a manufacturing company, making up accounts to 31 March each year.

The following information relates to the year to 31 March 2016:

- The company had tax adjusted trading profits (before taking into account the items below) of £1,000,000.

- On 15 May 2015, the company sold debenture stock for £45,000 in S Ltd which it had acquired for £22,400 on 1 April 1998 as an investment.

- On 31 July 2015, the company issued £200,000 of 6% loan stock for the purpose of raising finance for its trade. The cost of issuing the loan stock was £16,000.

- On 31 January 2016, it paid £900 interest on overdue corporation tax to HMRC for the period from 1 January 2016 to 30 January 2016.

- On 31 March 2016, it received bank interest accrued for the year ending on that date of £5,000.

Requirement

Compute the taxable total profits for Z Ltd for the year ended 31 March 2016.

2   Rogers Ltd bought a foreign investment property costing WAL $150,000 when the rate of exchange was £1 = WAL $4.8. Rogers Ltd sold the property for WAL $350,000 when the rate of exchange was £1 = WAL $8.4. The money was left on deposit in a Walgallesian bank. By the time the proceeds were remitted to the UK the exchange rate was £1 = WAL $9.

Requirement

Ignoring Indexation allowance, what foreign exchange gains or losses arise?

3   Gamma Ltd is currently owned 100% by Kathryn. Kathryn also owns 75% of the shares in Delta Ltd. Gamma Ltd has a 100% UK subsidiary, Beta Ltd.

In order to fund further trade expansion Gamma Ltd needs to raise £1,500,000. The cash will be used for trade purposes. Gamma Ltd is therefore considering two options:

- Issuing new shares; **or**
- Issuing new debentures.

Any issue of new shares would dilute Kathryn's holding in Gamma Ltd. Kathryn will retain just 44% of the total shares after any new share issue.

Kathryn has approached some prospective lenders (debenture purchasers) and investors (share purchasers) and has identified some relevant facts:

- Any debenture loan is likely to have an interest rate of at least 7.6% pa and require interest to be paid twice yearly.

- The capital on any debenture loan would be repayable in 10 years' time.

- Possible lenders are all large UK financial institutions.

- Possible investors are large UK public listed companies which would expect healthy dividends as well as capital growth in the future.

- Investors would look to sell some or all of their shareholding after three years.

- Investors would only be prepared to purchase up to 30% of the total shares. So Kathryn would need to find at least two investors if she decided to dilute her shareholding.

Kathryn has confirmed that the current asset value of Gamma Ltd is less than £5 million.

Requirement

Explain the tax implications of both options to Kathryn. You should only consider the implications to Gamma Ltd and any investor/lender.

Now, go back to the Learning objectives in the Introduction. If you are satisfied you have achieved these objectives, please tick them off.

Technical reference

Legislation

All references are to Corporation Tax Act 2009 (*CTA 2009*)

Loan relationships

Taxation of loan relationships	s.295
Bringing amounts into account	s.296
Meaning of loan relationship	s.302
Incidental costs	s.307(4)
Foreign exchange gains and losses	s.328
Connected party loans: late interest rule	s.373

Leasing

Long funding leases of plant or machinery	s.359 CTA 2010
Capital allowances for long funding leases	ss.70F-W CAA 2001
Tax treatment of finance leases	Statement of Practice 3/91

HMRC manual references

Company Taxation Manual (Found at www.hmrc.gov.uk/manuals/ctmanual/Index.htm)

This technical reference section is designed to assist you when you are working in the office. It should help you to know where to look for further information on the topics covered in this chapter.

Answer to Interactive question

Answer to Interactive question

	£'000
Trading income (W1)	12,065
Profit on non-trading loan relationships (W2)	24,875
Taxable total profits	36,940

WORKINGS

(1) Trading income

	£'000
Profit	80,605
Adjusted for:	
capital element for lease payments of long-funding leases (Note)	1,250
capital allowances on aircraft as long life assets at 8% via purchase under long-funding leases	(4,760)
capital allowances on aircraft via hire-purchase as long life assets at 8%	(40,000)
capital allowances	(3,000)
depreciation	2,200
interest receivable	(27,875)
interest payable	3,000
client entertaining	645
staff party – reasonable and therefore allowable	Nil
Trading income	12,065

Note. The long funding leases are operating leases. In the financial accounts they will therefore have been capitalised and depreciated by the lessor. This depreciation will be disallowed in the lessor's tax computation. Instead the lessor will be taxed on the rentals received less the periodic adjustment. For WIM this capital element of the lease rentals (ie the periodic adjustment) is disallowed for tax purposes and instead capital allowances are given.

(2) Profit on non-trading loan relationships

	£'000
Interest receivable	27,875
Interest payable	(3,000)
	24,875

1

		£
Trading income (W1)		976,000
Profit on non-trading loan relationships (W2)		26,700
Taxable total profits		1,002,700

WORKINGS

(1) Trading income

	£	£
Tax adjusted trading profit		1,000,000
Less: trading loan relationship debits		
incidental costs of finance	16,000	
interest payable (1.8.15 – 31.3.16)		
£200,000 × 6% × 8/12	8,000	(24,000)
Trading income		976,000

(2) Profit on non-trading loan relationships

	£
Non-trading loan relationship credits:	
Profit on sale of debenture stock	
(£45,000 – £22,400)	22,600
Bank interest receivable	5,000
	27,600
Less non-trading loan relationship debit:	
Interest on overdue corporation tax	(900)
Net credit taxable	26,700

2 Forex gains and losses

	£
Proceeds 350,000/8.4	41,667
Cost 150,000/4.8	(31,250)
Gain	10,417

The movement in the exchange rate simply forms part of the capital gain as the asset is a non-monetary asset which is not hedged.

As the proceeds were held on deposit overseas a foreign monetary asset was created at the date of disposal. This monetary asset will be assessed under the loan relationship rules. When the money is remitted exchange movements are crystallised and a loss of £2,778 will be included as a non-trading loan relationship debit, ie £41,667 – £38,889 (ie WAL $350,000/9).

3   Kathryn, Gamma Ltd and potential investors should be advised of the following issues with regard
     to the issue of debentures or shares:

	Debentures	Shares
Gamma Ltd	Issue costs are deductible as a trading expense.	Issue costs will not be deductible as a share issue is considered to be capital.
	Interest will also be an allowable trading deduction on an accruals basis.	Dividends are not deductible for corporation tax purposes.
	Debenture interest is paid gross to UK companies.	
Lender/ Investor	The interest receivable would be chargeable to tax as trading income as received by a financial institution.	Exempt dividends received from companies which are not related 51% group companies are treated as FII for corporation tax purposes.
	Any gain or loss on disposal would be included in trading income for the financial entity rather than as a gain under the loan relationship rules.	Any future sale of the shares would be exempt from chargeable gains as the substantial shareholding exemption (SSE) would apply. Would need to own ≥10% of the shares for at least 12 months and be a trading company.

CHAPTER 12

Corporation tax losses

Introduction

Examination context

Topic List

1 Revision from Tax Compliance

2 Change in ownership

3 Choice of loss relief

Summary and Self-test

Technical reference

Answers to Interactive questions

Answers to Self-test

Learning objectives

- Determine, explain and calculate the corporate tax liabilities for corporate entities ☐

- Explain and evaluate the tax implications of business transformation and change ☐

- Explain and calculate the tax implications involved in the cessation of trade ☐

- Identify legitimate tax planning measures to minimise tax liabilities ☐

- Evaluate and advise on alternative tax strategies relating to corporate transformations ☐

- Recognise, explain and communicate opportunities to use alternative tax treatments arising from past transactions ☐

Specific syllabus references for this chapter are 1f, 1l, 1m, 2a, 2c and 2d.

Syllabus links

The mechanics of relief for corporation tax losses and deficits on non-trading loan relationships is covered in the Tax Compliance study manual. This is extended at Business Planning: Taxation to include the implications of a change in ownership of the company and giving advice to clients on the most appropriate form of loss relief.

Examination context

In difficult trading conditions, the accountant must be able to advise on the most appropriate method of loss relief for all different types of loss. In addition they must take into account any factors that may lead to a restriction of the loss relief, for example certain changes in trading conditions.

In the examination candidates may be required to:

- Explain the trading loss relief options open to a company
- Explain the relief available for deficits on non-trading loan relationships
- Calculate the taxable total profits after the losses are relieved
- Determine when loss relief may be restricted on a change in ownership

The use of losses is often a discriminating factor between good and weaker candidates. Candidates must fully explain the loss reliefs available and their objectives in giving the loss relief.

Candidates must also remember to be very precise in their use of language. Stating that 'losses may be carried forward' is rarely sufficient to gain marks. Instead candidates should state that 'losses may be carried forward and set against the first available trading income from the same trade'.

1 Revision from Tax Compliance

Section overview

- A property loss is set against total profits of the current AP and then of future APs.

- A capital loss is set against gains of the current AP and then of future APs.

- A net loss from non-trading IFAs may be set against total profits of the same AP or carried forward and treated as a non-trading debit of the following accounting period.

- Trading loss relief is available to set off a loss against total profits of the current or earlier AP or by carrying it forward against future trading income.

- A deficit on non-trading loan relationships can be offset in the current year against total profits, offset in the previous year against profits on non-trading loan relationships, or carried forward against non-trading income.

- S.45 trading loss relief applies unless an alternative claim is made.

- Under s.45 trading losses must be carried forward and set against the first available trading income of the same trade.

- The amount of the loss must be shown in the corporation tax return.

- S.37 trading loss relief first sets off a trading loss against total profits in the same accounting period.

- Any remaining loss may then be carried back and set against total profits of the preceding 12 months.

- Total profits are income plus gains but before qualifying donations.

- Qualifying donations may become unrelieved.

- If more than one accounting period falls within the 12-month carry back period, relief is given on a LIFO basis.

- Terminal loss relief is given under s.37, but the carry back period is extended to 36 months.

- S.459 relief allows a claim to be made to set off a deficit on a non-trading loan relationship wholly or partly against any profits of the same accounting period.

- Alternatively or in addition, the deficit may be wholly or partly group relieved (see later in this Study Manual).

- Alternatively or in addition, the deficit may be set off against non-trading loan relationship profits of the previous 12 months.

- If no s.459 claim is made or if there is any unrelieved deficit, the deficit is carried forward to be set against non-trading profits (including chargeable gains) in future accounting periods.

1.1 Property losses

A property loss is first set off against total profits for the accounting period in which the loss arose. Any remaining loss is carried forward to the next accounting period as if it were a property loss of that accounting period (ie can be offset against total profits of that accounting period, not just against property income) and so on, until the loss is completely relieved.

Group relief is also available for a property loss (see Chapter 14).

1.2 Capital losses

A capital loss is first set off against other gains for the accounting period in which the loss arose. Any remaining loss is carried forward to be set against the first available gains. A capital loss incurred by a trading company cannot be set against income.

There are ways in which capital losses may be set against gains in a group. These are discussed later in Chapter 14.

1.3 Non-trading intangible fixed asset losses

If a net loss arises from non-trading IFAs, all or part of it may be set against total profits of the same accounting period or group relieved. Otherwise it is carried forward and treated as a non-trading debit of the following accounting period. In the first instance it would therefore be deducted from income from non-trading IFAs, but if there is an overall loss on non-trading IFAs in the following accounting period a claim could again be made to offset it against total income for that period.

1.4 Trading losses

A company may incur a trading loss where the company's adjusted trading income after capital allowances for an accounting period produces a negative result.

A trading loss has two main consequences:

- The trading income taxable amount will be NIL; and
- The company may be able to claim tax relief for the trading loss.

The loss may be relieved by setting it off against:

- Total profits of the current accounting period; then
- Total profits of an earlier accounting period.

Alternatively, or if there is any remaining loss, the loss can be carried forward to be set against future trading income of the same trade.

Group relief is also available for a trading loss (see Chapter 14).

The trading loss reliefs in this chapter are referred to by their statutory section numbers in the Corporation Tax Act 2010 (CTA 2010). Knowledge of section numbers is not required in the exam.

1.5 Deficit on non-trading loan relationships

A deficit on non-trading loan relationships can be relieved in a similar way to trading losses. This is discussed later in this section.

Group relief is also available for a deficit on non-trading loan relationships (see Chapter 14).

The relief for non-trading loan relationship deficits is referred to in this chapter by its statutory section number in Corporation Tax Act 2009 (CTA 2009). Again, knowledge of this section number is not required in the exam.

1.6 Overview of use of losses

	Property business losses	Capital losses	Trading losses	Deficits on non-trading loan relationships
Current year (c/y)	Set off against total profits in current AP – s.62 CTA 2010	Set off against gains in current AP – s.2 TCGA 1992	Set off against total profits in current AP – s.37(3)(a) CTA 2010	Set off (wholly or partly) against any profits in current AP after b/f trading loss relief but before a c/y or c/b claim for trading losses and prior to any property loss set off for c/y – s.459(1)(a) CTA 2009
Carry back (c/b)	N/A	N/A	Set off against total profits in previous 12 months (must make a c/y claim first) – s.37(3)(b) CTA 2010	Set off against profits on non-trading loan relationships in previous 12 months after other reliefs – s.459(1)(b)

	Property business losses	Capital losses	Trading losses	Deficits on non-trading loan relationships
			C/b extended to 36 months for terminal loss relief – s.39 CTA 2010	Carry back the lower of: • Deficit after c/y and group relief claims, and • Credits of the earlier period as reduced by c/y or b/f debits, qualifying charitable donations, trading losses and expenses etc of a company with an investment business
Carry forward (c/f)	Excess – set off against total profits in future APs	Excess – set off against gains in future APs	Alternatively or for remainder after c/y and c/b claims, carry forward against first available trading income from the same trade – s.45 CTA 2010	Alternatively or for remainder after c/y and c/b claims, carry forward against non-trading profits (incl chargeable gains) of future APs
Claim required?	No	No	c/y or c/b claims made within 2 years of end of AP of loss c/f claim automatic but must agree amount	c/y or c/b claims made within 2 years of end of AP of deficit c/f claim automatic but loss may be excepted from set-off
Group relief?	Yes – excess only – ss.99 & 102 CTA 2010 Claim within 2 years of end of loss making company's AP end	No – but can elect to transfer a gain or loss to another group company – s.171A TCGA 1992	Yes – including amounts allowable as qualifying charitable donations – ss.99-100 CTA 2010 Claim within 2 years of end of loss making company's AP end	Yes – s.99 CTA 2010 Claim within 2 years of end of loss making company's AP end

1.7 Carry forward of trading losses (s.45 CTA 2010)

If a company does not claim any specific form of loss relief, trading losses are carried forward under s.45 and relieved against future trading income of the same trade.

Trading losses carried forward must be set against the first available trading income arising and the maximum amount of the loss must be relieved.

No claim needs to be made for s.45 relief to apply; it applies automatically if no other claims are made. [Hp147]

However, the company must show the amount of the loss which is available for relief in its corporation tax return.

1.8 Setting trading losses against total profits (s.37 CTA 2010)

Under s.37(3)(a), a trading loss arising in an accounting period may be set (ie it is optional) against the company's total profits (ie all income and gains before deduction of qualifying donations) in the same accounting period.

Under s.37(3)(b), any remaining loss may then be carried back (ie it is optional) and set against the company's total profits of the preceding twelve months.

Note that the loss can only be carried back after a current accounting period claim is made. However, it is possible to make a claim to set the loss off only in the current period. In both cases, the maximum amount of loss relief must be taken.

As a result of making a loss relief claim, qualifying donations may become unrelieved.

Worked example: s.37 loss relief

G plc has the following results:

	y/e 31.3.14 £	y/e 31.3.15 £	y/e 31.3.16 £
Trading income/(loss)	10,000	(21,000)	14,000
Property income	2,000	2,000	2,000
Chargeable gains	3,000	Nil	Nil
Qualifying donation	1,000	1,000	1,000

G plc has unrelieved trading losses brought forward of £4,000 from the year ended 31 March 2013.

Requirement

Compute the taxable total profits for all years, assuming that the company wishes to claim loss relief as early as possible, and show any qualifying donations that become unrelieved.

Solution

	y/e 31.3.14 £	y/e 31.3.15 £	y/e 31.3.16 £
Trading income	10,000	Nil	14,000
Less s.45	(4,000)₁		(8,000)₄
	6,000	Nil	6,000
Property income	2,000	2,000	2,000
Chargeable gains	3,000		
	11,000	2,000	8,000
Less s.37(3)(a)		(2,000)₂	
s.37(3)(b)	(11,000)₃		
	Nil	Nil	8,000
Less qualifying donation	Nil	Nil	(1,000)
Taxable total profits	Nil	Nil	7,000
Unrelieved qualifying donations	1,000	1,000	

Note: subscripts above are reference markers ($_1$, $_2$, $_3$, $_4$).

Trading loss working

	£
y/e 31.3.13 loss	4,000
Less used under s.45 y/e 31.3.14	(4,000)
	Nil
y/e 31.3.15 loss	21,000
Less used under s.37(3)(a) y/e 31.3.15	(2,000)
	19,000
Less used under s.37(3)(b) y/e 31.3.14	(11,000)
	8,000
Less used under s.45 y/e 31.3.16	(8,000)
Loss c/f	Nil

Normally, the previous twelve months correspond with one twelve month accounting period.

However, there may be more than one accounting period falling into the twelve months before the start of the loss-making period. In this case, relief is carried back on a LIFO basis (ie to later accounting periods before earlier accounting periods).

If the accounting period falls partly outside the twelve months carry back period, loss relief is limited to the proportion of the period's total profits that fall within that twelve month period.

A claim for s.37 loss relief must be made within two years of the end of the accounting period in which the loss is made. [Hp147]

1.9 Terminal loss relief

S.37 loss relief is also available where a trading loss is incurred in the 12 months before the trade ceases.

In this case, the loss may be carried back against the company's total profits for the preceding 36 months.

If there is a loss in the penultimate accounting period and the final accounting period is less than 12 months long, then some of the terminal loss will be in the penultimate accounting period. That part of the terminal loss can be carried back to 36 months before the start of the penultimate accounting period.

For example if a company stopped trading on 31 March 2016, but had a trading loss of £120,000 for the year ended 31 December 2015, then 9/12 of that loss (ie £90,000) forms part of the terminal loss ie from 1 April 2015 to 31 December 2015. This loss can be carried back to 1 January 2012 ie 36 months before the beginning of the year ended 31 December 2015. Any loss of the final three months to 31 March 2016 can be carried back to 1 January 2013 ie 36 months before the start of the final accounting period.

Worked example: Terminal loss relief

Count Ltd ceased to trade on 30 June 2016. Its recent results are:

	Y/E 31.3.13	Y/E 31.3.14	Y/E 31.3.15	Y/E 31.3.16	P/E 30.6.16
Trading income	65,000	81,000	34,000	(250,000)	(129,000)
Chargeable gains	–	22,000	–	–	12,000
Profit on non-trading loan relationships	15,000	15,000	17,000	18,000	10,000

Requirement

Show how the losses should be relieved using terminal loss relief.

Solution

As the company has ceased to trade, its losses cannot be carried forward. Thus the best use must be made of the losses under current year, carry back and terminal loss relief rules.

Note that losses of earlier accounting periods must be used before losses of later accounting periods. It therefore follows that in exam questions losses should be dealt with in chronological order.

Terminal loss relief

Losses occurring in the final twelve months of trade are eligible for carry back against total profits of the previous three years on a LIFO basis. Some of the loss of the Y/E 31.3.16 occurred in the final twelve months of trade and is eligible for terminal loss relief (TLR). As some of the losses of the last twelve months occurred in the period 1.4.15 – 31.3.16, they may be carried back for three years from the start of that period which means that the terminal losses may be carried back against profits arising in the full period 1.4.12 – 31.3.13.

The loss of the last 12 months is:

Y/E 31.3.16 = 9/12 × £250,000 = £187,500

P/E 30.6.16 = £129,000

Loss of Y/E 31.3.16

The losses relating to the Y/E 31.3.16 must be dealt with first:

- £62,500 of the loss is not eligible for TLR and should be offset in the current year and then carried back under s.37(3)(a) and (b) CTA 2010.

- The remaining £187,500 of the loss may be carried back to the previous three years under s.39 CTA 2010.

Loss of P/E 30.6.16

The losses relating to the P/E 30.6.16 can be dealt with next:

- The full loss of £129,000 is eligible for TLR but there are no profits left in the prior three years and so it cannot be carried back.

- Instead £22,000 of the loss may be offset in the current accounting period and the remaining loss is unrelieved.

Trading loss

	Y/E 31.3.13	Y/E 31.3.14	Y/E 31.3.15	Y/E 31.3.16	P/E 30.6.16
Trading income	65,000	81,000	34,000	–	–
Chargeable gains	–	22,000	–	–	12,000
Profit on NTLR	15,000	15,000	17,000	18,000	10,000
	80,000	118,000	51,000	18,000	22,000
CY – s.37(3)(a) – Y/E 31.3.16				$(18,000)_1$	
CB – s.37(3)(b) – Y/E 31.3.16			$(44,500)_2$		
TLR – s.39 – Y/E 31.3.16	$(63,000)_5$	$(118,000)_4$	$(6,500)_3$		
CY – s.37(3)(a) – P/E 30.6.16					$(22,000)_6$
Taxable total profits	17,000	–	–	–	–

Loss of Y/E 31.3.16	£
Loss	250,000
1 Set off in current year – s.37(3)(a) CTA 2010	(18,000)
2 Set off in prior year – s.37(3)(b) CTA 2010	(44,500)
3 TLR – Y/E 31.3.15	(6,500)
Note this amount could have been offset under s.37(3)(b) instead, reducing the amount available for TLR but giving exactly the same result	
4 TLR – Y/E 31.3.14	(118,000)
5 TLR – Y/E 31.3.13	
Note there is no need to prorate the profits, the profits of the whole accounting period are available to offset the loss	(63,000)
Remaining loss unrelieved	Nil

Loss of P/E 30.6.16	
Loss	129,000
6 Set off in current year – s.37(3)(a) CTA 2010	(22,000)
NB TLR is not possible as no profits remaining in the three years prior to the start of the AP	-
Remaining loss unrelieved	107,000

1.10 Relief for deficit on non-trading loan relationships (s.459 CTA 2009)

A company which has a non-trading loan relationship deficit has four options for relieving its deficit.

1.10.1 Setting off the deficit in the same year

The non-trading loan relationship deficit may set off the whole or part of that deficit against any profits of the same accounting period. Note the difference between this relief and other loss reliefs which do not allow a partial relief claim.

Relief is given **after** any trading loss relief under s.45 CTA 2010 for trading losses brought forward from an earlier accounting period but **before**:

- Relief under s.37 CTA 2010; and
- Relief under s.459 CTA 2009 for a deficit carried back from a later accounting period.

1.10.2 Group relief

Alternatively, or in addition, any remaining deficit may be wholly or partly surrendered to another company in the group (see Chapter 14).

1.10.3 Carrying back 12 months

Alternatively, or in addition, if there is any remaining deficit not relieved in the current accounting period and/or surrendered as group relief, it may be set against profits on non-trading loan relationships of the previous 12 months. The amount which is offset is the lower of:

(i)   The deficit for the year as reduced by any current year claim and any group relief claim, and

(ii)   The non-trading loan relationship credits of the earlier period as reduced by a current year set off; brought forward deficits; qualifying charitable donations; relief for trading losses of the current year or carried back; and management expenses, capital allowances and qualifying charitable donations of an investment company.

The current year and group relief claims can be for any amount, ie partial claims are possible. A carry back to the previous year is for a prescribed amount, if it is not reduced by the set-off in (ii) it effectively becomes an all or nothing claim.

1.10.4 Carrying forward the deficit

Any remaining balance is then carried forward and may be set against non-trading profits (including chargeable gains) of future accounting periods. A claim may be made to except all or part of the loss from set-off in an accounting period, so that the excepted loss continues to be carried forward.

Note that unlike other loss reliefs, it is possible to make **partial claims** to use a non-trading loan relationship deficit. This may be useful to preserve the use of double tax relief credits or other corporation tax reliefs.

A claim for s.459 relief must be made within two years of the end of the accounting period in which the deficit arose. [Hp148]

1.11 Priority of loss relief claims

Within an accounting period, current period losses are set against total profits in the following order:

- Deficits on non-trading loan relationships
- Property business losses
- Trading losses of the current period

2 Change in ownership

Section overview

- Restrictions on loss relief apply where there is a change in ownership and a change in the trade of the company.

- The change in trade must either be a major change within three years of the change in ownership or a considerable revival in a small or negligible trade.

- The restriction applies to pre-acquisition losses which would be relievable under s.45 against profits arising after the change in ownership.

- It also applies to post-acquisition losses which would be relievable under s.37 against profits arising prior to the change in ownership.

- If a 'shell company' changes ownership, loan relationship and IFA non-trade debits, deficits and losses cannot be carried forwards or backwards through the date of change in ownership.

2.1 Change of ownership and conduct of trade

Restrictions on the use of losses apply where there is a change in ownership of a company and either:

- There is a major change in the nature or conduct of the trade within three years before or three years after the change in ownership; or

- After the company's trading activities have become small or negligible, there is a change in ownership followed by a considerable revival of the trade.

A change in ownership occurs if more than half of the ordinary share capital of the company is acquired by a single person or by two or more persons where each holds at least 5%.

Examples of a major change in the nature or conduct of the trade include a change in:

- Services or facilities provided in the trade (eg company owning public house switches to operate disco in the same premises)

- Nature of customers of the trade

- Nature of assets traded in (eg company operating dealership in cars switches to dealership in tractors – but not eg where the dealership switches to a new brand of cars)

- Location of business premises (but not, eg, where manufacturing in three old factories is moved to one new factory to increase efficiency)

- Identity of suppliers, management or staff

- Methods of manufacturing (but not, eg as a result of keeping pace with developing technology or rationalising the product range)

- Pricing or purchasing policies

HMRC will 'consider sympathetically' the application of s.673 (denial of losses when change in ownership and change in trade) where it arises as a result of a demerger. It recognises that the purpose of the demerger is to allow the trade being demerged to be 'managed more dynamically' and that this may involve a major change in the nature or conduct of the trade.

2.2 Restrictions on losses

The restriction applies to:

- S.45 CTA 2010 loss relief where the losses were made before the change in ownership (**pre-acquisition losses**). The pre-acquisition losses cannot be set against post-acquisition trading profits.

- S.37(3) CTA 2010 loss relief where the losses were made after the change in ownership (**post-acquisition losses**). The post-acquisition losses cannot be set against pre-acquisition profits.

- The restriction also applies to property business losses brought forward.

- The restriction does not apply to capital losses.

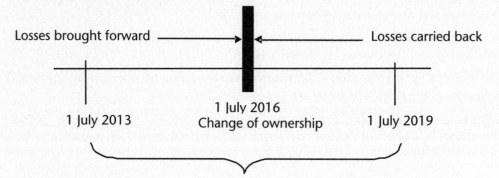

Major changes in nature or conduct of the trade within this six-year period

Interactive question 1: Change in ownership   [Difficulty level: Intermediate]

AB Ltd is a company which sells plumbing equipment to specialist trade outlets. It has a 31 December year end.

On 1 May 2015 the company is sold to XYZ plc. Over the next 12 months the following take place:

(1)   The board of directors of AB Ltd is replaced by XYZ plc appointees.

(2)   The company's name is changed to Alphabet Ltd.

(3)   The purchasing and administration functions are transferred to the group's central departments.

(4)   An increasing proportion of AB Ltd's sales is made to mass market retail DIY stores. At the end of 12 months approximately 35% of sales are made in this way.

Requirement

State what effect the above changes will have for AB Ltd.

See **Answer** at the end of this chapter.

2.3   Shell companies

Where there is a change in ownership of a shell company, non-trade debits or deficits on loan relationships and non-trade debits and losses on IFAs cannot be carried backwards or forwards through the date on which the ownership of the company changes.

A shell company is defined as a company which has:

- No trade;
- No investment business; and
- No UK property business.

For these purposes, the accounting period in which the change in ownership occurs is split into two parts, the first ending with the change in ownership. Debits and credits are allocated to the part of the period to which they relate, and are not generally time apportioned unless they accrue evenly through the period.

3   Choice of loss relief

Section overview

- A company will have a choice of loss reliefs.
- Historically the most important factor has been the rate of tax at which relief will be obtained.
- The next most important factor is the timing of the relief.
- Another factor is the loss of relief for qualifying donations.

3.1   Factors affecting the choice of loss relief

The company will usually have a choice of which loss reliefs to use. Loss relief claims reduce the taxable total profits and therefore the corporation tax payable by the company in the accounting period in which the relief is used. If a carry back claim is made, the corporation tax for the previous period will be recalculated and a repayment of any corporation tax paid may arise, together with interest.

In choosing which loss relief to use, the following factors should be taken into account:

- The rate of tax at which relief will be obtained
- The timing of the relief
- The loss of relief for qualifying donations

Until FY2014 the reduction of taxable total profits may have resulted in a different rate of tax becoming payable, for example, a reduction from the main rate to the small profits rate or marginal relief becoming payable. Where there has been a change in the rate or limits for corporation tax in a previous accounting period, this also needs to be taken into account, as do the projected rates of corporation tax in the future. For FY2015 there is a unified main rate of corporation tax so tax rates are less of an issue, although rates in previous financial years are slightly higher, so tax rates still have some bearing on the decision making process.

Usually the rate of tax at which the relief will be obtained will be the most important factor. However, if the company has cash-flow problems, it may be necessary to obtain relief as soon as possible, irrespective of the rate of tax. The projected level of future profits arising from the same trade will also be a factor.

Worked example: Losses, saving tax and cash flows

LM Ltd is a trading company. It has made up its accounts to 31 March each year, but changed its accounting date, making up accounts for the six months to 30 September 2015.

The company had the following results:

	y/e 31.3.15 £	p/e 30.9.15 £
Trading profit/(loss)	506,500	(417,485)
Profit on non-trading loan relationships	30,749	6,289
Chargeable gain	Nil	17,595
Qualifying charitable donation paid	(11,250)	(8,750)

The company has losses brought forward at 1 April 2014 of £15,400. LM Ltd anticipates making tax adjusted trading profits in the year ended 30 September 2016 of £845,000.

Requirement

Show how the loss for the six months to 30 September 2015 may be used and calculate the tax saving for each option for the year ended 31 March 2015.

Solution

Use of loss relief – CY then PY

LM Ltd must first make a claim under s.37(3)(a) to set its loss for the period ended 30 September 2015 against its total profits for that period before it is able to make a claim under s.37(3)(b) to carry back the loss to the prior year:

	p/e 30.9.15 £
Profit on non-trading loan relationships	6,289
Chargeable gain	17,595
	23,884
Less s.37(3)(a) loss relief	(23,884)
Taxable total profits	Nil
Qualifying charitable donation unrelieved	8,750
Loss available for carry back: (£417,485 – £23,884)	393,601

This would waste the tax relief on the qualifying charitable donation and would therefore only save tax at 20% on £15,134 of the loss (£23,884 – £8,750). The overall tax saving would be £3,027.

It could then make a claim under s.37(3)(b) to carry back the remainder of the loss to the year ended 31 March 2015:

	y/e 31.3.15
	£
Trading profit	506,500
Less b/f trading losses	(15,400)
Trading income	491,100
Profit on non-trading loan relationships	30,749
	521,849
Less s.37(3)(b) loss relief	(393,601)
	128,248
Qualifying charitable donation paid	(11,250)
Taxable total profits	116,998

This would save corporation tax at the marginal rate of 21.25% on the first £210,599 (ie after taking account of the qualifying charitable donation) and then at 20% on the balance of £183,002. Overall it would save tax of £81,352.

A current year claim followed by a carry back claim would therefore save total tax of £84,379 (£3,027 + £81,352). It would, however, mean there would be no corporation tax liability for the period ended 30 September 2015 and lead to a repayment of a substantial part of the corporation tax liability for the year ended 31 March 2015, if it has been paid yet. The liability for the year ended 31 March 2015 was due to be paid on 1 January 2016.

Use of loss relief – carry forward

The whole loss could be carried forward and set against future profits from the same trade. This would allow the whole loss to be offset at the unified main rate of 20%. This would therefore save tax of £83,497 (£417,485 x 20%). This tax is not due to be paid until 1 July 2017.

Conclusion

A current year claim and a carry back claim is 'all or nothing' ie you cannot choose how much loss to offset in any year. The maximum amount of loss must be offset. There is insufficient loss to make a current year and prior year claim and then allow some loss to be carried forward. The whole loss would be offset by a current year/prior year claim saving total tax of £84,379.

Given the low rate of tax saving in the current year, there is no tax advantage in making a current year claim and then carrying forward the remainder. However, if cash flow is a serious problem this may be preferable to having to borrow cash in order to pay the tax due on 1 July 2016.

Carrying forward the whole loss saves the tax of £83,497.

As this is a smaller amount of saving plus later relief, it is much better to obtain the cash flow advantages of a current year/prior year claim.

Interactive question 2: Use of loss relief
[Difficulty level: Easy]

T plc makes up its accounts to 31 March each year. Recent results are as follows:

	y/e 31.3.14	y/e 31.3.15	y/e 31.3.16
	£	£	£
Trading income/(loss)	237,000	(593,000)	700,000
Loan relationships	5,000	5,000	5,000
Chargeable gain	Nil	352,000	Nil
Qualifying charitable donation	(2,000)	(2,000)	(2,000)

Requirement

Using the standard format below, show the choices for loss relief and identify the option which will save the maximum amount of corporation tax and be the most beneficial.

Position before loss relief

	y/e 31.3.14 £	y/e 31.3.15 £	y/e 31.3.16 £
Trading income			
Loan relationships			
Chargeable gain			
Less qualifying donation	(_____)	(_____)	(_____)
Taxable total profits			

Limits for marginal relief (for FY2013 and FY2014)

Upper limit £.......................................

Lower limit £.......................................

Size of company ....

Options for loss relief

(1) *Carry forward (s.45)*

y/e 31.3.16

Tax saving:

£ _____ @ ....% £ _____

Total saving

(2) *Current year claim (s.37(3)(a)) and Carry forward (s.45)*

y/e 31.3.15

Tax saving:

£ _____ @ ....% £ _____
  @ ....%

Unrelieved qualifying donation £ _____

Loss available for c/f

 (£...................... – £......................) £ _____

y/e 31.3.16

Tax saving:

£ _____ @ ....% _____

Total saving

(3) *Current year claim (s.37(3)(a)) and Carry back (s.37(3)(b))*

y/e 31.3.15

Tax saving:

£ _____ @ ....% £ _____
  @ ....%

Unrelieved qualifying donation £ _____

Loss available for c/b

 (£...................... – £......................) £ _____

y/e 31.3.14

Tax saving:

£ _____ @ ....% _____

Total saving

Conclusion

The maximum amount of corporation tax is saved by

....

....

....

....

See **Answer** at the end of the chapter.

Interactive question 3: Losses [Difficulty level: Easy]

R Ltd is a trading company with no associated/ related 51% group companies. It has made up its accounts to 30 June each year, but changed its accounting date, making up accounts for the six months to 31 December 2013.

It has been breaking even for a number of years and in the year to 31 December 2015, following significant investment in restructuring the business, it made a trading loss.

The company had the following results:

	y/e 30.6.12 £	y/e 30.6.13 £	p/e 31.12.13 £	y/e 31.12.14 £	y/e 31.12.15 £
Trading profit/(loss)	9,000	10,000	15,000	50,100	(217,485)
Profit on non-trading loan relationships	8,000	2,000	4,000	8,749	6,289
Chargeable gain	Nil	Nil	Nil	Nil	17,595
Qualifying charitable donation paid	(8,250)	(8,250)	(8,250)	(11,250)	(8,750)

The company had no losses brought forward.

Requirements

Show how the loss for the year to 31 December 2015 may be used, assuming that the company wishes to claim relief as early as possible, and calculate the tax saved.

See **Answer** at the end of this chapter.

Summary

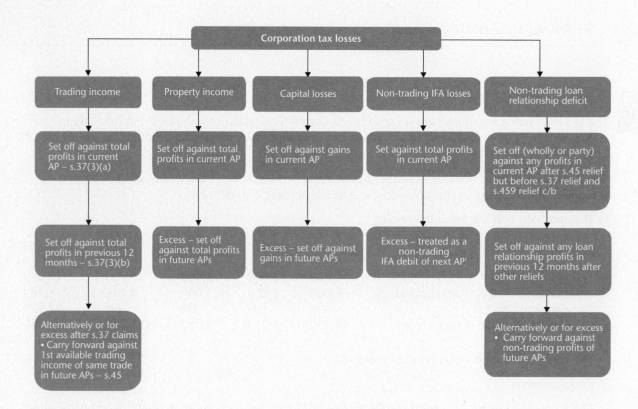

Self-test

Answer the following questions.

1   W plc has the following results:

	y/e 31.3.15 £	y/e 31.3.16 £
Trading income	285,000	1,990,000
Non-trading loan relationship credit/(deficit)	20,000	(15,000)

What is the maximum amount of corporation tax that can be saved by using relief under s.459 Corporation Tax Act 2009?

A   £3,188
B   £3,063
C   £3,150
D   £3,000

2   M plc made a substantial trading loss in the year to 31 December 2015.

Which **one** of the following factors will usually be the most important in deciding how it should use the loss?

A   Loss of relief for qualifying donations
B   Future profits of the company
C   Rate of tax at which relief will be obtained
D   Obtaining of relief as soon as possible

3   Z Ltd is a trading company. It has made up its accounts to 30 June each year, but changed its accounting date, making up accounts for the six months to 31 December 2015.

The company had the following results:

	y/e 30.6.15 £	p/e 31.12.15 £
Trading income/(loss)	491,100	(417,485)
Loan relationships	30,749	6,289
Chargeable gain	Nil	17,595
Qualifying donation paid	(11,250)	(8,750)

The company had no losses brought forward.

Requirements

(a)   Calculate the corporation tax payable by the company for the year ended 30 June 2015 before any loss relief.

(b)   Show how the loss for the six months to 31 December 2015 may be used, assuming that the company wishes to claim relief as early as possible, and calculate the tax saving for the year ended 30 June 2015.

Now, go back to the Learning objectives in the Introduction. If you are satisfied you have achieved these objectives, please tick them off.

Technical reference

> This technical reference section is designed to assist you when you are working in the office. It should help you to know where to look for further information on the topics covered in this chapter.

Answer to Interactive question 1

Changes (1), (2) and (3) do not, in themselves, amount to a major change in the nature or conduct of the trade.

However, taken together with (4) (a major change in customers), it is likely that HMRC would view this as a major change in the nature or conduct of the trade.

Trading losses incurred prior to the change in ownership on 1 May 2015 would not be available to carry forward against profits made after that date.

Answer to Interactive question 2

Position before loss relief

	y/e 31.3.14 £	y/e 31.3.15 £	y/e 31.3.16 £
Trading income	237,000	Nil	700,000
Loan relationships	5,000	5,000	5,000
Chargeable gain	Nil	352,000	Nil
	242,000	357,000	705,000
Less qualifying donation	(2,000)	(2,000)	(2,000)
Taxable total profits	240,000	355,000	703,000

Limits for marginal relief (for FY 2013 and FY2014)

Upper limit £1,500,000
Lower limit £300,000

Size of company	Small	Marginal relief	Unified main rate

Options for loss relief

(1) *Carry forward (s.45)*

   y/e 31.3.16

   Tax saving:

	£		£
Unified main rate	593,000	@ 20%	118,600
	593,000		
Total saving			118,600

(2) *Current year claim (s.37(3)(a)) and carry forward (s.45)*

   y/e 31.3.15

   Tax saving:

	£		£
Marginal band	55,000	@ 21.25%	11,688
Small profits rate	300,000	@ 20%	60,000
	355,000		71,688
Unrelieved qualifying donation	£2,000		
Loss available for c/f			
(£593,000 – £357,000)	£236,000		

   Note that tax is only saved on £355,000 of the loss. However, as the loss is set-off before deducting the qualifying donation, £357,000 of the loss is set-off leaving only £236,000 of loss to carry forward.

y/e 31.3.16

Tax saving:

Unified main rate	£236,000	@ 20%	47,200
Total saving			118,888

(3) *Current year claim (s.37(3)(a)) and carry back (s.37(3)(b))*

y/e 31.3.15

Tax saving:

			£
Marginal band	55,000	@ 21.25%	11,688
Small profits rate	300,000	@ 20%	60,000
	355,000		71,688
Unrelieved qualifying donation	£2,000		
Loss available for c/b			
(£593,000 – £357,000)	£236,000		

y/e 31.3.14

Tax saving:

Small profits rate	£236,000	@ 20%	47,200
Total saving			118,888

Conclusion

The maximum amount of corporation tax is saved by either option 2 or 3. However option 3 is earlier loss relief, leading to a repayment of tax and is therefore preferable.

Answer to Interactive question 3

R Ltd – Use of loss relief

R Ltd must first make a claim under s.37(3)(a) CTA 2010 to set its loss for the year ended 31 December 2015 against its total profits for that period. It can then make a claim under s.37(3)(b) CTA 2010 to carry back the loss to the year ended 31 December 2014:

	y/e 31.12.14	y/e 31.12.15
	£	£
Trading income	50,100	
Profit on non-trading loan relationships	8,749	6,289
Chargeable gain		17,595
Total profits	58,849	23,884
Less s.37(3)(a) loss relief		(23,884)
Less s.37(3)(b) loss relief	(58,849)	
Taxable total profits	Nil	Nil
Qualifying charitable donation unrelieved	11,250	8,750

Loss unrelieved (£217,485 – £23,884 – £58,849) = £134,752

Corporation tax saved – small profits rate applies throughout	£
– year ended 31 December 2015: (£23,884 – £8,750) × 20%	3,027
– year ended 31 December 2014: (£58,849 – £11,250) × 20%	9,520
Total tax saved	12,547

Answers to Self-test

1 B – £3,063

The optimum claim is to make a claim for £15,000 in y/e 31 March 2015 against the loan relationship profits as this saves tax at the then marginal rate of 21.25% on £5,000 followed by 20% on £10,000. This saves more tax than making a claim of £15,000 in the y/e 31 March 2016 to save tax at the unified main rate of 20%. The reduction in rate from FY 2014 to FY 2015 means that a prior year claim at the marginal/ small rate saves more tax than a current year claim at the unified main rate. (Alternatively relief could be £5,000 in y/e 31 March 2015 followed by £10,000 in y/e 31 March 2016, giving the same savings but this would be later relief.)

	£
y/e 31 March 2015	
£5,000 × 21.25%	1,063
£10,000 × 20%	2,000
	3,063

2 C – Rate of tax at which relief is obtained

3 **Z Ltd**

(a) **Corporation tax payable before loss relief for year ended 30 June 2015**

	£
Trade profit	491,100
Loan relationships	30,749
	521,849
Qualifying donation paid	(11,250)
Taxable total profits	510,599

Limits for marginal relief are:

Upper limit £1,500,000

Lower limit £300,000

Marginal relief applies in FY 2014

	£
FY2014:	
£510,599 × 21% × 9/12	80,419
Marginal relief	
(£1,500,000 – £510,599) × 1/400 × 9/12	(1,855)
FY2015: £510,599 × 20% × 3/12	25,530
Corporation tax payable	104,094

(b) **Use of loss relief**

Z Ltd must first make a claim under s.37(3)(a) to set its loss for the period ended 31 December 2015 against its total profits for that period before it is able to make a claim under s.37(3)(b) to carry back the loss to the prior year:

	p/e 31.12.15
	£
Loan relationships	6,289
Chargeable gain	17,595
	23,884
Less s.37(3)(a) loss relief	(23,884)
Taxable total profits	Nil
Qualifying donation unrelieved	8,750
Loss available for carry back:	
(£417,485 – £23,884)	393,601

It can then make a claim under s.37(3)(b) to carry back the remainder of the loss to the year ended 30 June 2015:

	y/e 30.6.15
	£
Trading income	491,100
Loan relationships	30,749
	521,849
Less s.37(3)(b) loss relief	(393,601)
	128,248
Qualifying donation paid	(11,250)
Taxable total profits	116,998

Revised computation of corporation tax payable for the year ended 30 June 2015

Small profits rate applies	£
£116,998 × 20%	23,400
Tax saving for y/e 30 June 2015 = (£104,094 – £23,400)	£80,694

CHAPTER 13

Anti-avoidance for owner-managed businesses

Introduction

Learning objectives

- Evaluate the tax implications of the choice of business structures, including provision of services through a company

- Identify and evaluate the impact of close companies on the taxation of companies and individuals

Specific syllabus references for this chapter are 1g, and 1i.

Syllabus links

Anti-avoidance legislation stems from the utilisation of taxation law for unintended purposes. The abuse of employment status and the use of personal service companies and managed service companies aim to manipulate the amount of taxation paid by some owner-managed businesses. Close company legislation aims to prevent abuse of the corporate structure (Chapter 10).

Examination context

Accountants have become adept at legally avoiding tax for the benefit of their clients, for example until 2002 many smaller traders were advised to incorporate to suffer lower levels of tax and NIC than they would have done as an unincorporated business. Legislation has over time developed to attack such tax avoidance techniques (intermediaries legislation to tackle the example given). In addition promoters of avoidance schemes are required to disclose schemes to HMRC for early detection so that new legislation can be drawn up on a timely basis to prevent too great a loss of tax revenue.

In the examination candidates may be required to:

- Explain whether an individual is an employee or self-employed and the implications for his tax liabilities

- Explain whether a company is affected by the use of intermediaries legislation and the implications for the company's and owner's tax liabilities

- Explain whether a company is a close company and explain the implications for the company's and participators' tax liabilities

1 Employment versus self-employment

Section overview

- The status of an individual as employed or self-employed has tax and legal implications.

- A number of factors need to be taken into account to determine the status of an individual, including how work is offered, how it is paid for and whether there is a financial risk for the individual.

- Generally, there is a lower tax burden on the self-employed, due to both differences in the way income subject to income tax is calculated and lower NICs for a self-employed person.

1.1 Importance of the distinction between employment/self-employment

The distinction between employment and self-employment is very important, not only for tax, but also for legal considerations. For example, an employee may claim holiday and sick pay, unfair dismissal, and may receive redundancy payments (including tax free lump sums) which are not available to a self-employed individual.

In terms of income tax and NIC liabilities, a self-employed person usually has a lower tax burden, which partially compensates for the risk of running a business. As a consequence many individuals claim self-employed status which is often challenged by HMRC.

In most instances the distinction between employment and self-employment is clear and is decided by common sense. However, this is a grey area for a number of individuals. For example, there is a problem in distinguishing between those acting as freelance consultants for several clients and as an employee with many part-time roles with different organisations.

The Employment Status Indicator (ESI) is an online tool provided by HMRC and is used to help determine whether a person is employed or self-employed. The ESI gives guidance based purely on information provided in response to set questions. The ESI tool can give a legally binding opinion in certain circumstances. This is the case if the answers to the ESI questions accurately reflect the terms and conditions under which the worker provides their services and if the ESI has been completed by an engager. If the worker completes the ESI tool the result is only indicative.

1.2 Criteria to determine employment status

To determine the employment status of an individual, HMRC will first consider the terms of the relationship between the individual and the person paying for the work performed.

An employee usually has a contract of service, whereas self-employed individuals are usually contracted for services.

The difference in wording suggests that if a contract for services exists, the individual is deemed to be in business on his own account providing services to clients. However, if a contract of service exists, the individual is deemed to work under the direction of an employer and is dependent on the payer for the service.

In practice there can be considerable difficulty in deciding whether a contract of service or for services exists. It has been left to the courts to interpret these terms in given circumstances.

As a result a number of factors which can be indicative of an employment relationship have been identified by a number of judgements in cases where there has been doubt over the employment status of an individual.

The following factors should be considered:

	Employees	Self-employment
Degree of control	Expect employer to: • Control/supervise work • Determine tasks to be performed • Instruct how to do work • Determine when and where to do work and length of working hours	Expect: • To control own work • To be contracted to produce a result • Not to be instructed how to do work • Work when decide to
Mutuality of obligations	• Perform assigned tasks • Have the right to expect further work when tasks completed • Have an obligation to perform future tasks when asked	• Are contracted to perform a task • Have no right to expect further work • Have no obligation to perform further tasks • Have the ability to delegate duties to others and freedom to hire own staff or subcontractors
Correction of work	• Are not personally liable for the cost of mistakes or correction of poor work	• Are personally responsible or liable for mistakes or correction of poor work
Provision of financial capital (ie degree of financial risk)	• Do not risk own capital • Are remunerated whether employer profitable or not	• Risk losing own capital if business fails (can insure against some risk) • Can operate at a loss
Provision of own equipment	• Expect employer to provide materials or equipment needed	• Expect to provide own equipment and materials
Payment and disciplinary rules	Entitled to: • Regular agreed fixed level of remuneration • Holiday and sick pay • Pay via PAYE system • Subject to disciplinary rules	• Only paid for work done • No holiday or sick pay • Paid gross on submission of invoice • Not subject to disciplinary rules
Client portfolio/ exclusivity	• Usually work for single employer • Often precluded from working for others	• Usually have a number of clients/customers

Many of these factors (eg conditions of pay, ability to hire own staff, provision of own equipment) require consideration of whether the individual has been integrated into the business organisation.

If the work is performed as an integral part of the business, this suggests employment. If the work performed is an accessory to the main part of the business, this suggests self-employment.

It is important to appreciate that these factors cannot be used as a simple checklist. There is no one clear and decisive test. However, the case law does indicate that where there is a genuine right of substitution (which could be used in practice) the relationship will almost certainly not constitute employment.

Where there is any doubt, the detailed facts in each individual case must be considered, along with the guidance from all of the factors/criteria in other cases to form an overall impression before a decision is made.

1.3 Tax consequences of individual tax payer's status

	Employed	Self-employed
Type of income	Employment income	Trading income
Basis of assessment	Receipts basis	Current year basis, with special rules in opening and closing years
Income assessed	Earnings received from the employment including taxable benefits for private use	All trading profits including adjustments for private use
Allowable expenses	Wholly, exclusively and necessarily incurred in the performance of the duties of the employment	Wholly and exclusively incurred for the purposes of the trade
National insurance contributions	• Class 1 primary • Class 1 secondary • Class 1A • Class 1B	• Class 2 • Class 4
Payment of income tax and national insurance contributions	Monthly via PAYE system	• Self-assessment for IT, class 2 and class 4 NICs – payment by payments on account and balancing payment

2 Use of intermediaries

Section overview

- Personal service companies were created by individuals to provide services via an intermediary company and remunerate themselves via dividends instead of salary.

- Less overall tax and NIC was payable as a result.

- IR35 personal service company rules counteract this by treating income from 'disguised' employment (ie services which would have been employment if not provided through a company) as deemed employment income.

- Managed service company rules apply where services are provided through a company and there is a managed service provider involved with the company. These automatically treat all non-employment income payments as deemed employment income (regardless of whether or not there is a 'disguised' employment).

2.1 Overview

It is generally more beneficial for taxation purposes to be classified as self-employed rather than as an employee when working for a business.

Where self-employment status was hard to prove an alternative method of minimising tax and national insurance liabilities was to set-up an intermediary company (or partnership) also known as a personal service company.

Anti-avoidance legislation therefore applies to block the provision of services to a client via an intermediary being used to reduce tax and national insurance liabilities.

There are two different sets of anti-avoidance legislation which can apply in this context. The first is the personal service company or 'IR35' legislation. The second is the rules which apply to managed service companies: these are companies which are effectively run for the worker (or group of workers) by an external service provider.

Thus a worker providing services via a company may be taxed in one of three ways:

- As a limited company within the scope of IR35;
- As a managed service company; or
- As a limited company to which neither IR35 nor the managed service company rules apply.

2.2 Personal service companies

If the worker is genuinely self-employed, IR35 does not apply. If, but for the intermediary, the worker would be an employee of the client then IR35 applies. The tax advantages of operating via an intermediary will then be reversed by the application of IR35.

2.2.1 Remuneration

Personal service companies employ the worker and invoice the client company for his work. The tax consequences are as follows:

- The client company therefore avoids payment of employer's national insurance as the worker is not its employee.

- The personal service company also avoids paying employer's national insurance as the worker will pay himself a minimum salary which maintains entitlement to social security benefits but is less than the earnings threshold.

- The remaining profits are either retained in the company (corporation tax payable at the small profits rate) or paid out as dividends with additional income tax of 25% of the cash dividend for a higher rate taxpayer or 30.6% for an additional rate taxpayer.

2.2.2 Scope of IR35 legislation

IR35 applies where an individual provides services to a client through an intermediary and would be treated as an employee of the client but for the existence of the intermediary, or where the individual is acting as an officer of a company and the services relate to the office. These situations are referred to as a relevant engagement.

Where an individual provides services to more than one client it is possible that some or all of the services will be treated as relevant engagements on a case by case basis.

In determining whether a worker would be an employee but for the existence of the intermediary, the employee/self-employed case law has to be considered for each separate contract.

Where the intermediary is a company, the provisions only apply where the individual controls at least 5% of the ordinary share capital. If the intermediary is a partnership, the individual plus his associates must control 60% of the partnership profits for the rules to apply.

The rules do not apply where the individual only receives earnings from the intermediary and has no right to capital; ie employees of service companies or consultancy firms who do not own shares are not within the scope of the legislation.

From 6 April 2014 arrangements using offshore employment intermediaries are also subject to IR35 legislation.

2.2.3 Application of IR35 legislation

Any employment income paid to the worker by the intermediary is paid in the normal way via PAYE.

Where the amount paid as employment income is less than the amount received from relevant engagements, the excess (less allowable expenses) will be treated as a deemed employment income payment on the 5 April of the tax year.

The deemed employment payment is subject to income tax and NIC even if it is not actually paid.

The deemed employment payment (and the employer's NIC) is deductible for corporation tax purposes in the accounting period in which it is deemed to have been paid. An accounting year end of 5 April may therefore be preferred.

Any dividends paid out of income which has been taxed as a deemed employment payment will be treated as reduced by the amount which has already been taxed. This is to ensure that the income is not taxed twice.

2.2.4 Allowable expenses

The deemed employment payment is reduced by:

- A flat 5% of the gross relevant engagement fees received;

- Expenses paid by the intermediary which would be deductible under employment income rules;

- Capital allowances on items provided by the intermediary which would be deductible from employment income in relation to assets used in his employment;

- Employer NIC paid during the year including NIC due on the deemed employment income payment; and

- Employer pension contributions.

Interactive question: Deemed employment income   [Difficulty level: intermediate]

W Ltd has the following results:

Steve is a computer consultant trading through a personal service company, XYZ Ltd, in which he owns 99% of the shares. During 2015/16 he is engaged by ABC Ltd under a contract between XYZ Ltd and ABC Ltd to the value of £60,000.

During 2015/16 Steve draws a salary of £25,000 from XYZ Ltd which is taxed via PAYE and employer's national insurance of £331 is due.

If XYZ Ltd did not exist Steve would be treated as an employee of ABC Ltd.

Requirement

Calculate Steve's deemed employment income payment and the income tax and the employee national insurance contributions due thereon for 2015/16.

Employment income	£	£
Total earned		
Less 5% allowable deduction	_____	
Less salary		
Employer's NIC	_____	
	_____	
Deemed employment income = £	_____	
Employer's NIC		=====
Income tax		
£ × 20%		
£_____ × 40%		_____
	=====	

Income tax on deemed employment income

Employee national insurance

£ _____ × 12%

£ _____ × 2%

Employee national insurance on deemed employment income

See **Answer** at the end of this chapter.

2.3 Managed service companies (MSCs)

2.3.1 Application of MSC legislation

Definition

Managed service company: A managed service company is one which:

- Supplies the services of individual workers to third party clients; and

- The worker receives the majority of the payments received by the managed service company from the client in relation to the worker's services; and

- The worker receives payments which are more than they would have been if they had been treated as employment income paid after deduction of IT and NIC via PAYE; and

- A managed service company provider is 'involved' with the company.

A managed service company provider is 'involved' if it takes a percentage of income, or arranges contracts, controls bank accounts or controls the company's finances generally. Recruitment agencies and persons providing legal and accounting services are excluded from being managed service company providers.

If the definition of a managed service company is met then:

- Any non-employment income paid out to the workers is to be treated as earnings for both IT and NIC purposes.

- There is no need to prove the existence of a disguised employment.

- A deemed employment payment will arise on any actual payments made to the workers which are not paid out after deduction of IT and NIC via PAYE.

- The payment is chargeable when the payments are made (unlike a personal service company when they are taxed at the end of the year).

- The only deductions from the deemed employment payment are expenses which would be allowed under normal employment income rules and the employer's NIC due on the deemed employment income.

This is generally a higher charge than would apply under the IR35 rules set out above. The reason for this is that workers in managed companies are assumed not to be really in business on their own account, because they are only operating through a company because the service provider deals with all of the associated administration.

2.3.2 Recovery of IT and NIC

If the IT and NIC due is not paid by the managed service company itself, HMRC can instead seek to recover the debt from any of:

- The directors of the managed service company;

- The managed service company provider; or

- Any person who directly or indirectly has encouraged, facilitated or otherwise been actively involved in the provision of the services of individuals through the managed service company.

This is a very broad definition and leaves managed service company providers in particular open to huge potential liabilities.

3 Close companies

Section overview

- A close company is one which is controlled by five or fewer participators or any number of directors. In essence close companies are generally family owned companies and participators are simply the shareholders.

- Loans to participators and their associates are subject to s.455 CTA 2010. A tax charge of 25% of the value of the loan is payable with the corporation tax liability. If the loan is written off the tax charge is repaid but the write off is treated as a net distribution in the hands of the participator/associate.

- Where a loan is made to a participator who is also an employee, then an employment income charge may also apply if the interest rate is less than the HMRC official rate.

- Where a benefit is provided to a participator who is not an employee, then an employment income charge cannot be made. Instead the benefit is treated as a net distribution.

3.1 Definition of a close company

A close company is one which is under the control of:

- Five or fewer participators; or
- Participators (any number) who are also directors.

A company is not close where it is:

- A quoted company with at least 35% of the voting power controlled by the public, or
- Controlled by one or more other companies which are themselves not close companies.

In general, close companies are family owned and controlled companies. In general, the participators are simply the shareholders.

Definitions

Participator: A person who has a share or interest in the capital or income of the company including:

- Any person who possesses, or is entitled to acquire, share capital or voting rights in the company;

- Any loan creditor of the company;

- Any person who possesses, or is entitled to acquire, a right to receive or participate in distributions of the company or any amounts payable by the company (in cash or in kind) to loan creditors by way of premium on redemption; and

- Any person who is entitled to secure that income or assets (present or future) of the company will be applied directly or indirectly for his benefit.

Director: Includes:

- Any person occupying the position of director (whatever name is given to that position);

- Any person in accordance with whose directions or instructions the directors are accustomed to act (shadow director);

- Any person who is:

    - A manager of the company or otherwise concerned with the management of the company; and

    - Is, either on his own or with one or more associates, the beneficial owner of, or able to control (directly or indirectly), 20% or more of the ordinary share capital of the company.

3.1.1 Associates

The interests of associates of a participator are added to the interest of the participator when determining whether control of the company exists.

Definition

Associate: Means:

- Any relative or business partner of the participator. Relative means spouse/civil partner, parent or remoter forebear (eg grandparent), child or remoter issue (eg grandchildren) and brother and sister; and

- The trustees of any settlement of which the participator or any relative of his was the settlor; and

- The trustees of any trust or personal representatives of an estate which has shares or obligations of the company where the participator has an interest in those shares or obligations.

Note that this definition does not include uncles, aunts, nephews or nieces. An associate of an associate of a participator is also not included.

Worked example: Close company

The share capital of Happy Families Ltd is 30,000 ordinary shares of £1 each, with each share carrying one vote. The shareholdings, which have been unchanged for several years, are as follows:

	No. of shares
George Bunn	4,500
Gladys Bunn (wife of George Bunn)	2,000
Mary Sole (sister of Gladys Bunn)	800
Brian Tape	2,400
Alfred Soot	3,000
Jean Brush (sister of Alfred Soot's wife)	1,700
Eileen Over (business partner of Jean Brush)	400
40 other equal shareholders	15,200

George and Gladys Bunn are the only directors of the company.

Requirement

Determine whether Happy Families Ltd is a close company.

Solution

The votes of the directors and their associates (George Bunn, Gladys Bunn and Mary Sole) total only 7,300. This does not make the company close. Therefore the next step is to consider the number of participators who control the company:

		No. of shares	
1	Gladys Bunn (is associated with her spouse and her sister)	2,000	
	George Bunn	4,500	
	Mary Sole (sister)	800	
			7,300
2	Alfred Soot		3,000
3	Brian Tape		2,400
4	Jean Brush (not an associate of Alfred Soot)	1,700	
	Eileen Over (Jean's business partner)	400	
			2,100
5	Any other single shareholder (15,200/40)		380
			15,180

Because five participators exercise control with 15,180 votes out of a total of 30,000 votes, Happy Families Ltd is a close company.

Note If the partnership between Jean Brush and Eileen Over were dissolved, they would cease to be associates. The largest number of votes controlled by five or fewer participators would then be 14,800 and Happy Families Ltd would cease to be a close company.

3.2 Loans to participators

3.2.1 Overview

When a close company makes a loan to

- One of its participators or to an associate of a participator, or

- To the trustees of a settlement where either trustee or beneficiary is a participator or an associate of a participator, or

- To an LLP or partnership in which a participator or an associate of a participator is a partner.

It must make a payment of notional tax to HMRC under s.455 CTA 2010. You do not need to know this section number in the examination. However, it is commonly used in practice and serves as a useful label.

The notional tax payable is 25% of the loan. The notional tax is subject to the same due dates as the corporation tax liability. So companies which pay corporation tax in instalments will also pay the notional tax in instalments. For all other companies (which will include most close companies), the tax is due for payment nine months and one day after the end of the accounting period in which the loan is made. [Hp141]

3.2.2 Definition of loan

A loan for these purposes includes:

- A debt owed to the company
- A debt owed by a participator or his associate which is assigned to the company
- An advance of money

3.2.3 Excluded loans

S.455 tax does not apply to:

- A loan made in the ordinary course of the company's business of money lending; or

- Money owed for goods or services supplied by the company in the ordinary course of its trade or business unless the credit given exceeds six months or is longer than that normally given to the company's customers; or

- A loan to a director or employee if:

  - Loans to that borrower do not exceed £15,000; and

  - The borrower works full-time for the close company; and

  - The borrower (on his own or with his associates) does not have a material interest (over 5% of the ordinary shares or the assets of the company on a winding up) in the company.

If the borrower did not have a material interest at the time the loan was made but later acquires one, the company is treated as making the loan at the time he acquires the material interest.

3.2.4 Loan repaid or written off

If the loan is repaid or written off, the tax charge is repaid on the normal corporation tax due date. Where the loan is repaid before the corporation tax is due, no s.455 tax is payable. However this is subject to anti-avoidance rules which prevent a loan being repaid just prior to the corporation tax due date and a new loan being issued very soon thereafter to avoid the payment of the s.455 charge.

The anti-avoidance rules apply such that if:

- There is both a repayment of at least £5,000 of a loan made in an earlier accounting period, and a new loan of at least £5,000 is made within the same 30-day period then the repayment is treated as a repayment of the new loan.

- The loan balance before a repayment was at least £15,000, and at the time of the repayment it was intended that a new loan would be made then the repayment is treated as a repayment of the new loan.

In either case, the repayment is only taken into account to the extent that it exceeds the amount of the new loan.

If the loan is written off, a net distribution of that amount is treated as having been made to the participator. The normal dividend income rules apply ie if he is a starting or basic rate taxpayer there is no further tax to pay. If he is a higher rate taxpayer an extra 22.5% on the grossed-up value is due (25% of the net distribution). If he is an additional rate taxpayer an extra 27.5% on the grossed-up value is due (30.6% of the amount received).

Although for income tax purposes the loan is treated as a distribution, it is not actually a distribution. The write off of the loan cannot be treated as a non-trading loan relationship debit. A deduction is specifically prohibited.

Worked example: Loan repayments

David Paul set up a company to provide IT services, called DP Tech Ltd, of which he is the sole shareholder.

It has a 30 September year end. From April to September 2015 he borrowed £5,000 per month from the company. On 15 January 2016 the loan balance was cleared by a payment out of David Paul's personal savings account. However, at the time he made the repayment, David intended to borrow a further £38,000, from the company to pay his tax via self-assessment at the end of January 2016.

Requirement

Explain how much tax will be payable by DP Tech Ltd under the loans to participators rules as a result of these transactions.

Solution

The maximum amount outstanding at any time is £30,000 (at the end of September 2015). A repayment is made prior to the date that DP Tech Ltd would have had to pay a s.455 charge under the loans to participators rules. However as the loan balance was at least £15,000 and, at the time of the repayment, it was intended that a new loan would be made, the repayment is treated as a partial repayment of the new £38,000 loan not the original loan. Therefore penalty tax of £7,500 (25% x £30,000) will fall due on 1 July 2016.

These anti-avoidance rules do not apply if the repayment gives rise to a charge to income tax on the person who received the chargeable payment. In other words, If in the above example the repayment had been by way of a dividend declared by DP Tech Ltd, the dividend would be treated as a repayment of the original loan and the penalty tax would not fall due.

3.2.5 Participator is also an employee

If the participator is an employee, there may be two charges to tax when the loan is made (s.455 and taxable benefit if cheap taxable loan).

If the participator is an employee and the loan is written off, the company is treated as making a net distribution of that amount, in priority to employment income rules; ie it is treated as a net distribution not an employment income charge for income tax purposes. However, where the participator (or associate) is also an employee, the amount written off will be liable to Class 1 NIC.

Worked example: Loans to participators

Pilling Ltd (a close company) lent Marvin, a participator, £118,000 on 1 May 2014. Marvin repaid £37,000 on 1 May 2015 but because of his financial position, the company agreed to waive the balance of the loan in December 2015. The company's year-end is 30 June, it has augmented profits of approximately £500,000 each year and no associated/ related 51% group companies. Marvin has total taxable income of £50,000 pa excluding the loan related transactions.

Requirement

Calculate and explain the taxation consequences of the loan. Assume that 2015/16 tax rates and rules apply in future periods.

Solution

	£
Loan made on 1 May 2014	
Pilling Ltd pays tax charge (25% × £118,000)	29,500
Paid on normal payment date – 1 April 2015	
Instalment repaid on 1 May 2015	
Pilling Ltd recovers tax charge (£37,000 × 25%; or £29,500 × $^{37}/_{118}$)	9,250
Recovered on normal payment date – 1 April 2016	

Loan waived in December 2015

Pilling Ltd recovers the remaining £20,250 on 1 April 2017.

Marvin is assessed on dividend income of £90,000 (£81,000 × $^{100}/_{90}$) in 2015/16. He is treated as having paid income tax of £9,000 (10% × £90,000).

Note. If Marvin were not liable for tax, he could not recover the tax credit. Grossing up is at the dividend rate (10% for 2015/16).

3.3 Benefits for participators

Where a close company provides a benefit to a participator or his associate who is not an employee, it cannot be taxed as employment income; instead the company is treated as making a distribution (like a dividend paid) to the participator.

The amount of the distribution is the amount that would be taxed as earnings under the Benefits Code if provided to an employee who is not in excluded employment.

The participator is then taxed on the grossed-up distribution. No further tax will be paid by a starting rate or basic rate taxpayer, but further tax will be payable by a higher or additional rate taxpayer.

The actual cost of providing the benefit is a disallowable expense for the company in its corporation tax computation.

A targeted anti-avoidance rule applies if a benefit is conferred directly or indirectly on a participator or an associate of a participator as part of a tax avoidance arrangement, and an income tax charge would not otherwise apply. In such cases, a charge of 25% of the taxable value of the benefit applies. This is treated as if it were corporation tax payable by the company, in the same way as s.455 tax. A claim can be made to reduce the tax charge, in whole or in part, if a payment is made to the company for the benefit. The claim must be made within four years of the end of the financial year in which the payment is made to the company.

Worked example: Benefits for participators

Jonathan is a participator of a close company, but is neither a director nor employee. During 2015/16 he is provided with a car by the company for which the equivalent benefit is £5,200. Jonathan is required to make a contribution of £700 to the company towards the benefit of using the car. Jonathan is a higher rate taxpayer, and the provision of the benefit is not part of an arrangement to avoid tax.

Requirement

Calculate and explain the taxation consequences of providing the car.

Solution

Jonathan will have a deemed distribution of £4,500. This will be grossed up by 100/90 in order to give a dividend income of £5,000. As a higher rate taxpayer the effective tax rate is 25% of the net ie £1,125.

This will not be a deductible expense for the close company and no Class 1A national insurance contributions are payable.

3.4 Qualifying interest

If a participator who owns at least 5% of the share capital or works full-time in the management of a close company (or, from 2014/15, an EEA resident company that would be close if resident in the UK) takes out a loan to buy shares in or make a loan to a 'close company', then income tax relief is available on any interest paid. Such qualifying interest is deductible from total income to give net income.

This relief is not available if the shares have already been given relief under the Enterprise Investment Scheme.

Amounts deductible under these provisions are subject to the restriction on income tax reliefs against total income, which is covered in Chapter 4.

3.5 Temporary non-residence

As set out in Chapter 8, if an individual is non-UK resident for any period of five years or fewer, certain types of income and gains which arise during the period of non-residence are taxed in the year in which he returns to the UK.

Income within the scope of these rules includes:

- Dividends from close companies where, at some time in the year of departure or one of the three previous tax years, the individual and his associates had a 5% interest. This does not apply to dividends paid out of trading profits which accrue after the individual ceases to be UK resident, and

- Income relating to the writing off of loans from close companies.

3.6 Jointly held shares

Distributions in respect of shares in close companies held jointly by spouses/civil partners are taxed according to their actual ownership rather than in equal shares.

3.7 Close investment holding companies

A close investment holding company is any close company except one which:

- Lets land, other than to connected persons; or
- Holds shares in or co-ordinates the administration of companies carrying out such activities.

The consequences of being a close investment holding company are:

- Prior to FY 2015 taxable total profits are always taxed at the main rate regardless of the level of augmented profits;

- Participators will not receive income tax relief for interest on loans taken out to make loans to or purchase shares in a close investment holding company.

A close company will become a close investment holding company after it ceases to trade.

Where a close company appoints a liquidator it will not be treated as a close investment holding company for the first accounting period after the liquidator is appointed, provided it was not a close investment holding company prior to the liquidator being appointed.

3.8 Capital gains tax on disposal of UK residential property

From 6 April 2015 non-UK resident companies controlled by five or fewer persons are subject to capital gains tax on disposals of UK residential property. The taxable gain is that part of the gain arising after 5 April 2015, based on the market value at that date. Alternatively an election can be made for the total gain over the whole period of ownership to be time apportioned and only the post 5 April 2015 gain charged to tax. The rate of CGT applying to companies is 20%.

This does not apply if the non-UK resident company is a 'qualifying institutional investor'. The provisions also apply to non-UK resident individuals and trusts (see Chapter 8).

CHAPTER

13

Anti-avoidance for owner-managed businesses   335

Summary and Self-test

Summary

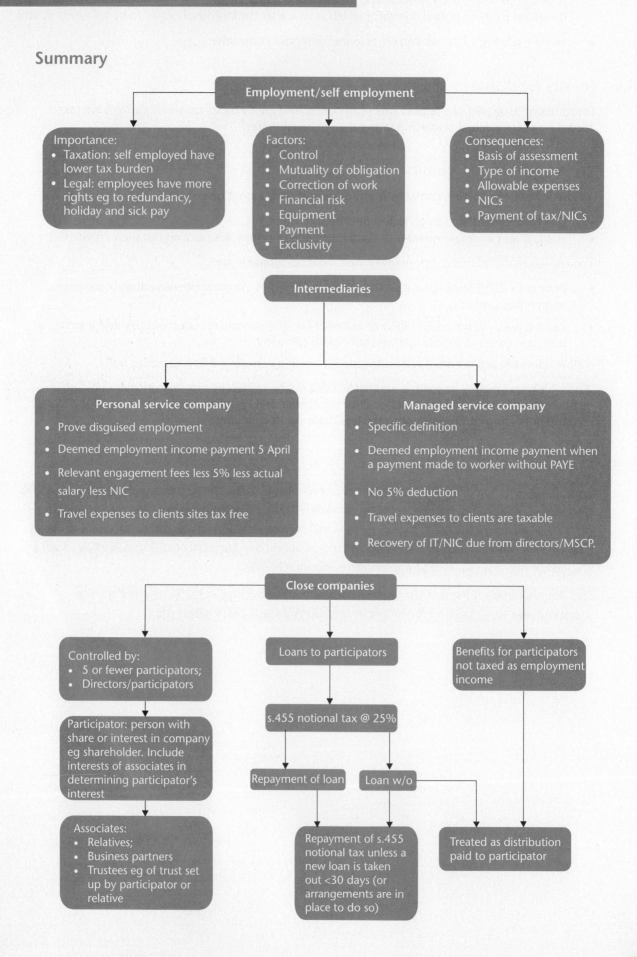

Employment/self employment

Importance:
- Taxation: self employed have lower tax burden
- Legal: employees have more rights eg to redundancy, holiday and sick pay

Factors:
- Control
- Mutuality of obligation
- Correction of work
- Financial risk
- Equipment
- Payment
- Exclusivity

Consequences:
- Basis of assessment
- Type of income
- Allowable expenses
- NICs
- Payment of tax/NICs

Intermediaries

Personal service company
- Prove disguised employment
- Deemed employment income payment 5 April
- Relevant engagement fees less 5% less actual salary less NIC
- Travel expenses to clients sites tax free

Managed service company
- Specific definition
- Deemed employment income payment when a payment made to worker without PAYE
- No 5% deduction
- Travel expenses to clients are taxable
- Recovery of IT/NIC due from directors/MSCP.

Close companies

Controlled by:
- 5 or fewer participators;
- Directors/participators

Participator: person with share or interest in company eg shareholder. Include interests of associates in determining participator's interest

Associates:
- Relatives;
- Business partners
- Trustees eg of trust set up by participator or relative

Loans to participators

s.455 notional tax @ 25%

Repayment of loan

Repayment of s.455 notional tax unless a new loan is taken out <30 days (or arrangements are in place to do so)

Loan w/o

Treated as distribution paid to participator

Benefits for participators not taxed as employment income

ICAEW

Self-test

Answer the following questions.

1 Jennifer is considering setting up in business as a freelance IT consultant. She cannot decide whether to operate as a sole trader or via a company.

Jennifer dislikes administration and has therefore decided to purchase a company 'off the shelf' from a management company. The management company also offers an on-going service whereby it ensures compliance with company law, prepares tax returns and advice, offers payroll services, prepares client contracts and will assist in the finding of clients. Jennifer is unsure whether to take advantage of the on-going service offered.

Jennifer will primarily work for her former employer, Chambers Ltd. She anticipates that 70% of the time she will work for Chambers Ltd. The remainder of the time she will work for a varied number of clients on an ad-hoc, short-term basis. Jennifer does not anticipate employing staff other than possibly a personal assistant for at least three years and will therefore need to fulfil all contracts personally.

Jennifer anticipates business income of between £100,000 and £150,000 per annum and costs (excluding her salary and travel costs) of £9,000 per annum. Travel to and from clients' premises is a considerable expense at £8,000 per annum.

Requirements

(a) Assuming that neither personal service company nor managed service company legislation applies, calculate the net disposable income for 2015/16 which would be generated from:

- Paying a salary of £25,000 from tax adjusted profits of £105,000 and the balance of retained profits paid as a dividend if trading via a company; or

- Having tax adjusted trading profits of £105,000 if trading as a sole trader.

(b) Explain whether Jennifer's company will be treated as a managed service company.

(c) State the definition of a personal service company and explain the taxation implications of falling within the scope of either personal service company or managed service company legislation.

2 S Ltd is a close company and paid corporation tax at the small profits rate prior to FY 2015. The company makes up accounts to 31 October. On 1 April 2015, it made a loan of £30,000 to Toby, a participator. On 1 August 2015, Toby repaid £5,000 of the loan. On 15 January 2016, he repaid a further £10,000. On 1 September 2016, he repaid £12,000 of the loan.

What is the actual amount of s.455 notional tax payable by S Ltd on 1 August 2016 in respect of the loan, assuming all relevant claims are made?

A £750
B £3,750
C £6,250
D £7,500

3 T Ltd is a close company. It provides a car for private use to Zara, a participator, for the whole of 2015/16. Zara is not a director nor an employee of the company.

The car has a list price of £23,400 and CO_2 emissions of 151g/km. Zara paid T Ltd £100 per month for use of the car. No private petrol is provided.

What is the taxable amount that Zara will enter on her tax return for 2015/16 in respect of the provision of the car?

A £4,650
B £5,167
C £5,850
D £6,500

4 J Ltd is a close company making up accounts to 30 September. It paid corporation tax at the small profits rate prior to FY 2015. On 1 March 2015, it made a loan of £50,000 to Matthew, one of its participators. Matthew repaid £20,000 of the loan on 1 January 2016 and then a further £10,000 of the loan on 1 August 2016.

Requirements

(a) Compute the amount of s.455 notional tax actually payable by J Ltd, stating when it is due for payment.

(b) Compute the amount of s.455 notional tax repayable to J Ltd, stating when it is due for repayment.

5 L Ltd is a close company making up accounts to 31 March each year. On 1 February 2015, it makes a loan of £75,000 to Simon, a participator. On 1 February 2016, L Ltd writes off £27,000 of the loan.

Simon is aged 50 and has property income of £125,000 in 2015/16.

Requirements

Compute:

(a) The amount of s.455 notional tax payable by L Ltd, stating when it is due for payment
(b) The amount of s.455 notional tax repayable to L Ltd, stating when it is due for repayment
(c) Simon's income tax payable for 2015/16

6 **Inferno Ltd**

Since 1 June 2013, Inferno Ltd shares have been owned as follows:

Shareholder	Number of shares held
Edward Dante (director)	150
Victor Dante (Edward's son)	25
Hugo Dante (Edward's son)	75
Hercule Christie (director)	100
Poirot Christie (Hercule's son)	25
Agatha Marple	100
Bertie Woodhouse	65
Jeeves Woodhouse (Bertie's uncle)	55
Laura Woodhouse (Bertie's aunt and wife of Jeeves)	55
Other parties (no more than 1% each)	350
Total	1,000

Inferno Ltd, an unquoted trading company with no associates/ related 51% group companies, prepares its accounts to 31 May each year. For the year ended 31 May 2015 its total profits were £1,345,000. Inferno Ltd has yet to announce any dividend for the year ended 31 May 2016 but it did undertake two transactions with its shareholders during this accounting period.

Jeeves Woodhouse, who is neither an employee nor a director, was provided with a London flat by Inferno Ltd from 1 February 2016. Inferno Ltd rents the flat for Jeeves at a cost of £1,700 per month. The flat has an annual value of £11,900.

Victor and Hugo Dante are employees of Inferno Ltd. On 1 November 2015 they received a loan from Inferno Ltd for £250,000 each to help settle the inheritance tax liability from their mother's estate. Interest was paid on the loans at 2.25% per annum. The loans were still outstanding on 31 May 2016 and are to be repaid in December 2018.

Requirement

Explain, with supporting calculations, the tax implications of the flat in London and the loans.

Assume an official rate of interest of 3%.

Now, go back to the Learning objectives in the Introduction. If you are satisfied you have achieved these objectives, please tick them off.

Technical reference

Legislation

Use of intermediaries

All references are Income Tax (Earnings & Pensions) Act 2003 *(ITEPA 2003)* unless otherwise stated

Personal service company – relevant engagements	s.49
Deemed employment payment	s.54
Meaning of managed service company	s.61B
Deemed employment payment	s.61D

Close companies

All references are Corporation Tax Act 2010 *(CTA 2010)* unless otherwise stated

Definition of close company	s.439
Exceptions	s.442
Control	s.450
Associates	s.448
Directors	s.452
Participators	s.454
Loans to participators	s.455
Exceptions from s.455	s.456
Repayment or release of loans	s.458 and s.464C
Benefits for participators	s.1064
TAAR applying to benefits for participators	s.464A
Disposal of UK residential property by non-residents	Sch. 7 FA 2015

HMRC manual references

Intermediaries Legislation (IR35) – Working through an intermediary, such as a service company (Found at www.hmrc.gov.uk/ir35/). This includes a deemed payment calculator which can be found at www.hmrc.gov.uk/ir35/ir35.xlt.

Managed Service Companies – www.hmrc.gov.uk/employment-status/msc.htm

Company Taxation manual (Found at www.hmrc.gov.uk/manuals/ctmanual/index.htm)

> This technical reference section is designed to assist you when you are working in the office. It should help you to know where to look for further information on the topics covered in this chapter.

Answer to Interactive question

	£	£
Employment income		
Total earned		60,000
Less 5% allowable deduction		(3,000)
		57,000
Less salary	25,000	
Employer's NIC	331	
		(25,331)
		31,669
Deemed employment income = £31,669 × 100/113.8		(27,829)
Employer's NIC		3,840

Income tax
£17,385 × 20% (£31,785 – (£25,000 – £10,600))   3,477
 £10,444 × 40%   4,178
 £27,829

| **Income tax on deemed employment income** | | 7,655 |

Employee national insurance
£17,385 × 12% (£42,385 – £25,000)   2,086
 £10,444 × 2%   209
 £27,829

| **Employee national insurance on deemed employment income** | | 2,295 |

1 (a) Tax efficient remuneration

			Sole trader £	Company £
Employment income				25,000
Trading profits			105,000	
Dividends £63,735 × 100/90 (W1)				70,817
Total income			105,000	95,817
Less personal allowance (W2)			(8,100)	(10,600)
Taxable income			96,900	85,217

Income tax	£	£	£	£
Basic rate band @ 20%	31,785		6,357	
Higher rate band @ 40%	65,115		26,046	
Basic rate band @ 20%		14,400		2,880
Basic rate band @ 10%		17,385		1,739
Higher rate band @ 32.5%		53,432		17,365
	96,900	85,217		
			32,403	21,984
Less dividend tax credit				(7,082)
Income tax payable			32,403	14,902

Note: The dividend tax credit is only recoverable to the extent that the dividend itself is taxable. As the personal allowance is offset against the employment income the whole dividend of £70,817 is taxable. The dividend tax credit deducted from the tax liability is therefore £7,082.

	Sole trader £	Company £
Cash (£63,735 + £25,000)	105,000	88,735
Less: income tax liability	(32,403)	(14,902)
NIC (W3)	(4,487)	(2,033)
Net cash	68,110	71,800

WORKINGS

(1)

	£
Employment income	25,000
Class 1 secondary NIC = ((£25,000 – £8,112) × 13.8%) – £2,000 employment allowance	331
Total employment cost	25,331
Corporation tax	
Trading profits	105,000
Less total employment cost	(25,331)
Taxable profits	79,669
Corporation tax liability @ 20%	(15,934)
Retained profit	63,735

(2)

	£
Personal allowance	10,600
Restricted by £1 for every £2 of income in excess of £100,000	(2,500)
Restricted personal allowance	8,100

(3)		£
	Sole trader NIC	
	Class 2: 52 weeks @ £2.80	146
	Class 4: (£42,385 – £8,060) × 9%	3,089
	(£105,000 – £42,385) × 2%	1,252
		4,487
	Employee NIC	
	Class 1 primary: (£25,000 – £8,060) × 12%	2,033

(b) Managed service company?

A managed service company is one which:

(i)   Supplies the services of individual workers to third party clients;

(ii) The worker receives the majority of the payments received by the managed service company from the client in relation to the worker's services;

(iii) The worker receives payments which are more than they would have been if they had been treated as employment income paid after deduction of IT and NIC; and

(iv) A managed service company provider is 'involved' with the company.

Jennifer's company would be supplying Jennifer to third party clients and would receive all the payments as she would be the sole shareholder. Assuming Jennifer also decides to pay herself in the form of dividends rather than salary, her company would have met criteria (i) to (iii).

The only criteria that is subjective is whether there is a managed service company provider 'involved' with the company. This would depend on whether Jennifer decided to utilise the additional services offered by the management company. Assuming she did make use of the additional services, she would be treated as owning a managed service company.

(c) Personal service company legislation

If Jennifer's company is not treated as a managed service company, ie if she decides not to use the additional services offered, then it would appear to still fall within the scope of personal service company legislation.

As Jennifer is providing a personal service to her former employer, HMRC is likely to challenge this as being a disguised employment. Assuming that using the normal employment status case law Jennifer is treated as having a disguised employment with Chambers Ltd, then she will fall within the scope of personal service company legislation.

To prove a disguised employment HMRC must prove that but for the existence of her company, she would be treated as an employee of Chambers Ltd. There is insufficient information in the question to make a definitive decision as to her employment status. However, the absence of a power of substitution and the amount of time she will spend working for Chambers Ltd are strong indicators that this is a disguised employment.

Where a disguised employment exists, all income from that employment is treated as earnings from a 'relevant engagement'.

A flat rate of 5% is deducted as overhead expenses regardless of the level of actual expenses. Thus 95% of income from all relevant engagements less any actual salary, employer's NIC, employer pension contributions and amounts which would have been deductible from employment income will be taxable as a deemed employment income payment. This deemed payment is treated as being made on the 5 April each year and is liable to income tax and NIC.

The income from relevant engagements will have been taxed as employment income and the benefit of operating via a company and receiving remuneration as dividends will have been lost.

However, there is still some benefit to operating as a personal service company:

•   Firstly, only the income from relevant engagements is subject to income tax and NIC under the personal service company legislation. The other 30% of Jennifer's income from her other clients can still benefit from lower rates of corporation tax and then being paid out as dividends.

- Secondly, Jennifer is treated as an employee of her company and therefore her company can reimburse her for travel to clients' offices as travel to and from a temporary workplace. This will not be taxable. If, however, she were an employee of the client this would be a permanent workplace and home to work travel which would be taxable if paid by the employer.

Managed service company legislation

If Jennifer's company is treated as a managed service company profits not extracted as employment income will be taxable as deemed employment payments each time a payment is made. There are thus some differences compared to personal service company legislation:

- Firstly, all the income is potentially subject to income tax and NIC as employment income. The other 30% of Jennifer's income from her other clients will also be treated as deemed employment income if paid out, ie the only way to avoid a deemed employment income charge is to pay out the whole of the income as employment income or to retain profits in the company.

- Secondly, for expenses purposes only, Jennifer is treated as an employee of each client and therefore each client's workplace is treated as a permanent workplace. Any travel expenses paid will be taxable income.

- Thirdly, the deemed employment income payment will be liable to income tax and NIC at the time it is triggered ie at the time Jennifer receives a payment from her company which has not already been subject to IT and NIC via PAYE.

- Finally, there is no flat rate deduction of overhead expenses for a managed service company. Thus any expenses not wholly, necessarily and exclusively incurred for the purposes of an employment would not be deductible. It is likely that only some of the trading expenses incurred would be deductible as the word 'exclusively' means that many trading expenses are not allowable for employment purposes.

Conclusion

It would be preferable for Jennifer to ensure that she does not fall within the scope of managed service company legislation. This could be done by ensuring that only normal tax planning and business advice is sought rather than the whole of the company's administration being outsourced. Although she would still fall within personal service company legislation her deemed employment income payments would at least be lower than if her company were a managed service company.

2   B – £3,750

S.455 notional tax y/e 31 October 2015:

	£
£30,000 × 25%	7,500
Less: claims for discharge	
£5,000 × 25%	(1,250)
£10,000 × 25%	(2,500)
Actual s.455 tax due	3,750

A claim can be made to discharge the s.455 liability to the extent that the loan is repaid before the due date of payment (1 August 2016).

3   B – £5,167

CO_2 emissions are 151g/km, round down to 150g/km

Appropriate percentage:

(150 – 95) = 55 g/km in excess of threshold

55/5 = 11%

14% + 11% = 25%

		£
List price £23,400 × 25%		5,850
Less contribution for use £100 × 12		(1,200)
Distribution		4,650
Grossed-up £4,416 × 100/90		£5,167

4 (a) s.455 notional tax y/e 30 September 2015:

	£
£50,000 × 25%	12,500
Less claim for discharge £20,000 × 25%	(5,000)
Actual s.455 tax due	7,500

Due date for payment 1 July 2016

(b) s.455 notional tax repayment y/e 30 September 2016:

£10,000 × 25%	£2,500

Due date for repayment 1 July 2017

5 (a) s.455 notional tax y/e 31 March 2015:

£75,000 × 25%	£18,750

Due date for payment 1 January 2016

(b) s.455 notional tax repayment y/e 31 March 2016:

£27,000 × 25%	£6,750

Due date for repayment 1 January 2017

(c)

	Non-savings income £	Dividend income £	Total income £
Property income	125,000		125,000
Distribution:			
£27,000 × 100/90		30,000	30,000
Net income	125,000	30,000	155,000
Less PA (Note)	Nil		Nil
Taxable income	125,000	30,000	155,000

Tax

	£
£31,785 × 20%	6,357
£93,215 × 40%	37,286
£25,000 × 32½%	8,125
£5,000 × 37½%	1,875
£155,000	
Tax liability	53,643
Less tax credit on distribution £30,000 × 10%	(3,000)
Tax payable	50,643

Note:

Simon's personal allowance is tapered to £nil as his income exceeds £121,200. The full personal allowance of £10,600 is not available for individuals with an adjusted net income of more than £100,000. The personal allowance is reduced by £1 for every £2 that the individual's adjusted net income exceeds £100,000. The personal allowance will be withdrawn completely for adjusted net income of £121,200 and above.

6 Inferno Ltd

Close company

Inferno Ltd is a close company as its shares are controlled by five or fewer participators including their associates (spouse, children, siblings):

	Number of shares held
Edward Dante (including children)	250
Hercule Christie (including son)	125
Agatha Marple	100
Jeeves Woodhouse (including wife)	110
	585

As a close company, payments to shareholders will be subject to close company rules.

London flat

The value of the flat equivalent to its taxable benefit will be treated as a distribution taxable on Jeeves. The cost of the flat will therefore be a disallowed expense in Inferno Ltd's adjustments to profits.

The distribution is its value as a taxable benefit for employment purposes ie the greater of the annual value and the rental paid by Inferno Ltd.

For 2015/16 this will be:

Net dividend 2 × £1,700	£3,400
Gross dividend £3,400 × 100/90	£3,778

Loans

Loans to participators are subject to tax. Inferno Ltd must pay a notional tax of 25% of the loans:

(2 × £250,000) × 25%	£125,000

This tax will be paid with the normal corporation tax liability for the year ended 31 May 2016. As Inferno Ltd did not pay corporation tax by instalments, this will be due nine months and one day after the chargeable accounting period end ie 1 March 2017.

The tax will be repaid to Inferno Ltd when the loans are repaid.

Victor and Hugo will be subject to income tax and Inferno Ltd will have to pay Class 1A national insurance contributions on the benefit of the low interest rate on the loans.

The benefit for each of Victor and Hugo for 2015/16 is the official rate of interest less the actual rate of interest:

(3% – 2.25%) × £250,000 × 5/12	£781

Inferno Ltd will be subject to corporation tax on the interest receivable as a non-trading loan relationship.

CHAPTER 14

Groups and consortia

Introduction

Examination context

Topic List

Summary and Self-test

Technical reference

Answers to Interactive questions

Answers to Self-test

Learning objectives

- Determine, explain and calculate the corporation tax liabilities for corporate entities ☐

- Explain and evaluate the tax implications of group structures ☐

- Identify legitimate tax planning measures to minimise tax liabilities ☐

- Evaluate and advise on alternative tax strategies relating to corporate transformations ☐

- Recognise, explain and communicate opportunities to use alternative tax treatments arising from past transactions ☐

Specific syllabus references for this chapter are 1f, 1j, 2a, 2c and 2d.

Syllabus links

The mechanics of issues relating to groups are covered in the Tax Compliance study manual. Group losses generally interact with group gains, liquidations (Chapter 17) and group transformations (Chapter 23). Group gains also interact with group transformations, but a liquidation has no impact on a gains group. This area is extended at Business Planning: Taxation to encompass overseas aspects, consortia and tax planning aspects including giving advice to clients on the best use of losses and gains.

Examination context

Additional tax planning for effective loss relief can be implemented within groups of companies. In these scenarios many types of loss can be passed around a group to ensure the groups objectives are achieved. These may include:

- Improving the group cash flow by obtaining relief as early as possible, and/ or
- Obtaining the maximum possible tax saving for the group as a whole (the normal group aim).

Further group tax planning can be undertaken in relation to gains. The timing of share disposals can lead to gains being fully exempt. Assets can be freely passed around a group for trading purposes with no corporation tax implications provided there are no underlying avoidance issues.

In the examination candidates may be required to:

- Identify to which group companies a loss may be surrendered and how much may be surrendered
- Give loss relief achieving the group's objectives
- Advise on the ways of reducing chargeable gains within a group

Candidates can do well on group questions if they work methodically through the issues identified in the questions. The area of groups is a discriminating factor between weak and good candidates.

1 Revision from Tax Compliance: group relief

Section overview

- A group relief group exists where one company is a 75% direct or indirect subsidiary of another company.

- Members of a group relief group may surrender trading losses, deficits on non trading loan relationships, excess qualifying charitable donations, excess property business losses and excess expenses of management.

- Losses of an overseas permanent establishment (PE) of a UK company which cannot be relieved overseas may be surrendered to any UK member of the group. If, however, the operations of the overseas PE amount to a separate trade which is wholly carried on overseas, the profits will be assessed separately and losses may only be carried forward against future profits from the same trade.

- It is not possible to surrender losses of an overseas PE of a UK company if an irrevocable election may be made to completely exempt the profits/losses of the UK company's overseas PE from corporation tax.

- Losses of a UK PE of a non-UK resident company which cannot be relieved overseas may be surrendered to any other UK member of the group. Similarly losses of any UK group member may be surrendered to the UK PE.

- A 'qualifying overseas loss' of an EEA company or PE which is a member of the group is available for group loss relief to other companies in the UK group.

- Only losses of the current year may be surrendered and must be used by the claimant company in the same accounting period. Where accounting periods are not the same, losses and profits must be prorated eg where a company joins or leaves the group or where group members have different year ends.

- Members of a 51% group where more than one member is liable to pay tax by instalments may elect to form a group for corporation tax payment purposes – a group payment group.

- A member is nominated to make payments by instalment on behalf of the whole group.

- Once all the member's tax returns have been filed, the nominated member allocates payments made to member companies. Any shortfall will then be sought by HMRC.

- HMRC will allocate the shortfall between the members in such a way as to maximise the tax geared penalties payable.

- It is also possible to surrender payments of corporation tax between members of a loss relief group. This is less flexible and now less popular than a group payment arrangement.

1.1 Group relief

A group relief group exists where:

- One company is a 75% subsidiary of another company; or
- Both companies are 75% subsidiaries of a third company.

Note that to be in a group, ownership must be via a company.

Consider the following group of companies:

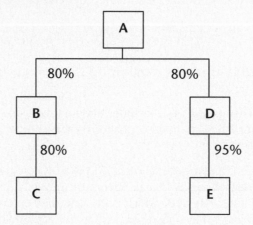

There are two group relief groups here:

(i) B and C
(ii) A, B, D and E (C is not a member of this group as A's indirect interest is 80% × 80% = 64%)

One member of a group relief group can surrender qualifying losses to other members of that group in any proportion it wishes. Thus C could surrender a loss to B (or vice versa). A could surrender a loss to B, D or E etc.

A group relief group may include non-UK resident companies. Losses may be surrendered between UK resident companies, but not, generally, between UK and non-UK companies (but see below). For example, if D in the above example were non-UK resident, D and E would still be part of the A, B, D, E group, but it would not be possible to surrender losses to/from D.

1.2 Operation of the relief

Group relief is obtained by setting off the loss of the surrendering company against the total profits of the claimant company after the deduction of:

- Trading losses brought forward under s.45;

- Deficits on non-trading loan relationships;

- Property business losses of the same period; and

- Any current period trading losses (s.37(3)(a)) regardless of whether a claim is actually made;

  but before deducting

- Any relief carried back from a subsequent accounting period.

1.2.1 Losses of the surrendering company

Group relief can be surrendered for the current year in respect of the following:

(i)   Trading losses
(ii) Deficit (ie net debit) on non-trading loan relationships
(iii) Excess qualifying charitable donations
(iv) Excess property business losses
(v)   Excess expenses of management of a company with investment business

Brought forward losses and losses carried back cannot be group relieved.

A surrendering company can surrender any amount up to the whole of items (i) and (ii) above. It need not use these items against its own profits first.

However, items (iii), (iv) and (v) may only be group relieved to the extent that they exceed the surrendering company's current period total other income (this includes amounts apportioned under the controlled foreign companies rules. These are covered in Chapter 16). They must be surrendered in the stated order: excess qualifying charitable donations, excess property business losses and finally excess expenses of management.

The amount surrendered is not restricted to the percentage interest of the parent in the subsidiary, ie it is possible for a 75% subsidiary to surrender 100% of its loss to another group company. It is usual, particularly where there is a minority shareholder, for the claimant company to pay for group relief. Such payments, up to a maximum of £1 for every £1 of loss surrendered, are ignored for tax purposes.

1.2.2 Available profits of the claimant company

Group relief is restricted to the amount of the claimant company's available profits.

The claimant company's available profits are its taxable total profits **after** deducting:

- Trading losses brought forward under s.45;
- Current period trading losses (regardless of whether a claim is actually made under s.37(3)(a));
- Non-trading loan deficits brought forward;
- Non-trading loan deficits for the current period;

but **before** deducting:

- Trading losses carried back under s.37(3)(b);
- Non-trading loan deficits carried back.

1.3 Overseas aspects of group loss relief

1.3.1 Overseas permanent establishment of UK resident company

Provided the losses are not relievable overseas and an election has not been made to exempt the profits/losses of PEs, group relief may be claimed for losses arising in an overseas PE of a UK resident company providing the trade of that PE does not amount to a separate trade carried out wholly overseas.

1.3.2 UK permanent establishment of non-resident company

A non-UK resident company which is within the charge to UK corporation tax (ie it trades in the UK through a PE) can claim group relief against its chargeable profits from other group members and surrender trade losses, and other amounts relating to chargeable UK activities, to group members.

However, a loss arising in a UK PE of a non-EEA resident company may only be surrendered to other companies in the UK group if those losses are not relievable in the overseas country.

For UK PEs of EEA companies, the surrender of the loss is only prohibited if it is actually relieved in the overseas country (if it is possible to claim relief overseas, but none is actually claimed, it is then possible to claim relief in the UK).

1.3.3 Qualifying overseas loss of non-resident 75% subsidiary

A 'qualifying overseas loss' of a non-UK resident 75% subsidiary is available for group loss relief to other companies in the UK group. The non-resident 75% subsidiary to which this applies is either

- Resident in the European Economic Area (EEA), or
- Resident elsewhere but carrying on a trade in the EEA through a PE.

The 'qualifying overseas loss' is relievable in the UK where, at the time when the claim for relief is made, there is no realistic possibility that relief will be obtained overseas either in the period of the loss or in later periods. In order to obtain relief against UK profits, the overseas loss is recomputed using UK tax principles.

The claim required in respect of overseas losses of non-resident companies is to be made by the UK claimant company. The claimant company is responsible for demonstrating that the losses meet the conditions.

Loss relief will be denied where arrangements exist the main purpose of which is to obtain UK relief.

1.4 Overlapping (corresponding) accounting periods

Only profits and losses arising in corresponding accounting periods may be group relieved. Where the accounting periods are not identical, then both the losses and the profits are scaled down:

- The loss available for surrender is A/S × the loss of the surrendering company
- The profit against which relief can be claimed is A/C × the profits of the claimant company

Where

- A is the time common to both accounting periods, ie the overlapping (or corresponding) period;
- S is the length of the surrendering company's accounting period; and
- C is the length of the claimant company's accounting period.

The maximum amount of group relief which can be claimed is the lower of the loss and the profit for the overlapping period.

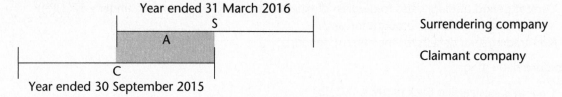

1.5 Group relief claim

The rules for claiming group relief under self-assessment are in Schedule 18 FA 1998:

- The time limit for making or withdrawing a group relief claim is normally the first anniversary of the filing date for the corporation tax return ie two years from the end of the loss making accounting period [Hp148].

- Regulations effectively permit group wide claims and surrenders. Where the arrangements are in force, an authorised company may make and withdraw group relief claims and surrenders on behalf of all participating companies by providing only one copy of the statement containing details of the claims and surrenders, and of the effects on the self-assessment of all the companies concerned.

- The actual claim for group relief is made on the filing of the company tax return if made at the time at which it is filed. Otherwise a claim is made via an amendment to a previous company tax return.

1.6 Group payment arrangements

Where more than one company in a group is liable to pay tax by instalments, arrangements may be made for the instalments to be paid by one company (the nominated company), and allocated amongst the participating companies in the group.

The arrangements mean that:

- Groups still have to pay the right amount of CT at the right time;

- When estimating what is due to be paid, groups can forecast for the participating companies as a whole rather than for each individual company; and

- The effect on a group of the differential in interest rates on over and underpaid tax is mitigated.

A group payment arrangement is more flexible than a repayment surrender under s.963 for neutralising the effect of the credit and debit interest rates differential (see Section 1.7).

For a group payment arrangement to exist, at least one member of the group must pay its tax by instalments. However, a group payment arrangement can include companies which do not pay by instalments. Such companies do not then become liable to pay corporation tax by instalments simply because they have become members of a group payment arrangement.

The arrangements are as follows:

- Eligible companies are parent companies and their 51% subsidiaries, and the 51% subsidiaries of those subsidiaries and so on. It is not necessary to include all group members, and it is possible to have several group payment arrangements for subgroups.

- The arrangements apply to the period of account of the nominated company, and this will normally be the same accounting period for all participating companies.

- The nominated company agrees to pay all the instalments due by all of the companies covered by the arrangement. This includes the requirement to adjust the payments on the basis of amended profit forecasts, and the right to reclaim any amount it considers to be overpaid. HMRC will not seek payment of tax from any other participating company before the closing date.

- After all the members have filed their tax returns, the nominated company must allocate the payments between the participating companies as it thinks fit. HMRC may then seek payment of any shortfall from companies with liabilities exceeding allocated payments.

- If any of the participating companies are liable to a tax geared penalty for the late filing of their returns, any shortfall at the relevant date will be reallocated by HMRC for the purpose of calculating the tax geared penalty. The shortfall will be allocated first to companies liable to a 20% penalty, and then to companies liable to a 10% penalty, and finally to companies not liable to a tax geared penalty. This maximises the tax geared penalty that can be charged.

1.7 Group tax surrenders

The different interest rates charged on underpaid tax and earned on overpaid tax could operate unfairly where tax is unpaid by some companies in the group, but overpaid by others. Although the group may have made an overall payment sufficient to cover the group's tax liabilities there would, in these circumstances, be a net interest charge. It is therefore possible for a company to surrender a tax repayment to another company which is a member of the same group (same definition as a group loss relief group).

These rules are in addition to the group payment arrangements discussed above. However these rules are less flexible than group payment arrangements and are less popular since the introduction of group payment arrangements. Group tax surrenders are likely to be utilised only where no member of the group is liable to pay tax by instalments, which is unlikely.

2 Tax planning and group relief

Section overview

- Losses should be utilised in such a way as to minimise the overall corporation tax liability of the group, or to improve cash flow.

- Losses may be restricted if there is a change in ownership and either a major change in the nature or conduct of the trade, or a revival of the trade.

2.1 Tax planning

There is often more than one way in which a loss can be relieved. It will be important, both in practice and in the examination, that you can identify the optimal relief available from a number of possible alternatives.

In general, your approach should be to set the loss against profits that would otherwise suffer the highest marginal rate of tax. Until FY2014 a company suffered its highest marginal rate of tax on profits between the lower and upper limits. For FY2015 corporation tax rates have been unified at 20%.

The highest marginal rate of tax on a company in FY2014 is not 21%, the main rate, but 21.25%, being the effective rate in the marginal relief band:

FY2014	Profits £	Rate %	Tax £
Upper limit	1,500,000	21	315,000
Lower limit	(300,000)	20	(60,000)
	1,200,000	21.25*	255,000

* Effective rate for a company with no FII on band of profits between £300,001 and £1,500,000 =

$(255,000/1,200,000) \times 100\% = 21.25\%$

When planning the use of losses, consider the following for accounting periods falling wholly or partly into FY2014:

- If you are considering only current year profits, once all profits otherwise suffering tax at 21.25% have been utilised to relieve a loss, set the loss against profits suffering tax at 21%.

- Finally set a loss against any profits suffering tax at the small profits rate.

- Note that for FY2008 to FY2010 this marginal rate was 29.75%. For FY2011, the marginal rate was 27.5%. For FY2012, the marginal rate was 25%. For FY2013, the marginal rate was 23.75%.

- The exception to the above strategy concerns a group with overseas income. In this instance it is important not to waste double tax relief, and therefore sufficient taxable profits should be left in charge after group relief to ensure full double tax relief is available (Chapter 15).

- A company may disclaim capital allowances to reduce the amount of a loss for a particular year. This may be preferable where not all the loss can be relieved and would otherwise be carried forward. Disclaimed capital allowances in the current year will increase capital allowances in future years. If this generates a loss in future years, this may be offset against total profits (including chargeable gains).

Interactive question 1: Tax planning with group relief [Difficulty level: intermediate]

U Ltd owns 100% of V Ltd and W Ltd. All group companies have been members of the group for several years. All prepare accounts to 31 December each year and the results for the year ended 31 December 2015 are as follows:

	U Ltd £	V Ltd £	W Ltd £
Trading income/(loss)	130,000	550,000	(60,000)
Property income	5,000	20,000	Nil
Chargeable gains	Nil	Nil	65,000
Qualifying donations	(3,000)	(4,000)	Nil

Requirement

Using the standard format below, show the options for using the loss made by W Ltd, identify the most tax efficient use of the loss, assuming that the loss is to be relieved as soon as possible, and show the taxable total profits for each company after relief.

Taxable total profits before loss relief

	U Ltd £	V Ltd £	W Ltd £
Trading income			
Property income			
Chargeable gains			
Less qualifying donations	( )	( )	( )
Taxable total profits			

Marginal relief limits (all companies associated)

Upper limit: ....

Lower limit: ....

Size of company ....

Options for loss relief

(1) **Relieve loss under s.37(3)(a)**

Tax saving: £........................... × ....%   £_____

(2) **Group relief – most efficient claim**

First, surrender losses to ....

Available loss	£	
Available profits	£	
Surrender £................. to save tax at .... rate		
Tax saving: £................. × ....%		£

Next, surrender losses to ....

Available loss	£	
Available profits	£	
Surrender £....................... to save tax at .... rate		
Tax saving: £....................... × ....%		£
Total tax saving		£

Conclusion

The most tax efficient use of the loss is to make a claim for ....

Taxable total profits after group relief

	U Ltd £	V Ltd £	W Ltd £
Trading income			
Property income			
Chargeable gains	_____	_____	_____
Less qualifying donation	(_____)	(_____)	(_____)
Less group relief	(_____)	(_____)	_____
Taxable total profits	======	======	======

See **Answer** at the end of this chapter.

Interactive question 2: Group tax planning [Difficulty level: Intermediate]

Blake Ltd has two wholly-owned subsidiaries, Avon Ltd and Cally Ltd. All three companies are UK resident. In the year ended 31 December 2015, the companies have the following results:

	£
Blake Ltd	
Trading loss	(156,000)
Other profits	33,800
Avon Ltd	
Trading profit	767,000
Cally Ltd	
Trading profit	191,000

Requirement

Show how the loss of Blake Ltd can best be utilised.

See **Answer** at the end of this chapter.

2.2 Group transformations

Restrictions on the use of losses may apply where there is a change in ownership of a company and either:

- There is a major change in the nature or conduct of the trade within three years before or three years after the change in ownership; or

- After the company's trading activities have become small or negligible, there is a change in ownership followed by a considerable revival of the trade.

In addition, where arrangements exist for a company to leave a group it is no longer possible to surrender losses to or claim losses from the departing company.

Once a liquidator has been appointed to liquidate a holding company any loss relief groups with its subsidiaries will be terminated. No further losses may be surrendered from or to the holding company nor between the subsidiaries which were in a group together because they were owned by the holding company.

3 Consortium relief

Section overview

- A consortium exists where 20 or fewer companies (consortium members) each own at least 5% and jointly own at least 75% of a UK company (consortium company).

- Losses of the consortium members can be surrendered to the consortium company and vice versa.

- It is always the consortium member's percentage interest in the consortium company's profit or loss which dictates the amount which may be surrendered to or claimed from the consortium company.

- Regardless of whether the consortium company makes a current year loss claim, its loss available for surrender to the consortium members is always restricted by the amount of the possible current year loss claim.

- A group/consortium company exists where the consortium company is also a member of a group. Again, its loss available for surrender to the consortium member is always restricted by a notional current year loss claim and also by a notional group surrender claim to companies in the group/consortium company's group.

- A link company exists where the consortium member is also a member of a group. Losses can flow through the link company to and from the consortium company as if the members of the link company's group were in fact the consortium members.

3.1 Main principles

The group relief provisions described in Section 1 above also apply, with modifications, to consortia. Therefore any amount eligible for group relief can also be surrendered from or to a consortium company.

Definition

Consortium: A consortium exists where 20 or fewer companies ('consortium members') each own at least 5% and jointly own at least 75% of the ordinary share capital of another UK resident company ('consortium company').

- A company which is a 75% subsidiary cannot also be a consortium company, since in that case the normal group relief rules would apply.

- All companies, whether resident or non-resident, may be taken into account in establishing a consortium relationship (shareholdings held by individuals do not count).

- Shareholders with holdings of less than 5% are not treated as consortium members and will not be eligible to partake in consortium relief.

Losses may be surrendered, in either direction, between a consortium member and the consortium company. Losses may not be surrendered between the consortium members.

3.1.1 Loss in consortium company

Where the consortium company makes a loss, the maximum surrender is the lower of:

- Available loss = consortium member's % holding in the consortium company × consortium company loss

- Available profits = all of the taxable total profits of the consortium member

In other words, it is always the consortium member's percentage interest in the consortium company's profit or loss which dictates the amount which may be surrendered to or claimed from the consortium company.

Worked example: Consortium relief – Loss in the consortium company

Purcell Ltd is owned by a consortium of companies as follows:

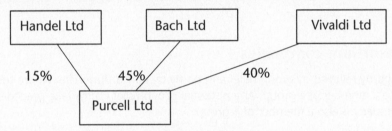

In the year ended 31 March 2015, these companies' results are:

	Tax adjusted trading profit/(loss)
Handel Ltd	£28,000
Bach Ltd	£48,000
Vivaldi Ltd	£96,020
Purcell Ltd	£(36,000)

Requirement

What is the maximum amount of consortium relief that Purcell Ltd can surrender to each of the consortium members?

Solution

The maximum consortium relief surrenders which Purcell Ltd may make to the consortium members are:

Handel Ltd	£36,000 × 15%	=	£5,400
Bach Ltd	£36,000 × 45%	=	£16,200
Vivaldi Ltd	£36,000 × 40%	=	£14,400

If the consortium company has a trading loss and other profits against which a current year claim could be made, it is assumed that such a claim is made in priority to the consortium relief claims. No current year claim need actually be made.

By contrast, a company surrendering group relief is not treated as having first made use of the loss via a current year claim.

If Purcell Ltd, in the worked example above, had property income of £20,000 in the year ended 31 March 2015, as well as the trading loss of £36,000, each consortium member would be entitled to claim its share of £16,000 (£36,000 – £20,000) only.

3.1.2 Loss in consortium member

Conversely, where the consortium member incurs a loss, the maximum surrender is the lower of:

- Available loss = all of the loss of the consortium member
- Available profits = consortium member's % holding in the consortium company × consortium company taxable total profits

Worked example: Consortium relief – Loss in the consortium member

Following on from the previous example, in the year ended 31 March 2016, Handel Ltd makes a tax adjusted trading loss of £100,000 and Purcell Ltd makes a taxable trading profit of £50,000.

Requirement

What is the maximum amount of loss that Handel Ltd can surrender to Purcell Ltd?

Solution

The maximum amount of loss which Handel Ltd may surrender to Purcell Ltd is restricted to £50,000 × 15% ie £7,500.

3.2 Group/consortium companies

A loss may be partly relieved by group relief and partly by consortium relief where the consortium company is also a member of a group. Any potential group relief claims take precedence when the consortium company is also a member of a group.

Note: the rules regarding when losses of a subsidiary of a consortium company can be surrendered to a consortium member are not examinable, and are therefore not included in the material below.

Definition

Group/consortium company: When the consortium company is also a member of a group ie it has 75% subsidiaries it is described as a 'group/consortium company'.

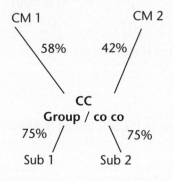

3.2.1 Loss in group/consortium company

Where a group/consortium company makes a loss, the consortium relief available to the consortium members is calculated by:

- First assuming that the loss is set against any of the group/consortium company's other profits via a current year claim; and

- Then assuming that the maximum potential group relief claims are made to surrender the loss to other group companies for the corresponding accounting period (but taking into account any other actual group relief claims for other losses in the group); and

- The balance can then be surrendered in the appropriate proportions to the consortium members.

Again no actual current year claim or group relief surrender need be made by the group/consortium company for the amount of loss eligible for consortium relief to be restricted.

Worked example: Group/consortium company surrenders loss

Global Ltd is owned in equal shares by W Ltd, X Ltd, Y Ltd and Z Ltd. Global Ltd is a trading company with two 75% subsidiaries, Alpha Ltd and Delta Ltd. For the year ended 31 December 2015 the companies had the following results:

Global Ltd:	Trading loss	(£90,000)
	Bank interest	£10,000
Alpha Ltd:	Trading loss	(£8,000)
Delta Ltd:	Trading profit	£25,000

Requirement

Show the amount of loss each of the consortium members may claim.

Solution

The amount available for consortium relief will depend on whether Alpha Ltd's loss is in fact group relieved and to what extent. If it were fully relieved against Delta Ltd's profit then the balance of £25,000 – 8,000 = £17,000 would be deemed to be available for relieving Global Ltd's loss.

Global Ltd's loss would then be analysed as follows:

	£
Total loss	90,000
Notional current year claim	(10,000)
	80,000
Notional group relief claim: Delta Ltd	(17,000)
Available for consortium members	63,000

Thus each consortium member (W Ltd to Z Ltd) could claim up to 25% × £63,000 = £15,750.

If no claim were made to relieve Alpha Ltd's loss against Delta Ltd then the total amount would be reduced since the notional group relief claim against Delta Ltd would then be £25,000. Hence each consortium member would be entitled to claim up to 25% × £55,000 = £13,750.

3.2.2 Loss in consortium member

Where a consortium member makes a loss, the maximum that can be surrendered to the group/consortium company is determined by the relevant percentage of the group/consortium company's profits less any potential group relief claims that the group/consortium company could make to utilise losses of other companies in its group.

Worked example: Consortium member surrenders loss

Same companies as in the last example. Results:

Global Ltd:	Trading profit	£90,000
Alpha Ltd:	Trading loss	(£15,000)
Delta Ltd:	Trading profit	£10,000

Requirement

What is the maximum consortium relief that can be surrendered to Global Ltd by one of the consortium members?

Solution

Global Ltd could claim group relief for Alpha Ltd's loss of £15,000. This would leave £90,000 – 15,000 = £75,000 of which 25% is £18,750, and this is the maximum loss that, say, W Ltd could surrender to Global Ltd.

Alternatively, if £10,000 of Alpha Ltd's loss were surrendered to Delta Ltd then Global Ltd's available profit would be £90,000 – 5,000 = £85,000 of which 25% is £21,250.

Until FY 2014 tax rates often determined the optimum claims within a consortium.

3.3 Link companies

Consortium relief can also be surrendered via a 'link company'.

Definition

Link company: A company which is both a member of a group and a consortium member.

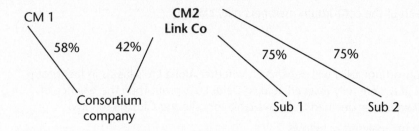

Any UK related member of the consortium member's group can claim consortium relief on behalf of the link company and can surrender its losses to a UK related company owned by the link company's consortium.

A link company must either be UK related or established in the EEA. However, if it is merely 'established in the EEA' then it must be possible to establish that it is in the same group as the claimant company or surrendering company without the involvement of a company that is not 'established in the EEA'.

A company is UK related if it is either UK resident or trading through a UK permanent establishment.

There is no order of priority of group relief and consortium relief where the consortium member is also a member of a group. Therefore a group company which is also a consortium member can:

- Surrender its loss to other companies in its group, and/or
- To the consortium company in any order.

The effect of these rules is that where the link company has insufficient profits to absorb a loss made by the consortium company, those losses can be used by a fellow group company. In addition, where the link company has insufficient profits to absorb a loss made by a fellow group company, those losses can be used by the consortium company.

Worked example: Link company, consortium company makes a loss

Dynasty Ltd is a member of a consortium which owns a trading company Ming Ltd. Dynasty Ltd's shareholding in Ming Ltd is 25%. Dynasty Ltd is a 75% subsidiary of Porcelain plc which also owns 75% of Xiao Ltd. The results for the year ended 31 March 2016 are:

Dynasty Ltd:	Trading profit	£36,000
Ming Ltd:	Trading loss	(£240,000)
Xiao Ltd:	Trading profit	£120,000

Requirement

Show how Ming Ltd's loss can be relieved.

Solution

The loss of 25% × £240,000= £60,000 can be shared between Dynasty Ltd and Xiao Ltd in various different ways. For instance, Dynasty Ltd could relieve all of its profit of £36,000 leaving a balance of £24,000 loss to be set against Xiao Ltd's profit of £120,000. Alternatively, Dynasty Ltd might claim only £20,000 and Xiao Ltd £40,000.

Worked example: Groups, losses, consortia and foreign companies

AVC Ltd, a UK resident company, owns 61% of the shares in P Ltd, 78% of the shares in Q Ltd, 88% of the shares in R SpA, and 82% of the shares in S Ltd.

All five companies prepare accounts to the 31 March each year. All of the companies are UK resident except R SpA which is resident in Italy. The shares in all companies except Q Ltd have been owned since their incorporation. The shares in Q Ltd were acquired on the 1 April 2015.

S Ltd holds 89% of the shares in T Ltd; R SpA also holds 8% of the shares in T Ltd; and SD Ltd holds 16% of the shares in P Ltd.

The tax adjusted trading results for each company for the year ended 31 December 2015 are as follows:

		£
AVC Ltd	Profit	77,000
P Ltd	Profit	96,000
Q Ltd	Loss	(40,000)
R SpA	Loss	(82,000)
S Ltd	Profit	8,000
T Ltd	Profit	302,000
SD Ltd	Loss	(84,000)

AVC Ltd has a brought forward trading loss of £15,000.

R SpA has been trading poorly and it is not anticipated that it will become profitable again in the near future.

Requirement

Calculate the UK corporation tax liability for all companies for the year ended 31 December 2015 assuming all losses are used as quickly as possible.

Solution

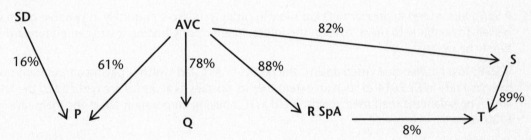

Associates (FY 2014)

There are six associated companies ie AVC, P, Q, R, S and T. The upper and lower limits for FY2014 are:

£0 – £50,000	20%
£50,001 – £250,000	21% less MR (marginal rate = 21.25%)
over £250,000	21%

Loss relief group

There is one loss group for group relief purposes ie AVC, Q, R, S and T.

Note that AVC's effective interest in T Ltd is (82% × 89%) + (88% × 8%) = 80%

As Q Ltd was not acquired until 1 March 2015 it may only surrender losses to other members of the group for the post acquisition period ie 1 March 2015 to 31 December 2015. Thus it may surrender the lower of 9/12 of its loss and 9/12 of the claimant company's profit.

Consortium

There is also a consortium consisting of SD and AVC as consortium members owning P as the consortium company. AVC is a link company as it is both a member of a group and a consortium member. The losses of any member of AVC's loss relief group could be offset against P's profit.

SD Ltd's interest in the profits of P Ltd is 16% × £96,000 = £15,360. Thus SD can surrender the lower of its actual loss of £84,000 and its interest in P's profits ie £15,360. SD can surrender £15,360 of its loss to P.

Qualifying overseas loss of non-UK resident 75% subsidiary

As R SpA is resident in Italy which is within the EEA, its loss may be surrendered to any company within its UK group. This assumes that the loss cannot be relieved overseas either now or in the future.

	P Ltd	AVC Ltd	S Ltd	T Ltd
	£	£	£	£
Trading profit	96,000	77,000	8,000	302,000
B/f loss		(15,000)		
Taxable total profits pre loss relief	96,000	62,000	8,000	302,000
Initial marginal CT rate – FY2014	21.25%	21.25%	20%	21%
Consortium relief SD Ltd (Note 1)	(15,360)			
R SpA loss (Note 2)		(12,000)₁		(70,000)₂
Q Ltd loss (Note 3)				(30,000)
Taxable total profits	80,640	50,000	8,000	202,000
Revised CT rate – FY2014	21% less MR	20%	20%	21%
FY2014 (3 months):				
CT (3/12)	4,234	2,500	400	10,605
Less marginal relief				
(250,000 – 80,640) × 1/400 × 3/12	(106)			
FY2015: @ 20% × 9/12	12,096	7,500	1,200	30,300
	16,224	10,000	1,600	40,905

Notes:

(1) SD Ltd can only surrender its loss to P Ltd. As AVC Ltd is a link company, P Ltd could use Q's loss or R's loss to reduce its profit. The losses can only be used to reduce 61% of P's profit (ie £58,560). Given that AVC Ltd's shareholding in P Ltd is lower than its holdings in the companies within its own group, it would be more advantageous for the group to utilise the losses internally.

(2) R SpA's loss is used in priority to Q Ltd's loss in order to utilise it as quickly as possible given that it is likely to continue to make losses in the future. In effect, any trading losses carried forward would simply be wasted.

R SpA's loss has first been used against the profits of AVC Ltd which is paying corporation tax at the marginal rate in FY 2014 to such an extent that its taxable total profits are reduced to the lower limit. The balance is then used against T Ltd as it is paying corporation tax at the main rate in FY2014.

(3) Q Ltd's loss can then be set against T Ltd's taxable total profits. The maximum amount of the loss available for offset is the lower of 9/12 of the loss and 9/12 of the remaining unrelieved profit:

9/12 of T Ltd's taxable total profits of (£302,000 – £70,000) = £174,000

9/12 of Q Ltd's loss of £40,000 = £30,000

Note:

As a group relief claim has already been made to offset R SpA's loss against T Ltd's taxable total profits, T Ltd's remaining unrelieved profit in the above calculation must also be reduced accordingly. Although it makes no difference in this case, such a restriction could be avoided if the group relief claim between Q Ltd and T Ltd were submitted prior to those claims in respect of R SpA's losses.

If Q Ltd's loss claim had been made first there would still only be £30,000 in total to offset. Q Ltd could therefore surrender to AVC Ltd the lower of:

9/12 of AVC Ltd's taxable total profits of £62,000 = £46,500

9/12 of Q Ltd's loss of £40,000 = £30,000

It would still only choose to offset £12,000.

It could then surrender to T Ltd the lower of:

9/12 of S Ltd's taxable total profits of £302,000 = £226,500

9/12 of Q Ltd's loss of £40,000 = £30,000 − £12,000 already offset = £18,000

R SpA could then surrender all of its loss to T Ltd.

4 Revision from Tax Compliance: chargeable gains groups

Section overview

- A chargeable gains group exists where a principal company owns at least 75% of its direct subsidiaries and has an effective interest of more than 50% in each sub-subsidiary. Each link has to have a minimum direct holding of 75%. A company may not be in two gains groups simultaneously.

- Assets transferred between members of a chargeable gains group are transferred at nil gain/nil loss.

- A degrouping charge arises where a company leaves a chargeable gains group within six years of a nil gain/nil loss transfer where the departing company still owns the asset transferred.

- Pre-entry capital losses are generally only available for use against gains on pre-entry assets and assets used by the company with the loss in a pre-entry trade.

- Rules exist to prevent the acquisition of companies with capital losses purely for tax avoidance purposes. These rules are more restrictive than the normal pre-entry losses rules.

- The substantial shareholding does not apply to intra-group transfers which are at nil gain/nil loss. However, the ownership period for the purposes of a subsequent disposal outside of the group will be from the date of acquisition by the original purchaser within the group.

- When a company is a member of a group (a >50% shareholding for these purposes) then the holdings of the shares in companies which may potentially qualify for the SSE exemption can be aggregated within the group.

- Where a newly incorporated subsidiary receives assets from another group company, the new company will qualify for the substantial shareholding exemption providing that the assets transferred were held and used in the trade of another group company for the 12 months before the transfer.

- Where assets are transferred from one group company to another and one company uses the asset as a capital asset and the other as trading stock then trading profits or chargeable gains may arise. The asset is always transferred as a capital asset as a nil gain/nil loss transfer.

- Pooled plant and machinery is transferred between companies at the actual transfer price charged (unless it is within the mandatory successions rules or a succession election is made).

- Intangible fixed assets acquired since 1 April 2002 are transferred between group companies in a similar way to other capital assets.

- A group is treated as carrying on a single trade for rollover relief purposes. Gains on assets disposed of by one group company may be rolled over into acquisitions by any other member of the gains group.

- Rollover relief also applies to intangible fixed assets acquired by the group since 1 April 2002.

4.1 Chargeable gains groups

A chargeable gains group comprises a 'principal company' and its 75% subsidiaries and their 75% subsidiaries and so on. However, each subsidiary must also be an 'effective 51% subsidiary' of the principal company.

All companies, regardless of UK residency status, may belong to a chargeable gains group. However reliefs applying to such groups are restricted to UK resident companies, and chargeable assets owned by non-resident companies where the gain would be within the charge to corporation tax eg UK assets used in a trade carried on by a UK branch of an overseas company.

4.2 Intra group transfers of assets at nil gain/nil loss (s.171)

Where one group company transfers a chargeable asset to another group company, it is deemed to take place at such a price as gives no gain and no loss to the transferor company ie deemed proceeds are equal to allowable expenditure plus indexation allowance up to the date of the transfer.

The nil gain/nil loss treatment will apply where both the transferor and transferee company are part of the same group at the time of transfer, and are either both UK resident or the asset is chargeable both before and after the transfer (eg asset in a UK branch).

However shares transferred under a group reorganisation or reconstruction (which is treated under s.127 or s.135 as not involving a disposal) are prevented from being a transfer at nil gain, nil loss under s.171(1).

S.171 is mandatory; it does not require an election.

On a future disposal outside the group the transferee's base cost is the original cost of acquisition by the group plus indexation allowance to the date of transfer. This indexed base cost is deducted from the proceeds to calculate the unindexed gain and then an indexation allowance to the date of disposal is deducted to calculate the indexed gain.

4.3 Company leaving the group – degrouping charge

4.3.1 Calculation of the degrouping charge

A degrouping charge arises if within six years of a nil gain/nil loss transfer:

- A company ceases to be part of a gains group, and

- The departing company, or an 'associated company' (associated if they could form a separate gains group) leaving the group at the same time, still owns an asset (or owns a replacement asset against which a gain on the first asset has been rolled over).

The degrouping charge will be calculated as a deemed disposal by the departing company at the time the original intra-group transfer took place, ie based on the market value at the time of the original transfer and thus charging to tax the gain avoided at the time of the transfer.

For any future disposal of the asset, the departing company (or its associate) will then be treated as having a base cost equivalent to the market value on the date of the original transfer.

4.3.2 Degrouping charge as a result of a qualifying share disposal

Where the degrouping arises from a qualifying share disposal (ie within the corporation tax regime or made by a non-resident company which could have claimed the substantial shareholding exemption had it been subject to UK corporation tax), the resulting degrouping gain or loss is treated as follows:

- A degrouping gain is added to the sales proceeds received on the disposal of the shares.
- A degrouping loss is added to the allowable cost on the disposal of the shares.

4.3.3 Interaction with substantial shareholding exemption

Where the qualifying share disposal which results in the company leaving the group is exempt as a result of the substantial shareholding exemption (or would be exempt if the company making the disposal were UK resident), the degrouping charge will also be exempt (see Section 4.6.4 below).

Summary

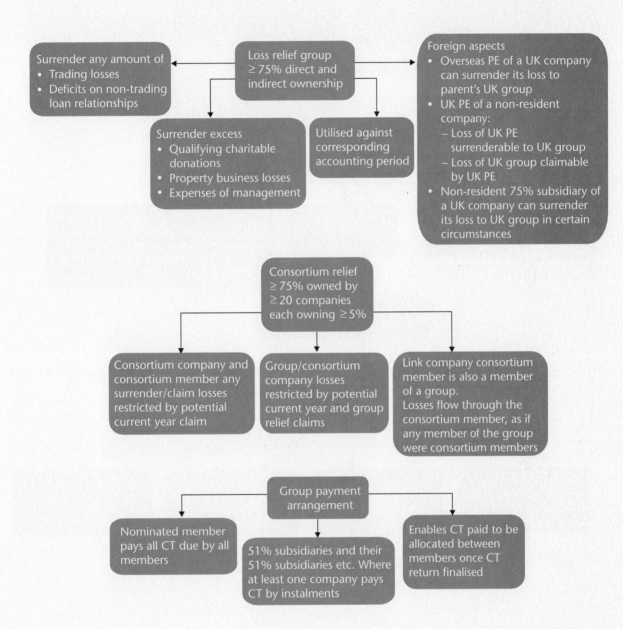

CHAPTER

14

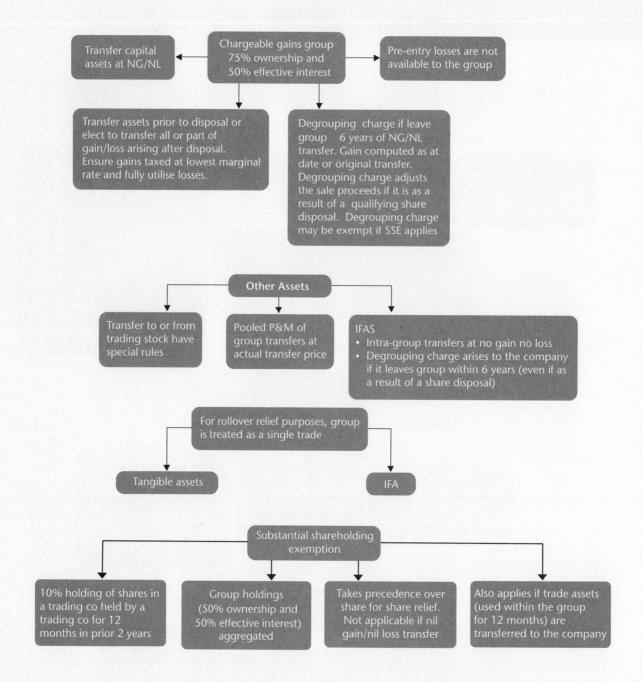

Self-test

Answer the following questions.

1   Flax Ltd, a manufacturing company, has three wholly owned subsidiaries. Stem Ltd and Source Ltd are trading companies and Nile Ltd is a property investment company.

The taxable total profits for the three trading companies for the year ended 31 December 2015 are as follows:

	£
Flax Ltd	480,000
Stem Ltd	380,000
Source Ltd	100,000

Nile Ltd had taxable total profits of £550,000 in the year ended 31 December 2014 due to capital gains on the sale of most of its properties in that year. In the year ended 31 December 2015 it has property income of £24,000, a profit on non-trading loan relationships of £21,000 and expenses of management of £85,000.

Requirement

Explain how the expenses of management of Nile Ltd should be relieved.

2   Indigo Ltd was formed two years ago to manage Sportax, a project for the marketing and advertising of a major tennis event in the UK. Indigo Ltd is owned by Alpha Ltd, Beta Ltd and Delta Ltd in the ratio of 60:30:10 respectively.

Unfortunately the event was not a success and Indigo Ltd suffered £150,000 of trading losses in the year ended 31 December 2015. Indigo Ltd had £20,000 of investment income for the same period.

The taxable total profits of Indigo Ltd's shareholders for the year ended 31 December 2015 were:

	£
Alpha Ltd	100,000
Beta Ltd	80,000
Delta Ltd	10,000

Requirement

Show how relief may be claimed for the trading loss of Indigo Ltd.

3   Assume from question 2 that Delta Ltd instead made a trading loss of £10,000 for the year ended 31 December 2015 and that Indigo Ltd had total profits of £130,000.

Requirement

How much loss could be surrendered by Delta Ltd?

4   Yellow Ltd owns 100% of Scarlet Ltd and 56% of Blue Ltd. The remaining 44% of Blue Ltd is owned by Purple Ltd, an unconnected UK resident company. Blue Ltd has two 76% subsidiaries, Taupe Ltd and Orange Ltd.

All the companies are UK resident trading companies and prepare accounts to 31 December. The forecast results for the year ended 31 December 2015 are as follows:

	Yellow Ltd £	Scarlet Ltd £	Blue Ltd £	Taupe Ltd £	Orange Ltd £
Trading profit	482,000	(60,000)	(140,000)	106,000	(58,000)
Profit on non-trading loan relationships	20,000		22,000		
Property income		96,000			
Qualifying charitable donation	(15,000)	(10,000)	(10,000)		

It is expected that in the year ended 31 December 2016, Scarlet Ltd will make modest profits, Blue Ltd will make trading profits of around £150,000 and its profit on non-trading loan relationships will be covered by qualifying charitable donation payments and Orange Ltd will continue to make losses.

In recent periods Purple Ltd has paid tax at the main rate of corporation tax.

Requirement

Explain the most beneficial way of relieving Blue Ltd's losses. Assume that FY 2015 tax rates continue into the future.

5   Branch Ltd has been a wholly-owned subsidiary of Tree Ltd since 1 January 1993. On 1 December 1993, Branch Ltd made a chargeable disposal of an asset acquired in January 1992 which gave rise to a capital loss of £95,833. The company has not made any other chargeable disposals since 1 January 1993. All companies in the Tree Ltd group have a year end of 31 December.

Branch Ltd carries on a trade of manufacturing car seats and assembling pushchairs. These activities are regarded by HMRC as a single trade. Tree Ltd has decided to dispose of the manufacturing activities, which are loss-making, thereby enabling the company to concentrate on its assembly business. A potential purchaser (a UK company) has now been identified.

The proposal is as follows:

(1)   The assets, including stock, of Branch Ltd related to its manufacturing operations will be transferred into a new wholly-owned subsidiary of Branch Ltd, Leaf Ltd. Leaf Ltd will also have a year end of 31 December.

(2)   Payment for the assets acquired by Leaf Ltd will be left outstanding as intra-group loans.

(3)   All of the share capital of Leaf Ltd will be acquired for a nominal sum by the purchaser, which will then lend sufficient funds to Leaf Ltd to enable the amount due to Branch Ltd to be repaid.

As at 31 December 2015, Branch Ltd had unused trading losses of £246,000.

It is expected that the transfer of assets to Leaf Ltd will take place on 1 February 2016 and the sale of shares on 1 March 2016. The purchaser anticipates that Leaf Ltd will become profitable by the end of 2016.

Requirements

(1)   Detail the corporation tax implications of the present proposal for the Tree Ltd group.

(2)   State the advice you would give to the purchaser regarding the future activities of Leaf Ltd.

(3)   Identify the drawbacks for Leaf Ltd, from a corporation tax point of view, of the present proposal and make any suggestions for its improvement.

Now, go back to the Learning objectives in the Introduction. If you are satisfied you have achieved these objectives, please tick them off.

Technical reference

C
H
A
P
T
E
R

14

Company Taxation Manual (Found at www.hmrc.gov.uk/manuals/ctmanual/Index.htm)

CTM80000 – Groups & consortia

CTM97400 – Corporation Tax self assessment: group payment arrangements

CTM02250 – Corporation Tax: chargeable gains

CTM06060 – Corporation Tax: company reconstructions: transfers of trade

Capital Gains Manual (Found at www.hmrc.gov.uk/manuals/cgmanual/Index.htm)

CG40200 – Companies and groups of companies

CG45400 – The degrouping charge

> This technical reference section is designed to assist you when you are working in the office. It should help you to know where to look for further information on the topics covered in this chapter.

Answer to Interactive question 1

Taxable total profits before loss relief

	U Ltd £	V Ltd £	W Ltd £
Trading income	130,000	550,000	Nil
Property income	5,000	20,000	Nil
Chargeable gains	Nil	Nil	65,000
	135,000	570,000	65,000
Less qualifying donation	(3,000)	(4,000)	(Nil)
Taxable total profits	132,000	566,000	65,000

FY2014 (3 months): Marginal relief limits (all companies associated)

Upper limit: £1,500,000/3 = £500,000

Lower limit: £300,000/3 = £100,000

Size of company (FY2014 part of the accounting period)	Marginal relief	Main rate	Small

Options for loss relief

(1) Relieve loss under s.37(3)(a)

Tax saving: £60,000 × 20% £12,000

(2) Group relief – most efficient claim

First, surrender losses to U Ltd

Available loss	£60,000
Available profits	£132,000

Surrender £32,000 to save tax at marginal rate in FY14

	£
FY2014: Tax saving: £32,000 × 21.25% × 3/12	1,700
FY2015: Tax saving: £32,000 × 20% × 9/12	4,800
	6,500

Next, surrender losses to V Ltd

Available loss (£60,000 – £32,000)	£28,000
Available profits	£566,000

Surrender £28,000 to save tax at main rate

FY2014: Tax saving: £28,000 × 21% × 3/12	1,470
FY2015: Tax saving: £28,000 × 20% × 9/12	4,200
Total tax saving	£12,170

Conclusion

The most tax efficient use of the loss is to make a claim for group relief as shown in Option (2).

Taxable total profits after group relief

	U Ltd £	V Ltd £	W Ltd £
Trading income	130,000	550,000	Nil
Property income	5,000	20,000	Nil
Chargeable gains	Nil	Nil	65,000
	135,000	570,000	65,000
Less qualifying donation	(3,000)	(4,000)	(Nil)
	132,000	566,000	65,000
Less group relief	(32,000)	(28,000)	
Taxable total profits	100,000	538,000	65,000

Answer to Interactive question 2

In FY2014

Lower limit: $\dfrac{300,000}{3}$ = £100,000

Upper limit: $\dfrac{1,500,000}{3}$ = £500,000

Loss relief strategy:

(a) The 'other profits' of Blake Ltd are chargeable at 20% only.

(b) Avon Ltd has a rate of tax of 21% in FY2014.

(c) Cally Ltd has a rate of tax of 21.25% in FY2014 on profits above £100,000, the rate of tax will then fall to 20%.

(d) Therefore the loss should be surrendered to Cally Ltd first, to set against profits otherwise taxable at 21.25% for FY 2014, then to Avon Ltd for relief at 21% in FY2014. No s.37(3) claim to offset the losses against the other income of Blake Ltd in the current year should be made.

		Blake Ltd £	Avon Ltd £	Cally Ltd £
Trading profit		Nil	767,000	191,000
Other profits		33,800		
Less group relief		NA	(65,000)(ii)	(91,000)(i)
Taxable total profits		33,800	702,000	100,000
Tax rate (FY2014 part of acc period)		20%	21%	20%
Trading loss		(156,000)		
To Cally Ltd (£191,000 – 100,000)	(i)	91,000		
To Avon Ltd (balance)	(ii)	65,000		
Unrelieved loss		Nil		

Answer to Interactive question 3

For FY 2014 there are four associated companies in the Paper plc group.

For FY2014 the upper limit is therefore £1,500,000/4 = £375,000, and the lower limit £300,000/4 = £75,000.

Excluding the chargeable gain for the part of the accounting period falling in FY2014, Paper plc and Scissors Ltd have a marginal rate of corporation tax of 21.25%, Stone Ltd has a marginal rate of 20% and Water Ltd has a marginal rate of 21%. For the FY2015 part of the accounting period all companies re subject to the unified tax rate of 20%.

Stone Ltd has £55,000 (£75,000 – £20,000) of its small profits rate band for FY2014 unutilised. £55,000 of Paper plc's gain should therefore be reallocated to Stone Ltd to be taxed at 20% in the FY2014 part of the accounting period.

The balance of the gain and the whole of Scissors Ltd's loss should then be reallocated to Water Ltd, giving a net chargeable gain of £26,500 (£97,500 – £55,000 – £16,000) to be taxed at 21% in the

FY2014 part of the accounting period and 20% in the FY2015 part of the accounting period (overall tax rate of 20.25%).

The total corporation tax payable on the gain is then (20% × £55,000) + (20.25% × £26,500) = £16,366.

This compares with a corporation tax rate of 20.31% ((21.25% × 3/12) + (20% × 9/12)), and so corporation tax of of 20.31% ×(£97,500 – £16,000) = £16,555 if the net gain had been taxed in either Paper plc or Scissors Ltd.

C
H
A
P
T
E
R

14

1 Nile Ltd must offset £45,000 of the expenses of management against its income for the year. The remaining expenses of £40,000 can be carried forward for relief in the future or surrendered as group relief. They cannot be carried back against the profits (ie the gains) arising in the previous year as they are not trading losses.

In deciding which group company to surrender the excess expenses to, the rates of tax paid by each of the group companies in FY2014 and consequently the tax limits must be determined.

Lower limit £300,000 ÷ 4 = £75,000

Upper limit £1,500,000 ÷ 4 = £375,000

Flax Ltd and Stem Ltd are main rate companies and Source Ltd is a marginal company in FY2014.

£25,000 of the expenses of management should be surrendered to Source Ltd for relief at 20.31% ((21.25% × 3/12) + (20% × 9/12)). This reduces the profits of Source Ltd to the lower limit in FY2014.

The balance should be surrendered to Stem Ltd where £5,000 will be relieved at 20.25% ((21% × 3/12) + (20% × 9/12)) and the remaining £10,000 will be relieved at 20.31%.

2 The loss could be relieved as follows:

(i) **Relief under s.37(3)**

£20,000 relieved in Indigo Ltd under s.37(3)(a) against other income and gains of the same period. This claim need not actually be made, however it will still be treated as a notional claim and restrict the amount surrenderable to the consortium members.

This leaves £130,000 loss.

(ii) **Consortium relief**

Alpha Ltd – is entitled to 60% × £130,000 = £78,000.

Its available profits are £100,000, so it can take all £78,000 of the available loss.

Beta Ltd – is entitled to 30% × £130,000 = £39,000.

Its available profits are £80,000, so it can also take all the loss available, ie £39,000.

Delta Ltd – is entitled to 10% × £130,000 = £13,000.

Its available profits are £10,000, so it cannot take its full entitlement; it can only take £10,000.

The remaining £3,000 loss (ie the amount to which Delta Ltd was entitled but could not take because its available profits were too low) cannot be given to the other members of the consortium.

Instead, it will have to be relieved by Indigo Ltd in some other way, eg carry back or carry forward.

3 Delta Ltd can surrender its total loss of £10,000 as its share of Indigo Ltd's profits is greater than £10,000 ie £13,000 (10% × £130,000).

4 **Group structure**

Yellow Ltd and Scarlet Ltd form a loss relief group. Blue Ltd, Taupe Ltd and Orange Ltd form a second loss relief group. Blue Ltd is also a consortium company owned by two consortium members: Yellow Ltd and Purple Ltd.

Blue Ltd is thus a group/consortium company.

Yellow Ltd is a link company because it is both a consortium member and a member of a loss relief group.

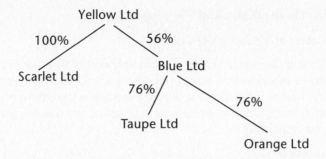

As a group/consortium company, Blue Ltd's loss available for surrender to the consortium members is restricted by all potential current year and group relief claims that Blue Ltd could make even if such a claim is not actually made. Any actual group relief surrender by other companies is taken into account first ie Orange Ltd could surrender its loss to Taupe Ltd reducing the amount of loss Blue Ltd could surrender to Taupe Ltd and maximising the amount available as consortium relief.

As Yellow Ltd is a link company, either Yellow Ltd or Scarlet Ltd can claim Blue Ltd's loss.

Associated companies (FY2014)

5 (not Purple Ltd: not under common control)

Lower limit £300,000 ÷ 5 = £60,000

Upper limit £1,500,000 ÷ 5 = £300,000

Blue Ltd loss

Blue Ltd's loss of £140,000 may be used as follows:

(a) Current year relief against Blue Ltd's own profits of the year: £22,000 of loss may be used, saving tax at 20% (and creating excess qualifying charitable donations of £10,000).

(b) Group relief to Taupe Ltd. Assuming Orange Ltd has already surrendered £58,000 of its loss to Taupe Ltd, Blue Ltd could only surrender a further £48,000 of the loss, saving tax at 20%.

(c) Consortium relief to Yellow Ltd and Purple Ltd. The maximum consortium relief available to Yellow Ltd and Purple Ltd is as follows:

Loss available*: £140,000 – 22,000 – 48,000 = £70,000

Yellow Ltd (56%) £39,200 saving tax at 21%

Purple Ltd (44%) £30,800 saving tax at 21%

*The total loss is reduced by deemed current year and group relief claims assuming that Orange Ltd has already surrendered its loss to Taupe Ltd. If Orange Ltd had not surrendered its loss to Taupe Ltd, only £12,000 of Blue Ltd's loss would be available for consortium relief £(140,000 – 22,000 – 106,000).

The loss available to Yellow Ltd could be claimed wholly or in part by Scarlet Ltd. This would depend on how Scarlet Ltd decided to utilise its own loss.

(d) Carry forward relief against Blue Ltd's future profits from the trade. It is anticipated that the whole loss would be relieved in the year ended 31 December 2016, saving tax at 20% (the unified rate).

Therefore options (a) and (b) should be rejected as the rate of tax saving is relatively low. Option (c) is attractive, as the loss is utilised quickly and efficiently. Option (d) is not as attractive, as there is a slightly lower tax rate saving and there is a cash-flow disadvantage from not using the loss as quickly. As Orange Ltd is expected to make losses next year which can be group relieved to Blue Ltd, it appears that the relief in respect of Blue Ltd's loss is (c):

• ie £70,000 of the loss is used now as consortium relief (ie the maximum as calculated above, assuming this is beneficial for Purple Ltd).

• £70,000 is used in the current year against its own profits and Taupe Ltd profits.

This maximises the cash-flow relief of the loss and relieves profits at an efficient rate.

5 (1) **Corporation tax implications of the proposal**

(a) Application of the successions rules

Even though Branch Ltd is transferring only part of its trade to Leaf Ltd, the provisions relating to successions to trades potentially apply. The basic conditions appear to be met, because part of the trade is beneficially owned to the extent of at least 75% by the same person at some time within the one year before the transfer and at some time within the two years following.

In that event:

- Capital allowances are given on a continuation basis, so that allowances for the accounting period in which the succession takes place are apportioned between Branch Ltd and Leaf Ltd (ie total WDAs for y/e 31.12.16 are apportioned 1:11) and

- Trading losses arising from the part of the trade transferred can potentially be used by Leaf Ltd against future profits from that trade (the capital loss however is not transferred with the trade).

The following will need to be established:

- That Branch Ltd will have beneficial ownership of the shares in Leaf Ltd when the trade is transferred.

- That Leaf Ltd does in fact take over the manufacturing activities of Branch Ltd as its trade and continues to carry on that trade.

- The extent to which the trading losses of £246,000 relate to those manufacturing activities rather than the assembly activities.

- Whether any reduction in those losses is required under the rules which apply when the transferor retains liabilities. If, after the succession, the remaining assets of Branch Ltd (including the amount of consideration due from Leaf Ltd) are insufficient to meet its remaining liabilities (eg trade creditors), then the amount of the shortfall must be deducted from the losses carried forward and relievable by Leaf Ltd.

(b) *Capital assets*

Since Branch Ltd and Leaf Ltd are within the same group for capital gains purposes at the time of the succession, any capital assets will pass at nil gain/nil loss. Any potential gain is therefore effectively passed to Leaf Ltd and will crystallise as a degrouping charge when the shares in that company are sold. The degrouping charge will be added to the disposal proceeds from the sale of the shares in Leaf Ltd.

(c) *Sale of shares*

The sale by Branch Ltd of the shares in Leaf Ltd is a chargeable disposal, but since they are to be sold for a nominal amount a gain is unlikely to arise. The increase in the value of the sale proceeds by the amount of any degrouping charges will however mean that there is a gain. However, as Leaf Ltd is a newly incorporated subsidiary which has received the assets of another group company which are used in its trade at the time of the share sale, the shares in Leaf Ltd will qualify for the substantial shareholding exemption as the assets transferred to it were held and used in the trade of Branch Ltd for the 12 months before the transfer.

(2) **Advice to purchaser**

The trading losses transferred to Leaf Ltd under the successions rules may only be used against future profits from the same trade (under s.45 CTA 2010). If the activities of the company are drastically altered, HMRC may argue that the original loss-making trade has ceased and a new trade commenced. In that case, relief for the brought forward losses is denied.

However, even if the original trade continues, the brought forward losses are at risk under the rules which apply on a change of ownership. The sale of the shares in Leaf Ltd constitutes a change in ownership of that company. If there is then a major change in the nature or conduct of its trade within the three years after the change in ownership (or indeed the three years before), then the losses cannot be used against post acquisition profits. Any necessary apportionments are made where the change in ownership takes place part way through an AP.

The difficulty with these rules lies in determining what constitutes a 'major change in the nature or conduct of trade'. The statute defines a major change as including major changes in:

- The type of property dealt in or services or facilities provided, and
- The company's customers, outlets or markets,

even if the change is gradual.

(3) **Drawbacks**

Although the succession rules apply, it is in the interests of both the purchaser and the vendor to ensure that the trading losses relating to the manufacturing activities are used to the maximum extent before the sale of the shares in Leaf Ltd. For the purchaser, this reduces the amount at risk under the rules which apply where there is a change in ownership and a major change in the nature or conduct of the trade, and may therefore enable the vendor to secure a higher price. There may be some scope for disclaiming capital allowances in the periods prior to the change in ownership, so long as obtaining the capital allowances is not one of the main purposes of the sale.

CHAPTER 15

International expansion

Introduction
Examination context
Topic List
Summary and Self-test
Technical reference
Answer to Interactive question
Answers to Self-test

Introduction

Learning objectives

- Evaluate the tax implications of the choice of business structures
- Explain the issues relating to business start-ups
- Calculate the impact of international expansion on UK tax liabilities
- Explain the tax implications of inward investment in the UK
- Recognise the implications of double tax treaties and the OECD Model Tax Convention
- Apply and advise on double taxation relief
- Identify legitimate tax planning measures to minimise tax liabilities
- Evaluate and advise on tax strategies to meet business objectives

Specific syllabus references for this chapter are 1g, 1h, 1n, 1o, 1p, 1q, 2a and 2b.

Syllabus links

E-commerce also has considerable implications for VAT (Chapter 18) as well as residency. The use of losses (Chapter 12 and 14) is also critical in the decision as to the choice of business structure when first expanding overseas.

Double taxation relief for companies interacts with the corporation tax computation (Chapter 10).

Examination context

Overseas operations need careful tax planning to ensure that excess amounts of UK tax are not paid. Accountants need to obtain as much information as possible in order to advise on the setting up of an overseas entity to determine whether it is better to set up as a subsidiary or as a branch (permanent establishment). In addition consideration may need to be given to changing from a branch to a subsidiary at a later point in time.

In the examination candidates may be required to:

- Advise whether a company is UK resident
- Advise and calculate the UK taxation liabilities of non-UK resident companies
- Advise companies on the implications of migrating overseas
- Advise on the alternative methods of establishing an overseas business
- Calculate the double taxation relief available in a given scenario and advise on the optimum use of losses and qualifying charitable donations in a group eligible for double taxation relief
- Advise on the implications of the OECD Model Tax Convention

1 Company residence

Section overview

- A company is liable to UK corporation tax on its world-wide profits if it is resident in the UK.

- A company is resident in the UK if it is incorporated in the UK or if its real business is carried on in the UK (ie its central management and control is exercised from the UK).

- A company resident in the UK can make an irrevocable election for all its foreign PEs to be exempt from UK corporation tax on their profits.

- E-commerce presents difficulties in establishing the location of a business and its residence for corporation tax purposes.

- The OECD considers that the location of a server could determine the residency of the business. The UK does not currently accept that a server alone can determine the residency of a business.

1.1 UK residence

A company is liable to UK corporation tax on its world-wide profits if it is resident in the UK.

Definition

UK resident: A company is UK resident if either:

- It is incorporated in the UK; or

- Its real business is carried on in the UK, and the real business is carried on where central management and control actually resides. This test is therefore relevant for companies incorporated overseas. An HMRC Statement of Practice explains that case law attaches importance to the place where the company's board of directors meet, but the location of central management and control is wholly a question of fact, hence there can be no single conclusive test.

In addition, regardless of whether it is incorporated or managed and controlled in the UK, a company is not resident in the UK for all tax purposes if it is treated as non-UK resident by any double taxation arrangement.

Companies which are UK resident are liable to UK corporation tax on their world-wide profits. Those profits arising overseas are likely to have already been subject to taxation in accordance with the overseas country's rules. Double taxation relief exists to ensure that profits are not taxed twice.

A system of double taxation treaties between many countries exists, many of which are based on the Organisation for Economic Co-operation and Development's (OECD) model agreement. Generally the UK follows the OECD model (see Section 6).

1.2 Implications for UK taxation liability

A company which is resident in the UK is charged to corporation tax on the full amount of its world-wide profits. In the case of overseas profits it is irrelevant whether they are remitted to the UK.

Although world-wide profits are taxable, it is possible for a company to make an irrevocable election for all its foreign permanent establishments (PEs), located anywhere in the world, to be exempt from UK corporation tax on their profits. If an election is in force no relief is available for foreign PE losses.

The exemption from tax for foreign PEs taken together with the distribution (dividend) exemption means that in effect, where an election applies, profits earned through foreign operations of UK resident companies will not generally be taxed in the UK except by reason of the controlled foreign company rules, the equivalent exclusions from the PE exemption, or other rules intended to prevent the artificial diversion of profits from the UK (Chapter 16).

A non-UK resident company is charged to corporation tax only if it carries on a trade in the UK through a PE. The chargeable profits are restricted to those which, broadly, are derived from the PE. Note that other UK-source income may be subject to income tax.

1.3 Residence and e-commerce

Increased activity in internet sales overseas creates difficulty in determining the residence status/location of e-business. Consequently there is a need to determine which country should levy:

- Direct tax on the profits derived from such sales (eg corporation tax); and
- Indirect taxes, such as VAT, on the sales.

This section looks at the recent decisions made to ensure this income does not escape tax and is taxed in the most appropriate location.

For corporation tax purposes, a country will charge tax on the profits of a PE based in that country. The current situation for corporation tax purposes may be summarised as follows:

	Website software/data location	*Server equipment location*
OECD model agreement	Not PE	Could be a PE
UK	Not PE	Not PE

1.3.1 Residence and e-commerce

Residence based taxation involves taxing trading income in its source country. It has become generally accepted that the key determinant of the source of income is the country in which a physical presence has been established.

Instead of 'physical presence', UK tax legislation and most double tax treaties use the term 'permanent establishment', stating that profits derived from a PE in a country should be taxed in that country (see Section 2).

When business is carried out over the internet, the application of the principles of physical presence and permanent establishment are difficult to apply. HMRC in the UK and the OECD internationally are both attempting to relate the 'old rules' to the new technology of e-commerce.

1.3.2 The views of the OECD and the UK

E-commerce activities are carried out through a combination of a website and a server.

The website is a combination of software and electronic data that is operated by a server. The server is the physical equipment that hosts the website.

The OECD makes a clear distinction between a website and the server on which the website is stored and used. Its view is that a website is a combination of software and electronic data, and does not of itself constitute tangible property. Hence it does not have a location. On the other hand, a server is a piece of equipment with a physical location, which could be regarded as a fixed place of business.

The view of the OECD is that:

- A website cannot of itself constitute a PE.

- If a business pays an Internet Service Provider (ISP) to host its website, this does not normally create a PE.

- If a business owns or leases its own server, then the place where the server is located could be a PE. However, it will not be a PE if the activities performed at that location are 'preparatory or auxiliary', such as advertising or providing information to potential customers. Activities such as taking orders, processing payments and arranging delivery of goods are not preparatory or auxiliary, and could lead to the server being treated as a PE.

The UK disagrees with the OECD view of servers. In the view of the UK, a server, whether owned or rented, is 'insufficient of itself to constitute a PE'. This issue is one of those being considered in detail in the base erosion and profit shifting (BEPS) action plan (Chapter 1).

2 Non-UK resident companies

Section overview

- A non-UK resident company is only liable to UK corporation tax if it is carrying on a trade in the UK through a PE.

- A PE exists where there is a fixed place of business in the UK or an agent has habitually worked in the UK on behalf of the non-resident company.

- The main rate of corporation tax is normally charged on the profits of a PE.

- Where a non-UK resident company carries on a trade in the UK without having a PE, any profits will be chargeable to income tax.

2.1 Corporation tax charge

A non-UK resident company is liable to corporation tax in the UK only if it is carrying on a trade in the UK through a PE.

Definition

Permanent Establishment: A company has a PE when either:

- It has a fixed place of business through which the business of the company is wholly or mainly carried on; or

- An agent acting on behalf of the company has, and habitually exercises, authority to do business on behalf of the company.

The main rate of corporation tax is normally charged, regardless of the level of profits arising in the PE. Up to FY2014 the small profits rate of corporation tax could be claimed where the appropriate double taxation treaty contained a non-discrimination clause.

Self assessment rules apply to UK PEs.

For the purposes of collection of tax, a PE will be treated as the UK representative through which the non-UK resident company carries on a trade in the UK. The PE is treated as a distinct and separate person to the non-UK resident company.

2.2 Charge to corporation tax

Profits charged to corporation tax comprise:

- Trading income arising directly or indirectly through or from the PE;
- Income from property or rights used by, held by or held for the PE; and
- Chargeable gains falling within s.10B TCGA 1992

2.3 Charge to tax on capital gains

Capital gains are charged to corporation tax, where the company carries on a trade in the UK through a PE, if they arise on:

- Assets situated in the UK used in or for the purposes of the trade at or before the time when the gain accrued; or

- Assets situated in the UK held or used for the purposes of the PE at or before the time when the gain accrued.

2.4 Charge to income tax

Income from sources within the UK which is not subject to corporation tax is subject to income tax. This could arise, for example, if a non-UK resident company carries on a trade in the UK without having a PE, or receives letting income from a UK property.

The charge to income tax on savings income and on dividends from UK companies is limited to the tax deducted at source. (This includes tax paid, treated as paid, or where there is an entitlement to a tax credit.)

2.5 Societas Europaea

The European Company or Societas Europaea (SE) was created in 2001 as a new form of corporate structure. Although registered in a single member state, it is able to operate in any member state without any further registration, authorisation, certification or licence to operate in that other member state.

As far as taxing a SE is concerned, it does not have any special tax status. Therefore, a SE will be subject, in the first instance, to the tax regime of the country in which it is registered. In order to prevent there being any significant tax disadvantage (or advantage) to the establishment of a SE by merger between two or more companies, not all of which are resident in the same EU member state, such mergers are tax neutral.

A SE is regarded as UK resident for tax purposes if it is incorporated in the UK (either as an SE or as a normal UK company which is then converted to an SE) or if it transfers its registered office from another EU member state to the UK. Any other place given by rule of law is disregarded in determining its residence status. In addition, it will not cease to be regarded as UK resident merely because of a subsequent transfer of its registered office out of the UK, although as with other companies if an SE is treated as non-UK resident under the terms of a double tax agreement it will cease to be UK resident for all other purposes.

3 Company migration

Section overview

- A company incorporated in the UK cannot normally cease to be UK resident.

- When a company 'migrates' by ceasing to be UK resident, chargeable gains and allowable losses arise on any assets leaving the scope of UK corporation tax ie those which will no longer be used in a UK trade.

- When a company migrates, the total net gains arising on trading assets leaving the scope of UK corporation tax can be deferred if there is a 75% UK resident parent company.

- If an asset on which a gain is deferred at migration is subsequently sold within six years of the migration, a proportion of the total net gain previously deferred becomes chargeable on the UK parent company.

- If a company migrates to another EEA member state, it can also defer the exit charge under an exit charge payment plan. The charge can be paid in six annual instalments, or on the earlier of the date on which the asset is sold or the 10th anniversary of the migration.

3.1 Overview

A company is treated as 'migrating' from the UK if it ceases to be resident here. This can arise:

- In the case of a company which is incorporated outside the UK but managed and controlled in the UK, where central management and control is relocated away from the UK, or

- In the case of a company which is UK incorporated, if it arranges things so that it is treated as resident in another territory under that territory's tax law **and** so that it is treated as not resident in the UK under the terms of a double taxation agreement with that other territory.

What this entails will vary according to the terms of the relevant double taxation agreement, but many of the UK's double taxation agreements follow the OECD model treaty (see section 6), and use a company's place of effective management to determine treaty residence where a company is otherwise resident in both states.

It is therefore generally harder for a UK incorporated company to migrate from the UK than a non-UK incorporated company. It is not possible for a UK incorporated company to migrate to a country with which the UK does not have a double taxation agreement.

As the company is becoming non-UK resident the corporation tax accounting period ends at the date of migration.

3.1.1 Chargeable gains on migration

When a company ceases to be UK resident, it is deemed for the purposes of TCGA 1992 to have disposed of and reacquired all of its assets at market value immediately before becoming non-UK resident. Accordingly, a liability to corporation tax on chargeable gains may arise (often referred to as an 'exit charge'). This is the case for both UK incorporated companies ceasing to be resident as a result of treaty tie-break provisions, and for non-UK incorporated companies which move their central management and control.

However, there is no deemed disposal of assets which:

- Are situated in the UK immediately after the company becomes non-UK resident, and
- Are used at any time thereafter in a trade carried on in the UK through a PE.

A charge to tax does not arise on these assets which remain within the UK trade until:

- The UK assets are actually disposed of, or
- The UK PE trade ceases, or
- The assets become situated outside the UK.

Thus the exit charge is confined to trading assets which leave the scope of UK corporation tax on migration, or assets which are held as investments.

 ### Worked example: Chargeable gains on migration

Melone SA, a company incorporated in Argentina, migrated from the UK on 1 October 2015 when its central management and control was moved from London to Buenos Aires. At that date it held two chargeable assets, both located in the UK. One was an investment property on which a gain of £335,000 would have arisen if sold for its market value. The other was the factory which it used for its trade and on which a gain of £784,000 would have arisen on an arm's length sale.

Requirement

State which, if either, of the gains becomes chargeable on the migration.

Solution

The gain on the investment property becomes chargeable on Melone SA immediately before it becomes non-UK resident. Provided the company continues to trade in the UK through a branch or agency, the gain on the factory is not chargeable. The factory will give rise to a chargeable gain at its then market value if it is actually sold or if the UK trade ceases.

Note that the question made no mention of the trade itself migrating, merely its management. Ensure that in the exam you consider assets used for investment purposes and assets used in the trade separately.

3.1.2 Deferring chargeable gains on migration

If the company which is migrating is a 75% subsidiary of a UK resident parent, the two companies may elect to defer part of the chargeable gain which would otherwise accrue. The election applies to net gains on assets situated outside the UK and used for the purposes of a trade carried on outside the UK.

3.1.3 Crystallising deferred gains

The deferred gain will crystallise in the UK parent company if the now non-UK subsidiary company disposes of any of the assets on which a gain was deferred within six years of migrating.

On the disposal of an asset the gain that will be chargeable is:

$$\text{Net Gain Deferred} \times \frac{\text{Gain at date of migration on asset sold}}{\text{Gross gains at migration}}$$

Note that whilst the gains and losses at migration are used to calculate the net gain to be deferred, it is the sum of the gains only (ie ignoring losses) that is used as the denominator in the fraction to calculate gross gains at migration.

Worked example: Deferring chargeable gains on migration

Cabernet SpA, a migrating company, is a wholly owned subsidiary of Sauvignon Ltd, a UK resident company. Cabernet SpA owns a warehouse situated in Utopia which it uses for its trade carried on abroad and on which a gain of £560,000 accrues in 2015 immediately before becoming non-UK resident. It also has goodwill (which relates to a pre-1 April 2002 trade) standing at a loss of £192,000 and fixed plant and machinery which will give rise to gains of £96,000. Cabernet and Sauvignon elect to hold over the total net gains of £464,000 under s.187 TCGA 1992. Cabernet SpA sells the warehouse in 2016 for £1,280,000.

Requirement

State the amount of any gain becoming chargeable in 2015 and 2016.

Solution

As Cabernet SpA is migrating, it would normally be liable to corporation tax on gains on any assets which are leaving the scope of UK corporation tax ie those which will not be used in a trade carried on in the UK. By election, the gains are deferred and none is chargeable in 2015.

Any gains arising after Cabernet SpA's migration will not be liable to UK corporation tax as it is no longer UK resident and will therefore only pay corporation tax on profits including gains from any UK trade. As it has no UK trade, it is completely outside the scope of UK corporation tax from 2015 onwards.

As the migrating company sells the asset subject to the election within six years of migrating, the

deferred gain of $£464,000 \times \dfrac{560,000}{656,000} = £396,098$ becomes chargeable in 2016 in Sauvignon Ltd.

The gain also crystallises if the UK parent company disposes of shares in the migrating company such that it ceases to be a 75% subsidiary or the parent company itself becomes non-UK resident. In both of these cases all of the gain not yet brought back will crystallise.

Similar provisions apply to intangible fixed assets which were originally acquired on or after 1 April 2002, which are taxed under the IFA rules.

3.2 EEA exit charge deferral

Where a company migrates from the UK to another EU member state, it can choose to defer the corporation tax payable in relation to the migration under an 'exit charge payment plan'.

This follows ECJ case law which concluded that it was a breach of a company's right to freedom of establishment under the EC treaties to collect the tax payable under exit charge provisions at the time of migration. This is because if the company had not migrated it would not have had to pay the tax until such time as the underlying asset was sold.

The charges which can be deferred under these provisions are not limited to chargeable gains exit charges. They also include profits on the disposal of trading stock on the cessation of the trade, and exit charges under the IFA and loan relationship provisions.

In order for the deferral to apply the company must make an application within nine months of migrating. On ceasing to be UK resident it must also carry on a business in an another EEA member state. The maximum amount of tax which can be deferred is the amount by which the corporation tax for the period ending with the migration is greater than it would have been without the exit charges.

The migrating company can choose the exit charge payment plan for one of two different deferral methods to apply to the amount of tax deferred (it is also possible to apply a mixture of the two methods).

- The standard instalment method

  The tax is then due in six equal instalments. The first instalment is payable nine months and a day after the end of the accounting period of migration. The rest of the instalments are payable on the following five anniversaries of that date. This method allows all assets to be taken together, without distinguishing between different classes, and without the need to track individual assets.

- The realisation method

  Under this method the tax is due on the earlier of the disposal of the asset and the tenth anniversary of the end of the accounting period of migration.

  For IFAs and loan relationship exit charges, the charge under this method is spread over 10 annual instalments, unless there is an earlier disposal of the asset. The first instalment is payable nine months and a day after the end of the accounting period of migration.

  This method requires a calculation of tax attributable to exit charges to be allocated on an asset by asset basis at the time of the exit.

Under both methods, the balance of the tax deferred under the exit charge payment plan becomes due if the company goes into liquidation or administration, or if it ceases to be resident in an EEA member state.

Where an exit charge payment plan is in place:

- Interest on late paid tax applies from the date on which the exit charge would normally fall due until the relevant instalment is paid. Each instalment of the tax is paid with the related interest charge, but

- No penalties apply unless an amount set out in the exit charge payment plan is paid late.

Worked example: EEA exit charge deferral

Pilsner BV, a Dutch incorporated company, has been UK resident for a number of years because its central management and control has been located in the UK although its business operations are all located in the Netherlands. On 1 February 2016 its central management and control is moved to the Netherlands. The company prepares accounts to 31 March each year.

At the time of migration it owns a factory site which is standing at a gain of £700,000, and goodwill (taxable under the IFA rules) which is standing at a gain of £500,000. It is also treated as realising a profit of £25,000 on its trading stock on cessation.

Requirement

Calculate the tax which could be deferred under an 'exit charge payment plan', and explain when it would be payable.

Solution

The exit charge which can be deferred is as follows (this assumes that it is not offset by losses etc, such that the total CT liability is less than the exit charge).

	£
Gain on deemed disposal of factory	700,000
IFA profit on goodwill	500,000
Profit on trading stock	25,000
Taxable profit	1,225,000
Corporation tax @ 20%	245,000

Under an exit charge payment plan:

- Under the standard instalment method, the tax would be payable in six equal annual instalments of £40,833. The first instalment would be due on 1 November 2016 (being nine months and one day after the end of the AP on 31 January 2016 – migration ends the AP), and the later instalments on the anniversary of that date.

- Under the realisation method, the tax relating to the factory and the trading stock would be deferred until the earlier of the asset being sold (which is likely to be soon in the case of the trading stock) and 31 January 2026, which is the tenth anniversary of the end of the accounting period of migration.

  The tax relating to the goodwill would be due in 10 annual instalments of £10,000 (1/10 × 20% × £500,000) starting on 1 November 2016, unless the goodwill is sold within ten years of migration in which case the balance of the tax is due immediately.

3.3 Migration procedures

Provisions exist to ensure that HMRC receives advance notification of the intended migration of companies, and to secure payment of all UK tax liabilities by companies which cease to be resident in the UK. There are penalties for non-compliance.

HMRC has published guidance notes on the procedures to be followed by migrating companies in Statement of Practice 2/90. The company which is migrating is usually required to provide a guarantee that any unpaid UK tax liabilities will be paid (either from a UK resident group company, or a bank). An accounting period also comes to an end when a company ceases to be resident in the UK. Where non-UK residence occurs during a period of account, an apportionment of profits must be made ie split between UK resident and non-UK resident accounting periods.

4 Establishing an overseas business

Section overview

- A UK company may choose to expand overseas either through a PE or via a subsidiary company incorporated overseas.

- Normally profits or losses of an overseas PE controlled from the UK are included in the overall trading profits of the parent company, thereby giving automatic loss relief.

- A company may make an irrevocable election to exempt the profits and losses of all its foreign PEs from UK corporation tax. This is subject to anti-avoidance rules which mirror the controlled foreign companies rules which apply to foreign subsidiaries, set out in Chapter 16.

- Non-UK resident subsidiary companies are not liable to UK corporation tax. The remittance of profits of a non-UK resident subsidiary, through dividends received by the UK parent company, will also usually be exempt from UK tax.

- Expanding overseas is often via a PE initially followed by incorporation when profits are anticipated.

- Incorporation of a PE will generate chargeable gains and allowable losses. However, a type of deferral relief is available which operates in a similar way to incorporation relief for capital gains tax purposes.

- Incorporation of EU PEs is subject to alternative relief in accordance with the EC Merger Directive.

- International expansion also has VAT implications which are considered in Chapter 18.

4.1 Permanent establishment abroad

Any company resident in the UK is liable to UK corporation tax on its world-wide income.

In addition, most other countries charge tax on the trading profits of UK resident companies if derived from a 'PE' in that foreign country. Thus a UK company will usually suffer double taxation on trading profits accruing to any 'PE' which it maintains abroad.

However, it is possible for a company to make an irrevocable election for all its foreign PEs, located anywhere in the world, to be exempt from UK corporation tax on their profits.

Where a treaty with a non-discrimination article is in place, the exempt income is the UK measure of the profits of the PE that are taxable by the other state in accordance with the relevant treaty. Otherwise the measure is based on the OECD Model Tax Convention. Exempt profits include any chargeable gains attributable to the foreign PE and taxable under the treaty.

If an election is in force no relief is available for foreign PE losses.

The phrase 'PE' is defined in the OECD model treaty which is used as the basis for many double taxation treaties.

4.2 Election to exempt income and losses

4.2.1 Introduction

A company may elect to exempt all its foreign PEs Taxable Total Profits or Losses from UK corporation tax. Once made, the election applies to all the foreign PEs of that company and is irrevocable from the start of the accounting period after the one in which the election is made.

4.2.2 Making an election

The election is effective from the start of the accounting period after the one in which the election is made.

Where an election is in force, the company must calculate its Taxable Total Profits or Losses excluding the 'foreign permanent establishments amount'. This is defined as the aggregate of the 'relevant profits amount' and 'relevant losses amount' for each foreign territory.

Where a treaty with a non-discrimination article is in place, the 'relevant profits amount' is the UK measure of the profits of the PE that are taxable by the other state in accordance with the relevant treaty. Otherwise the measure is based on the OECD Model Tax Convention.

Exempt profits include any capital gains attributable to the foreign PE and taxable under the treaty. If an election is in force no relief is available for foreign PE losses.

4.2.3 Capital allowances

The business carried on by the PE is treated as a separate activity whose profits and gains are not chargeable to tax. No actual capital allowances can be claimed by the UK parent company in respect of any past capital expenditure on assets being used for the purposes of PE activity.

This ensures that profits of a UK company which remain chargeable to UK tax cannot be reduced by any capital allowances in respect of any assets used by the UK company's exempt foreign PE.

4.2.4 Exclusions from the election

Payments subject to deduction of income tax

Where payments would be subject to Part 15 ITA 2007 (requiring the UK resident to deduct income tax), if they were made by a UK resident payer to a company resident in the territory where the PE is situated rather than paid to a PE, then the income is not exempted from UK corporation tax.

This is to ensure that the PE exemption does not create an incentive to arrange for payments that would otherwise be subject to the rules on deduction of tax to be received by PEs.

Deduction of income tax is required, for example, to the payment of yearly interest, annual payments or royalties to a non-resident company.

PE of a 'small company'

The profits of a PE of a 'small company' are only exempt where the PE is resident in a full treaty territory.

A company is 'small' if it has:

- Fewer than 50 employees, and
- Either:
    - An annual turnover not exceeding €10 million or
    - An annual balance sheet total not exceeding €10 million.

4.2.5 Anti-diversion rule

An anti-diversion rule prevents the branch exemption from being used to avoid taxation on the amount of profits arising in a UK resident company. It very closely mirrors the controlled foreign companies (CFC) rules. These are considered further in Chapter 16. In general, this should mean that there is no advantage to trading through a foreign subsidiary rather than an exempt PE (or vice versa).

Profits of a PE to which an election applies are not exempt if:

- They constitute 'diverted profits', which are profits which would pass through the CFC 'gateway' tests if the PE were a company incorporated in the territory in which it trades; and

- None of the specific exemptions applies.

The exemptions which apply to permanent establishments are:

- The excluded territories exemption, which applies to activities in 'high tax' jurisdictions listed in regulations issued by HMRC;

- The low profits exemption, which applies where the PE has either taxable profits (excluding chargeable gains) of no more than £50,000 in a 12 month accounting period, or taxable profits of no more than £500,000 including non-trading profits of less than £50,000. Note that, unlike for CFCs, there is no option to apply this rule on the basis of accounting profits;

- The low profit margin exemption, which applies where the accounting profit is no more than 10% of the PE's operating expenses, excluding amounts paid to related parties and the cost of goods other than those used by the PE in its local territory; and

- The low tax exemption, which applies if the tax which the PE pays in its local territory is at least 75% of the corresponding UK tax.

4.2.6 Transitional restriction for net losses

Under the credit relief system, loss relief in a foreign PE is clawed-back through a reduction in the amount of credit relief in subsequent years. If a loss arises in a foreign PE then it is relievable against the overall profits of the company. Typically, the source state (ie the PE territory) will allow the foreign PE losses to be carried forward in much the same way as happens in the UK, so that when the PE returns to profit, it will obtain relief from local taxation through that brought forward loss. This means that the UK corporation tax on the PE profits of the period when the loss is relieved locally in the PE is reduced to a lesser extent by credit relief, or maybe not at all if the loss cancels out the profits. This represents the claw-back mechanism.

4.2.7 Considerations in making an election

Because an election to exempt profits of foreign PEs is irrevocable once made, companies are likely to look at future profit projections in determining whether to make an election. The following points should also be considered:

- The fact that losses of PEs to which an election applies are not deductible for UK tax purposes removes one of the main advantages which normally applies to trading through a PE.

- The election is likely to be beneficial if the company has low tax PEs which do not fall foul of the anti-diversion rule. It would also be beneficial if a company had high tax PEs and UK losses, as in that case the election will preserve the losses for use against future UK profits.

- The detailed calculations needed to identify the exempt amount mean that there is unlikely to be any administrative saving from making the election.

4.3　Permanent establishment or subsidiary abroad?

	Overseas permanent establishment (PE)	Overseas subsidiary
Legal status	Part of UK company = single entity	Separate legal entity
Additional related 51% subsidiary?	No	Yes
Income taxed in the UK company	PE profits = Trading profits unless election made to exempt profits from UK CT	Dividends received = Usually not taxable (see Section 5)
Basis of assessment	Arising (accruals) basis	Remittance basis if in unlikely event dividends are taxable.
Profits taxed overseas?	Yes DTR available in UK (see Section 5)	Yes DTR available in UK (see Section 5)
Overseas trading losses	Unrelieved losses offset against UK company's profits in accordance with UK loss relief rules if PE is part of UK trade and election to exempt not made If PE is separate trade operating wholly overseas, then losses may only be offset against future profits from that PE's trade	Overseas losses cannot be surrendered to a UK company Unrelieved losses of a 75% subsidiary resident in EEA may be surrendered to a UK parent company
Capital allowances	UK allowances available unless election to exempt profits made	Overseas allowances available as per local rules. No UK allowances available
Transfer of assets to the foreign entity	No gains or losses arise. No balancing adjustments	Gains/losses and balancing adjustments arise

Where the foreign country has a lower rate of company taxation than the UK, it can be beneficial for the UK company to conduct its foreign activities through a non-UK resident subsidiary or an exempt PE if profits are anticipated, and through a non-exempt PE if losses are likely to arise.

In the case of a foreign subsidiary which is not resident in the UK the repatriation of profits to the UK through dividend payments to the UK parent will in most cases be exempt from UK tax (see Section 5). Relief can only be obtained against the UK parent's profits for any losses of a non-UK resident subsidiary in certain limited circumstances (if the non-UK resident subsidiary is not resident in an EEA member state, and does not have a PE in an EEA member state, no loss relief will be possible unless the loss relates to a UK PE).

4.4　Losses of an overseas permanent establishment

Gross profits of a PE which is not a separate trade carried on wholly overseas, and which are not the subject of an exemption election, are included within total trading income. This therefore gives automatic loss relief where either the PE or the UK business is loss making. Where the UK business has brought forward trading losses, those losses can be set off against UK trading income in priority to those of the PE in order to maximise double taxation relief. However, if the losses are sufficient to entirely eliminate the trading profit, double taxation relief will inevitably be wasted.

Gross profits of a PE which amounts to a separate trade which is wholly carried on overseas, and which are not the subject of an exemption election, are also included within total trading income. However, these profits or losses are ring fenced such that loss relief between UK profits and the losses of this type of PE is not possible. Any loss realised by such a PE can only be offset against future profits of that PE.

4.5 Incorporating an overseas permanent establishment

4.5.1 Implications of incorporation

Where a foreign operation is likely to show a loss in the early years followed by a profit, it may be worthwhile to trade through a non-exempt foreign PE whilst losses arise (so that loss relief is available against the company's UK profits assuming the PE's trade is controlled from the UK) and then later to convert the PE into a non-UK resident subsidiary company (so that profits can be accumulated at potentially lower rates of foreign tax).

An overseas PE is incorporated by setting up a new company resident abroad and transferring the PE's net assets into the new company in exchange for shares. The PE will then cease to trade.

Incorporation will result in balancing adjustments arising on the branch assets transferred to the non-UK company.

Incorporation will also constitute a disposal of the assets of the PE giving rise to chargeable gains or losses in the hands of the UK company.

4.5.2 Incorporation relief for incorporation of an overseas permanent establishment

Relief exists for chargeable gains on incorporation to be postponed where:

- The trade of a foreign PE is transferred to a non-UK resident company with all the assets used for that trade except cash;

- The consideration for the transfer is wholly or partly securities (shares or shares and loan stock);

- The transferring company owns at least 25% of the ordinary share capital of the non-UK resident company; and

- A claim for relief is made.

There is full postponement of the net gains arising on the transfer where the consideration is wholly securities. Where part of the consideration is in a form other than securities, eg cash, that proportion of the net gains is chargeable immediately.

The postponement may be indefinite.

4.5.3 Crystallising of deferred gains

The gain becomes chargeable on the UK company which owned the PE only when:

- It at any time disposes of any of the securities received on the transfer; or

- The non-UK resident company within six years of the transfer disposes of any of the assets on which a gain arose at the time of the transfer.

Disposal of asset within six years

In the case of an asset disposal the proportion of the deferred gain brought back into charge is calculated as

$$\text{Remaining balance of net gain deferred} \times \frac{\text{Gain on asset at incorporation}}{\text{Gross gains at incorporation}}$$

Disposal of securities in subsidiary at any time

Where securities are disposed of, the gain previously deferred is chargeable in addition to any gain arising on the disposal of the securities themselves. Note that if the gain on the securities is exempt under the substantial shareholding exemption, the previously deferred gain remains chargeable.

Similar provisions apply to intangible fixed assets which were originally acquired on or after 1 April 2002.

Interactive question: Incorporating a foreign PE   [Difficulty level: Exam standard]

Grape Ltd, a UK resident company, used to trade through a foreign branch in Mexico. This trade was transferred to a US subsidiary, Raisin Inc, in 2011. The terms were that Raisin Inc would issue shares (valued at £600,000) for 90% of the consideration and pay the balance in cash. On transfer of the trade the chargeable capital assets gave rise to gains of £375,000 and losses of £75,000.

In 2013 Grape Ltd sold 55% of the shares it received in Raisin Inc for £825,000. In January 2016 Raisin Inc sold assets on which gains amounting to £150,000 arose on the transfer in 2011.

The substantial shareholding exemption does not apply.

Requirement

Show the amounts of any gains that become chargeable.

See **Answer** at the end of this chapter.

4.6 Incorporating an EU permanent establishment

4.6.1 Transfer of non-UK trade

Under the EC Merger Directive, relief applies where a UK company trading in another EU member state via a PE transfers the whole of the assets used in that trade or part trade to a company resident in an EU member state, other than the UK, wholly or partly in exchange for shares.

If a claim for relief is made, the exit gain remains taxable but credit is given (as if it were double taxation relief) for the tax which would have been payable in the jurisdiction in which the PE is located if the transfer to the company had been a taxable transfer. Detailed tax advice will therefore need to be obtained in the PE jurisdiction to determine the amount of the relief.

A claim will only be accepted if HMRC is satisfied that the transfer is for bona fide commercial reasons and is not for the purpose of tax avoidance.

Note that this is a 'permanent' relief, unlike the deferral relief outlined above. If a claim is accepted, the relief cannot be reversed on a later disposal of the shares or the underlying business.

Worked example

House Ltd, resident in the UK, operates a business in Italy through a permanent establishment which it then transfers to Casa SpA, resident in Italy, in exchange for shares.

Requirement

Describe the tax consequences of this transfer.

Solution

Note that the two companies need not be part of a world-wide group.

A gain is chargeable on disposal of the assets of the permanent establishment, but credit is given as double taxation relief for the foreign (EU) tax which would have been payable if the EC Merger Directive had not applied. In other words, in the example above any UK corporation tax charged would be reduced by the Italian tax which would have applied but for the EC Merger Directive.

4.6.2 Transfer of UK trade

Under the EC Merger Directive, there should also be no tax charge where a company resident in one member state transfers the whole or part of a UK trade to a company resident in another member state, subject to certain conditions being met.

This will often be the case in any event where a UK trade is transferred between two companies which are part of the same chargeable gains group, because the s.171 nil gain/nil loss transfer rules apply to transfers to and from UK trading PEs.

Where this is not the case, there is a further EU Merger Directive relief which can apply if a claim is made, under which a transfer of a UK trade between two companies which are not members of a chargeable gains group is treated as made at nil gain/nil loss. In order for it to be possible to claim under these provisions the transfer must be from a company in one EU member state to a company in another EU member state (which can be the UK). The consideration must be wholly in the form of the issue of shares or debentures, and the assets need to remain within the scope of UK corporation tax ie continue to be used in a UK trade.

A claim for the relief must be made by both companies, and is subject to HMRC clearance as mentioned above.

Similar provisions apply to intangible fixed assets which were originally acquired on or after 1 April 2002.

5 Double taxation relief

Section overview

- A UK resident company is liable to UK corporation tax on its world-wide profits.

- Where a UK resident company operates both in the UK and overseas, it may suffer both UK corporation tax and overseas tax on its overseas profits.

- Double taxation relief (DTR) gives relief for overseas tax borne on the income which is also taxable in the UK, by way of a credit against the UK resident company's corporation tax liability.

- Any overseas income received should be grossed up and included in the corporation tax computation of the UK company.

- Dividends received from overseas companies are usually exempt from tax. They may form part of franked investment income (FII). The dividend received is grossed up by 100/90 for the purposes of FII. Any overseas taxes suffered in respect of the dividend are ignored.

- Each overseas source of income is considered separately when calculating the amount of DTR available.

- Consideration should be given to the allocation of losses and qualifying charitable donations to UK income in priority to overseas income in order to maximise DTR available.

- Unrelieved foreign tax (UFT) on profits of an overseas PE which is treated as part of the UK trade may either be carried forward indefinitely against future UK tax liabilities of that PE or carried back three years on a LIFO basis against UK tax liabilities of that PE.

- UFT on other foreign sources of income is lost.

A UK resident company which also operates overseas will be liable to UK corporation tax on its world-wide profits. If it operates via a PE, UK corporation tax will apply to all the profits of the PE, unless it has made an irrevocable election to exempt the profits of its PEs from UK corporation tax.

A UK company may receive other income from overseas, for example rental income from an overseas property, which will be taxable in the UK. Many countries also deduct tax on income remitted overseas (withholding tax).

In both cases it is likely that the foreign income will be subject to both foreign and UK corporation tax. There are three principal ways in which double taxation relief can be given:

- Under the terms of a double tax treaty (treaty relief);
- Unilateral double tax relief where no double tax treaty exists (unilateral relief); or
- Expense relief.

5.1 Treaty relief

The UK has a network of double taxation treaties with a number of other countries. Most such treaties allow the UK company a credit for tax suffered on income and gains derived from the other country. The basic principles of treaty relief are as follows:

- Treaties always take precedence over UK tax law

- If double tax relief is given under a double tax treaty, then unilateral relief via the UK tax provisions cannot be given

- Most double tax treaties follow the standard OECD model.

5.2 Unilateral relief

Where no double tax treaty provision applies, unilateral relief allows double taxation relief (DTR) as a credit against the UK corporation tax liability on the foreign income.

5.3 Expense relief

Where a company has overseas income but, due to the availability of losses or qualifying charitable donations, its UK tax liability is nil or very small, the UK company can choose to treat the overseas tax as an expense and include the overseas income in the corporation tax computation net of the overseas tax.

5.4 Classification of overseas income

Overseas income is taxed as follows:

- Trading income:

    - Where an overseas PE does not have a separate trade carried on wholly overseas, its trading profits will be included in the total trading income of its UK resident parent company.

    - Where an overseas PE has a separate trade carried on wholly overseas its trading profits are also taxed as trading income but will be calculated separately from the UK trade as any losses incurred can only be offset against profits of the same overseas trade.

- Profits on non-trading loan relationships – this includes income from overseas securities eg interest from debentures in an overseas company.

- Property income eg foreign rental income.

5.5 Foreign dividend income

As we saw in Chapter 10:

- All dividends received, whether received from UK companies or overseas companies, are treated in the same way.

- All dividends received are exempt from corporation tax if they fall within the list of exemptions.

The list of exemptions available for dividends is wide ranging and in almost all cases foreign dividends received will be exempt dividends. The repatriation of profits of overseas subsidiaries is unlikely to be subject to UK corporation tax. The DTR position in cases where the exemptions do not apply is considered briefly below.

However, exempt foreign dividends received from non-associated companies/ companies which are not related 51% group companies are included in franked investment income (FII) and therefore up to FY2014 are taken into account when determining the rate of tax charged (see Chapter 10), and to determine whether corporation tax should be paid in instalments. The amount included in FII is the amount of the dividend received grossed up by 100/90. Any overseas tax suffered in respect of the dividend is ignored.

5.6 Taxing overseas income

Overseas income is received by UK resident companies net of foreign tax, but the gross amount of this income is assessable to UK corporation tax. Overseas income must therefore be grossed up for any overseas tax suffered for inclusion in the UK corporation tax computation.

Foreign taxes are classified as either withholding tax (WHT) or underlying tax (UT):

- WHT is a direct tax on income and is always potentially recoverable on any source of income. It includes tax withheld on remittances of income to the UK and overseas taxes paid on the profits of a UK company's overseas PE.

- UT is the overseas tax suffered on an overseas company's profits out of which foreign dividends are paid. It is now largely irrelevant for UK tax purposes as almost all foreign dividends are now exempt from UK corporation tax and it is not included when calculating FII.

5.7 Calculating DTR

In computing the DTR available to a company, each source of income must be considered separately. The DTR is the lower of:

- The UK tax on the overseas income ie gross overseas income × company's average UK corporation tax rate; and

- The overseas tax suffered in respect of each separate source.

Each source of income is considered separately when calculating the amount of double taxation relief available.

5.8 Interaction of donations, loss reliefs, management expenses and DTR

Where a company has deductions from total profits, for example:

- Qualifying charitable donations;
- Group relief; or
- Expenses of management.

It can choose to offset them in such a manner as to maximise its DTR. This is achieved by offsetting the deductions against UK income first followed by foreign income which has suffered the lowest marginal rate of overseas tax.

Worked example: Unilateral relief, multiple sources of income

PAF Ltd has received rental income from two properties situated in Utopia and Overlandia. It also has trading losses of £210,000 that have been surrendered from another group company.

PAF Ltd has the following results for the year ended 31 March 2016:

	£
Trading income	200,000
Property income (gross Utopian rental income)	100,000
Property income (gross Overlandian rental income)	100,000
Foreign tax has been suffered as follows	
Property income (Utopian rental income)	10,000
Property income (Overlandian rental income)	40,000

Requirement

Calculate PAF Ltd's corporation tax liability for the year ended 31 March 2016.

Solution

Corporation tax computation – year ended 31 March 2016

	£
Trading income	200,000
Property income Utopia	100,000
Property income Overlandia	100,000
	400,000
Group loss relief	(210,000)
Taxable total profits	190,000
Corporation tax @ 20%	38,000
DTR (W)	(30,000)
Corporation tax liability	8,000

WORKING

	Trading income	Property income Utopia	Property income Overlandia	Total
	£	£	£	£
Profits	200,000	100,000	100,000	400,000
Group loss relief	(200,000)	(10,000)	–	(210,000)
Taxable total profits	–	90,000	100,000	190,000
Corporation tax @ 20%	–	18,000	20,000	38,000
Double tax relief				
Lower of – £18,000				
– £10,000	–	(10,000)	–	(10,000)
Lower of – £20,000				
– £40,000	–	–	(20,000)	(20,000)
Corporation tax payable	–	8,000	–	8,000

The unrelieved overseas tax of £20,000 (£40,000 – £20,000) from the Overlandian rental income is lost.

Note: If the surplus group losses of £10,000 had been offset against the Overlandian source of property income, the double tax relief would be reduced to £18,000 on that source.

5.9 DTR on taxable foreign dividends

As noted above, the majority of foreign dividends received by a UK company are exempt from corporation tax. However, if a UK company receives a non-exempt dividend, it may still be able to claim DTR to offset its corporation tax liability on the dividend.

DTR is available in respect of:

- Withholding taxes, and

- Where the UK company controls at least 10% of the voting rights in the foreign company, the underlying corporate tax paid by the company on the profits from which the dividend is paid.

The amount of the dividend is grossed up for both withholding tax and underlying tax to determine the amount of taxable income. The DTR calculation is then the same as for other sources of income.

5.9.1 Underlying tax

The amount of underlying tax which is taken into account is calculated as:

(Gross dividend received/Profit available for distribution per the accounts) × Tax paid

Where a dividend resolution specifies the period for which a dividend is paid, the calculation is done with reference to the tax paid and accounts for that period. Where it does not, you should look to the accounts and profits of the last period for which the paying company draws up accounts ending before the dividend was paid.

The amount of DTR which is attributable to a dividend is capped at the UK tax attributable to the dividend, under the 'mixer cap' provisions. In practice, this is only relevant where a dividend is paid through a chain of companies before reaching the UK. If a dividend is received directly in the UK, the limitation of the DTR to the lower of the foreign tax or the UK tax on the same income will achieve the same result.

Worked example: Underlying tax

Ball Ltd (a member of a large global group) has a 25% shareholding in Foot SA, which is a company resident in Fantopia. Dividends received from Foot SA are not exempt from corporation tax.

In the year ended 31 March 2016, Ball Ltd's only income was a dividend of £13,200 from Foot SA. This was after deduction of Fantopian withholding tax of 12%. The dividend was paid out of Foot SA's profits for the year ended 31 December 2015. Its accounts for that period showed distributable profits of £106,500, and its tax return shows a tax payment of £8,300.

Requirement

Calculate Ball Ltd's corporation tax liability for the year ended 31 March 2016.

Solution

Corporation tax computation – year ended 31 March 2016

	£
Net dividend	13,200
Add WHT (12/88 × £13,200)	1,800
Gross dividend	15,000
Underlying tax: (£15,000/£106,500) × £8,300	1,169
Taxable total profits	16,169
Corporation tax @ 20%	3,234
DTR lower of : UK tax of £3,234, and	
Overseas tax of (£1,800 + £1,169) = £2,969	(2,969)
Corporation tax liability	265

5.10 Unrelieved foreign tax

Where the overseas tax exceeds the amount of UK tax on the foreign income, unrelieved foreign tax (UFT) is created. The relief that may be available for the UFT depends on the source of foreign income.

UFT on profits of an overseas PE which does not have a separate trade carried on wholly overseas may either be carried forward indefinitely against future UK tax liabilities of that PE or carried back three years on a LIFO basis against UK tax liabilities of that PE.

UFT on other foreign sources of income is simply lost.

6 OECD Model Convention

Section overview

- The model treaty is the basis for many double tax treaties.

- The treaty only applies where a formal agreement has been signed between two 'Contracting States'.

- The term residence in the treaty basically follows the rules for company residence in the contracting states.

- Business profits are only taxable in a state where there is a 'permanent establishment', ie a fixed place of business.

- The model treaty sets a maximum rate of withholding tax for dividends (5% for holdings of 25% or more and 15% for smaller holdings) and interest (10%).

- Gains on disposals of immovable property are generally taxable where the property is situated.

- The model treaty sets out the method for eliminating a double taxation charge where a liability to tax arises in both Contracting States.

- Most income will be exempt in one of the two countries.

- Dividends will remain taxable in both states with a deduction in the form of a credit relief.

- This 'treaty relief' for dividends follows identical rules to unilateral relief.

6.1 Introduction

The UK has international taxation agreements with many countries. Once an agreement has been authorised by an Order in Council it has statutory effect.

Most of the treaties the UK has negotiated with other territories have followed the model draft treaty prepared by the Organisation for Economic Co-operation and Development (OECD). The model treaty is regularly revised to address new tax issues arising within the evolving global economy, and was last revised in July 2014. Further revisions are expected as a result of the BEPS action plan (Chapter 1).

This chapter explains and illustrates the provisions and workings of the OECD Model Convention as they affect the taxation of companies and groups of companies.

The OECD model, like tax legislation, is split into various chapters. These are as follows:

Chapter	Title	Containing articles
I	Scope of the convention	1 and 2
II	Definitions	3 to 5
III	Taxation of income	6 to 21 (Article 14 has been deleted)
IV	Taxation of capital	22
V	Methods for elimination of double taxation	23A and 23B
VI	Special provisions	24 to 29
VII	Final provisions	30 and 31

6.2 Scope of the model convention

Article 1 states that the agreement 'shall apply to persons who are residents of one or both of the Contracting States'. Contracting states simply refers to the two countries party to the treaty. [Article 1]

The agreement applies to taxes on income and on capital. If these taxes change after the treaty is signed it can also apply to any new similar taxes of each country. [Article 2]

6.3 Definitions

6.3.1 General definitions

The following are the most important general definitions:

(a) Person: 'includes an individual, a company and any other body of persons'. [Article 3(1)(a)]

This, for example, would include the recognition of a partnership or co-operative.

(b) Company: 'any body corporate or any entity which is treated as a body corporate for tax purposes'. This would include a charity or friendly society. [Article 3(1)(b)]

6.3.2 Residence

A company is 'resident of a contracting state' if under the laws of that state it is liable to tax in that State 'by reason of its place of management or any other criterion of a similar nature'. [Article 4(1) & (3)]

However, a company is not resident in another Contracting State if its liability to tax only derives from sources of income in that State.

For companies, there is a tie-breaker clause which states that a company will be deemed to be resident in the state which is the place of its effective management and control. The commentary to the treaty defines the place of effective management as the place where key management and commercial decisions are taken. It will ordinarily be the place where the most senior group of people are and where decisions affecting the operating of the company are taken. There can be more than one place of management but only one place of effective management and control at any given time.

A company must make a self-assessment of its UK residence status. Where the relevant treaty has a standard tie-breaker clause, the company will need to self-assess the location of its place of effective management.

6.3.3 Permanent establishment

A company has a permanent establishment in a Contracting State if it has a 'fixed place of business through which the business of an enterprise is wholly or partly carried on'. [Article 5(1)]

This will include: [Article 5(2)]

(a) A place of management
(b) A branch
(c) An office
(d) A factory
(e) A workshop
(f) A mine, oil or gas well, quarry or any other place of extraction of natural resources
(g) A building or construction/installation site if the project lasts for more than 12 months. [Article 5(3)]

A 'permanent establishment' shall not include:

(a) Facilities solely used for storage, display or delivery of goods [Article 5(4)]

(b) Storage facilities for stock and work-in-progress

(c) Premises used solely for the purpose of purchasing, collection of information, preparation or auxiliary activity of the enterprise

(d) A broker, general commission agent or similar where they are acting in the ordinary course of their business. [Article 5(6)]

Where a person other than an agent of independent status is acting on behalf of an enterprise and has, and habitually exercises, in a contracting state its authority to conclude contracts in the name of the name of the enterprise, there will be a PE.

6.3.4 The ambit of the agreement

The definitions given in Articles 1 to 5 of the OECD Model define the ambit of the agreement.

The definitions given by the treaty define the terms such as residence and 'permanent establishment' for the purposes of the application of the treaty only. The definitions do not replace the definitions of these terms for domestic legislation in any Contracting State (although the basis of the residence definition in the model treaty is the definition used in each State's domestic legislation). It does not therefore follow that just because a company is resident (or not) in one or other country under the terms of the agreement that it will (or not) be resident under the domestic rules of each country.

Note. The treaty definitions have been incorporated into UK legislation for determining a PE for the purpose of taxing a non resident company in the UK, and for the purposes of determining whether a company is non-resident.

6.4 Treaty exemption

6.4.1 Introduction

Much of the model agreement concentrates on the relief from tax in one or other of the Contracting States. Set out below are the rules relating to income receivable by companies.

6.4.2 Business profits

Under the OECD model, business profits of a company resident in the UK are taxable only in the UK unless the business is carried on in the other contracting state through a 'permanent establishment'. In this case the profits attributable to that permanent establishment are taxed only in the other territory. [Article 7]

The opposite also applies, so a non-UK resident company will only be taxed in the UK where profits arise from a permanent establishment situated in the UK.

6.4.3 Dividends

The treaty sets a maximum limit on the rate of withholding tax as follows: [Article 10]

Company holds at least 25% of the shares	5%
Company holds < 25%	15%

6.4.4 Interest

The maximum withholding tax rate is 10% subject to interest being at an arm's length commercial rate. [Article 11]

6.4.5 Royalties

Patent and copyright royalties arising in one country but payable to a person resident in another country are taxed only in the country of residence unless the beneficial owner carries on business through a permanent establishment in the first country. [Article 12]

Note that electronic ordering and downloading of goods may give rise to a royalty if the ordering and downloading is for commercial exploitation by the recipient.

6.5 Capital gains

6.5.1 Immoveable property

Gains on the disposal of immoveable property (eg land and buildings) are generally taxable in the territory in which the property is situated. [Article 13]

6.5.2 Moveable property

Gains on the disposal of moveable property are taxable as follows:

(a) Gains accruing through a permanent establishment are taxable in the country where the permanent establishment is situated.

(b) Other gains are taxable in the country of residence of the chargeable person. [Article 13]

6.6 Elimination of a double taxation charge

The OECD model treaty sets out two ways in which double taxation may be avoided, the exemption and credit methods. It is up to the Contracting States to agree which method they will adopt. It is possible for the two states to adopt different methods, or for different methods to be adopted for different types of income. The UK generally adopts the credit method of relief.

6.6.1 Exemption method

Where this method applies, if a person resident in one Contracting State derives income or owns capital in the other Contracting State that, in accordance with the OECD agreement is taxed in that other State, the income is exempt from tax in the Contracting State in which the person is resident. [Article 23A(1)]

However, this exemption shall not apply to interest or dividends taxable in both Contracting States. In this situation, the country of residence of the recipient must allow a deduction in the form of credit relief of the amount of tax paid in the other Contracting State up to a maximum of the tax payable in the country of residence. [Article 23A(2)]

6.6.2 Treaty relief by credit

This is the approach typically adopted in the UK. Tax relief is available in the UK for withholding and underlying tax on profits arising in another country where, subject to the terms of the treaty, they are taxable in the UK. Where the UK has an agreement with another country this tax is known as 'treaty relief'. [Article 23B]

Unilateral relief is also available where the UK does not have such an agreement or where an agreement does not cover a particular type of income.

6.7 Special provisions

6.7.1 Non-discrimination

This clause basically ensures that foreign nationals taxable in another country shall not be charged any more tax than individuals native to that country on income received from similar sources. [Article 24]

6.7.2 Mutual agreement procedure

This enables any UK national taxable in another Contracting State to apply to HMRC, where the UK national feels that the action of one or other State will result in income or capital being taxed not in accordance with the treaty. [Article 25]

It is then the responsibility of HMRC, where it feels the case is justified, to make a mutual agreement with the other Contracting State to resolve the situation.

The case must be notified to HMRC within three years of the action taken by either authority that results in taxation not in accordance with the terms of the particular treaty.

Summary

UK Resident if:
- Incorporated in UK
- Centrally managed and controlled in UK
- Liable to UK corporation tax on worldwide profits
- Can elect to exempt profits/ losses of overseas PEs from UK CT

Non-UK Resident companies
- Liable to UK corporation tax on profits of a UK PE
- Chargeable at main rate
- Liable to income tax on other UK income

Company migration

- Company ceases to be UK resident
- Incorporated outside the UK, and management and control moves from the UK, or
- UK incorporated and becomes non-resident under a double tax treaty

Chargeable gains and losses on any assets no longer used in UK trade (foreign assets)

Total net gains on foreign assets can be deferred if has a 75% UK parent company

Exit charge payment plan can defer tax on migration to EEA
- 6 annual instalment, or
- Earlier of realisation and 10 years

Deferred gains become chargeable if asset sold within 6 years or shares sold at any time

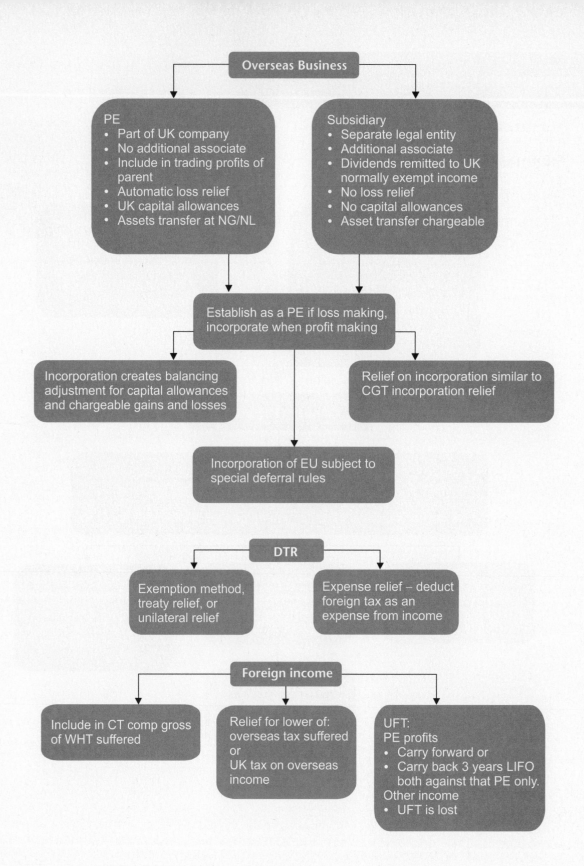

Overseas Business

PE
- Part of UK company
- No additional associate
- Include in trading profits of parent
- Automatic loss relief
- UK capital allowances
- Assets transfer at NG/NL

Subsidiary
- Separate legal entity
- Additional associate
- Dividends remitted to UK normally exempt income
- No loss relief
- No capital allowances
- Asset transfer chargeable

Establish as a PE if loss making, incorporate when profit making

Incorporation creates balancing adjustment for capital allowances and chargeable gains and losses

Relief on incorporation similar to CGT incorporation relief

Incorporation of EU subject to special deferral rules

DTR

Exemption method, treaty relief, or unilateral relief

Expense relief – deduct foreign tax as an expense from income

Foreign income

Include in CT comp gross of WHT suffered

Relief for lower of:
overseas tax suffered
or
UK tax on overseas income

UFT:
PE profits
- Carry forward or
- Carry back 3 years LIFO both against that PE only.
Other income
- UFT is lost

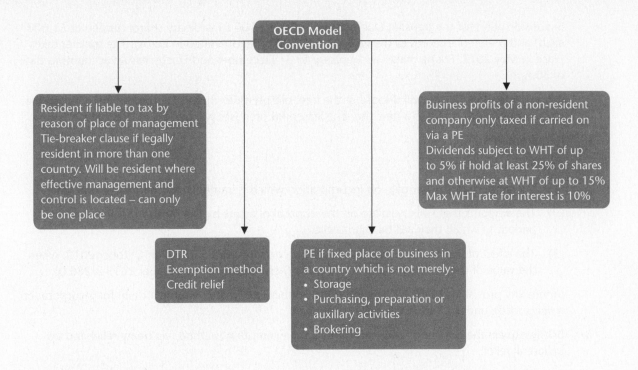

Self-test

Answer the following questions.

1 When is a company UK resident?

2 Tahuna plc is the UK resident holding company of a multinational group. One of its wholly owned subsidiaries, Beach Ltd, operates a manufacturing facility in Pacifica. The tax system in Pacifica is broadly the same as that in the UK.

Beach Ltd was incorporated in Pacifica in 2004 but due to production and marketing problems has always been managed and controlled from the UK. The company is regarded as UK resident under the UK/Pacifica double tax treaty.

As a result of legislation introduced in Pacifica to give locally resident companies certain commercial advantages, it has been decided to transfer the management and control of Beach Ltd to Pacifica.

Requirements

Summarise the taxation implications of the following:

(a) Making Beach Ltd resident in Pacifica; or instead

(b) Transferring the trade and assets of Beach Ltd (whilst still UK resident) to a new subsidiary of Tahuna plc resident in Pacifica in exchange for shares.

3 When might a non-UK resident company come within the scope of UK corporation tax?

4 Frame Ltd (Frame) is a company incorporated in the UK, which carries on a trade of manufacturing pushchairs. In 1994, it set up a manufacturing operation in Luxembourg, which was treated as a PE by the Luxembourg authorities. The operation is now making substantial profits, and so the trade of the PE is to be transferred to a company, Duchy Gmbh (Duchy), which is resident in Luxembourg.

On incorporation, the following chargeable gains and allowable losses arise on assets held by the PE:

	£
Freehold land and buildings	112,500
Leasehold land and buildings	(22,500)
Goodwill	52,500
Net chargeable gain	142,500

In consideration for the transfer, Duchy issues to Frame 100 £1 ordinary shares (valued at £1,000 each) and preference shares to the value of £350,000 (denominated in euros). The transfer takes place in May 2012. Frame makes accounts up to 31 December and Duchy has an accounting date of 30 April.

It is expected that Duchy will dispose of the freehold premises during September 2016, when the trading operations move to a new site. The leasehold premises will be sold in late 2017.

Requirements

Calculate:

(1) The amount of the net gain on incorporation which is immediately chargeable on Frame.

(2) The amounts that will crystallise on the disposal of assets by Duchy and the accounting periods in which they will be chargeable.

(3) The effect of Frame disposing of the preference shares for £550,000 in October 2019, when the value of the ordinary shares is £450,000 (Assume the RPI in October 2019 is 280.0).

Ignore any provisions of the UK/Luxembourg Double Tax Treaty. Assume a claim for incorporation relief is made under s.140 TCGA 1992.

5   Briefly explain the difference between DTR via the exemption method, via treaty relief and via unilateral relief.

6   LMN Ltd's UK business has suffered from increasing competition and has suffered a trading loss in the current year. It also received rental income from an overseas property. In the year ended 31 March 2016 LMN Ltd has the following results:

	£
Trading loss	(50,000)
Gross property income (gross of 25% WHT)	20,000

LMN Ltd will make a s.37(3)(a) CTA 2010 current year loss relief claim.

Requirements

Show LMN Ltd's corporation tax liability and trading loss carried forward for the year ended 31 March 2016 assuming:

(a) Credit relief is taken.
(b) Expense relief is taken.

7   Holmes Ltd is a large UK resident company with the following results for the year ended 31 March 2016.

	£
Trading income	550,500
Profits from overseas PE controlled from UK (overseas tax paid on profits £50,000)	150,000
Dividends received from foreign companies in different tax territories (no double tax treaty applies to any of the territories)	
Reichenbach Ltd (after £10,000 WHT)	250,000
Lestrade Ltd (after £13,500 WHT)	76,500
Qualifying charitable donations paid	50,500

Note:

Holmes Ltd owns the following holdings in the ordinary share capital of the following foreign companies:

	%
Reichenbach Ltd	100
Lestrade Ltd	5

Holmes Ltd has not made an election to exempt the profits of its overseas PE from UK corporation tax.

Requirement

Calculate the UK corporation tax payable by Holmes Ltd for the year ended 31 March 2016, explaining the relief for foreign tax suffered.

8   Bucks SHg is a company incorporated in Utopia, and tax resident there by virtue of its incorporation. The board of Bucks SHg often holds its board meeting in Monaco. The board often fly from London to Monaco taking the opportunity to have a meeting with management in the UK before making their journey to Monaco. The meetings in the UK often discuss items to be decided at the meetings in Monaco.

In the UK, the company has an office which acts as a distributor for goods manufactured in Utopia. No manufacturing takes place in the UK. The contracts for sale of goods are negotiated directly from Utopia. The UK merely acts as the delivery agent ensuring that once the goods arrive in the UK they are transported rapidly to the final destination. To this end, the UK office deals directly with local shipping companies to arrange and monitor the transfer of the goods.

Bucks SHg is a 100% subsidiary of Windsor Ltd, a UK resident company. During the year, Windsor Ltd received interest income of £60,000 net of 7.5% withholding tax and a dividend of £150,000 net of 5% withholding tax from Bucks SHg.

Requirements

(a)   Discuss whether Bucks SHg will be held to be resident in the UK under the double tax treaty between the UK and Utopia. The treaty is based on the OECD guidelines. Does Bucks SHg have a permanent establishment in accordance with the treaty?

(b)   Explain the rules for withholding tax on dividends and interest, as set down in the treaty.

Now, go back to the Learning objectives in the Introduction. If you are satisfied you have achieved these objectives, please tick them off.

ICAEW

Legislation

All references are to Corporation Tax Act 2009 (*CTA 2009*) unless otherwise stated

UK resident company chargeable on worldwide profits	s.5
Central management and control	Statement of practice 1/90
Companies treated as non-UK resident under double taxation agreements	s.18
Exemption for profits or losses of foreign PEs	ss.18A-S
Chargeable profits of non-UK resident company with a PE in UK	s.19
Non-UK resident companies income subject to IT if no PE or not trading	s.3
Definition of a PE	s.1141 CTA 2010
Deemed disposal of assets on company ceasing to be resident in UK	s.185 TCGA 1992
Deferral of charge on deemed disposal under s.185	s.187 TCGA 1992
Deemed disposal of IFAs on company ceasing to be resident in UK	ss.859-862 CTA 2009
Exit charge payment plans	s.59FA & Sch.3ZB TMA 1970
Penalties for non-compliance with migration procedures	ss.109B-F TMA 1970
Procedures to be followed by migrating companies	Statement of practice 2/90
Incorporation relief for incorporation of an overseas PE	s.140 TCGA 1992
Incorporation relief for IFAs for incorporation of an overseas PE	ss.827-830 CTA 2009
Transfer of UK trade	s.140A TCGA 1992
Transfer of IFAs with a UK trade	ss.819-820 CTA 2009
Treaty relief	ss.2 & 18 TIOPA 2010
Unilateral relief	ss.8 & 18 TIOPA 2010
Amount of DTR	s.42 TIOPA 2010

HMRC manual references

International Manual (Found at www.hmrc.gov.uk/manuals/intmanual/index.htm)

INTM120000 – Company Residence

INTM120120 – Company residence: when to question residence

INTM120180 – Company residence: how to review residence

INTM150000 – Principles of Double Taxation Relief and Introduction to Double Taxation Agreements

INTM260000 – Non-UK residents trading in the UK

Company Taxation Manual (Found at www.hmrc.gov.uk/manuals/ctmanual/Index.htm)

CTM80300 – Groups: group relief: the international aspect: overview

HMRC Digest of double taxation treaties (August 2010 publication found at www.hmrc.gov.uk/cnr/dtdigest.pdf)

> This technical reference section is designed to assist you when you are working in the office. It should help you to know where to look for further information on the topics covered in this chapter.

Answer to Interactive question

Chargeable gains of Grape Ltd	£

	£
In 2011: Gains on disposal of assets	375,000
Less losses on disposal of assets	(75,000)
Net gains on transfer of trade	300,000
Less net gains deferred (90% × £300,000)	(270,000)
Immediately chargeable gain	30,000
Balance of net gains deferred	270,000

In 2013, Grape Ltd disposed of 55% of its holding in Raisin Inc. 55% of the remaining balance of net gains deferred became chargeable. in addition to the gain on the disposal of the shares.

	£
Sale proceeds of 55% of the shares received in Raisin Inc	825,000
55% × £600,000	(330,000)
Chargeable gain (before indexation)	495,000
Deferred gain now chargeable (55% × £270,000)	148,500
Total amount taxable	643,500
Balance of net gains deferred £270,000 – £148,500	121,500

In January 2016, Raisin Inc disposed of assets on which gains were deferred at incorporation within six years of that incorporation. The proportion of the remaining balance of net gains deferred which relates to that asset became chargeable on Grape Ltd.

In January 2016: Proportion of balance of deferred gains

$$\frac{150,000}{375,000\,*} \times £121,500$$

	£
Chargeable gain	48,600
Deferred gains c/fwd (£121,500 – £48,600)	72,900

* Note that the denominator is the gross gains arising on the transfer of trade before deducting losses.

1　A company is UK resident if either it is incorporated in the UK or it is centrally managed and controlled from the UK.

2　(a)　**Implications of making Beach Ltd resident in Pacifica**

This involves the migration of a UK resident company (see Section 3).

A company is resident in the UK if it is incorporated in the UK or managed and controlled from the UK. Once Beach Ltd is managed and controlled from Pacifica it will cease to be UK resident.

As a UK resident company, Beach Ltd is subject to corporation tax on its world-wide income. Once it is resident in Pacifica it will no longer have a UK tax liability as it does not have any UK sources of income.

Although the change in the location of management and control has no effect on the activities of Beach Ltd or the ownership of its assets, the company is deemed to have sold its assets at market value on the date of migration. However, any capital gains arising can be deferred via an election made by Tahuna plc and Beach Ltd.

The deferred gains will be charged on Tahuna plc if:

- Tahuna plc sells shares in Beach Ltd such that it is no longer a 75% subsidiary; or
- Tahuna plc becomes non-UK resident; or
- The assets giving rise to the gains are sold by Beach Ltd within six years.

A corporation tax computation will need to be prepared as migration brings about the end of an accounting period.

Beach Ltd must notify HMRC that it intends to transfer its residence to Pacifica and make arrangements for any outstanding corporation tax to be paid.

(b)　**Transfer of trade and assets of Beach Ltd to new subsidiary resident in Pacifica**

This involves the transfer of a trade from a UK resident company to a non-UK resident company (see Section 4.5).

The commercial effect is the same as transferring the residency of Beach Ltd although it may be more complicated to achieve, as the legal ownership of assets together with the benefits of existing contracts will have to be transferred to the new company.

The shares received by Tahuna plc will have a cost for the purposes of chargeable capital gains equal to the value of the assets transferred.

A corporation tax computation will need to be prepared as Beach Ltd, having sold its trade and assets, will have ceased trading and an accounting period will end.

Capital gains and balancing adjustments must be computed in respect of the assets sold. Because the consideration will all be in the form of shares, it is possible to claim relief under the s.140 TCGA branch incorporation provisions in relation to chargeable gains and IFA profits arising. If such a claim is made, the related profits and gains will only become chargeable if the assets are sold by the company within six years of the transfer, or if the shares in the company are sold.

3　A non-UK resident company will become liable to UK corporation tax if it trades in the UK through a PE. It will be liable on all income and gains of the PE.

4   (1)   Assuming that Frame owns at least 25% of the ordinary share capital of Duchy and that a claim is made under s.140 TCGA 1992 and the provisions relating to IFAs, the amount immediately chargeable = nil, since the consideration comprises entirely shares.

    (2)   (a)   Disposal of freehold premises within six years after incorporation

$$\frac{£112,500}{£165,000} \times 142,500 = £97,159$$

           (Postponed gain c/f = £45,341)

           AP in which chargeable y/e 31.12.16, chargeable to Frame

        (b)   Disposal of leasehold premises – irrelevant, since a loss arose on incorporation.

    (3)   Balance of gain $\times \dfrac{A}{B}$

        where   A = MV of securities disposed of

               B = total MV of securities held immediately before disposal.

        ie £45,341 × 550,000/1,000,000 = <u>£24,938</u>

        (Postponed gain c/f = £20,403)

        Chargeable gain on sale of preference shares:

        In addition to some of the deferred gain becoming chargeable, the disposal of the securities will realise a chargeable gain unless the substantial shareholding exemption applies.

	£
Proceeds	550,000
Less cost	(350,000)
Less indexation	
$\dfrac{275.0 - 235.2}{235.2} \times 350,000$	(54,290)
Chargeable gain	145,710

5   Where the UK has negotiated a double tax treaty, double taxation relief is given either via the exemption method or via treaty relief. The exemption method simply means that the terms of the treaty dictate that certain types of income (principally business profits) will only be liable to corporation tax in either one country or the other.

    For interest, royalties and gains which are not subject to the exemption method, relief will instead be given via treaty relief. Treaty relief means that a credit is given against UK corporation tax to relieve the foreign tax paid. The maximum amount of relief is restricted to the UK corporation tax due on the foreign income.

    Unilateral relief is given for income not covered by a double tax treaty, or where treaty relief is disclaimed, or for income from a country with which the UK has not negotiated a double tax treaty. Unilateral relief and treaty relief work in exactly the same way.

6 Corporation tax computation – year ended 31 March 2016

	(a) Credit relief £	(b) Expense relief £
Property income	20,000	15,000
s.37(3)(a) CTA 2010	(20,000)	(15,000)
Taxable total profits	–	–
Corporation tax @ Nil %	–	–
DTR	–	–
Corporation tax liability	–	–
Trading loss in the year	(50,000)	(50,000)
s.37(3)(a) CTA 2010 – current year loss relief	20,000	15,000
Loss available to carry forward or back	(30,000)	(35,000)

Note:

In part (a), where the company claims credit relief, there is unrelieved foreign tax (UFT) of £5,000 as no DTR is claimable. As the UFT arises on property income it cannot be relieved in earlier or later periods. The foreign tax should therefore be treated as an expense ie as in part (b).

In part (b) the gross income of £20,000 less expensed foreign tax of £5,000 gives taxable property income of £15,000. There are £5,000 of additional losses available for relief in earlier or later periods. The losses will reduce taxable profits and consequently save tax at the company's marginal rate in the future.

7 Corporation tax computation – year ended 31 March 2016

	Trading income UK £	Trading income PE £	Total £
Trading profits	550,500	150,000	700,500
Qualifying charitable donations	(50,500)		(50,500)
Taxable total profits	500,000	150,000	650,000
Corporation tax @ 20%			130,000
Double tax relief			
Lower of – UK tax (@ 20%) £30,000			
– Overseas tax £50,000			(30,000)
Corporation tax payable			100,000

The unrelieved foreign tax of £20,000 (£50,000 – £30,000) may either be carried forward indefinitely against future UK tax liabilities of that PE or carried back three years on a LIFO basis against UK tax liabilities of that PE.

Note:

The calculation of the UK taxation suffered on foreign income is much simpler for corporation tax purposes than it is for income tax purposes. The rules for income tax are set out in s.36 TIOPA 2010. The income tax rules require that each source of foreign income is stripped out one by one and a full income tax computation redone with one source less of foreign income each time in order to calculate how much income tax would be payable without that source of income. The difference between the previous income tax computation and the revised computation therefore being the amount of UK income tax payable on that source of foreign income. See Chapter 8 for more details.

8 (a) A company is resident in a country if, according to the laws of that country, it is liable to tax in that country by reason of incorporation or place of management. Therefore, this excludes situations where the liability merely arises from a source of income in that state. The first question is therefore whether Bucks SHg is resident in the UK as a matter of UK law. As it is not a UK incorporated company, this comes down to whether central management and control takes place in the UK. It will be a matter of fact whether this is at the meetings in Monaco, or at the pre-meetings in the UK.

If it is resident in both Utopia and the UK, the model treaty has a tie breaker clause for situations where a company may be resident in more than one country. The tie breaker clause states that a company will be held to be resident where its effective management and control is carried on. The test of effective management and control is a lower level test than the test of central management and control used in UK tax law which looks at where the highest level of control is exercised often focusing on board meetings. The test under the treaty looks more at the day to day operations of the company as to where the key management and commercial decisions take place. As the company would appear to be mainly based in Utopia with only a distribution office in the UK, it is likely that the effective management and control is in Utopia.

Article 5 of the model treaty defines a permanent establishment (PE) as a fixed place of business through which the business of the enterprise is wholly or mainly carried on. The article states that a PE includes a place of management, a branch, an office, a factory, a workshop and construction sites under certain circumstances. However, facilities purely for the storage, display or delivery of goods will not be a PE. Premises used merely to undertake preparatory or auxiliary activities will also not give rise to a PE. Here the UK activities are solely related to the delivery of the goods (where the business of the company as a whole is their manufacture), so there would seem to be a good case that they do not constitute a PE for the purposes of the treaty.

(b) The treaty sets limits for withholding tax on interest on dividends. The limit for dividends depends on the percentage shareholdings. As Windsor Ltd has a 100% shareholding, the maximum withholding permitted under the treaty is 5% which conforms with the amount withheld. Where a shareholding is less than 25%, the maximum is 15%. For interest the maximum withholding is 10% subject to the interest being at an arm's length rate, which is met as the rate is 7.5%.

CHAPTER 16

Corporate anti-avoidance

Introduction

Examination context

Topic List

    1 Value shifting

    2 Controlled foreign companies (CFCs)

    3 Transfer pricing

    4 Thin capitalisation

    5 Diverted profits tax (DPT)

    6 Worldwide debt cap

Summary and Self-test

Technical reference

Answer to Interactive question

Answers to Self-test

Learning objectives

Tick off

- Determine, explain and calculate the corporation tax liabilities for corporate entities ☐

- Evaluate the tax implications of the choice of business structures ☐

- Explain and evaluate the tax implications of group structures ☐

- Apply, explain and evaluate issues relating to transfer pricing ☐

- Explain and evaluate the tax implications of business transformations and change ☐

Specific syllabus references for this chapter are 1f, 1g, 1j, 1k and 1l.

Syllabus links

Corporate anti-avoidance legislation stems from the utilisation of taxation law for unintended purposes. The value shifting rules are intended to counter transactions which are designed to reduce or eliminate chargeable gains. CFC legislation aims to prevent shifting profits offshore to benefit from the way in which foreign subsidiaries are taxed (Chapter 15). Transfer pricing legislation also aims to prevent profit shifting, whilst thin capitalisation and the worldwide debt cap legislation aim to prevent abuse of interest as a deductible expense (Chapter 11). Diverted profits tax aims to tax the double non-taxation of profits by large multinational groups.

Examination context

In order to tackle tax avoidance schemes developed over many years by tax professionals, many different pieces of legislation have been implemented in an attempt to block tax avoidance via companies eg when UK and overseas companies sell goods to each other at prices above/below market rate in order to avoid UK tax. As a result, transfer pricing legislation was introduced to counteract any consequent reduction in UK tax. In additional the OECD has developed an action plan in conjunction with the G20 countries to tackle issues such transfer pricing and diverted profits.

In the examination candidates may be required to:

- Recognise when a transaction falls within the scope of the provisions relating to value shifting and depreciatory transactions and be able to explain the tax implications arising

- Recognise when a company is a CFC and in broad terms explain whether its profits attributable to UK activities and non-trading finance income will be liable to a CFC charge in the UK

- Recognise when the transfer pricing rules apply to a given scenario and evaluate and explain the tax implications arising

- Recognise when the thin capitalisation rules apply to a given scenario and evaluate and explain the tax implications arising

- Recognise when the diverted profits tax rules apply to a given scenario and evaluate and explain the tax implications arising

- Recognise when the worldwide debt cap rules apply to a given scenario and evaluate and explain the tax implications arising

1 Value shifting

Section overview

- Certain transactions can effectively reduce the consideration taken into account on a share disposal. This includes pre-sale dividends from shareholdings which do not qualify for the substantial shareholding exemption, where the shareholder may be seeking a reduction in their overall tax liability because in such cases a dividend is likely to be exempt whereas the chargeable gain would be taxable at the company's marginal rate of corporation tax.

- The value shifting legislation counteracts this where the transactions are tax-motivated, by requiring an adjustment must be made to the consideration from a share disposal under the value shifting rules.

- Capital losses may also be adjusted on a 'just and reasonable' basis if a depreciatory transaction has added to or created the loss.

1.1 Introduction

Legislation ensures that a company can pay out its dividends as exempt income to corporate shareholders thereby preventing double taxation of that income. If a company pays a pre-sale dividend out of distributable reserves which represent earned profits, it will reduce the value of the company and hence the gain on its disposal. However, the profits have already been subject to corporation tax and the timing of the distribution should not affect the overall aim to prevent double taxation.

However, where a company pays a dividend out of unearned profits, then it is attempting to avoid tax by reducing the value of the company by distributing increases in the value of capital assets as exempt dividends.

The aim of the legislation is to ensure that transfers of value, such as the payment of an inflated pre-sale dividend, are not used to convert chargeable gains into exempt income. It is not intended to affect the payment of a pre-sale dividend of earned income. It is also intended to counteract other transactions which would achieve a similar result, such as intra-group sales of assets for less than their market value or transactions designed to increase the base cost of the shares which are to be sold.

The consideration received is increased by a 'just and reasonable amount'; the provisions can therefore restrict a loss, or create or augment a gain.

1.2 When an adjustment is required

An adjustment must be made to the consideration from a share disposal which is subject to corporation tax if:

- Arrangements have been made which materially reduce the value of the shares or securities disposed of or any asset owned by a member of the same group as the company being disposed of; and

- The main purpose, or one of the main purposes, of the arrangements is to obtain a tax advantage (meaning the avoidance of a liability to corporation tax on chargeable gains); and

- The arrangements do not consist solely of the making of an exempt distribution.

1.3 When an adjustment is not required

Given that the payment of a pre-sale dividend will by definition reduce the amount of gain subject to corporation tax, unless there is simply an exempt distribution and no other associated transaction prior to the disposal of the shares a value shifting adjustment will be required. The only exception to this would be if a tax saving was not one of the main reasons for the arrangements.

It seems unlikely that there will ever be an arrangement whereby the only transaction is the payment of a dividend. The availability of distributable profits does not equate to an availability of cash. Therefore the payment of a dividend may require loan finance which would, from a strict interpretation of the legislation, require a value shifting adjustment.

However, HMRC guidance states that a normal pre-sale transaction that reduces the value of a target company is not an arrangement with a main purpose of obtaining a tax advantage, providing the disposal consideration for the shares is a true measure of the value passing from the vendor group.

In addition, where the share disposal is exempt as a result of the substantial shareholding exemption, there will be no adjustment. In that case reducing the value of the shares would not secure a tax advantage.

1.4 Depreciatory transactions

The depreciatory transaction rules only apply to companies which are members of a gains group. If the rules apply they will reduce the allowable loss on disposal of shares to an amount equal to the true commercial loss on a 'just and reasonable basis'. They will apply where there has been a disposal of shares and their value has been materially reduced by a depreciatory transaction. Thus there is no requirement for a scheme or arrangement to avoid tax.

Suppose company X buys company Y for £15m which is the value of Y's assets. If X extracts value from Y by a transaction which does not take place at market value it is able to manipulate the value of Y's underlying asset values (ie at the 'asset tier') which will then affect the value of X's holding in Y (ie at the 'share tier').

These rules do not apply on a disposal of shares or securities if there is a period of at least six years between the reduction in value of the asset and the crystallisation of the loss.

Depreciatory transactions can arise where there is a movement of assets around a group not at market value.

In addition transactions treated as depreciatory include:

- The cancellation of a loan or a debt;
- Payments to fellow group members for services or products not at market value; and
- Excessive payments for group relief.

This includes the payment of dividends where a company has at least a 10% interest in the company paying the dividend. Payment of dividends out of post-acquisition profits are not treated as depreciatory transactions.

Amounts being left outstanding on loan account should not give rise to a depreciatory transaction so long as the debtor has the resources to pay the debt at the time it is created.

Worked example: Depreciatory transactions

Company A bought company B for £24m. Since acquisition the value of B's assets has declined from £24m to £17.6m for genuine commercial reasons. B sells to A for £5m a property with a current market value of £9.8m. A then sells the shares in B at their market value £12.8m.

Requirement

Explain how much of the loss on the disposal of the shares is an allowable loss.

Solution

A has realised a commercial loss of £11.2m (£12.8m – £24m) on the disposal of the shares in B. Of the total loss of £11.2m, £6.4m (£24m – £17.6m) represents the decline in value of B's assets attributable to external commercial factors, and £4.8m (£9.8m – £5m) results from the depreciatory transaction whereby A extracted value from B.

Legislation does not allow such distortion by reducing capital losses to the extent that these result from depreciatory transactions. Thus A's allowable capital loss is restricted on a 'just and reasonable' basis to £6.4m.

The depreciatory transaction rules can only disallow a loss, not create a gain. The value shifting rules can, however, turn a loss into a gain. They would apply if arrangements have materially reduced the value of the shares, and one of the main purposes of those arrangements is to obtain a tax advantage. As with value shifting the loss will be adjusted on a just and reasonable basis. However, a loss cannot become a gain under this rule, it will merely be extinguished.

In the case of a loss, where both the value shifting rules and the depreciatory transaction rules apply, and the addition to the consideration for the disposal under the value shifting provisions still leaves a capital loss, a further adjustment restricting or eliminating the loss may in theory be made under the depreciatory transactions rules. However, as they do not require a tax avoidance purpose, the depreciatory transactions rules will also apply to non-tax motivated transactions which are not within the scope of the value shifting rules.

1.5 Other value shifting provisions

The provisions set out above only apply to disposals of shares by companies. However, there are two other value-shifting provisions which can apply to disposals by both companies and individuals:

- If a controlling shareholder uses his control so that value passes out of his shares in a company, into other shares or rights over the company, this is treated as giving rise to a taxable disposal with consideration equal to the amount which would have been paid between third parties.

  For example, suppose a controlling shareholder arranged for a change to the rights attached to his shares, such that his shares decreased in value and those of another family member increased as a result. The change in rights will be treated as a disposal at market value.

- Where the value of an asset has been materially reduced, and the person disposing of it (or someone connected with him) has received value in such a way that it has not been taxed as part of an arrangement which had tax avoidance as one of its main purposes, just and reasonable adjustments can be made to the disposal calculation to eliminate the tax benefit. (This provision does not apply to share disposals which are within the rules set out in Sections 1.2 and 1.3).

2 Controlled foreign companies (CFCs)

Section overview

- Anti-avoidance legislation exists to prevent UK companies from diverting income away from the UK to low-taxed companies in other countries.

- A CFC exists where a non-UK resident company is controlled by UK resident persons.

- Where a CFC exists, so much of its profits as pass through the 'gateway' test are apportioned to its UK resident corporate owners with a holding in the CFC of at least 25%, and taxed at the main rate of corporation tax.

- By election, only 25% of the interest income on loans to other non-UK group companies passes through the gateway, and there is no charge if the group as a whole has no net UK interest deductions.

- A number of exemptions exist whereby profits will not be apportioned. These include a list of excluded territories, and an exemption for companies which pay local tax of at least 75% of the UK corporation tax which would be payable if the company was UK resident.

2.1 Introduction

This section sets out the CFC rules and defines the extent to which the CFC rules are examinable. The next three sections give an overview of the rules; the rest of this section explains the rules in more detail.

As set out in Chapter 15, a UK resident shareholder is not generally taxable on the income of its foreign subsidiaries. It is not taxed on the income when it arises, and in most cases dividends will be exempt. This means that if assets or activities can be located in foreign companies which pay a rate of tax which is lower than the UK rate, a tax saving can be achieved.

The CFC rules are an anti-avoidance measure which can apportion the profits of affected companies amongst their shareholders. If the shareholders are UK resident companies, these profits are charged to UK corporation tax at the main rate. The rules aim to identify and apportion only those profits which have been diverted from the UK.

2.2 Consequence of being a CFC

The CFC rules focus on the artificial diversion of profits from the UK, using 'gateway' provisions to specify those profits which are potentially within the scope of the rules. Where a CFC's profits fall within the gateway provisions and are not otherwise excluded by any of the entry conditions, safe harbours or exemptions, they are apportioned to the UK, and any UK resident company with at least a 25% holding in the CFC will be required to self-assess a CFC charge at the main rate. Any foreign tax attributable to the apportioned profits can be credited against the CFC charge.

The regime also includes an exemption for certain intra-group loans. Where the 75% exemption applies, it equates to an effective UK tax rate on such profits of 5% from FY2015. Complete exemption is available in certain circumstances.

2.3 What is a CFC?

Definition

CFC: A company is within the scope of the CFC rules if it is:

- Resident outside the UK; and
- Controlled by persons resident in the UK.

A company is under UK control if:

- A UK person, or persons, controls the company (ie >50%, or de facto control), or

- Is at least 40% controlled by a UK resident and at least 40% but no more than 55% by a non-UK resident.

A number of different factors are considered in determining control, including whether the company would be a subsidiary of a UK resident company in accordance with FRS2.

Worked example: The control test

Alpha AG is resident in Germany and is owned as follows:

Orange Ltd ⎤	35%
Lemon Ltd ⎬ UK resident companies	15%
Lime Ltd ⎦	25%
Pomegranate Ltd (Resident in the Bahamas)	25%
	100%

Beta Ltd is resident in Ireland and is owned as follows:

Apple GmbH (resident in Switzerland, 80% owned by Orchard plc which is UK resident)	60%
Pear SpA (resident in Italy)	40%
	100%

Gamma Ltd is resident in Jersey and is owned as follows:

Tiny SA (also resident in Jersey)	56%
Big plc (UK resident)	42%
Mr Average (resident in Guernsey)	2%
	100%

Requirement

Explain which of the companies are CFCs.

Solution

Alpha AG is a CFC because it is 75% owned by UK residents.

Beta Ltd is a CFC because, although Orchard plc only has a 48% 'effective' interest, Orchard plc can control it as a matter of fact. This is because it controls Apple GmbH, which in turn controls Beta Ltd.

Gamma Ltd is not a CFC. This is because although there is a UK shareholder (Big plc) with a shareholding of at least 40%, and also a non-UK shareholder with a shareholding of at least 40% (Tiny SA), the non-UK shareholder has a holding of more than 55%.

Note that if Tiny SA's shareholding had been 55% or less, Gamma Ltd would be a CFC under the 40% test.

2.4 Does a CFC charge apply?

Once it is established that a foreign company is a CFC you then need to determine whether a CFC charge arises. There is a CFC charge if (and only if):

- No CFC exemptions apply;
- The CFC has 'chargeable profits'; and
- There is a UK company which (together with connected companies) holds an interest of at least 25%.

These conditions may be applied in any order, so that (for example) if one of the CFC exemptions applies to a CFC it is not necessary to consider whether it has any chargeable profits.

If a CFC charge arises, it is charged on each 'chargeable company' holding a relevant interest.

2.4.1 Exemptions

These are largely entity-level tests that entirely exempt the profits from apportionment.

If a company falls entirely within one of the exemptions it is not necessary to consider 'chargeable profits' (the gateway tests).

2.4.2 Chargeable profits

A CFC charge can only apply if the CFC has chargeable profits that pass through the gateway tests. These tests identify:

- Business profits that have been diverted from the UK through tax avoidance arrangements, and
- Certain finance profits.

Only the part of the foreign company's profits that 'passes through' the gateway are 'chargeable profits' potentially subject to apportionment.

Chargeable gains are always excluded from a company's chargeable profits.

In addition, property income does not pass through the 'gateway', so is not chargeable.

2.5 The exemptions

2.5.1 Introduction

The exemptions are largely entity-level tests. If any one of them is met it entirely exempts the profits of a foreign company from the CFC rules. The five exemptions are each considered below

2.5.2 Exempt period

This is intended to give companies coming within the UK CFC rules time to restructure so that they are not subject to a charge.

The exempt period exists only for the first 12 months after the company first comes under the control of UK residents, and then only if

- It was already carrying on a business before coming under the control of UK residents; or
- It was formed as an acquisition vehicle for an existing non-UK resident company,

and the UK company was not a chargeable company (a UK resident company with an interest of at least 25% in a CFC) in the 12 months before the exempt period commences.

An accounting period ending within the exempt period is exempt (with periods falling partly within the exempt period being partly exempt). To qualify for exemption, the company must be within the scope of the CFC rules in its first accounting period after the end of the exempt period, but with none of its profits in that subsequent accounting period subject to an apportionment.

HMRC has the discretion to extend an exempt period for longer than 12 months at the request of the company's UK shareholder. HMRC guidance indicates that this will only be granted where the company is prevented from restructuring within the usual 12 month time limit as a result of factors which are beyond its control.

2.5.3 Excluded territories

HMRC has issued regulations setting out a list of 'good' territories, where a company's profits are not generally subject to a low rate of tax. A company which is resident and fully taxable in a listed territory will not generally be subject to a CFC charge unless it has income which derives from intellectual property which originated from a UK connected party.

2.5.4 Low profits

A company is exempt from an apportionment where its profits are:

- No more than £50,000, or
- No more than £500,000, of which no more than £50,000 is non-trading profits.

Profits can be determined on either a tax or accounts basis, and the limits are scaled down for accounting periods of less than 12 months.

2.5.5 Low profit margin

A company is exempt from an apportionment if its accounting profits are no more than 10% of its relevant operating expenditure. This is the operating expenditure shown in its accounts, less amounts paid to related parties and the cost of goods sold (unless they are used by the CFC in its local territory).

2.5.6 Tax exemption

A company is exempt from an apportionment if its tax paid in its territory of residence is at least 75% of the UK corporation tax which would have been payable if it had been resident in the UK.

The local tax must be adjusted for items which are taxed locally but not in the UK, and expenditure which is allowed locally but is not allowed in the UK computation. The exemption is not available if the foreign tax is paid under designer rate provisions.

2.6 Chargeable profits

If none of the exemptions apply, the company must then calculate the amount of its chargeable profits potentially subject to apportionment.

A CFC's chargeable profits are the part of its profits that pass through the 'CFC charge gateway'. The gateway tests are intended to identify and tax only those profits which have been diverted from the UK.

Different gateway tests apply to different types of profits. Of relevance for your exam are:

- Profits attributable to UK activities (ie trading profits and non-trading IFA profits)
- Non-trading financing profits

In essence, the effect of the gateways should be to ensure that chargeable profits only comprise:

- Business profits (excluding chargeable gains) attributable to activities in the UK that arise in a CFC through arrangements lacking any substantial non-tax value and that would not have been entered into by independent companies, and

- Certain finance profits.

2.6.1 Gateway for profits attributable to UK activities

2.6.1.1 Introduction

The gateway for profits attributable to UK activities applies to all of a company's profits except its non-trading finance profits and its property business profits (which are always exempt). In practice, the profits likely to come under this heading are trading profits and profits on non-trading IFAs.

2.6.1.2 Does the CFC charge gateway apply?

Profits will pass through the gateway and become chargeable profits unless a company meets at least one of the following entry conditions:

- The company has not been a party to arrangements, one of the main purposes of which is to reduce or eliminate a charge to UK or overseas tax at any time in the accounting period.

- None of the company's assets or risks are managed or controlled from the UK to any significant extent at any time in the accounting period.

- If the company does have assets or risks that are managed or controlled from the UK, it has the commercial capability to ensure that the company's business could continue if the UK managed assets and risks were no longer being managed from the UK. This is intended as a test of how reliant the CFC is on UK management.

2.6.1.3 Trading profits exemption

Certain other trading profits are also excluded from being chargeable profits even though they pass through the CFC charge gateway. In essence this excludes companies which have only a limited UK connection.

2.6.1.4 Quantifying chargeable profits

Where the entry conditions are not met and the trading profits exemption does not apply, ie profits pass through the gateway, the company must determine to what extent profits have been diverted from the UK.

To do this, the company must analyse its activities (excluding any property business and any non-trading finance activities) and identify the assets and risks that significantly impact its profits, and identify any 'significant people functions' (SPFs) which relate to those assets and risks.

If any SPFs are carried out in the UK, by either a related party or by the CFC itself other than through a UK PE, the CFC's profits are recalculated as if it does not have the assets and risks relating to the UK SPFs. The difference between the CFCs total trading profits and the trading profits excluding the UK SPFs is the amount that passes through the CFC gateway.

Worked example: CFC gateway entry conditions

Gladbags plc had carried out manufacturing operations in Overland for a number of years through a branch. On 1 January 2014 it incorporated the branch into a company, Gladbags Manufac SA, which was incorporated in Overland. Companies which are incorporated in Overland are regarded as tax resident there, and are taxed at a headline rate of 11%.

The company's operations are manufacturing bags and other accessories for both group companies and third parties. All of the services are provided through its two factories in Overland, and all of its customers are based either there or in nearby Underland. It also sources its materials locally.

The UK group management has some involvement in the strategic direction of the company, and is critical in negotiating agreements with several other groups with which the Gladbags group works on a global basis (local subsidiaries of which provide nearly 50% of Gladbags Manufac SA's turnover).

However, this is largely limited to board level input and the related costs are only a small fraction of the company's overall management costs.

Requirement

Explain whether Gladbags Manufac SA meets the entry conditions which would result in none of its trading profits passing through the CFC gateway.

Solution

It is unlikely that Gladbags Manufac SA meets the entry conditions which would result in none of its trading profits passing through the CFC gateway. This is because the incorporation of the original Overland branch is likely to constitute an arrangement designed with the main purpose of reducing UK tax. Its assets and risks are managed from the UK to some extent. It will be a matter of fact whether the company could continue to run its business without the UK management input, but the nature of that involvement suggests that it could not.

2.6.2 Non-trading financing profits

2.6.2.1 Exclusions

A separate set of gateway tests apply to non-trading finance profits.

If none of a CFC's trading profits pass through the CFC gateway, its non-trading finance income from funds held for its trade are not treated as non-trading finance profits for these purposes, and are also excluded from the CFC charge. This exclusion is intended to cover cash retained to fund day-to-day working capital requirements.

There are also exclusions for amounts held:

- To pay dividends more than 12 months after the end of the accounting period;
- With a view to investing in shares or making a capital contribution; and
- For contingencies or in order to reduce a tax liability.

2.6.2.2 The 5% test

In a case where the company's non-trading finance profits are incidental, ie no more than 5% of its trading profit, none of its non-trading finance profits pass through the CFC gateway.

The same rule applies to companies with a property business where the non-trading finance income is no more than 5% of the property income.

For holding companies where a substantial part of their business is holding share or securities in 51% subsidiaries, no non-trading finance profits pass through the gateway if they represent no more than 5% of the company's exempt distribution income.

2.6.2.3 Quantifying chargeable profits

Where the CFC's non-trading finance profits are not incidental they will pass through the gateway and become chargeable profits if they are derived from:

- Assets and risks in relation to which any relevant significant people functions are carried out in the UK (in the same way as for profits attributable to UK activities)

- Capital investment from the UK

- Specified arrangements in lieu of dividends (typically loans) with the UK

- UK finance leases

It should be noted that HMRC believes that in a UK parented group, an analysis of the significant people functions will always result in a significant proportion of intra-group loans being allocated to the UK.

2.6.3 Qualifying loan relationships

2.6.3.1 Introduction

The qualifying loan relationships rules can significantly reduce, and in some cases eliminate, the CFC charge on intra-group financing income where certain conditions are met. They apply both to finance companies, and to other companies which happen to hold loan receivables in addition to having other operations.

In order for these rules to apply:

- The CFC must have non-trading finance profits which would otherwise pass through the gateway;

- The non-trading finance profits must include profits from qualifying loan relationships; and

- The CFC must have business premises in its territory of residence which are intended to be occupied and used with a reasonable degree of permanence, and from which the CFC's activities in the territory are wholly or mainly carried on.

The rules apply on a period by period basis by election. The election must be made in the corporation tax return of the UK company to which an apportionment is made (each company must elect separately if profits are apportioned to more than one UK company). The UK company must make the election within 12 months of the normal filing date for the return or, if later, 30 days after the conclusion of an enquiry or appeal is concluded, or 30 days after the issue of a notice of amendment.

2.6.3.2 Definition

A loan is a qualifying loan relationship if:

- The CFC is the creditor; and

- The ultimate debtor is a connected company which is controlled by the same UK resident person or persons who control the CFC; and

- The loan is not part of an arrangement which has a tax avoidance purpose; and

- The ultimate debtor is not:

    - A UK resident company (unless the debit is within an exempt PE), or a UK PE; or

    - A CFC if the debits on the loan reduce the amount which is chargeable under the CFC provisions.

2.6.3.3 75% exemption

Where an election is in place and the company has qualifying loan relationships, 75% of the profit on those loan relationships is exempt.

2.6.3.4 Qualifying resources exemption

Where a loan is funded out of qualifying resources it will be fully exempt.

Where it is funded only partially from qualifying resources only that part is fully exempt and the balance may be exempt under the matched interest rule (the 75% exemption does not apply to the part which is not fully exempt).

In essence, qualifying resources are a source of funds that place no demands on group resources outside the borrower's territory of residence ie are derived from the CFC's own assets in the territory to which the new loan is made or represent new group capital.

Specifically, qualifying resources are profits earned by the CFC from lending to members of the CFC group within the relevant territory that are used for the purposes of the business being carried on in that territory. Profits from lending to a particular territory can only constitute qualifying resources to the extent that they are used to reinvest in that same territory.

To qualify, the ultimate debtor must remain resident in the same territory at all times throughout the period.

The matched interest rules apply to the amount of income on qualifying loan relationships which is not exempt as a result of the qualifying resources or 75% exemption.

This residual profit from qualifying loan relationships is fully exempt where UK members of the group do not have any net finance expense under the worldwide debt cap rules – ie the tested income amount (TIA) before taking account of any finance profits subject to a CFC charge is greater than or equal to the tested expense amount (TEA).

The residual profit on qualifying loan relationships is partially exempt to the extent that the CFC charge would otherwise cause the TIA to exceed the TEA. The result of making this proportion exempt is to cause the TEA to be exactly equal to the TIA (see Interactive question 1 for an example).

While the worldwide debt cap rules only apply to 'large' groups, these rules apply to smaller groups too. A calculation of their net interest and expense amounts under those rules may therefore be required.

Worked example: Financing Income

The JKL plc group has a Luxembourg resident financing company called DEC Financing SA which pays tax at an effective rate of 6%. All of DEC Financing SA's capital was originally provided by JKL plc.

Its interest income for the year ended 31 December 2015 is as follows:

	£'000
Loan to JKL plc	2,100
Loan to Jumble Inc (Cayman Island resident group company)	4,170
Loan to AH GmbH (German resident group company)	960
Bank deposit	2,400
	9,630

The JKL group as a whole had net UK interest deductions of £1,500,000, and there are no other CFCs in the group with interest income. None of the investments has been funded out of DEC Financing SA's retained profits, which have all been paid out as dividends.

DEC Financing SA is a CFC and under the basic rules all of its profits are likely to pass through the CFC gateway for non-trading finance profits because the profits arise from relevant UK funds (original capital provided by JKL plc) and to the extent that they do not they are managed from the UK to a significant extent. Therefore, DEC Financing SA has elected for the qualifying loan relationships rules to apply.

Requirement

Calculate the amount of DEC Financing SA's chargeable profits, on the assumption that it elects for the group financing income rules to apply

Solution

	£'000	£'000
Loan to JKL plc (no reduction as ultimate debtor is a UK company)		2,100
Bank deposit (no reduction as not a group borrower)		2,400
Qualifying loan relationships:		
Loan to Jumble Inc £4,170,000 × 25%	1,043	
Loan to AH GmbH £960,000 × 25%	240	
	1,283	
Amount which passes through the gateway is the lower of £1,283,000 and		
the net UK interest deduction of £1,500,000		1,283
Chargeable profits		5,783

If the group financing income rules apply then at least some of the profits arising on qualifying loan relationships will be exempt. Only the loans which are made intra-group to non-UK resident debtors are qualifying loan relationships.

Neither of the loans can qualify for the qualifying resources exemption as all of DEC Financing SA's retained profits have been paid out as dividends. However, as qualifying loan relationships, 75% of the interest will be exempt.

Then the matched interest exemption potentially applies to amounts arising from qualifying loan relationships which are not exempted by the qualifying resources or 75% exemptions. In this case DEC Financing SA has £1.283 million remaining which could potentially be exempted by the matched interest exemption. However, the group's net expense amount under the debt cap rules of £1.5m is larger than the residual profit on the company's qualifying loan relationships (ie the TIA would still not exceed the TEA), so there is no reduction of the amount passing through the gateway under the matched interest rules.

2.6.3.6 Qualifying loan relationship (QLR) exemptions not available

The QLR exemptions are not available if the CFC's non-trading finance profits derive from an arrangement with the main purpose of artificially diverting into a CFC non-trading finance profits currently received by a UK resident company ie where a UK company effectively exports a loan receivable to a non UK company in order to benefit from the rules, anti-avoidance legislation takes effect to ensure that there is no loss to the exchequer.

Worked example: QLR exemptions not available

In January 2015 a UK parent company lent £200 million to a Utopian resident subsidiary. Interest of £8 million was due to be received annually by the UK parent and is subject to corporation tax at the main rate. On 1 July 2015 the UK parent set up a new CFC and transferred the loan to the CFC in exchange for shares in the CFC.

Requirement

Explain how the interest is taxable on the UK parent company.

Solution

The UK credits of the UK parent are reduced from 1 July 2015 as a result of the arrangement, and the main purpose was to achieve the reduction. Therefore the creditor relationship of the CFC cannot be a qualifying loan relationship.

The profits arising in the CFC in respect of its creditor relationship with the Utopian resident company fall within the gateway for non-trading finance profits, but cannot benefit from QLR exemptions. In effect the interest that would have been subject to UK corporation tax is subject to a CFC charge, and so there is no change in the amount of tax paid.

2.7 The CFC charge

2.7.1 Apportionment of profits

UK companies which own at least 25% of a CFC will be taxed on their share of the CFC's profits which represent its chargeable profits. The UK company is responsible for self-assessing the corporation tax due on the CFC's chargeable profits.

The chargeable profits of the CFC are taxed at the main rate of UK corporation tax.

2.7.2 Creditable tax

Where CFC profits are apportioned, the UK tax payable may be reduced by the amount of apportioned creditable tax. Creditable tax includes any DTR which would be available if the foreign company's chargeable profits were chargeable to UK corporation tax under normal rules, ie the lower of the UK corporation tax payable and actual foreign corporation tax paid.

Interactive question: Controlled foreign companies   [Difficulty level: Exam standard]

The Fizz plc group's main business is the production and sale of soft drinks. The following companies are its wholly owned subsidiaries:

Bubble Ltd is a group financing company which is resident in Jersey. Its income for the year ended 31 December 2015 is as follows:

	£'000
Dividends received from Jersey-resident property investment company (100% owned)	2,500
Interest on loan to Pop AG (Group company, resident in Germany)	10,800
Interest on loan to Bottle Inc (Consortium-owned trading company, in which Fizz plc has a 40% shareholding)	6,400
Interest on US treasury bonds	4,200
	23,900

Bubble Ltd has no retained profits, as it pays regular dividends to Fizz plc. Both Pop AG and Bottle Inc used the loans to invest in their trades.

Slurp SA is resident in Switzerland. It is the group's main trading company, and is expected to make a profit for the year ending 31 December 2015 of £22 million. Four years ago a number of trademarks were transferred to Slurp SA from Fizz plc, as part of a plan to reduce the group's overall tax liability. While the majority of the staff needed to carry on its operations also relocated to Switzerland, the legal team and two senior designers (responsible for the 'look' of the brands) remain employed by Fizz plc in the UK. Fizz plc charges Slurp SA for the brand designers' services. Slurp SA pays an effective rate of tax of 10% on its profits.

Cheers plc is resident in Ireland. It manufactures and sells the Bubblepop brand in the UK and Ireland, and also licenses the brand to other group companies worldwide. It owned and developed the brand itself, and was an independent company quoted on the Irish stock exchange until ten years ago. In addition to its trading income, it has made a number of loans to Fizz plc. The interest on those loans in the year ended 31 December 2015 amounts to £3.5m. Cheers plc pays tax in Ireland at a rate of 12.5%.

The Fizz plc group as a whole has net UK interest deductions of £2 million for the year ended 31 December 2015. There are no other CFCs in the group with qualifying loan relationships.

Requirement

Explain (with calculations where you have the information to do so) how the chargeable profits which will be apportioned to Fizz plc under the controlled foreign companies rules will be determined for each of these companies.

See **Answer** at the end of this chapter.

---

3 Transfer pricing

Section overview

- Where large companies enter into transactions other than at arm's length such that one company gains a tax advantage, transfer pricing rules may apply.

- The company which gains a tax advantage (defined as lower profits or higher losses) is required to adjust its corporation tax self-assessment by substituting an arm's length price for the original price.

- Transfer pricing rules apply to wholly UK transactions and to transactions between UK and non-UK companies.

- It is normal for the other party to the transaction to then make an equal and opposite adjustment, if it is a UK company.

- In some cases it may be possible to enter into an Advance Pricing Agreement (APA) with HMRC to agree the transfer pricing method to be used before returns are filed.

Transactions can take place between connected parties at a price other than the arm's length price due to their special relationship. This could facilitate the transfer of profits from one party to another to take advantage of, for example, losses brought forward or a lower effective rate of tax. Prices may also be set for performance management reasons or perhaps to simplify intra-group costing procedures.

Regardless of the reason for the price chosen, the transfer pricing legislation applies where such a transaction results in a tax advantage to one of the parties. The legislation requires the income, expenditure, profits and losses of the advantaged party to be adjusted where prices are not at arm's length.

Definitions

Arm's length price: The price which might have been expected if the parties had been independent persons dealing with each other in a normal commercial manner unaffected by any special relationship.

Tax advantage: A tax advantage arises simply where either profits used to calculate UK tax are reduced or losses are increased as a result of the transfer price set.

Connected companies: Two companies are connected if either:

- One company directly or indirectly participates in the management, control or capital of the other company; or

- A third party directly or indirectly participates in the management, control or capital of both companies.

Transfer pricing rules apply equally to transactions between two UK companies or between a UK and a non-UK company.

3.1 Transfer pricing rules

The rules cover the supply of goods and services as well as the provision of loan finance. Remember that the transfer pricing rules are equally relevant to groups of companies based wholly in the UK.

The rules apply to all large companies.

Definitions

Large company: A company is large if it has:

- At least 250 employees; or

- Revenue of at least €50 million (approximately £40 million) and total assets of at least €43 million (approximately £34 million).

Where the company is a member of a group, it is large if the group as a whole breaches the above limits.

The rules can also apply to smaller companies but only in certain limited circumstances.

The transfer pricing rules require profits for tax purposes to be computed as if the transactions had been carried out at arm's length. The rules only apply to the company gaining the tax advantage, however normally UK parties to the transaction would make equal and opposite adjustments for tax purposes.

Worked example: Transfer pricing

JJ Ltd has two wholly owned subsidiaries, H Ltd and O Inc. They are manufacturing companies operating in the automotive industry.

O Inc is an overseas company and pays a low rate of corporation tax of 12% in its overseas tax jurisdiction.

During the year ended 31 March 2016 JJ Ltd's revenue is as follows:

Sales to:	£'000	Gross profit margin %
H Ltd	14,650	25
O Inc	22,400	10
Other UK customers	3,950	25
	41,000	

The board of directors of JJ Ltd agreed to sell goods to O Inc at a lower gross profit margin than normal to take advantage of the low rate of tax paid by O Inc.

Requirement

Explain the transfer pricing consequences of the sales to O Inc and calculate the necessary transfer pricing adjustment.

Solution

The group is large for the purpose of the transfer pricing rules as JJ Ltd's revenue exceeds £40m and the requirement is that the revenue for the group as a whole must exceed this limit. Therefore a transfer pricing adjustment must be made by JJ Ltd to adjust for the tax advantage it has gained by selling goods to O Inc at a lower profit margin than in an arm's length sale.

The sales revenue of JJ Ltd to O Inc is understated by $[(£22,400k \times 0.9)/0.75] - £22,400k = £4,480,000$.

JJ Ltd's sales revenue and hence taxable profit should be increased by this amount. This will result in additional tax of £896,000 payable by JJ Ltd.

Under corporation tax self-assessment JJ Ltd must self-assess the additional tax liability as a result of this transfer pricing adjustment.

3.2 Advance pricing agreements (APAs)

In order to remove the uncertainty that comes with the risk of transfer pricing adjustments, a taxpayer can enter into an Advance Pricing Agreement (APA) with HMRC which sets out how particular transactions will be treated before a return is submitted.

An APA is usually only granted where the issues involved are complex, or there is a high risk of double taxation (ie that the taxpayer will be taxed on the same profits in two jurisdictions). HMRC recommends that taxpayers contact it informally in the first instance, and make an 'expression of interest' before a formal application is submitted to establish whether HMRC is likely to be willing to enter into an APA and what analysis the business needs to do to support the application.

An APA can be 'unilateral', meaning that it is simply an agreement between HMRC and the taxpayer. However, HMRC generally recommends that where possible they should be 'bilateral' agreements, including the tax authority of the jurisdiction in which the other party to the transactions is resident. Bilateral agreements are entered into under the terms of double tax agreements.

There are a number of rules relating to applying for and administering APAs:

- A formal application must be in writing by the taxpayer and include a declaration that it is made for the purposes of the APA legislation.

- They are typically for a term of three to five years.

- HMRC can revoke an APA where the business does not comply with the terms and conditions of the agreement, or where the assumptions which have been identified as critical when the APA was entered into cease to be valid.

- A penalty of up to £10,000 can apply where false or misleading information is provided fraudulently or negligently in connection with an application for an APA.

4 Thin capitalisation

Section overview

- There are a number of anti-avoidance provisions which may restrict the amount of loan interest which is deductible for tax purposes, such as the transfer pricing provisions and the worldwide debt cap provisions.

- Thin capitalisation is where a company is financed by a greater proportion of debt to equity than would be normal if the loan had been provided via an arm's length transaction.

- Transfer pricing rules apply to the provision of loan finance between large companies both to the rate of interest and (in cases where a company is thinly capitalised) the amount of the loan.

- Where a company is thinly capitalised, the amount of the loan which is deemed to be excessive is discounted and no interest relating to that amount of the loan will be allowable for tax.

- Where interest is set at an excessive rate only the interest payable at an arm's length rate is allowable.

4.1 Introduction

When establishing a subsidiary the parent has two basic methods of funding the investment:

(1) Equity
(2) Debt

A detailed analysis of debt versus equity is provided in Chapter 11.

To understand the key issues in financing from a taxation point of view, it should be remembered that dividends are not deductible in the payer's tax computation, whereas interest payments are normally deductible and hence attract tax relief.

Anti-avoidance provisions exist, such as the transfer pricing rules and the worldwide debt cap provisions which may disallow, for tax purposes, part of the interest cost of a UK company.

4.2 Transfer pricing

The transfer pricing rules and rules relating to APAs, covered in the previous section, also apply to the provision of loan finance between large connected companies. The rules apply to both the amount of the loan and the rate of interest charged.

4.3 Thin capitalisation

Thin capitalisation is the term used to describe the situation where a company has been provided with loan finance by a connected company and the amount of the loan exceeds that which an independent third party would have been willing to provide.

HMRC will consider a number of different factors in determining whether a company is thinly capitalised. These include consideration of both the company's ability to service the loan (looking at interest cover on an EBIT or EBITDA basis), and debt cover ratios (including both simple debt to equity measures, and the maximum loan to asset value ratios which a third party lender would accept on particular types of asset). Which factors are most important in a particular case will depend on the nature of the business and the loan, much as banks will look at different factors in determining whether they will lend.

The transfer pricing rules disallow the interest on the part of the loan that an independent third party would not have been willing to provide.

In determining what would have happened at arm's length, the borrowing capacity of the individual company and its subsidiaries is considered without reference to the position of other companies in the group, ie without the benefit of any potential guarantees another member of the group could make.

These rules also apply to a UK branch of an overseas company as if it were a stand-alone company.

Worked example: Thin capitalisation

Chelsea Ltd is a UK resident subsidiary of Little Rock Inc, a company resident in the US. It is in the process of expanding its operations and intends to acquire machinery at a cost of £2,700,000.

It will finance the acquisition via a loan of £1,800,000 at 8.5%, from a UK branch of Barclays Bank, with the balance being provided by Little Rock Inc. It is currently financed wholly by equity.

Barclays' lending criteria restricts its loan to a maximum such that the interest cover (profit before tax divided by interest paid), based on Chelsea Ltd's forecast results for the year ended 30 June 2016, is 2:1.

Little Rock Inc will provide as much as possible of the additional £900,000 in the form of debt.

The forecast results of Chelsea Ltd for the year ended 30 June 2016 are:

	£'000
Revenue	2,220
Profit before taxation	390
Taxation on profits	117

Requirement

State, with reasons, the amount of additional finance that Little Rock Inc should provide in the form of debt.

Solution

Chelsea Ltd will not be allowed a tax deduction for the interest on the loan from Little Rock Inc if it is regarded as thinly capitalised.

In considering this issue, HMRC will review the company's gearing and interest cover in order to determine how much it could borrow from a third party on an arm's length basis. It is reasonable to use the lending criteria of Barclays Bank to determine an acceptable level of third party borrowings.

The maximum that Barclays would be willing to loan, such that its lending criteria are satisfied, is £2,294,000 (½ × £390,000/8.5%).

Accordingly, the loan from Little Rock Inc must not exceed £494,000 (£2,294,000 – £1,800,000) if the interest is to be allowable. Interest on the balance of the finance will not be tax deductible, so it is likely to be preferable to provide it as equity.

4.4 Excessive interest

Where the rate of interest charge is not at arm's length such that a tax advantage is obtained in the UK, a market rate of interest must be substituted when preparing the company's corporation tax computation.

4.5 Guaranteed loans

Where a third party such as a bank lends to a member of a group, the third party will often require the group parent to guarantee the loan. In some cases, the third party may also (or instead) require guarantees from the group's main trading companies. This is to ensure that if the borrower has difficulty repaying the loan, the third party will have access to the assets of the group as a whole rather than just the individual company.

The thin capitalisation rules apply to third party loans which are supported with a guarantee from a group member in the same way as they apply to intra-group loans. The result can therefore be that interest on a 'real' bank loan is disallowed.

In addition, the rules require that a company's borrowing capacity should be determined on a stand-alone basis, without taking guarantees into account. This specifically includes consideration of:

- The level or extent of the debt;
- Whether, without the guarantee, the loan would have been made; and
- The interest rate and other terms of the loan.

Where interest on a loan to a UK company is disallowed, and another UK group company has provided a guarantee, it may be possible for the guarantor (rather than the borrower) to claim a corresponding adjustment to its profits. This is only possible if the guarantor would have been able to borrow the amount in question, and is never possible where the guarantor is a subsidiary of the borrower.

Where a guarantee is in place, consideration also has to be given to whether the fees (if any) paid for the guarantee itself are on arm's length terms. This is relevant both to borrower companies, and to group parents or other substantial companies within groups who provide guarantees to other group members.

5 Diverted profits tax (DPT)

Section overview

- Anti-avoidance legislation exists to prevent companies (mainly large multinationals) from diverting profits away from the UK without paying tax in either the UK or overseas.

- DPT applies when either
  - Arrangements exist to avoid having a UK PE, or
  - Transactions lack economic substance.

- DPT is 25% of 'taxable diverted profits'.

- Companies must notify HMRC if they expect to be within the scope of DPT. The tax is not self-assessed.

This section is new.

5.1 Introduction

Finance Act 2015 introduced the diverted profits tax (DPT), from 1 April 2015, which for the first time may subject overseas companies to UK tax simply for doing business with the UK ie even without the presence of a PE. It tackles artificial/contrived arrangements, with the Government forecasting revenue from DPT of £300m per annum. The DPT, otherwise known as the 'Google tax', was developed in response to the actions of a number of high profile multinational entities who have avoided UK tax, and is imposed ahead of similar issues targeted by the OECD BEPS action plan (Chapter 1).

5.2 When does DPT apply?

5.2.1 Introduction

DPT will apply if either of the following situations applies:

- Arrangements avoiding a UK permanent establishment (PE).

  A person ('the avoided PE') is carrying on activity in the UK in connection with supplies of goods and services by a non-UK resident company to customers in the UK, and the detailed conditions are met ('the first rule'); or

- Transactions with a 'lack of economic substance'.

  Where a company which is taxable in the UK creates a tax advantage using certain arrangements which lack economic substance, and the detailed conditions are met ('the second rule').

In both situations DPT does not apply if both parties are SMEs.

5.2.2 The first rule: non-UK resident companies

The first rule applies where all of the following conditions are met:

- There is a non-UK resident company carrying on a trade;

- A person ('the avoided PE') is carrying on an activity in the UK in connection with supplies of services, goods or other property by the non-UK resident company;

- It is 'reasonable to assume' that the activity of the avoided PE is designed to ensure the non-UK resident company does not carry on a trade in the UK for corporation tax purposes; and

- The 'mismatch condition' or the 'tax avoidance condition' is met.

There is an exception to the rule if total sales revenues from all supplies of goods and services to UK customers do not exceed £10m, or total expenses relating to the UK activity do not exceed £1m.

The 'mismatch condition'

The 'mismatch condition' is met if arrangements are in place between the two parties by way of a transaction/series of transactions and the two parties are connected (defined as for transfer pricing). There must be an 'effective tax mismatch outcome' as a result of the arrangements, and the arrangement must have 'insufficient economic substance'.

The 'tax avoidance condition'

This condition is met if arrangements in place relate to the supply of goods, services or property, with the main purpose/one of the main purposes being the avoidance of/reduction to a charge to corporation tax.

5.2.3 The second rule: UK resident companies or UK PEs

The second rule applies where all of the following conditions are met:

- There is a UK resident company or a UK PE of a non-UK resident company carrying on a trade;

- The company has an arrangement by way of a transaction or series of transactions with another person;

- The two parties are connected (defined as for transfer pricing);

- The arrangement causes an 'effective tax mismatch outcome' between the two parties which is not a loan relationship; and

- The 'insufficient economic substance condition' is met.

The other party to the arrangements will usually be a non-UK resident person although it equally applies if they are UK resident.

5.2.4 'Effective tax mismatch outcomes'

Arrangements have an 'effective tax mismatch outcome' where for an accounting period they result in an increase in expenses/deductions or a reduction in income for one party and the reduction in that party's liability is greater than any resulting increase in the other party's total liability to tax (UK corporation tax, income tax or any other non-UK tax).

The 'effective tax mismatch condition' does not apply in either of the following situations, if:

- The tax paid by one party is at least 80% of the reduction in the other party's liability; or

- Certain payments are made which would give a mismatch due to them not being taxed (eg payments by an employer into a pension scheme or payments to a charity).

The 'effective tax mismatch outcome' does not apply to a loan relationship outcome (ie DPT specifically excludes financing arrangements).

5.2.5 'Insufficient economic substance condition'

The condition is satisfied if it is reasonable to assume that either:

- The arrangements were designed to obtain a tax reduction arising from the tax mismatch outcome, unless it was reasonable to assume that the overall non-tax financial benefits would exceed the overall financial benefit of the tax reduction. Any non-financial benefits are ignored; or

- The involvement of a person who is party to the transaction was designed to secure a tax reduction.

The second of these conditions is not satisfied if either it was reasonable to assume that the non-tax financial benefits arising as a result of the contribution of the person's staff would exceed the financial benefit of the tax reduction, or the income arising from the contribution of the person's staff in an accounting period exceeds other income attributable to the transaction.

5.3 Consequences of DPT

DPT is calculated as 25% of 'taxable diverted profits'.

No deduction or other relief is available for diverted profits tax, nor is it a distribution.

The valuation of 'taxable diverted profits' depends on which of the rules apply.

5.3.1 Arrangement avoiding a UK PE (the first rule)

'Taxable diverted profits' are based on the 'notional PE profits'.

Definition

Notional PE profits: Notional PE profits of an accounting period are the profits that would have been the chargeable profits of the non-UK resident company attributable to the 'avoided PE' had it been a UK PE through which the company carried on a trade.

The non-UK resident company must consider the 'relevant alternative provision' ie the arrangement that it is just and reasonable to assume would have been made or imposed had tax (UK and overseas) not been a consideration. In practice this will lead to a lot of uncertainty and is likely to be heavily disputed between taxpayers and HMRC.

Where the 'mismatch condition' is met, the 'taxable diverted profits' are notional PE profits plus any UK taxable income of a connected company (if any) that would have resulted from the 'relevant alternative provision'.

Where only the 'tax avoidance condition' is met the 'taxable diverted profits' are notional PE profits.

5.3.2 Transactions with a 'lack of economic substance' (the second rule)

If on applying the 'relevant alternative provision' expenses of the same type and for the same purpose arise and there would have been no resulting UK taxable income then 'taxable diverted profits' are nil if either:

- The arrangements are at arms-length; or
- A transfer pricing adjustment is made before the end of the DPT review period.

Otherwise 'taxable diverted profits' are the profits of the transfer pricing adjustment plus UK taxable income (if any).

Double tax relief is available on a just and reasonable basis.

5.4 Administration

Unlike most taxes DPT is not self-assessed. A company must notify HMRC within three months of the end of the relevant accounting period if it is potentially within the scope of DPT (six months for accounting periods ending on or before 31 March 2016).

Where HMRC determines that a DPT liability arises the company is issued with a preliminary notice, including an estimate of the 'taxable diverted profits'. Following receipt the company has 30 days to make representations. Following receipt of representations HMRC then issues a charging notice or confirms that there will be no charging notice.

DPT must then be paid within 30 days. The taxpayer is free to make an appeal as normal, but this does not delay the due date for payment of the tax.

All charging notices must be reviewed by HMRC within one year (the review period), at which point representations are looked at again and the original best estimate may be revised.

Worked example: Diverted profits tax

During the year ended 31 March 2016, Apricot Inc, a large company resident in Utopia (a tax haven), bought goods from an unconnected company to sell to UK customers via, Mango Ltd, a UK company within the same group. For tax purposes, Apricot Inc ensures that Mango Ltd never concludes these contracts with the UK customers, although some support services are offered to customers. Apricot Inc generates income of approximately £15m in sales to UK customers.

Requirement

Explain whether DPT applies to this arrangement.

Solution

It appears that arrangements are in place to avoid having a UK PE. Mango Ltd is taking on the role of the 'avoided PE' by carrying on an activity in the UK in connection with supplies of goods by Apricot Inc, a non-UK resident company.

It is 'reasonable to assume' that the activity of Mango Ltd is designed to ensure the non-UK resident company does not carry on a trade in the UK for corporation tax purposes ie Apricot Inc ensures that Mango Ltd never concludes a contract on its behalf, and so the tax avoidance condition (and possibly the mismatch condition) is fulfilled.

As Apricot Inc is not an SME and the income generated exceeds £10m, DPT will apply to the taxable diverted profits.

6 Worldwide debt cap

Section overview

- Under the worldwide debt cap provisions, the amount of interest deductible in the UK cannot exceed the total amount of interest expense incurred by the worldwide group as a whole.

- The rules only apply to groups where at least one member of the worldwide group is large at any time in the accounting period.

- The rules also only apply where there is at least one relevant company in the group. A company is a 'relevant group company' if it is resident in the UK or carrying on a trade in the UK through a UK PE.

- A 'gateway' test disapplies the debt cap where average UK net debt is less than 75% of the average worldwide gross debt.

- The total disallowed amount in any period is the difference between:
  - The 'tested expense amount', and
  - The 'available amount'.

- When a group suffers a debt cap disallowance, and a UK group member has net finance income, some or all of the net finance income will be exempt from tax.

- When considering the deductibility of interest by a company within a large group, if applicable the transfer pricing rules are applied before the worldwide debt cap rules.

6.1 Overview

UK group companies may suffer a restriction in the amount of finance cost they can deduct in calculating their UK taxable profits under the worldwide debt cap provisions.

The basic premise of the debt cap is that the maximum amount of interest deductible in the UK should not exceed the total amount of interest expense incurred by the worldwide group as a whole.

The rules apply to large groups with at least one relevant group company.

6.2 The definition of large

The rules only apply where at least one member of the worldwide group is 'large' at any time in the accounting period. Thus companies which move between being medium sized and large may move the whole group into and out of the scope of the rules from one accounting period to the next. 'Large' is defined as a company which is not within the definition of a small or medium sized enterprise (SME) under EU rules.

A SME is defined as an enterprise with:

(a) Less than 250 employees, and
(b) Either:

– An annual turnover of not more than €50 million; or
– An annual balance sheet total of not more than €43 million.

Therefore a company is large if it has at least 250 employees irrespective of its annual turnover or balance sheet total.

6.3 Relevant group company

The rules also only apply where there is at least one relevant company in the group. A company is a 'relevant group company' if it is resident in the UK or carrying on a trade in the UK through a UK permanent establishment and is the member of the worldwide group and is either the ultimate parent of the worldwide group or one of its effective 75% subsidiaries.

A 'relevant group company' includes a UK resident company that does not have share capital (eg a company limited by guarantee). In addition the 75% subsidiary rule allows ownership to be traced through intermediary entities without ordinary share capital (eg trusts).

A stand-alone company cannot, by definition, be within the scope of the rules as it is not a member of a group. To be a UK member of a group the company must be a 75% subsidiary of the ultimate parent. Thus a joint venture company will not be affected.

Worked example: Relevant company

For the year ended 31 December 2015, U Inc, which is resident in the USA, has interests in various group companies: J Ltd, K Ltd, L Ltd, M Ltd and N Ltd.

All subsidiaries are 100% owned by U Inc except for M Ltd which is 75% owned, and N Ltd which is 51% owned. J Ltd and M Ltd are UK resident trading companies. K Ltd is resident in Germany but carries on all its trading activities through a UK permanent establishment. L Ltd is dormant.

Requirement

State which companies are relevant companies for the year ended 31 December 2015.

Solution

All the companies except for N Ltd are at least 75% owned by U Inc and are therefore potentially UK relevant group companies. As N Ltd is only 51% owned by Z Inc, it cannot be a UK relevant group company.

Although K Ltd is non-resident, as it trades exclusively via its UK permanent establishment, it is a UK relevant group company.

As L Ltd is dormant it is not a trading company and is therefore not a UK relevant group company.

Therefore, for the purposes of the world wide debt cap, the companies affected by the rules are: U Inc, J Ltd, K Ltd and M Ltd.

6.4 Gateway test

A 'gateway' test disapplies the debt cap where average UK net debt is less than 75% of the average worldwide gross debt.

UK net debt is the sum of the average net debt amounts (relevant liabilities less relevant assets) for each relevant UK company with net debt. The test excludes:

- Companies with net financial assets
- Companies with a net debt of less than £3m
- Dormant companies

Worldwide gross debt is calculated based on the average of the group's relevant liabilities at the beginning and end of the period as reported in the worldwide group's financial statements.

Where UK-headquartered groups have significant UK intra-group loans, they will almost certainly fail the gateway test. This will therefore require them to carry out a comprehensive review of the debt cap provisions even if they have no overseas operations at all.

6.5 Disallowance of deductions

The total disallowed amount in any period is the difference between:

- The 'tested expense amount' (TEA), and
- The 'available amount' (AA).

The TEA is the sum of the net financing deductions (ie financing expense less financing income) of each relevant UK group company.

If there is no excess (the financing income amount exceeds the financing expense amount) then a nil value is given for that relevant UK group company.

If the net figure for a UK relevant company is small, defined as less than £500,000 or negative, the amount for that relevant company included in the TEA is nil.

The AA is the worldwide group's gross consolidated finance expense, ie both UK and non-UK.

The disallowance is deducted from the financing expense amounts of relevant group companies as the group sees fit.

6.6 Exempting income

When a group suffers a debt cap disallowance, and a UK group member has net finance income, some or all of the net finance income will be exempt from tax.

Where a group has one or more companies with net financing income (ie financing income amounts exceed financing expense amounts), the total of the net financing incomes of UK group companies is the 'tested income amount' (TIA). However, if the net figure for a UK relevant company is small, defined as less than £500,000 or negative, the amount for that relevant company included in the TIA is nil. Therefore if each company's net financing income is less than £500,000 then the total TIA will be nil.

The lower of the TIA and the total disallowed amount is exempt from corporation tax. The exempt amount is deducted from the financing income amounts of relevant group companies as the group sees fit.

In addition, financing income received from other group companies resident in the EEA (other than the UK) is exempt income for the UK recipient where those companies are denied a deduction for the income paid to the UK.

Thus, overall, a net disallowance should only arise on a group-wide basis where the net UK interest expense exceeds the gross interest expense in the consolidated financial statements.

Worked example: Disallowance of deductions and exempting income

Continuing from the previous worked example, for the year ended 31 December 2015, U Inc has the following interest expense and interest income for its group of companies:

	Finance expense £m	Finance income £m
U Inc consolidated	(1.70)	11.00
J Ltd	(2.20)	1.86
K Ltd	(3.10)	0.25
M Ltd	(1.10)	2.30
N Ltd	(2.10)	1.30

Requirement

Calculate the total disallowed amount for the year ended 31 December 2015, and the amount of any exempt financing income.

Solution

Start by calculating the TEA:

Company		Net financing deduction £m
J Ltd	Less than £500k	Nil
K Ltd	Expense less income	2.85
M Ltd	Net income therefore treated as nil	Nil
Total TEA		2.85

(N Ltd is excluded because it is not a relevant group company)

Compare with AA:

The worldwide interest expense is £1.7 million, TEA exceeds AA therefore disallowance is:

£2.85 million – £1.7 million = £ 1.15 million.

Disallowance:

The disallowance can be allocated as the group chooses, although any single company can only have a disallowance up to the extent of its net finance expense.

Exempting income:

Insofar as there are disallowances, financing income up to the lower of the disallowance and the TIA is exempted from tax. Of the relevant group companies, only M Ltd has net financing income (£1.2 million) and therefore the TIA is £1.2m. As the disallowance is less than the TIA, the exemption will be restricted to the disallowed amount. Therefore £1.15 million of M Ltd's net financing income will be exempted from tax.

6.7 Election to disapply the £500,000 de minimis limit

A group can elect to disapply the £500,000 de minimis limit. This is the limit which applies both in determining the TEA and the TIA.

The election is beneficial where there is a debt cap disallowance and the total of the amounts of interest income in UK companies which would be ignored as a result of the £500,000 limit is more than the deductions which are ignored as a result. An example of where this will usually be the case is where an entirely UK based group suffers a disallowance because of the application of the de minimis limits.

The election must be made within 12 months of the end of the period of account to which it is first intended to apply, and remains in place until withdrawn. A notice to withdraw the election also has to be given within 12 months of the end of the period of account to which it is intended to apply.

Worked example: Disallowance of income and disapplying the de minimis limit

Continuing from the previous worked example, for the year ended 31 December 2016, U Inc has the following interest expense and interest income for its group of companies. Note that 100% of the shares in BB Ltd, a UK resident company, were purchased on 1 January 2016.

	Finance expense £m	Finance income £m	Net income £m	Net expense £m
U Inc consolidated	(2.20)	11.20	9.00	
BB Ltd	(0.80)	1.20	0.40	
J Ltd	(2.30)	1.95		(0.35)
K Ltd	(3.20)	0.45		(2.75)
M Ltd	(1.80)	2.10	0.30	
N Ltd	(2.40)	1.55		(0.85)

Requirement

Calculate the total disallowed amount for the year ended 31 December 2015 and the amount of any exempt financing income, assuming that (i) the group has not made an election to disapply the de minimis limit; and (ii) the election has been made.

Solution

Without an election

Start by calculating the TEA

Company		Net financing deduction £m
BB Ltd	Net income therefore treated as nil	Nil
J Ltd	Less than £500k	Nil
K Ltd	Expense less income	2.75
M Ltd	Net income therefore treated as nil	Nil
Total TEA		2.75

(N Ltd is again excluded because it is not a relevant group company)

Compare with AA:

The worldwide interest expense is £2.2 million, TEA exceeds AA therefore disallowance is:

£2.75 million – £2.2 million = £ 0.55 million.

Disallowance:

The disallowance can be allocated as the group chooses, although any single company can only have a disallowance up to the extent of its net finance expense.

Exempting income:

Insofar as there are disallowances, financing income up to the lower of the disallowance and the TIA is exempted from tax. Of the relevant group companies, the application of the de minimis limit means that there is no net financing income and therefore the TIA is £nil. As the disallowance is greater than the TIA, the exemption will be restricted to the TIA ie £nil. Therefore, despite there being a disallowance of £0.55m, none of the net financing income will be exempted from tax.

With an election

Start by calculating the TEA

Company		Net financing deduction £m
BB Ltd	Net income therefore treated as nil	Nil
J Ltd	Expense less income	0.35
K Ltd	Expense less income	2.75
M Ltd	Net income therefore treated as nil	Nil
Total TEA		3.10

Compare with AA:

The worldwide interest expense is £2.2 million, TEA exceeds AA therefore disallowance is:

£3.10 million – £2.2 million = £ 0.9 million.

Disallowance:

The disallowance can be allocated as the group chooses, although any single company can only have a disallowance up to the extent of its net finance expense.

Exempting income:

Insofar as there are disallowances, financing income up to the lower of the disallowance and the TIA is exempted from tax. Of the relevant group companies, BB Ltd and M Ltd have net financing income (£0.4m + £0.3m) and therefore the TIA is £0.7m. As the disallowance is more than the TIA, the exemption will be restricted to the TIA. Therefore the full £0.7 million of UK group net financing income will be exempted from tax.

Overall

Without an election the group suffers a disallowance of £0.55m of interest expense but the full £0.7m of interest income remains taxable in the UK. Overall the UK group companies have a net interest expense of £2.7m (0.35m + 2.75m + 0.85m – 0.55m – 0.4m – 0.3m).

However, with an election although the disallowed interest expense increases to £0.9m, all of the UK interest income is exempted. Overall the UK group companies have a net interest expense of £3.05m (0.35m + 2.75m + 0.85m – 0.9m). The election is therefore beneficial.

6.8 Business combinations or demergers

The worldwide debt cap also applies where a group is party to a business combination or demerger, as a result of which the identity of the ultimate group parent company changes.

In such cases, the rules are applied as if there were two separate periods of account. The first deemed period of account ends immediately prior to the merger or demerger. The rules are then applied separately to each deemed period of account.

Worked example: Business combinations

Racquet plc acquires 100% of the Shuttlecock plc group with effect from 1 July 2016. The Racquet plc group draws up accounts for the year ended 31 December 2016

Explain how the worldwide debt cap rules apply to the Racquet plc group in the year ended 31 December 2016.

Solution

The acquisition is a business combination for the purposes of the worldwide debt cap rules. They therefore apply as if the Racquet plc group has one period of account for the six months to 30 June 2016, and a second period of account for the six months from 1 July to 31 December 2016.

The gateway test therefore applies to each six month period of account separately. If the gateway test is failed, the tested expense amount, available amount and exempt income are also calculated separately for each period of account. Note that the £500,000 de minimis applied in calculating the tested expense and income amounts is not reduced for the short periods of account.

6.9 Interaction of transfer pricing and worldwide debt cap

When considering the deductibility of interest by a company within a large group, if applicable the transfer pricing rules are applied before the worldwide debt cap rules.

If for example the interest receivable on a loan by one group company to another group company is adjusted because of the transfer pricing rules, it is the adjusted amount which is used as the interest income or interest expense for the purposes of the worldwide debt cap.

Similarly where the loan amount itself is excessive, HMRC's view is that only the arm's length amount is included when calculating the UK net debt.

Worked example: Interaction with transfer pricing rules

A Ltd has borrowed £100m from a group company resident in South America. The interest on the loan is charged at a rate of 15%. An arm's length interest rate would be 6.5% and an external organisation would only have been prepared to lend A Ltd £80m. A Ltd has benefitted from a tax advantage as a result of the loan being with a group company.

Requirement

What loan value will be used to determine the UK net debt for the purpose of the gateway test?

Calculate the interest expense for A Ltd which will be used to determine its financing expense for the purposes of the worldwide debt cap.

Solution

HMRC's view is that the UK net debt will be based on the £80m arm's length value.

The excessive interest will be disregarded. Only the arm's length interest on the arm's length loan value will be used to determine the financing expense, ie 6.5% × £80m = £5.2m.

6.10 Targeted anti-avoidance rules

There are also detailed targeted anti-avoidance rules which aim to prevent schemes which seek to circumvent the debt cap rules. These are not examinable.

Summary and Self-test

Summary

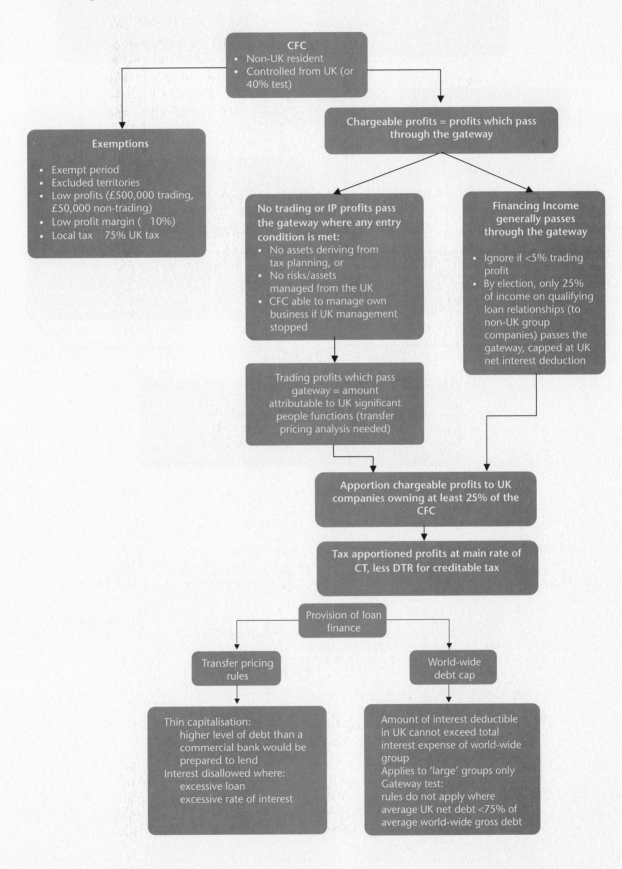

CFC
- Non-UK resident
- Controlled from UK (or 40% test)

Chargeable profits = profits which pass through the gateway

Exemptions
- Exempt period
- Excluded territories
- Low profits (£500,000 trading, £50,000 non-trading)
- Low profit margin (10%)
- Local tax 75% UK tax

No trading or IP profits pass the gateway where any entry condition is met:
- No assets deriving from tax planning, or
- No risks/assets managed from the UK
- CFC able to manage own business if UK management stopped

Financing Income generally passes through the gateway
- Ignore if <5% trading profit
- By election, only 25% of income on qualifying loan relationships (to non-UK group companies) passes the gateway, capped at UK net interest deduction

Trading profits which pass gateway = amount attributable to UK significant people functions (transfer pricing analysis needed)

Apportion chargeable profits to UK companies owning at least 25% of the CFC

Tax apportioned profits at main rate of CT, less DTR for creditable tax

Provision of loan finance

Transfer pricing rules

World-wide debt cap

Thin capitalisation:
  higher level of debt than a commercial bank would be prepared to lend
Interest disallowed where:
  excessive loan
  excessive rate of interest

Amount of interest deductible in UK cannot exceed total interest expense of world-wide group
Applies to 'large' groups only
Gateway test:
  rules do not apply where average UK net debt <75% of average world-wide gross debt

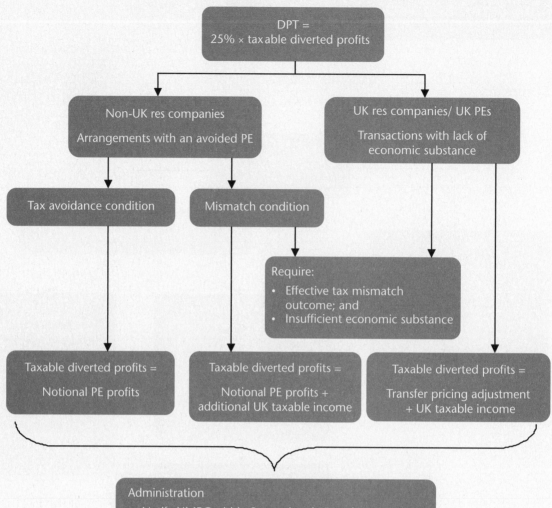

DPT =
25% × taxable diverted profits

Non-UK res companies

Arrangements with an avoided PE

UK res companies/ UK PEs

Transactions with lack of economic substance

Tax avoidance condition

Mismatch condition

Require:
• Effective tax mismatch outcome; and
• Insufficient economic substance

Taxable diverted profits =

Notional PE profits

Taxable diverted profits =

Notional PE profits + additional UK taxable income

Taxable diverted profits =

Transfer pricing adjustment + UK taxable income

Administration

• Notify HMRC within 3 months of AP end
• Pay tax within 30days of HMRC charging notice
• Appeal within 30 days
• HMRC review all charging notices within 12 months

Self-test

Answer the following questions.

1   Mele SA is a company resident in Switzerland. Shareholdings in Mele SA are as follows:

	Local CT/IT rate	%
Apple Ltd, UK resident company	20%	25
Banana Ltd, UK resident company	20%	25
Emily, a UK resident individual	40%	25
Fragola SpA, an Italian resident company	33%	25

In the year ended 31 March 2016 Mele SA had total profits of £2,000,000. Of these £1,000,000 related to interest on loans to Apple Ltd and Banana Ltd, with the balance being other financing income. It paid corporation tax in Switzerland of £280,000.

Requirement

Calculate the total UK corporation tax payable on the profits of Mele SA, if any.

2   Damson Ltd and Elderflower Ltd are both owned by Plum plc. Plum plc alone has 500 employees. During the year ended 31 December 2015 Damson Ltd sold Elderflower Ltd 100,000 manufacturing components worth £5 each at its standard internal transfer price of £4 each. Elderflower completed the parts at a cost of £1.50 each and then sold the parts to an unconnected third party for £8 each. All parts had been sold at the end of the year. Damson Ltd pays corporation tax at the main rate. In the FY 2014 part of the accounting period Elderflower Ltd pays corporation tax at a marginal rate of 21.25% although its average rate of tax in that financial year is 20.7%.

Requirement

Explain whether a tax advantage has been gained from the transfer and if so what action should be taken when preparing the corporation tax returns of both Damson Ltd and Elderflower Ltd.

3   Explain what is meant by the term 'thin capitalisation' and how its use can reduce the amount of UK corporation tax payable.

4   Traveria plc, resident in Ireland, intends to set up a wholly owned UK based subsidiary, Green Ltd, financed via debt with just £1,000 of £1 nominal value shares. Some of the finance will be provided by a major UK bank guaranteed by Traveria plc and the remainder will be via a loan from Traveria plc.

The UK bank has agreed to lend Green Ltd £1,000,000 at a commercial rate of 6.7%. Under the bank's normal rules it would only be prepared to lend £1,350,000 in total based on Green Ltd's own assets and ability to pay the interest.

The remaining £800,000 of finance required will be provided by Traveria plc at a rate of interest of 12%.

Traveria plc has no other UK subsidiaries.

Requirement

Calculate the amount of interest which will be allowable as a trading deduction each year in Green Ltd.

Now, go back to the Learning objectives in the Introduction. If you are satisfied you have achieved these objectives, please tick them off.

Legislation

Value shifting

All references are to Taxation of Chargeable Gains Act 1992 *(TCGA 1992)* unless otherwise stated

Value shifting – disposal of shares or securities by a company	s.31
Depreciatory transactions within a group	ss.176-7

CFCs

All references are to Taxation (International & Other Provisions) Act 2010 *(TIOPA 2010)* unless otherwise stated

Definition of a CFC	s.371AA and 371RA-RG
CFC entity level exemptions	ss.371JF-NE
Excluded territories regulations	SI 2012/3024
Does Chapter 4 apply?	s.371CA
CFC charge gateway for profits attributable to UK activities	Chapter 4
Does Chapter 5 apply?	s.371CB
CFC charge gateway for non-trade financing profits	Chapter 5
Qualifying loan relationship exemptions	s.371IA

Transfer pricing

All references are to Taxation (International & Other Provisions) Act 2010 *(TIOPA 2010)* unless otherwise stated

Arm's length price	s.147
Advance pricing agreements	Statement of Practice 2/10
Excessive interest	s.152

Diverted profits tax

All references are to Finance Act 2015 unless otherwise stated

Charge to tax	s.79
Transactions lacking economic substance	ss.80-1
Non-UK company avoiding a UK taxable presence (avoided PE)	ss86-87
Calculation of taxable diverted profits	ss.82-85 & 88-91
Administration	ss.92-105

Worldwide debt cap

All references are to Taxation (International & Other Provisions) Act 2010 *(TIOPA 2010)* unless otherwise stated

Large company	s.344
Relevant group company	s.345
Gateway test	s.261
UK net debt	s.262
Worldwide gross debt	s.264
Disallowance of deductions	s.274

Tested expense amount	s.329
Available amount	s.332
Exempting income	s.293
Election to disapply the £500,000 de minimis limit	s.261
Gateway test	s.331ZA

HMRC manual references

International Manual (Found at www.hmrc.gov.uk/manuals/intmanual/index.htm)

INTM410500 – What is transfer pricing all about?

In due course, the current CFC guidance should also be updated for the new CFC rules:

www.hmrc.gov.uk/manuals/intmanual/INTM200000.htm

Corporate Finance Manual (Found at www.hmrc.gov.uk/manuals/cfmmanual/index.htm)

CFM90000 – Debt cap

This technical reference section is designed to assist you when you are working in the office. It should help you to know where to look for further information on the topics covered in this chapter.

Answer to Interactive question

Bubble Ltd

Assume it elects for the group financing income rules to apply where relevant.

	£'000
Dividends – not chargeable because they would be exempt if received by a UK company	-
Interest on US Treasury Bonds – no reduction because borrower is not a group company	4,200
Interest on loan to Bottle Inc – no reduction because borrower is not a group company	6,400
Qualifying loan relationships:	
Amount of interest on the loan to Pop AG included in chargeable profits is the lower of (25% × £10,800,000) = £2,700,000 and the net UK interest deduction of £2,000,000	2,000
Total chargeable profits	12,600

The only qualifying loan is the loan to Pop AG:

- It will automatically qualify for the 75% exemption – ie only 25% of the interest will be taxable.

- It will not meet the qualifying resources exemption as the loan is not provided from qualifying resources – ie profits of the CFC.

- Therefore the remaining 25% of the interest can only be exempted under the matched interest rules. In this case the TIA after taking into account the residual profit is £2.7m which exceeds the TEA of £2m. Therefore £0.7m of the residual interest is exempted such that the TIA and the TEA become equal.

Slurp SA

- Does not appear to qualify for any of the exemptions (Switzerland would not be included in a list of 'high tax' excluded territories).

- As it has assets deriving from a tax planning scheme and it appears that some of its assets are managed from the UK, it does not satisfy any of the 'entry conditions' and therefore some of its trading profits will pass through the gateway.

- It does not fall within any of the safe harbours.

- It will therefore need to carry out an analysis of the significant people functions which are relevant to its operations. To the extent that those functions are carried on in the UK (for example, under the arrangements with Fizz plc), the profits attributable to those functions are the chargeable profits which will be apportioned to Fizz plc.

Cheers plc

- Also does not appear to qualify for any of the exemptions.

- From the information given it seems likely that it will satisfy at least one of the 'entry conditions' such that its trading profits will not pass through the gateway. This assumes that it does not have assets derived from tax planning, or that it does not have assets which are managed from the UK, which should be confirmed. Assuming this is the case, none of its trading profits are chargeable profits.

- The interest on its loans to Fizz plc does, however, constitute chargeable profits. The rules relating to qualifying loan relationships can apply to loans which are held by trading companies, but they are not relevant here because the borrower is UK resident. The chargeable profits are therefore £3,500,000.

1 Mele SA appears to be a CFC as:

- It is not resident in the UK; and

- It is controlled by UK resident persons – UK residents own 75% of the shares which is greater than 50% required for control.

It does not appear to qualify for any of the exemptions. In particular, its profits are greater than the £500,000 de minimis, the fact that the cost of goods sold has to be excluded in applying the profit margin test means it is very unlikely to be satisfied here, and the effective rate of tax in Switzerland is 14% (£280,000/£2,000,000) which is less than 75% of the UK rate of 20%.

Therefore so much of profits as pass through the gateway will be apportioned to its UK resident corporate owners with a holding of at least 25%. As none of the interest arises on a 'qualifying loan' to another non-resident group company the full amount of its profits are chargeable. The apportioned profits will be taxed at the main rate of corporation tax less relief for the actual Swiss tax paid ie the creditable tax:

	UK CT on apportioned profits £	apportioned creditable tax £	Net UK CT payable £
Apple Ltd (£2,000,000 × 20% × 25%)	100,000	(70,000)	30,000
Banana Ltd (£2,000,000 × 20% × 25%)	100,000	(70,000)	30,000
Emily	0	0	0
Fragola SpA	0	0	0

2 Damson Ltd and Elderflower Ltd may be affected by transfer pricing rules if they are large companies which have gained a tax advantage from a transaction made other than at arm's length.

In determining whether they are large, the position of the group is considered as a whole. As Plum plc alone exceeds the employee threshold to be considered large, then all three companies in the group are large by definition as together the number of employees will exceed the limit of 250.

If Damson Ltd had sold the parts to Elderflower Ltd at the arm's length price of £5 per unit, its total profit would be £100,000 higher than it is currently stated. A tax advantage has therefore accrued to Damson Ltd (the tax rates of the companies involved are irrelevant).

Damson Ltd must therefore restate its profits to reflect its true profit position by increasing its profit by £100,000. Elderflower Ltd is then advised to make a corresponding opposite adjustment to reduce its profits by £100,000.

3 Thin capitalisation is the term used to describe the situation where a company has been provided with loan finance by a connected company and the amount of the loan exceeds that which an independent third party would have been willing to provide.

Companies utilise thin capitalisation in order to claim the tax deduction available in respect of interest payments. This makes debt finance preferable to equity finance in certain circumstances. This is particularly true where an overseas company is investing in a UK subsidiary.

The transfer pricing rules disallow the interest on the part of the loan that an independent third party would not have been willing to provide.

4   Thin capitalisation rules will prevent part of the interest on the loan by Traveria plc from being allowed. As under normal commercial rules it would appear that only a further £350,000 would be lent to Green Ltd only that amount of the interest would be allowable, ie £350,000 × 12% = £42,000 pa.

Furthermore, as the amount of interest seems to be excessive and is not the rate which would apply in an arm's length transaction, a commercial rate will need to be substituted. This would reduce the allowable interest to: £350,000 × 6.7% = £23,450.

We also need to consider whether the worldwide debt cap provisions apply.

The annual interest cost in Green Ltd (the UK company), applying the transfer pricing rules first is £90,450 ((£1,000,000 × 6.7%) + (£350,000 × 6.7%)). As this is less than £500,000 the net financing deductions of the UK are deemed to be £nil and therefore there is no restriction on the deductibility of interest in Green Ltd under the debt cap rules. It would not be beneficial to elect to disapply the £500,000 limit in this case, as the election would mean Green Ltd's interest could be disallowed where it otherwise could not.

CHAPTER 17

Companies – special situations

Introduction

Examination context

Topic List

Summary and Self-test

Technical reference

Answers to Interactive questions

Answers to Self-test

Learning objectives

- Explain and evaluate the tax implications of business transformations and change

- Explain and calculate the tax implications involved in the cessation of trade

- Evaluate and advise on tax strategies to meet business objectives

- Evaluate and advise on alternative tax strategies relating to corporate transformations

Specific syllabus references for this chapter are 1l, 1m, 2b and 2c.

Syllabus links

Some owner managers choose to liquidate their company in order to revert to an unincorporated status. Colloquially this is known as a 'disincorporation' and is considered further in Chapter 22. Other liquidations may also arise as a result of corporate transformations or reorganisations (Chapter 23).

Examination context

In practice companies often undergo significant changes, for example a management fall out may lead to one shareholder/director disposing of his shares, or a failing company may go into liquidation. Professional accountants must be able to advise the shareholders and the companies to ensure that this is done in the most tax efficient manner. Standard tax planning may mean that a shareholder is taxed on a capital gain at 10% rather than suffer income tax at more than three times that rate of tax.

In the examination candidates may be required to:

- Advise on the correct treatment of and calculate the tax liabilities arising as a result of a company purchase of own shares

- In relation to a liquidation or winding up of a company give relevant advice and calculate the tax liabilities arising

1 Company purchase of own shares

Section overview

- A company may choose to repurchase its own shares or a shareholder may wish to sell his own shares back to the company.

- Where the shareholder is a company it will always be treated as making a chargeable capital disposal giving rise to a chargeable capital gain or allowable capital loss unless the substantial shareholding exemption applies.

- Where the shareholder is an individual the disposal will automatically be treated as a capital distribution if all the necessary conditions are met.

- To be treated as a capital distribution there must be a repurchase of unquoted shares for the benefit of the trade or to settle an IHT liability. Where the disposal is for the benefit of the trade, the vendor must be a UK resident individual who will substantially reduce his shareholding after the sale and hold no more than 30% of the issued shares after the repurchase.

It is possible for a shareholder to sell shares back to the company, rather than to an external third party.

Subject to certain formalities of the Companies Act, companies may issue shares which may be repurchased by the company at a later date. When the shares are repurchased they are normally cancelled.

A company may make a payment out of capital on the purchase of its own shares. The calculation of a permissible capital payment is shown below, but this is still subject to the company having sufficient capital reserves.

Permissible capital payment

The permissible capital payment (PCP) is the amount by which a private company can reduce capital on a purchase of own shares. It is calculated as follows:

	£
Cost of redemption/purchase	X
Less: proceeds of fresh share issue	(X)
available distributable profits	(X)
PCP	X

A PCP can only be made if various stringent requirements of the directors are met. Members or creditors objecting to the payment may apply to the court for cancellation/review of the payment.

Where a company chooses to hold repurchased shares as 'treasury shares', they are still treated as having been cancelled as, from a tax point of view, treasury shares are treated as if they do not exist.

Definition

Treasury shares: A company which buys back and then holds its own shares will hold them as treasury shares. [Companies (Acquisition of own shares) (Treasury Shares) Regulations 2003]

The shares can later be sold, transferred to an employee share scheme or cancelled. At buy back, the shares will be treated as if they had been cancelled although ad valorem stamp duty will be payable by the company. The company's nominal share capital will be reduced. If sold the shares are treated as being a new issue to the purchaser (although income tax relief will not be available to an individual on the sale of treasury shares by a Venture Capital Trust).

1.1 Repurchase of shares from a corporate shareholder

Where a corporate shareholder sells shares back to the issuing company it will always be treated as a capital transaction. Unless the substantial shareholding exemption applies, a chargeable gain or allowable loss will arise.

1.2 Repurchase of shares from an individual shareholder

The payment to an individual for the repurchase of his shares by the company may be treated for taxation purposes either:

- As an income distribution (and thus subject to income tax in the hands of the individual shareholder); or

- As a capital distribution (thereby giving rise to a capital gain).

The treatment depends on the circumstances at the time of repurchase.

An individual shareholder cannot choose whether he will be taxed to income or capital. If conditions are satisfied, the capital route is mandatory. If any condition is not satisfied, the income route will apply. However, he may be able to plan to ensure he meets the conditions if he would prefer the capital rather than the income distribution route. Similarly he is likely to be able to plan to ensure he fails a condition if the income route is preferred.

Income distribution route	Capital distribution route
Applies unless conditions for capital distribution route met	Applies automatically if conditions are met
Excess over original subscription cost is treated as an income distribution: (Proceeds – Subscription price) × 100/90	Entire disposal treated as a capital transaction
Deemed 10% tax credit available (not repayable)	A chargeable gain or allowable loss using normal CGT disposal rules
An allowable capital loss may also arise as the shares are treated as being disposed of at original subscription cost, ie where base cost > original subscription cost there will be a loss	

Worked example: Purchase of own shares from the original subscriber

Bina has owned 45% of the £1 ordinary shares in Sonnalple Ltd, which is a property investment company, since she subscribed for them in January 1990. She wished to sell her shares but the other shareholders did not want outside shareholders to own shares in the company. The company agreed to a purchase of own shares. Bina has never worked for the company.

4,500 shares, representing Bina's entire holding, were repurchased by the company. Bina is a higher rate taxpayer. The relevant details relating to the shares are as follows:

1 January 1990	Subscription (ie at a £2 premium)	£3
1 January 2016	Sale to company	£23

Requirement

Compare the tax consequences of the purchase of own shares under the income and capital distribution routes.

Solution

Income distribution route

Dividend income = 100/90 × 4,500 × (£23 – £3) = £100,000

Tax charge (higher rate taxpayer) = 22.5% × £100,000 = £22,500

Allowable loss

	£
Proceeds (4,500 × £23)	103,500
Less net distribution (4,500 × (£23 – £3))	(90,000)
Deemed proceeds	13,500
Less cost (4,500 × £3)	(13,500)
Gain/loss	Nil

Ie there will be no chargeable gain/allowable loss under the income distribution route if the shareholder is the original subscriber.

Capital distribution route

Chargeable gain

	£
Proceeds (4,500 × £23)	103,500
Less cost (4,500 × £3)	(13,500)
Gain	90,000

Tax charge = 28% × (£90,000 – £11,100) = £22,092

Note. As Bina is a higher rate taxpayer, none of the basic rate band is available to tax the gain at 18%. Therefore, after deduction of the annual exempt amount, the balance of the gain is taxable at 28%.

Worked example: Purchase of own shares – shareholder not the original subscriber

The facts are the same as in the previous example except that Bina was not an original subscriber. She purchased her shares in January 1996.

1 January 1990	Subscription	£3
1 January 1996	Purchase by Bina	£5
1 January 2016	Sale to company	£23

Requirement

Compare the tax consequences of the purchase of own shares under the income and capital distribution routes.

Solution

Income distribution route

Dividend income = 100/90 × 4,500 × (£23 – £3) = £100,000

Tax charge (higher rate taxpayer) = 22.5% × £100,000 = £22,500

Allowable loss

	£
Proceeds (4,500 × £23)	103,500
Less net distribution (4,500 × (£23 – £3))	(90,000)
Deemed proceeds	13,500
Less cost (4,500 × £5)	(22,500)
Allowable loss	(9,000)

Note. This allowable loss only arises under the income distribution route where the shareholder originally paid more for the shares than their subscription price.

Capital distribution route

Chargeable gain

	£
Proceeds (4,500 × £23)	103,500
Less cost (4,500 × £5)	(22,500)
Gain	81,000

Tax charge = 28% × (£81,000 – £11,100) = £19,572

The advantage of the income distribution route is that there is no further tax to pay if the shareholder will remain a basic rate taxpayer after the distribution. The capital distribution route will benefit from the annual exempt amount and possibly entrepreneurs' relief (see Chapter 6), subject to the various conditions.

1.3 Capital distribution route

The capital distribution route is mandatory where:

- The repurchase is for the benefit of the trade; or

- The proceeds are used to settle an inheritance tax liability; or

- The shares are employee shareholder shares, and they are repurchased by the issuing company after the individual to whom they were issued has ceased to be an employee (see Chapter 3).

1.3.1 Repurchase for the benefit of the trade

Where the repurchase is for the benefit of the trade, all of the following conditions must be met for the capital route to apply:

- The company (purchaser) must

  - Be an unquoted trading or holding company of a trading group (AIM = unquoted);
  - Be purchasing the shares for the benefit of the trade; and
  - Not be using the purchase as part of a scheme to avoid tax.

- The shareholder (vendor) must

  - Be resident in the UK;

  - Have owned the shares for at least five years prior to sale (three years if inherited including ownership of personal representatives and deceased);

  - Not hold more than a 30% share (including associates) in the purchaser or any other company in the same 51% group immediately after the sale; and

  - Have substantially reduced his shareholding (including associates) by holding 75% or less of the pre sale holding.

Associate includes spouse/civil partner and minor children.

Benefit of the trade

The purchase will benefit the trade where:

- Disagreement over the management of the company has an adverse effect on the running of the trade. The condition will clearly be satisfied if the dissenting shareholder sells his entire shareholding to the company;

- A temporary investor wishes to realise his investment;

- A proprietor of a company is retiring to make way for new management; or

- A shareholder dies and his PR or beneficiary does not wish to retain the shares.

Substantial reduction in shareholding

In many cases the entire shareholding will be repurchased by the company. Thus the vendor will automatically fulfil both the shareholding criteria. The following should be noted:

- If the shareholder wishes to retain an interest in the company, his shareholding must be substantially reduced, and, after selling the shares, he must not be connected with the company.

- In calculating whether the shareholder has reduced his interest in the company to 75% or less of his percentage share before the purchase, remember that the company cancels the shares bought back and therefore the total share capital will be reduced.

Worked example: Substantial reduction in shareholding

Wilma owns 16,000 of the 32,000 issued shares in A Ltd. The company buys back 4,000 of Wilma's shares.

Requirement

Is the substantial reduction in shareholding test met?

Solution

		Wilma £	Others £	Total £
Before		16,000	16,000	32,000
Purchase by company		(4,000)	-	(4,000)
After		12,000	16,000	28,000
Percentage before:	16,000/32,000			50%
Percentage after:	12,000/28,000			43%
75% of percentage before				37½%

As the post sale holding is more than 75% of the pre-sale holding the test is not met and the income distribution treatment will apply instead.

1.3.2 Repurchase in order to settle IHT liability

Where the repurchase is primarily to raise cash to pay an IHT liability, and the following conditions are satisfied, the capital route must apply:

- The person receiving the payments must use all, or virtually all, of the proceeds to pay an IHT liability falling on him as a result of a death; and

- The IHT paid could not otherwise have been paid without causing undue hardship, ie the sale of the shares back to the issuing company is the last resort; and

- The payment of the tax must be within two years of the death.

2 Tax implications of administration or liquidation

Section overview

- A company which is in financial difficulty may proceed in one of four ways:

  1. Enter into a voluntary arrangement;
  2. Have an administrative receiver appointed;
  3. Enter administration; or
  4. Liquidate.

- The appointment of a corporate voluntary arrangement (CVA) supervisor or an administrative receiver has no taxation implications.

- The appointment of an administrator terminates the current accounting period. Future accounting periods will end on the normal accounting date.

- The commencement of winding up has significant taxation implications both for the taxation of the company and how any assets of the company can be distributed to the shareholders.

A company which is in financial difficulty or is insolvent may proceed in one of four ways: enter into a voluntary arrangement; have an administrative receiver appointed; enter administration; or liquidate. Detailed study of these procedures was included in the Knowledge Level Law syllabus and is not repeated here; a brief revision of the definition of each procedure is provided below.

Definitions

Company voluntary arrangement (CVA): A CVA allows a financially troubled company to reach a binding agreement with its creditors about payment of all, or part of, its debts over an agreed period of time. The directors remain in control of the company.

Administrative receivership: An administrative receiver is appointed by a secured debenture holder (provided the charge was set up pre 15 September 2003) who has the right to appoint an administrative receiver to realise the charged assets and pay off the debt. The administrative receiver does not have any rights over assets other than those on which the debt was secured.

Administration: A company will normally enter administration voluntarily. Once an administrator is appointed he will effectively take over control of the company as a whole and seek to rescue the company as a going concern. If that is not possible he will aim to achieve a better outcome for the creditors than a winding up.

Liquidation: A liquidation is the process of terminating a company's existence via its winding up. A company may choose to liquidate (where it is solvent as a members' voluntary winding up) or may be forced into a liquidation (as a creditors' voluntary winding up or court appointed liquidation). Once a liquidator is appointed he will take over control of the company as a whole.

From a tax perspective only the appointment of an administrator or liquidator is relevant. Neither the appointment of a supervisor to administer a CVA nor the appointment of an administrative receiver has any effect on the company's accounting periods or tax position. The corporation tax due on the company's profits remains the responsibility of the company.

The taxation consequences of appointing an administrator or a liquidator are considered in the rest of this section.

2.1 Tax implications of appointing an administrator

On the appointment of an administrator, the current accounting period ends and a new period begins. Future accounting periods end on the company's accounting date and when the company ceases to be in administration.

2.2 Tax implications of winding up a company

A company is liquidated when its affairs are wound up. The winding up process normally commences when the members pass a resolution to wind up a company or a court winding up order is granted. A liquidator will then be appointed to manage the process.

2.2.1 Tax implications

The date on which the winding up of a company commences has the following important taxation consequences:

- The liquidator becomes responsible for fulfilling the company's obligations under the Taxes Acts, and must pay all corporation tax liabilities arising after the commencement of winding up.

- Corporation tax is charged on the profits arising during the winding up of a company.

- Thereafter, accounting periods end ONLY on each anniversary of the commencement to wind up the company. The final accounting period will end when the winding up is complete ie all assets have been distributed. Ceasing to trade after a winding up has commenced will not bring an accounting period to an end.

- The liquidator becomes the beneficial owner of the company's assets. This is not treated as a disposal for chargeable gains purposes.

- The final distribution of cash/assets to the shareholders on a winding up of a company will have income tax, capital gains tax and corporation tax implications.

2.2.2 Ceasing to trade

A company will cease to trade at some point during the winding up process. It is therefore worth reviewing the implications of ceasing to trade:

- Balancing adjustments must be calculated in respect of plant and machinery on which capital allowances have been claimed, as the assets will either be sold or scrapped.

- Trading losses may be carried back three years under terminal loss relief (see Chapter 12).

- If when trading the company was a close company it will become a close investment company after the cessation of trade. As such participators will not receive income tax relief on loans to purchase shares in the company, and prior to FY2015 it paid corporation tax at the main rate from cessation onwards. Where the cessation occurs in the first accounting period of the liquidation, the company is a close investment company from the start of the next accounting period.

3 Tax planning when winding up a company

Section overview

- Not all company liquidations are the result of insolvency. Some liquidations are voluntary and involve companies with significant assets which need to be extracted.

- The planning involved in the winding up of a company which is insolvent is very different to the process where a company is still solvent.

- Consideration should be given to the timing of commencing a winding up and of ceasing to trade where possible in order to maximise the use of losses.

- Distributions made before the commencing of winding up are normally treated as a dividend whereas distributions made after the commencing of winding up are normally treated as a disposal for chargeable gains purposes.

- When a winding up commences the company loses the beneficial ownership of its assets. Shareholdings in subsidiary companies are therefore no longer treated as belonging to the company. Any loss relief group or consortium created via the shareholdings of the liquidating company will cease to exist.

- Disincorporation relief can be claimed where a business is transferred to shareholder(s), and the total value of goodwill and interests in land transferred is less than £100,000. If claimed, goodwill and land are transferred at the lower of cost and market value (lower of TWDV and market value for post-2002 goodwill).

Liquidating a company is the final stage of winding up the company during which the life span of the company is brought to an end and its assets, if any, are distributed. It must be remembered that not all liquidations are the result of a company's insolvency. A solvent company may be liquidated for a number of reasons.

3.1 Uses of losses on winding up

A company facing the possibility of voluntary or compulsory liquidation is often trading at a loss. Once the company ceases to trade, the following points should be noted:

- Trading losses cannot be carried forward.

- Current year trading losses can be offset against total profits including gains. It is therefore advantageous to realise gains prior to cessation, if possible, in order to offset the losses.

- Balancing adjustments may arise on the deemed disposal of assets as at the date of cessation.

- Redundancy costs will only increase the current year losses.

- Terminal loss relief is available upon cessation. Under terminal loss relief, the trading loss of the final 12 months of trade may be carried back up to 3 years against total profits.

- The winding up will mean that only losses accrued up to the date of commencement of the winding up can be group relieved.

Interactive question 1: Losses on cessation   [Difficulty level: Intermediate]

Crash Ltd, a UK company, has been trading for many years. The present market conditions have affected Crash Ltd severely and it is essential that substantial investment in new machinery be made. The shareholders/directors are unwilling to authorise this expenditure and propose instead to liquidate the company. Crash Ltd ceased trading on 31 October 2015.

Its recent tax adjusted trading results were as follows:

	£
Y/E 31 July 2012	114,000
Y/E 31 July 2013	112,000
Y/E 31 July 2014	28,000
Y/E 31 July 2015	(62,000)
P/E 31 October 2015	(47,000)

Requirement

Show the final taxable total profits for each of the accounting periods, assuming appropriate claims are made to relieve the losses. State any amounts unrelieved.

See **Answer** at the end of this chapter.

Interactive question 2: When to wind up a company   [Difficulty level: Intermediate]

John Brown owns and runs Browns Ltd, a car repair business. John wishes to sell the company but has been unable to find a buyer. He is now considering commencing winding up the company during the next few weeks.

Although the company has been profitable, John has lost interest, with the result that heavy trading losses are now being sustained. The main asset of the company is the workshop, which a developer is interested in buying as this is situated next to a new shopping centre.

Requirement

What advice would you give John regarding the commencement of winding up and what additional information would you need in order to advise him fully?

See **Answer** at the end of this chapter.

3.2 Distribution of assets in a winding up

Where a liquidation is not a result of insolvency, then tax planning for the distribution of assets is very important.

Distributions are treated as follows:

- Distributions made after the winding up has started are capital and are treated as a part disposal of the shares by the shareholder. This is true even if the distribution is cash from accumulated net profits out of which a dividend could have been paid.

- Individuals will be taxed at a maximum of 28% after any possible reliefs and the annual exempt amount. A company will be subject to corporation tax but with the possibility of a substantial shareholding exemption applying (minimum holding 10% held for at least 12 months in the past 2 years).

- Distributions made prior to the winding up commencing are an income distribution and will be taxed as a dividend. Distributions of no more than £25,000 made in contemplation of a striking off can be treated as capital if certain criteria are met.

- Consideration should therefore be given as to whether it would be more beneficial to make a distribution prior to or subsequent to the commencement of winding up.

In the case of a voluntary liquidation, where the shareholders/directors can plan the timing of distributions, it may be preferable to declare a dividend prior to entering liquidation via a pre-liquidation dividend strip. Whether this is advantageous depends on the personal circumstances of the shareholders.

In a voluntary liquidation it is possible to mix and match pre and post liquidation distributions to minimise the tax liabilities of the shareholders. However, HMRC will not allow pre-liquidation distributions that would artificially create a capital loss (depreciatory transactions). The distributions must be paid out of commercially generated distributable profits.

Entrepreneurs' relief may be available on a post-liquidation capital distribution. It applies to the disposal by an individual of shares held in his personal company (broadly ≥5% shareholding) where the individual is an employee/director of the company and has owned the shares for one year prior to the disposal. The relief (up to an overall lifetime limit of gains of £10 million) means that the gains will be taxed at a reduced rate of 10%. The detailed rules are given in Chapter 6.

3.2.1 Striking off

Where a company's directors want to dissolve a company without the expense of a formal liquidation they may instead apply to the Registrar of Companies to be struck off the Register.

This cannot be done until three months after the company has ceased to trade.

It is therefore possible for solvent companies to distribute their assets to their shareholders prior to applying to be struck off, hence avoiding the need to appoint a liquidator.

The distribution of funds prior to the dissolution of a company is generally an income distribution unless a liquidator has been appointed.

However, there is an exception to this rule where distributions are made either during or in contemplation of a striking off providing certain conditions are met:

- The company intends to collect its debts and pay off its creditors in full (or has already done so); and

- The total amount of the distributions potentially within the scope of these provisions is no more than £25,000.

The treatment is withdrawn if the company has not been struck off, or has not collected its debts and paid its creditors, within two years of the date of the distribution.

If a distribution is made when there is already an intention to strike the company off, this seems to be automatically treated as within the scope of the statutory rules, making it difficult to pay an income distribution before the striking off begins in order to reduce the assets to be distributed as capital to £25,000.

Under company law, distributions of undistributable reserves cannot be made in the course of a winding up unless it is a formal liquidation. Thus the value of the share premium account and the share capital account should not form part of this pre-striking off distribution.

Leaving the undistributable reserves until after striking off the company theoretically presents a risk as the company's remaining assets after striking off are technically bona vacantia and belong to the Crown. However the Treasury Solicitor has confirmed that no action will be taken.

Interactive question 3: Voluntary liquidation   [Difficulty level: Intermediate]

Parker Ltd is an unquoted trading company owned by three individuals. The father, Paul, aged 55, has run the business with his son, Peter, and daughter, Penelope, but he now wishes to retire. Neither Peter nor Penelope wants to continue in business and they all want to realise the cash from the company to pursue their own interests in the future.

The company was put into liquidation and the net asset value for distribution is as follows:

	£
Factory	255,000
Inventories, receivables, cash	171,000
	426,000
Payables	(21,000)
	405,000

The share capital of the company is held as follows:

	Number	Cost £	Acquisition
Paul	150,000	60,000	May 1984
Peter	42,000	26,000	August 1992
Penelope	8,000	1,800	September 1994

In January 2016 the liquidators distributed the net assets of Parker Ltd.

Paul is an additional rate taxpayer and claimed £9.9m of entrepreneurs' relief on a gain realised in October 2012. The October 2012 claim was the first time Paul had claimed entrepreneurs' relief. Peter is a higher rate taxpayer and has no other gains in 2015/16. Penelope has no other income or gains for 2015/16.

Assume the RPI for January 2016 is 259.5.

Requirement

(a) Explain the tax consequences of the liquidation for Paul, Peter and Penelope.

(b) Consider whether the tax liabilities could have been reduced via a pre-liquidation dividend payment.

(c) Outline the difference in treatment if a UK company had owned the 8,000 shares instead of Penelope.

See **Answer** at the end of this chapter.

3.3 Disincorporation relief

Where a trade is transferred to a company's shareholders on, or in preparation for, the winding up of a company this will generally constitute a taxable disposal of all of the company's assets. Where the companies are members of the same group, the nil gain nil loss rules should apply to the transfer of chargeable gains assets and IFAs.

Disincorporation relief provides relief for some of the company-level gains on the disincorporation of the smallest businesses. The relief applies to disposals between 1 April 2013 and 31 March 2018.

In order to qualify for relief:

• The business must be transferred to individuals who have held shares in the company for at least twelve months ending with the transfer date.

• The business must be transferred as a going concern.

• All of the assets of the business (or all of the assets excluding cash) must be transferred.

• The total market value of the goodwill and interests in land transferred must be no more than £100,000.

Note that there is no requirement for the company to be subsequently liquidated or struck-off, although in practice this will often happen.

Disincorporation relief applies only to goodwill and interests in land. Where it is claimed:

• Interests in land and pre-2002 goodwill which falls within the chargeable gains rules are treated as transferred at the lower of their chargeable gains base cost and their market value. The base cost taken into account for these purposes is after any claims for gift relief made on the transfer of the assets to the company, but before indexation allowance.

• Post-2002 goodwill falling within the IFA rules is treated as transferred for the lower of its TWDV and its market value.

Relief must be claimed jointly by the company and the shareholder(s) to whom the trade is transferred within two years of the date of the transfer.

Worked example: Disincorporation relief

Ruth has owned 100% of the shares in Evermax Ltd since its incorporation on 1 January 2010, when she transferred to it a trade which she had previously operated as a sole trader. She has now decided that the administrative burden of running a company outweighs its benefits, and wishes to revert to being a sole trader.

With effect from 1 January 2016 she therefore intends to transfer the trade back into her personal ownership, and then appointed a liquidator. The assets currently owned by the company are as follows

	Expected MV at disincorporation £
Goodwill	40,000
Storage facility	50,000
Other net assets	38,000
Total	128,000

The goodwill was worth £30,000 at the time of incorporation. No gift relief was claimed. Ruth's original trade started in 2004, so relief has been claimed (on a 4% straight line basis) under the IFA rules.

The storage facility was acquired in 2004 for £20,000, and was worth £35,000 at incorporation. A claim for gift relief was made.

Ruth believes that there will be taxable income of approximately £6,000 arising on the other assets (on the disposal of trading stock , and capital allowances balancing charges)

Requirement

What is the impact of a claim for disincorporation relief?

You should assume an RPI for January 2016 of 259.5.

Solution

Although the total value of assets transferred is more than £100,000, Ruth and Evermax Ltd can claim disincorporation relief because the value of the goodwill and the interest in land (ie the storage facility) is only £90,000.

If no relief is claimed, the overall taxable profit on the transfer of the trade would be:

	£	£
Value of goodwill	40,000	
Less: TWDV (£30,000 – 6 × (£30,000 × 4%))	(22,800)	
		17,200
Value of storage facility	50,000	
Less cost (after gift relief claim)	(20,000)	
Less indexation ((259.5 – 217.9)/217.9) = 0.191 × £20,000	(3,820)	
		26,180
Profit on other assets		6,000
Taxable profit on disincorporation		49,380

If disincorporation relief is claimed, the goodwill will be treated as transferred to Ruth for its TWDV of £22,800, and the storage facility will be treated as transferred for its base cost (after the adjustment for gift relief) of £20,000. The only profit left in charge would be the profit of £6,000 on other assets.

However, Ruth's base cost for later disposals of the assets will be significantly lower as a result, and the benefit of the indexation allowance on the storage facility would be permanently lost.

3.4 Group relationships

On the commencement of a winding up a company ceases to be the beneficial owner of its assets. Thus where those assets include shareholdings it is no longer the beneficial owner of those shares. For group loss relief purposes this means that a holding company will no longer be the beneficial owner of its shareholdings and any loss relief groups formed via its share holdings will be broken up.

However, commencement of winding up does not break up the chargeable gains group. Even if gains are realised after cessation of trade or the commencement of winding up, group gains tax planning may still mitigate the tax payable.

Liquidation of a holding company		Liquidation of a subsidiary company

Group relief group

- No longer in a group with its subsidiaries

- Group relief ceases to be available both to and from subsidiaries
- The timing of the commencement of winding up must be chosen in order to maximise relief for group losses

Capital gains group

- The group is preserved

- All the benefits of being in a group continue

Liquidation of a subsidiary company

- The subsidiary's parent company owns the shares until the final dissolution of the subsidiary
- The subsidiary remains part of the group for all purposes until that date

CHAPTER

17

Summary

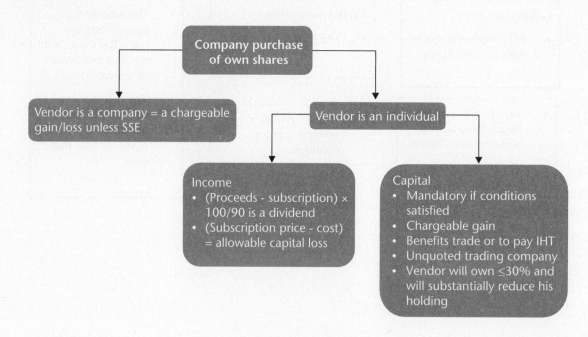

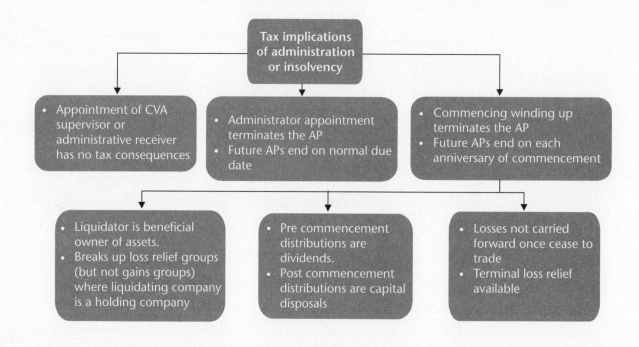

Self-test

Answer the following questions.

1   Winterbourne Ltd, a company with a 31 July year end, ceases to trade on 18 September 2014. The members pass a resolution to wind up the company on 31 January 2015 and the winding up is complete on 8 April 2016.

    Requirement

    From 1 August 2014 what are the dates of Winterbourne Ltd's accounting periods?

2   Bridgford Ltd, a UK resident company, with a 31 March year end has traded for a number of years.

    Bridgford Ltd incurred trading losses of £6m in the year ended 31 March 2015. Bridgford Ltd last made a profit in the year ended 31 March 2013 with total profits of £1m.

    On 30 June 2015, Bridgford Ltd ceased to trade. The company commenced winding up proceedings on 1 January 2016.

    The company's balance sheet as at 30 June 2015 showed substantial cash balances of £15m compared to total liabilities of just £4m.

    The £15m was realised on the disposal on 30 June 2015 of Bridgford Ltd's entire 20% shareholding in a UK quoted trading company which had been held for a number of years. The cash is currently held in high interest deposit accounts pending distribution.

    The company's profit and loss account for the three months to 30 June 2015 showed a trading loss of £2m and a dividend paid out of retained earnings on 30 April 2015 of £9m.

    Requirement

    Draft a brief report to the liquidator of Bridgford Ltd about the corporation tax position for the three month accounting period to 30 June 2015 and for later accounting periods including any recommendations.

3   Ben Cartwright was the founder of Bonanza Ltd and has owned 6,200 shares (62%) for the last 30 years.

    Ben wishes to withdraw from the day-to-day management of the company. A partial repurchase of Ben's shares by the company will benefit its trade.

    Requirements

    (a) How many shares must Bonanza Ltd repurchase from Ben for the purchase to satisfy the conditions for chargeable gains treatment?

    (b) What would the answer be if Ben's shareholding in Bonanza Ltd were only 3,400 shares (34%)?

4   The shareholders of Waterstripe Ltd have decided that the company should be wound up. The trade is to be transferred to Eva Partridge (one of the shareholders, who has owned a 40% stake in the company since it was set up in 2000) on 30 September 2015.

The assets to be transferred are as follows:

	Cost	Expected MV at disincorporation
	£	£
Goodwill	Nil	75,000
Patent rights	20,000	50,000
Trading stock	15,000	25,000
Total		150,000

The patent rights were acquired on 1 October 2010, and are being amortised on a straight line basis over a period of 10 years. Eva has always owned the premises out of which the business operates: the company's lease is due to expire on 30 September 2015. She will pay the company market value for the assets which are transferred to her.

Requirement

Calculate the taxable profit arising in Waterstripe Ltd on the transfer of the trade, assuming all possible reliefs are claimed.

5   Your firm acts as business advisors to Soup Ltd and you are a senior in the tax department.

The three full-time director shareholders have approached your partner following bitter arguments and irreconcilable differences between themselves concerning the management of the company.

As a result Mr Broth and Mr Consommé have agreed to sell their shares. However, Mr Soup does not have the necessary funds.

It has therefore been decided that the company, which has surplus cash, will buy back the shares of Mr Broth and Mr Consommé on 31 March 2016 at £9.00 per share.

From the client files you find the following information.

- Issued share capital of Soup Ltd is 10,000 £1 ordinary shares owned as follows:

    - Mr Soup 60%
    - Mr Broth 25%
    - Mr Consommé 15%

- Mr Broth, aged 42, had subscribed for his shares at par in May 1988.

- Mr Consommé, aged 43, had bought his shares at £4 per share in June 1991.

- Both Mr Broth and Mr Consommé pay higher rate income tax, and regularly make gains which use up the annual exempt amount.

Your partner is meeting with the directors next week to discuss the purchase of shares. He has asked you to prepare some notes highlighting the taxation consequences resulting from the purchase of shares, assuming both that HMRC does not allow the transaction to be treated as a capital transaction, and that the transaction is treated as a capital transaction.

Requirement

Draft the notes required by your partner for the meeting.

Now, go back to the Learning objectives in the Introduction. If you are satisfied you have achieved these objectives, please tick them off.

Legislation

Purchase of own shares

All references are to Corporation Tax Act 2010 *(CTA 2010)* unless otherwise stated

Repurchase for the benefit of the trade	ss.1033-1043
Benefit of trade	Statement of Practice 2/82
Repurchase in order to settle IHT liability	s.1033(3)

Administration & liquidation

All references are to Corporation Tax Act 2010 *(CTA 2010)* unless otherwise stated

Taxation of profits during winding up	s.6(2) CTA 2009
Ceasing to trade after winding up commences does not terminate AP	s.12 CTA 2009
Terminal loss relief	s.39
CIC from start of next AP if cease to trade in first AP of liquidation	s.34(5)
Distributions post winding up starting are capital	ss.1000 & 1030
Distributions made in contemplation of striking off are capital	s.1030A
Striking off	ss.1000-1008 CA 2006
Disincorporation relief	ss.57-60 FA 2013

HMRC manual references

Company Taxation Manual (Found at www.hmrc.gov.uk/manuals/ctmanual/index.htm)

CTM36100 – Particular topics: company winding up etc

CTM17500 – Distributions: purchase of own shares

> This technical reference section is designed to assist you when you are working in the office. It should help you to know where to look for further information on the topics covered in this chapter.

Answer to Interactive question 1

	Y/E 31 July 2012 £	Y/E 31 July 2013 £	Y/E 31 July 2014 £	Y/E 31 July 2015 £	P/E 31 Oct 2015 £
Taxable total profits	114,000	112,000	28,000	–	–
Loss of Y/E 31/7/15					
– s.37(3)(b) against PY			(28,000)		
– TLR		(34,000)			
Loss of P/E 31/10/15					
– TLR		(47,000)			
Taxable total profits	114,000	31,000	–	–	–

Utilisation of losses

(1)	Loss of Y/E 31 July 2015	(62,000)
	s.37(3)(b) against Y/E 31 July 2014	28,000
	TLR against Y/E 31 July 2013	34,000
	Unrelieved	Nil

(2)	*Terminal loss relief*		
	Loss of last 12 months trading		
	P/E 31 October 2015		(47,000)
	Part of Y/E 31 July 2015		
	Max = 9/12 × £62,000	(46,500)	
	Limited to amount unrelieved	(34,000)	(34,000)

Each terminal loss may be offset against profits of the previous 36 months. Each loss must be dealt with in turn, dealing with the earlier loss first. Thus the terminal loss of £34,000 arising in the Y/E 31 July 2015 must be dealt with first. It is carried back 24 months to the Y/E 31 July 2013 and fully relieved. If more losses had remained, it could have been carried back a further 12 months against all profits arising between 1 August 2011 to 31 July 2012. This is 36 months from the beginning of the loss making period which commenced on 1 August 2014.

The terminal loss arising in the period ended 31 October 2015 is dealt with next. It can be carried back 36 months from the start of that loss making period ie against profits arising since 1 August 2012 on a LIFO basis.

Answer to Interactive question 2

If a developer buys the workshop it is likely to result in a chargeable gain. Passing a resolution to commence winding up the company will cause the accounting period to end. As long as the company is still trading at this point, the trading losses could be used against any subsequent gain realised in the same accounting period prior to cessation. However, if the company ceases to trade prior to the sale of the workshop, trading losses arising in the accounting period prior to cessation cannot be set against the gain arising in a subsequent accounting period.

In order to advise Mr Brown fully, it is necessary to know the following information:

- The likely amount of the gain and whether there are any capital losses within the company which can be set against this gain.

- The level of trade losses and whether these can be relieved via a terminal loss claim.

Answer to Interactive question 3

(a) Tax consequences of liquidation on individual shareholders

A chargeable gain arises on the disposal of shares

	Paul £	Peter £	Penelope £
Consideration (£405k × 75%/21%/4%)	303,750	85,050	16,200
Cost	(60,000)	(26,000)	(1,800)
Gains	243,750	59,050	14,400
Less annual exempt amount	(11,100)	(11,100)	(11,100)
Gains	232,650	47,950	3,300

Paul has a further £100,000 of the entrepreneurs' relief lifetime limit remaining which he may use to offset against this gain. The first £100,000 of the gain will therefore be taxed at 10%. The balance will be taxed at 28%

Peter's entire gain will be taxable at 10% as it is eligible for entrepreneurs' relief.

Penelope is not eligible for entrepreneurs' relief as her holding is less than 5%. However, as she has no other income and the whole of her gain falls within the basic rate band, it will be taxable at 18%.

	Paul	Peter	Penelope
Capital gains tax	47,142	4,795	594

Note. The rules on entrepreneurs' relief are covered in detail in Chapter 6.

(b) If a pre-liquidation dividend had been paid to the shareholders

- Each individual would have been assessed on the dividend income. Penelope would have no further tax to pay as she would be a basic rate taxpayer. Peter would have further tax to pay at 22.5% of the gross or 25% of the net or cash received. Paul would have further tax to pay at 27.5% of the gross or 30.6% of the net or cash received.

- The company would have then had less net assets to distribute after the commencement of the winding up, which would have reduced the chargeable gain on the final distribution.

- The effective rate of tax on Paul's and Peter's gains is less than 19.4%/8.2% respectively taking into account the effect of entrepreneurs' relief and the annual exempt amount. This is preferable to the effective rate of tax of 30.6%/25% that would have been charged on a pre-liquidation dividend received by an additional rate/higher rate taxpayer respectively.

- Therefore Paul and Peter would be worse off if they received a pre-liquidation dividend. Penelope would be better off as she would have no tax liability if a pre-liquidation dividend were paid.

(c) If a UK company owned 8,000 shares in Parker Ltd

- On a final distribution a chargeable gain of £12,979 would arise on the company as indexation allowance runs to the date of disposal:

	Company £
Consideration (£405k × 4%)	16,200
Cost	(1,800)
	14,400
Indexation to disposal, January 2015	
259.5– 145.0/145.0 × £1,800	(1,421)
Indexed gain	12,979

- The gain would be subject to corporation tax (20% for FY2015). If the UK company had owned at least 10% of Parker Ltd for 12 months out of the previous 2 years, the substantial shareholding exemption would have been available to exempt the gain. However, as this is only a 4% holding the gain would be taxable.

- If a pre-liquidation dividend payment were made, the dividend receipt would not be taxable in the hands of the company, although it could affect the rate of tax payable as it would be treated as franked investment income.

- As a result, the final distribution gain would also be reduced, saving corporation tax.

- However, if Parker Ltd were to make a pre-liquidation dividend payment, it could not be discriminatory. All shareholders would receive a dividend, which in this case is not in the best interests of Paul or Peter.

Answers to Self-test

1   01.08. 14 – 18.09.14 To the date trade ceases.

     19.09. 14 – 31.01.15 The commencement of a winding up brings an AP to an end.

     01.02. 15 – 31.01.16 AP cannot exceed 12 months.

     01.02.16 – 08.04.16 Final AP ends when winding up complete.

2   **Report to Liquidators of Bridgford Ltd should cover:**

Although the company has made a loss, given its assets and liabilities it is clearly not insolvent and a substantial amount of money will need to be distributed to the shareholders once the creditors have been paid. As the company has already ceased to trade and has already commenced winding up proceedings, there are only limited tax planning opportunities available.

(1) *Accounting period to 30 June 2015*

As the company ceased to trade on 30 June 2015 for taxation purposes an accounting period will have ended. Thus the company has an accounting period of three months from 1 April 2015 to 30 June 2015.

During this three month period, the company made a loss of £2m. As a result no corporation tax will be payable.

The company will be entitled to terminal loss relief (TLR) as a result of the cessation. This gives relief for losses incurred in the last 12 months of trade by carrying them back up to three years. As the final accounting period is short, the loss of the final 12 months of trade is eligible for carry back.

Losses for the period 1 July 2014 – 31 March 2015 may be carried back against total profits arising since 1 April 2011 as the loss may be carried back three years from the start of the first accounting period of the loss. In other words it may be carried back three years back from 1 April 2014 being the first accounting period in which part of the loss of the final 12 months arose. The amounts eligible for terminal loss relief are £2m and £4.5m (ie 9/12 × £6m).

The £4.5m arising in the year ended 31 March 2015 will be offset first. This will fully offset the profits arising in the year ended 31 March 2013. So unless there are profits arising in the year ended 31 March 2012, £3.5m of this loss will remain unrelieved.

The £2m arising in the period ended 30 June 2015 will be offset next. It can be carried back against profits arising since 1 April 2012. However, as all profits have been fully relieved, this £2m will remain unrelieved.

The remaining £1.5m from the year to 31 March 2015 which was not eligible for TLR cannot be carried forward as the trade has ceased and there are no profits in either the current or prior year against which it can be set.

The £15m proceeds on disposal of a shareholding of at least 10% in a trading company should be exempt under the substantial shareholding exemption.

The company paid a dividend of £9m on 30 April 2015. This has no tax consequences for the company.

(2) *Accounting period to 31 December 2015*

The commencement of winding up proceedings will result in the end of an accounting period and the commencement of a new accounting period (s.12 CTA 2009).

Thus Bridgford Ltd will have a six month accounting period 1 July 2015 to 31 December 2015.

During this accounting period the company will not have a trade. The company will not be able to utilise any losses carried forward from its trade.

At 1 July 2015 the company had cash on deposit of £15m. This will result in bank interest which will be taxable as a non-trading loan relationship profit. This interest receipt will not be eligible for loss relief as it arises after cessation from deposits of money.

· The company will not be able to receive deductions for expenses as it does not have a trade nor is it making and managing investments which would entitle it to deduct management expenses.

(3) *Accounting periods during liquidation*

As stated above, the commencement of winding up will result in the commencement of a new accounting period. The accounting period will run to the anniversary of the appointment or to the date the liquidation is completed. The only exception to this rule is that an accounting period will end before 12 months should the company cease to be in liquidation without being wound up.

The tax position of the company will be as stated above; interest received will be taxed as a non-trading loan relationship profit with no relief for losses brought forward or expenses.

Expenses of the liquidator will not qualify for relief. The expenses will be incurred as part of the winding up, not as part of the company's trade which ceased in June 2015.

Advice to reduce tax

The company should pay its creditors as soon as possible and then make distributions to the shareholders.

The distributions to the shareholders will be capital distributions and will not result in any tax consequences for the company.

The tax position of the shareholders will depend on how much they paid for their shares. Each shareholder will be making a capital disposal or part disposal on receipt of sums from the liquidator.

3 (a) **Ben holds more than 40% of the company's shares (30% test relevant)**

For the purchase to satisfy the conditions for chargeable gains treatment, Ben's holding must be reduced to 30%, so that he is not connected with the company after the purchase.

This will require a reduction in his holding of more than 75% such that the substantial reduction rule is also satisfied.

For Ben's shareholding to be 30%, the other shareholders must hold 70%.

This means that the total share capital is 3,800/0.7 = 5,428.

The reduction in the total share capital of 4,572 (10,000 – 5,428) is the number of shares to be sold by Ben.

Ben's new holding is 1,628 (6,200 – 4,572) or 30% of 5,428.

(b) **Ben holds less than 40% of the company's shares (75% substantial reduction test relevant)**

For the purchase to satisfy the conditions for chargeable gains treatment, Ben must satisfy the 75% substantial reduction rule. This will also ensure that he is not connected with the company after the purchase.

Ben's new holding must be reduced to 75% × 34% = 25.5%.

For Ben's shareholding to be 25.5%, the other shareholders must hold 74.5%.

This means that the total share capital is 6,600/0.745 = 8,859.

The reduction in the total share capital of 1,141 (10,000 – 8,859) is the number of shares to be sold by Ben.

Ben's new holding is 2,259 (3,400 – 1,141) or 25.5% of 8,859.

4   Because the value of the goodwill is less than £100,000 (the business has no interests in land), disincorporation relief can be claimed. This would result in the goodwill being transferred for its cost of nil, and Eva then having no base cost in the goodwill going forward.

The profits/gains on the other assets would remain fully taxable:

	£	£
Value of patent rights	50,000	
Less TWDV (£20,000 – 5 × (£20,000/10))	(10,000)	
		40,000
Profit on disposal of stock (£25,000 – £15,000)		10,000
Taxable profit on transfer of trade		50,000

5   **Notes for forthcoming meeting**

To	A partner
From	A tax senior
Client	Soup Ltd
Date	Today
Subject	Purchase of own shares

If the transaction is treated as an income distribution

Taxation consequences for the company

	£
Consideration (4,000 × £9.00)	36,000
Subscribed amount (4,000 × £1.00)	(4,000)
Net distribution	32,000

The cost to the company is £36,000.

Taxation consequences for individual shareholders

Mr Broth and Mr Consommé will be treated as having received dividends as follows.

Income tax

	Mr Broth £	Mr Consommé £
Consideration	22,500	13,500
Original subscription price (£1 per share)	(2,500)	(1,500)
Net distribution	20,000	12,000
Gross dividend (£20,000/£12,000 × $^{100}/_{90}$)	22,222	13,333
Income tax payable [£22,222/£13,333 × 22½% (ie 32½% – 10%)]	5,000	3,000

Capital gains tax

There are no capital gain tax consequences for Mr Broth as he originally subscribed for the shares at par.

For Mr Consommé an allowable loss arises as he purchased the shares for more than par after the original subscription.

	£
Consideration	13,500
Less net distribution taxed as income	(12,000)
	1,500
Less cost of purchase (1,500 × £4)	(6,000)
Allowable loss	(4,500)

If the transaction is treated as a capital distribution

Taxation consequences for the company

The cost to the company is £36,000, as before.

Taxation consequences for the individual shareholders

Income tax

There are no income tax consequences for Mr Broth and Mr Consommé.

Capital gains tax

Mr Broth and Mr Consommé will be assessed to capital gains tax as follows.

	Mr Broth £	Mr Consommé £
Proceeds	22,500	13,500
Cost	(2,500)	(6,000)
Gain	20,000	7,500
Less annual exempt amount (used)	–	–
Gain	20,000	7,500
Capital gains tax:		
£20,000/7,500 × 10%	2,000	750

Both Mr Broth and Mr Consommé are eligible for entrepreneurs' relief and will therefore pay CGT at 10%.

CHAPTER 18

VAT

Introduction

Examination context

Topic List

Introduction

Learning objectives

- Determine, explain and calculate the VAT liabilities for individuals and corporate entities ☐

- Explain and evaluate the tax implications of group structures ☐

- Explain and evaluate the tax implications of business transformations and change ☐

- Explain and calculate the tax implications involved in the cessation of trade ☐

- Evaluate and advise on tax strategies to meet business objectives ☐

- Evaluate and advise on alternative tax strategies relating to corporate transformations ☐

Specific syllabus references for this chapter are 1f, 1j, 1l, 1m, 2b and 2c.

Syllabus links

VAT on property interacts with Stamp Duty Land Tax (Chapter 19). VAT within a corporate transformation will be critical as VAT on property, or the sale of a trade within the scope of VAT, is often considerable.

Examination context

VAT can often amount to a significant sum of money, for example in a property transaction. With careful planning VAT liabilities (especially on property) can be reduced to nil. If such care is not taken a client can be exposed to a substantial additional tax liability. The use of options to tax and transfers of a going concern can be complex areas for many advisers. It is often important in practice to be able to identify when VAT may be a significant issue in a transaction so that it can be passed on to a VAT specialist.

In the examination candidates may be required to:

- Advise on the correct treatment of and calculate the tax liabilities arising as a result of the acquisition, intra-group transfer, or disposal of property

- Advise on the correct treatment of and calculate the tax liabilities arising as a result of a transfer of a going concern

- Advise on the interaction of the transfer of a going concern rules, option to tax and capital goods scheme

- Advise on the implications and advantages of group registration

- Advise on the VAT implications of international trade

1 Revision from Tax Compliance

Section overview

- The following topics were covered at Tax Compliance:

  1. VAT rates
  2. Partial exemption
  3. VAT on property
  4. Capital goods scheme
  5. Overseas aspects

- Property transactions may be exempt, zero rated or standard rated depending on the nature of the supply.

- The capital goods scheme governs the recovery of input tax on land and buildings; ships and aircraft; and computers which may be used over a period of time to make both taxable supplies and exempt supplies.

- The scheme applies to purchases of land and buildings costing at least £250,000 or single ships and aircraft or computing items (excluding software) each costing at least £50,000.

- An adjustment is made to the recovery of input tax over

  - Ten years for land and buildings
  - Five years for ships, aircraft and computers

  This is called the adjustment period.

- On sale an adjustment is made for the remaining adjustment period, assuming current usage is 100% taxable if the sale itself is taxable and current usage is 0% taxable if the sale itself is exempt.

- Companies under common control can apply for group registration for VAT.

- A VAT group is treated as a single VAT entity which submits one VAT return.

- Not all the companies eligible for group registration need be included in the group registration eg exempt or partially exempt companies may be excluded.

- No VAT is charged on intra-group supplies.

1.1 VAT rates

The standard rate of VAT has fluctuated as follows:

- 1 April 1991 to 30 November 2008   17.5%
- 1 December 2008 to 31 December 2009   15%
- 1 January 2010 to 3 January 2011   17.5%
- From 4 January 2011   20%

For the purposes of the exams in 2016 you should use the correct rate of VAT based on the date of the transaction.

1.2 VAT on property transactions

The following points are important from your earlier studies:

- Sales and leases of land and buildings are generally exempt.

- There is an option to make otherwise exempt supplies standard rated. This does not apply to the sale of residential buildings.

- Sale and leases of new residential buildings are zero rated.

- Sale of the freehold of a new (less than three years old) commercial building is standard rated.

- The supply of services relating to land or buildings is either standard rated or taxable at the reduced rate.

1.2.1 Residential buildings

The sale of a new building for residential or charitable purposes is zero rated ie it is a taxable supply and the input tax relating to the supply can be recovered.

The sale of an existing residential building or the lease of a residential building are generally exempt and there is no option to tax in relation to residential buildings. Any input tax in relation to the supply is irrecoverable.

Work on existing residential buildings is generally standard rated.

1.2.2 Commercial buildings

The following supplies are standard rated:

- Construction of commercial buildings
- Sale of the freehold of a new (less than three years old) commercial building
- Work on existing commercial buildings

The following supplies are exempt, but subject to the option to tax:

- Sale of the freehold of an old (three years old or more) commercial building
- Lease of any commercial building

1.2.3 Option to tax – basic principles

Owners of interests in land and buildings may opt to charge VAT on supplies which would otherwise be exempt (except in relation to residential property). Once the option to tax is exercised, it applies to all future supplies relating to that land/ building.

The tax consequences are:

- VAT at the standard rate must be charged on the sale or lease (premium and rents) of the property. This may be a problem if the purchaser/tenant makes wholly or partially exempt supplies since there may be a restriction in recovering this input tax.

- Any inputs relating to the supply may be recovered eg heating costs, cleaning, repairs etc.

1.2.4 Option to tax – additional points

The following points should be noted about the option to tax:

- The option to tax relates to individual land or buildings, not to all the land and buildings owned by the person opting to tax. However, if made, the option applies to the whole building. This may be a problem if there are a number of tenants, some of whom are either not registered for VAT or make exempt supplies.

- An option to tax is made by the owner of the land or building and does not transfer with the land or building on any future disposal except transfers between VAT group members. Transfers of assets between VAT group members are disregarded for VAT purposes and therefore the option to tax will continue to bind the other members of the VAT group.

- The option may be revoked within a six month 'cooling off' period provided the option to tax has not been put into practical effect eg by charging VAT on rent.

- An option to tax will be automatically revoked once the person who opted has held no interest in the property for six years.

- In any event, the option to tax may be revoked after 20 years with the consent of HMRC.

1.2.5 Option to tax – planning issues

When deciding whether to opt to tax a building, consideration must be given to the likely VAT status of any future purchaser.

For example:

- Once the option is exercised, any future disposal of the building will be standard rated.

- If potential purchasers are exempt traders, the cost of the building will be higher.

- The purchase of an 'opted' building may be less desirable than one upon which the option to tax has not been exercised.

- Where potential purchasers are likely to be partially exempt the building will be subject to the capital goods scheme and only some of the VAT will be recoverable.

In addition, consideration must be given to the proposed use of the building.

For example:

- If a landlord purchases a new commercial building it is a taxable transaction and the landlord will therefore pay VAT on the value of the whole building. Unless he opts to tax the building, renting it out would be an exempt supply and the input tax suffered would be irrecoverable. Opting to tax the building converts the renting out of the building into a taxable supply and thus means the input tax suffered on the purchase price is recoverable.

- If a VAT registered trader purchases a new commercial building for use in his taxable trade the input VAT suffered will be recoverable.

- If an exempt trader purchases a new commercial building for use in his exempt trade the input VAT suffered is irrecoverable. It would be meaningless for the exempt trader to make an option to tax the building as it would still be used in his exempt trade and the input VAT would still be irrecoverable.

1.2.6 VAT and stamp duty land tax (SDLT)

Where VAT is charged on property it may or may not be recoverable. Where it is recoverable it merely represents a cash flow timing difference. However SDLT will be charged on the VAT inclusive price and thus SDLT is a significant cost.

1.3 Capital goods scheme

1.3.1 Introduction

Normally input tax recovery depends on the immediate use of the item purchased ie input VAT may be recovered where it is first used to make taxable supplies and is irrecoverable where it is first used to make exempt supplies. The capital goods scheme amends this treatment for capital items which are:

- Buildings and land costing £250,000 or more;

- Aircraft, ships, boats and other vessels that are bought after 31 December 2010 costing £50,000 or more; or

- Single computer items (excluding software) each costing £50,000 or more.

It is recognised that these items may be used for different purposes over a period of time, and therefore:

- Initial recovery on these items is calculated as normal; but

- The initial recovery is revised over an 'adjustment period' to reflect changes in use during that time including the sale of the item.

Where a capital item within the scope of the scheme is purchased by a wholly taxable business, the capital goods scheme still applies. However, providing the items are used purely for taxable purposes throughout the adjustment period, no actual adjustments will be required. [Hp 270]

1.3.2 Initial recovery

Where a capital item within the scope of the scheme is purchased, initial recovery of input tax will be based on its initial use:

- Wholly taxable business – 100% of the input tax will be recoverable.

- Partially exempt business – input recovery will be based on its use in the quarter of purchase and then adjusted at the end of the VAT year. The input tax recovered for the first year as adjusted at the year end is the initial recovery.

- Wholly exempt business – no input tax may be recovered initially.

1.3.3 Adjustments for use

An adjustment is required for ten intervals for buildings and five intervals for aircraft, ships and computers. For each interval the use within that VAT interval is compared to the initial recovery. Where the usage differs, that difference leads to an adjustment in respect of that interval's share of the total VAT:

$$\left(\frac{\text{Total input VAT}}{\text{10 or 5 intervals}}\right) \times (\text{taxable \% usage now} - \text{initial taxable \% usage})$$

Where taxable usage has increased, an additional amount of input tax can be recovered. Where taxable usage has reduced, some of the original input tax recovered will be clawed back.

The first interval will run from the date of acquisition to the end of that VAT return year. Subsequent intervals generally coincide with the VAT year.

Worked example: Adjustments for use

Diverse plc acquired a new ten-floor office block incurring £100,000 of input tax. It uses four floors in connection with its insurance broking trade (an exempt supply) and the rest in connection with its retail trade (a taxable supply).

Five years after the acquisition it ceases its insurance broking trade and from then on it uses the whole of the building in its retail trade.

Requirement

Explain how Diverse plc will recover the input tax.

Solution

Diverse plc will initially recover £60,000 (60% × £100,000) in the first interval.

Additional input tax can be reclaimed from year 6 onwards as follows:

(£100,000/10) × (100% – 60%) = £4,000 per year

Interactive question 1: Adjustments for use [Difficulty level: Intermediate]

A company purchases a new building for £2m plus VAT on 1 July 2010. The company immediately rents it out without opting to tax the building. HMRC grants permission for the company to opt to tax the building from 1 April 2016. The company prepares VAT returns to 31 March each year.

Requirement

Calculate the initial recovery of input VAT and subsequent adjustments required in later years, if any.

See **Answer** at the end of this chapter.

1.3.4 Adjustments for sale

If a capital item is sold within the adjustment period, two adjustments are made:

- For the year of sale the normal adjustment is made as if the item had been used for the whole year; and

- A further adjustment for the complete intervals following the year of sale, assuming 100% taxable use if the sale itself was taxable and 0% taxable use if the sale itself was exempt. Any additional input VAT recoverable may be limited to the output VAT charged on the taxable sale where tax avoidance is in point.

Thus where a new commercial building is sold after three years it will be an exempt sale. However, if it is sold within 10 intervals of acquisition it will be subject to a claw back of input tax on the original purchase price.

Worked example: Adjustments for sale

Haddock plc purchased a new computer for £200,000 plus VAT on 15 November 2013 and used it 55% for taxable purposes each year until 31 March 2016. It then used the computer 75% for taxable purposes and finally sold it for £22,000 plus VAT on 18 June 2016. Haddock plc prepares VAT returns to 31 March.

Requirement

Calculate the initial input tax recovery and adjustments required for all subsequent years.

Solution

Haddock plc will initially recover £22,000 (55% × £40,000) in the first interval to March 2014.

In the intervals to March 2015 and March 2016 no adjustment is required as the taxable usage has remained constant.

Additional input tax can be reclaimed in interval four (to March 2017) as taxable usage has increased:

(£40,000/5) × (75% − 55%) = £1,600

As the computer is sold in the fourth interval there is also an adjustment on disposal. This is calculated based on 100% taxable use for any remaining intervals of the adjustment period as it was a taxable sale. As this is a computer the adjustment period is five intervals and only one interval remains to be adjusted for:

(£40,000/5) × (100% − 55%) × 1 interval = £3,600

1.4 VAT groups

1.4.1 Introduction

Two or more companies are eligible to be treated as members of a group provided that each is established or has a fixed establishment in the UK and:

- One of them controls each of the others;
- One person (individual or holding company) controls all of them; or
- Two or more persons carrying on a business in partnership control all of them.

Control means that there must be a shareholding of greater than 50%.

An application for group registration results in the group being treated as a single taxable person for VAT purposes, registered in the name of the representative member (one of the group companies).

The representative member is responsible for accounting for VAT on behalf of the VAT group and submitting the VAT returns. The total input VAT suffered by the group is deducted from the total output VAT, and the excess paid to HMRC by the representative member.

1.4.2 Choice of group companies

Group registration is optional and not all group companies have to join the VAT group. More than one VAT group can be registered as well as separate single company registrations within a large group of companies.

Issues affecting the choice of group companies:

- Exclude a company in a net repayment situation (making mainly zero-rated supplies).
  It can make monthly VAT returns and receive regular cash repayments from HMRC, rather than lose the cash flow advantage by 'netting off' the repayment against other group liabilities.

- Exclude a company making wholly exempt supplies.
  Including them would make the group 'partially exempt' and may restrict the recoverability of input VAT for all group companies.

1.4.3 Advantages and disadvantages

The main advantages of group registration are:

- No VAT is charged on intra-group supplies

- Only one VAT return is required (ie administrative costs savings possible)

- If a relatively small wholly exempt company is included in the group, it may be possible to recover its input tax under the de minimis partial exemption rules for the group as a whole

The main disadvantages of group registration are:

- All companies in the group are jointly and severally liable for the VAT of the group as a whole

- Having to make one return may cause administrative difficulties in collecting and collating the information required for the return

- Bringing in an exempt or partially exempt company may lead to a restriction of input tax

2 Transfer of a going concern (TOGC)

Section overview

- If a business is transferred as a going concern (TOGC), there is no taxable supply and so no VAT is chargeable.

- If the transferor is VAT registered, the transferee must also be VAT-registered before or immediately after the transfer.

- If the transferee is not VAT-registered before the transfer, the transferor's VAT registration number may also be transferred with the business.

- Taxable land included within a TOGC is subject to special rules.

- VAT on property transactions, VAT on property within a TOGC and property within the capital goods scheme are linked topics and it is important that the interaction between these three aspects of VAT is fully understood at Business Planning: Taxation.

2.1 The relief

If an unincorporated business is transferred (eg as a gift when a business is passed down from parent to child, on incorporation or on sale to a third party), without special rules output tax would have to be charged by the transferor on standard–rated assets transferred to the new owner. If the transferee will be making wholly taxable supplies, this will be tax-neutral as he will be able to recover the VAT paid as input tax, although this may cause cash-flow problems if the amount is substantial.

However, a special rule applies so that if a business is transferred as a going concern (TOGC), there is no taxable supply of goods or services and so no output tax is chargeable on the assets transferred.

For transfers of assets within a VAT group, like most supplies between the members of a VAT group, the transfer will be disregarded for VAT purposes. The TOGC rules do not need to be considered.

2.2 Conditions

For the relief to apply, all of the following conditions must be satisfied:

- The whole of the business of the transferor or part of the business which is capable of separate operation is transferred as a going concern.

- The assets are to be used by the transferee in the same kind of business as that carried on by the transferor.

- If the transferor is VAT registered, the transferee is also VAT registered when the transfer takes place or will immediately become VAT registered after the transfer.

- There is no significant break in trading.

2.3 Incorrect application of TOGC

If the transfer is treated as a TOGC but fails to satisfy the conditions, the transferor may be assessed by HMRC for the output tax he should have charged on the transfer of assets. The sale contract should cover this possibility, by stating that the purchase price is VAT-exclusive and that VAT may be chargeable on that price, so that the transferor can recover this tax from the transferee. Otherwise, the purchase price will be treated as VAT inclusive and the transferor cannot recover anything in excess of this price.

If the transferor incorrectly charges output tax where the transaction is, in fact, a TOGC, the transferee cannot recover this as input tax because there was no supply to him. The transferee may recover this amount from the transferor, but may be unable to do so if the transferor has disappeared or has become insolvent.

2.4 Transfer of VAT registration number

If the transferee was not VAT registered immediately before the transfer instead of registering in his own right, he may apply to have the transferor's VAT registration number transferred to him with the business.

The transferee will also take over outstanding VAT liabilities. However, he will also be eligible for bad debt relief on the transferor's bad debts.

The transfer of the VAT registration number is therefore not usually made on a commercial sale but may be useful where the transferor and transferee are closely connected (eg on passing of a business from parent to child or on incorporation). If the VAT registration number is transferred, the transferor's VAT records must also be transferred.

2.5 Land and buildings

The special rule for the TOGC will not cover:

- Buildings aged three years or less
- Land or buildings which the transferor has opted to tax

unless the transferee opts to tax these assets.

Remember that the option to tax does not automatically transfer with the land or buildings.

If the transferee does not make an option to tax then VAT must be charged on the transfer of these assets (although all the other assets being transferred as part of the TOGC remain subject to the special rule).

2.5.1 Land and buildings – rental properties

A building generating rental income and capable of independent operation constitutes a business. Its sale would therefore qualify as a TOGC. However if the building is less than three years old or the vendor has opted to tax the building, the purchaser is still required to opt to tax the building (see above). Otherwise VAT would be charged on the sale of the building.

If the purchaser does not opt to tax the building and uses the building in his taxable business (ie he occupies the building personally for trade purposes) the input VAT on the purchase is recoverable but the building will not be a taxable supply on any subsequent sale (assuming it is more than three years old by the time of disposal).

2.6 Interaction of the capital goods scheme and TOGC rules

Where an item is transferred as part of a TOGC then its disposal represents neither a taxable supply nor an exempt supply so no adjustment on sale is required. Instead the new owner assumes responsibility for any adjustments of input tax required under the scheme for the remainder of the adjustment period.

Purchasers should therefore:

- Establish whether any of the assets being transferred are within the scope of the scheme and obtain details of any adjustments already made.

- Be aware of the need to repay some of the input tax claimed by the original owner. Conversely, he may be entitled to recover more tax than that originally claimed.

If the seller has been fully taxable since the acquisition of the capital item and the buyer is and remains fully taxable until the expiry of the adjustment period, then no adjustments are required under the scheme.

2.7 Option to tax, TOGC and the capital goods scheme

Where commercial property which is less than three years old or on which an option to tax has been exercised is transferred as part of a TOGC, the purchaser must also opt to tax the property or pay VAT on the purchase price of the property.

An exempt trader may opt to tax the building and therefore not pay any input tax on the purchase of the property. However, where the property is within the scope of the capital goods scheme, adjustments will then need to be made for the remainder of the adjustment period, if any.

Interactive question 2: Opting to tax in a TOGC   [Difficulty level: Easy]

For many years Charlotte has run a public house in a freehold building that she owns in London. Charlotte purchased the building new 15 years ago. She has opted to tax this building for VAT purposes.

On 31 December 2015 which was also the last day of her VAT accounting quarter, she sold the pub business, including the freehold building, to Edmund. During the two months ending on that date, the pub had been closed for renovations. Charlotte had originally intended to reopen the pub after the renovations but a sudden bereavement in the family caused her to change her plans.

The terms of the sale to Edmund were as follows:

	£
Value of the property	1,800,000
Goodwill	1,350,000
Chattels	72,000
Stock	225,000

Requirements

(a) State the conditions that must be met for the business transfer to be a transfer of a going concern for VAT purposes.

(b) Compute, giving your reasons, the amount of output VAT chargeable on Edmund in respect of the transfer.

See **Answer** at the end of this chapter.

Thus, if the property is less than ten years old at the time of the TOGC the exempt trader acquires the property as part of a TOGC and although he pays no input VAT he instead accepts responsibility for any future adjustments required under the capital goods scheme. If the property was previously used for taxable purposes and is now wholly used for exempt purposes the VAT clawed back by the annual capital goods scheme adjustments may be substantial.

However, the claw back of VAT may still be preferable to the payment of VAT on the purchase price if the option to tax had not been exercised. Also extra stamp duty land tax would have been payable on the purchase. In addition, the remainder of the capital goods scheme adjustment period will be shorter than a new adjustment period which would have arisen if the acquisition had not been part of a TOGC.

Worked example: Option to tax, TOGC and the capital goods scheme

Bray plc, a fully taxable company, constructs new business premises for £1.5m plus VAT on 1 July 2010. Bray plc uses the premises for 100% business use until 31 March 2013.

From 1 April 2013 Bray plc rents out 60% of the premises to an unconnected tenant. Bray plc decides not to opt to tax the building.

On 1 April 2015 Bray plc sells the premises (with the tenant still renting out 60% of the building) to a VAT registered property company, Dean plc, for £2m.

Dean plc also decides not to opt to tax the building and continues to rent the building to both the existing and some new tenants.

Both Bray plc and Dean plc prepare VAT returns to 31 March.

Requirement

Explain, with supporting calculations, the VAT implications of the property transactions.

Solution

At the time of acquisition of a new commercial property, Bray plc will have suffered input VAT of £262,500 (£1.5m × 17.5%). As the building is used wholly for taxable supplies it is fully recoverable. However, as the building cost at least £250,000 it will be subject to the capital goods scheme.

No capital goods scheme adjustments are required for the first three intervals ie March 2011, March 2012 or March 2013.

From 1 April 2013 part of the building is rented out as an exempt supply as no option to tax has been made. The interval to 31 March 2014 will therefore require a capital goods scheme adjustment:

£262,500/10 × (40% − 100%) = (£15,750)

£15,750 of the original input VAT recovered will have to be repaid to HMRC. The same adjustment will be required for the interval to 31 March 2015.

As the building is sold with a tenant in situ it will probably constitute a TOGC. As the commercial property is now more than three years old and no option to tax was made by Bray plc, no option to tax is required by Dean plc for it to be included within the TOGC ie the transfer is not subject to VAT.

As the transfer is part of a TOGC no adjustment on sale is required by Bray plc. However, Dean plc assumes responsibility for the remainder of the capital goods scheme adjustment period. As Dean plc is now using the building exclusively for exempt supplies (no option to tax has been made) an adjustment will be required for each of the remaining five intervals to 31 March 2020:

£262,500/10 × (0% − 100%) = (£26,250)

This will lead to a total input VAT recovery of £131,250 payable by Dean plc.

---

3 Overseas aspects of VAT

Section overview

- Zero rating applies to dispatches of goods to another EU state where the customer is VAT registered and certain other conditions are met.

- Other dispatches within the EU are subject to VAT in the state of origin.

- A VAT-registered trader must account for output tax on acquisitions made by him but he will also be able to recover input tax on the supply.

- Imports from outside the EU are usually liable to VAT on entry. This VAT may be recovered by a registered person.

- Exports to outside the EU are zero rated.

- VAT usually applies to supplies of services in the country of origin if the supply is to a non-business customer. If the customer is a relevant business person, VAT applies in the destination country instead and is charged using the reverse charge system. There are certain exceptions such as land related services and electronically supplied services.

- VAT on electronically supplied services by any overseas trader to a UK non-business customer is levied in the UK. For supplies to business customers VAT is normally levied in the destination country but may be levied where the services are used and enjoyed if either:

  - The place of supply would be the UK (because the supplier or the customer belongs in the UK) but the services are effectively used and enjoyed outside the EU – treated as supplied in the non-EU state.

  - The place of supply would be outside the EU (because the supplier or the customer belongs outside the EU), but the services are effectively used and enjoyed in the UK – treated as supplied in the UK.

The following points are important from your earlier studies:

- A sale of goods within the EU is called a dispatch. The purchase of goods within the EU is called an acquisition.

- A sale of goods to a country outside the EU is an export. The purchase of goods from a country outside the EU is an import.

- Zero rating applies to dispatches of goods to another EU state where the customer is VAT registered and certain other conditions are met.

- Other dispatches are subject to VAT in the member state of origin ie a dispatch from the UK is taxable at the appropriate UK rate.

- A VAT-registered trader must account for output tax, at the appropriate rate, on acquisitions made by him ie it is treated as if the trader has made a supply of the goods to himself. The output tax is then recoverable as input tax based on the taxable use of the acquisition. These self-supplies are also taken into account when determining whether the trader has exceeded the registration thresholds.

- Imports from outside the EU are liable to VAT on entry. The goods will be held at the port of arrival until the VAT is paid, ie it is not a self-supply unlike acquisitions from the EU. The VAT paid on entry becomes recoverable input VAT if the goods becomes stock or an asset of a taxable business.

- Exports to outside the EU are zero rated provided evidence that the goods have actually been exported is obtained.

3.1 Supplies of services

3.1.1 General provisions

The basic rule is that most services are supplied:

- Where the customer has established his business, if supplied to a relevant business person; and
- Otherwise where the supplier has established his business.

A 'relevant business person' is defined as:

- A taxable person within the scope of Article 9 of the Principal VAT Directive, or
- Registered for VAT in the UK, another Member State, or the Isle of Man.

A person is a taxable person within the scope of Article 9 of the Principal VAT Directive if he carries out any economic activity. Therefore supplies of services to any business customer, even if not registered for VAT, will be taxed where the customer is established.

Therefore, the UK supplier of a service to a non-business customer accounts for any output VAT due on the supply, regardless of whether the customer is inside the EU. The origin basis therefore applies to such supplies of services.

Where services are received by a UK VAT registered trader from another country (EU or non-EU) for the purposes of his business, under the basic rule above the supply is deemed to be made in the UK. VAT is charged in the UK under the reverse charge system. This changes the basis of the VAT charge from the origin system to the destination system and is called a tax shift.

The UK customer must account for VAT on the supply to him because he is treated as making the supply. This amount will also be his input tax for the supply. The effect is tax-neutral unless the trader is making some exempt supplies.

The actual supplier of the services will not be treated as making a VAT supply where the reverse charge rules apply.

There are some exceptions to the basic place of supply rule above. For example for land related services, the service is deemed to be supplied wherever the land is situated. There are also special rules for electronically supplied services.

3.1.2 EC Sales Lists (ESL)

Businesses need to file an ESL where they are supplying services to business customers in other EU countries where the place of supply is the customer's country and where the customer is required to account for VAT under the reverse charge procedure.

ESLs also apply to supplies of goods.

3.1.3 Time of supply rules

The supplier is required to report the supply of the service on an ESL at the same time as the customer is required to report the reverse charge on his VAT return.

For single supplies, the tax point is when the service is completed or when it is paid for if earlier.

For continuous supplies, the tax point is the end of each billing or payment period. Where the service is not subject to billing or payment periods, the tax point is 31 December each year unless a payment has already been made.

3.1.4 Electronic refund procedure for VAT incurred in other EU Member States

An electronic VAT refund procedure exists across the EU. The system requires UK businesses to submit claims for overseas VAT electronically on a standardised form to HMRC rather than direct to the Member State from which the refund is due.

3.2 VAT and e-commerce

E-commerce transactions fall into two categories:

- Physical goods ordered over the internet and delivered direct to business and private customers; or
- Services, including digitised products provided online (eg music downloads).

3.2.1 Physical goods

Existing rules ensure that tax arises in the country to which the goods are delivered.

Low Value Consignment Relief applies to exempt goods, which are physically imported into the UK from outside the EU, from VAT where the value of the goods is less than £15. This relief does not apply to imports from the Channel Islands under distance selling arrangements. This is to counter the tax-avoidance strategy that was being undertaken by online suppliers of goods such as DVDs and CDs, who had set up subsidiaries in Jersey and Guernsey to import low-value goods to the UK without paying VAT.

3.2.2 Services supplied via e-commerce

Non-business customers

The place of supply of services to non-business customers is normally where the supplier is established. However, the rules differ for electronically supplied services (e-services).

E-services supplied from anywhere in the world (ie EU or non-EU) to non-business customers in the EU (including the UK) are deemed to be supplied where the customer belongs. This ensures that UK consumers of e-services pay UK VAT no matter where the supplier of the services belongs.

Business customers

The place of supply of services to relevant business customers is normally where the customer is established. However, for e-services additional rules apply instead in the following two circumstances:

- If the place of supply would be the UK (because the supplier or the customer belongs in the UK) but the services are effectively used and enjoyed outside the EU – they are treated as supplied in the non-EU state.

- If the place of supply would be outside the EU (because the supplier or the customer belongs outside the EU), but the services are effectively used and enjoyed in the UK – they are treated as supplied in the UK.

For example,

- E-services by a business based in Italy to a UK business customer, but the services are actually used in Canada – Treated as supplied in Canada (where used) and there are therefore no UK VAT implications.

- E-services by a business based in Italy to a Canadian business customer, but the services are actually used in the UK – Treated as supplied in UK (where used). The UK registered business using the services must account for UK VAT using the reverse charge procedure.

The effect of the rules are that:

- Non-EU suppliers to private individuals in the EU must register and account for VAT in the EU;

- EU suppliers to private individuals in the another EU country must register and account for VAT in the second EU country (eg a supplier in France to a customer in UK must register in the UK);

- EU businesses do not have to charge VAT on supplies used and enjoyed outside the EU; and

- UK registered customers using/enjoying e-services in the UK must account for VAT using the reverse charge procedure.

A mechanism, known as a Mini-One Stop Shop (MOSS), gives both EU and non-EU businesses supplying e-services the option to register for VAT, and to make returns and payments with as little bureaucracy as possible. Such businesses can register for VAT electronically with one member state and make all returns and payments to that state. The VAT return has an entry for each member state. The receiving member then sends details to other relevant member states along with payment.

Worked example: E-commerce and place of supply

Triangle SpA, an Italian business supplied electronic services to Square Ltd, a UK company. Square Ltd's subsidiary company, Octagon GmbH, based in Germany actually uses the services.

Pear Ltd, a UK business, purchased electronically supplied services from a company based in Luxembourg. The actual services were used by Pear Ltd's subsidiary company based in Australia.

Steak GmbH, based in Germany, supplied electronic services to Pepper Inc, a US company. The services were used by Pepper Inc's UK subsidiary, Salt Ltd.

Laura, who lives in the UK, purchased electronic services from Apollo Inc, an American company, for her personal use.

Requirement

Explain the location of the place of supply for each of the above transactions and the UK VAT implications, if any.

Solution

The services supplied by Triangle SpA will be treated as supplied in the UK. Square Ltd will need to charge itself VAT under the reverse charge procedure. Although the services are not used in the UK, as they are used in the EU the additional rules for electronic services do not apply.

The services supplied by the Luxembourg company have been used in Australia. The place of supply will be where the supply was used ie Australia. There are no UK VAT implications.

The services supplied by Steak GmbH have been used in the UK and will therefore be treated as supplied in the UK. Salt Ltd must use the reverse charge procedure to account for input VAT on the supply.

Laura is a non-business customer who has purchased an electronic supply from an overseas supplier for use in the UK. This will be treated as a supply made in the UK and she will therefore be liable to UK VAT on the purchase.

Summary

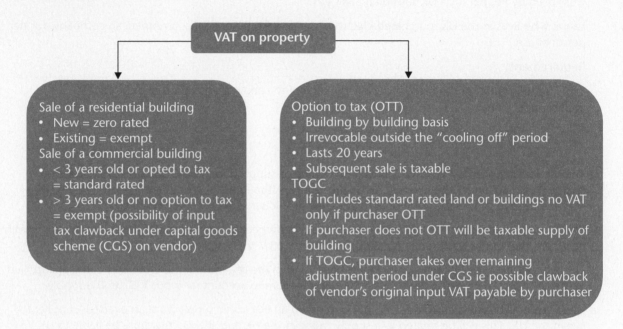

VAT on property

Sale of a residential building
- New = zero rated
- Existing = exempt

Sale of a commercial building
- < 3 years old or opted to tax = standard rated
- > 3 years old or no option to tax = exempt (possibility of input tax clawback under capital goods scheme (CGS) on vendor)

Option to tax (OTT)
- Building by building basis
- Irrevocable outside the "cooling off" period
- Lasts 20 years
- Subsequent sale is taxable

TOGC
- If includes standard rated land or buildings no VAT only if purchaser OTT
- If purchaser does not OTT will be taxable supply of building
- If TOGC, purchaser takes over remaining adjustment period under CGS ie possible clawback of vendor's original input VAT payable by purchaser

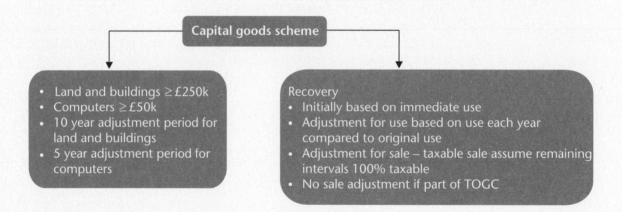

Capital goods scheme

- Land and buildings ≥ £250k
- Computers ≥ £50k
- 10 year adjustment period for land and buildings
- 5 year adjustment period for computers

Recovery
- Initially based on immediate use
- Adjustment for use based on use each year compared to original use
- Adjustment for sale – taxable sale assume remaining intervals 100% taxable
- No sale adjustment if part of TOGC

Transfer of business as going concern: no supply for VAT if:
- Whole of the business of the transferor is transferred as a going concern or part of the business capable of separate operation
- Assets used by transferee in the same kind of business as carried on by the transferor
- If transferor VAT registered, the transferee also VAT registered before or immediately after transfer
- No significant break in trade

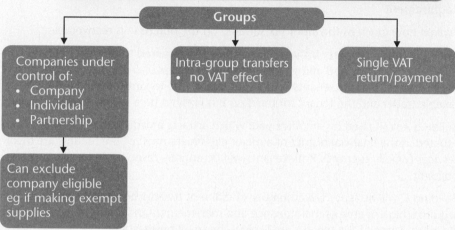

Groups

Companies under control of:
- Company
- Individual
- Partnership

Intra-group transfers
- no VAT effect

Single VAT return/payment

Can exclude company eligible eg if making exempt supplies

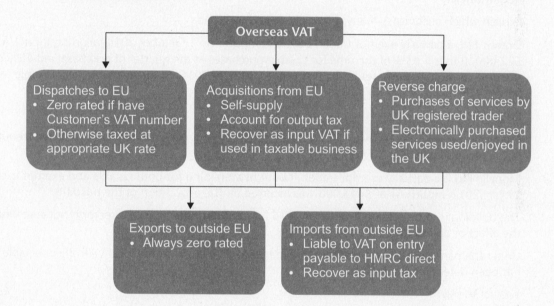

Overseas VAT

Dispatches to EU
- Zero rated if have Customer's VAT number
- Otherwise taxed at appropriate UK rate

Acquisitions from EU
- Self-supply
- Account for output tax
- Recover as input VAT if used in taxable business

Reverse charge
- Purchases of services by UK registered trader
- Electronically purchased services used/enjoyed in the UK

Exports to outside EU
- Always zero rated

Imports from outside EU
- Liable to VAT on entry payable to HMRC direct
- Recover as input tax

Self-test

Answer the following questions.

1   Table Ltd is a wholly exempt trader. On 1 January 2016 Table Ltd purchased a new freehold commercial property for £2.5m and immediately opted to tax the building. Table Ltd occupied the premises on 1 January 2016 for the purposes of its trade.

Requirement

Explain how much of the input tax suffered on the purchase is recoverable.

2   Chair plc runs a property business. It has recently acquired three new freehold commercial buildings (Buildings A, B and C) each costing in excess of £1m. It has decided to rent out two of the buildings to single tenants on 15 year leases. The tenant for building A is likely to be a wholly taxable trader and the tenant for building B is likely to be a wholly exempt trader.

Building A is situated on an office park which attracts a wide variety of tenants. Building B is situated in the financial district of a major city where most of the tenants are involved in financial services (wholly exempt). Both tenants will be entirely responsible for all costs associated with the building.

Building C will be rented to a number of different tenants on short term leases. It will therefore require a high degree of maintenance and management including redecoration costs, security and cleaning. Some of the tenants are likely to be small businesses.

Requirement

Explain which building(s), if any, Chair plc should opt to tax.

3   Drawer Ltd, a partially exempt trader, buys a computer on 1 October 2014 incurring input VAT of £22,000. It uses it 63% of the time for taxable purchases in the quarter of purchase and 60% of the time for taxable purposes in the first year to 30 April 2015. In the following year taxable use falls to 45%.

Requirement

Calculate the input tax recovery for the first interval to 30 April 2015 and the adjustment required in the second interval to 30 April 2016.

4   Monello Ltd is a partially exempt trader. It bought a building for both taxable and exempt use on 29 July 2012. Input VAT of £445,000 was incurred on the acquisition of the building.

The building is to be sold on 2 October 2016 for £2.286m; the finance director is not sure what the effect of opting to tax the sale would be.

Under the partial exemption method agreed by Monello Ltd with the local VAT office, taxable use has been determined as follows:

Year to 31 March	Rate
2013	67%
2014	75%
2015	70%
2016	55%
2017	88%

Requirement

Calculate the input tax recoverable each year under the capital goods scheme both with and without an option to tax being made.

5   Calcolo Ltd, a manufacturing company, has the following relevant financial information for the quarter to 31 December 2015:

Sales

	£
Sales in the UK (standard rated)	245,687
Sales in the UK (zero rated)	43,989
Sales in Italy (VAT registered customers)	68,144
	357,820

Purchases

	£
Raw materials	43,888
Distribution expenses	15,177
Accountancy services in UK	4,500
Accountancy services in Italy	6,999
Other expenses	56,853
	127,417

All the purchases are standard rated. All figures exclude VAT.

Requirement

Explain how the VAT on the sales to Italy and the accountancy services provided by the Italian supplier should be treated.

6   The freehold interest in Oggadoon House, a new commercial building, was purchased by Umbrella plc in April 2008 incurring a substantial amount of input VAT. In January 2009 it was transferred to a 75% subsidiary of Umbrella plc, Wellington Ltd.

The option to tax Oggadoon House was exercised at the time of its original purchase in April 2008 by Umbrella plc.

Wellington Ltd has decided to sell Oggadoon House to an unconnected third party in December 2016 for £3.25m.

Oggadoon House has been let to tenants since its acquisition under the terms of a short lease. No information has been obtained as to whether the tenants would remain in the property following the sale. However, under the terms of the lease, the tenants have the right to terminate the lease should the ownership of the freehold change.

Requirement

Explain the VAT implications of the above transactions. No supporting calculations are required.

Now, go back to the Learning objectives in the Introduction. If you are satisfied you have achieved these objectives, please tick them off.

Legislation

All references are to Value Added Tax Act 1994 *(VATA 1994)* unless otherwise stated

Option to tax land	Sch 10
Sale of new commercial building	Sch 9, Group 1
Capital goods scheme	SI 1995/2518 Regs 112-6
Transfer of business as a going concern	s.49
	SI 1995/1268 Reg 5
VAT groups	ss.43-43B
Value Added Tax Regulations	SI 1995/2518

HMRC manual references

Transfer of a Going Concern Manual (Found at www.hmrc.gov.uk/manuals/vtogcmanual/index.htm)

VTOGC2000 – What is the transfer of a going concern

VTOGC5000 – Transfers and VAT groups

VTOGC6000 – Land and property

Place of Supply of Services Manual (Found at www.hmrc.gov.uk/manuals/vatpossmanual/index.htm)

Not all of the VAT information available on the HMRC website has been organised into VAT manuals since the merger of the Inland Revenue and Customs & Excise to form HMRC.

Information about VAT is not available in the same format as that for direct taxes. This is because following the merger of the two departments, the former Customs & Excise pages have not yet been redesigned.

To find out more practical information about VAT, access the relevant section of the HMRC website through the main home page (www.hmrc.gov.uk/) and then following the link, or access it direct at

www.hmrc.gov.uk/vat/index.htm?_nfpb=true&_pageLabel=pageVAT_InfoGuides

A series of information and guides is available by clicking on the various links.

> This technical reference section is designed to assist you when you are working in the office. It should help you to know where to look for further information on the topics covered in this chapter.

Answer to Interactive question 1

The input VAT on the building is £350,000 (£2m × 17.5%) . The building cost at least £250,000 and is therefore within the scope of the capital goods scheme. Annual adjustments are required for 10 intervals.

From 1 July 2010 to 31 March 2016 the building is rented out as an exempt supply. Thus, initially, no input VAT can be recovered. The initial interval is to 31 March 2011. No adjustment is required for March 2012, March 2013, March 2014, March 2015 or March 2016 as taxable use is still 0%.

From 1 April 2016 onwards the rental has become a taxable supply and each year an additional amount of input VAT can therefore be recovered:

£350,000/10 × (100% – 0%) = £35,000

In total therefore 4 intervals of adjustments will be required totalling £140,000 (March 2017, March 2018, March 2019, March 2020).

Answer to Interactive question 2

(a) The business (or part of a business) that is being transferred must be capable of separate operation.

It must be capable of being immediately operated by the purchaser.

The business must be transferred as a going concern, therefore there must have been no significant break in trading. It is a question of fact whether the two months in this case is significant.

Edmund must use the assets in the same kind of business.

As Charlotte is a taxable person, Edmund must already be, or immediately become as a result of the transfer, a taxable person.

(b) The effect of a transfer of a going concern is that assets are mandatorily transferred without VAT being charged.

It is wrong to charge VAT in these circumstances, and can result in penalties, and the loss of the purported 'input VAT' by the purchaser.

In the case of a building that has been the subject of an option to tax, VAT will still be chargeable on it unless Edmund has also opted to tax it.

The sale of goodwill is taxable in principle, but will be subject to the TOGC rules if they apply.

Therefore: if no TOGC, all assets are chargeable: £3,447,000 at 20% = £689,400. Stamp duty land tax will be payable at 4% on the VAT inclusive value of the building ie a cost of £86,400.

If a TOGC and Edmund opts to tax, there will be no VAT chargeable to him. Stamp duty land tax will be payable at 4% on the value of the building ie a cost of £72,000.

If a TOGC and Edmund does not opt to tax, he will pay VAT on the sale of the building: £1.8m at 20% = £360,000. In addition the stamp duty land tax will be payable on the VAT inclusive price at 4% ie a cost of £86,400 (generating an additional cost of £14,400).

1   Opting to tax the building does not in itself make the input VAT on the purchase of the building recoverable. Opting to tax the building cannot make Table Ltd's supplies taxable. Therefore, as Table Ltd is using the building wholly to make exempt supplies, none of the input VAT can be recovered.

2   The purchase of a new freehold commercial building is a standard rated purchase and Chair plc has thus incurred a significant amount of input VAT which may or may not be recoverable depending on whether it opts to tax each building. The decision to opt to tax or not opt to tax can be made on a building by building basis. Once made, it applies to the whole building and after the cooling off period is irrevocable for 20 years. Consideration must therefore be given to both the short-term and long-term.

As the tenant for building A will be wholly taxable it will simply recover any input tax suffered on the rent if Chair plc decided to opt to tax the building. Opting to tax the building is unlikely to deter any future purchasers from buying the building given its location as it could attract taxable traders who could recover the input VAT on the purchase price. It will also enable the recovery of the considerable amount of input VAT suffered by Chair plc on the purchase.

Building B is to be rented by a wholly exempt trader who will consider any VAT on the rent to be an additional expense as it will not be recoverable. In addition, as future tenants are also likely to be exempt traders it may make the building harder to rent or the rent may have to be reduced to ensure the gross rent remains competitive with that of neighbouring buildings. Any future purchaser is also likely to be exempt and would be unable to recover the input VAT.

The effect of charging VAT on the rent if an option to tax is made for building B needs to be compared to the inability to recover the input VAT suffered on the purchase if the option to tax is not made.

As input VAT suffered by Chair plc on building C is likely to be ongoing and substantial this may make it financially viable to opt to tax the building even if some of the tenants are not VAT registered. This may make the building less attractive to some tenants or require Chair plc to reduce the rent. However, the additional recovery of substantial input VAT may make this worthwhile. It will also enable the recovery of the input VAT paid on the purchase price.

3   As the input VAT equates to a VAT inclusive purchase price of £132,000 the acquisition is within the scope of the capital goods scheme. For the first interval, the recovery (after the annual partial exemption adjustment) is:

£22,000 × 60% = £13,200.

For the second year, the capital goods scheme adjustment is:

£22,000/5 × (45% − 60%) = (£660) payable to HMRC.

4

Year	To	Adjustment calculation	Amount
1	March 2013	£445,000 × 67%	£298,150
2	March 2014	£445,000/10 × (75% − 67%)	£3,560
3	March 2015	£445,000/10 × (70% − 67%)	£1,335
4	March 2016	£445,000/10 × (55% − 67%)	(£5,340)
5 use	March 2017	£445,000/10 × (88% − 67%)	£9,345
5 sale	Opt	£445,000/10 × (100% − 67%) × 5	£73,425
	Do not opt	£445,000/10 × (0% − 67%) × 5	(£149,075)

The total difference between opting to tax and not opting to tax is £222,500 or 5/10 × £445,000. However the output tax charge on a sale price of £2.286m is £457,200 (or £2.286m × 1/6 = £381,000 if the purchaser is exempt and will not accept the addition of VAT to the purchase price). The loss of input tax may be less of a problem than the charging of output tax.

5   The supply of goods to the Italian VAT registered customers is zero rated (assuming the other conditions have been satisfied).

The receipt of accountancy services from Italy is treated as supplied in the UK (where the business customer is established). Calcolo Ltd must account for output VAT on the supply under the reverse charge system. This amount will also be the company's input tax for the supply. The effect is tax-neutral as Calcolo Ltd is not making any exempt supplies.

6   **Oggadoon House**

The original VAT at the time of acquisition by Umbrella plc would have been reclaimed in full as the option to tax converted the rental business from an exempt supply into a taxable supply.

The VAT treatment at the time of the transfer to Wellington Ltd would depend on whether the two companies were part of a VAT group:

- If they were part of a VAT group the transfer would be disregarded for VAT purposes and the option to tax would continue to apply.

- If they were not part of a VAT group then the transfer would be chargeable to VAT as a disposal of a taxable building (still less than three years old). The OTT would not have transferred to Wellington Ltd.

    However, as the transfer appears to have been a transfer of a business it would have qualified as a TOGC and no VAT would have been charged provided Wellington Ltd also opted to tax the building.

The VAT implications of the subsequent disposal outside of the group would depend upon whether an option to tax was in force at that time. It would be a taxable supply if either:

- Umbrella plc and Wellington Ltd were part of a VAT group in January 2008 as the option to tax would continue to apply at the time of its sale; or

- Umbrella plc and Wellington Ltd were not part of a VAT group in January 2008 but Wellington Ltd had subsequently opted to tax the building prior to its disposal.

Otherwise it would be an exempt supply as the building is more than three years old by the time of its sale. However, this would lead to a claw back of input VAT under the capital goods scheme as it is still less than 10 years since its acquisition by the vendor.

The sale could avoid being treated as a taxable supply if it qualified as a TOGC and the purchaser opted to tax the building. No VAT would then be charged.

As part of a TOGC, the purchaser would take over the remainder of the capital goods scheme adjustment period and potentially be liable to repay some of the input VAT on the original purchase recovered by the vendor. This would only apply if the purchaser used the building for less than 100% taxable use.

However, if the tenants were to terminate their lease prior to, or as a result of a sale to a new owner, then it would no longer qualify as a TOGC.

If it is a taxable supply, the potential recoverability of the input tax suffered by the purchaser may affect the price negotiations. In addition, stamp duty land tax will be payable on the VAT at 4% which may also impact the price negotiations as this increases the purchase price (as it is never recoverable) by 0.8% (20% × 4%).

CHAPTER 19

Stamp taxes

Introduction

Examination context

Topic List

Introduction

Learning objectives

Tick off

- Determine, explain and calculate the liability for individuals and corporate entities to stamp taxes ☐

- Explain and evaluate the tax implications of group structures ☐

- Explain and evaluate the tax implications of business transformations and change ☐

- Explain and calculate the tax implications involved in the cessation of trade ☐

- Evaluate and advise on tax strategies to meet business objectives ☐

- Evaluate and advise on alternative tax strategies relating to corporate transformations ☐

Specific syllabus references for this chapter are 1f, 1j, 1l, 1m, 2b and 2c.

Syllabus links

Both stamp duty and stamp duty land tax are likely to be relevant in any corporate transformation. The impact of stamp duty land tax on incorporation can be significant. Stamp duty land tax also interacts with the calculation of VAT due.

Examination context

Similarly to VAT, stamp taxes add significant sums of money to the cost of a transaction and must not be overlooked. For tax professionals the interaction of VAT and stamp taxes on property can become tax planning nightmares if not correctly dealt with.

In the examination candidates may be required to:

- Advise on the correct treatment of and calculate the tax liabilities arising as a result of the acquisition, intra-group transfer, or disposal of property

- Advise on the correct treatment of and calculate the tax liabilities arising as a result of the acquisition, intra-group transfer, or disposal of shares

Worked example: Transfer between group companies

Sparrow Ltd owns 88% of the ordinary share capital of Vulture Ltd, which in turn owns 86% of the ordinary share capital of Cuckoo Ltd.

Shares are transferred from Sparrow Ltd to Cuckoo Ltd under an instrument executed on 1 November 2016.

Requirement

Is the transfer liable to stamp duty?

Solution

Stamp duty is not payable as the transaction qualifies for relief. Both Sparrow Ltd and Cuckoo Ltd are part of a group. Sparrow Ltd owns at least 75% (88% × 86% = 75.7%) indirectly in Cuckoo Ltd.

1.6 Administration of stamp duty

Stamp duty is administered by HMRC Stamp Taxes.

The stock transfer form must be presented to HMRC within 30 days of execution and the duty paid at that time.

Interest may be charged if the duty is paid late. Interest runs from the end of the 30-day period to the day before the duty is paid. Interest is rounded down to the nearest multiple of £5 and is not charged if the amount is less than £25.

In addition, a penalty may be imposed if the transfer is presented late for stamping.

If the transfer is presented up to one year late, the maximum penalty is the lower of: [Hp 249]

- £300; and
- The amount of the unpaid duty.

If the transfer is presented more than one year late, the maximum penalty is the greater of:

- £300; and
- The amount of the unpaid duty.

The penalty can be reduced, for example if there is a reasonable excuse for the delay.

There are no plans to bring stamp duty within the common penalty regime for the late filing and late payment of tax introduced by Finance Act 2009.

2 Stamp duty reserve tax

Section overview

- Stamp duty reserve tax (SDRT) is payable at 0.5% on the paperless electronic transfer of shares and securities.

- There are few direct exemptions from SDRT but if a transaction is exempt from stamp duty then normally no stamp duty reserve tax is payable.

- SDRT is payable on the seventh day of the month following the month of sale if not made through CREST.

- SDRT is payable 14 days after the trade date if via CREST.

2.1 Charge to stamp duty reserve tax

Stamp duty depends on there being a document which can be stamped. It is not able to cope with paperless transactions. For that reason, Stamp Duty Reserve Tax (SDRT) was introduced in 1986. SDRT is now the largest source of stamp duty revenue on share transfers. SDRT is payable on the paperless ie electronic transfer of shares and securities. Most such transfers are executed via the CREST system.

The principal charge to SDRT is on agreements to transfer 'chargeable securities' (most stocks and shares) for consideration in money or money's worth. SDRT applies instead of stamp duty where the transfer is not completed by an instrument of transfer (ie by a stock transfer form stamped with ad valorem duty).

The rate of duty is 0.5% of the consideration. Unlike stamp duty, there is no rounding. [Hp 253]

2.2 Exemptions from stamp duty reserve tax

If there is no consideration in money or money's worth there is usually no SDRT charge.

2.3 Cancellation of stamp duty reserve tax

To prevent a double charge to both stamp duty and SDRT, any SDRT paid on an agreement to transfer shares will be repaid if the transaction is subsequently completed by a stamped stock transfer form. Normally, if the subsequent stock transfer form is exempt from stamp duty it will also be exempt from SDRT and any SDRT paid will still be repaid.

2.4 Exemptions

Securities admitted to trading on a recognised growth market (eg AIM) but not listed on that or any other market are exempt from SDRT.

In addition, where a duly stamped transfer document can be produced which states that the transfer is free from stamp duty it will lead to the cancellation of the stamp duty reserve tax. Thus an intra group transfer qualifying for stamp duty relief will also be exempt from SDRT.

2.5 Administration of stamp duty reserve tax

Stamp duty reserve tax is administered by HMRC Stamp Taxes but is actually collected automatically via stock brokers.

Stamp Duty Reserve Tax has to be reported by and is payable on the seventh day of the month following the month in which the agreement was made or became unconditional. If, however, the payment is capable of being made via CREST it should be paid over by 14 calendar days after the trade date.

3 Stamp duty land tax

Section overview

- Stamp duty land tax (SDLT) is payable on the transfer of land and buildings at various rates depending on the title transferred (freehold or leasehold) and the use to which the land is put.

- Where there is chargeable consideration, SDLT is charged as a percentage of the consideration.

- The rate of SDLT depends on whether the land is residential or non-residential.

- There is also a charge to SDLT on a grant of a lease based on the Net Present Value of the rents receivable over the term of the lease.

- SDLT is not charged where the transfer is made between members of a 75% group for bona fide commercial reasons.

- A land transaction form must usually be delivered to HMRC within 30 days of the transaction and the SDLT paid at that time.

- Interest is payable on late paid SDLT.

- There are penalties for late delivery of a land transaction form.

3.1 Charge to SDLT

Stamp duty land tax (SDLT) is chargeable on land transactions. Examples include the transfer of freehold land, the assignment of a lease and the grant of a lease.

Where a land transaction is made for chargeable consideration (payment in money or money's worth), there is a charge to SDLT based on the amount of that consideration. It is based on the VAT inclusive amount.

SDLT is payable by the purchaser.

The rate of SDLT depends on whether the land is used for residential purposes or non-residential purposes. [Hp243]

Stamp duty land tax on the purchase price, lease premium or transfer value is calculated as a percentage of chargeable consideration according to the following table:

%	Residential	%	Non-residential
0	£Nil – £125,000	0	£Nil – £150,000[2]
2[1]	£125,001 – £250,000	1	£150,001 – £250,000
5[1]	£250,001 – £925,000	3	£250,001 – £500,000
10[1]	£925,001 – £1,500,000	4	£500,001 or more
12[1]	£1,500,001 and over		

Notes:

1 These rates and thresholds apply from 4 December 2014. Prior to this the rates and limits were as for non-residential property, except that the first threshold was £125,000 (rather than £150,000) and additional rates of 5% and 7% applied to residential property in excess of £1m and £2m respectively.

2 For non-residential property, where the transaction involves a grant of a lease, the zero rate band is not available if the annual rent exceeds £1,000.

For non-residential property, once the rate of SDLT has been determined, the rate then applies to the whole of the consideration, not just the amount over the relevant threshold.

For residential property, from 4 December 2014, SDLT applies to consideration at the relevant rate for each threshold. Prior to this date. SDLT was calculated in the same way as for non-residential property.

For leases, the lease premium is charged under the normal rules as if the lease premium were the chargeable consideration. However, if the rent is £1,000 pa or more and the land is non-residential property, the 0% rate is not available and the whole of the premium will be chargeable at 1% or higher.

The threshold for notification of non-leasehold transactions is £40,000.

There is relief for purchasers of residential property who acquire more than one dwelling via linked transactions. Where the relief is claimed, the rate of SDLT on the consideration attributable to the dwellings is determined not by the aggregate consideration but instead is determined by the mean consideration (ie by the aggregate consideration divided by the number of dwellings), subject to a minimum rate of 1% of the total consideration.

Worked example: SDLT on sale of freehold land

Harold sells his house to Lily for £375,000 on 10 April 2015.

Requirements

(i) Compute the SDLT payable by Lily.
(ii) Compute the SDLT payable if Lily had disposed of a non-residential property for £375,000.

Solution

(i) SDLT is calculated as follows:

	£
£125,000 × 0%	0
(£250,000 – £125,000) × 2%	2,500
(£375,000 – £250,000) × 5%	6,250
SDLT payable is	8,750

(ii) SDLT would have been £375,000 × 3% = £11,250.

Interactive question: SDLT on lease premium   [Difficulty level: Easy]

G plc is granted a lease of a factory by T plc. The lease is for seven years. The premium payable by G plc is £45,000 and the annual rent is £3,000.

Requirement

Compute the SDLT payable by G plc in respect of the premium.

See **Answer** at the end of this chapter.

3.2 Lease rentals

On the grant of a lease, in addition to any SDLT payable on the premium (using SDLT table in Section 3.1) SDLT is payable on the rental. The rental charge is based on the net present value of the rent payable to the landlord over the term of the lease. This is the total rent payable, discounted by 3.5% each year.

For examination purposes, you may take the NPV to be the total rents payable over the term of the lease, ie ignore discounting.

The rate of SDLT payable on the NPV of the rent is charged according to the following table. [Hp245]

%	Residential	Non-residential
0	Up to £125,000	Up to £150,000
1	Excess over £125,000	Excess over £150,000

Note that the thresholds for lease premiums and lease rentals may work differently. For lease premiums on non-residential property the whole of the premium is charged if it is above the relevant threshold. For lease rentals (residential and non- residential property) only the excess over the threshold is chargeable at 1%.

Worked example: SDLT on rental

Donald is granted a 25-year lease of a factory by Simon on 1 August 2015. He pays an annual rental of £9,000 per year for the term of the lease.

Requirement

Compute the SDLT payable by Donald.

Solution

	£
Rental payable over term of lease	
£9,000 × 25	225,000
Less non-residential threshold	(150,000)
Amount chargeable	75,000
SDLT £75,000 × 1%	£750

Note the difference between this calculation (on the excess consideration over the threshold) and the main SDLT calculation (on the whole consideration) for non-residential property.

3.3 Exemptions from SDLT

There are a number of exemptions from SDLT including transfers:

- For no chargeable consideration (eg gifts)
- On divorce
- Effecting a variation of a will

In these cases, no land transaction form needs to be submitted to HMRC.

If land is transferred to a company which is connected with the transferor in exchange for shares, the transaction is not exempt. It is deemed to be made for chargeable consideration at least equal to the market value of the land. This situation could occur on the incorporation of a business.

Note that where responsibility for a debt is assumed by the purchaser, the value of the debt is treated as consideration and not an outright gift eg an intra spouse transfer where the property transferred is subject to a mortgage.

3.3.1 Group relief

An exemption from SDLT also applies on a transfer of land between members of a group of companies (75% ownership directly or indirectly, and 75% right to profits and right to 75% of assets on winding up) where:

- One company is the parent company of another company; or
- Both companies have a common parent company.

Relief will be denied where at the time of the transfer arrangements exist for the two companies to cease to be members of the same group. Relief will also be denied where the transaction is not for bona fide commercial reasons or if the transaction forms part of arrangements of which the main purpose is tax avoidance.

SDLT will be charged retrospectively based on market value at the date of transfer if the transferee company leaves the group within three years whilst still owning the land transferred. This will be an issue where property is transferred as part of a hive down and the new company leaves the group within three years.

A land transaction form must be submitted in the usual way where there is a group transfer.

3.4 Higher rate for transfers to companies

Where an interest in a single dwelling is sold for an amount in excess of the 'higher threshold interest' the rate of SDLT is 15% (rather than the usual 7%) if the buyer is:

- A company;
- A partnership where at least one partner is a company; or
- A collective investment scheme.

The 'higher threshold interest' is £500,000 (£2m prior to 20 March 2014).

This measure is designed to combat SDLT tax avoidance where increasingly 'expensive' properties were being transferred to companies, so that after a one-off charge to SDLT further transfers only attracted stamp duty at a rate of 0.5%. The 15% rate does not apply where a property developer acquires the dwelling solely for the purpose of developing and reselling the land.

Where a residential property has been transferred to a company, partnership or collective investment scheme and the 15% rate of stamp duty has applied, the Annual Tax on Enveloped Dwellings, and related CGT charge, will often apply. These are explained at the end of this chapter.

4 Stamp duty on incorporation or liquidation

Section overview

- On incorporation, the company is liable to pay SDLT on any land or buildings transferred to it. However, the sole trader is not liable to pay stamp duty on an issue of new shares received.

- If land or buildings are transferred to the shareholders as part of a liquidation, SDLT is not payable by the shareholder providing no consideration is given.

4.1 Incorporation

For further details on the taxation implications of incorporation see Chapter 22.

The stamp duty costs of incorporation cannot be overlooked. When a business is incorporated, its assets are sold to the newly formed company.

The new company must therefore pay SDLT (at up to 4%) on the value of any commercial land or buildings included in the sale.

The percentage used will be based on the total value of any land transferred eg if five separate buildings are transferred each worth £200,000 the total value is £1m and therefore 4% SDLT applies.

Ownership of the land or buildings may be retained by the individual personally to avoid payment of the SDLT but this would then prevent the application of s.162 TCGA 1992 incorporation relief. However, gift relief under s.165 TCGA 1992 could be claimed instead.

If the transfer qualifies as a transfer of a going concern (TOGC) it will not be liable to VAT and the SDLT will be calculated only on the actual value of the land transferred. If the transfer does not qualify as a TOGC, then SDLT will be payable on the VAT inclusive value of the land (see Chapter 20).

When the sole trader receives shares in exchange for the assets transferred to the company, no stamp duty will be payable assuming the shares are a new issue of shares. Stamp duty is only payable on the transfer of existing shares.

4.2 Liquidation

For further details on the taxation implications of liquidations see Chapter 17.

SDLT may be payable on any land transferred to the shareholders, if any consideration is given. If the land is simply distributed to the shareholders under the liquidation, no SDLT will be payable.

The shares will then be cancelled by the company and no stamp duty is payable.

5 High value properties

Section overview

- This is anti-avoidance legislation, reflecting the fact that SDLT was being avoided by transferring expensive residential properties to companies so that later transfers only attracted 0.5% stamp duty rather than higher rate SDLT.

- The Annual Tax on Enveloped Dwellings (ATED) applies an annual charge based on the value of the property, to dwellings worth more than £2 million.

- Where ATED applies, any disposal of the property is subject to CGT. The special CGT charge only applies to the gain since 5 April 2013 (unless a non-rebasing election is made).

5.1 Background

The Annual Tax on Enveloped Dwellings (ATED) and the related CGT charge were introduced by FA 2013 because a significant number of residential properties had been transferred to companies in order to avoid SDLT on their later sale. Both UK resident and non-UK resident companies (as well as collective investment schemes and certain partnerships) are potentially within the scope of the rules if they own an interest in a dwelling in the UK worth more than £1 million (previously £2 million).

The 15% stamp duty charge (see above) was intended to reduce the number of future transfers of residential property to companies. However, ATED and the related CGT charge apply to both newly transferred properties, and properties which have been owned by companies for a number of years.

5.2 Annual Tax on Enveloped Dwellings (ATED)

ATED is charged from 1 April 2013, for years which run from 1 April to 31 March.

5.2.1 Scope

ATED applies to: [Hp139]

- Owners of interests in an individual dwelling worth more than £1 million, where

- The owner is a company, collective investment scheme, or partnership where at least one of the partners is a company or collective investment scheme.

5.2.2 Valuation

The value of the interest in the property which is taken into account is generally its market value at the later of 1 April 2012 and the date on which the owner acquired the interest. For newly built or converted properties, it is the value at the earlier of the date when the property is entered onto the Council Tax valuation lists and the date on which it is first occupied.

The 1 April 2012 values will be revalued every five years. The first revaluation for properties which have not been sold in the interim will therefore be on 1 April 2017, with the new valuation to be inserted onto the return for the period beginning on 1 April 2018.

Property values must be self-assessed. HMRC will confirm that a property has been placed in the appropriate charging band if the taxpayer applies for a pre-banding check. This will only apply where taxpayers believe that the valuation falls within 10% of one of the banding thresholds.

5.2.3 Amount of charge

The annual charge is as follows: [Hp139]

Property value	Annual charge 2015/16	Annual charge 2014/15
Up to £1,000,000	N/A	N/A
£1,000,001 – £2,000,000	£7,000	N/A
£2,000,001 – £5,000,000	£23,350	£15,400
£5,000,001 – £10,000,000	£54,450	£35,900
£10,000,001 – £20,000,000	£109,050	£71,850
£20,000,001 or more	£218,200	£143,750

The threshold is to be reduced further to £500,000 from 1 April 2016.

Where a property is acquired or sold part way through the year, the charge is pro-rated based on the number of days when it is owned.

5.2.4 Reliefs

There are a number of reliefs which eliminate the ATED charge. These include reliefs for:

- Properties exploited as part of a property rental business.

- Property developers and traders.

- Heritage properties which are open to the public as part of a trade for at least 28 days each year.

- Certain farmhouses.

- Properties held for charitable purposes.

- Unoccupied properties where steps are being taken to sell, demolish or convert them without undue delay.

Worked example: ATED

Jayhome Ltd owns two properties, one in London and one in Manchester. The freehold of the Manchester property would be worth £2,100,000 but Jayhome Ltd only owns a twenty year lease worth £800,000. The freehold is owned by an unrelated property investment company.

The London property was bought in February 2011 for £4,300,000. Its value on 1 April 2012 was estimated at £4,500,000. It was rented out as part of a property rental business from the time of its acquisition until 31 December 2015. Since that time, the property has been lived in by Jake Hughes, the sole shareholder of Jayhome Ltd.

Requirement

Determine the ATED payable by Jayhome Ltd for the year to 31 March 2016.

Solution

There is no charge in relation to the Manchester property. Although the freehold is worth more than £1 million, the interest owned by the company is worth less than that. If Jayhome Ltd had been connected with the company owning the freehold it might have been necessary to consider the combined value of the interests, but as they are not connected this is not relevant.

The charge for the London property will be based on its market value at 1 April 2012, so the full annual charge would be £23,350. However, as an exemption applies for the period from 1 April to 31 December 2015, the charge will be reduced to 3/12 × £23,350 = £5,838.

5.2.5 ATED administration

In general an ATED return has to be completed and returned, and the tax paid, within 30 days of the beginning of the chargeable year. The return for the year from 1 April 2016 to 31 March 2017 must therefore be submitted by 30 April 2016, and the tax payment made by the same date.

If you acquire an ATED dwelling part way through the chargeable year, the return and tax are due 30 days after the date of purchase (90 days where the dwelling is newly built). If you dispose of an interest part-way through a chargeable year, or an exemption starts to apply, an amended return must be submitted before a refund can be claimed.

From the chargeable period beginning on 1 April 2015, a 'relief declaration return' can be submitted instead of a normal ATED return where a relief (see Section 5.2.4) is available to eliminate the ATED charge. The return is much less detailed than the normal ATED return, and is intended to reduce the administrative burden where there is no charge payable. This is particularly important as the ATED threshold is falling. For the first year of implementation the 'relief declaration return' filing deadline is extended to 1 October 2015 , with the 30 April deadline for future years. Prior to this period a normal ATED return had to be submitted even where there was no ATED payable as a result of the exemptions.

Penalties apply to:

- Errors in returns;
- Late filing of returns; and
- Late payment of ATED (in addition to interest).

The penalties are based on the same rules as those which apply for most other taxes. Penalties of between 30% and 100% of the tax due can apply for late filing and incorrect returns, depending on whether or not the failure was deliberate and whether it was concealed. Penalties for late paid tax are 5% of the tax at each of 30 days after the payment was due, and five months and 30 days after the payment was due, and eleven months and 30 days after the payment was due.

5.3 CGT charge on high value properties

5.3.1 Overview

Where the owner of a property is subject to a charge to ATED, a disposal of the property on or after 6 April 2013 for consideration of at least £1 million (£2 million before 1 April 2015) will also be subject to capital gains tax. The limit is reduced further to £500,000 from 1 April 2016.

This applies even if the owner is a non-UK resident company (which would normally not be within the charge to either capital gains tax or corporation tax on its chargeable gains). In the case of a UK resident company, it may be necessary to split the chargeable gain between the part which is subject to corporation tax in the normal way, and the part which is subject to the CGT charge.

5.3.2 Calculation

The charge is calculated as follows:

- The starting point is a normal capital gains tax computation, of proceeds less allowable cost. Because it is a capital gains tax calculation not a corporation tax one, there is no indexation allowance.

- For properties which are within the ATED rules from 6 April 2013, the allowable cost is generally the market value on 5 April 2013 because gains accruing before that date are not within these rules. For later acquisitions, the normal capital gains tax rules apply to determine the deductible cost.

- CGT is charged at the rate of 28%, with no annual exempt amount.

- Where the consideration is only marginally more than £1 million the amount of the gain falling within these rules is capped at 5/3 × (taxable consideration – £1,000,000).

- Losses arising on enveloped dwellings can only be offset against gains on enveloped dwellings in the same tax year or later ones (as with normal capital losses, no carry back of losses is allowed). Capital losses on other assets cannot be offset against gains on enveloped dwellings.

Where a property is not within the ATED rules for the whole of the ownership period since 5 April 2013, the amount which is taxed under these provisions is determined by pro-rating the gain on a time basis.

The taxpayer can elect for the 5 April 2013 rebasing to market value not to be used in computing the gain. Where an election is made, the gain is computed over the full period of ownership and then pro-rated on a time basis to determine the amount attributable to the period during which the ATED rules applied.

Worked example: CGT charge on high value properties

Howard Ltd is a company incorporated and resident in Jersey. Its only asset is the freehold of a house in Hampshire, which it purchased on 1 August 1994 for £700,000. On 3 March 2016 it sells the house for £5,870,000. A surveyor has confirmed that the market value of the house on 5 April 2013 was £5,500,000.

The company's interest in the house has been within the ATED rules since 5 April 2013.

Requirement

Compute the capital gains tax payable by Howard Ltd, and explain whether the company should elect to disapply the 5 April 2013 rebasing.

Solution

As the interest has been within the charge to ATED for the whole of the period since 5 April 2013, if no election is made the full amount of the gain, computed using the 5 April 2013 market value as cost, will be subject to CGT rule for high value properties.

	£
Proceeds	5,870,000
Allowable cost (MV at 5 April 2013)	(5,500,000)
Taxable gain	370,000
CGT £370,000 × 28%	£103,600

If the election to disregard rebasing is applied, the gain over the whole period of ownership is calculated and then pro-rated on a time basis.

	£
Proceeds	5,870,000
Allowable cost	(950,000)
Taxable gain	4,920,000
Prorated (2 years 11 months)/(21 years 7 months) = 35/259 × £4,920,000	£664,865
CGT £664,865 × 28% =	£186,162

The election therefore results in a high CGT charge, so should not be made

---

Where a UK resident company owns a property which is within the ATED rules, the gain may need to be split between the ATED element and the amount which is subject to corporation tax in the normal way. Where this is the case, the ATED element is computed in the normal way. The amount subject to corporation tax is computed as follows:

- The pre-5 April 2013 chargeable gain is calculated in the normal way (including indexation allowance), assuming a disposal on 5 April 2013 at the property's then market value.

- If any amount of the post-5 April 2013 gain, as computed under the ATED rules, is not subject to a CGT charge (eg because an exemption applied for part of the post-5 April 2013 period). This is adjusted for indexation allowance and added to the pre-5 April 2013 chargeable gain.

Worked example: CGT charge on high value properties, interaction with corporation tax

MarkOne Ltd is a UK resident company, which has acquired a house in London for £1,760,000 in March 2002. On 21 July 2016 it sells the house for £7,800,000. The market value of the house on 5 April 2013 was £7,700,000.

The interest in the house has been subject to an ATED charge from 1 April 2013 to 21 July 2016.

Requirement

Compute the capital gains tax and corporation tax payable by MarkOne Ltd on the disposal of the house.

Assume no election is made to disapply the 5 April 2013 rebasing, that FA 2015 tax rates and allowances continue to apply.

Solution

The CGT charge is:

	£
Proceeds	7,800,000
Allowable cost (MV at 5 April 2013)	(7,700,000)
Taxable gain	100,000
CGT £100,000 × 28%	£28,000

Because the full amount of the post-5 April 2013 gain is subject to CGT, the amount subject to corporation tax will be limited to the pre-5 April 2013 gain.

	£
Proceeds (MV at 5 April 2013)	7,700,000
Less: allowable cost	(1,760,000)
indexation (249.5 – 174.5)/174.5) = 0.430 × £1,760,000	(756,800)
Gain subject to corporation tax	5,183,200
CGT £5,183,200 × 20%	£1,036,640

5.3.3 Administration

For administrative purposes, the capital gains tax charge on companies etc owning high value properties is subject to the normal capital gains tax rules. The charge is on a tax year basis. The return must be submitted and payment made by 31 January following the end of the tax year (ie by 31 January 2017 for 2015/16).

Summary

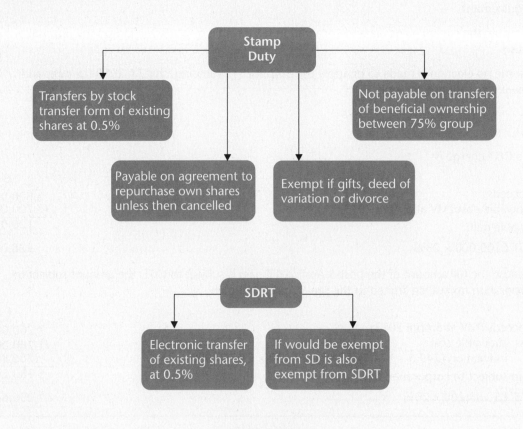

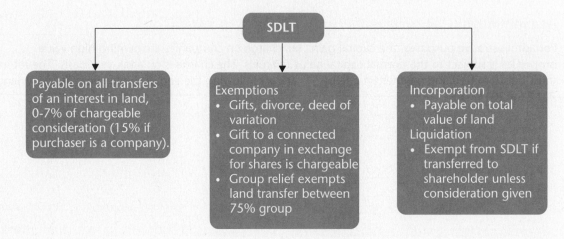

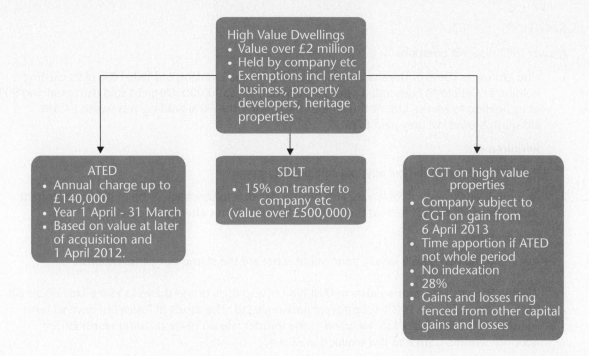

High Value Dwellings
- Value over £2 million
- Held by company etc
- Exemptions incl rental business, property developers, heritage properties

ATED
- Annual charge up to £140,000
- Year 1 April - 31 March
- Based on value at later of acquisition and 1 April 2012.

SDLT
- 15% on transfer to company etc (value over £500,000)

CGT on high value properties
- Company subject to CGT on gain from 6 April 2013
- Time apportion if ATED not whole period
- No indexation
- 28%
- Gains and losses ring fenced from other capital gains and losses

Self-test

Answer the following questions.

1   Dog Ltd owns 100% of the shares in Cat Ltd and Mouse Ltd. Dog Ltd sells 10% of its existing holding in Cat Ltd to Edmund, a private individual, for £500,000. Dog Ltd sold the remaining 90% of its holding to Mouse Ltd. At the time of the transfer the 90% holding was worth £4.5m although Mouse Ltd only paid £2m.

   Requirement

   Calculate the stamp duty, if any, payable on the disposals.

2   As a result of excess cash balances, Fish plc has decided to buy back some of its shares from its shareholders. It intends to hold the shares as treasury shares after the repurchase.

   Requirement

   Assuming the purchase is legally permissible, what are the stamp duty implications?

3   Whale plc owns 78% of the shares in Dolphin Ltd and 85% of the shares in Plaice Ltd. Whale plc has just formed a new 100% subsidiary, Kilmarnock Ltd. The assets of Plaice Ltd have all been transferred to Kilmarnock Ltd. Included in the transfer was an office building worth £2.5m, goodwill worth £1.5m and stock valued at £0.4m.

   Requirement

   Explain the stamp duty land tax implications of the transfer of assets.

4   **Hawks Ltd and Huxley House**

   Leopard Ltd is considering the following transactions, both of which would occur on 1 February 2016.

   (1) The purchase of existing shares in Hawks Ltd, a small UK trading company, for £53,000. Leopard Ltd would purchase 5% of the shares in this company, the remainder being held by individuals.

   (2) Entering into a five year lease on Huxley House. Leopard Ltd would use Huxley House as office premises. The terms of the lease involve Leopard Ltd paying a premium of £72,500 on 1 February 2016 and rent of £29,600 pa, payable quarterly in advance. The landlord, Hepburn Ltd, has owned Huxley House for many years and also prepares accounts to 31 January each year.

   Requirements

   Describe the corporation tax and any stamp taxes consequences of the proposed transactions, using calculations to illustrate your answer.

5   Charlotte has decided to incorporate her business and will thus transfer ownership of the following assets to the newly formed company. In exchange Charlotte will receive 1,000 new shares issued at par £1.

	£
Freehold office building	180,000
Freehold warehouse	400,000
Goodwill	333,450
Current assets:	
Stock	35,000
Cash	24,000
Debtors	12,000
Fixtures and fittings	98,341
Total	1,082,791

   Requirement

   Calculate the stamp duty and stamp duty land tax payable on incorporation.

6   Pigsty Properties Ltd bought a house in the Cotswolds for £1,050,000 on 1 March 2016. The value of the house on 1 April 2012 was £850,000.

On 1 June 2017 the house is sold to an unrelated third party for £1,150,000.

Requirement

Calculate any ATED charges due, and any tax charges due on the disposal of the house. You should assume FA2015 rates and allowances continue unchanged in future years.

Now, go back to the Learning objectives in the Introduction. If you are satisfied you have achieved these objectives, please tick them off.

Technical reference

Legislation

Stamp Duty

Ad valorem duty on shares	Sch 13 para 3 Finance Act 1999
Exempt Instruments Regulations	SI 1987/516
Transfers between group companies	s.42 FA 1930
Exemption for transfer of assets in consideration of shareholder rights in a liquidation if shareholder assumes no liabilities of liquidating company	SI 1987/516
Interest on late stamping	s.15A Stamp Act 1891
Penalties on late stamping	s.15B Stamp Act 1891

Stamp Duty Reserve Tax

References are to Finance Act 1986 (*FA1986*)

The principal charge	s.87
Exceptions	s.90
Repayment or cancellation of tax	s.92
Definition of chargeable securities	s.99

Stamp Duty Land Tax

References are to Finance Act 2003 (*FA 2003*) unless otherwise stated

Land transactions	s.43
Deemed market value to be used where involves connected company	s.53
Rates of SDLT	s.55
Disadvantaged areas relief	s.57
Leases – amount of tax chargeable on rent	Sch 5 para 2
Exemptions:	
• No chargeable consideration	Sch 3 para 1
• Divorce	Sch 3 para 3A
• Variations	Sch 3 para 4
Filing of land transaction form	s.76
Payment of SDLT	s.86
Interest on late payment	s.87
Penalties on failure to deliver return	Sch 10 paras 3, 4

High value properties

Annual Tax on Enveloped Dwellings (ATED)	ss.94-174 FA 2013
Capital gains tax charge on disposal of ATED properties	Sch 25 FA 2013

Stamp Duty Land Tax (Found at www.hmrc.gov.uk/manuals/sdltmanual/SDLTM00010.htm)

SDLTM00010 – Introduction to stamp duty land tax

SDLTM00050 – Introduction to stamp duty land tax – rates of tax

SDLTM10000 – Leases

See also Stamp Taxes Manual (Found at www.hmrc.gov.uk/so/index.htm)

See also Stamp Taxes: Stamp Duty Reserve Tax (Found at www.hmrc.gov.uk/sdrt/index.htm)

> This technical reference section is designed to assist you when you are working in the office. It should help you to know where to look for further information on the topics covered in this chapter.

Answer to Interactive question

Answer to Interactive question

The rate of SDLT on the premium on the grant of a non-residential lease between £0 and £150,000 is 1% where the annual rent exceeds £1,000.

SDLT is therefore £45,000 × 1%   £450

1   Edmund has purchased an existing holding of shares and will therefore be personally liable to stamp duty at 0.5% ie £2,500.

Mouse Ltd has purchased an existing holding of shares from a connected company. Under the rules for transfers between group companies the transfer will be exempt from stamp duty where one company is the parent (75%) company of the other and the beneficial interest is transferred. In this case, Dog Ltd owns at least 75% in Mouse Ltd and therefore the transfer will be exempt from stamp duty.

2   Stamp duty is payable on a repurchase of a company's own shares where they are not cancelled immediately. Treasury shares are shares which have been repurchased and not cancelled. Although the repurchase does not require a stock transfer form, the notification to the Registrar of Companies is stampable at 0.5% instead.

3   SDLT is only payable on the transfer of land as the goodwill and stock are both exempt.

Where land is transferred between members of a 75% group the transfer will be exempt from SDLT. However, relief will be denied if the transfer is not for bona fide commercial reasons. Relief will also be retrospectively denied if Kilmarnock Ltd is subsequently sold outside of the group within three years whilst still owning the office building.

4   **Hawks Ltd and Huxley House**

(1)   **Purchase of shares in Hawks Ltd**

Corporation tax

The purchase represents an acquisition of a chargeable asset, upon which corporation tax will be payable on sale by the vendor, unless the shareholding is sold in circumstances where the substantial shareholding exemption applies. This would require the shareholder to have owned a 10% holding for at least 12 months in the previous two years.

Stamp duty

Stamp duty of 0.5% on the consideration for the purchase of shares in Hawkes Ltd is payable ie £53,000 × 0.5% = £265

(2)   **5 year lease on Huxley House**

Hepburn Ltd – Landlord

Corporation tax

The rent receivable for the year ended 31 January 2017 of £29,600 will be subject to corporation tax as property income for Hepburn Ltd.

The income element of the premium received will also be subject to tax as property income for Hepburn Ltd in the year ended 31 January 2017 as follows:

$$£72,500 \times \frac{50-4}{50} \qquad\qquad £66,700$$

Leopard Ltd – Tenant

Corporation tax

The rent payable of £29,600 will be deductible as an allowable trading expense for Leopard Ltd for the year ended 31 January 2017.

Leopard Ltd will also be entitled to a deduction against its trading profits for part of the lease premium paid. The trading profits deduction is calculated as the income element to the landlord spread over the life of the lease = £66,700/5 years = £13,340 pa.

CHAPTER

19

Stamp duty land tax

Stamp duty land tax (SDLT) is payable on leases at the rate of 1% of the NPV of rent charged.

There is no charge where the NPV is less than £150,000. In this case as the NPV of the rent charged is £29,600 × 5 = £148,000, no SDLT is payable on the rental.

However, SDLT is payable on the premium @ 1% × £72,500 = £725 as the annual rental exceeds £1,000.

5   Charlotte will not pay stamp duty on the acquisition of the shares as it is not a transfer of an existing holding.

The company will pay SDLT on the composite value of all property transferred to it as it is connected to Charlotte and the transfer is made in exchange for shares. The total value of the (non-residential) land transferred is £580,000 and SDLT is therefore payable at 4% ie £23,200.

All other assets are exempt from stamp taxes.

6   Because the house was acquired after 1 April 2012, the taxable value for ATED is the purchase price rather than the 1 April 2012 value. Pigsty Properties will therefore be liable for an ATED charge from the time when the property is acquired until the time of its disposal.

The annual charge is £7,000, but this is reduced where the property is only owned for part of the year. The ATED charges are therefore as follows:

Year ended 31 March 2016 – 1/12 × £7,000	£583
Year ended 31 March 2016 – full year's charge	£7,000
Year ended 31 March 2017 – 2/12 × £7,000	£1,167

Because the consideration is more than £1,000,000 and the property has been within the charge to ATED throughout the period of ownership, capital gains tax will apply to the disposal as follows:

	£
Proceeds	1,150,000
Less cost	(1,050,000)
Taxable gain	100,000

Capital gains tax £100,000 × 28% = £28,000

Note: (£1,150,000 – £1,000,000) × 5/3 = £250,000, so the taxable gain is not capped.

CHAPTER 20

Communication skills

Introduction
Examination context
Topic List
Summary and Self-test
Answer to Interactive question
Answers to Self-test

Learning objectives

- Communicate in a format appropriate to the recipient who may be an external client, a fellow professional or an internal colleague

- Prepare suitable advice to explain tax liabilities with supporting calculations

- Recommend appropriate tax-planning advice

- Identify further information required to complete tax computations and finalise tax advice

- Give advice which is appropriate, technically correct, and within the law and the ICAEW Code of Ethics

Specific syllabus references for this chapter are 1a, 1b, 1c, 1d and 1e.

Syllabus links

In the Principles of Taxation and Tax Compliance syllabuses you developed the basic knowledge and application skills for a number of tax rules. You have extended these knowledge and application skills in chapters 1 to 19 of this Study Manual. This chapter will help you to consider how the format of your answer and the way in which you explain yourself will demonstrate to the examiner that you have the ability to exercise your judgement and give advice. The final three chapters use scenarios to draw together various aspects of your tax studies to date and help you to understand the interaction of the taxes. The final three chapters are revision of your earlier studies.

In the advanced level papers you will be faced with further scenario questions where you will be required to identify and resolve more complex issues. The skills that you have begun to develop in this paper will help to prepare you for the advanced level papers.

Examination context

In the examination you will be faced with questions based upon 'real life' scenarios. The questions will often be 'open-ended'. You will be required to deconstruct the scenario given and then reconstruct the facts, issues and judgements as part of your answer. Ethical issues and professional judgement are regular features in these types of questions.

The questions involve a significant proportion of higher-level skills as they involve analysing events and formulating the most appropriate tax treatments.

In the examination candidates may be required to:

- Discuss the tax treatment for the issues arising from a business event or series of events

- Quantify the effects of the tax implications for the client

- Advise on the most appropriate course of action

- Recognise the ethical, legal and professional issues for a professional accountant undertaking work in tax and giving advice on tax issues

- Prepare and present tax computations from structured and unstructured data

- Explain in non-technical language the application of tax rules to information provided

- Develop and advise upon tax policy for an organisation

1 Scenario questions

Section overview

- In this exam you are being tested on your ability to communicate in addition to whether you have the technical knowledge.

- In the examination you will meet questions that are based closely upon 'real life' scenarios. The scenarios are based upon the tax implications of common business events.

- It is important that you learn how to deal with a scenario question. You need to start by deconstructing the question into manageable sections, then plan your answer, before you start to actually write your answer.

1.1 Introduction

In this exam you are being tested on your ability to communicate in addition to whether you have the technical knowledge.

Does it really matter how you communicate the answer, though? Surely as long as you have answered the technical requirements of the question, that is good enough. As an illustration, consider the following paragraph from a letter to a client:

> If some of your NTLR are qualifying and they're not already exempt under the exemptions I mentioned above, then they will be automatically exempted under the matched interest rules as long as we elect for the Chapter 9 rules to apply in the first place. So, what this means is that if your company's tested income amount exceeds the tested expense amount then all the remaining profits are completely exempted. Whereas if it's the other way round, then only some of them will be exempted. We work out how much is exempt by using the formula: $100\% \times E/(I + R)$. You can see by referring to appendix A, that in your case only £1m of qualifying loan relationships profits are in fact subject to the CFC charge.

A better consideration of format and communication skills in general would have helped to ensure that the client could understand what was written. A better section of the letter might be:

Qualifying loan interest – matched interest rules

Where you have remaining qualifying loan interest after the application of the 75% and the qualifying resources exemptions discussed above, the residual profits relating to qualifying loan relationships may be exempted under the matched interest rules.

Unlike the 75% exemption and the qualifying resources exemption, the matched interest exemption applies automatically if you elect for your loan relationships to be treated under the qualifying loan relationship rules – ie no additional claim is required.

The matched interest rules use some of the principles from the worldwide debt cap rules to determine how much, if any, of the residual profits are exempt:

- If the tested income amount (TIA) equals or exceeds the tested expense amount (TEA) (before taking account of the residual qualifying loan relationships profits), then the residual profits of those qualifying loan relationships are fully exempted.

- If the TIA including the residual qualifying loan relationships profits exceeds the TEA, then some of the residual profits will be exempted. The exempt amount will be the amount which makes the TIA equal to the TEA.

Appendix A sets out the detailed calculations in relation to the profits for the year ended 31 December 2016. You will see that £1m of your qualifying loan relationships remain subject to the CFC charge after the application of all possible exemptions. You should self-assess this amount on your CT600 tax return and note that it is subject to UK corporation tax at the main rate.

1.2 Common business events

Common business events that may occur in scenario questions **could** include:

- Business start up
- Business transformation
- Mergers and acquisitions
- Demergers and disposals
- Life changing events such as marriage, divorce and death
- Bankruptcy and liquidation

These questions will test the technical knowledge that you have developed through the Principles of Taxation, Tax Compliance and Business Planning: Taxation modules. However, clients and employers expect ICAEW Chartered Accountants to provide advice, solutions to complex issues and options about strategy, in addition to technical excellence. These scenario questions test your ability to identify issues as well as apply technical knowledge when providing solutions.

1.3 Skills

Strong answers to scenario style questions require methodology and planning. This mirrors the way that you should approach challenges in the workplace.

The examiners are looking for the following characteristics in **strong** answers:

- Well structured and planned answers addressing the **key issues** in a logical format.

- **Technical excellence** through identifying the relevant business issues and the related tax issues.

- Focused **discussion** of the issues arising with arguments applied to the specific circumstances of the scenario in the question.

- **Quantification** of the issues and where necessary preparation of tax computations.

- Advice where a **range of solutions** is available by discussing a range of factors rather than simply one solution.

- Answers that demonstrate **higher skills** by synthesising, integrating, analysing and evaluating the material in the question.

- Demonstration of professional scepticism where information or computations presented in the question, perhaps by a junior colleague or a client, are inappropriate or inaccurate.

Weaker answers would fail to display many or all of the above characteristics. **Weaker** answers may have the additional features:

- Points made are merely **repetition** from the question, without any 'added value' in the form of analysis or drawing of inferences.

- Points are made **randomly** without any focus or argument.

- The **requirements are not addressed** directly or fully.

- **Failure** to provide a clear explanation of the point or **to communicate** a clear understanding.

- **Lack of any consideration** of the broader aspects of an issue and its wider implications.

- Technically incorrect solutions or answers that include **content copied** from the set text without a focus on the scenario.

- Too much **emphasis on demonstrating knowledge** as opposed to problem solving.

- Lack of prioritisation of the key, as opposed to **peripheral**, parts of the question.

1.4 Deconstruct the question

1.4.1 Focus on the requirements

It is essential that before you begin to answer the question you take a few minutes to understand the requirements and develop a plan.

In this exam you will be given the total marks available for a question but will not be given a breakdown of marks. One of the skills you therefore need to develop is an ability to judge the relevant importance of each sub-requirement – ie the level of detail you should write for each answer.

Firstly you should read and consider the requirement. Ask yourself the following.

- What am I being asked to do?
- Am I required to give advice in a particular context (for example reporting to a third party)?
- Is there a particular format such as a report or memorandum?
- Is there anything I need to be aware of in formulating my answer?

1.4.2 Read the question thoroughly

Now that you have read the requirements you know why you are reading the information. Read it actively, not passively. For example, if one of the requirements relates to inheritance tax and then in the information an asset is an 'unquoted trading company', you can immediately think 'BPR'. Without reading the requirements the fact it was an 'unquoted trading company' would have been meaningless and may have related to any number of different issues.

Highlight key facts and annotate the question paper in the margins with the implications of the information you are given. The likelihood is that if you are specifically told something by the examiners it is for a reason.

Note the requirements which are stand-alone and the ones which interact. Note also any other factors which interact, eg your advice regarding capital gains tax will also impact on your inheritance tax advice.

1.4.3 Consider the marks allocations

In practice you would need to consider how best to utilise the time available to help your client. In this exam, now you have read the information you can consider the relative weightings of each requirement in order to decide how much time to allocate to each part. As you do not know the marks allocations you have to use your own judgement to decide how much time to allocate, just as you would in practice.

1.4.4 Plan your answer

The next challenge is to identify the key aspects of your answer by identifying the key business and tax issues. The following questions will assist you in developing a plan of your answer and the key points that the examiners are seeking.

- **Business issues**
    - What is the business issue(s) in the question?
    - How is this reflected in the scenario?

- **Tax issues**
    - What are the tax issues?
    - Are any of the issues linked or are they independent of one another?

- **Ethical issues and judgements**
    - Are there any that need considering?
    - Are there any areas where significant judgement has been or needs to be applied?

- **Additional information**

    Is there any additional information that may be required to complete my analysis of the issues identified?

Before you start to write your answer you should plan your answer to each requirement. Considering each requirement in turn should ensure that your answer to part (a) does not also answer most of part (b).

Worked example: Question 1 from sample paper two

Tutorial note:

The following question is taken from one of the two sample papers issued by the ICAEW when the BPT paper was introduced in 2013. Work through the question following the steps set out above.

TT Ltd is a UK resident company which imports music technology systems and other electrical products for distribution in the UK. TT Ltd has a projected taxable profit of £18 million for the year ending 31 December 2016. The year end for all the companies in the TT group is 31 December. You are a tax assistant working in a firm of ICAEW Chartered Accountants, and the TT group of companies is a client of your firm.

Briefing received from the newly appointed TT Group Tax Director:

'My predecessor has left some handover notes concerning the potential purchase of shares in Circon Ltd (**Exhibit 1**) and the incorporation in July 2015 of TT Ltd's permanent establishment in Grania as GG Inc (**Exhibit 2**). GG Inc is now a subsidiary of TT Ltd.

Jo Sun, a TT Group tax assistant, is currently on secondment at GG Inc. Jo Sun is in the final year of her training contract and is expected to qualify as an ICAEW Chartered Accountant next year. She has sent me an email in which she has identified issues which may have ethical implications for both herself and for the TT Group (**Exhibit 3**).'

Requirements

Prepare a working paper, addressed to the Tax Director of the TT Group of companies that includes:

(a) With reference to the potential purchase of shares in Circon Ltd (Exhibit 1):

    (i) An explanation and determination of the maximum trading loss that Circon Ltd would be able to surrender to TT Ltd in the year ending 31 December 2016, taking account of any possible claims for allowances and reliefs; and

    (ii) A brief analysis of the factors that TT Ltd needs to consider in response to Alan Fleurie's suggestion (Exhibit 1) regarding the price for his Circon Ltd shares.

(b) With reference to the incorporation of GG Inc (Exhibit 2), a summary of the UK tax implications of transferring the trade and assets of TT Ltd's permanent establishment in Grania to GG Inc.

(c) With reference to the email from Jo Sun (Exhibit 3), an explanation of the ethical and legal implications of the entertaining costs. Draft appropriate advice for Jo Sun and recommend the action TT Ltd should take.

(40 marks)

Exhibit 1 – Handover notes – potential purchase of shares in Circon Ltd

Alan Fleurie a major shareholder in Circon Ltd has offered to sell 45% of the ordinary share capital of Circon Ltd to TT Ltd, from his own personal shareholding. TT Ltd is currently in negotiations with him.

Circon Ltd produces circuit boards in the UK and has two subsidiaries, Cafee Ltd, a music system retailer and WebAd Ltd, an on-line retailer.

The proposed date of the share purchase is 1 January 2016, although no agreement has been reached yet on the price for the shares.

Alan has suggested that 'the price for my Circon Ltd shares should take into consideration Circon Ltd's projected trading loss which, after the share purchase, TT Ltd will be able to offset against its taxable profits for the year ending 31 December 2016.'

Following the proposed share purchase, the shareholders of Circon Ltd would be as follows:

Shareholder	% shareholding in Circon Ltd	Tax residency
TT Ltd	45	UK
Alan Fleurie	10	UK
DL Corporation	45	China

Circon Ltd

The company has been breaking even for a number of years, but is projecting its first tax trading loss (£8 million before capital allowances) for the year ending 31 December 2016. Circon Ltd has a potential claim for capital allowances of £2 million and also has projected taxable property income of £1 million for the year ending 31 December 2016.

Cafee Ltd

Circon Ltd owns 100% of the ordinary shares in Cafee Ltd which operates a small chain of specialist music systems shops. Cafee Ltd has projected taxable trading profits of £6.8 million for the year ending 31 December 2016.

WebAd Ltd

Circon Ltd owns 75% of the ordinary shares in WebAd Ltd, which sells a low-cost range of music products on-line. WebAd Ltd was incorporated on 1 January 2015 and immediately purchased the trade and assets of Alan Fleurie's sole trader business for £5.5 million. The remaining 25% of WebAd Ltd's shares are owned by Alan.

WebAd Ltd is projected to make a tax trading loss of £3 million for the year ending 31 December 2016.

Exhibit 2 – Handover notes – Incorporation of TT Ltd's permanent establishment in Grania as GG Inc.

In 2012 TT Ltd set up a permanent establishment in Grania, an overseas tax jurisdiction, to manufacture TT Ltd's own brand of music systems. As a permanent establishment, its profits and losses formed part of TT Ltd's taxable total profits subject to UK corporation tax. No election had been made to exempt the permanent establishment from the charge to UK taxation.

The venture in Grania has not been a success for TT Ltd and the board is seeking an exit strategy. On 1 July 2015, in preparation for disposal of the Granian operation, TT Ltd transferred the trade and assets of its permanent establishment in Grania to a newly incorporated Granian subsidiary, GG Inc, in exchange for 100% of the shares issued. The only significant asset transferred with the trade was the freehold property in Grania which had cost £250,000 in October 2012. The property's market value at the date of incorporation had increased to £600,000.

GG Inc is tax resident in Grania. It is still the intention for TT Ltd to sell the shares in GG Inc, as soon as a suitable buyer can be found.

(Assume the retail price index for July 2015 is 257.5)

Exhibit 3 – Email from Jo Sun

To: Group tax director
From: Jo Sun, tax assistant at GG Inc
Subject: GG Inc
Date: 26 October 2015

GG Inc has made a £100,000 payment to an export company and I have been instructed to include this in entertaining costs. However, there is no supporting documentation for this payment. I have asked the export department to send the paperwork, but I have been told that these types of payments are 'normally' permitted for tax purposes in Grania as they ensure that GG Inc's goods are not held up at the port. However, there are rarely receipts available.

My manager here at GG Inc has told me not to worry about this payment as there have been other similar payments in the past which have not presented any difficulties for TT Ltd in the UK. He has told me that this is a cultural issue and that I will be 'very unpopular' if I ask too many questions. I would really appreciate your advice.

Solution

1. First analyse the requirements

> Professional document, but no particular format

> Addressee not clueless about tax

Prepare a working paper, addressed to the Tax Director of the TT Group of companies that includes:

> Needs calculation

(a) With reference to the potential purchase of shares in Circon Ltd (Exhibit 1):

> Relatively small part of qu? Knowledge needs to be applied to facts.

(i) An explanation and determination of the maximum trading loss that Circon Ltd would be able to surrender to TT Ltd in the year ending 31 December 2016, taking account of any possible claims for allowances and reliefs; and

(ii) A brief analysis of the factors that TT Ltd needs to consider in response to Alan Fleurie's suggestion (Exhibit 1) regarding the price for his Circon Ltd shares.

(b) With reference to the incorporation of GG Inc (Exhibit 2), a summary of the UK tax implications of transferring the trade and assets of TT Ltd's permanent establishment in Grania to GG Inc.

(c) With reference to the email from Jo Sun (Exhibit 3), an explanation of the ethical and legal implications of the entertaining costs. Draft appropriate advice for Jo Sun and recommend the action TT Ltd should take.

> (a)(i) – co-terminous APs?

> Two different addressees for this part

> (a)(i) – loss capacity unlikely to be limited

2. Read and annotate the question

TT Ltd is a UK resident company which imports music technology systems and other electrical products for distribution in the UK. TT Ltd has a projected taxable profit of £18 million for the year ending 31 December 2016. The year end for all the companies in the TT group is 31 December. You are a tax assistant working in a firm of ICAEW Chartered Accountants, and the TT group of companies is a client of your firm.

Briefing received from the newly appointed TT Group Tax Director:

'My predecessor has left some handover notes concerning the potential purchase of shares in Circon Ltd (**Exhibit 1**) and the incorporation in July 2015 of TT Ltd's permanent establishment in Grania as GG Inc (**Exhibit 2**). GG Inc is now a subsidiary of TT Ltd.

Jo Sun, a TT Group tax assistant, is currently on secondment at GG Inc. Jo Sun is in the final year of her training contract and is expected to qualify as an ICAEW Chartered Accountant next year. She has sent me an email in which she has identified issues which may have ethical implications for both herself and for the TT Group (**Exhibit 3**).'

> (c) – junior staff member

Requirements

Prepare a working paper, addressed to the Tax Director of the TT Group of companies that includes:

(a) With reference to the potential purchase of shares in Circon Ltd (Exhibit 1):

(i) An explanation and determination of the maximum trading loss that Circon Ltd would be able to surrender to TT Ltd in the year ending 31 December 2016, taking account of any possible claims for allowances and reliefs; and

(ii) A brief analysis of the factors that TT Ltd needs to consider in response to Alan Fleurie's suggestion (Exhibit 1) regarding the price for his Circon Ltd shares.

(b) With reference to the incorporation of GG Inc (Exhibit 2), a summary of the UK tax implications of transferring the trade and assets of TT Ltd's permanent establishment in Grania to GG Inc.

(c) With reference to the E-mail from Jo Sun (Exhibit 3), an explanation of the ethical and legal implications of the entertaining costs. Draft appropriate advice for Jo Sun and recommend the action TT Ltd should take.

(a)(i) – <75%, so consortium relief?

(40 marks)

Exhibit 1 – Handover notes – potential purchase of shares in Circon Ltd

Alan Fleurie a major shareholder in Circon Ltd has offered to sell 45% of the ordinary share capital of Circon Ltd to TT Ltd, from his own personal shareholding. TT Ltd is currently in negotiations with him.

(a)(i) – relief for whole AP?

Circon Ltd produces circuit boards in the UK and has two subsidiaries, Cafee Ltd, a music system retailer and WebAd Ltd, an on-line retailer.

The proposed date of the share purchase is 1 January 2016, although no agreement has been reached yet on the price for the shares.

Alan has suggested that 'the price for my Circon Ltd shares should take into consideration Circon Ltd's projected trading loss which, after the share purchase, TT Ltd will be able to offset against its taxable profits for the year ending 31 December 2016.'

(a)(ii) – linked to (a)(i) (why wouldn't it pay Circon for the losses??)

Following the proposed share purchase, the shareholders of Circon Ltd would be as follows:

Shareholder	% shareholding in Circon Ltd	Tax residency
TT Ltd	45	UK
Alan Fleurie	10	UK
DL Corporation	45	China

(a)(i) – 90% owned by cos, so consortium relief applies.

(a)(i) – DL unable to claim consortium relief as NUKR

(a)(i) – £8m loss Reliefs = CAs?

(a)(ii) – co may be able to utilise loss in future?

(a)(i) – APs are coterminous

(a)(i) – consortium relief is after offset against property income.

Circon Ltd

The company has been breaking even for a number of years, but is projecting its first tax trading loss (£8 million before capital allowances) for the year ending 31 December 2016. Circon Ltd has a potential claim for capital allowances of £2 million and also has projected taxable property income of £1 million for the year ending 31 December 2016.

(a)(i) – cons. relief: assume max surrender to group members first

Cafee Ltd

Circon Ltd owns 100% of the ordinary shares in Cafee Ltd which operates a small chain of specialist music systems shops. Cafee Ltd has projected taxable trading profits of £6.8 million for the year ending 31 December 2016.

(a)(i) – GR group with Circon

WebAd Ltd

Circon Ltd owns 75% of the ordinary shares in WebAd Ltd, which sells a low-cost range of music products on-line. WebAd Ltd was incorporated on 1 January 2015 and immediately purchased the trade and assets of Alan Fleurie's sole trader business for £5.5 million. The remaining 25% of WebAd Ltd's shares are owned by Alan.

WebAd Ltd is projected to make a tax trading loss of £3 million for the year ending 31 December 2016.

(a)(i) – cons. relief will be higher if W loss surrendered to Cafee first

CHAPTER

20

Exhibit 2 – Handover notes – Incorporation of TT Ltd's permanent establishment in Grania as GG Inc.

In 2012 TT Ltd set up a permanent establishment in Grania, an overseas tax jurisdiction, to manufacture TT Ltd's own brand of music systems. As a permanent establishment, its profits and losses formed part of TT Ltd's taxable total profits subject to UK corporation tax. No election had been made to exempt the permanent establishment from the charge to UK taxation.

The venture in Grania has not been a success for TT Ltd and the board is seeking an exit strategy. On 1 July 2015, in preparation for disposal of the Granian operation, TT Ltd transferred the trade and assets of its permanent establishment in Grania to a newly incorporated Granian subsidiary, GG Inc, in exchange for 100% of the shares issued. The only significant asset transferred with the trade was the freehold property in Grania which had cost £250,000 in October 2012. The property's market value at the date of incorporation had increased to £600,000.

GG Inc is tax resident in Grania. It is still the intention for TT Ltd to sell the shares in GG Inc, as soon as a suitable buyer can be found.

(Assume the retail price index for July 2015 is 257.5)

S.140 could be claimed for 100% gain on incorporation

SSE? Deferred gains will crystalise

Info to calculate gain

Exhibit 3 – Email from Jo Sun

All/ only relates to (c)

To:	Group tax director
From:	Jo Sun, tax assistant at GG Inc
Subject:	GG Inc
Date:	26 October 2015

Bribery Act? Professional integrity? (could also be a money laundering issue)

GG Inc has made a £100,000 payment to an export company and I have been instructed to include this in entertaining costs. However, there is no supporting documentation for this payment. I have asked the export department to send the paperwork, but I have been told that these types of payments are 'normally' permitted for tax purposes in Grania as they ensure that GG Inc's goods are not held up at the port. However, there are rarely receipts available.

My manager here at GG Inc has told me not to worry about this payment as there have been other similar payments in the past which have not presented any difficulties for TT Ltd in the UK. He has told me that this is a cultural issue and that I will be 'very unpopular' if I ask too many questions. I would really appreciate your advice.

Used local channels – now going to HO (if still unhappy then resign?)

Personal pressure

3. Consider the mark allocation

If there are no other ethics or legal elements in the paper, the ethics element (c) has to be worth between five and ten marks. Here you are asked to consider the position of both the company and an individual, and the position is not entirely straightforward, so it is likely to be nearer to ten marks than five.

Part (b) is reasonably straightforward – a calculation of the gain on incorporation, identifying the possibility of s.140 TCGA 1992 relief and the consequences of disposal. It is unlikely to be worth more than eight to ten marks.

The rest of the marks (say 20-25) therefore have to be allocated to part (a), with the majority allocated to (a)(i).

Tutorial note:

The actual mark allocation given with the sample paper was as follows (remember that there are almost always more marks available across the different requirements than the maximum for the question):

Part (a) (no split given between the elements)	24
Part (b)	9
Part (c)	10

4. Plan your answer

Brief bullet points to ensure that you do not forget key issues might be as follows:

(a)(i)
- Consortium relief not group relief, incl implications (max 45% of loss)
- Accounting periods (whole y/e 31.12.16)
- Circon's own results – claim CAs, offset against property income
- Impact of subs: position with and without GR surrender from W to Cafee

(a)(ii)
- Available loss limited (per (i))
- Loss reliefs usually determined by effective tax rates – benefit in Circon if c/f?
- Other shareholders will expect company to be paid (risk that they would be paying twice?)

(b)
- General consequences of incorporation (cessation/ balancing charges/ disposals)
- Calculate gain
- s.140 branch incorporation relief
- Disposal (SSE/gain on branch assets becomes chargeable)

(c)
- Two issues – the potential illegal payment and the pressure on Jo Sun not to act with integrity (Question asks for advice for Jo and for the company)
- Jo
  - Ensure she has all of the facts
  - Refuse to be involved if has concerns
  - If Head Office do not resolve the position, may need to take external advice/resign

- TT
  - Bribery Act – procedures?
  - Take legal advice?
  - Money laundering issue if there are proceeds from illegal activities.
  - No UK tax deduction for illegal payments.

1.5 Reconstruction

1.5.1 Writing your answer

You are now in a position to start writing your answer. Because the examiner will have ordered the requirements in the given order for a reason, it will in most cases be a good idea to answer them in that order. This is consistent with how you have planned the question. Lay your answer out using headings that relate to the requirements.

Before you make an attempt at writing an answer, it is important that you think through how the points you make will be assessed. It is important that you understand why one script would obtain a better mark on the points made than another.

Strong answers will address the requirements of the question. They will identify the issues. For each issue candidates should ensure that their answers:

- **Identify the issue** and **discuss the tax treatment**. The analysis should be appropriate to the context of the question. It should refer to the facts given in the question and relate these to the tax treatment. Alternative treatments should be discussed and where possible a conclusion drawn as to the most appropriate.

- **Quantify the effects**. In quantifying the effects, you may be required to consider the cash effects of a particular strategy or perhaps whether the implications for other taxes mean that the original strategy cannot be achieved. You should always consider whether anything can be done to mitigate the tax cost – ie are any reliefs available, or can the tax payable be (legally) delayed. Where appropriate, your answers could mention the impact of the conclusions you draw. For example, the timing of the disposal of a property pre and post liquidation can have implications for the use of trading losses to offset against the resulting chargeable gain.

In most cases, **good points pass the 'because' test**. When suggesting a solution to the tax issue you should explain 'why', ie your reason for suggesting it. For example, the loss cannot be carried forward because …., the company should elect for amortisation at 4% because… The word '**because' changes a 'what' into a 'why'**. In other words you can demonstrate what approach is most appropriate and why.

You should try to relate the 'why' to the specific business issues given in the question. The reader (in your case the examiner) will then appreciate that you understand the **relationships between** the **tax treatment** and the **business issues**.

1.5.2 Answer the actual question set

It is important when writing your answer to consider the depth that you will need to go into. This is where you can demonstrate your understanding and added value. As a general rule, you will be able to demonstrate more 'added value' where the issues are of significant magnitude and where judgement is required in discussing the issue and developing solutions.

Before you write your answer check the requirements one last time by re-reading them in full, ie word for word; do not skim read them. Spending a few extra minutes re-reading the requirements word for word is time well spent. Noticing in the last 15 minutes that you have actually missed one of the two issues of relevance is too late.

Interactive question: Sample paper question   [Difficulty level: Exam standard]

Using the plan which you prepared in the worked example, write up your answer to the TT Ltd sample paper question.

This is a 40 mark question, meaning the total time allocated was one hour. You are likely to have spent 10-15 minutes analysing the question and preparing your answer plan. You should therefore attempt to write up your answer in 45-50 minutes.

See **Answer** at the end of this chapter.

2 Formatting your answer

Section overview

- Communication involves the format of your answer as well as the language, tone and style of your answer.

- Remember that marks for the format of your answer should be the easiest marks on the paper. Set out your answer in the format requested: examples could include a report, letter, memorandum or meeting notes.

- Adjust your language to suit the recipient. Technical language might be acceptable for your tax partner but is not appropriate in a letter direct to a personal tax client.

2.1 Introduction

In the exam you may be asked to prepare a draft report or a draft letter for a client or fellow professional. The format itself is likely to only be worth a few marks, but they should be easy marks to achieve. This section will highlight how to format your answer in an exam scenario.

2.2 Report writing

2.2.1 Overview

A formal report that you might prepare in practice is too detailed for the exam. A basic report format is all that is required. Do not go over the top in the exam and do not waste time on excessive presentation at the expense of detailed content.

In essence your report should be in a recognisable format and should be easy to navigate. Each part of the report should be clearly identified and have headings with effective use of subheadings. Any appendices should be referred to in the main body of the report.

A report is perhaps more likely to be for other professionals or a corporate client than a personal tax client.

2.2.2 A design suggestion

The following is a suggested report format:

Section	Skill level
Title block • Who the report is written for (eg 'Board of XYZ plc') • Who has written the report • Date • Title	Low
Introduction • A few lines introducing the report; it should set the scene and explain what will be discussed in the report. • Avoid explaining or evaluating issues.	Low
Executive summary • Briefly set out what is covered in the report.	Medium It may be a useful tool to help plan your answer to the question before you start writing
Discussion and prioritisation of main issues • If there is more than one requirement to be dealt with in the report, deal with them, in order, in separate parts of the report. So Part 1 would relate to requirement (a), Part 2 would relate to requirement (b) etc. • Discuss the most important issues within each requirement first. • Explain background and potential consequences of each issue including any potential to mitigate likely charges. • Use headings and sub-headings to organise and help break up your report. It may also be useful to number each heading and sub-heading within each part of your report but this is not essential. So the first heading would be 1.0, the first sub-heading would be 1.1, the second sub-heading would be 1.2 then the second heading would become 2.0 etc. The headings within Part 2 would begin again at 1.0 etc. This allows easy cross-referencing. • Numerical values stated and referenced to appendix where they can be found (eg 'the amount that should be paid as the first instalment of corporation tax is £3.6m (Appendix 3)'). • Less important issues can be grouped as 'other issues' at end. • Leave recommendations until the end of the report. These should be written as you write the main analysis if possible; just write them on a separate page. Then they are easy for the examiner to see and mark. Alternatively put the recommendation for each part at the end of the section to which it relates and then move on to the next requirement.	High Critical section of the report as you are answering the requirements; it will be where the majority of the marks are awarded. Most of the skills marks will be awarded here as you demonstrate that you can bring together disparate facts, recognise the interaction of taxes, identify embedded points and apply your technical knowledge to a novel scenario.

Section	Skill level

Recommendations

This is where you give advice.

- Each section states what decision you recommend, explains why you recommend it, and then tells the client how to do it. For example:

  'Y plc is clearly subject to the transfer pricing rules. Y plc therefore needs to ensure that its tax adjusted profits are restated to take account of an arm's length price. As discussed above, this increases its taxable total profits by £1.25m and will give an increase in the corporation tax liability of £0.25m.'

- It is not acceptable to avoid making recommendations on grounds such as 'need more information'. These should be included as a list in the main section of the report and used as a caveat for the recommendation. For example:

  'Subject to any of the further information listed above as being required to make a definitive decision, I am of the opinion that business property relief will not apply to the transfer of the furnished holiday accommodation. The chargeable lifetime transfer is therefore liable to inheritance tax at a rate of 20% which is payable by the trustees. This should be paid by 31 December 2016 to avoid interest and penalties becoming due. '

High

This section is also important and will also enable you to gain the skills marks available as it demonstrates your ability to reach a judgement based on your reasoning and evaluation skills.

Appendices

- Put at back of answer and include all workings here in separate cross referenced appendices.

- Only summary figures or tables should be included within the main body of the report.

- There should be no data in the appendices which is not referred to and discussed in the main body of the report.

Medium/High

The topic of the question and in particular whether the topic is new at this paper or brought forward knowledge from Tax Compliance will determine to what extent there will be large computations to undertake.

Normally there will be at least some requirement to undertake computations to justify your answer and demonstrate your ability to apply your technical skills.

Your ability to recognise where to utilise your time and what computations are required is also a skill being tested in this paper.

2.3 Letter

2.3.1 Overview

A letter is most likely to be the required format for contacting a personal tax client directly. It should be suitably formal and use professional language.

If you were writing a letter in practice, the use of legislation in the answer itself would be minimal if it is for a personal tax client rather than another professional.

Where an address is given in the question, ensure you set out the letter formally with your full address in the top right, then the date below on the left, and then the recipient's address below that and also on the left.

2.3.2 A design suggestion

The structure of a letter is broadly similar to that of a report and could be formatted as follows.

Section	Skill level
Top of the first page	**Low**
• Your address on the right • Date • Recipient's address on the left • Dear Mr/Mrs/Miss/Ms etc – address the letter to the recipient specified in the question • Subject eg RE: PROPOSED DISPOSAL OF SHARES	
Introduction	**Low**
• A few lines introducing the letter, it should set the scene and explain what will be discussed in the letter.	
Discussion and prioritisation of main issues	**High**
• If there is more than one requirement to be dealt with in the letter, deal with them, in order, in separate parts of the letter. So Part 1 would relate to requirement (a), Part 2 would relate to requirement (b) etc. • Discuss the most important issues within each requirement first. • Explain background and potential consequences of each issue including any potential to mitigate likely charges. • Use headings and sub-headings to organise and help break up your letter unless it will be very short. • Numerical values stated and referenced to appendix where they can be found (eg 'the amount that should be paid as the first instalment of corporation tax is £3.6m (Appendix 3)'). • Less important issues can be grouped as 'other issues' at end. • You could put recommendations at the end of the letter – just write them on a separate page as you work through the requirements. Alternatively, you can put a recommendation at the end of the section to which it relates.	Critical section of the letter as you are answering the requirements; it will be where the majority of the marks are awarded. Most of the skills marks will be awarded here too as you demonstrate that you can bring together disparate facts, recognise the interaction of taxes, identify embedded points and apply your technical knowledge to a novel scenario.
Recommendations	**High**
• Your recommendations should follow the same basic format as specified for a report above.	As per report above.
Sign off	**Low**
• You should end your letter with a suitable closing sentence (eg 'Please let me know if you require any further information regarding the matters covered in this letter.') • Finally you should sign off with 'Yours sincerely' and then state underneath who you are meant to be according to the question, eg 'Tax Manager'.	
Appendices	**Medium/High**
• Your appendices should follow the same basic format as specified for a report above.	As per report above.

2.4 Memorandum or briefing notes

A memorandum or set of briefing notes is a less formal document than either a report or a letter and is most likely to have an internal recipient.

In both cases you should maintain a professional standard of English.

There is no generally accepted structure for either format. However you could use the following as a guide:

Memorandum

- Use a heading which includes: who it is to and from; the date; and subject.

- Introduction – just one or two sentences to explain what the memorandum will cover.

- Use headings and sub-headings to break-up the main body.

- Put all workings at the end of the memorandum and ensure they are cross referenced to the main body.

- Ensure there are recommendations and that they are clearly highlighted as such.

Meeting notes

The only difference between the memorandum and the meeting notes is likely to be the heading. For meeting notes it is sufficient to state simply the meeting for which they were prepared and the subject title.

2.5 Language

Your use of language should reflect the intended recipient. For example, technical language is not appropriate for a recipient with a non-tax background. Your use of language should also be suitably professional.

Beware of jargon, overly technical terms and specialist knowledge the user may not share. Keep your vocabulary, sentence and paragraph structures as simple as possible, without patronising an intelligent user.

In reports and letters in particular, impersonal constructions should be used rather than 'I', 'we' etc, which carry personal and possibly subjective associations. In other words, use of the first person should be replaced with the third person. For example, avoid saying 'I/We found that'. Instead the sentence can be framed as 'It became clear that' or 'Mr X found that' or even 'Investigation revealed that'.

Colloquialisms and abbreviated forms should be avoided in formal written English. Informal words such as 'I've', 'don't' and so on should be replaced by 'I have' and 'do not'. You should not use colloquial expressions like 'blew his top'; instead formal phrases should be used, such as 'showed considerable irritation'.

Make the report easy to understand by avoiding technical language and complex sentence structures for non-technical users.

	Example	
Rule	**No**	**Yes**
Keep words simple	Expenditure	Cost
Short words are quicker to write	Aggregate	Total
	Terminate	End
Avoid words you do not need to write	I should be grateful	Please
	Due to the fact that	Because
	In the not too distant future	Soon (better: say when)
	At this point in time	Now (or currently)
	In the majority of instances	In most cases
	It is recommended that A Ltd should consider	A Ltd should consider

3 Use of legislation

Section overview

- An ability to use the legislation in practice is critical.

- The tax legislation is divided into three main sections: primary legislation (acts of Parliament), secondary legislation (primarily statutory instruments) and non-statutory materials.

- The contents pages and footnotes in the primary legislation plus the indices are the most useful way of accessing information. Ensure that you are using the correct index.

- Read the legislation carefully to ensure you interpret it correctly.

3.1 Introduction

This section is included to enable you to utilise the technical reference sections at the end of each chapter in this study manual. In addition, whilst the use of legislation is not specifically examinable, it is an essential skill for all ICAEW members to develop.

In practice, the ability to refer to the source legislation is an important skill for any tax professional. Most tax professionals use either CCH or Tolley's tax legislation either in soft copy or hard copy as a reference tool. The aim of this section is to give you an overview of the tax legislation published by both CCH and Tolley's so that you could investigate a technical point if necessary. For ease of reference these two published sets of legislation will be referred to herein as the 'tax legislation'.

There are two basic types of legislation: primary and secondary included in the tax legislation. In addition, both CCH and Tolley's also publish various types of extra-statutory material.

3.2 Primary legislation

3.2.1 Statute

Primary legislation is defined as Acts of Parliament. For taxation purposes the most important primary legislation is the annual Finance Act. There are various other Acts which are of particular importance:

- **Taxes Management Act 1970** (TMA 1970)

  Details of responsibilities of taxpayers, administrative deadlines, penalties and interest.

- **Inheritance Tax Act 1984** (IHTA 1984)

- **Income and Corporation Taxes Act 1988** (ICTA 1988 or TA 1988)

  For corporation tax purposes this has been superseded by CTA 2009 and CTA 2010 and TIOPA 2010. For income tax purposes this has largely been superseded by the ITA 2007.

- **Taxation of Chargeable Gains Act 1992** (TCGA 1992)

- **Value Added Tax Act 1994** (VATA 1994)

- **Capital Allowances Act 2001** (CAA 2001)

  This rewrote tax legislation relating to capital allowances for all businesses.

- **Income Tax (Earnings and Pensions) Act 2003** (ITEPA 2003)

  This rewrote tax legislation relating to income from employment, pensions and social security.

- **Income Tax (Trading and Other Income) Act 2005** (ITTOIA 2005)

  This Act commenced the separation of the income tax and corporation tax legislation for unincorporated and incorporated businesses. It therefore covers income tax rules relating to trading, property and investment income of individuals.

- **Income Tax Act 2007** (ITA 2007)

  This rewrote the remaining income tax legislation. It includes the income tax computation and liability, reliefs, eg loss reliefs, EIS, and VCT, interest paid, Gift Aid, specific rules relating to settlements and trustees, manufactured payments, tax avoidance and deduction of tax at source.

- **Corporation Tax Act 2009** (CTA 2009)

  This rewrote some of the corporation tax legislation previously in ICTA 1988. It includes the corporation tax computation and liability, property income, loan relationships, derivatives, intangible fixed assets, intellectual property, exempt distributions, miscellaneous income, employee share schemes, research and development, and companies with investment business.

- **Corporation Tax Act 2010** (CTA 2010)

  This rewrote some of the corporation tax legislation previously in ICTA 1988. It includes losses, group relief, qualifying donations, reliefs and distributions.

- **Taxation (International and Other Provisions) Act 2010** (TIOPA 2010)

  This rewrote some of the corporation tax legislation previously in ICTA 1988. It includes the foreign aspects of corporation tax such as double taxation relief; transfer pricing; advance pricing agreements; tax arbitrage and CFCs.

3.2.2 Annual Finance Act

It should be noted that the version of all the primary legislation included in the tax legislation is not the version of the Act as originally enacted. Instead it is as amended by subsequent Finance Acts. So although the Taxes Management Act was originally introduced in 1970 it should more accurately be referred to as the Taxes Management Act 1970 (as amended by subsequent Finance Acts).

This is why it is particularly important that you always ensure you use the most recent version of the legislation in practice. Remember, though, that for the purposes of the exams you are often one Finance Act out of date: 2016 exams are based on Finance Acts 2015.

3.2.3 The Tax Law Rewrite Project

The Tax Law Rewrite Project was established to rewrite, simplify and codify various aspects of tax law. Largely this has involved a change in terminology and the application of consistency to make tax law easier to understand. The project's remit did not give it the power to make substantive changes to the law itself. CAA 2001, ITEPA 2003, ITTOIA 2005, ITA 2007, CTA 2009, CTA 2010 and TIOPA 2010 were all introduced by this project.

3.3 Secondary legislation

Due to the volume and increasing complexity of tax law it is not possible for it all to be enacted via an Act of Parliament. Secondary legislation enables Parliament to delegate its legislative powers to another body via an enabling Act. Examples of secondary legislation include:

- Statutory instruments including regulations, directions made under regulations, rules and Treasury Orders;

- Bye-laws; and

- Orders in Council.

Statutory Instruments form the biggest single type of secondary legislation.

Providing the delegated legislation is within the legislative powers conferred by its parent statute (ie it is intra vires), it has the force of law.

HMRC directions are made in accordance with regulations and give the detailed conditions for using online services, electronic payment and for qualifying for incentives.

3.4 Extra-statutory material

3.4.1 Introduction

HMRC publishes various other documents which are valuable in reaching an understanding of the legislation. These documents do not have the force of law.

3.4.2 Statements of practice (SP)

Statements of practice set out HMRC's interpretation of particular issues, outlining how they will be dealt with in practice. Generally, HMRC will use these to clarify how it will approach a particular technical point or deal with a particular point of ambiguity.

3.4.3 Extra-statutory concessions (ESC)

Extra-statutory concessions set out a position, possibly contrary to primary legislation which, as a concession, HMRC is prepared to accept. This may be, for example, a situation where it is prepared not to tax certain benefits which would otherwise be caught by the legislation under first principles.

It should be noted that the ability of HMRC to make such ESC was questioned by the House of Lords in 2005 in R (on the application of Wilkinson) v IRC. The House of Lords upheld that HMRC did not have the power to concede an allowance which Parliament could have granted but did not grant. Since 2005 HMRC has been reviewing the legality of every ESC as only some would have been made unlawful by the 2005 case. Finance Act 2008 has given HMRC the power to enact, by Treasury Order, all ESC in existence at the date Finance Act 2008 came into force.

3.4.4 Press releases

These cover many topics and are issued by HMRC throughout the year.

3.4.5 Revenue & Customs briefs

These were introduced in January 2007 to replace business briefs (issued by the former Customs & Excise) and tax bulletins (issued by the former Inland Revenue). Business briefs included announcements advising of policy changes resulting from legislation, litigation or internal policy reviews and notification of some consultation exercises.

Note that in CCH, tax bulletins issued before January 2007 are in a separate section of the legislation.

Tax bulletins contained decisions, HMRC interpretations, and articles. See below for how these are referenced in CCH and Tolley's.

3.4.6 Notices

These relate to VAT and detail how VAT rules and regulations work in practice.

3.4.7 Other materials

This can include extracts from correspondence with other bodies such as the Law Society, CIOT or ICAEW on technical areas, extracts from HMRC pamphlets or selected accounting standards which have an impact on tax. Also included are extracts from Hansard, which records the original Parliamentary debate regarding the introduction of each Act.

Note also that the footnotes to the tax legislation may refer to HMRC manuals. Manuals are an important source of information. They are not reproduced in the tax legislation but may be accessed from HMRC's website.

3.5 Navigation through the legislation

3.5.1 Overview

The legislation will only be useful to you in an exam context if you can find material easily and efficiently.

Both CCH and Tolley's organise the legislation in a similar way. Firstly, material is grouped together by subject matter, eg all information relating to income, corporation and capital gains tax is kept together, and the material relating to VAT is located together.

Within a particular section, all primary legislation will be reproduced first (always in chronological order). This is then followed by the secondary legislation and finally the extra-statutory material.

Using NIC as an example, all the material will relate purely to NIC and is ordered as follows:

- Statutes (in chronological order)
- Statutory instruments (also in chronological order)
- HMRC Directions (CCH only)
- European material
- Extra-statutory material (Press releases etc in Tolley's)
- Tables of destinations (CCH only)
- Index to NIC
- NIC list of definitions and meanings (Words and phrases in Tolley's)

3.5.2 Statutory instruments

Delegated legislation for taxation is typically by statutory instrument. Statutory instruments are arranged by year, and then numerically.

Regulations and Treasury Orders are enacted via a statutory instrument, so in order to find them in the legislation, you need to know which statutory instrument brought it into force. For example, the Income Tax Act (Amendment) Order 2007 was enacted via SI 2007/940, and is reproduced with all the other statutory instruments in 2007. Note that not all of the statutory instruments are reproduced in the legislation.

3.5.3 Extra-statutory materials

The extra-statutory material is arranged by type and then chronologically, within each section. Tolley's and CCH have slightly different ordering.

Extra-statutory concessions

ESCs are listed alphabetically and then by number. ESCs are categorised in both books as follows:

A   Concessions applicable to individuals (income tax and interest on tax)

B   Concessions applicable to individuals and companies (income tax and corporation tax)

C   Concessions applicable to companies etc (corporation tax and income tax)

D   Concessions relating to capital gains (individuals and companies)

E   Concessions relating to Estate Duty – note that these have been superseded by IHT and are therefore no longer relevant

F   Concessions relating to Inheritance Tax (and capital transfer tax where relevant)

G   Concessions relating to Stamp Duties

H   Concessions relating to Development Land Tax (now obsolete)

I   Concessions relating to Petroleum Revenue Tax

J   Concessions relating to Capital Transfer Tax only (now obsolete)

ESCs in categories A – D will be found within CCH Volume 1E or Tolley's Part 2. ESCs in categories E, F and J will be found in the IHT section, ie CCH Volume 1F or Tolley's Part 3. ESCs in category G will be found in CCH Volume 1G or Tolley's Orange handbook Part 2.

Tolley's indices

As for CCH, there is no single index covering all the taxes.

Parts Ic and 2 of the yellow volume both have an identical index at the back covering all the material relating to income tax, corporation tax and capital gains tax.

Part 1 of the orange volume has its own index at the back relating to VAT.

Part 3 of the yellow volume and the orange volume part 2 also each have indices behind each of the taxes covered. Therefore, to find an item of relevance to IHT in the index, you must ensure that you are using the IHT index.

3.5.7 Acts' contents pages

Overview

Often the easiest way to find something within an Act is to use its contents page. This is probably quicker if you know which Act you are most likely to be dealing with, eg CTA 2009, CTA 2010 or TIOPA 2010 is most likely to be relevant to anything specific to corporation tax.

The contents page at the beginning of every Act lists every section and paragraph and its title. This may be sufficient to answer your query.

Structure of an Act

An Act is organised as follows:

- Contents page

- Parts and chapters – an Act is subdivided into parts which are further subdivided into chapters. We do not normally refer to parts or chapters and generally just reference the legislation by the specific section or paragraph of relevance

- Sections – within each chapter there will be various sections. Each section has a title and is generally broken down into sub-sections. Notation when referring to a section is: 's.3(5) IHTA 1984'. This refers to section 3, sub-section 5 of IHTA 1984

- Schedules are the equivalent to appendices and are always at the end of an Act after all the sections. Schedules are broken down into paragraphs and sub-paragraphs. Notation when referring to a paragraph is: 'para1(3), Sch 5 IHTA 1984'. This refers to paragraph 1, sub-paragraph 3 of Schedule 5 of IHTA 1984

3.6 Interpreting legislation

It is important to read the legislation carefully in order to ensure that you have understood it correctly.

The following extracts from the legislation highlight the importance of critical words:

- 'This section **shall** apply...' (s.162 TCGA 1992)
- '...the company **may** surrender...' (s.99(2) CTA 2010)

The use of the word 'shall' indicates that a provision is mandatory and must be used. Although, take care, as Finance Act 2002 subsequently inserted s.162A which allows a taxpayer to make an election for s.162 to not apply.

In contrast, the word 'may' shows that the company has an option. Generally, where there is an option the taxpayer (and the taxpayer's agent) are required to take some action in order to receive a relief.

Other words to consider include:

- '...then, **subject to** subsection (3) **and** sections 166, 167, 169, 169B **and** 169C, subsection (4) **shall** apply in relation to the disposal.' (s.165(1) TCGA 1992)

  – indicating that conditions must be satisfied or exclusions apply.

- '...'relative' means spouse **or** civil partner; parent **or** remoter forebear; child **or** remoter issue; **or** brother **or** sister...' (s.448(2) CTA 2010)

  – indicating that any of the relatives listed will satisfy the requirement.

- '...paragraph 13 **does not apply if** (a), (b) **and** (c).' (para 15(1) Sch 10 PCA 2002)

  – indicating that all conditions must be satisfied.

- 'A claim under any provision of the Corporation Tax Acts for a relief, an allowance or a repayment of tax **must** be for an amount which is quantified at the time when the claim is made...' (Para 54 Sch 18 FA 1998)

  – a mandatory provision.

- 'Property **shall be treated** as satisfying the condition in section 106 above **if-**...' (s.107(1) IHTA 1994)

  – indicating a deeming provision – be careful to identify for what purposes this is held to be true – it may only affect small parts of the legislation.

Summary

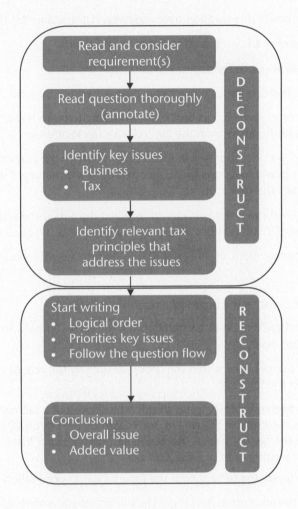

Self-test

Answer the following questions.

1   Set plc is a large company incorporated in the UK. It owns 100% of the ordinary share capital of three subsidiaries – Deuce Ltd, Advantage Ltd and Love Ltd. All companies prepare accounts to 30 June each year and the figures discussed at the meeting relate to the year ended 30 June 2016.

   The finance director of Set plc, Venus Wimbledon, met recently with your audit partner, Greg Henman, and expressed her concern about some group corporation tax issues.

   Greg took some notes at the meeting and, following a request from Venus, he promised to send a report to the board of directors of Set plc setting out the implications.

   The notes Greg took at the meeting were as follows:

   • Deuce Ltd is a manufacturing company, based in Hull.

      – It has trading losses of £1m brought forward and an estimated loss of £2m for this year.

      – Due to innovations and efficiency measures that are to be implemented, it expects to be profitable within the next three years.

      – Profits are then anticipated to be in the region of £4m per annum.

   • Advantage Ltd is incorporated in the UK.

- Provides financial services and has two branches, one in Wokingham, England and one in Utopia where its board meetings are also held.

- Both branches are very profitable, with trading profits this year of £3m for each branch.

- Due to poor exchange rates none of the overseas branch profits is remitted to the UK.

- The overseas branch suffers tax at 19%.

- There is no double taxation treaty between Utopia and the UK.

- A dividend of £1.5m is paid to Set plc every year.

- Love Ltd deals in goods for delivery to and from the UK.

  - Very profitable – expects profits for the year ended 30 June 2016 to be £750,000.

  - Set up some years ago as part of an overall scheme to reduce the group's tax liability by shifting profits away from the UK to lower tax locations.

  - Love Ltd was incorporated in Overseasland where the corporation tax rate is 10% and holds its board meetings there. Its operations are managed locally, with no significant input from the UK.

- Set plc's only income is from dividends received from its three subsidiary companies and rental income of £100,000 per annum from investment properties.

  It incurred management expenses of £50,000 in the current year.

Requirement

Draft a report to be sent to the board of directors explaining:

- The scope and calculation of corporation tax for each company in the group, including double taxation relief, and

- The possible use of losses within the group, assuming the rate of corporation tax remains unchanged in the future.

2   Rectangle Ltd needs to raise cash. It has decided to dispose of a factory to an unconnected property investment company, House Ltd, for £4.5m on 31 March 2016. House Ltd will then immediately lease the factory back to Rectangle Ltd on a 22 year lease. The annual rental will be £241,500 plus a lease premium of £432,000.

If House Ltd were to sell the factory with the tenants still in occupation it would be worth £4.3m.

The factory has a historic cost in Rectangle Ltd's financial statements of £945,000 (including land of £535,000) and its net book value is £725,000 as at 31 March 2016. The factory was originally purchased on 1 April 2009 as a newly constructed building.

Both Rectangle Ltd and House Ltd prepare their accounts and their annual VAT returns to 31 March. Rectangle Ltd is VAT registered making wholly standard rated supplies.

Requirement

Explain the tax implications of:

- The sale and purchase for both Rectangle Ltd and House Ltd.
- The lease back for just Rectangle Ltd.

Assume an RPI for March 2016 of 260.2.

3   **Svetlana Lucas [taken from Sample Paper 1]**

Svetlana Lucas is an entrepreneur with many business interests. She is a new personal tax client of your firm and has provided you with some background information (**Exhibit 1**). Your firm has already completed its client acceptance procedures in respect of Svetlana.

Svetlana prepared and filed her own tax return for the tax year ended 5 April 2016 and has recently attended a meeting to discuss a number of tax issues. Your firm has agreed to advise Svetlana with regard to her 2016/17 tax return.

Svetlana is also the finance director of Galileo Ltd, a corporate tax client of your firm. Information concerning Galileo Ltd's taxable profits is in **Exhibit 2**, together with the draft estimated results for the nine months ending 31 December 2015. Galileo Ltd ceased trading on 31 December 2015.

The tax partner has left some notes for you on your desk from the meeting with Svetlana, prepared by a junior associate.

Notes from the meeting:

Business expansion plans for Newton Cards

Svetlana wishes to expand Newton Cards to include on-line sales and requires finance of £25,000. On 1 December 2015 she ordered £25,000 of computer software and hardware. Svetlana has negotiated an instalment payment plan with the computer supplier such that she will spread the cost of the equipment over 18 months, with the first payment due six months after successful delivery and operation of the on-line sales system. Additional payments will be made in monthly instalments. The hardware is due to be delivered on 1 July 2016 and the supplier has guaranteed that the system will be operating from 1 August 2016.

Svetlana claimed 100% capital allowances on the equipment from the date that she placed the order and is not willing to revise her income tax return for the year ending 5 April 2016.

In order to raise the £25,000 required to implement her plans, Svetlana will sell shares in Kepler Ltd. Another shareholder in Kepler Ltd is willing to purchase 5,000 of her shares for £6 per share, provided the sale occurs by September 2016. Other than the existing shareholders, there is no real market for Svetlana's Kepler Ltd shares. Should there be any shortfall in funding, Svetlana will use her overdraft facility, incurring an arrangement fee of £500.

IT support required by Newton Cards

Svetlana recently announced her expansion plans to the employees of Newton Cards. Freda Hoyle works part-time for Newton Cards, but was head of IT solutions for a small on-line trading company until she took voluntary redundancy in October 2014. Freda has told Svetlana that she would be willing to provide the required on-going IT support for the expansion of the business.

Svetlana would like to compare the total tax cost of employing Freda at a higher salary or using an independent IT consultant based on the following assumptions:

- Fee to be paid for IT consultancy services: £1,000 per month (VAT exclusive).

- The IT consultant would be based in the EU and would be liable for all UK and overseas income tax and national insurance as a result of the engagement.

- Extra salary for Freda: £10,000 pa.

- Freda currently earns an annual salary of £14,000 from Newton Cards.

Requirements

Prepare notes for the tax partner which address the following issues:

For Galileo Ltd:

(1) Determine, using appropriate calculations, how the trading loss for the nine months ending 31 December 2015 could be utilised by Galileo Ltd to obtain a repayment of corporation tax. You are not required to calculate the tax repayment.

For Svetlana:

(2) Explain the tax implications of Svetlana's business expansion plans for Newton Cards. Include comments on any ethical implications for your firm.

(3) Using the assumptions provided by Svetlana, compare the annual total after tax cost of employing Freda at a higher salary or using an independent IT consultant.

(30 marks)

Exhibit 1 – Background information on Svetlana Lucas

Personal information:	Born 3 May 1965.
	UK resident, UK domiciled, and a higher rate taxpayer.
Kepler Ltd:	UK resident graphic design company.
	Svetlana subscribed for 20,000 ordinary shares in December 2014 for £86,000. This represented a 20% shareholding. Svetlana does not work for Kepler Ltd. Svetlana claimed EIS income tax relief in respect of the purchase of these shares in the tax year ended 5 April 2015.
	EIS reinvestment relief was also claimed to defer a chargeable gain of £76,000 in the tax year ended 5 April 2015.
Newton Cards:	An unincorporated business set up by Svetlana in 2000 producing hand-made greetings cards and stationery. The business is registered for VAT and has four employees.
Capital transactions:	Svetlana had a capital loss brought forward of £8,000 at 6 April 2015 and has made no disposals of chargeable assets during 2015/16.

Exhibit 2 – Information concerning Galileo Ltd – Actual and estimated tax adjusted results for Galileo Ltd

	Year ended 31 March 2013 £	Year ended 31 March 2014 £	Year ended 31 March 2015 £	Nine months ending 31 Dec 2015 £
Trading profits/(losses)	243,900	171,600	41,300	(78,000)
Overseas permanent establishment profits (gross)	–	4,200	6,950	9,300
Property income	13,200	15,100	5,450	2,200

Galileo Ltd has an overseas permanent establishment in a jurisdiction where the tax rate on trading profits of permanent establishments is 18%. The permanent establishment was established in February 2014 and is controlled from the UK by Galileo Ltd. There is no tax treaty between the UK and the overseas jurisdiction and no election has been made to exempt the profits of the permanent establishment.

Galileo Ltd has two associated/ related 51% group companies and ceased trading on 31 December 2015.

Now go back to the Learning objectives in the Introduction. If you are satisfied you have achieved these objectives, please tick them off.

Answer to Interactive question

The suggested solution to the sample paper question is set out below. You are unlikely to have been able to produce this in the time suggested, but it is still a good indication of the points a strong answer would cover.

Working paper for the attention of the Tax Director TT Group

(a) (i) (1) *Explanation of the maximum surrender of Circon's trading loss to TT*

Although TT will not have a 75% shareholding in Circon, sufficient to claim group loss relief, its acquisition of 45% of the shares will ensure that it forms a consortium with DL. The two companies together would own more than 75% of the ordinary shares. Circon would therefore be a consortium company. The fact that DL is an overseas company does not affect this.

Losses of the consortium company can be surrendered to the consortium members in proportion to the consortium members' shareholdings. However, as DL is an overseas company, no loss relief will be surrendered to DL.

Circon is a group consortium company, because it is also a member of a 75% group with Cafee and WebAd. Circon's consortium loss surrender to TT will therefore be restricted by a notional current year loss claim and also by notional group relief surrender to its subsidiaries.

(2) *Determination of the maximum trading loss from Circon available to TT*

If the 'maximum surrenderable loss' is to be calculated, a claim for capital allowances should be made in the individual tax computations of Circon as follows:

	£m
Trading loss	8.0
Add capital allowances	2.0
Revised trading tax loss	10.0

The amount of loss available to be surrendered to the consortium members is as follows:

Circon would first make a notional current year loss relief claim against its property income profits.

The amount available for consortium relief to TT will then depend on whether WebAd's loss is group relieved to Cafee and, if so, to what extent. If it were fully relieved against Cafee's profit then the balance of £3.8 million (£6.8 million – £3 million) would be deemed to be available for relieving Circon's loss.

Circon	£m
Revised tax loss	10.0
Less notional current year loss relief claim	(1.0)
notional group relief claim	(3.8)
Available for consortium members	5.2

Thus a maximum consortium loss claim of 45% × £5.2 million = £2.34 million would be available to TT.

If no claim is made to relieve WebAd's loss against Cafee's profit, then the available loss for the consortium members would be notionally reduced by the total of Cafee's profits of £6.8 million.

Circon	£m
Revised tax loss	10.0
Less notional current year claim	(1.0)
notional group relief claim	(6.8)
Available for consortium members	2.2

Thus a maximum consortium loss claim of 45% × £2.2 million = £0.99 million would be available to TT.

(ii) *A brief analysis of the factors TT needs to consider in response to Alan Fleurie's suggestion (Exhibit 1) regarding the price for his Circon shares.*

Alan is presumably suggesting that the value of the loss to TT is taken into account as a negotiating factor in order to increase the price TT are willing to pay for his shares. Circon is arguably worth more to TT than Alan Fleurie, given its 2016 losses can potentially be used by TT, but not by Alan. However, TT would need to consider this carefully as there is considerable uncertainty over the amount of loss relief that TT can claim.

- *Timing of relief*

Surrender of the loss to TT may prove to be the most effective use of the Circon loss, as the rate of corporation tax is unified at the main rate of 20%. It would appear that Circon has not been paying tax so a carry back claim may not be possible. An alternative is for Circon to carry forward the loss against future profits of the same trade, but this will be later relief.

- *Consortium members may not agree to the use of consortium loss – DL and Alan have different priorities regarding use of Circon's loss.*

DL, the other consortium member, is not able to claim consortium relief because it is an overseas company. However, a claim for consortium relief requires the permission of the consortium members. Surrendering part of the trading loss to TT is effectively giving away a future asset of Circon. DL may require that TT pays for the consortium relief, which would therefore result in any additional amount paid to Alan Fleurie being greater than the tax value TT receives from the use of the losses

Given the uncertainties regarding the use of the loss, using the losses as a negotiation factor in the price to be paid for Alan's shares is questionable.

(b) *A summary of the UK tax implications of transferring the trade and assets of TT's permanent establishment in Grania to GG Inc.*

As no election for the exemption of the profits from the charge to UK tax has been made, the profits of the PE would be included in TT's taxable total profits for the six months prior to incorporation.

Incorporation of the permanent establishment as a limited company created balancing adjustments for capital allowances and a chargeable gain on the freehold property in Grania.

The gain on the freehold property can be postponed as the consideration for the transfer of the trade and the assets was in the form of shares (securities). Potentially there will be a claw back of the relief if the shares in GG are sold within six years, when any gain will be taxed in TT's hands.

If the shares in GG are sold, the chargeable gain on the freehold property in Grania of £338,000 (600,000 – 250,000 = 350,000 less £12,000 indexation allowance ie (257.5 – 245.6/245.6 = 0.048 × £250,000) will be chargeable on TT, together with any gain on the disposal of the shares themselves. However, the gain on the sale of the shares themselves may be eligible for the substantial shareholding exemption.

SDLT will not apply as it is generally payable on the purchase or transfer of property or land in the UK. This is property/assets based overseas.

It is unclear whether there are any risks regarding the residence position of GG: if its central management and control are in the UK, it will be UK resident. This should be clarified: if there is any uncertainty it may be possible to confirm the position with HMRC.

GG will pay Granian corporation tax and must comply with Granian indirect tax and other regulations.

Dividends paid by GG to TT in the UK will not be taxable in the UK.

(c) *Ethical and legal implications:*

Jo's e-mail raises ethical and legal issues both for the employee, Jo Sun and for TT.

Jo potentially is in a different position from TT. The officers of TT should consider carefully their actions in order to avoid 'tipping off' those committing the illegal acts under the money laundering regulations.

For Jo Sun

She feels pressure to hide the payments because, in the first instance, the request to do so was made by her superior. Financially she would like to keep her job and personally, she is away from home and wants to feel part of the culture and environment in which she is working. Potentially if she performs well on her secondment there is the possibility of future rewards.

Action by Jo Sun

Jo should:

Determine the facts, and the extent of the payments and document her findings and discussions.

As she has concerns regarding the legality of the payments she has correctly initially discussed this further with her line manager in Grania.

As this avenue has proved ineffective she has brought the matter to the attention of head office in the UK.

If she has suspicions over the legality of the payments, she should refuse to be involved in the authorisation of the payments.

Clearly if head office is complicit in the treatment of these items then Jo will need to seek help from outside the organisation. In any case Jo should seek help from her professional body and also consider taking legal advice locally in Grania regarding her own position. Ultimately resignation may be the only option.

For TT

This issue raises a number of points:

- There is the potential that illegal payments are being made from one of TT's subsidiaries. Payments made to officials who are in a position to influence the decision to permit GG's goods to enter the country quickly would contravene the Bribery Act.

Action: TT needs to ensure that it has policies and procedures necessary to ensure that all employees and agents understand the Bribery Act and the requirement to comply with its provisions.

- As the tax department at TT is now aware of the issue, we should contact Jo to discuss the payments and determine further action. Dependent on the outcome of the discussions, TT should seek legal advice both in the UK and in Grania.

- If satisfactory explanations are not forthcoming, the matter should be brought to the attention of the TT board and should be considered within the company's own procedures for identifying and reporting money laundering.

- If other payments had been made, when the permanent establishment was within the charge to UK corporation tax, ie prior to incorporation, such payments are not permitted for tax deduction in the UK and TT should consider disclosure to HMRC and revision of past corporation tax computations.

1 **Report to the board of directors of Set plc**

Prepared by Greg Henman
Date Today
Subject Group corporation tax issues

Group structure

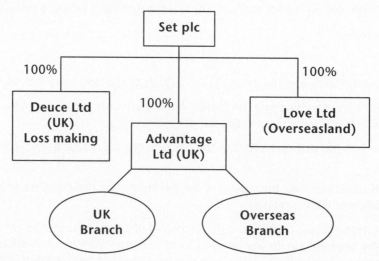

Implications of the group structure

Love Ltd is not resident in the UK as it is both incorporated and controlled overseas. As Love Ltd only trades overseas, its profits will not be taxed in the UK unless it is treated as a controlled foreign company.

It will be treated as a controlled foreign company because it is resident overseas and controlled from the UK. Unless it satisfies one of the exemptions from the CFC rules, to the extent that it has chargeable profits which pass through the CFC gateway these will be apportioned to Set plc as its sole shareholder. Those profits are subject to corporation tax in the UK, less credit for the Overseasland tax paid on those profits.

It is likely here that although Love Ltd has assets which derive from a tax planning scheme, none of its trading profits will pass through the CFC gateway because none of its assets or risks are managed from the UK. If this is right, none of its profits will pass through the gateway, and there will be no amount to be apportioned. Any financing income included in its profits would need to be considered separately, unless it represented less than 5% of the company's trading profits.

Set plc, Deuce Ltd and Advantage Ltd will be assessed to UK corporation tax.

Group loss relief claims are possible between Set plc, Deuce Ltd and Advantage Ltd. Losses cannot be group relieved to Love Ltd as it is not resident in the UK and does not carry on a trade in the UK.

Set plc

Set plc only receives dividends from other companies in the group; not all of the dividends are UK dividends. As Set plc is a large company and the dividends are all received from 100% subsidiaries both the UK and overseas dividends from Love Ltd are exempt from tax. Thus Set plc's only taxable income for the year is its property income.

As Set plc carries on an investment business, the expenses of management of £50,000 are deductible from the company's total profits, ie £100,000, leaving taxable profits of £50,000, which are liable to UK corporation tax at 20%.

Set plc could claim losses from Deuce Ltd.

Deuce Ltd

The £1m trading losses brought forward cannot be surrendered within the group; they can only be carried forward and set off against future trading profits of the same trade in Deuce Ltd.

The innovations and efficiency measures do not in themselves constitute a change in trade; thus the losses should be relieved at some point in the future, provided its existing trade continues.

The current year losses can be surrendered via group relief to Set plc and/or Advantage Ltd, but not to Love Ltd (see implications of group structure).

Advantage Ltd

As the company is incorporated in the UK it is UK resident, and will pay corporation tax on its worldwide profits. It will therefore be liable to tax on both the UK and overseas branch profits. The location of the board meetings is irrelevant in determining whether the company is UK resident.

The profits of the UK branch will be assessed as trading profits. As the Utopian branch is an entirely separate trade carried on wholly from Utopia, ie where the board meets, its profits will also be assessed as trading profits but they are treated as ring fenced for the purposes of offset of trading losses. The profits of the branch in Utopia are assessed in full, regardless of whether they are actually remitted to the UK.

As the profits will be translated into sterling, relief will be given for the low exchange rate.

For future years, it is possible for Advantage Ltd to make an irrevocable election for all its foreign permanent establishments to be exempt from UK corporation tax on their profits. The profits of the Utopian branch would be exempt and this would reduce Advantage Ltd's UK tax liability. It is not possible to make this election for the current accounting period as the election only becomes valid from the start of the accounting period after the one in which the election is made.

Utilisation of trading losses within the group

The trading losses of Deuce Ltd can all be surrendered to Advantage Ltd. Deuce Ltd has current year losses of £2m. The whole amount can be surrendered to Advantage Ltd as it has profits of £6m.

Group relief is set against total profits including any profits arising overseas. In other words, for the purposes of group relief of a loss against the profits of a foreign PE, it is not relevant whether the PE is carrying on a separate trade controlled wholly overseas. However, if the loss is set against the profits arising in the foreign PE, the amount of DTR would be reduced. It is therefore important to allocate the losses against the UK branch profits in preference to the overseas branch profits, as this will ensure that double taxation relief is not wasted.

Advantage Ltd – corporation tax computations with group loss relief

	Total £'000	UK £'000	Utopia £'000
Trading profit	6,000	3,000	3,000
Group loss relief	(2,000)	(2,000)	
Taxable total profits	4,000	1,000	3,000
Corporation tax at 20%	800	200	600
Basic DTR – lower of			
(i) UK tax = £630,000			
(ii) Overseas tax (£3m × 19%) = £570,000	(570)		(570)
Corporation tax liability	230	200	30

From a cash flow point of view, it is clearly advantageous to obtain relief for the losses now via group relief, rather than waiting for relief in the future. It is assumed that all losses are relieved in Advantage Ltd rather than Set plc.

The claim for group relief needs to be made 12 months after Advantage Ltd's filing date. This is likely to be two years after the end of its accounting period.

2 Sale and lease back – taxation implications

Rectangle Ltd – vendor

The disposal of the factory will give rise to a chargeable gain of £3,337,650 (Working 1). This will give rise to additional corporation tax of £667,530 meaning that the sale will only generate cash of £3,832,470 (£4,500,000 – £667,530).

It may be possible for the gain to be rolled over into the purchase of other qualifying business assets such as property or fixed plant and machinery between 1 April 2015 and 31 March 2019.

As the factory is more than three years old and assuming the option to tax was not exercised, there is no VAT to be charged on the sale. However, as the building is only seven years old and originally cost more than £250,000 it falls within the capital goods scheme. Therefore on an exempt disposal before 1 April 2019 there will be a claw back of some of the initial input VAT recovered:

Original input VAT recovered = £945,000 × 15% = £141,750

The sale adjustment under the capital goods scheme will be:

(£141,750/10) × (0% – 100%) × 3 intervals = £42,525 repayable to HMRC

Rectangle Ltd could opt to tax the building prior to its disposal. This would make the sale a standard rated supply. There would then be no sale adjustment under the capital goods scheme.

However, this may affect the purchase price payable by House Ltd, depending on whether House Ltd is prepared to opt to tax the building in order to recover the input tax paid. As House Ltd will be renting out the property it will be an exempt supply and the input tax would be irrecoverable unless House Ltd also opted to tax the building.

House Ltd – purchaser

If both companies opt to tax the building, the VAT payable will simply be a timing difference for House Ltd. However, stamp duty land tax is payable on the VAT inclusive price. This is a permanent increase in price.

Opting to tax would enable House Ltd to recover any input VAT incurred on the expenses of the business. House Ltd would need to charge VAT on the lease premium and the annual rental. As Rectangle Ltd is VAT registered, this will simply represent a cash flow timing difference. However, it will increase the SDLT payable by House Ltd, if applicable.

Stamp duty land tax will be payable on the purchase price of the factory at 4% ie £180,000 if a VAT exclusive sale or £216,000 if the purchase price is £4.5m plus VAT.

Rectangle Ltd – lessee

SDLT at 3% will be payable on the lease premium inclusive of VAT. In addition SDLT will also be payable at 1% on the net present value of the total lease rentals inclusive of VAT in excess of £150,000. Assuming there is no VAT on the lease, this will give total SDLT payable on the lease of £64,590 (W2).

Some of the lease premium will be treated as rental income for House Ltd and will therefore be allowed as additional deemed rent for Rectangle Ltd. The additional annual rent allowable as an expense for corporation tax purposes will be £250,560/22 = £11,389 (W3).

The lease rentals will be a tax deductible expense.

Note. The SDLT payable on the lease back may be exempt under s.57A of Finance Act 2003. There is insufficient information in the question to determine whether it is exempt and this exemption is also outside the scope of the syllabus. However, credit would be given for any candidate stating it as a possibility.

WORKINGS

(1) **Chargeable gain on sale of factory**

	£
Proceeds	4,500,000
Less cost	(945,000)
Less IA April 2009 to March 2016	
$\dfrac{260.2 - 211.5}{211.5} = 0.230 \times £945,000$	(217,350)
Chargeable gain	3,337,650

(2) **SDLT on lease**

	£
SDLT on lease premium at 3%	12,960
SDLT on NPV of lease premiums (assume NPV is as stated in question)	
22 × £241,500 = £5,313,000 – £150,000 = £5,163,000 @ 1%	51,630
Total SDLT	64,590

(3) **Deemed additional rent**

	£
Deemed rent = £432,000 × [(50 – 21)/50]	250,560

3 **Svetlana Lucas**

Briefing note for the partner

(1) **Use of Galileo Ltd's trading loss**

	Year ended 31 March 2013	Year ended 31 March 2014	Year ended 31 March 2015	9 months ending 31 December 2015
	£	£	£	£
Trading profits	243,900	171,600	41,300	Nil
Overseas profits (Note)	–	4,200	5,699	7,626
Property income	13,200	15,100	5,450	2,200
Total profits	257,100	190,900	52,449	9,826
Less loss relief		(15,725)	(52,449)	(9,826)
Taxable total profits	257,100	175,175	Nil	Nil

Therefore a repayment of corporation will be available for the year ended 31 March 2014 and 2015.

Note:

Double tax relief is available for the overseas tax on the profits of the permanent establishment. However, no credit relief will be available in the year ended 31 March 2015 and the nine month period to 31 December 2015 because the profits are eliminated by losses. The overseas tax can instead be treated as an expense and deducted from the overseas profits as follows:

Nine months ended 31 December 2015: £9,300 – 1,674 = £7,626

Year ended 31 March 2015: £6,950 – 1,251 = £5,699

The post-cessation trading receipts will have been accrued for in the results for the nine months ended 31 December 2015 and therefore no further adjustment is required.

(2) **Tax implications of Svetlana's expansion plans**

Financing options – option 1

Interest payable on the bank borrowing will be deductible as a business expense in calculating the tax adjusted profits of Newton Cards. The £500 arrangement fee is an incidental cost of raising loan finance and deductible as an expense in arriving at the tax adjusted profits of Newton Cards.

Financing options – option 2

As the EIS shares in Kepler Ltd are being sold within three years of purchase, a gain will arise. In addition, the deferred gain of £19,000 will crystallise.

Svetlana's annual exempt amount of £11,100 and also her capital loss brought forward of £8,000 are available to offset this gain as follows:

	£
Proceeds £6 × 5,000	30,000
Less cost £86,000 × 5,000/20,000	(21,500)
	8,500
Add deferred gain £76,000 × 5,000/20,000	19,000
	27,500
Less:	
Capital loss b/f	(8,000)
Annual exempt amount	(11,100)
	8,400
Capital gains tax: £8,400 × 28%	2,352
Add withdrawal of EIS relief, lower of:	
Relief already given: £21,500 × 30% = £6,450	
Relief on the value received = £30,000 × 30% = £9,000	6,450
	8,802

Therefore the funds available for Svetlana are £30,000 – 8,802 = £21,198

The remaining £(25,000 – 21,198) = £3,802 will need to be funded from Svetlana's overdraft facility, the interest on which will be deductible for the purposes of computing her tax adjusted trading profits.

New computer equipment

The order for the new equipment was placed on 1 December 2015. For capital allowances purposes, expenditure is deemed to be incurred on the date on which the obligation to pay becomes unconditional. However, if any part of the payment is not due until four months after that date, that part of the expenditure is treated as having been incurred on the due date for payment.

Therefore, capital allowances would not be available on the computer equipment until 2016/17 and Svetlana's tax return for 2015/16 is incorrect.

Ethical issues for the firm – refusal to amend the 2015/16 income tax return

By claiming capital allowances that are not due on the computer equipment, Svetlana is evading tax which is illegal. She should be informed of the need to amend her tax return, in writing. She should also be informed of the possible interest payment on underpaid tax and also penalties, which are also influenced by her behaviour, which appears to be deliberate.

If Svetlana continues to refuse to amend her return, the engagement letter should be checked for any agreed conditions under which the firm may disclose information to HMRC.

Consideration should also be given as to whether the firm should cease to act for Svetlana. HMRC should then be informed of the decision not to act, without reasons.

As she has filed her tax return, the tax evasion means that she has paid less tax and therefore this constitutes proceeds of crime for money laundering purposes. A report should be made to the MLRO with consideration as to whether a SAR should be submitted.

(3) **Annual cost of employing Freda or using an IT consultant**

Employing Freda

	£
Additional salary	10,000
Employers' NI: £10,000 × 13.8%	1,380
	11,380
Less IT relief £11,380 × 42%	(4,780)
After tax cost	6,600

Using an independent IT consultant

	£
Fees: £1,000 × 12 × 120%	14,400
Reverse charge: £1,000 × 12 × 20%	(2,400)
	12,000
Less IT relief £12,000 × 42%	(5,040)
After tax cost	6,960

The after tax cost of employing Freda is slightly lower.

CHAPTER 21

Choice of business structure

Introduction
Examination context
Topic List
Summary and Self-test
Answers to Interactive questions
Answers to Self-test

Introduction

Learning objectives

- Communicate in a format appropriate to the recipient who may be an external client, a fellow professional or an internal colleague ☐

- Prepare suitable advice to explain tax liabilities with supporting calculations ☐

- Recommend appropriate tax-planning advice ☐

- Identify further information required to complete tax computations and finalise tax advice ☐

- Give advice which is appropriate, technically correct, and within the law and the ICAEW Code of Ethics ☐

- Determine, explain and calculate the tax liabilities for individuals and corporate entities, including income tax, national insurance, corporation tax, stamp taxes and VAT ☐

- Evaluate the tax implications of the choice of business structures ☐

- Explain the taxation issues relating to business start-ups ☐

- Explain and evaluate the tax implications of group structures ☐

- Explain and evaluate the tax implications of business transformations and change ☐

- Explain and calculate the tax implications involved in the cessation of trade ☐

- Identify legitimate tax planning measures to minimise tax liabilities ☐

- Evaluate and advise on tax strategies to meet business objectives ☐

- Evaluate and advise on alternative tax strategies relating to corporate transformations ☐

- Recognise, explain and communicate opportunities to use alternative tax treatments arising from past transactions ☐

Specific syllabus references for this chapter are 1a, 1b, 1c, 1d, 1e, 1f, 1g, 1h, 1j, 1l, 1m, 2a, 2b, 2c and 2d.

Syllabus links

The choice of business structure is very important for determining the way in which profits are taxed and where (owner, employee, company, shareholder). Careful consideration should therefore be given to selecting the most appropriate structure.

Examination context

Selecting the best type of trading entity for a client, identifying when that may need to change and the most appropriate method of profit extraction is a fundamental part of the tax advice accountants give to many owner managed businesses year after year.

In the examination candidates may be required to:

- Advise on the most appropriate business structure for a given scenario
- Advise on the most tax efficient method of withdrawing profits from a business for a given scenario
- Advise on the most appropriate corporate structure for a given scenario

1 Choice of trading entity

Section overview

- A trade may be operated as an unincorporated business (sole trader or partnership) or a corporate business (company).

- When considering which type of entity to use, consider the taxation of the owner, the business and the tax effect of extraction of profits.

- Deciding how to structure a business will, however, depend on both tax and non-tax considerations.

- Establishing a business as an unincorporated trader is administratively easier and all of the profits and gains of the business are taxable on the trader personally.

- Establishing a business as a company requires adherence to company law and reporting procedures. It also means that the shareholders are potentially taxable on income and gains extracted from the company which have already been subject to corporation tax. Whether the overall tax effect of trading as a company is beneficial depends on the level of forecast income and gains.

1.1 Types of trading entity

An individual who wishes to set up his own business must consider the choice of trading entities available. It is advisable to select the most suitable permanent trading medium for a new business at the commencement of operations. This is due to the problems and costs of changing the trading entity at a later stage (eg by incorporation of an existing business – see later in this chapter).

The two main choices available are:

- Unincorporated business (ie sole trader or partnership)
- Corporate business (company – individuals are shareholders and/or directors)

In many cases taxation is the key factor in choosing the appropriate trading medium. However, there are some relevant non-tax matters which should also be taken into consideration (eg an unincorporated business has flexibility of business arrangements, no statutory filing requirements, reduced reporting requirements but unlimited liability).

1.2 Unincorporated or corporate business?

In your previous studies, you considered the implications of establishing a business as either a sole trader/partnership or as a company. The tax implications of the two choices are important both in the short-term and long-term. The tax effects of the choice will affect how the profits of the business are taxed and then extracted and how the business will be taxed on a subsequent disposal.

When considering the tax implications of different structures and transactions it is important to also consider, where possible, known future changes to tax rates and the tax system (see Section 2.2).

	Unincorporated business	Company
Status	• Sole trader or partnership	• Corporate body
		• Probably a close company – liable to penalty tax on loans to participators

	Unincorporated business	Company
Taxation of profits	• All profits subject to income tax at maximum of 45%	• Profits of the company subject to corporation tax at 20% • Extracted profits subject to income tax in the hands of the shareholders (see below) • Gains on the sale of shares subject to CGT for individual shareholders
NIC	• Class 2 & 4 at 9% and then 2% max	• Class 1 at 12% max employee + 13.8% employer • Overall NIC bill is higher
Payment of tax	• Payments on account 31 January in tax year, 31 July following tax year end • Balance 31 January following tax year end	• Operate PAYE on employment income, payable monthly • Corporation tax payable 9 months + 1 day after AP end
Pension	• Personal pension scheme (PPS) only	• Company can contribute to a PPS and/or an occupational pension scheme (OPS) • If a Small Self Administered Scheme (SSAS) may lend money to the company (the PPS equivalent, a SIPP, cannot lend money)
Losses	• Use of losses is more flexible eg losses in first four tax years of trade can be set against total income of previous three years (subject to overall cap on deductions)	• Use of losses is normally against total profits of CY and PY and then carry forward against trading profits only
Disposal of assets	• The trader owns the assets so it is a disposal by him which will be taxed at a maximum of 28% • If entrepreneur's relief is claimed, this reduces to 10% on the first £10m (lifetime limit) of gains	• Disposal of assets owned by the company will be subject to corporation tax at 20% • If the funds are then extracted they will be subject to tax again in the hands of the individual shareholder, ie double taxation charge
Exit strategy	• Disposal of business as a going concern and cease to trade • Disposal of separate assets and cease to trade • Simply cease to trade	• Sell shares back to company • Sell shares to a third party • Solvent liquidation • Insolvent liquidation
Disposal of business	• Disposal of each individual asset for CGT purposes • Entrepreneurs' relief may be available	• Disposal of shares by individual shareholders is subject to CGT • Entrepreneurs' relief may be available

	Unincorporated business	Company
IHT	• A transfer of the whole business is eligible for BPR at 100% • A transfer of an asset used in a partnership is only eligible for BPR at 50%. • A transfer of an asset used in a business or partnership may qualify for 100% BPR if HMRC accepts that transfer results in reduction of net value of the business. [Nelson case]	• A transfer of shares in an unquoted trading company will always be eligible for BPR at 100% (NB if quoted, BPR is at 50% providing transferor has control) • A transfer of an asset owned personally and used in a company he controls is only eligible for BPR at 50%.

2 Withdrawing profits from the business

Section overview

- A sole trader pays tax on all profits from the business whether or not he extracts the funds.

- It is possible to extract profits from a company in a number of ways; the extraction of profits in a tax efficient manner is of paramount importance.

- It may be more tax efficient to extract profits from a company through a dividend rather than as earnings, but this depends on the rate of tax payable by the company.

2.1 Extracting profits from a company

A sole trader pays tax on all the profits of the business and on gains on the disposal of any assets used in the business. There are no issues in extracting funds from the business as they have already been taxed on the individual in full.

An owner managed company needs to carefully consider the way in which funds are extracted in order to minimise the taxation implications. The business profits may only be subject to corporation tax, probably at the small profits rate, but any monies paid to the shareholders will be subject to further taxation.

2.1.1 Ongoing methods of extracting profits

Shareholders (who may also be employees) of an owner managed company, who wish to extract the profits of the business, may do so in the form of:

- Dividends
- Remuneration ie cash or benefits
- Pension contributions, or
- Loans.

2.1.2 Exit route for investors

Shareholders of an owner managed company who wish to extract their share of the company's assets may do so in one of four ways:

- Sell their shares to a third party (see Chapter 23);
- Sell their shares back to the company (see Chapter 17);
- Liquidate an insolvent company (see Chapter 17); or
- Liquidate a solvent company (see Chapters 17 and 22).

2.1.3 Tax efficient remuneration

Director/shareholders of an owner-managed company will seek to extract profits from the company in the most tax efficient way possible.

Method of extracting funds	Treatment for company	Treatment for individual shareholder/director
Salary, bonus, commission, benefits	• Gross amount (plus employer NIC) deductible as trading expense. Reduces CT • Cost to company is gross amount plus employer NIC less CT relief • Can discriminate and make payments to selected directors only • Employer's NIC applies to salary and benefits with no upper limit	• Income tax payable at max 45% • Employee's NIC at max 12% • Employment income treated as part of relevant earnings for pension purposes
Dividend	• Not an allowable deduction for CT purposes • Cost to company is dividend paid • Must be paid to all shareholders of same class, including minority shareholders. Cannot discriminate payments between shareholders (unless different classes of shares are issued) • Must be paid out of retained earnings. If the company never makes a profit, dividends may not be payable • No employer's NIC	• Subject to income tax at a max rate of 37.5% with a tax credit of 10% • Effective tax rate for a higher rate taxpayer is 25% of the cash dividend • Effective tax rate for an additional rate taxpayer is 30.6% of the cash dividend • Not part of relevant earnings for pension purposes • No employee's NIC
Pension	• Employer's contributions are an allowable deduction for CT purposes. Reduces CT payable • Cost to the company is gross contribution less CT relief • Can discriminate between individual employees • No employer's NIC	• Employer's contributions are an exempt benefit • Funds in scheme grow tax-free • No employee's NIC • Pension income is taxable on retirement although max 25% may be taken as a tax free lump sum

2.1.4 Allocating dividend income

Spouses and civil partners can own shares in a company jointly and pay out income as dividends. The transfer of shares is treated as an outright gift and the dividend income will be taxed on each shareholder independently.

In Jones v Garnett (2007) the House of Lords ruled that a gift of shares between spouses should be treated as a gift and the income therefore taxed on each spouse independently. In this case (also known as Arctic Systems) Mr Jones earned most of his company's revenue and paid himself a low rate of pay. The shares were owned jointly by Mr and Mrs Jones and most of the profits were paid out as dividends. HMRC tried to argue that Mr Jones should be taxed on all the dividend income as the transfer of shares was not a true gift, but a settlement.

The Treasury had intended to introduce specific anti-avoidance legislation, in the form of 'income shifting' rules, to target this perceived abuse, although its initial proposals were shelved after consultation. This topic remains very topical and is of critical importance to the thousands of owner managed companies it affects.

2.2 Future tax rates

From 2016/17 the basic income tax personal allowance will be increased by £200 to £10,800 and, the basic rate limit will be increased by £115 to £31,900. The corporation tax rates will stay unified at the main rate of 20%.

Interactive question 1: Dividend or bonus [Difficulty level: Intermediate]

D Ltd is an owner-managed company making up +accounts to 31 March each year.

Delia is the sole director/shareholder and receives a salary of £50,000 a year. As the company has had a very profitable year, she is considering withdrawing a further £12,000 in the year to 31 March 2016.

The company would prefer to pay a bonus of £12,000 (inclusive of class 1 secondary NICs). As an alternative it would consider paying a dividend which overall still costs the company the same as the bonus.

Requirement

Using the standard format below, compute the net income receivable by Delia if D Ltd pays her:

(1)   A dividend; or
(2)   A bonus.

	(1) Dividend	(2) Bonus
	£	£
Payments made by company:		
Bonus		
Secondary class 1 NICs		
CT on additional profits		
Dividend paid	_____	_____
Total payments	_____	_____
Amount received by owner		
Gross bonus		
Gross dividend		
Income tax @.......%		
NICs		
Income tax @.......%	_____	_____
Income net of tax	_____	_____

See **Answer** at the end of this chapter.

Interactive question 2: Salary/bonus or dividend [Difficulty level: Intermediate]

Grant and Steve are directors of Klub Ltd, a company in which they each own 50% of the shares. They receive salaries from Klub Ltd of £44,000 and £11,000 respectively and have no other income.

Klub Ltd's taxable total profits for the year ending 31 March 2016, ignoring any additional payments made, are £40,000. No dividends have yet been paid in the year to 31 March 2017.

Requirement

Calculate the cost to Klub Ltd of paying additional salary or a dividend to Grant and Steve in 2016/17 such that they receive additional income, net of all taxes and deductions, of £6,000, and recommend a course of action.

See **Answer** at the end of this chapter.

3 Corporate structure

Section overview

- A company operating more than one trade may operate as a single company or as a group. This may involve corporation tax and value added tax considerations.

- There are a number of different corporate structures: group, consortium, corporate partnership, limited liability partnership, joint venture, parallel company or divisional structure.

- The choice of corporate structure will depend on both tax and commercial considerations.

- Where companies are associated/ related 51% group companies, the corporation tax limits are reduced accordingly.

- Companies within a group are taxed separately although tax reliefs are available to members of the same group such as the treatment of the transfer of capital assets, gains and losses, and the surrender of trading losses via group relief.

3.1 Taxation of corporate structures

The choice of a corporate business structure will depend on both tax and non-tax considerations.

Within a group structure, each separate company is taxed separately. However, the group structure affords advantages regarding the transfer of assets and losses within the group. The corporation tax limits are divided according to the number of related 51% group companies, so that each company is more likely to pay corporation tax in instalments.

3.2 Single company v group of companies

Another aspect of types of trading entity that needs to be considered is whether it is more advantageous to operate as a single company with a divisional structure or through the medium of a group with a holding company and several subsidiaries.

	Single company	Group of companies
Corporation tax – income aspects	• All profits in one computation of taxable total profits • Automatic set-off of all income and losses between divisions in accounting period of loss • Money and other assets can be transferred between divisions with no effect for corporation tax	• Separate computation of taxable total profits for each company • Group relief can be used (may be limited by receiving company's taxable total profits and non-coterminous accounting periods) • Intra-group dividends are not franked investment income and so are ignored for corporation tax
Corporation tax – chargeable gains aspects	• On all assets owned by the company • All gains and losses automatically matched • Rollover relief for replacement of business assets will apply, regardless of which division uses asset • Sale of division will be sale of assets, which could give rise to capital gains or intangible fixed asset profit	• Intra-group change of ownership of asset on no gain/no loss basis • Election can be made to transfer a gain or loss from company making a disposal to a third party, to another group company to match gains and losses • Rollover relief for replacement of business assets – group treated as single entity regardless of which company owns/uses asset • Sale of subsidiary company, ie shares could give rise to capital gain, but substantial shareholding exemption could apply
Corporation tax – administrative aspects	• One corporation tax return • One payment of corporation tax	• One corporation tax return for each company • Can elect for group payment of corporation tax instalments, otherwise each company pays own corporation tax
Value added tax	• Company is a single entity for VAT: only one return required and supplies intra-division are ignored • Exempt supplies made, eg by one division, may restrict recovery of input tax	• Group can register as single entity: only one return required and supplies intra-group are ignored • Can exclude companies making exempt supplies so no restriction on recovery of input tax

Worked example: Single company v group of companies

E Ltd carries on two trades. It makes fabrics for soft furnishings and also restores original antique material. In the year ended 31 March 2016 it makes profits of £1,000,000 on the first trade and £140,000 on the second trade, and anticipates similar profit levels in the future. There are no dividends received.

Requirement

Advise which of the following will be the more effective structure in relation to payments of tax in future years:

(1) A single company with two divisions.
(2) A holding company with two wholly owned subsidiaries each operating one of the trades.

Solution

(1) **Company with two divisions**

	£
Manufacturing	1,200,000
Restoration	140,000
Taxable total profits = augmented profits	1,340,000

Limit for instalment payments:

Upper limit £1,500,000

As the augmented profits are less than £1.5 million, corporation tax of £268,000 (£1.34m × 20%) is payable by 1 January 2017.

(2) **Group of companies**

Manufacturing company

Taxable total profits £1,200,000

Restoration company

Taxable total profits £140,000

Limit for instalment payments – with two related 51% group companies:

Upper limit £1,500,000/2 = £750,000

The manufacture company has augmented profits in excess of the limit. If this is the first year of trading then the tax of £240,000 will be payable by 1 January 2017, but for the following year will be payable in four equal instalments starting with £60,000 on each of 14 October 2016, 14 January 2017, 14 April 2017 and 14 July 2017.

The restoration company has augmented profits less than £750,000, so corporation tax of £28,000 is payable by 1 January 2017.

Conclusion

It would be more tax efficient for E Ltd to operate as a single company on these level of profits, in order to prevent the early payment of corporation tax for the second and future years of the manufacturing company.

3.3 Taxation advantages and disadvantages of different trading structures

Type	Description	Advantages	Disadvantages

Group	Usually consists of holding company with controlling interests in a number of other companies.
	
	Companies can be UK resident or overseas resident but only UK companies or companies trading in the UK can generally enjoy reliefs.
		Depends on % of shares held.
		
		>50% – Companies with a trading presence in UK can form VAT group and avoid VAT on intra-group sales.
		
		≥75% – Group loss relief
		
		   – No gain/no loss transfers
		
		   – Transfer of capital gains and losses.
			Group accounts will usually be required.

Consortium	UK company at least 75% owed by other companies each of which owns ≥ 5%.	Consortium members can claim their % share of losses of consortium company. Exempt dividends paid up to members by the consortium company are not FII. Useful for large, speculative ventures as spreads risk and financing, or for high-tech ventures.	If not correctly structured the losses of the consortium company will be trapped within that company.
Corporate partnership	An unincorporated trading entity in which the partners can all be companies or a mix of companies and individuals. The profits/losses of the partnership are computed as if the partnership were a separate company using corporation tax rules.	Partnership losses available for offset against other profits (and c/b 12 months). Flexible – can be in any format agreed by partners. Confidential – limited disclosure requirements (but see IAS27 in cases of significant influence).	Partnership will be treated as a separate entity for VAT and may require registration. Members have joint and several liabilities.
Limited liability partnership (LLP)	Business structure which in law is regarded as a body corporate, but for tax will generally be treated as 'transparent', ie members will be taxed as if they were partners carrying on a business in partnership.	Conceived as a vehicle to allow professional partnerships to seek the protection of limited liability.	Significant anti-avoidance legislation where the LLP is not involved in a trade or profession (eg investment business).

Type	Description	Advantages	Disadvantages
Joint venture (JV)	If the JV vehicle is a company = a consortium (eg two companies owing 50% each of a UK company).	See advantages above.	See disadvantages above.
	If the JV vehicle is a separate unincorporated body = a corporate partnership.	See advantages above.	See disadvantages above.
	If the JV arrangement is merely contractual, the members will automatically account for the income and expenses of the venture through their own records.	Flexible. No joint and several liability. No restrictions on the use of losses (as they will arise directly in own accounts). No need to register for VAT.	Probably not suitable for long-term arrangements. May be difficult to control the activities of others in the JV.

Interactive question 3: Choice of business structure   [Difficulty level: Intermediate]

Two training companies decide to save costs by closing their in-house publishing operations and instead set up a joint venture publishing house to produce their own training material and material for external sale. The directors of each company are considering the following options:

1   Incorporate a separate company to be owned 50:50 by the two training companies;

2   Set-up an unincorporated business in which the two training companies will be equal partners; or

3   Split the publishing activities between the two companies, with one company responsible for writing and editorial functions and the other for printing and delivery. Any imbalance in costs is to be cross-invoiced at the year end.

Requirement

Explain to the directors the tax effect of each proposal.

See **Answer** at the end of this chapter.

Summary and Self-test

Summary

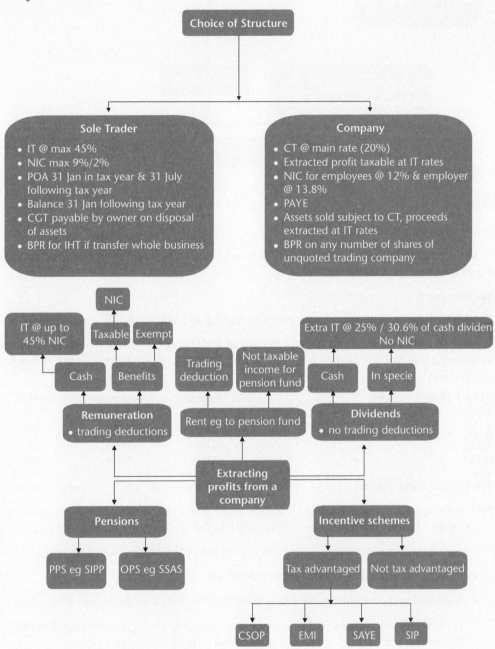

Choice of Structure

Sole Trader
- IT @ max 45%
- NIC max 9%/2%
- POA 31 Jan in tax year & 31 July following tax year
- Balance 31 Jan following tax year
- CGT payable by owner on disposal of assets
- BPR for IHT if transfer whole business

Company
- CT @ main rate (20%)
- Extracted profit taxable at IT rates
- NIC for employees @ 12% & employer @ 13.8%
- PAYE
- Assets sold subject to CT, proceeds extracted at IT rates
- BPR on any number of shares of unquoted trading company

NIC

IT @ up to 45% NIC

Taxable **Exempt**

Extra IT @ 25% / 30.6% of cash dividend No NIC

Cash **Benefits**

Trading deduction

Not taxable income for pension fund

Cash **In specie**

Remuneration
- trading deductions

Rent eg to pension fund

Dividends
- no trading deductions

Extracting profits from a company

Pensions

Incentive schemes

PPS eg SIPP **OPS eg SSAS**

Tax advantaged **Not tax advantaged**

CSOP **EMI** **SAYE** **SIP**

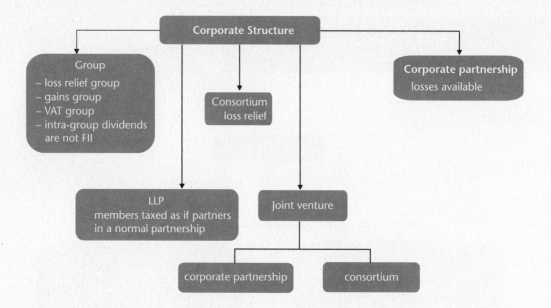

Self-test

Answer the following questions.

1 Stuart is considering setting up in business as a publisher. He cannot decide whether to operate as a sole trader or via a company.

Requirement

Explain to Stuart the taxation implications of trading as a sole trader or via a company.

2 Saoirse, Ruaraidh, Callum and Iain St Clair are all the children and sole beneficiaries of Jeannie St Clair. Jeannie St Clair died recently and left each child a shareholding in each of her four companies:

Class 1 ordinary shares	Saoirse	Ruaraidh	Callum	Iain
A Ltd	70%	10%	10%	10%
B Ltd	10%	70%	10%	10%
C Ltd	10%	10%	70%	10%
D Ltd	10%	10%	10%	70%

Prior to her death Jeannie St Clair owned 100% of the shares in each company personally.

Each company is currently worth £10 million and has annual profits of between £500,000 and £1,000,000. All four companies are trading companies and operate in different business sectors.

The four children are considering the best way to hold their shares from a tax perspective.

Alternative structures currently being considered are:

* Transferring their holdings between themselves so that they each own 25% of each company.

* Transferring their shares to a single holding company, H Ltd, in exchange for 25% of the shares in H Ltd each. H Ltd would then own 100% of all four companies.

Requirement

Explain the tax implications of the ownership structure created by the will and the two alternatives proposed by the children. Suggest how the children could effect the transfer of their holdings if they chose either of the two alternatives.

3 **Donald and Lauren [taken from Sample Paper 2]**

Background information:

Your firm, ABC & Co Chartered Accountants, is co-sponsoring a competition run by the NorthWest Business School. Your firm is to provide the two finalists, Donald Hand and Lauren Hepburn, with tax planning advice on how to structure their businesses. The two finalists are expected to commence in business on 1 April 2016.

As part of the prize, the two finalists are coming into your offices for their first meeting with your manager.

Your manager has passed over to you the following information concerning Donald and Lauren.

Name and Age: Donald Hand aged 55

Recent employment history:

Donald was made redundant from his job as a data control manager with a bank on 1 October 2015. He received a redundancy package of £160,000. Donald will continue to receive fees of £45,000 pa as a non-executive director of a computer software company.

Business:

Donald has developed a data-handling program which will revolutionise certain data routines in the banking environment. Donald already has contracts with his former employer to commence on 1 April 2016 but is looking for support to widen the application to other sectors. Donald has been offered finance by an investor who is looking to make an equity investment in Donald's business in 2019.

Finalist 1: Profit and asset projections: year ended 31 March

	2017 £	2018 £	2019 £
Revenue	200,000	500,000	750,000
Trading profit	38,000	76,000	103,000
Closing net asset value (excluding goodwill)	155,000	340,000	380,000
Closing goodwill value	45,000	200,000	350,000
Research and development expenditure	10,000	15,000	30,000

Research and development costs are included in the pre-tax profit calculation

---

Name and Age:	Lauren Hepburn aged 35		

Recent employment history:

A production manager working for a confectionery company on a salary of £35,000 per annum. On unpaid maternity leave since 1 April 2015, Lauren has decided not to return to her previous employment.

Business:

Manufacturing of hand-made chocolates. Lauren has some contracts with local shops but is trying to establish sales to supermarkets. Consequently she is anticipating losses in the initial period due to marketing and advertising costs. Lauren is being financed in the early years by her parents. However she intends to purchase business premises for £180,000 during the year ended 31 March 2019 and will need to raise finance from a bank or an investor.

Finalist 2: Profit and asset projections: year ended 31 March

	2017	2018	2019
	£	£	£
Revenue	150,000	275,000	850,000
Trading (loss)/profit	(48,000)	10,500	200,000
Closing net asset value (excluding goodwill)	60,000	180,000	410,000
Closing goodwill value	10,000	90,000	200,000

Under the terms of the competition both finalists must agree that the maximum profit to be extracted in the first year to 31 March 2017 will be equivalent to a post-tax receipt of £10,000. The pre-tax (loss)/profit projections do not include any allowance for Donald or Lauren's extraction of profits.

Your manager leaves you the following note before lunch:

'The finalists will be asking us for advice on how to structure their businesses tax efficiently from the point of view of both profit extraction and utilisation of losses.'

Note: You may assume that the tax rates and allowances for 2015/16 and Financial Year 2015 apply throughout, to earlier and later periods.

Requirement

Prepare pre-meeting notes which, based on the information above, provide the following:

(a) For both Donald and Lauren, provide advice and recommendations including explanations, of the most appropriate structure for their businesses for tax reasons, for the years ended 31 March 2017 to 2019 inclusive. Include a discussion of any relevant claims or elections available to Donald, Lauren and any potential investors.

(b) Based on your recommendations, prepare a calculation of the tax implications for Donald and for Lauren, of extracting profits equivalent to a post-tax receipt of £10,000 in the year to 31 March 2017.

(30 marks)

Now, go back to the Learning objectives in the Introduction. If you are satisfied you have achieved these objectives, please tick them off.

Answer to Interactive question 1

	(1) Dividend	(2) Bonus
	£	£
Payments made by company:		
Bonus		10,545
Secondary class 1 NICs (£12,000 × $\frac{13.8\%}{113.8\%}$)		1,455
CT on additional profits (Note 1)	2,400	
Dividend paid (12,000 × $\frac{80}{100}$)	9,600	
Total payments (Note 2)	12,000	12,000
Amount received by owner		
Gross bonus		10,545
Gross dividend (£9,600 × 100/90)	10,667	
Income tax @ 40% (Note 3)		(4,218)
NICs (Note 4) £10,545 @ 2%		(211)
Income tax @ 32½% (Note 5)	(3,467)	
Income net of tax	7,200	6,116

Note

(1) If dividends are paid rather than a bonus, additional profits of £12,000 will be subject to corporation tax as dividends are not deductible for calculating taxable total profits.

(2) The cost to the company is the same under both options.

(3) Delia earns £50,000 a year and therefore any additional income will be taxed on her at higher rate.

(4) Class 1 primary NICs are payable on the bonus but not on dividends. As Delia's level of earnings are above the upper earnings limit, the bonus will be subject to class 1 primary NICs at 2%.

(5) The dividend will be taxable at 32.5% but subject to a 10% tax credit giving an effective tax rate of 25% of the net or 22.5% of the gross. The tax credit needs to be taken into account if we are to properly compare the after tax income of the bonus compared to a dividend. You should therefore either use the gross dividend income and the tax liability due (as above) or the net dividend received and the net tax payable.

Answer to Interactive question 2

Payment of dividend

	Grant £	Steve £
Net cost to the company		
Net dividend required	6,000	6,000
Gross income		
HR taxpayer (£6,000 × 100/67.5)	8,889	
BR taxpayer (£6,000 × 100/90)		6,667
Less income tax liability		
£8,889 @ 32 $^1/_2$%	(2,889)	
£6,667 @ 10%		(667)
Net income	6,000	6,000
Cash dividend to be paid by the company		
£8,889 × 90/100	8,000	
£6,667 × 90/100		6,000

Total net cost to company £8,000 + £6,000 = £14,000.

Payment of additional salary/bonus in 2016/17

Grant is a higher rate taxpayer and his earnings exceed the upper earnings limit for NIC purposes. Accordingly, his effective IT + NICs rate is 42% (40% + 2%). Therefore, gross up at 100/58.

Steve is a basic rate taxpayer. Accordingly his effective IT + NICs rate is 32% (20% + 12%). Therefore gross up at 100/68.

Net cost to the company	*Grant* £	*Steve* £
Net salary required	6,000	6,000
Gross employment income at effective IT and NIC rate		
HR taxpayer (£6,000 × 100/58)	10,345	
BR taxpayer (£6,000 × 100/68)		8,824
Less income tax payable		
(£10,345 @ 40%)	(4,138)	
(£8,824 @ 20%)		(1,765)
Less Primary Class 1 NICs		
(£10,345 × 2%)	(207)	
(£8,824 × 12%)		(1,059)
Net income	6,000	6,000
Payments to be made by the company		
Gross salaries	10,345	8,824
Employer's secondary Class 1 NICs		
£10,345/£8,824 × 13.8%	1,428	1,218
	11,773	10,042
Less corporation tax saving:		
£11,773/£10,042 × 20%	(2,355)	(2,008)
Net cost to the company	9,418	8,034

Total net cost to the company £9,418 + £8,034 = £17,452

Advice

It is cheaper for Klub Ltd to pay dividends as opposed to additional salary.

However, there is a slight problem, as the directors need to receive different amounts of dividend. This could be difficult in practice as they each own 50% of the company's shares.

Answer to Interactive question 3

Two training companies

1   This would be a consortium. The separate company would bear its own costs and sell its output to the training companies. It would be responsible for paying its own tax. Any after tax profits could be stripped out as dividends by the training companies and any losses shared equally as consortium relief.

2   This would be a corporate partnership. The profit or loss would be computed using corporation tax rules and would then be shared equally between the training companies. They would include these amounts in their own corporation tax computations.

3   The costs would arise directly in each company. They would each receive tax relief for their costs in their own corporation tax computation.

1 Company versus sole trader

Trading as a sole trader for tax purposes means that all the profits of the business will be subject to income tax in the tax year in which each accounting period ends.

Trading as a company means that the company's profits will be subject to corporation tax each year. Any profits extracted from the company will also be subject to income tax. The overall level of taxation may still be lower if operating as a company depending on how the profits are extracted from the business.

Operating as a company means that you will be an employee of the company and would therefore need to operate PAYE. Income tax and national insurance contributions (NIC) on any salary would be payable on the 19th of each month (22nd of the month if paid electronically) for the previous month. Income tax on dividends at the higher rate would be due in two instalments and one balancing payment on the 31 January following the tax year end. Dividends are not liable to NIC.

Operating as a sole trader means you would be liable to lower rates of NIC than as an employee of a company but income tax would be due on the same dates as for dividends. Any cash flow advantage from this later payment of tax for sole traders would be eroded if, when operating as a company, dividends were used instead of salary.

If you were a sole trader you could only make contributions to a personal pension scheme (PPS) although this could be a self-invested pension (SIP). A SIP is permitted to invest in commercial property. Any contributions would attract income tax relief at 40%.

If you operated via a company it could establish an occupational pension scheme (OPS) via a small self-administered scheme (SSAS). This has one advantage over a SIP in that a SSAS can lend money to its sponsoring company. This might be a useful way of raising finance for the business, if required.

Any pension contributions by the company would receive corporation tax relief at 20%. Employer contributions are not a taxable benefit on you. In addition, you could also make contributions to the scheme which would be paid from gross salary thereby receiving tax relief at 40%. However, tax relief will only be available for £40,000 of contributions each year. Alternatively you could simply operate a PPS and both you and the company could make contributions to it and receive the same level of tax relief.

Any gains from the subsequent disposal of a sole trader business would be taxable on you personally. As would any disposal of the shares. Both types of disposal would qualify for entrepreneurs' relief with a tax rate of 10% with at least one year's ownership.

2 Parallel companies – as created by the will

The shareholdings created by Jeannie St Clair's will has created parallel companies held by different members of the same family.

Given the number of shareholders, all four companies will be treated as close companies and within the scope of anti-avoidance legislation regarding the payment of loans and benefits to shareholders.

The companies do not form part of a group. Thus using this structure the companies cannot benefit from any of the advantages of being a member of a group explained below.

The advantage of this type of structure is that each child can financially benefit from the results of a single company. If the shares in each company were owned equally each shareholder would be entitled to the same dividend remuneration regardless of the amount of work undertaken as there is only one class of shares.

Parallel companies – own 25% each

Again each company would be treated as a close company.

Again the companies would not form a group.

As the shares in each company would be owned equally, each shareholder would be entitled to the same dividend income regardless of the amount of work undertaken as there would only be one class of shares.

Holding company group

If 100% of the shares in the four trading companies were held by a single holding company it would form a loss relief group and a capital gains group.

If the holding company received dividends from its subsidiaries they not be taxable nor would they be franked investment income.

As members of a loss relief group any non-capital losses within the group could be transferred to any other member of the group. In addition as members of a capital gains group any capital assets transferred within the group would be at nil gain/nil loss and capital gains and losses could be transferred around the group to minimise the overall net gains of the group. The group would also be treated as a single entity for rollover relief purposes.

Finally, the group could form a VAT group which avoids the need to account for VAT on intra-group sales. Also only one VAT return would be required.

Effecting the transfer

Assuming that Jeannie St Clair died within the past two years it is possible for the beneficiaries to execute a deed of variation to alter her will to give effect to either one of the proposed alternative structures.

A deed of variation is effective for both inheritance tax and capital gains tax and means that the transfer is treated as having been made on Jeannie's death ie it is as if the will has been rewritten. There would then be no inheritance tax or capital gains tax disposals by any of the children.

The deed of variation must be executed within two years of death, in writing and be signed by all the beneficiaries. It must state that it is to be effective for inheritance tax purposes and for capital gains tax purposes.

If it is more than two years since Jeannie St Clair's death it is too late to make a deed of variation. Instead the disposals would need to be made by the children themselves.

Given the equal value of the four companies, it would appear that neither of the proposed transfers would constitute a disposal of value for inheritance tax purposes for any of the children.

For capital gains tax purposes transferring their shares to a single holding company in exchange for shares would qualify as a share for share exchange and there would be no gain on the transfer. The new shares would be treated as having been acquired at the time of Jeannie's death for their probate value.

Transferring their holdings between themselves, however, would result in the chargeable disposal of shares by the children for capital gains tax purposes.

3 Donald and Lauren

Pre-meeting notes

Business structure

It is generally not a good idea to allow taxation considerations to totally dominate the choice of business structure. For example there are also non-tax, commercial considerations to consider.

The finalists should also consider other factors, for example, their primary sources of finance and whether their financial backers will require an equity stake or be prepared to offer debt finance.

In the case of fledgling businesses where cash flow is likely to be critical, generating a tax refund or minimising tax liabilities can assist cash flow immensely. A business structure should not therefore prevent the obtaining of an optimum tax position if possible.

Tax considerations

The two finalists are different in two respects:

- Donald Hand will be an additional rate tax payer in 2015/16 because of his redundancy package and his fees of £45,000. In 2016/17 he will be a higher rate taxpayer because of his director fees of £45,000 in addition to the maximum permitted post tax payment that he can withdraw from the business.

- Lauren Hepburn however is likely to be at most a basic rate payer in 2016/17 as she must abide by the conditions of the competition to withdraw a maximum post tax payment of £10,000 and she has no other income. She is unlikely to have profits to sustain any significant increases in remuneration in the near future.

Donald Hand

The most appropriate structure for Donald's business in terms of his financing needs would be a limited company. This would secure the support of his backer and also provide both him and his financial backer with an exit strategy in terms of selling shares.

Donald's investor is seeking an equity shareholding. Donald's company would appear to satisfy the conditions for a qualifying company under the Enterprise Investment Scheme. Although we do not act for Donald's investor he should be made aware that his investor could potentially be able to claim income tax relief for the investment in his company if he satisfies the conditions as a qualifying individual. Our firm would be able to advise his potential investor on this on completion of the appropriate client acceptance procedures.

As a company Donald would also be able to benefit from additional research and development expenditure. This would enable him to deduct 230% instead of 100% of the actual cost of research and development each year.

As an employee and shareholder in the company Donald could extract profits either as dividend, salary or pension contributions.

Donald will be a higher rate taxpayer and his other earnings exceed the upper earnings limit for NIC.

Payment of a dividend

	£
Net remuneration required	10,000
Effective tax for higher rate taxpayer at 25%	3,333
Cash dividend to be paid by company	13,333

Payment of salary

	£	£
Gross salary required = £10,000 × 100/58	17,241	
Less income tax at 40%	(6,896)	
Less NIC at 2%	(345)	
		10,000
Payments to be made by the company:		
Gross salary		17,241
Employer's NIC = (£17,241 – 8,112) × 13.8%		1,260
		18,501
Less corporation tax saving at 20%		(3,700)
Cash cost to the company		14,801

Payment of pension contribution

Since Donald has other income it may be appropriate for Donald to consider taking the £10,000 as a pension contribution if he has sufficient income outside his business to meet his needs.

A pension contribution by the company would attract corporation tax relief at 20% and would therefore only cost the company £8,000 (ie 80% × £10,000). The pension is an exempt benefit for Donald and is therefore exempt from income tax.

Advice

A dividend would cost less for the company than a salary. However, the company must have sufficient distributable reserves to make a dividend payment. Thus if the company were in fact to make a loss in its first year, it could not pay a dividend. A pension contribution is the cheapest option for the company.

Lauren Hepburn

As Lauren's business is likely to make a loss in the initial period, Lauren should consider carefully the structure of her business.

A loss made by a limited company in the initial years can only be carried forward against future trading profits, so if a company never becomes profitable the loss is locked in the company and may never be used. Also the loss is subject to anti-avoidance, such that if there were a change in the nature of the trade and a change in ownership, losses could potentially be unrelieved.

A more tax efficient structure in terms of the utilisation of tax losses for Lauren would be a sole trader structure. Losses could then be carried back against her total income including her employment earnings in the previous three tax years.

This would have the advantage of generating a tax refund of £7,480 (Working). Repayment interest will be added to this amount calculated from the 31 January following the end of the tax year of the loss ie from 31 January 2018 to the date of repayment.

Remuneration

Drawings by a sole trader are not a business expense for tax purposes. The full amount of the business profit (or loss) before drawings is taxable income (or relievable against other income) of the sole trader.

Lauren could withdraw £10,000, funds permitting, with no immediate income tax or NIC consequences. As she has made a loss there is no income tax or NIC liability. The £10,000 is not allowed as a business expense for tax purposes and thus will not increase the available loss.

Lauren should also consider disclaiming all or some of her capital allowances in the initial period if actual losses exceed her income in the previous three tax years.

Her forecast profits for 2017/18 of £10,500 will be fully taxed as Lauren's income regardless of the level of actual drawings taken. She should ensure that she has sufficient cash to pay the associated income tax and NIC liability on 31 January 2019, however this is likely to be covered by her personal allowance. Her first payment on account for 2017/18 will also fall due on 31 January 2019 being equivalent to 50% of her income tax and Class 4 NIC liability for 2017/18.

Future expansion

Lauren's business is expected to expand in Year 3 with profits predicted of £200,000. To attract investors and also to retain profits within the business, Lauren should seek to incorporate. Should she not incorporate, profits are subject to income tax and NIC regardless of the level of drawings.

Incorporation on 1 April 2018 would ensure that the first substantial profits are taxed within the company at 20%. Only extracted profits will be subject to a top rate of tax of up to 45%.

Incorporation will lead to chargeable gains arising on the goodwill and property transferred. The gain on the goodwill is £90,000. And the property will probably not yet have been purchased.

The transfer of the assets should be outside the scope of VAT as the transfer will qualify as a transfer of a going concern.

Utilising incorporation relief or gift relief would prevent capital gains tax crystallising on the transfer of the goodwill.

Incorporation relief would only defer the capital gains tax until the ultimate disposal of the shares and would give a base cost for the shares equivalent to the market value of the company less the gains deferred ie £270,000 (£180,000 + £90,000) less gain on goodwill of £90,000 = £180,000.

Gift relief is an alternative but would only defer the gain until the company disposed of the assets or the shares in the company were sold. Assuming that a gain only arises on the goodwill, shares would be issued in exchange for the net assets excluding goodwill, and the goodwill would be gifted to the company. This would mean that the base cost of the shares would be the net asset value excluding goodwill of £180,000, and the goodwill in the company would have nil cost.

Lauren could consider disclaiming incorporation relief and claiming entrepreneurs' relief rather than gift relief to permanently cancel part of the chargeable gain on incorporation. The base cost of the shares would then be the full market value of the assets transferred of £270,000. However as her only chargeable asset is goodwill and she is related to the company after incorporation (as a shareholder) entrepreneurs' relief would not apply to the gain on the goodwill.

Summary

	Gift relief	Incorporation relief	Disclaim incorporation relief
	£	£	£
Gain on goodwill	90,000	90,000	90,000
Deferral	(90,000)	(90,000)	(0)
	0	0	90,000
Less AEA			(11,100)
Taxable gain			78,900
Tax £31,785 @ 18%			5,721
Tax (£78,900 – £31,785) @ 28%			13,192
			18,913

	Gift relief	Incorporation relief	Disclaim incorporation relief
Base cost of shares	Market value of assets excluding goodwill	Market value of all assets less gains deferred	Market value of all assets
Base cost of goodwill for company	£180,000	£180,000	£270,000
	Market value less gain deferred	Market value	Market value
	£0	£90,000	£90,000

Incorporation relief is only available if Lauren transfers all of the assets of the business to the company.

In the year ended 31 March 2019, Lauren's company will then purchase a property. This could be purchased by the company or by Lauren personally.

If Lauren buys the property personally and then leases it to the company, this could be a further means of tax efficient extraction of profits. The rental expense would be allowable for corporation tax purposes but would be taxable income for Lauren at up to 45%. If market rent is charged, any gain on sale would not be eligible for entrepreneurs' relief even if it were a disposal associated with the share sale. Therefore the gain would be taxable at up to 28%. Alternatively the property could be purchased by Lauren's pension fund and then the rental income and any future gains on the disposal of the property would be tax free. However, this is a restrictive option and would limit what Lauren could do with the funds in the future.

Advice

Lauren would maximise her tax relief from the use of losses by commencing to trade as a sole trader and then incorporating before her first year of substantial profits.

She could utilise gift relief to transfer the goodwill to the company with no chargeable gain at the expense of a lower base cost for her shares. If all assets are transferred incorporation relief ensures a nil gain at incorporation but again at the expense of a lower base cost for her shares. The future relief of this gain needs to be considered.

A decision to disapply incorporation relief need not be made for 34 months from the end of the tax year of incorporation. If Lauren could delay incorporation until 6 April 2018 (ie in 2018/19) this would delay the need to make a decision regarding incorporation relief until 31 January 2022. However due to the inability to use entrepreneurs' relief this is unlikely to be a valid option due to high levels of capital gains tax.

- The process may assist them in the future to raise finance.

- ABC & Co should ensure that engagement procedures are followed and that quality is maintained despite the lack of fee.

WORKING

Loss relief

Lauren did not have any income in the previous year (2015/16) as she was on maternity leave so there is no scope for a claim for current year and prior year relief. However, under opening year loss relief rules the loss will be carried back to 2013/14 , 2014/15 and 2015/16. Carrying back the loss would lead to a full repayment of the 2013/14 tax liability and a repayment of some of the 2014/15 liability:

	£
2013/14	
£35,000 of the loss will be set off	
The amount of income tax which will be repaid is:	
Net income	35,000
Personal allowance (note)	(10,600)
Taxable income	24,400
Income tax	
£24,400 @ 20%	4,880
2014/15	
The remaining £13,000 of the loss will be set off	
Income tax repaid @ 20%	2,600
Cash refund	7,480

Note: Using 2015/16 rates and allowances as stated in the question.

As the total loss is less than £50,000, there is no limitation under the rules which restrict the offset of losses against total income

CHAPTER 22

Transformation of owner-managed businesses

Introduction

Examination context

Topic List

Summary and Self-test

Answers to Interactive questions

Answers to Self-test

Introduction

Learning objectives

Tick off

- Communicate in a format appropriate to the recipient who may be an external client, a fellow professional or an internal colleague ☐

- Prepare suitable advice to explain tax liabilities with supporting calculations ☐

- Recommend appropriate tax-planning advice ☐

- Identify further information required to complete tax computations and finalise tax advice ☐

- Give advice which is appropriate, technically correct, and within the law and the ICAEW Code of Ethics ☐

- Determine, explain and calculate the tax liabilities for individuals and corporate entities, including income tax, national insurance, corporation tax, stamp taxes and VAT ☐

- Evaluate the tax implications of the choice of business structures ☐

- Explain the taxation issues relating to business start-ups ☐

- Explain and evaluate the tax implications of group structures ☐

- Explain and evaluate the tax implications of business transformations and change ☐

- Explain and calculate the tax implications involved in the cessation of trade ☐

- Identify legitimate tax planning measures to minimise tax liabilities ☐

- Evaluate and advise on tax strategies to meet business objectives ☐

- Evaluate and advise on alternative tax strategies relating to corporate transformations ☐

- Recognise, explain and communicate ethical and professional issues in giving tax planning advice ☐

Specific syllabus references for this chapter are 1a, 1b, 1c, 1d, 1e, 1f, 1g, 1h, 1j, 1l, 1m, 2a, 2b, 2c and 2d.

Syllabus links

Incorporation has potential interaction with stamp duty land tax, VAT and chargeable gains. Disincorporation interacts with the same taxes but less favourably.

Examination context

The change in structure of a business entity requires the professional accountant to take careful consideration of the whole range of taxes that may be affected including income tax, corporation tax, the capital taxes, VAT and stamp tax. The accountant will need to look at the overall tax cost of alternative routes before presenting accurate advice.

In the examination candidates may be required to:

- Advise on and calculate the tax liabilities arising from the incorporation of an unincorporated business

- Advise on and calculate the tax liabilities arising from the disincorporation of a company

- Advise on and calculate the tax liabilities arising from the bankruptcy of an individual

1 Incorporation

Section overview

- Incorporating a sole trader or partnership business has significant tax implications.

- Capital gains tax may be payable on the disposal of the business assets to the company. The trader may be able to take advantage of incorporation relief, gift relief or entrepreneurs' relief.

- Where the gains are small, they may be covered by the capital gains tax annual exempt amount and therefore it may not be necessary to use any of the above reliefs. It is possible to manipulate the amount taken as cash consideration to utilise available entrepreneurs' relief, capital losses and the annual exempt amount in the year of incorporation.

- Incorporation relief defers the gains on incorporation providing all assets are transferred to the company. The gains are deducted from the base cost of the shares and will be taxed on the shareholder on any subsequent disposal of the shares.

- Gift relief is applied on an asset by asset basis and is therefore useful where some of the assets (eg property) are retained outside of the company. However, it means the base cost of the shares and the assets will be lower than with incorporation relief.

- Entrepreneurs' relief may be claimed, up to a lifetime limit of £10m.

- A trader may choose to disapply incorporation relief and not claim gift relief where the shares are likely to be sold within one year of incorporation or where he will not be an employee of the new company. In both cases entrepreneurs' relief would not apply to a sale of the shares. Instead he would choose to claim entrepreneurs' relief at incorporation (but not for goodwill).

1.1 Implications of incorporation

When a sole trader or partnership incorporates there are significant tax implications.

Income tax	• Closing year rules apply to the unincorporated business
	• Overlap profits deducted from final assessment
	• Choice of incorporation date may affect marginal rates of tax (ie start versus end of a tax year)
	• Losses can be carried back against trading profits of unincorporated business under terminal loss relief, or be offset against total income of the tax year of cessation and/or the preceding tax year
	• Alternatively, losses can be carried forward to be set off against income received from the company (eg salary, dividends) under s.86 ITA 2007
	• Need to operate PAYE on profits extracted as salary after incorporation
	• Personal service company or managed service company legislation may apply
Corporation tax	• If a new company is set up, it will commence to trade for corporation tax purposes
	• The new company may be a close company
Capital allowances	• Assets disposed of at market value at cessation, leading to balancing adjustments
	• Election to transfer assets at TWDV can be made as unincorporated business and company will be connected persons – succession election

Intangible fixed assets	• Where the trader commenced trading prior to April 2002, IFAs are dealt with under the old rules (capital gains treatment) if the company is a close company and the trader is a participator ie it is a purchase from a connected party. Amortisation of goodwill or any other IFA will not be an allowable expense
	• Where the trader commenced trading post April 2002, the amortisation of goodwill is not an allowable expense (for incorporations on/ after 3 December 2014).
Stock	• Disposal at market value gives rise to trading income or s.167 CTA 2009/s.178 ITTOIA 2005 election may be made to transfer stock at higher of cost and actual sales proceeds
Capital gains tax	• Assets disposed of at MV at cessation leading to capital gains or losses
	• Net gains will be deferred under incorporation relief into cost of shares acquired on incorporation if all assets are taken (other than cash) and business transferred as going concern (can elect to disapply)
	• Cash consideration may be manipulated to leave a gain covered by a capital loss and/or the annual exempt amount
	• If not all assets are transferred to company, can use gift relief for business assets to defer gains against cost of assets in company
	• Consider retaining appreciating property (will need to use gift relief instead of incorporation relief for any other assets transferred)
Stamp duty land tax	• Deemed transfer of land at market value, giving rise to SDLT charge even if no consideration
	• Retain property to save SDLT
Inheritance tax	• If unincorporated business attracted BPR and transfer is to unquoted company, 100% BPR will be available on the shares due to the replacement of business property rules (property owned at least 2 years out of 5 years before transfer of value)
	• No BPR on property used by but not owned by company unless owner has control of company. Then BPR is at 50%
Value added tax	• Transfer of assets will not be a supply of goods if transfer of a going concern (TOGC) treatment applies
	• As long as the goodwill of the business is transferred, other assets could be retained (ie business premises) and it would still qualify as a TOGC. A transfer of a going concern must involve transfer of the goodwill [IRC v Muller & Co Margarine Limited, (1901) AC 217]
	• Company can take over the VAT registration number of unincorporated business
	• Need to consider VAT implications of any property included in TOGC and the capital goods scheme if appropriate

1.2 When to disapply incorporation relief

Where the sole trader will not be an employee of the new company or the shares in the company are likely to be sold within one year of incorporation, entrepreneurs' relief would not apply to the later disposal of shares. It may therefore be preferable to not claim incorporation relief. Assuming the assets have been owned for at least one year, this will mean that:

- The maximum rate of tax on any gains will be 10% after entrepreneurs' relief, if this is available.
- The shares will have a base cost of the market value of the assets at transfer.

However, for incorporations on/ after 3 December 2014 entrepreneurs' relief cannot be claimed on goodwill, unless the disposal is by a retiring partner who will have no stake in the successor company.

A claim to disapply incorporation relief does not need to be made until 34 months from the end of the tax year of incorporation. It is therefore possible to choose to disapply the relief once the taxpayer knows whether the shares have been owned for at least one year.

Interactive question 1: Disapply incorporation relief?   [Difficulty level: Intermediate]

Thorne started a construction business on 1 April 2004. On 1 July 2015 he transferred the business to a newly formed company, Cullen Ltd, in exchange for shares. The value of the assets transferred and the gains arising are as follows:

	Value £	Gain £
Freehold property	260,000	80,000
Goodwill	70,000	70,000
Plant and machinery	150,000	–
Net current assets	20,000	–
	500,000	150,000

On 5 January 2016 Thorne sold his shares in Cullen Ltd for £680,000. Thorne has made no other chargeable disposals in 2015/16 and has taxable income in excess of £50,000.

Requirement

Determine whether Thorne should elect to disapply incorporation relief.

See **Answer** at the end of this chapter.

1.3 Incorporation relief or gift relief?

The most likely assets to give rise to a substantial chargeable gain on incorporation are goodwill and land and buildings, however:

- Where the gain on any goodwill is small, the gain on incorporation may be covered by the annual exempt amount.

- If the land and buildings were being retained outside of the business it may then only be necessary to use gift relief on any plant and machinery not otherwise exempt.

- Where incorporation relief is preferred it is possible to grant a lease on the property to the unincorporated business. The lease is then transferred to the company. The freehold is retained outside of the business.

The main advantage of gift relief is that it allows some assets to be transferred and others to be retained personally by the sole trader or partners. The most likely asset to be retained is land and buildings. This then:

- Avoids the payment of SDLT on incorporation.

- Avoids the potential double charge to taxation on the eventual sale of what is generally an appreciating asset.

- Enables a tax efficient form of profit extraction in the form of rent. However, the rent may restrict the availability of entrepreneurs' relief on the sale of the property as an associated disposal to the sale of the shares.

Rent is not subject to national insurance although it is subject to income tax at a maximum rate of 45% and is an allowable expense against corporation tax, unlike dividends.

	Incorporation relief	Gift relief
Conditions	All assets (other than cash) must be transferred	Applies on an asset by asset basis meaning that any asset(s) may be retained Possible VAT implications if it does not qualify as a TOGC
Consideration	Wholly or partly in exchange for shares Any cash consideration means some of the gain is chargeable immediately Cash consideration may be taken to ensure the annual exempt amount is fully utilised	Need not be transferred in exchange for shares ie could use loan stock or cash instead Any consideration received in excess of the original cost restricts the amount of relief
Claim required	Automatic, but may elect to disapply by the second anniversary of 31 January following the end of the tax year of incorporation ie 31 January 2019 if incorporate in 2015/16	Joint election required by transferor and transferee
Base cost of shares	The gain deferred reduces the base cost of the shares The base cost will therefore be the market value of the shares less the gains deferred	The shares are not reduced by the gain deferred The base cost will therefore be the nominal value of the shares ie lower than for incorporation relief
Base cost of assets transferred	The assets are transferred to the company at their market value	The deferred gain reduces the base cost of the assets transferred, giving a lower base cost Although this increases the effect of double taxation of chargeable assets (subject to corporation tax and then income tax when extract funds) it is not an issue if appreciating assets are not transferred
Deferred gain crystallises when	Shares sold	Assets sold
Crystallises on	Shareholder	Company
Advantages/ disadvantages	The assets transferred will be subject to double taxation on the increase in value from incorporation. If any appreciating assets are transferred this could be significant	Enables appreciating assets to be retained outside the company and therefore ensures the gain will only be taxed once Base cost of both assets and shares is lower than under incorporation relief
Statutory reference	s.162 TCGA 1992	s.165 TCGA 1992

2 'Disincorporation'

Section overview

- The majority of this section is merely revision of your Tax Compliance knowledge. The only new element is the disincorporation relief for very small companies.

- 'Disincorporation' describes a situation whereby an owner/director dissolves a solvent company in order to revert to sole trader status. The trade effectively continues under the same ownership.

- A 'disincorporation' creates numerous tax issues as there are no reliefs apart from VAT transfer of going concern rules and the new relief for very small companies.

- Where a property was included in the assets at incorporation or goodwill was created as a balance sheet asset at incorporation, capital gains tax may be substantial.

- Disincorporation relief can be claimed where a business is transferred to shareholder(s), and the total value of goodwill and interests in land transferred is less than £100,000. If relief is claimed, goodwill and land are transferred at the lower of cost and market value (lower of TWDV and market value for post-2002 goodwill).

If a 'disincorporation' scenario is set in the exam you will need to draw on various aspects of your tax knowledge and apply it to the question. There is little new knowledge in this area: it primarily requires you to think and apply your knowledge in a new way.

2.1 Turning back the clock

Since 2002 the trend has been to incorporate to benefit from tax advantages. The decision to incorporate should only be taken where it is beneficial overall, not just because of tax savings. However recent changes in legislation have attempted to reduce the attraction of incorporation from a pure tax perspective.

Managed service company legislation may discourage businesses from incorporating.

Some companies have decided to 'disincorporate' ie an owner/director liquidates the company and reverts to sole trader status. The trade continues under the same effective, although not legal, ownership. The new disincorporation relief is intended to facilitate this for the smallest of companies.

2.2 Tax advantages of corporate status

There can be significant overall tax saved (NIC, income tax and corporation tax) from operating as a company and extracting profits in tax-efficient ways compared to operating as a sole trader. Overall, the tax saved has to be balanced against the increased administration and legal formalities required to operate as a company.

However, there are other tax advantages of operating as a company. Many of the recent business tax incentives are available only to companies eg:

- Intangible fixed assets reliefs (although now restricted in relation to goodwill);
- Research and development expenditure and tax credits; and
- The substantial shareholdings exemption.

2.3 Implications of 'disincorporation'

On 'disincorporation' the company:

- Transfers all of its assets to its owner and hence generates chargeable gains subject to corporation tax; and

- The owner sells his shares generating a gain on disposal and will also realise any gains deferred if had previously taken advantage of incorporation relief.

VAT will also be charged if the TOGC conditions are not met and SDLT may be payable on any transfers of land and buildings.

2.4 Overview of 'disincorporation'

When a company 'disincorporates' there are significant tax implications. The following table assumes that the 'disincorporation' is undertaken to enable the owner/director to revert to being a sole trader and that it is a solvent company.

Corporation tax	• The company will cease to trade, triggering the end of an AP • The CT will be due 9 months and 1 day after cessation which may be earlier than projected • The company will probably be a close company and will therefore become a close investment holding company after cessation. Any loans to purchase shares/make loans to the company by the shareholder/director will no longer be eligible for relief as qualifying interest.
Trading losses (see Chapter 12)	• On cessation of trade, losses cannot be carried forward and will be lost. Unlike incorporation, there is no equivalent of s.86 ITA 2007 relief to carry forward losses against future income from the business • Carry back losses of final 12 months up to three years against total profits • Cannot be offset against gains realised after cessation – advisable to transfer assets prior to cessation if trading losses in final AP
Capital allowances	• Assets disposed of at market value at cessation, leading to balancing adjustments • If trade is transferring to the owner/shareholder, can elect to transfer at TWDV as shareholder and company are connected persons – succession election
Intangible fixed assets	• Assuming the goodwill is transferred to the owner/shareholder and not left in the company it will not be eligible for amortisation (amortisation of IFAs only applies to companies) • If disincorporation relief is claimed, goodwill is transferred at the lower of MV and TWDV. • May be able to rollover gains on other business assets into purchased goodwill
Stock	• Deemed disposal at market value gives rise to trading income or s.162 CTA 2009 election to transfer at higher of cost and actual sales proceeds if sold to connected person ie owner/shareholder
Income tax & NIC	• Commence trade – notify HMRC as soon as possible after commencement of trade for both IT and NIC to avoid a penalty. • Consider implications of overlap profits on choice of accounting date • Unlikely that large redundancy payments will be acceptable to HMRC as exempt from IT nor as allowable for CT purposes
Company's chargeable gains	• Assets are disposed of by company to a connected person, therefore deemed proceeds at market value at cessation leading to capital gains or losses • Net gains may be substantial if gift relief was used at incorporation as this results in low base costs for assets • Disincorporation relief available to very small companies on land/buildings and goodwill: transfer at lower of cost and MV.
Capital gains tax	• The disposal of the shares will give rise to a capital gain • The use of gift relief at incorporation will have reduced the base cost of the shares thereby increasing the gain on eventual disposal
Stamp duty land tax	• Depending on the assets transferred and the receipt of consideration, SDLT may be payable
Value added tax	• Transfer of assets will not be treated as supply of goods if transfer of going concern (TOGC) relief applies • If the goodwill of the business is retained in the company it will not be a TOGC and all the other assets sold will be subject to VAT

2.5 Disincorporation relief

Disincorporation relief can be claimed on a transfer of the trade of the smallest businesses, where the trade is transferred between 1 April 2013 and 31 March 2018. As set out in Chapter 17, the conditions for relief are:

- The business must be transferred to individuals who have held shares in the company for at least twelve months ending with the transfer date.

- The business must be transferred as a going concern.

- All of the assets of the business (or all of the assets excluding cash) must be transferred.

- The total market value of the goodwill and interests in land transferred must be no more than £100,000.

Where it is claimed:

- Interests in land and pre-2002 goodwill which falls within the chargeable gains rules are treated as transferred at the lower of their unindexed chargeable gains base cost and their market value.

- Post-2002 goodwill falling within the IFA rules is treated as transferred for the lower of its TWDV and its market value.

Note that the benefit of the indexation allowance which has built up in the company is effectively lost if disincorporation relief is claimed. However, as the individual will often be able to claim entrepreneurs' relief once the business has been operated as a sole trade for twelve months after disincorporation, this is only likely to be a significant consideration if the indexation eliminates most of the gain(s).

If the sole trader disposes of the land or buildings within a year of the transfer of trade, a calculation is likely to be needed to determine whether it is beneficial to claim disincorporation relief. If none of the trader's annual exempt amount or basic rate band is available, it will generally be preferable not to claim relief and to choose instead for the gain on disincorporation to be taxed in the company (at a rate of 20%) rather than taxed on the individual at a rate of 28%. However, where the annual exempt amount, losses, or the basic rate band are available this may not be the case.

2.6 Winding up the company

The owner/director has a number of choices as to what to do with the company:

- Allow the company to become dormant;
- Liquidation; or
- Striking off (see Chapter 17).

A dormant company still needs to comply with company law filing and administrative requirements. This option may therefore not be favoured.

Liquidation is time consuming and can be expensive as a liquidator must be appointed.

Striking off is a less expensive means of dissolving a company. The company applies to the Registrar of Companies under ss.1000-1008 CA 2006 to be struck off the register. This cannot be done until at least three months after the company has ceased to trade and the directors have to agree to a number of conditions.

The distribution of funds prior to the dissolution of a company is generally an income distribution unless a liquidator has been appointed. However, there is an exception to this rule where distributions are made either during or in contemplation of a striking off. This applies where:

- The company intends to collect its debts and pay off its creditors in full (or has already done so); and

- The total amount of the distributions potentially within the scope of these provisions is no more than £25,000.

The treatment is withdrawn if the company has not been struck off, or has not collected its debts and paid its creditors, within two years of the date of the distribution.

If a distribution is made when there is already an intention to strike the company off, this seems to be automatically treated as within the scope of the statutory rules, making it difficult to pay an income distribution before the striking off begins in order to reduce the assets to be distributed as capital to £25,000.

Under company law, distributions of undistributable reserves cannot be made in the course of a winding up unless it is a formal liquidation. Thus the value of the share premium account and the share capital account should not form part of this pre-striking off distribution unless there is a reduction in capital.

Leaving the undistributable reserves until after striking off the company could present a risk as the company's remaining assets after striking off are technically bona vacantia and belong to the Crown. However the Treasury Solicitor has confirmed that no action will be taken.

Interactive question 2: 'Disincorporation' [Difficulty level: Exam standard]

Helen has decided that she is tired of the increasing red tape and administration required to operate her company including the need to operate PAYE for just herself. She has therefore decided to revert to being a sole trader on 1 January 2016.

At incorporation on 1 January 2002, the only chargeable assets were the goodwill and the property used in the business. At incorporation Helen transferred all of the assets of the business in exchange for shares with a nominal value of £1,000. Helen is the sole shareholder.

Helen used incorporation relief to defer her gains.

Helen, who has always been an employee of her company, has decided to dissolve the company. She has appointed a liquidator and is therefore seeking to make a capital distribution of all the assets in the company.

	Cost	MV at incorporation	MV at disincorporation
	£	£	£
Property	25,000	80,000	130,000
Goodwill	-	40,000	70,000
Other net assets	18,000	30,000	65,000
Total	43,000	150,000	265,000

The property was originally purchased on 1 January 1991.

The other net assets of £65,000 available at disincorporation include a cash balance of £22,000 and an amount of corporation tax payable of £2,445 as a result of adjustments for the sale of stock to Helen and the balancing adjustments arising on the transfer of plant and machinery. Each item of plant and machinery included in the other net assets figure originally cost less than £6,000 and has not appreciated in value.

Helen has always been a higher rate taxpayer and has already used her annual exempt amount for 2015/16. Helen's company has an accounting reference date of 31 March.

Requirements

(a) Calculate the total value of the assets the company should transfer to Helen at disincorporation assuming all reserves are distributable.

(b) Calculate the capital gains tax payable by Helen on the disposal of the shares assuming incorporation relief of £85,975 was available and not disclaimed.

(c) Calculate the cash cost of disincorporation.

Ignore SDLT.

Assume an RPI of 259.5 for January 2016.

See **Answer** at the end of this chapter.

3 Bankruptcy

Section overview

- When a sole trader suffers financial difficulties he may become bankrupt as a result. Unlike a company, a sole trader does not have the advantage of limited liability and thus all his personal assets may be sold to pay creditors.

- An alternative to bankruptcy is an individual voluntary arrangement IVA. This is an arrangement available to an individual (including sole traders and partners) to reach a compromise with his creditors, with the aim of avoiding bankruptcy.

- From a tax perspective, where a sole trader or partner is in severe financial difficulties he may be forced to cease to trade. Cessation has a number of important tax implications.

A sole trader or partner who is in financial difficulty or is insolvent may proceed in one of two ways: enter into a voluntary arrangement or face bankruptcy. Detailed study of these procedures was included in the Knowledge Level Law syllabus and is not repeated here; a brief revision of the definition of each procedure is provided below.

Definitions

Individual voluntary arrangement (IVA): An IVA normally provides for the debtor to pay reduced amounts towards his total debt over a period of, usually, five years. Once approved, an IVA binds *all* of the debtor's creditors and none may pay petition for bankruptcy.

Bankruptcy: A person may become bankrupt either by petitioning the court himself or by his creditor petitioning the court for bankruptcy. Bankruptcy is effectively the equivalent for a sole trader or partnership (or other individual) of a compulsory winding up in the case of a company. It should be considered as a last resort after an IVA.

The trader may be able to sell the business as a going concern but if the financial difficulties are severe this is unlikely and he may instead simply cease to trade. From a tax perspective if a sole trader or partner ceases to trade the implications are as shown in the table below.

Income tax	• Closing year rules apply to unincorporated business
	• Overlap profits deducted from final assessment
	• Losses can be carried back against trading profits of unincorporated business under terminal loss relief or be offset against total income of the tax year of cessation and/or the preceding tax year (see Chapter 4)
Capital allowances	• Assets will be treated as having been disposed of at market value at cessation, leading to balancing adjustments
Stock	• Disposal at market value gives rise to trading income
Capital gains tax	• Any assets disposed of at market value at cessation leading to capital gains or losses
	• Net gains could be deferred using rollover relief although it would be unlikely for the trader to reinvest in the near future
Value added tax	• Transfer of assets will not be a supply of goods if transfer of going concern (TOGC) treatment applies
	• Any assets which are sold-off individually will be subject to VAT if the trader is VAT registered and it is a taxable supply
	• The trader will need to deregister for VAT and may be liable to a deregistration charge if there are assets/stock remaining on which input tax was recovered (de minimis limit of £1,000)

Interactive question 3: Terminal losses   [Difficulty level: Exam standard]

Wilson Smith, a small fruit and vegetable retailer, has operated his shop on Dovehouse Parade for many years. Due to the construction of a large supermarket close by with ample parking, his business has suffered in recent years. Disillusioned, Wilson has decided to close his business on 30 June 2016.

His trading income profits/(losses) have been as follows:

	£
Y/E 31 December 2013	14,850
Y/E 31 December 2014	11,880
Y/E 31 December 2015	8,000
P/E 30 June 2016	(9,800)

On commencement of trading, his overlap profits were £5,700.

Wilson has no other source of income.

Requirement

Calculate the terminal loss and show how it can be relieved.

See **Answer** at the end of this chapter.

Summary

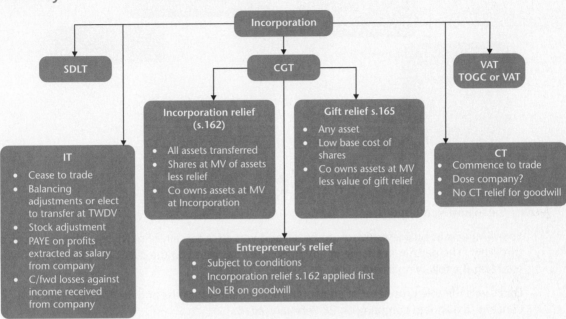

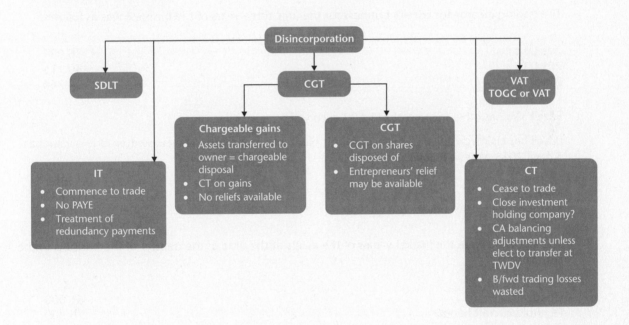

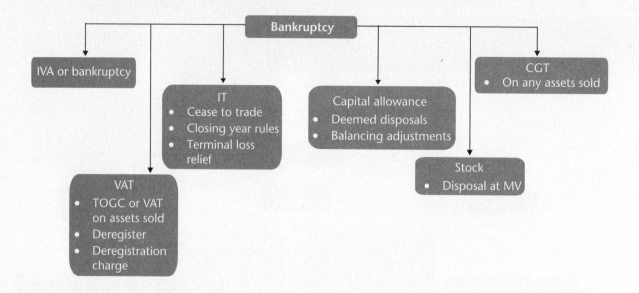

Self-test

Answer the following questions.

1   Your firm acts as business advisors to Edzell and you are a tax senior newly appointed to look after this client. The partner in charge of advising Edzell has sent you the client files, from which you ascertain the following information.

Edzell was the sole proprietor of an aircraft maintenance business until he transferred it as a going concern to a limited company on 28 February 2016.

Since founding the business in 1982 Edzell has always made up accounts to 5 April each year.

The trading income for Edzell's business for the final three years of the business was as follows.

	£
2013/14	36,039
2014/15	40,115
2015/16	34,764

Edzell also has other income of £11,500 each year.

Edzell has claimed capital allowances for his plant and machinery. The tax written-down values at 5 April 2015 were as follows.

	£
Main pool	12,637
Motor car with 10% private use	4,444

The following were the market values of the assets at the time of the transfer of the business to the company.

	£
Goodwill	61,000
Freehold aircraft hangar	76,300
Plant and equipment (not including any fixed plant) – no item sold for > cost	20,000
Motor car	5,000
Net current assets (excluding cash)	20,700
	183,000

The freehold aircraft hangar was acquired on 31 March 1982 at a cost of £30,000 and did not qualify for any form of capital allowances. The goodwill cost £25,000 on the same date.

All other assets are exempt assets for chargeable gains purposes.

For capital allowance purposes both Edzell and the company have jointly elected to transfer the assets at their tax written-down value.

The transfer of the business to the company was satisfied by the issue to Edzell of all of the authorised share capital of 100,000 ordinary shares of £1 each in Famosa Ltd (a company formed specifically for the purpose of the transfer) and the payment to him of £40,000 cash. Edzell was appointed managing director of the company.

Your partner has also sent you the following email.

From	Andrew, partner
To	Alan, tax senior
Date	10 May 2016
Subject	Edzell – Incorporation

Alan,

I need your input into advising Edzell of the consequences of incorporating his business.

Please draft some notes for me covering the following.

- The chargeable gain arising on the transfer of the business to Famosa Ltd and the capital gains base value of his shares in Famosa Ltd, on the assumption that no claim or election in respect of capital gains tax is made.

- The implications of making an election to disapply incorporation relief.

- The effect on both Edzell and Famosa Ltd if the election to transfer the assets for capital allowances purposes at their written-down value had not been made.

- The National Insurance and value added tax consequences for Edzell of transferring the business to the company.

- The consequences of Edzell retaining personally the aircraft hangar and renting it to the company.

I need to get back to Edzell on Friday, so please report back to me by then. Remember that he does not want to claim entrepreneurs' relief as he believes that capital gains tax rates will go up and he will save more money in the future.

Andrew

Requirement

Respond to Andrew's email.

2   Max Molyska and Klaus Ackerman are two undergraduates at Cambridge University, studying mathematics and statistics. They are currently in their final year. In their first year they set up a student website 'cambridgeuniparty.com' which includes lists of all the events happening in Cambridge over the forthcoming term.

The website has approximately 2,000 hits per day and is continuing to grow in popularity. Advertisers have been relatively easy to attract.

Advertisers (bars, clubs, shops, theatres, cinemas) pay £500 for their event to be listed on the site in the weeks leading up to 'the night'. When students click on the event icon, a whole page appears on screen with details of the event. Once they began advertising through this medium, the popularity and revenues of the venues began to increase steadily.

On average, over the last academic year, seven advertisements have been placed every week for approximately 35 weeks a year. Costs have amounted to approximately 40% of revenue earned. This year advertising has increased to about ten per week. The cost margin has remained the same.

As Max and Klaus have been treating this as merely 'a bit of fun', their required return is only 15%. They have been drawing only a modest salary.

However, now that their days at university are nearly over, they are considering their futures. It has been suggested that they expand their operation and consider working full-time for the website. The Anglia Polytechnic University (APU), the University of East Anglia (UEA) and the Suffolk College (SC) have already shown an interest in having such websites for their students.

The two friends have been running the site from the top floor of Max's three-storey freehold property. He had inherited this from his grandfather. They feel that they can continue to run the site from there but need to invest heavily in new hardware, software, other equipment and people. They also need to decide whether to continue operating in partnership or to incorporate their business so as to limit their liability. Under their current agreement, profits are shared equally but their interests in the capital reflect the fact that Max contributed the property. Max is therefore entitled to the value of the property plus 50% of the value of the other assets, and Klaus to 50% of the value of the other assets.

Profits of the business since commencement have been as follows.

	£
6 months ended 30 June 2014	40,564
12 months ended 30 June 2015	75,746
12 months ended 30 June 2016	105,000 (estimated)

Max has valued the business with the help of a friend of his father, Charlie, an ICAEW Chartered Accountant. They have put together the following summary of assets and liabilities.

	Value @ 30 June 2016 £	Cost £	Acquisition date
Property (3rd floor flat above Max's house)	100,000	50,000 (probate value)	1 Aug 2014
Computer equipment	2,500	4,000	30 Nov 2013
Furniture and fittings	600	(negligible)	
Jointly owned car	8,000	9,000	20 Apr 2015
Goodwill	250,000	Nil	1 Jan 2014
Bank account	2,000		
	363,100		

Max has recently seen an advertisement in the careers office about government grants available to new graduates to help them set up companies.

Upon registration by a new graduate, the company is instantly entitled to £2,000. A further £2,000 can be claimed for each person employed by the company as long as the employees are new graduates or previously unemployed. However, £1,000 is repayable if the employee is required by the company to leave within three years.

Max and Klaus have estimated that they need to invest £30,000 in new equipment in order to run the business on a full-time basis. They wish to raise the finance for this externally.

Max and Klaus realise that they can no longer rely on free help from Charlie and want to deal with a local firm of advisors. They have approached your firm, in which you are a manager.

You have had a 'brainstorming' meeting with them yesterday to discuss their plans, and you ascertained that they require advice on a wide variety of issues. You have agreed to send them a report addressing their concerns, but will produce some notes for your partner to review before writing a formal report.

These are the notes that you made at the meeting.

Meeting with Max Molyska and Klaus Ackerman
15 April 2016

Action points

- Max and Klaus will run the business on a full-time basis, will expand into APU, UEA and SC (with 10 advertisements for each per week), and will pay themselves salaries of £60,000 each per annum.

- Assuming the 2015/16 tax rates apply throughout, explain the taxation implications for Max and Klaus of incorporating their business on 30 June 2016. Preparing calculations where necessary, cover the following areas:

  - The effect of incorporation on their trading profits
  - Any gains arising on incorporation (before any reliefs)
  - Possible reliefs available to mitigate gains arising

- Highlight the key tax differences for Max and Klaus between operating as a partnership and operating through a company.

- Explain the options available to them in terms of extracting profits from the business in both the long term and the short term, and the taxation implications of these possibilities for the individuals and the company.

Requirement

Write briefing notes for your partner to review, covering the issues noted at your meeting with Max and Klaus.

3   David originally set up in business as a sole trader in January 2000. He has now decided that he wants to go back to being a sole trader on 1 July 2016 having incorporated on 1 April 2009.

David purchased a company 'off the shelf' with a nominal value for the shares of £500. David is the sole shareholder and a director of the company.

At incorporation the only chargeable assets were the goodwill and the property used in the business. At incorporation David gave the goodwill and other assets to the company but retained the property personally. David used gift relief to defer his gain on the goodwill.

David has appointed a liquidator who will now distribute the total assets of the company to David.

	Cost	MV at incorporation	MV at disincorporation
	£	£	£
Goodwill	-	48,000	72,000
Other net assets	6,000	36,000	78,000
Total	6,000	84,000	150,000
Property	30,000	96,000	144,000

The property was originally purchased on 1 April 2003.

The other net assets available at disincorporation include an adjustment for corporation tax due in respect of the sale of stock to David and balancing adjustments arising on the transfer of plant and machinery.

David has always been a higher rate taxpayer and has already used his annual exempt amount for 2016/17.

Requirements

(a)   Calculate the capital gains tax payable by David on the disposal of the shares, assuming any relevant reliefs are claimed.

(b)   Calculate the amount available for distribution and the capital gains tax payable by David assuming that at incorporation he had instead transferred both the goodwill and the property to the company using incorporation relief. Assume that David did not purchase the company off-the-shelf and instead made the transfer in exchange for an issue of shares.

(c)   Compare the cash cost of disincorporation having used gift relief at incorporation to the cash cost having used incorporation relief.

Assume all tax rates and allowances under FA 2015 will continue in the future.

Ignore indexation allowance.

4   You are a senior in the tax department of Rush & Co. You have received the following email from a client, Alan Walters, which was forwarded by your partner Sonia Dixon.

From	Alan Walters
To	Sonia Dixon
Subject	End of the road

Sonia,

As you know, for the last year or so my aunt has been extremely ill and much of my time has been spent looking after her. Last May I had my 60th birthday and decided that it was time I stopped working so hard.

I ceased trading on 30 June 2015 and sold the business assets. Not surprisingly, I made a trading loss of £8,100 in my last period of trading, but thankfully made a large gain of £200,000 on the disposal of the assets.

The trouble is that I now want to sort out all my tax affairs and put the whole business to bed. I therefore need your help to explain how to obtain optimum tax relief for the trading losses.

I should also tell you that from 2015/16 onwards I will not have any other source of income. I sold some shares in May 2015 and made a chargeable gain of £10,000.

Please can you help.

Alan

From your tax files you discover that Alan is a widower, has no children and has been in business as a sports retailer since 1 October 2011. He prepared accounts to 30 September each year until 30 September 2014.

His trading income results from his previous tax returns have been as follows:

	Adjusted profits £
Year ended 30 September 2012	8,780
Year ended 30 September 2013	10,150
Year ended 30 September 2014	4,200

Until the end of 2014/15 Alan received other income which ensured that he was a higher rate taxpayer for that year. However, according to his e-mail he will have no other source of income from 2015/16 onwards.

Requirement

Prepare notes for Sonia to use to respond to Alan Walters' e-mail.

5   **Medina and Andy [taken from Sample Paper 1]**

You work as a tax assistant for Galax and Co, a firm of chartered accountants. Medina Galen and Andy Dromeda are new tax clients of Galax and Co. Since 1999 Medina and Andy have traded as a partnership called 'Dromeda Solutions', providing web-based marketing services and are seeking tax advice regarding the proposed incorporation of their partnership. Both Medina and Andy are higher rate tax-payers.

Proposed incorporation

On 6 April 2016 the assets of the Dromeda Solutions partnership will be transferred to a newly-incorporated company, DS Ltd, in exchange for 100,000 ordinary £1 shares. The shares will be issued in the same proportion as that governing profit sharing in the partnership agreement of Dromeda Solutions. Under the terms of that agreement, Medina receives 60% and Andy 40% of any profit or loss. Capital gains and losses are allocated in the same proportion.

The projected assets and liabilities for Dromeda Solutions at 6 April 2016 are as follows:

	Market value £	Cost £
Antares House	950,000	431,000
Goodwill	320,000	Nil
Plant and machinery	19,000	31,000
Net current assets	28,000	10,000

Medina and Andy purchased a commercial property, Antares House (a newly constructed building) for £431,000 (VAT exclusive) in May 2010. Dromeda Solutions operates its business from Antares House. The option to tax was exercised at the time of purchase.

As an alternative to transferring Antares House to DS Ltd, Clowde Ltd, a property company with no connections to the partnership, has made an offer to purchase the property for £890,000 (VAT exclusive) at the time of incorporation. Clowde Ltd would then lease six floors of the building to DS Ltd under a 10-year lease. The remaining four floors would be leased to Saturn Ltd, an insurance company, for use as its administrative centre.

Expansion plans

Following incorporation of their partnership as DS Ltd, Medina and Andy plan to reward and motivate key employees. Medina and Andy have identified two potential new directors of DS Ltd. Following their recruitment and a suitable probationary period, they would like to grant options over shares to both of these individuals at an attractive discount. The aim is to encourage the two individuals to stay with the company for at least five years, but they do not wish to implement a company-wide scheme.

Medina's future plans

In addition to the above information, your firm also received an email from Medina, outlining her plans for the future, an extract of which is produced in **Exhibit 1**.

Requirements

Your manager has asked you to produce a briefing note in preparation for a meeting with Medina and Andy in which you:

(1) Determine (with supporting calculations) the tax implications for Medina and Andy of incorporating their partnership, Dromeda Solutions, as DS Ltd. Assume for this purpose that all assets are transferred on incorporation.

(2) Explain the tax implications of the offer by Clowde Ltd to purchase Antares House.

(3) Advise on a suitable share incentive scheme that may be implemented following incorporation.

(4) Prepare a reply to the email from Medina.

(30 marks)

Exhibit 1 – Email from Medina

'I should like independent advice on two issues regarding my own personal tax position.

1   After incorporation, I intend to remain as a director of DS Ltd for two years and then withdraw from the business. I would like to give my shares in DS Ltd to my daughter Andrea. I have discussed this with her and I would make the gift in either early 2017 or 2018. My daughter is currently working in New York but will be returning to the UK in April 2017.

Please advise me of the tax implications of gifting my shares to my daughter.

2   Before appointing your firm, Andy prepared and submitted the partnership tax return. Andy has told me that my unutilised share of the partnership tax loss is £81,700 as at 5 April 2016. I have been offsetting a trading loss from 5 April 2013 against partnership income for the last three years and this is what remains. He has also told me that I cannot use these losses in the future against my income.

I have attached a summary of my investment income for the current tax year and a projection of my investment income and employment income from DS Ltd for the tax years ending 5 April 2017 and 5 April 2018.

Please advise me on how I may utilise my partnership loss.'

Attachment to the email – Medina's summary of investment income and projected employment income from DS Ltd

	2015/16 £	2016/17 £	2017/18 £
Dividends from UK shares	21,900	30,000	30,000
Dividends from DS Ltd	–	26,000	26,000
Salary and bonus from DS Ltd	–	90,000	90,000

Now, go back to the Learning outcomes in the Introduction. If you are satisfied you have achieved these outcomes, please tick them off.

Answer to Interactive question 1

Assuming incorporation relief applies, the base cost of Thorne's shares would be:

	£
Total gains	150,000
Less incorporation relief	(150,000)
	Nil
Base cost of shares:	
Market value of assets transferred	500,000
Less incorporation relief	(150,000)
Base cost	350,000

The chargeable gain on disposal of the share would therefore be:

	£
Proceeds	680,000
Less cost	(350,000)
	330,000
Annual exempt amount	(11,100)
Taxable amount	318,900
Capital gains tax @ 28%	89,292

Entrepreneurs' relief is not available as the shares have been held for less than one year.

If Thorne elects to disapply incorporation relief the gain on incorporation would then be taxed at 10% (except for the gain on goodwill) but the gain on the sale of the company, in respect of which no relief is available, would be significantly less:

	Non-ER gains £	ER gains £
Gain on incorporation:		
– Freehold property		80,000
– Goodwill	70,000	
Gain on sale of shares (£680,000 − £500,000) (higher base cost for shares)	180,000	
Annual exempt amount (Note)	(11,100)	
Taxable amount	238,900	80,000
Capital gains tax @ 28% / 10%	66,892	8,000

The total CGT liability is £74,892. Therefore Thorne should elect to disapply incorporation relief.

Note: The AEA is offset in the most advantageous way ie against the gains taxed at the higher rate first.

Answer to Interactive question 2

(a) Helen can distribute all the assets of the business to herself as a capital distribution. This will constitute a disposal by the business of any chargeable assets giving rise to further corporation tax on any gains arising. She should transfer the assets less the corporation tax liability:

	£
Property	
Proceeds	130,000
Less cost (market value at incorporation)	(80,000)
Less IA 1 Jan 2002 to 1 Jan 2016 = 259.5 – 173.3/173.3 = 0.497 × £80,000	(39,760)
	10,240
Goodwill (Note)	
Proceeds	70,000
Less cost (market value at incorporation)	(40,000)
Less IA 1 Jan 2002 to 1 Jan 2016 = 0.497 × £40,000 (see above)	(19,880)
	10,120
Total gains = £10,240 + £10,120	20,360
CT @ 20%	4,072
Distributable assets to transfer = £265,000 – £4,072	260,928

Note: The goodwill arises prior to 1 April 2002 and is therefore a chargeable asset for chargeable gains purposes.

(b) Helen would also incur a gain on the disposal of the shares with deemed proceeds equal to the market value of the assets transferred:

	£
Proceeds	260,928
Less cost (W1)	(64,025)
	196,903
CGT @ 10% (Entrepreneurs' relief is available)	19,690
WORKING 1 – Base cost of shares	
Market value of assets transferred	150,000
Less incorporation relief (given)	(85,975)
	64,025

(c) There would thus be a cash cost of £2,445 + £4,072 + £19,690 = £26,207

Loss eligible for relief under s.89 ITA 2007 terminal loss relief

The loss arising in the final 12 months of trading may be carried back against the trading profits of the previous three years using terminal loss relief.

	£	£
Loss in last tax year		
6 April 2016 to 30 June 2016		
3/6 × £(9,800)	(4,900)	
Add overlap profits	(5,700)	(10,600)
Loss relief in penultimate tax year within 12 months of cessation		
1 January 2016 to 5 April 2016		
3/6 × £(9,800)	(4,900)	
1 July 2015 to 31 December 2015		
6/12 × £8,000	4,000	(900)
Available for s.89 ITA 2007 relief		(11,500)

Thus £4,000 of loss is not eligible for terminal loss relief ie £9,800 + £5,700 – £11,500 = £4,000. However, it could be used under any of the other possible loss relief claims ie not s.83 ITA 2007 as the trade has ceased. However, as there is no other income in 2016/17 or 2015/16 the £4,000 will be wasted.

Loss relief

	2013/14 £	2014/15 £	2015/16 £	2016/17 £
Trading income	14,850	11,880	8,000	Nil
Less s.89 ITA 2007 loss relief	(–)	(3,500)	(8,000)	(Nil)
Left in charge	14,850	8,380	Nil	Nil

Loss relieved under s.64 ITA 2007 and then under s.89 ITA 2007

Alternatively the loss could have been relieved under s.64 ITA 2007 first and then the remaining loss would have been eligible for relief under terminal loss relief rules. The TLR would be calculated as:

	£
Loss for PE 30 June 2016	9,800
Plus overlap profits from commencement	5,700
Loss for 2016/17	15,500
Less loss already utilised via s.64	(8,000)
Maximum TLR claim is therefore	7,500

Loss relief

	2013/14 £	2014/15 £	2015/16 £	2016/17 £
Trading income	14,850	11,880	8,000	Nil
s.64 ITA 2007 relief against PY total income			(8,000)	
Less s.89 ITA 2007 loss relief	(–)	(7,500)	(Nil)	(Nil)
Left in charge	14,850	4,380	Nil	Nil

Answers to Self-test

1 **Notes to partner**

To	Andrew, partner
From	Alan, tax senior
Client	Edzell
Subject	Incorporation of business

Chargeable gain on transfer of business

A chargeable gain arises on the disposal of every single chargeable business asset in the business (ie goodwill and the aircraft hangar). The other net assets are not chargeable assets for capital gains purposes.

	Goodwill £	Aircraft hangar £
Market value on transfer to company	61,000	76,300
Cost	(25,000)	(30,000)
Gains before incorporation relief	36,000	46,300

	£
Total gains (£36,000 + £46,300)	82,300
Less incorporation relief (W)	(64,311)
Gains after reliefs	17,989
Total chargeable gain – 2015/16	£17,989

Total consideration for business

100,000 ordinary £1 shares	143,000
Cash	40,000
Market value of business	183,000

Base cost of shares in Famosa Ltd

Market value of shares received	143,000
Less incorporation relief (W)	(64,311)
Base cost	78,689

WORKING

Incorporation relief

Incorporation relief automatically applies (without a claim or election) to roll over part of the gains against the base cost of the shares in Famosa Ltd.

$$\text{Deferred gain} = \frac{\text{MV of share consideration}}{\text{MV of total consideration}} \times \text{total gains before reliefs}$$

$$= \frac{£143,000}{£183,000} \times £82,300$$

$$= \underline{£64,311}$$

Election made to disapply incorporation relief

Incorporation relief will apply automatically unless an election is made. The consequences of electing to disapply incorporation relief would be as follows.

	£
Total gains for 2015/16 before reliefs (as before)	82,300
Capital gains base value of shares in Famosa Ltd	143,000

The effect of disapplying the relief is that the base cost of the shares in Famosa Ltd is £64,311 (£143,000 – £78,689) greater, while the chargeable gains increase by £64,311 (£82,300 – £17,989).

If Edzell were to change his mind and claim entrepreneurs' relief, then the gain on the freehold property would be liable to capital gains tax at 10% instead of 28%.

Election to transfer assets at tax written down value

If the election to transfer assets at tax written down value for capital allowances purposes had not been made, then since Edzell and Famosa Ltd are connected persons:

- Edzell would have been deemed to have disposed of the assets at open market value, and
- Famosa Ltd would be deemed to have acquired them at that value.

This would result in balancing charges on Edzell as follows.

Capital allowances computation – p/e 28 February 2016

	Main pool £	Motor car (10% private use) £	Total allowances £
TWDV b/f	12,637	4,444	
Disposal at market value – 28 February 2015	(20,000)	(5,000)	
Balancing charges	(7,363)	(556) × 90%	(7,863)

This increases Edzell's assessable profits by £7,863 in 2015/16.

It is therefore recommended that the election is made.

Edzell's National Insurance position

As a sole trader Edzell will have been liable to pay:

- Weekly flat rate Class 2 contributions

- Class 4 contributions of 9% of his profits between £8,060 and £42,385 and 2% of his profits in excess of £42,385.

If the business is transferred to the company, the National Insurance position is as follows.

- As a company director Edzell will be liable to pay employee's contributions at the rate of 12% on earnings between £8,060 and £42,385 a year and 2% on earnings in excess of £42,385.

- In addition the company, as his employer, will have to pay contributions at 13.8% on annual remuneration in excess of £8,112. This assumes that non-contracted out rate contributions are payable.

- The company's contributions will, however, be allowable expenses against the profit for corporation tax.

Edzell will be able to control how much of the profit is left in the company – to be charged to corporation tax at 20% (after charging the remuneration) – and how much to draw as remuneration.

VAT consequences

Incorporation has the following consequences for VAT.

- The transfer is not treated as a supply of goods or services, and no VAT will be payable on the assets transferred since the business is transferred as a going concern.

- HMRC must be notified within 30 days of the transfer.

- It is assumed that Famosa Ltd is VAT registered and that the business is transferred as a going concern.

Retention of chargeable property

If Edzell were to retain the aircraft hangar in private ownership, not all the assets would be transferred to the company, and therefore incorporation relief would not be available. As a result, the gain on the goodwill could not be rolled over against the base cost of the shares.

However, holdover relief (gift relief) for the goodwill could be obtained, as the transfer is a gift of a business asset to the company.

The advantage of the retention outside the company is that on the disposal of the aircraft hangar there will be one tax charge (on Edzell himself), rather than a corporation tax charge for the company (on the chargeable gain) and a further charge when profits are extracted from the company (by salary or dividend).

2	**To**	A Partner
	From	A Manager
	Date	17 April 2016
	Subject	Max and Klaus – expansion plans

Taxation implications

On incorporation Max and Klaus will cease to operate as sole traders and will transfer their trade and assets into a newly-formed company, probably in return for share capital in that company.

This will give rise to final trading income assessments and chargeable gains as follows.

Trading income profits

As they are ceasing to trade, final tax year rules will apply. The trading income profits of the business will be as follows.

	Total £	Max £	Klaus £
2013/14 (3 m/e 5 April 2014)			
$^3/_6$ × £40,564	<u>20,282</u>	<u>10,141</u>	<u>10,141</u>
2014/15 (12 m/e 31 December 2014)			
$^6/_6$ × £40,564	40,564		
$^6/_{12}$ × £75,746	37,873		
	<u>78,437</u>	<u>39,218</u>	<u>39,219</u>
2015/16 (12 m/e 30 June 2015)	<u>75,746</u>	<u>37,873</u>	<u>37,873</u>
2016/17 (12 m/e 30 June 2016)	105,000		
Less : Overlap relief			
(3 m/e 5 April 2014)	(20,282)		
(6 m/e 31 Dec 2014)	(37,873)		
	<u>46,845</u>	<u>23,423</u>	<u>23,422</u>

Chargeable gains arising on disposal of assets (before reliefs)

	£
Property	
Open market value (30 June 2016)	100,000
Cost (1 August 2014)	(50,000)
Gain	<u>50,000</u>
Goodwill	
Open market value (30 June 2016)	250,000
Cost (1 January 2014)	Nil
Gain	<u>250,000</u>

All other assets are exempt from capital gains tax.

Summary	Gains	Allocation	
		Max	Klaus
	£	£	£
Property	50,000	50,000	
Goodwill	250,000	125,000	125,000
	<u>300,000</u>	<u>175,000</u>	<u>125,000</u>

Possible reliefs available against gains

There are three methods of mitigating the gains arising.

- Incorporation relief
- Gift relief
- Entrepreneurs' relief

Incorporation relief

The gains are automatically deferred (unless an election is made to prevent this) against the base cost of the shares, provided all the assets (except cash) are transferred to the company in return, wholly or partly for shares.

Assuming that all assets, including cash, are transferred into the company, this will have the following effect for each partner.

	Max £	Klaus £
Market value of shares acquired (50% × £363,100)	181,550	181,550
Gains on incorporation	175,000	125,000
Less incorporation relief	(175,000)	(125,000)
Chargeable gains on incorporation	Nil	Nil
Base cost of shares (181,550 – 175,000/125,000)	6,550	56,550

- No gains are immediately chargeable.

- Entrepreneurs' relief is lost.

- The base cost of the new shares is reduced, leading to a larger capital gain on a future sale. These shares may qualify for entrepreneurs' relief, and so future gains should be taxable at 10%.

- Max may prefer to take a larger percentage of the shares in the new company to reflect his entitlement to the value of the property.

Holdover relief

Holdover relief is available to defer the gains against the base cost of the assets in the company. It can be particularly useful where incorporation relief is denied (eg if one or more of the assets are not transferred to the company).

The effect of the relief is as follows.

- Non-chargeable assets are transferred to the company in return for share capital.

Shareholders	Company	£
Base cost of shares £6,550 each	Computer equipment	2,500
	Furniture and fittings	600
	Car	8,000
	Cash	2,000
		13,100

- Chargeable assets are then gifted to the company and gift relief is claimed.

	Shareholders (total) £	Base cost of assets for the company £	£
Market value of individual assets		100,000	250,000
Gains on incorporation	300,000		
Less gift relief	(300,000)	(50,000)	(250,000)
Chargeable gain on incorporation	Nil		
Base cost of individual assets		50,000	Nil

- Small base cost of the shares in the hands of the shareholders gives possible large future gains (may be mitigated by entrepreneurs' relief in the future).

- No gains immediately chargeable.

- Small base cost of the assets in the company means large gains on a future sale by the company.

Entrepreneurs' relief

As this is a qualifying business disposal it will for entrepreneurs' relief. However as the incorporation is on/ after 3 December 2014 there is no entrepreneurs' relief on the gain on goodwill. Incorporation relief may be disclaimed. If entrepreneurs' relief is claimed as a result of disapplying incorporation relief, then chargeable gains will arise as follows:

	Max £	Klaus £
Gains on incorporation	175,000	125,000

- Of these gains only £50,000 of Max's gain will be subject to tax at 10%, with the annual exempt amount being available against the gain on goodwill which is subject to capital gains tax at 18% or 28%.

- The base cost of the shares would be £181,550 (ie £363,100 × 50%) and therefore any future gain would be lower. In addition, if the shares are held for at least one year, further entrepreneurs' relief may be available, subject to the relevant conditions for this relief being met when the shares are disposed of.

Key differences between operating as a partnership and operating through a company

Max and Klaus will now be treated as employees rather than self-employed individuals. This will mean the following changes to the way in which they are taxed.

	Self employed	Employed
Payment of salary	• Treated as drawings (see below)	• Taxed as employment income • IT deducted at source via PAYE • Class 1 NIC payable by both the employer and the employee • Gross salary and employer's NIC costs are tax deductible for the company
Drawings of profits	• Not allowed as a deductible expense • Profits of the business are taxed as trading income • Classes 2 and 4 NICs are payable • Tax and NIC is payable under self assessment (for 2016/17) as follows 1st instalment – 31 January 2017 2nd instalment – 31 July 2017 Bal. Payment – 31 January 2018	• Dividends are not allowed as a deductible expense in the company • The company will pay corporation tax on the business profits • Dividends subject to income tax on a receipts basis • Higher/additional rate tax on dividends is due under self assessment
Expenses borne privately	• Expenses must be incurred wholly and exclusively for the purpose of the trade to qualify for an income tax deduction.	• Expenses must be incurred wholly, exclusively *and necessarily* for the purpose of the employment to qualify for an income tax deduction.

Extraction of profits

Longer term options	Tax implications for the individual	Tax implications for the company
Sell the shares	• Gain on disposal chargeable to CGT • Entrepreneurs' relief may be available • Annual exempt amount and losses available to reduce the gain	• Change in ownership, but no other tax effect
Liquidate the company	• Income tax or capital gains tax due on the distribution (treatment dependent on whether distributions are made prior to the appointment of a liquidator)	• Disposal of assets giving rise to gains in the company – corporation tax due • Distribution of remaining reserves

Short and long term options	Tax implications for the individual	Tax implications for the company
Salary and bonuses	• Income tax on employment income at 20% and 40% (given level of income) • PAYE deducted at source • Receipts basis of assessment • Class 1 Primary NIC payable	• IT and NIC to be deducted • Class 1 Secondary NIC payable • Tax allowable expense, on the accruals basis
Dividends	• Income tax as dividend income • Higher rate tax liability (25% of dividend - given level of income) due under self assessment • Receipts basis of assessment • No NICs	• Not a tax allowable expense • No NIC cost
Benefits	• Income tax under employment income on the 'cash equivalent' • Tax collected via PAYE scheme • No NICs if benefits are not cash or convertible into cash	• Tax allowable expense • Class 1 Secondary or Class 1A NICs are payable
Pension contributions	• Not an assessable benefit on receipt (taxed instead on withdrawal from the fund)	• Tax allowable expense • No NICs due

3 (a) David can distribute all the assets of the business to himself as a capital distribution as a liquidator has already been appointed. This will constitute a disposal by the business of any chargeable assets giving rise to further corporation tax on any gains arising. He should thus transfer the assets less the corporation tax liability.

However, as the company does not have an interest in the property, the total value of the goodwill and interests in property to be transferred is £72,000. David has held the shares in the company for more than 12 months, and the business is to be transferred as a going concern, so disincorporation relief can be claimed. The goodwill (which is pre-2002, and so within the chargeable gains rules) will be treated as transferred for the lower of its market value of £72,000 and its base cost of nil (see Working), ie nil.

The full value of the business would therefore be the proceeds used to calculate the gain on disposal of the shares:

	£
Proceeds	150,000
Less cost (as purchased the company off the shelf is simply nominal value)	(500)
Chargeable gain	149,500
CGT @ 10%	14,950

WORKING
The base cost to the company of the goodwill is the market value at incorporation less the claim for gift relief:

	£
Proceeds	48,000
Less cost	(nil)
	48,000
Less gift relief	(48,000)
Chargeable gain	Nil
Base cost = £48,000 – £48,000	Nil

(b) If David had transferred both the property and the goodwill to the company at incorporation using incorporation relief to defer the gains, disincorporation relief would not be available because the total value of the goodwill and interests in land to be transferred back to him would have been more than £100,000. The assets available for distribution would therefore have been:

	£
Property	
Proceeds	144,000
Less cost (market value at incorporation)	(96,000)
	48,000
Goodwill	
Proceeds	72,000
Less cost (market value at incorporation)	(48,000)
	24,000
Total gains = £48,000 + £24,000	72,000
CT @ 20%	14,400
Distributable assets to transfer = (£150,000 + £144,000) – £14,400	279,600

The gain on the disposal of the shares would therefore be:

	£
Proceeds	279,600
Less cost (W1)	(66,000)
Chargeable gain	213,600
CGT @ 10%	21,360

WORKING – Base cost of shares

Market value of assets transferred (£84,000 + £96,000)	180,000
Less incorporation relief = £48,000 + £66,000	(114,000)
	66,000
Incorporation relief	
Gain on goodwill = market value at incorporation as cost is nil	48,000
Gain on property:	
Proceeds	96,000
Less cost	(30,000)
	66,000

(c) The cash cost of disincorporation having used gift relief at incorporation is £14,950.

The cash cost of disincorporation having used incorporation relief at incorporation is £35,760 ie £14,400 + £21,360.

However, under the first cost the base cost of the goodwill is nil, and the base cost of the property is £30,000. In the second scenario the base costs are uplifted to £72,000 for the goodwill and £144,000 for the property.

4 Alan Walters

EMAIL RESPONSE

To	Sonia Dixon
From	A Senior
Date	Today
Client	Alan Waters
Subject	Response to e-mail re cessation of business

Tax relief for trading losses

Options available

- Alan has ceased to trade, and hence cannot carry forward any losses.

- The trading loss of 2015/16 can be used in a claim (s.64 ITA 2007) against total income of 2015/16 and/or 2014/15. However, he has no income in 2015/16.

- The claim for 2015/16 can be extended (s.261B TCGA 1992) to cover the gains arising in that year.

- A terminal loss claim (s.89 ITA 2007) can be made for the loss of the last twelve months of trading against trading profits of the final year of trading and the three preceding years on a LIFO basis.

Overlap relief and trading income assessments

			£
2011/12	1 October 2011 to 5 April 2012	6/12 × £8,780	4,390
2012/13	Y/E 30 September 2012		8,780
2013/14	Y/E 30 September 2013		10,150
2014/15	Y/E 30 September 2014		4,200
2015/16	P/E 30 June 2015	Loss £8,100 + overlap £4,390	(12,490)

Terminal loss

The last 12 months of trading are split between the relevant tax years ie 1 July 2014 to 5 April 2015, and 6 April 2015 to 30 June 2015. For each of those periods the terminal loss comprises the following.

	£	£
Loss in last tax year-		
6 April 2015 to 30 June 2015		
3/9 × £(8,100)	(2,700)	
Add overlap profits	(4,390)	(7,090)
Loss relief in penultimate tax year within 12 months of cessation		
1 October 2014 to 5 April 2015		
6/9 × £(8,100)	(5,400)	
1 July 2014 to 30 September 2014		
3/12 × £4,200	1,050	(4,350)
Available for s.89 ITA 2007 relief		(11,440)

Optimum tax relief for trading losses

- Alan's level of income is such that up to and including 2014/15 he would have paid tax at 40% on income. He would have paid 28% on gains until 2014/15. In 2015/16 as he has no income the first £31,785 of gains will be taxed at 18% with the balance at 28%. However, if he claims entrepreneurs' relief the gain on disposal of the business will be taxed at 10%.

- He obtains the same level of tax relief on a terminal loss claim or a s.64 ITA 2007 claim.

- A terminal loss claim will save tax at 40% on £11,440 of loss.

- The loss of £1,050 (£12,490 – £11,440) not used in a terminal loss claim can be claimed under s.64 ITA 2007 for 2014/15 against other income, and also saves tax at 40%.

- Alternatively, the whole loss of £12,490 could be used against Alan's gains (arising on the sale of the business) for 2015/16. [s.261B TCGA 1992]

- However, the use of the trading loss against gains would save tax at 10% after the application of entrepreneurs' relief and is therefore not recommended.

5 **Medina and Andy**

Briefing note for the meeting with Medina and Andy

(1) **Incorporation of Dromeda Solutions**

On incorporation, capital gains will arise on the transfer of Antares House and the goodwill. No gain arises on the net current assets.

With regard to plant and machinery, no capital loss will arise on any items sold at a loss upon which capital allowances have been claimed. However, if any item has been sold for more than its original cost, and more than £6,000, then a capital gain may arise and would need to be quantified.

Capital gains:

The following gains arise on the transfer of Antares House and the goodwill:

Antares House	£	Medina £	Andy £
Proceeds	950,000		
Less cost	(431,000)		
	519,000		
Allocation: 60:40		311,400	207,600
Goodwill			
Proceeds	320,000		
Less cost	Nil		
	320,000		
Allocation: 60:40		192,000	128,000
Total gains		503,400	335,600

There are several potential ways of mitigating the gains arising on incorporation including incorporation relief, gift relief or disapplying incorporation relief in order to take advantage of entrepreneurs' relief, which will result in a 10% tax rate on the property gain arising (but not on the gain on goodwill as the incorporation is on/after 3 December 2014).

Incorporation relief

The gains are automatically deferred against the base cost of the shares (unless an election is made to prevent this). This relief is available as all of the assets of Dromeda Solutions are transferred in exchange for shares.

The effect for Medina and Andy is that the gains on incorporation are deferred against the cost of the shares as follows:

	Medina £	Andy £	Total £
Market value of shares (60:40)	790,200	526,800	1,317,000
Less incorporation relief	(503,400)	(335,600)	(839,000)
Base cost of the shares	286,800	191,200	478,000

No tax is payable on the incorporation of the partnership. However, incorporation relief may be disapplied. One reason for this may be for an individual to utilise entrepreneurs' relief on qualifying assets instead (ie not goodwill), whereby the gain is taxed at the time of incorporation at 10%, rather than the deferred gain being taxed at potentially higher rates in the future.

On the future sale of the shares, entrepreneurs' relief may be available, but Medina's future plans may jeopardise this (see below).

Stamp duty land tax (SDLT) and VAT on incorporation

SDLT at 4% is payable on the transfer of Antares House. If the building is retained personally (see below) then no SDLT is payable.

The transfer of the assets of Dromeda Solutions will be treated as a transfer of a going concern (TOGC) and therefore outside the scope of VAT. It seems that the conditions for TOGC treatment are met.

However, as the option to tax has been exercised on Antares House, the TOGC treatment will not cover the building, unless DS Ltd also opts to tax the property.

If DS Ltd opts to tax Antares House, then no VAT is charged. However, SDLT on the VAT exclusive amount will still be payable ie £950,000 × 4% = £38,000

If DS Ltd does not opt to tax Antares House, VAT should be charged on the consideration allocated to the building. In addition, SDLT will be charged on the VAT inclusive amount of:

£950,000 × 120% × 4% = £45,600

The input VAT incurred by DS Ltd will be recoverable if the building is used wholly in the production of taxable supplies. It appears that Antares House will be used as the business premises under this option.

Retention of Antares House

Should the partners retain Antares House, then incorporation relief would not be available to Medina and Andy as not all assets are transferred on incorporation.

However, the goodwill could be gifted to DS Ltd and the remaining non-chargeable assets transferred in exchange for shares.

The transfer of the non-chargeable assets would result in a total base cost of the shares of £(19,000 + 28,000) = £47,000, assuming no capital gains arise on plant and machinery.

The goodwill could be gifted to DS Ltd and gift relief claimed. The goodwill will have a zero base cost ie the market value of the asset at the time of the gift £320,000 minus the gift relief claimed of £320,000.

Should the business be sold in the future, the goodwill will have a zero base cost and the shares also have a low base cost. As the business has existed since 1999, it seems likely that the IFA rules do not apply and amortisation will not be deductible for DS Ltd. If the goodwill is deemed to be post April 2002 goodwill subject to IFA rules, amortisation is still not available due to the restrictions imposed by FA 2015.

Even if the building is not transferred, the transfer of the other assets should still qualify as a TOGC and no VAT would be payable.

If Medina and Andy retain Antares House and charge DS Ltd a market rent, the building will be treated as an investment property and the sale of the property in the future would not attract entrepreneurs' relief. Instead, the gain would be taxed at 28%/18% instead of 10%.

(2) **Offer from Clowde Ltd to purchase Antares House**

The sale to Clowde Ltd will be standard rated for VAT purposes as the option to tax has been exercised on the property. This will increase the cost to £1,068,000 but the VAT will be recoverable if Clowde Ltd opts to tax the building.

Potentially the VAT on the rent chargeable to Saturn Ltd will be irrecoverable if its business is exempt. This will effect Clowde Ltd's negotiation of a competitive rent.

The disposal of the building will result in a capital gain of £(890,000 – 431,000) = £459,000, split 60:40 between Medina and Andy. Capital gains tax at 10% will be payable on the gain as entrepreneurs' relief is available on the disposal of an asset which is in use when the business ceases.

Clowde Ltd will also pay SDLT on the VAT inclusive price of £(890,000 × 120%) × 4% = £42,720.

(3) **Suitable share schemes**

A tax-advantaged share option scheme would be a suitable long-term incentive for the two prospective directors. A Company Share Option Plan would not allow the granting of options at a discount. An Enterprise Management Incentive (EMI) share option scheme would allow options to be granted at a discount to key employees.

There are some conditions for EMI schemes, the most relevant to DS Ltd being that the employees must own no more that 30% of the share capital and work for a substantial amount of time for the company.

This would preclude part-time employees, but a separate scheme (not tax-advantaged) could be set up for these employees. There are no restrictions or conditions for such schemes, so this could be very flexible.

However, the tax treatment of the schemes is different. Under an EMI, any discount is taxable as employment income on exercise (or the difference between the MV of the shares at exercise and the exercise price, if lower). A capital gain will arise on disposal of the shares being the difference between the sales proceeds and the total of the exercise price and the amount taxable on exercise. So long as the company is a qualifying trading company, at least one year has elapsed between the time when the option was granted and the disposal of the shares, and the individual owning the shares is an officer or employee of the company at the time of the disposal, entrepreneurs' relief should apply to reduce the capital gains tax rate to 10% (subject to a £10 million lifetime cap).

If DS Ltd is confident in the potential rise in its share price, it might be willing to forgo the discount, in which case, no tax will be payable until disposal.

Under a scheme that is not tax-advantaged there will be income tax charge on exercise based on the difference between the MV of the shares on exercise and grant and then a capital gain will arise on disposal based on the difference between the proceeds and the market value of the shares on exercise. The entrepreneurs' relief conditions are also stricter for non-EMI shares. It would only apply to reduce the tax rate applicable to the capital gain if the individual owned at least a 5% interest in the company, and the shares had been held for at least a year from the time of issue (not from the date of the grant of the option). In order for the relief to apply, the company would again have to be a qualifying trading company and the individual would have to be an officer or employee of the company at the time of the disposal.

(4) **Reply to Medina's email**

Dear Medina,

Gift of shares

If you are planning to give your shares to your daughter in 2017, then it would be advisable to ensure that the gift is after 6 April, to ensure that the required one year minimum ownership period is met in order to claim entrepreneurs' relief, meaning that your capital gain would only be taxed at 10%, rather than 18%/28%. You have confirmed that you will remain a director of the company for two years and your position as a director is essential at the time that you claim entrepreneurs' relief.

If entrepreneurs' relief is not available because you gift your shares before 6 April, gift relief is still available on the disposal of your shares to your daughter, providing she is UK resident or at the time. However, this is a deferral of the gain, ultimately charged on your daughter, rather than an absolute relief.

The gift of shares to your daughter is a potentially exempt transfer for inheritance tax (IHT) purposes. This means that there will be no inheritance tax on the date of the gift, but were you to die within seven years of the gift, then IHT may arise.

However, business property relief (BPR) will be available on the gift of your shares. Whilst you may not hold the shares for the required two year period, the shares are replacement property for your stake in the partnership and the ownership periods are therefore added together. As a result, BPR at 100% will be available on the gift to your daughter. Therefore, unless she sells the shares before your death no IHT should be payable.

Use of your trading losses from the partnership

As the business is ceasing, terminal loss relief would normally allow your remaining loss on cessation to be offset against partnership income in the year of cessation and the previous three tax years. However, it appears that you have already eliminated previous partnership profits.

However, on incorporation, your remaining trading loss may be carried forward and offset against future income arising from DS Ltd. The loss of £81,700 may be offset against your salary and bonus, reducing that to £8,300 in 2016/17.

Best wishes

CHAPTER 23

Corporate reorganisations

Introduction

Examination context

Topic List

Summary and Self-test

Answers to Interactive questions

Answers to Self-test

Note: All statutory references are to CTA 2010 unless otherwise stated

Introduction

Learning objectives

Tick off

- Communicate in a format appropriate to the recipient who may be an external client, a fellow professional or an internal colleague ☐

- Prepare suitable advice to explain tax liabilities with supporting calculations ☐

- Recommend appropriate tax-planning advice ☐

- Identify further information required to complete tax computations and finalise tax advice ☐

- Give advice which is appropriate, technically correct, and within the law and the ICAEW Code of Ethics ☐

- Determine, explain and calculate the tax liabilities for individuals and corporate entities, including income tax, national insurance, corporation tax, stamp taxes and VAT ☐

- Evaluate the tax implications of the choice of business structures ☐

- Explain and evaluate the tax implications of group structures ☐

- Explain and evaluate the tax implications of business transformations and change ☐

- Explain and calculate the tax implications involved in the cessation of trade ☐

- Identify legitimate tax planning measures to minimise tax liabilities ☐

- Evaluate and advise on tax strategies to meet business objectives ☐

- Evaluate and advise on alternative tax strategies relating to corporate transformations ☐

- Identify and communicate ethical and professional issues in giving tax planning advice ☐

Specific syllabus references for this chapter are 1a, 1b, 1c, 1d, 1e, 1f, 1g, 1j, 1l, 1m, 2a, 2b, 2c and 2d.

Syllabus links

The use of losses; the effect on loss relief groups and chargeable gains groups; and the possible application of stamp taxes and VAT all need to be considered in a corporate reorganisation. Successions may also be important (Chapter 14).

The substantial shareholding exemption (Chapters 10 and14) may apply to a sale by a corporate vendor. Share for share relief may apply to the reorganisation of shares owned by a private individual or a company (Chapters 6 and 10).

Examination context

Sales of trades or shares within groups of companies can take place using several different vehicles. Substantial planning and preparation time takes place between teams of advisers to ensure the best possible deal for all parties involved.

In the examination candidates may be required to:

- Advise on and calculate the tax liabilities arising from the disposal of a corporate business
- Advise on and calculate the tax liabilities arising from the transfer of a trade intra-group
- Advise on and calculate the tax liabilities arising from hive down of a trade
- Advise on and explain the tax implications of a management buy out

1 Disposing of a corporate business

Section overview

- A corporate business can only be disposed of in one of two ways: via a share sale; or via the sale of its assets.

- A share sale will create a chargeable gain or an allowable loss for the vendor. For a corporate vendor this may be exempt under the substantial shareholding exemption. For an individual, relief may be given via entrepreneurs' relief or EIS or SEIS reinvestment relief.

- The sale of assets will create chargeable gains for the company which will be subject to corporation tax. It will also create balancing adjustments for capital allowances purposes.

- A corporate shareholder could extract the proceeds as a dividend and pay no further tax. An individual shareholder will pay tax on the extracted proceeds whether they are extracted as income (unless a basic rate taxpayer) or capital.

1.1 Overview of two methods of disposing of a business

Sale of shares	Sale of assets
Consequences for individual & corporate shareholders	*Consequences for company selling the assets*
• Capital gain/loss arises on sale of shares	• The company sells its assets resulting in capital gains/losses and capital allowances balancing adjustments
• Capital losses may be available to reduce gain	• Taxable credits or allowable debits will arise on the sale of intangible assets
• The gain may be reduced via a pre-sale dividend strip (see below)	• Where the purchaser and the company are connected, it is possible to elect to transfer assets at TWDV to avoid balancing adjustments
• The gain may be deferred via a share for share exchange	• Rollover relief may be available for gains/taxable credits if new qualifying assets are purchased
	• If the company sells its only trade, it will cease to trade and an accounting period will end. Trading losses will lapse
• Stamp duty at ½% is payable on share purchases by the purchaser	• SDLT at up to 4% (assuming non-residential) is payable by the purchasers on the purchase of land and buildings (including VAT if applicable)
• A share sale is exempt from VAT	• For VAT, the transfer will be not be a supply of goods if it fulfils the TOGC conditions. Otherwise VAT will be payable on the assets sold
	• Property may still be subject to VAT even if part of a TOGC (see Chapter 18)
	• Items subject to capital goods scheme may be subject to usage adjustments by vendor and/or purchaser

Sale of shares	Sale of assets
Further consequences for corporate shareholders	*Consequences for corporate shareholders of the company*
• A corporate shareholder's gain may be exempt if it is from a substantial shareholding (see Chapters 10 and 14)	• The after-tax proceeds from the sale can be extracted from the company as a dividend. The dividend may be FII but normally will not be subject to corporation tax
• For a corporate shareholder there may be group implications of the sale: – Loss of group relief – Degrouping charges	
Further consequences for individual shareholders	*Consequences for individual shareholders of the company*
• An individual vendor may be able to relieve the gain with EIS or SEIS reinvestment relief and/or entrepreneurs' relief	• An individual owner can choose to take out the funds as income (dividend) or capital if part of a liquidation. • Further tax will be due ie there is a double taxation charge (see Chapter 17)

1.2 Comparison of shares versus asset purchase

1.2.1 Advantages and disadvantages of a share deal

	Vendor	Purchaser
Advantages	• Only the gain on the shares is taxed (no double charge unlike when extract funds after an asset sale) • Exemption for gains on sales from qualifying substantial shareholdings for corporate shareholders • No cessation of AP • No balancing adjustments	• Losses of the target company continue to be available subject to s.673 • Stamp duty at 0.5% (but on whole consideration) • All legal contracts pass with company, legally straight forward
Disadvantages	• Degrouping charges (but share sale consideration is adjusted for the degrouping charge. It may then be exempt if the share sale qualifies for SSE)	• Assets acquired at tax written down value for the purpose of capital allowances and goodwill amortisation • Contingent liabilities pass with company, subject to indemnities

Interactive question 2: Group relief

[Difficulty level: Intermediate]

Pilot Ltd is a UK resident holding company that owns many wholly owned subsidiaries, one of which is Sky Ltd. On 1 April 2015, Pilot Ltd sold 30% of the share capital of Sky Ltd. Sky Ltd is currently a loss-making entity.

Sky Ltd has always prepared accounts to 30 September and Pilot Ltd to 31 December. Recent results have been as follows:

	£
Sky Ltd – year ended 30 September 2015	(9,000)
Pilot Ltd – year ended 31 December 2015	20,000

Requirement

If Pilot Ltd wishes to claim maximum group relief from Sky Ltd, state the amounts that can be claimed.

See **Answer** at the end of this chapter.

Interactive question 3: Degrouping charges

[Difficulty level: Intermediate]

Academy plc is the holding company of a large group.

On 1 March 2011 it sold an office block to Dax Ltd, a 100% subsidiary, for its then market value of £3 million. The office block had been acquired in 1989 and had an indexed cost of £2.5 million on 1 March 2011.

In December 2015 Academy plc sold the shares in Dax Ltd for £10 million to raise cash to reduce its borrowings. Dax Ltd still owns the office block in December 2015. Dax Ltd prepares accounts to 31 December.

Requirement

What is the degrouping charge and how is it taxed?

See **Answer** at the end of this chapter.

Worked example: Degrouping charge – intangible fixed asset

Q Ltd purchased a licence for £100,000 and charged the income statement £10,000 per year for three years. At the start of period 4 it sold the licence to W Ltd, its wholly owned subsidiary, for £70,000 (its book value) when its market value was £90,000.

Two years later, at the end of period 5, Q Ltd sold W Ltd. W Ltd continues to own the licence.

Requirement

Calculate the taxable credit arising as a result of the sale of W Ltd.

Solution

Originally, W Ltd takes over the licence at its written down value and its amortisation continues unaffected. Thus it would continue to charge its income statement with £10,000 per annum. This charge would be made in year 4. W Ltd is sold during year 5 and hence the amortisation would be calculated as shown below. W Ltd is treated as having sold and reacquired the licence for £90,000 on the date it was acquired from Q Ltd. The licence would have a remaining life of 7 years.

	£	£
Deemed sale proceeds		90,000
Cost		(70,000)
		20,000
Amortisation for period 4 (£10,000 × £90,000/£70,000)	12,857	
Already claimed	(10,000)	
		(2,857)
Amortisation for period 5 (£10,000 × £77,143/£60,000)		(12,857)
Net credit		4,286

23

2.2.5 Demerger relief

The demerger provisions aim to make it easier to divide and put into separate ownership the trading activities of a company or group of companies when no new controlling owner is involved.

The tax effects of the legislation are as follows:

- The distribution is treated as exempt and hence not treated as income or FII in the hands of the recipient.

- Degrouping charges do not apply to a company leaving a group solely as a result of the demerger.

- HMRC will 'consider sympathetically' the application of s.673 (denial of losses when change in ownership and change in trade). It recognises that the purpose of the demerger is to allow the trade being demerged to be 'managed more dynamically' and that this may involve a major change in the nature or conduct of the trade.

Examples of a demerger:

A plc owns 100% of the shares in X Ltd.

- A plc distributes the shares in X Ltd to its own shareholders. Thus A plc shareholders now own 100% of the shares in both A plc and X Ltd directly:

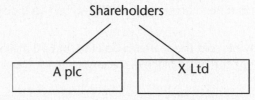

- A plc creates a new company, Newco Ltd, and transfers the shares in X Ltd to Newco Ltd. In exchange Newco Ltd issues shares in itself to the shareholders of A plc:

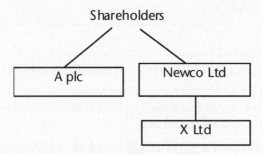

2.3 Implications for the company being sold

Taxation consequences of share sale for company being sold	
Pre-entry trading losses	• Brought forward trading losses will continue to be carried forward and can be set against future profits from the same trade.
	• If s.673 applies, losses brought forward will be wasted as they will not be available for future offset.
	• Pre-entry trading losses are not eligible for surrender to a new loss relief group, if applicable.
Pre-entry capital losses	• Brought forward capital losses will continue to be carried forward and can be set against future gains within the company being sold.
	• Pre-entry capital losses cannot be relieved against gains on assets owned by a new chargeable gains group, if any (eg by deemed transfers before sale).

Taxation consequences of share sale for company being sold		
Degrouping charges	•	Degrouping charges arise where a company leaves a gains group in the accounting period in which it leaves the group. The gain taxed is the original gain avoided on the nil gain/nil loss transfer. The charges are passed on to the vendor if it is a qualifying share sale, and the substantial shareholding exemption may apply (see above). Otherwise they will arise in the departing company.
Capital allowances	•	Assets stay with the company being sold at their tax written down value and will continue to receive allowances as normal.

2.4 Purchase of shares by a company

Taxation consequences of share purchase by a company		
Stamp duty	•	Stamp duty will be payable on the transfer of shares at 0.5%.
Dividends	•	Assuming the acquiring company holds at least > 50% of the shares any dividends received are unlikely to have any corporation tax implications. Most dividends are exempt from corporation tax and exempt dividends from 51% related companies are not included in franked investment income.
Pre-entry trading losses	•	Pre-entry trading losses are not eligible for group relief.
	•	The acquisition of a company with brought forward trading losses is subject to anti-avoidance legislation in s.673 (see Chapter 12).
	•	Any brought forward losses cannot be carried forward after the date of the change in ownership if either:
		– There is a major change in the nature or conduct of the trade within three years before or three years after the change in ownership; or
		– After the company's trading activities have become small or negligible, there is a change in ownership followed by a considerable revival of the trade.
	•	Consider the implications of proposed changes on the future availability of losses.
Pre-entry capital losses	•	Affects all realised capital losses at the time of the change in ownership.
	•	Pre-acquisition losses may only be used against:
		– Gain made before the company is acquired;
		– Gain on asset owned at the time the company is acquired; or
		– Gain on asset purchased from a third party since joining the group and used in the trade it carried on at the time it joined the group.

Where a company changes ownership as part of an arrangement which is designed to give rise to a tax advantage in relation to the offset of capital gains and losses, a targeted anti-avoidance rule applies instead of the pre-entry loss rules outlined above. Under these rules no losses can be offset against pre-entry gains, and pre-entry losses are not allowable losses.

3 Sale of trade and assets

Section overview

- The sale of the trade and assets of an unincorporated business or of a company will result in balancing adjustments for capital allowances and gains on chargeable assets.
- The sale of the trade and assets of an unincorporated business will generate capital gains or losses

and balancing adjustments for income tax purposes. Gains may be deferred by rollover relief, gift relief, EIS reinvestment relief or SEIS reinvestment relief or tax reduced by entrepreneurs' relief

- The sale of the trade and assets of a company will generate chargeable gains or losses and balancing adjustments for corporation tax purposes. Gains may be deferred via rollover relief.

- Companies which are members of a group can utilise group wide purchases to utilise rollover relief.

- The purchase of the trade and assets of a company may be preferable to the purchase of shares. It could be used to create balance sheet goodwill and it leaves any legal liabilities with the vendor.

- Irrecoverable VAT may be incurred and SDLT may be payable at a higher cost than if the shares had been purchased.

3.1 Sale of trade and assets

3.1.1 Taxation implications

The sale of individual assets will lead to capital gains/losses for tangible assets; profits/losses for intangible assets; and balancing adjustments for capital allowances purposes.

There may also be VAT consequences. If the disposal of assets is not a transfer of a going concern, there may be VAT due on the proceeds. Even if the disposal is a transfer of a going concern, the implications of the inclusion of property in the transfer and any option to tax still need to be considered. Capital goods scheme adjustments must also be considered especially where assets are used by the purchaser in a partially exempt or exempt business (see Chapter 18).

Capital and revenue implications arising from sale of trade and assets

Asset	Capital	Revenue
Land and buildings	• Gain or loss	• None
Plant and machinery	• Gain may arise, but no capital losses are available on assets qualifying for any allowance in CAA 200	• Balancing adjustment unless succession election under either s.948 CTA 2010 or s.266 CAA 2001
	• Wasting assets exempt if bought and sold ≤ £6k	
Goodwill		
Acquired pre 1.4.02	• Gain or loss	• None
Acquired post 1.4.02 (companies only)	• None	• Taxable profit or allowable loss
Investments (for companies only)	• Gain or loss unless exempt (eg SSE)	• None except for profits or losses on loan stock taxable under loan relationship rules
Inventories	• None	• Write down of inventories reduces profit or increases loss
Receivables	• None	• Write off of receivables reduces profit or increases loss

3.1.2 Allocation of consideration

The allocation of consideration between assets can be done in a tax efficient manner, but must also be commercially justifiable. It is advisable to seek professional valuations as HMRC has the power to make a 'just and reasonable' apportionment.

Vendors may prefer commercially justifiable allocations biased towards buildings and investments in the following cases:

- Assets have high base costs and hence low gains;

- Capital losses are available;
- Rollover or other reliefs are available.

Vendors may prefer commercially justifiable allocations biased towards 'new' intangible assets, capital allowance assets, inventories and receivables in the following cases:

- Trading losses brought forward are available to relieve higher trading profits produced by the disposal of the above assets;

- Where most items of plant and machinery, inventories, and receivables produce no capital gains;

- Assets qualifying for capital allowances are to be transferred at their TWDV for tax purposes so that no balancing adjustments arise. This is true where the vendor and purchaser are connected and have elected to transfer at TWDV (see Chapter 4); or where the transfer is part of a corporate reorganisation without a change in ownership (see Chapter 14).

Where the disposal includes property which contain fixtures the vendor and purchaser may jointly elect to treat some of the consideration as relating to the fixtures. A s.198 CAA 2001 election may only be made where capital allowances have been claimed on the fixtures and the allocated consideration cannot exceed the original cost. The advantage is that the vendor will end up with balancing charges which can then be offset against brought forward or current year trading losses. Whereas any gains arising on the disposal of the building can only be offset by current year trading losses.

Where consideration is not in the form of cash, its value will be equal to the market value of the assets transferred.

For example, X Ltd sells a property to Y Ltd. The property is worth £500,000. Y Ltd issues 100 £1 shares to X Ltd as consideration. These shares have a value of £500,000 and would be regarded as issued at a premium of £499,900.

3.2 Sale of trade and assets of an unincorporated business

When an unincorporated business is sold by an individual, it is taken to be a disposal of the underlying assets of the business including any goodwill. This has significant capital gains and income tax implications.

Capital gains tax	Income tax
• Gains/losses on each chargeable asset eg property and goodwill	• Cessation of trade rules apply. Any overlap profits from commencement or transitional overlap can be used
• Consideration includes any deferred consideration (see Chapter 5)	• Balancing charges or allowances on assets qualifying for capital allowances
• May be eligible for rollover relief if reinvest in qualifying business assets (not shares)	• Losses in the last 12 months of trading can be relieved under terminal loss rules against trading income of the tax year of cessation and the three preceding tax years.
• If partial business use of old or new asset, only partial relief granted	
• If new asset is depreciating (UEL <60 years) the gain is deferred (not rolled into the base cost of the new asset) for a maximum of 10 years	
• May allocate the gain between more than one new asset. Allocating to non-depreciating assets defers the gain for longer.	
• May be eligible for EIS or SEIS reinvestment relief if purchase new shares in a qualifying unquoted trading company for cash	
• Deferred gain is held over until disposal of	

shares (and is still eligible for entrepreneurs relief if original disposal on/after 3.12.15)

- May be eligible for entrepreneurs' relief

- Gains may be reduced with capital losses

Worked example: Rollover relief

Mr Smith acquired an office block to use in his stockbroker business on 31 March 1987. Two of the three floors were occupied for trade purposes, with the other floor let. The building was sold on 30 September 2015 for £840,000, as part of Mr Smith's disposal of the business. The gain arising was £278,100.

Mr Smith then immediately started to trade as an insurance agent and acquired a new property for £600,000 which was used entirely for the trade. He had already used his lifetime entitlement to entrepreneurs' relief as a result of a disposal in July 2015.

Requirement

Show the gain eligible for rollover relief and the base cost of the new asset if the relief is claimed.

Solution

Gain on old office block	£278,100
Gain qualifying for rollover relief = $^2/_3 \times$ £278,100	£185,400

The gain may be fully rolled over as proceeds reinvested (£600,000) were at least $^2/_3 \times$ £840,000 = £560,000

Base cost of replacement premises	£
Cost	600,000
Gain rolled over	(185,400)
	414,600

Worked example: Rollover relief – acquisition of depreciating asset

A gain is made on the disposal of a freehold office on 31 October 2003. A rollover relief claim is made to defer the gain against expenditure on fixed plant acquired on 1 September 2006.

The fixed plant ceases to be used for trading purposes on 30 November 2015 and was sold on 1 January 2016.

Requirements

(a) When will the deferred gain become chargeable?

(b) Is the gain eligible to be deferred again?

Solution

(a) The deferred gain will become chargeable on the earliest of:

    (i) 10th anniversary of acquisition of replacement = 1 September 2016

    (ii) Date of disposal of replacement = 1 January 2016

    (iii) Date when replacement asset ceases to be used in the business = 30 November 2015

    ie 30 November 2015.

(b) The gain could be rolled over against the cost of a non-depreciating asset, provided the new asset was purchased prior to the deferred gain crystallising ie pre 30 November 2015.

3.3 Sale of trade and assets of a company

This section looks at the taxation implications specific to the sale of the trade and assets of a company:

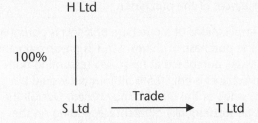

H Ltd

100%

S Ltd ——Trade——▶ T Ltd

S Ltd sells its trade to a third party, T Ltd. This will have implications for all three companies.

Implications for H Ltd

Assuming S Ltd then becomes a dormant company it will no longer be a related 51% company used to determine whether the instalments basis applies for paying corporation tax.

Implications for S Ltd

When a company sells all of its assets and trade, it will generate chargeable gains or losses and it will cease to trade.

Chargeable gains	Trading profits
• Gains/losses on each chargeable asset eg property and pre April 2002 goodwill	• Cessation of trade ends the accounting period • Profit or loss on post April 2002 goodwill
• Eligible for rollover relief • If part of a gains group eligible on a group wide basis	• Balancing charges or allowances on assets qualifying for capital allowances
• Capital losses continue to carry forward after cessation of trade	• Unused trading losses will lapse unless terminal loss relief is available or losses are transferred with the trade under s.944 (see Chapter 14)

In addition, the transfer of the business as a going concern means it is not a supply of goods for VAT (see Chapter 18).

Implications for T Ltd

Many of the assets acquired will result in tax deductions for the purchaser by way of capital allowances, amortisation or allowable trading expenses (eg on trading stock). The purchase of individual assets also enables the creation of tax deductible goodwill. Goodwill arising on consolidation on a purchase of shares does not give rise to a tax deduction.

The split of the consideration between the individual assets will affect the total deductions available to the purchaser and their timing.

The purchase of trade and assets rather than shares means that no new related 51% group company is created and that all potential pre-existing legal liabilities remain with the vendor company.

Taxation consequences of purchase of a company's assets for transferee	
VAT	• The acquisition of individual assets may give rise to irrecoverable VAT depending on the circumstances of the purchaser.
SDLT	• The stamp duty land tax implications of a purchase of assets is potentially more significant than for the purchase of shares. SDLT is payable on any property included in the assets purchased at up to 4% (assuming non-residential). Stamp duty on shares is only 0.5% although it would be payable on the full market value of the business purchased. Overall the amount payable may not be substantially different depending on the nature of the assets included in the business.
Commencement of trade	• Where the acquiring company is not already trading, the acquisition and subsequent commencement of a trade brings about the end of an accounting period and the start of a new one.

3.4 Implications for capital and revenue

The purchase of individual assets, whether by an individual or a company, has capital and revenue taxation consequences as summarised below.

Asset	Capital	Revenue
Land and buildings	• Price paid is base cost for future disposal • Qualifying business assets for rollover relief if used for trade purposes	• None
Plant and machinery	• Price paid is base cost for future disposal • Fixed plant or fixed machinery qualifies for rollover relief	• Capital allowances based on the price paid
Goodwill (companies only)	• Qualifying asset purchase for deferral of profits on sale of any intangibles	• 4% straight line tax relief based on the price paid (if not amortised through the income statement), unless purchased from a connected individual on/after 3 December 2014
Investments	• Price paid is base cost for future disposal	• None except for profits or losses on loan stock taxable under loan relationship rules
Inventories	• None	• Part of future cost of sales
Receivables	• None	• None

4 Transfer of a company's trade within a 75% group

Section overview

- A transfer of the trade of one company to another company within a 75% group is subject to special rules (see Chapter 14).

- Most significantly, trading losses transfer with the trade, SDLT is not payable on the transfer of any land and buildings, and assets will transfer at nil gain/nil loss.

4.1 Introduction

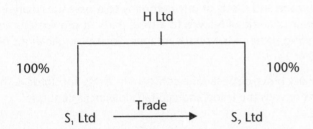

Special rules apply to the transfer of a trade within a 75% group (see Chapter 14).

Implications for H Ltd

If S_1 Ltd becomes dormant, then H Ltd will have one fewer related 51% group company.

Implications for S_1 Ltd

Taxation consequences of transfer of trade for transferor	
Nil gain/nil loss	• As it is a 75% group, the assets will transfer at nil gain/nil loss.
Capital losses	• Unrelieved capital losses remain with S_1 Ltd.
Trading losses	• Trading losses are transferred to S_2 Ltd (reduced by net liabilities remaining in S_1 Ltd – see Section 5 below).
Capital allowances	• Assets transfer at their TWDV so no balancing adjustments in the accounting period of transfer.

Implications for S_2 Ltd

Taxation consequences of transfer of trade for transferee	
SDLT	• As it is a 75% group, SDLT is not payable on the transfer of any land and buildings. However a subsequent sale of S_2 Ltd within three years will mean the withdrawal of this exemption and the SDLT will then have to be paid.
Nil gain/nil loss	• Degrouping charges will arise on S_2 Ltd if it is sold within six years of the transfer. If it is as a result of a qualifying share disposal the degrouping charge will adjust the sale proceeds of the sale of S_2 Ltd, passing the cost on to H Ltd, however it may be exempt if the substantial shareholding exemption applies.
Trading losses	• Trading losses are transferred to S_2 Ltd but are ring fenced and can only be set against future profits from that trade.

5 Hive downs

Section overview

- A hive down is the transfer of a trade and assets to a new subsidiary (Newco) prior to a sale of Newco to a third party.

- A hive down provides some of the advantages of a share sale (preservation of trading losses, no balancing adjustments) whilst avoiding some of the main disadvantages eg exposure to contingent liabilities.

5.1 Introduction

A hive down typically involves the transfer of trade and assets of one company to a new subsidiary in which it has beneficial ownership (Newco) prior to a sale of Newco to a third party. It provides some of the tax advantages of a share sale whilst avoiding some of the disadvantages. The tax implications of a hive down were considered in detail in Chapter 14.

The most significant difference compared to any other disposal of a company's assets and trade is that under ss.944 and 948 any trading losses transfer with the trade and capital allowances continue unaffected ie no balancing adjustments arise.

5.2 Transfer of trading losses

Trading losses transferable are subject to two restrictions:

- Where the transferring trade and the acquiring company's existing trade are merged in the acquiring company, the losses transferring must be ring-fenced and can only be set against future profits from the trade that is transferred; and

- Where the transferring company is left technically insolvent, full transfer of losses is not permitted if all liabilities are not transferred to the transferee (see Chapter 14).

The second limitation prevents relief for the deficit both as a trading loss transferred to the successor company and also as a bad debt in the hands of the creditors of the transferor company.

Worked example: Restriction of losses

Stone Ltd and Rubble Ltd are both wholly-owned subsidiaries of Epsilon plc. Stone Ltd has incurred substantial trading losses. Epsilon plc has decided that a transfer of Stone Ltd's trade to Rubble Ltd is the only way to prevent future trading losses.

Stone Ltd's statement of financial position (using market value at time of transfer) is given below.

	£'000
Non-current assets	100
Current assets	10
Current liabilities	(120)
Other liabilities	(50)
	(60)
Trading losses	(100)

The non-current assets are transferred to Rubble Ltd for £90,000 and the other items on the balance sheet remain in Stone Ltd.

Requirement

Compute the losses relievable in Rubble Ltd under s.944 CTA 2010.

Solution

Losses relievable in Rubble Ltd	£'000	£'000
Losses in Stone Ltd		(100)
Less: relevant liabilities (£120,000 + £50,000)	170	
relevant assets (£10,000 + £90,000)	(100)	
		70
Losses relievable		(30)

5.3 Taxation consequences

A hive down provides some of the advantages of a share sale (preservation of trading losses, no balancing adjustments) whilst avoiding the main disadvantage (exposure to contingent liabilities).

- Purchaser acquires a 'clean' company containing the assets it requires. The company's tax and commercial history, together with any contingent liabilities, are left behind.

- Unrelieved trading losses are available in Newco (subject to s.673) for relief in the future.

- Capital losses, deficits on non-trading loan relationships and losses on non-trading IFAs are not transferred.

- Tangible assets are transferred at no gain/no loss but degrouping charges may arise on the sale of Newco within six years of the transfer. However, if the assets transferred were held and used in the trade of another group company for the 12 months before the transfer, and were used in the trade of the new company at the time of the share sale, the shares in the new company will be treated as having been held for 12 months and it will be treated as having traded for the previous 12 months. If the vendor is a member of a trading group, the shares in the new company will qualify for the substantial shareholding exemption. The degrouping charges will be added to the proceeds on the sale of the shares and hence be exempt.

- The transfer of an intangible asset will be at its original cost and acquisition date. The sale of Newco may then give rise to a degrouping charge.

- A gain may arise on the sale of the Newco shares.

- The exemption from stamp duty land tax on any land and buildings in respect of transfers between companies in the same 75% group will not be available due to the sale of Newco within three years of the transfer.

Interactive question 4: Hive down   [Difficulty level: Intermediate]

Zek Ltd, an internet bookseller, began trading in 2001. Its only chargeable assets for capital gains purposes are as follows:

	Market value £m	Indexed cost £m
Warehouse	1.5	0.9
Goodwill	1.0	Nil

Its other net assets are worth £0.5 million. Zek Ltd has been trading at a loss and has accumulated losses brought forward of £2 million.

Zek Ltd's parent company, Duke plc, wishes to sell Zek Ltd and has found a possible purchaser, Alpha plc, which is prepared to pay £3 million. Alpha plc would like the benefit of Zek Ltd's brought forward losses but is not keen on buying the shares of Zek Ltd due to a negligence claim pending against the company.

Requirement

Explain how a hive down may provide a suitable method for sale.

See **Answer** at the end of this chapter.

6 Management buy out

Section overview

- A management buy out is a transaction whereby ownership of the business is transferred to its existing managers.

- The new company is likely to be a close company and the buy out is likely to raise employment income issues for the managers and financing issues for the company.

6.1 Introduction

A management buy out (MBO) is a transaction where the business of an existing company is bought by its managers, with or without the assistance of external financiers. The transaction normally follows the hive down route and therefore the same taxation consequences mentioned earlier are relevant.

This section covers the following additional taxation consequences of transferring a business to the managers.

(1) **Employment income consequences**

If favourable terms are given to managers (as is usually the case) there are income tax consequences for those managers.

(2) **Financing**

The MBO team will almost certainly need to raise finance to purchase an interest in the business and the company may also need to borrow to continue operations. This section covers the taxation consequences of financing the deal.

(3) **Close company status**

The new company formed will often satisfy the definition of a close company.

6.2 Taxation consequences of issuing shares to managers

The issue to the managers of shares in the new company may cause income tax implications and a NIC liability, since any advantage may be due to employment.

If the shares are acquired at less than the perceived market value, the difference will give rise to assessable employment income.

If the shares are acquired partly paid, this will be deemed to be due to employment, and the amount outstanding will be treated as a beneficial loan. This continues until the notional loan (undervalue) terminates, eg by paying the outstanding amount.

The managers may be issued with share options to acquire shares in the new company. These are subject to the normal share option rules.

6.3 Relief available for financing a MBO

A MBO requires managers to purchase shares in the new company. However, they may not be able to finance the purchase of these shares personally.

It is common for the individual managers to need to raise finance to purchase a stake in the new company. Similarly, to facilitate change and expand in the future, the new company may need to raise finance to run the business.

Managers

Income tax relief will be available in respect of loan interest on a loan taken out to buy shares in the new company, provided the company is close at the time the loan is applied. In order to qualify for this relief:

- The managers must hold more than 5% of the ordinary share capital; or

- The managers must be full-time working officers or employees involved in the management of the company and own some shares; or

- The company must be employee-controlled.

Amounts deductible are subject to the restriction on income tax reliefs against total income (Chapter 4).

Note that this relief is not given if income tax relief has been claimed under the Enterprise Investment Scheme.

Company

Interest on any finance raised by the company will either be allowable as a trading expense or non-trading loan relationship debit (according to normal loan relationship rules).

Summary

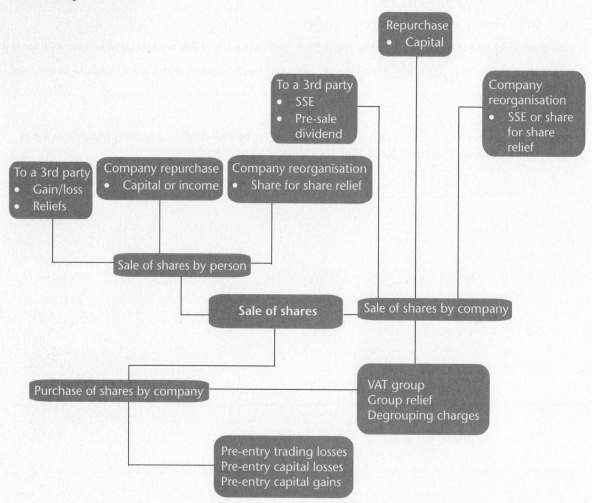

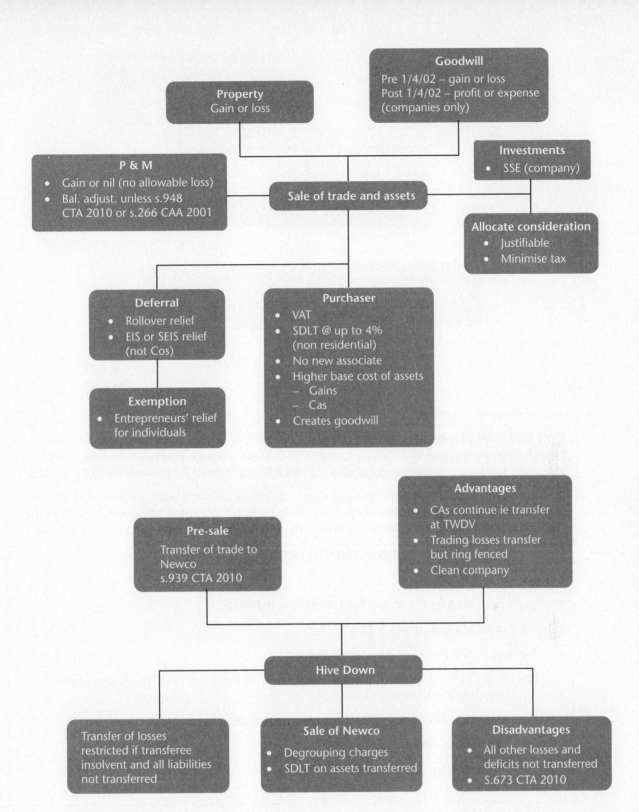

Property
Gain or loss

Goodwill
Pre 1/4/02 – gain or loss
Post 1/4/02 – profit or expense
(companies only)

P & M
- Gain or nil (no allowable loss)
- Bal. adjust. unless s.948 CTA 2010 or s.266 CAA 2001

Sale of trade and assets

Investments
- SSE (company)

Allocate consideration
- Justifiable
- Minimise tax

Deferral
- Rollover relief
- EIS or SEIS relief (not Cos)

Exemption
- Entrepreneurs' relief for individuals

Purchaser
- VAT
- SDLT @ up to 4% (non residential)
- No new associate
- Higher base cost of assets
  - Gains
  - Cas
- Creates goodwill

Advantages
- CAs continue ie transfer at TWDV
- Trading losses transfer but ring fenced
- Clean company

Pre-sale
Transfer of trade to Newco
s.939 CTA 2010

Hive Down

Transfer of losses restricted if transferee insolvent and all liabilities not transferred

Sale of Newco
- Degrouping charges
- SDLT on assets transferred

Disadvantages
- All other losses and deficits not transferred
- S.673 CTA 2010

CHAPTER

23

ICAEW

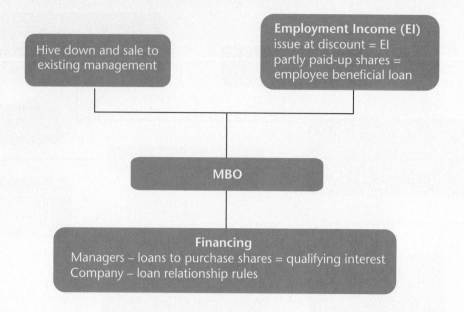

Self-test

Answer the following questions.

1 On 1 May 2004 Jane Bennett set up a company, PP Ltd, specialising in the sale of high quality organic produce through two specialist shops and over the internet. Internet sales have been extremely successful, and company profits of £750,000 are forecast for the year to 30 April 2016.

Jane has been a tax client of your firm and a personal friend for many years. In December 2015 Jane received an offer to purchase her business from Hurst plc, a quoted company. As soon as she received this she sent you the following note with information about the offer.

PROPOSED OFFER FROM HURST PLC

Key points

- Hurst plc is keen for me to join the company as a director.

- Total consideration offered of £8 million.

- Three options for providing the consideration.

    (1) Shares in Hurst plc worth £6.4 million, plus £1.6 million in cash. The shares would constitute a 3% holding in Hurst plc.

    (2) As (1) but with £1.6 million of 6% loan stock instead of cash.

    (3) £8 million in cash.

- Planned completion date – 1 March 2016.

Jane

From the client files you know that Jane is the sole shareholder and director of PP Ltd. Her shares cost £100 on their issue in May 2004; this is so small in relation to the consideration that it can be ignored.

Jane is 36 and is currently drawing a salary of £51,475 per annum. She made chargeable gains of £11,100 in June 2015.

Jane has sent you the following email today

To	John Gordon
From	Jane Bennett
Date	28 January 2016
Subject	Offer from Hurst plc

Hi John

Please help me! I am really undecided whether to accept a post as a full-time director of Hurst plc or to get out, retire and write novels!

To help me to decide, I need some answers to a few questions about the taxation effects of this proposal. Therefore can we please meet to discuss the following.

- What capital gains tax will I have to pay for each of the three options offered?

- Can I take some of the consideration out of PP Ltd in the form of a pre-sale dividend, with a corresponding reduction in the sum received from Hurst plc?

- What effect would this have on my tax position?

- What factors would need to be considered in respect of the payment of a dividend?

- If I were to retire now, what effect would this have on my future capital gains liabilities?

- Are there any reliefs available to me to reduce any capital gains liabilities?

How about discussing this over dinner on Thursday?

Jane

Requirement

Prepare notes for your forthcoming dinner with Jane.

2   Delta Ltd is a company which manufactures small pleasure boats. Poor weather throughout 2014 and 2015 has resulted in declining sales, with the result that Delta Ltd ceased trading on 1 January 2016. Its net assets at that date were as follows.

	£'000	£'000
Freehold boatyard		80
Freehold office		40
Plant and machinery		30
Motor vehicles		30
		180
Current assets		
Inventory	125	
Receivables	375	
Cash	1	
	501	
Current liabilities		
Trade payables	425	
Bank overdraft (unsecured)	375	
Hire purchase liabilities	31	
	(831)	
Net current liabilities		(330)
Non-current liabilities		
Loan secured on freehold office		(35)
		(185)

There were unrelieved trading losses at 1 January 2015 amounting to £290,000. The company has incurred substantial losses in each of the last three years, and has an adjusted loss of £60,000 in the year ended 31 December 2015.

You are the audit senior for Delta Ltd. Two weeks ago the directors informed you of the following.

- A receiver was appointed by the hire purchase company at the request of the directors on 18 December 2015.

- A wholly-owned subsidiary, Flood Ltd, was formed, and on 1 January 2016 the assets and undertaking of Delta Ltd were hived down. All assets were transferred to Flood Ltd, except the freehold office which the receiver sold to a third party on 10 January 2016. No liabilities were transferred to Flood Ltd other than the hire purchase liabilities, which relate entirely to plant and motor vehicles. The consideration for the trade transferred was the issue of shares in Flood Ltd, which were quickly sold by the receiver to a third party for £475,000.

The directors have contacted you today with queries relating to the use of Delta Ltd's tax losses.

Requirement

Prepare a draft response to the directors in which you:

- Calculate the tax losses available to Delta Ltd for the year ended 31 December 2015.
- Indicate the amount of unrelieved trading losses available to be transferred to Flood Ltd.

3 Holland plc, a major client of your firm, is the parent company of a large UK group engaged in the manufacture of reproduction regency furniture. You are the tax senior in charge of the client.

Holland plc has a wholly-owned subsidiary, Carlton House Ltd, which owns a chain of 30 high street shops. The shops carry a range of products, including furniture, soft furnishings and carpets.

On 1 January 2016 Holland plc acquired the entire share capital of Hope Ltd from Pavilion plc. Hope Ltd owns a small chain of ten specialist porcelain and glass shops.

To reduce costs Holland plc plans to centralise the purchasing, administration and distribution functions of both chains of shops to include a full range of all products, and progressively over a period of a year or so to change the name of the Hope shops to Carlton House. To minimise administrative inconvenience and cost, Holland plc would like to transfer all the shops and trade to Carlton House Ltd and merge the two chains.

The finance director has approached you for some advice regarding the use of losses and the proposed merger of the trades.

You ascertain that Hope Ltd has trading losses of £270,000 brought forward at 1 April 2015. Its estimated losses for the first nine months (to 31 December 2015) of the year ended 31 March 2016 were £144,000, but it plans to surrender these to Pavilion plc as group relief. Hope Ltd has continued to make losses since the acquisition, but Holland plc's finance director tells you that the proposed cost-cutting exercise is expected to make its trade profitable, so that the losses of £270,000 can be utilised within a few years.

Requirement

Draft notes in preparation for a meeting with the finance director in which you:

- Explain how the tax losses of Hope Ltd can be relieved, assuming that the trade of Hope Ltd continues unchanged.

- Set out the factors that could be interpreted as a major change in the nature or conduct of Hope Ltd's trade for taxation purposes.

- Explain the difference in tax terms of transferring the trade of Hope Ltd to Carlton House Ltd or vice versa.

4   Hive plc is a UK trading company which holds 100% of Dawn Ltd.

The companies had the following tax results in the year ended 31 March 2016.

	Hive plc £	Dawn Ltd £
Trading profit	803,000	(240,000)

Dawn Ltd had found recent trading difficult and had trading losses of £178,000 brought forward at 1 April 2015. On 1 January 2016 the management of Dawn Ltd commenced negotiations with the board of Hive plc with a view to a management buyout, and HMRC has indicated that it believes that arrangements exist for Dawn Ltd to leave the group. These negotiations have been protracted due to difficulties in raising the finance needed, so that the sale will not be completed until 1 November 2016.

Dawn Ltd's main asset is a freehold retail unit which was acquired on 1 January 1998 for £800,000. It is expected to be worth £1,429,600 at 1 November 2016.

Dawn Ltd also owns a freehold office block which had been acquired from Bull Ltd in January 2011 for £103,250, its market value at the time. The building was originally acquired by Bull Ltd in January 1992 for £50,000. Bull Ltd is also a 100% subsidiary of Hive plc.

The managers of Dawn Ltd believe that they could trade profitably without the restrictions placed on them by the board of Hive plc. They are considering establishing a company to take over the trade and assets of Dawn Ltd, with or without the company itself. Their projections show that in the period ended 31 March 2017 they will make a trading profit of £80,000, rising to £200,000 in the year ended 31 March 2018 and later years, these profits approximating to the tax adjusted trading profits.

Requirements

(a) Calculate the trading losses that Dawn Ltd has available to carry forward at 1 April 2016 after maximum group relief has been surrendered to Hive plc.

(b) Calculate the degrouping charge that would arise if the managers were to purchase the share capital of Dawn Ltd.

(c) State three tax effects of a purchase of the trade and assets of Dawn Ltd, rather than its share capital.

(d) Explain the advantages of a transfer of assets and trade from Dawn Ltd to a newly-formed subsidiary (hive down) prior to the sale of the subsidiary to the managers.

Note. Ignore VAT. The RPI for November 2016 can be taken as 263.0.

5   **Rossetti Ltd [taken from Sample Paper 1]**

Rossetti Ltd is a company that manufactures plastics for the aero-space industry. Rossetti Ltd is based in Wales and is a client of your firm. The engagement includes a review of the corporation tax computations prepared by the financial controller and advice on tax issues, as requested by the client during June 2016. Your firm also acts for the directors of Rossetti Ltd in respect of their personal tax affairs.

Background information on Rossetti Ltd

The shareholders and their holdings of £1 ordinary shares are as follows:

	Notes	£m
Bill Roscoe	1	0.55
Christina Stone	1	0.40
Tomaz Kinsella	2	0.30
Pebble plc	3	1.75
WB Inc	4	0.45
TSE Ltd	5	1.55
		5.00

Notes:

(1) Bill Roscoe and Christina Stone are directors of Rossetti Ltd.

(2) Tomaz Kinsella was the only other director of the company. He was made redundant on 1 February 2016 and received compensation for loss of office of £10,700. An interest free loan of £5,100 was made to Tomaz on 1 January 2015. The loan was written off in Rossetti Ltd's income statement on 1 February 2016. Tomaz is an additional rate taxpayer.

(3) Pebble plc is a UK resident listed company. Three directors of Pebble plc each own 20% of the ordinary shares in the company and the remaining 40% of the ordinary shares are publicly owned.

(4) WB Inc is a US resident trading company.

(5) TSE Ltd is a UK resident company whose ordinary share capital is owned equally by three directors and has made taxable total profits of £42,000 for the year ended 31 March 2016.

Pebble plc and WB Inc both made taxable total profits in excess of £2 million for the year ended 31 March 2016.

Rossetti Ltd – Draft corporation tax computation for the year ended 31 March 2016 and notes prepared by the financial controller

The financial controller of Rossetti Ltd has prepared a draft corporation tax computation for the year ended 31 March 2016 and has identified two issues where he is unsure of the correct tax treatment.

	£
Profit before tax (Issues 1 and 2)	369,895
Add disallowable expenses	82,900
Less bank interest receivable	(2,150)
Less capital allowances	(51,800)
Tax adjusted trading profit	398,845

Issue 1

The profit before tax of £369,895 includes a deduction for £443,900, which represents revenue expenditure incurred by Rossetti Ltd, directly related to researching and developing a new polymer which withstands extremely low temperatures. Rossetti Ltd is an SME for research and development purposes.

Issue 2

Finance costs of £57,274, as described below, were deducted in arriving at the profit before tax of £369,895.

	£
Write off of loan to Tomaz	5,100
Interest on loan from Spanish bank	52,174
	57,274

On 1 January 2016 Rossetti Ltd borrowed €2 million from a Spanish bank to fund the polymer research. The loan is for two years at an interest rate of 12% pa and the amount received was immediately converted to £ sterling at the exchange rate on 1 January 2016 of £1 = €1.30. The liability in respect of the loan was recognised in the financial statements at the same exchange rate, but no adjustments have since been made in respect of this liability.

The interest charge of £52,174 shown above is an accrual for interest of €60,000 for the first three months, translated at the exchange rate on 31 March 2016 of £1 = €1.15.

The financial controller has also provided information regarding the divestment of Shelly Ltd, Rossetti Ltd's 100% owned subsidiary (**Exhibit 1**). Shelly Ltd sells medical equipment, employs 25 staff and operates from premises in Wales. It started trading in 1999. Rossetti Ltd has decided to sell its interest in Shelly Ltd and initial consultations have taken place with Marvell plc, the potential purchaser.

Exhibit 1 – Email from Antonia Loga

Date: 1 May 2016
Subject: Letter from executor of grandfather's will

My grandfather owned a 10% shareholding in SloeStep Ltd, an unquoted manufacturing company. In August 2014, my grandfather gave me these shares when they were worth £150,000. I still hold these shares and they are now worth £200,000.

Sadly my grandfather has died recently and I have received a letter from the executor of his will. The executor is asking me whether I still hold the shares in SloeStep Ltd. Please could you advise me on whether there are any tax implications for me arising from grandfather's gift to me of his shares in SloeStep Ltd.

I do not require any calculations on this matter.

Antonia

Now, go back to the Learning objectives in the Introduction. If you are satisfied you have achieved these objectives, please tick them off.

Answer to Interactive question 1

(a) (i) Capital gains tax liability

	£'000
Proceeds	4,200
Cost	(1,200)
Gain	3,000
Capital gains tax @ 28%	840

(ii) **Additional tax due to pre-sale dividend**

	£'000
Proceeds (£4.2m – £1.8m)	2,400
Cost	(1,200)
Gain	1,200
Capital gains tax @ 28%	336
Income tax (£1.8m × $^{100}/_{90}$ × (37.5 – 10) %)	550
Total tax	886
Part (a) – Capital gains tax	(840)
Additional tax	46

(b) **The effect of Janner Ltd being a trading company**

The disposal of the shares in Janner Ltd would qualify for entrepreneurs' relief. The capital gains tax liability would be calculated as follows:

	£'000
Gain (as before)	3,000
Capital gains tax @ 10%	300

The availability of entrepreneurs' relief has reduced the CGT payable by £540,000 (£840,000 – £300,000).

In situation (a) the effect of paying a pre-sale dividend of £1.8m is to replace a gain taxed at 28% with dividend income taxed at an effective rate of 30.6% $\left[\dfrac{100}{90} \times \left(37\frac{1}{2}\% - 10\%\right)\right]$ and is not therefore advisable. In situation (b) the payment of a pre-sale dividend will replace a gain taxed at 10% with dividend income taxed at an effective rate of 30.6% and therefore is not desirable.

(c) **Corporate shareholders and pre-sale dividends**

Where a company makes a disposal out of a substantial shareholding, no gain or loss arises. In this situation the payment of a pre-sale dividend is irrelevant.

Where the exemption is not available, the payment of a dividend will reduce the gain and save tax at the main rate of 20%. The dividend itself is tax free in the hands of the company.

A pre-sale dividend cannot be used to create or increase a capital loss.

Answer to Interactive question 2

Corresponding APs end for both companies on 1 April 2015

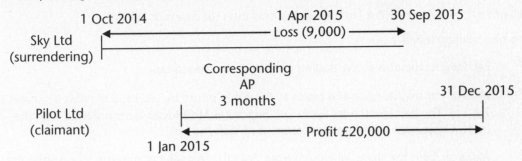

Sky Ltd's loss is dealt with as follows.

$^6/_{12}$ (1 April 2015 – 30 September 2015) £4,500 is 'ring fenced'. This can only be relieved by Sky Ltd against its own profits.

$^6/_{12}$ (1 October 2014 – 31 March 2015) £4,500 is available for group relief.

The amount of the loss arising in Pilot Ltd's year ended 31 December 2015 is for the period 1 January 2015 – 31 March 2015 ie £2,250 ($^3/_{12}$ × £9,000). Since Pilot Ltd's available profit for this period is £5,000 ($^3/_{12}$ × £20,000) the whole of the £2,250 loss may be surrendered by Sky Ltd and used by Pilot Ltd against the profits of the year ended 31 December 2015.

The remainder of the £4,500 loss available for group relief can be offset against Pilot Ltd's profits in the year ended 31 December 2014. This is provided Pilot Ltd has at least £2,250 of profits in the last three months of that year.

Answer to Interactive question 3

A degrouping gain arises because Dax Ltd leaves the group within six years of an earlier no gain/no loss transfer. It is calculated as follows.

	£m
Market value of the office block (1 March 2011)	3.0
Cost and indexation to 1 March 2011	(2.5)
Degrouping gain	0.5

As the sale of the shares by Academy plc is a disposal of shares within the charge to corporation tax, it is a qualifying share disposal. Therefore the degrouping gain will be added to the sales proceeds from the disposal of the shares of £10m.

The proceeds will therefore become £10.5m. However, if Dax Ltd is a trading company the disposal of the shares is likely to be exempt under the substantial shareholdings rules.

The base cost carried forward by Dax Ltd is £3m (deemed acquisition date of 1.3.11).

Answer to Interactive question 4

Alpha plc does not wish to buy shares in Zek Ltd.

Alpha will not get the benefit of Zek Ltd's losses if it only buys the assets of Zek Ltd.

A compromise solution is a hive down.

Step 1 Zek Ltd incorporates a new trading company, say Newco Ltd.

Step 2 Zek Ltd transfers its trade and assets to Newco in return for the issue of Newco's shares to Zek Ltd. The succession rules apply and hence Zek Ltd's losses are transferred with the trade. Chargeable assets are transferred at no gain/no loss.

Step 3 Alpha plc buys the shares of Newco from Zek Ltd. This will not give rise to a gain as the base cost of Newco will equal its market value.

Step 4 Newco is now a subsidiary of Alpha plc. It has the trade, assets and losses of Zek Ltd but none of its 'history'.

Step 5 When Newco is sold, a degrouping charge arises on the assets transferred from Zek Ltd.

Warehouse (£1.5m – £0.9m) = £0.6 million

Goodwill = £1.0 million

These gains will be added to the sale proceeds of the shares in Newco. Zek Ltd will have increased proceeds of £1.6m.

As the trade and assets had been used in the trade of Zek Ltd for 12 months before the transfer, the shares in Newco will be treated as having been held for 12 months and it will be treated as having traded for the previous 12 months. The shares in Newco will qualify for the substantial shareholding exemption.

The degrouping charges which are added to the proceeds on the sale of the shares will be exempt.

The goodwill is an 'old' intangible asset as Zek Ltd began trading prior to 1 April 2002.

Factors to watch

(1) Newco has undergone a change of ownership. If major changes are made to the nature or conduct of the trade carried on, the losses brought forward will lapse (s.673).

(2) A transfer of assets between 75% group members is normally free of stamp duty land tax. However, the relief is not available where there are arrangements in place for the company to be sold or if the company actually leaves the group within three years of the transfer.

(3) It should be noted that where a sale of the transferee company has been agreed prior to the hive down, the benefits of the succession rules may be lost.

(4) Stamp duty is payable on the purchase of the shares of Newco at 0.5%.

1

Subject: Offer from Hurst plc

Capital gains tax payable for each option

Option 1 – shares and cash

- The share element of the consideration would be treated as a share-for-share exchange with no capital gain arising at this time.

- As the shares from Hurst plc constitute 80% of the consideration, they would be regarded as taking over 80% of the cost of the original shares, ie £80.

- Gains on the Hurst plc shares would only arise on a future disposal.

- The cash element would be treated as a chargeable disposal, giving a gain of £1.6m (less £20 of cost which can be ignored).

- Entrepreneurs' relief is available on the gain of £1.6m as follows:

	£
Chargeable gain	1,600,000
Capital gains tax:	
£1,600,000 × 10%	£160,000

Option 2 – shares and loan stock

- As in Option 1 the share element would be treated in the same way.

- The loan stock element would be treated as a chargeable disposal giving rise to a chargeable gain of £1.6m (as Option 1). However, this is not charged at the time of the receipt of loan stock. The gain is deferred until the loan stock is sold/redeemed. As the deferred gain is unlikely to be eligible for entrepreneurs' relief in the future when it becomes chargeable, it will be taxed at 28%. It may be preferable to elect to treat the transaction as a disposal on 1 March 2016 so it is taxed at 10% as entrepreneurs' relief is available at that date.

Option 3 – cash only

- If the consideration is all in the form of cash, a chargeable gain arises immediately.

- The gain of £8m will be taxed at 10% (as it is within the lifetime limit of £10m) as entrepreneurs' relief is available.

Pre-sale dividend

- A pre-sale dividend would be taxed on Jane as income. The first £98,525 (£150,000 – £51,475) of the gross dividend would attract income tax at 25% of the net cash received. The balance of the dividend would attract income tax at 30.6% of the net cash received. In addition because her total income would be more than £120,000, her personal allowance would be withdrawn resulting in additional tax of £4,240 (£10,600 × 40%) on her other income.

- Receipt of cash for her shares is taxed as a gain as in Option 3 above. This has an effective tax rate of 10%.

- Hence a pre-sale dividend will increase the tax payable by Jane and would not be recommended.

- Furthermore, a dividend can only be paid out of distributable profits as defined for company law purposes. This course of action would need to be agreed with Hurst plc beforehand.

Retirement now

- Hurst plc is a quoted company. Jane's shareholding will be only 3% which is insufficient to qualify for entrepreneurs' relief even if she continued to work for the company.

- Her future gain will be taxed at 28%.

Other tax reliefs available

- The only other way in which Jane could shelter gains on the sale of her shares in PP Ltd is reinvestment relief. This requires a subscription in eligible shares in a qualifying company.

- Up to £50,000 of the gain would be exempt if she invested £100,000 in shares on which Seed Enterprise Investment Scheme relief was claimed in 2015/16. However, this would still leave most of the gain in the charge to tax.

- The best option is therefore likely to be to invest in shares in a company which qualifies under the Enterprise Investment Scheme (EIS), although it is not necessary for Jane actually to receive such EIS relief.

- The relief allows deferral of the gain until the EIS shares are disposed of, and as the disposal is on/after 3 December 2014 the deferred gain will be eligible for entrepreneurs' relief when realised.

- To obtain full relief Jane would need to reinvest an amount equal to the gain, which seems unlikely.

2

DRAFT RESPONSE TO DIRECTORS' QUERIES

Prepared by A Senior
Subject Hive down of Delta Ltd assets to Flood Ltd – use of losses

Losses available to Delta Ltd for the year to 31 December 2015

	£'000
Unrelieved losses at 1 January 2015	290
Trading loss for y/e 31 December 2015	60
Unrelieved losses at 31 December 2015	350

As Delta Ltd has no taxable profits, all losses are unrelieved.

Losses available for transfer to Flood Ltd

For intra-group transfers of trades, the losses transferred with the trade are restricted by the excess of 'relevant liabilities' over 'relevant assets' as follows (see tutorial note below).

	£'000	£'000
Relevant assets (not transferred)		
Freehold office		40
Less relevant secured loan		(35)
		5
Consideration received from Flood Ltd		475
		480
Relevant liabilities		
Current liabilities of Delta Ltd		831
Less hire purchase liabilities (transferred)		(31)
		800
Trading losses transferred		
Unrelieved losses at 31 December 2015		350
Relevant liabilities	800	
Relevant assets	(480)	
		(320)
Losses available for transfer to Flood Ltd		30

3

NOTES RE HOLLAND PLC MERGER OF TRADES

Prepared by: A Senior

Relief of trading losses of Hope Ltd

- Hope Ltd has trading losses brought forward of £270,000 at 1 April 2015. However, this must be increased by the portion of the planned group relief surrender of £144,000 to Pavilion plc which will be disallowed.

- Group relief is denied where 'arrangements' are in existence, which means that, at some time during or after the end of the accounting period, the surrendering company could cease to be a member of the group, or become a member of another group, or become controlled by a third party.

- Under case law only the loss arising after arrangements come into existence will be excluded from a group relief claim.

- It is likely that, for the sale on 1 January 2016, arrangements will have existed for several weeks.

- If arrangements were made on, say, 1 December 2015, one-ninth of the £144,000 loss (ie £16,000) would be excluded from the group relief claim. Hope Ltd's losses brought forward would therefore be increased by £16,000 to £286,000.

Factors that could be interpreted as major changes

Section 673 CTA 2010 disallows a trading loss where, within a period of three years, there is both a change in ownership of a company and a major change in the nature or conduct of a trade carried on by it.

- Firstly, the proposal to change the administration, purchasing and distribution of Hope Ltd could be regarded as a major change in the 'conduct' of the trade.

- Secondly, the proposal to widen significantly the range of goods stocked in Hope Ltd's shops could constitute a major change in the 'nature' of the trade.

- Thirdly, a change of name could be construed as a major change in Hope Ltd's outlets, and hence be regarded as a major change in the 'nature or conduct' of the trade.

Both qualitative issues (ie whether a change has occurred) and quantitative issues (ie whether the change is sufficient to constitute a major change) are considered.

The effect of the above would be to cancel the trading losses brought forward from the date of acquisition.

Tax effect of transfer of the trade from Hope Ltd to Carlton House Ltd

Assuming that the above proposals are not implemented for at least three years so that s.673 CTA 2010 is avoided, the effect of a transfer of a loss-making trade to a profitable trade is as follows.

- The trading losses of Hope Ltd could be transferred to Carlton House Ltd, together with the trade, under s.944 CTA 2010. However, they would be 'ring fenced'.

- The losses can be utilised against future profits but only those from the same trade (ie those of ex-Hope Ltd).

- Future profits of Carlton House Ltd would therefore need to be split between the two trades until the losses are fully utilised.

Tax effect of transfer of the trade from Carlton House Ltd to Hope Ltd

The effect of a transfer of a profitable trade to a loss-making trade is as follows.

- Carlton House Ltd is a profitable company, therefore no losses are transferred with the trade.

- Provided Hope Ltd now carries on a single merged trade, Hope Ltd's losses can be set off against ex-Carlton House Ltd's trade profits as there is no 'ring fencing' of profits.

- If there were in fact two distinct trades the set-off of losses brought forward by Hope Ltd would still be restricted to profits from the same (ie Hope Ltd's) trade.

4 (a) **Trading losses**

After a maximum group relief surrender of £180,000 (W1) to Hive plc, Dawn Ltd will have an unrelieved current year loss of £60,000 (£240,000 – £180,000) for the year ended 31 March 2016.

This will increase Dawn Ltd's unrelieved trading losses to carry forward to £238,000 (£178,000 b/f + £60,000 current year) at 1 April 2016.

(b) **Degrouping charge**

As Dawn Ltd would be leaving the group within six years of the transfer of the office block, the gain that would have arisen in 2011 is treated as arising in the year ended 31 March 2016.

This will result in a chargeable gain of £18,800 (W2). This would be added to the sale proceeds received by Hive plc on the sale of the shares in Dawn Ltd. The sale of the shares in Dawn Ltd should qualify for the substantial shareholding exemption and the degrouping charge will therefore be exempt.

(c) **Purchase of individual trade and assets**

No relief will be available to the management for the unrelieved trading losses of £238,000.

A chargeable gain of £110,400 (W3) will arise on the disposal of the retail unit, but it would be possible for the group as a whole to claim rollover relief for this gain if investment is to be made/has been made in other qualifying assets within the 12 months before and three years after the disposal of the retail unit.

A chargeable gain will arise on disposal of the office block. As the office block is being sold outside the group, a gain will crystallise in Dawn Ltd based on its value in November 2016. Provided that the office block had been used for the purpose of Dawn Ltd's trade, it is also possible to claim rollover relief for this gain if the group has qualifying investments.

(d) **Transfer of trade and assets to a new company, followed by sale of shares in the new company**

The main attraction of this option is that the new company is a 'clean' company, ie it will not have old liabilities of which the management could not be aware.

Brought forward trading losses are preserved on the transfer of trade and assets to the new company, provided that 75% of the new company is controlled by the same persons who had control of the old company. This is subject to there being no major change in the nature or conduct of the trade during the three years following the acquisition of the new company.

Plant and machinery will be transferred at tax written-down value for capital allowances purposes, so that no balancing charge will arise.

WORKINGS

(1) **Group relief from Dawn Ltd**

As 'arrangements' for Dawn Ltd to leave the group commenced on 1 January 2016, there will be the end of an accounting period on 1 January 2016 for the purposes of the calculation of group relief to the Hive plc group.

The loss available to Hive plc for group relief for the period 1 April 2015 to 1 January 2016 is thus £180,000 (£240,000 × 9/12).

(2) Gain on transfer of office block – January 2011

	£
Proceeds – market value (January 2011)	103,250
Less cost (January 1992)	(50,000)
Unindexed gain	53,250
Less indexation allowance 229.0 – 135.6/135.6 = 0.689 × £50,000	(34,450)
Chargeable gain	18,800

(3) Gain on disposal of retail unit

	£
Proceeds (November 2016)	1,429,600
Less cost (January 1998)	(800,000)
Unindexed gain	629,600
Less indexation allowance 263.0 – 159.5/159.5 = 0.649 × £800,000	(519,200)
Chargeable gain	110,400

5 Rosetti Ltd

Briefing paper

Recommendation with supporting calculations for the appropriate tax treatment of two issues

Issue 1 – Research and development costs

As Rossetti is an SME for research and development (R&D) purposes, an additional 130% of research and development expenditure may be deducted from its trading profit.

The development of the new polymer would appear to meet the definition of R&D in the guidelines issued by the Department of Business Innovation and Skills, but this should be confirmed.

Qualifying expenditure incurred on R&D for the year ended 31 March 2016 is £443,900.

Therefore an additional deduction of 130% × £443,900 = £577,070 is available for Rossetti Ltd.

Issue 2 – Finance costs

(i) *Loan write off*

Rossetti Ltd appears to be a close company as it is controlled (>50%) by five or fewer participators ie Bill Roscoe, Christina Stone, Tomaz Kinsella and TSE Ltd (which is a close company). Pebble plc is not a close company as >35% of the shares are publicly owned.

As Tomaz is a participator of Rossetti Ltd at the time of the write-off, the amount written off will be treated as a net distribution, taxed as a normal dividend in his hands.

A deduction for the write off is specifically disallowed as the loan was made to a participator and £5,100 should be added back to the trading profit.

(ii) *Forex adjustment required on Spanish loan*

	£
€2m @ £1:€1.3	1,538,462
€2m @ £1:€1.15	(1,739,130)
Loss on translation of the loan	(200,668)

Revised computation of the tax adjusted trading loss for the year ended 31 March 2016 and possible surrenders to consortium members

The revised computation of the tax adjusted trading loss is as follows:

	£
Tax adjusted trading profit per the financial controller	398,845
Less:	
R&D expenditure – additional 125%	(577,070)
Forex adjustment on the Spanish bank loan	(200,668)
Add:	
Loan write off for Tomaz Kinsella	5,100
Tax adjusted loss	(373,793)

Pebble plc, WB Inc and TSE Ltd own a combined shareholding of 75% and therefore a consortium exists. Whilst WB Inc's shareholding is considered in meeting the consortium criterion that Rossetti Ltd is at least 75% owned by companies, as a non-UK resident company it cannot benefit from the surrender of losses by Rossetti Ltd.

However, both TSE Ltd and Pebble plc, with the consent of the consortium members may benefit from the surrender of Rossetti Ltd's trading loss of £373,793, after a notional offset against its profit on non-trading loan relationships of £2,150. Consortium relief claims are therefore based on available losses of £371,643.

It is usual for consortium relief to be paid for at the marginal rate of the claimant company (ie 20%).

TSE Ltd can claim up to £42,000 of consortium relief for the trading loss (being lower than 31% × £371,643 = £115,209).

Pebble plc can claim up to 35% × £371,643 = £130,075

The unused losses may be carried forward.

Calculation of the tax credit available in respect of R&D expenditure and a recommendation as to the whether the claim should be made

As RSL is a SME and has a surrenderable loss in an accounting period in which it is entitled to an additional deduction from trading profits, it may convert all or part of the loss into an R&D tax credit.

The surrenderable loss is the lower of:

- The amount of the unrelieved loss in the period ie £371,643; and
- 225% of the related R&D expenditure ie £443,900 × 230% = £1,020,970

Clearly the trading loss is the lower number.

Note: Although Rossetti Ltd's loss was £373,793 it has any other income £2,150 of bank interest against which to set the loss, the offset needs to be deducted first. It is therefore be offset against the non-trading loan relationship profit to give a net loss of £371,643.

In addition, any other relief obtained for the loss ie the possible consortium relief described above should also be deducted from the unrelieved trading loss for the purposes of the tax credit.

The R&D tax credit is 14.5% of the surrenderable loss:

14.5% × (£371,643 – (42,000 + 130,075)) = 14. 5% × £199,568 = £28,937

Recommendation

Assuming payment is made for the consortium relief surrenders, that would result in Rossetti Ltd receiving non-taxable income. If the claim for the tax credit is not made, the unrelieved loss of £199,568 would be carried forward. The cashflow delay in the tax saving should be weighed against the amount of tax saved in the future, depending on RSL's future taxable total profits. It should be determined whether the carry forward is likely to save more tax than the saving generated by the current tax credit.

Income and corporation tax treatment of the amounts received by Tomaz on termination

The loan written off must be grossed up and taxed as a distribution ie £5,100 × 100/90 = £5,667

As Tomaz is an additional rate taxpayer, the personal allowance is completely withdrawn and the distribution will be taxed at 37.5% minus the 10% tax credit.

The termination payment of £10,700 is exempt as it is covered by the £30,000 exemption for non-contractual termination payments for loss of office.

As discussed above, no corporation tax deduction is available for the loan write off, but the termination payment of £10,700 will be fully deductible for corporation tax purposes.

Divestment of Shelly Ltd

Option One: Purchase of Shelly Ltd's share capital

Sale of shares

The sale of 100% of the shares in Shelly Ltd will result in a potential chargeable gain arising in RSL as follows:

	£
Proceeds	750,000
Less cost	(120,000)
Chargeable gain	630,000

However, the gain is exempt under the substantial shareholding exemption (SSE), all of the conditions being met.

Use of losses

The trading loss of £120,800 for the year ended 31 March 2017 arises in an accounting period where the ownership of Shelly Ltd has changed. The current period loss of £120,800 will available for carry forward, or by means of a current year claim to offset the loss against any other profits in the year ended 31 March 2017, subject to the provision described below.

A proportion of the current year trading loss may also be surrendered to Marvell plc as Shelly Ltd will be in a group with that company from 30 November 2016. The maximum loss that can be surrendered is 4/12 × £120,800 = £40,267.

Any trading losses carried forward in Shelly Ltd may not be available to offset against future trading profits of that company as there will be a change in ownership on 30 November 2016.

If there has been a major change in the nature or conduct of Shelly Ltd's trade within three years before or after the date of the change in ownership (30 November 2016), then no trading losses may be carried forward beyond 30 November 2016.

There are indications of an anticipated change in both the nature and conduct of Shelly Ltd's trade following its acquisition by Marvell plc on 30 November 2016.

Marvell plc's plans to re-focus the business to include selling to the public health sector, as well as the existing private sector, indicates a change in the nature of the trade. In addition, the new sales and marketing support provided by Marvell plc to include a new on-line sales strategy constitutes a change in the way that Shelly Ltd has previously conducted its business.

The sale of shares is an exempt supply, so no VAT is chargeable.

Option Two: Purchase of the trade and assets

The sale of the trade and assets of Shelly Ltd will result in chargeable gains arising in Shelly Ltd as follows:

Goodwill:	£
Proceeds	590,000
Less cost	–
Total gains	590,000

The chargeable gains will be subject to corporation tax at the main rate of 20%. However, any loss incurred for the accounting period to cessation can be offset against the gain.

The cessation of Shelly Ltd's trade on 30 November 2016 will bring about an accounting period end for corporation tax purposes. Any tax payment deadlines should be calculated with regard to this date.

Any unrelieved trading losses will lapse, as Shelly Ltd has ceased to trade.

For VAT purposes, the transfer will be a TOGC and outside the scope of VAT but subject to the condition that Marvell plc carries on the same trade following the transfer, which may be subject to scrutiny.

Tax issues affecting the negotiation

The purchase of the trade and assets of Shelly Ltd results in a clean purchase of assets without associated liabilities.

The purchase of the shares in Shelly Ltd means that Marvell plc acquires the entire company, with any associated liabilities or risks, which may include tax liabilities and/or risks. However, a due diligence process should identify these issues and appropriate warranties and indemnities should be included in the sale and purchase agreement.

Whilst a sale of the trade and assets may be simpler for Marvell plc, there may be fiscal tension between the vendor and purchaser as the sale of shares would be exempt from corporation tax for RSL.

The treatment of the goodwill may also affect the negotiation as to whether the trade and assets or the shares should be purchased.

6 **Eclipze plc**

Briefing Note

(a) (b) and (c) **Subject: Antonia Loga's income tax calculation, use of trading loss and explanation of treatment of termination payment.**

The following is a calculation of Antonia's income tax payable:

Antonia Loga – tax computation for the tax year ended 5 April 2016

	Total £	Non Savings Income £	Dividends £	Termination payment £
Dividends				
46,800 × 100/90	52,000		52,000	
Salary – Eclipze	110,000	110,000		
Compensation for loss of office (£75,000 + £25,000 – £30,000)	70,000			70,000
Net income before loss relief	232,000	110,000	52,000	70,000
s.64 Loss relief	(40,000)	(40,000)		
	192,000	70,000	52,000	70,000
No personal allowance				
31,785 @ 20%		6,357		
38,215 @ 40%		15,286		
	70,000			
52,000 @ 32.5%	52,000	16,900		
28,000 @ 40%		11,200		
42,000 @ 45%	70,000	18,900		
Tax liability	247000	68,643		
Less dividend tax credit		(5,200)		
PAYE		(62,000)		
Income tax payable		1,443		

Use of the trading loss for 2014/15 given the information available.

Trading loss

	£
2015/16	
Basis period	
1 June 2015 to 5 April 2016	
Loss £(44,000) × 10/11	(40,000)
2016/17	
Basis periods (First 12 months of trading)	
1 June 2015 to 31 May 2016	
Loss £(44,000) less used 2015/16 £(40,000)	(4,000)
Profit £144,000 × 1/12	12,000
Profit	8,000

There is no information regarding earlier years, however Antonia is an additional rate tax payer in the current year 2015/16. Given the information available, the most efficient use of the loss would be, given the information available, to utilise in the current year against general income (s 64 loss relief) – as the loss is less than £50,000, there should be no restriction under the rules which limit the offset of losses and deductions from total income. Carrying forward the loss would only be available against profits of the same trade which are only £8,000 for the tax year 2016/17. This would therefore be inefficient in terms of cash flow.

Tax treatment of termination payment

Provided the compensation for loss of office was not contractual, £30,000 should be treated as tax-free. The company car should be included at its market value as part of her termination payment. Her termination payment is treated as the top slice of her income and is taxed after savings income and dividends at her marginal rate of tax. Her termination payment therefore comprises of £75,000 + £25,000 – £30,000 = £70,000.

(d) **Chargeable gain on paper for paper/share for share exchange**

Antonia has incorrectly calculated the gain on the disposal of the Dezine shares. The Dezine shares were exchanged for shares in Eclipze. This is a 'paper for paper' or 'share for share' exchange and no gain was chargeable to capital gains tax at the time of the exchange, but this was because the new Eclipze shares took over the Dezine shares cost. So, if the Eclipze shares are sold in future a gain will arise on the difference between the market value of the Eclipze shares on sale and the original cost of the Dezine shares.

The disposal of her shares in Dezine would probably have qualified for entrepreneurs' relief. However as she now holds less than 5% of the shares in Eclipze, her new shares will not qualify for entrepreneurs' relief when she sells them in the future.

I would recommend that she disapply the takeover rules and take advantage of the 10% tax rate available if a gain is eligible for entrepreneurs' relief, particularly if she anticipates selling the Eclipze shares. The rate of CGT she would pay in the future on the sale of the Eclipze shares would be higher, because entrepreneurs' relief would not be available.

The cost of her shares in Eclipze would then become the market value of the shares at the time of the 'paper for paper' exchange and not the cost of the Dezine shares.

Therefore if she wishes to crystallise her entrepreneurs' relief, she would pay chargeable gains tax of:

	£
Disposal proceeds	
30 × 5,500 × £8 =	1,320,000
Less cost	1,200,000
	120,000
Less annual exempt amount	(11,100)
	108,900
Tax @ 10%	10,890

Additional information required to make a recommendation:

Does Antonia have the cash available to pay the CGT now?

Does Antonia have any brought-forward capital losses?

What are her future plans – will she be selling or holding her shares in Eclipze?

(e) **Reply to Antonia's email**

Dear Antonia

Tax implications of gift of shares in SloeStep from your grandfather

We would need to confirm whether your grandfather was resident and domiciled in the UK. If this is the case, then his worldwide assets would be liable to inheritance tax (IHT) at 40% in the UK. The gift of the shares to you in SloeStep is a potentially exempt transfer (PET) which, as he has unfortunately passed away within seven years of the date of the gift, may now be liable to IHT (subject to taper relief). The amount payable could be reduced by taper relief if the shares had been gifted to you at least three years before the date of your grandfather's death. In this case the gift was within three years of your grandfather's death, so no taper relief was available.

The shares might have qualified for business property relief (BPR) at 100% at the time of the gift as the shares were unquoted. BPR reduces the amount of the gift charged to tax by 100%. In general BPR will still apply to the transfer if you still own the shares transferred at the date of your grandfather's death. As you still own the shares this should apply and there should be no tax liability arising from the gift.

We suggest you contact the executor and confirm that you still own the shares and request more details.

If you have any further queries, please do not hesitate to contact me.

Regards   ,

Index

ICAEW

Notes

REVIEW FORM – BUSINESS PLANNING: TAXATION STUDY MANUAL

Your ratings, comments and suggestions would be appreciated on the following areas of this Study Manual.

	Very useful	Useful	Not useful
Chapter introductions	☐	☐	☐
Examination context	☐	☐	☐
Worked examples	☐	☐	☐
Interactive questions	☐	☐	☐
Quality of explanations	☐	☐	☐
Technical references (where relevant)	☐	☐	☐
Self-test questions	☐	☐	☐
Self-test answers	☐	☐	☐
Index	☐	☐	☐

	Excellent	Good	Adequate	Poor
Overall opinion of this Study Manual	☐	☐	☐	☐

Please add further comments below:

Please return completed form to:

The Learning Team
Learning and Professional Department
ICAEW
Metropolitan House
321 Avebury Boulevard
Milton Keynes
MK9 2FZ
E learning@icaew.com